Washington Real Estate Fundamentals

23rd edition

Kathryn J. Haupt
David L. Rockwell
David L. Jarman
Megan Dorsey
Jennifer Gotanda

Rockwell Institute
13218 N.E. 20th St.
Bellevue, WA 98005
www.RockwellInstitute.com

Published 2025. Printed in the United States of America

978-1-59844-562-6
27 26 25 1 2 3

For more information please visit www.RockwellInstitute.com

Table of Contents

Chapter 1: *The Nature of Real Property*

I. **What is Real Property?**
II. **Appurtenances**
   A. Air rights
   B. Water rights
   C. Solid mineral rights
   D. Oil and gas rights
   E. Other appurtenant rights
III. **Attachments**
   A. Natural attachments
   B. Man-made attachments (fixtures)
   C. Distinguishing fixtures from personal property
      1. Written agreement
      2. Method of attachment
      3. Adaptation to the property
      4. Intention of the annexor
      5. Relationship of the parties
   D. Manufactured homes as fixtures
IV. **Land Description**
   A. Metes and bounds
   B. Government survey
   C. Lot and block
   D. Other methods of description

Key Terms

Real Property
Personal Property
Appurtenance
Emblements
Trade Fixtures
Riparian Rights
Riparian Land
Littoral Land
Appropriative Rights
Lateral Support
Subjacent Support
Metes and Bounds
Monument
Point of Beginning
Course
Distance
Government Survey
Principal Meridian
Range
Township
Section
Government Lot
Lot and Block
Air Lot

Real estate agents are concerned not just with the sale of land and houses, but with the sale of real property. Real property includes the land and improvements, and it also encompasses the rights that go along with ownership of land. The first part of this chapter explains those rights, which are known as appurtenances. It also explains natural attachments and fixtures, which are sold as part of the land, and the distinction between fixtures and personal property, which is not ordinarily transferred with the land. The second part of this chapter explains methods of land description—the different ways in which a parcel of land may be identified in legal documents to prevent confusion about its boundaries or ownership.

What is Real Property?

There are two types of property: **real property** (realty) and **personal property** (personalty). Real property can be described as land, anything affixed to the land, and anything incidental or appurtenant to the land. Sometimes it is described as "that which is immovable." Personal property, on the other hand, is usually movable. A car, a sofa, and a hat are simple examples of personal property. Anything that is not real property is personal property.

The distinction between real and personal property is very important in real estate transactions. When a piece of land is sold, anything that is considered part of the real property is transferred to the buyer along with the land, unless otherwise agreed. But if an item is personal property, the sellers can take it with them when they move out, unless otherwise agreed.

Of course, the principal component of real property is land. But real property is more than just the surface of the earth. It also includes everything beneath the surface down to the center of the earth, and everything above the surface, to the upper reaches of the sky.

Fig. 1.1 The Inverted Pyramid

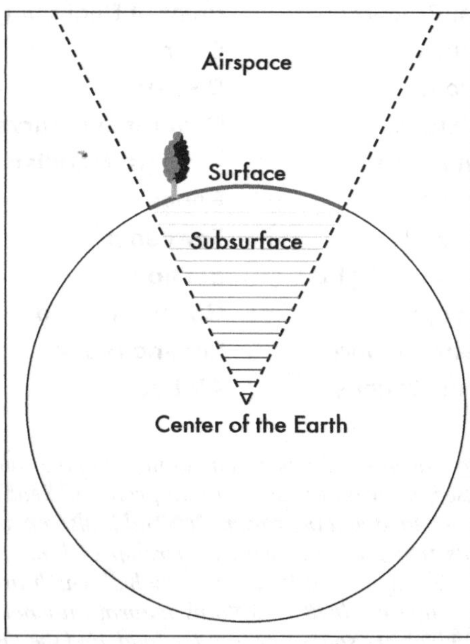

A parcel of real property can be imagined as an inverted pyramid, with its tip at the center of the globe and its base above the earth's surface. The landowner owns not only the earth's surface within the boundaries of the parcel, but also everything under or over the surface.

The rights and privileges associated with land ownership are also considered part of the real property. Think of real property as the land plus a bundle of rights. The owner's bundle of rights includes the rights to possess, use, enjoy, encumber, will, sell, or do nothing at all with the land.

Appurtenances

In addition to the basic bundle of ownership rights, a landowner has appurtenant rights. An **appurtenance** is a right or interest that goes along with or pertains to a piece of land. A landowner's property may include any or all of these appurtenances:

- air rights,
- water rights,
- solid mineral rights,
- oil and gas rights, and
- support rights.

Appurtenances are usually transferred along with the land, but the landowner can sell certain appurtenant rights separately from the land. For example, the owner may keep the land but sell her mineral rights to a mining company.

Air Rights

Air rights are the right to use the airspace above a particular parcel of land. In theory, a landowner's air rights extend to the upper limits of the sky, but that's not true in practice. Congress gave the federal government complete control over the nation's airspace. Landowners have the exclusive right to use the lower reaches of the airspace over their property, but may do nothing that would interfere with normal air traffic.

On the other hand, sometimes air traffic interferes with a landowner's right to the normal use of his land. If aircraft overflights cause substantial harm to a landowner, he may sue the government for compensation. The classic example is an airport built right next to a chicken farm. The noise and vibrations from overflights are so severe that the chickens no longer lay eggs. If the land can't be used for any other reasonable purpose, the value of the land is significantly diminished. The landowner may be able to force the government to condemn the property and compensate him for its fair market value.

Water Rights

Water is found both on the surface of the earth and beneath the surface. Surface water may be confined to a channel or basin, or it may be unconfined water, such as runoff or flood water. The water beneath the surface may also be "confined" in the sense that it runs in recognizable underground streams, or it may collect in porous ground layers called aquifers.

In regard to confined surface waters, two main systems are used to govern water rights in the United States:

1. the riparian rights system, and
2. the prior appropriation system.

Riparian Rights. Riparian rights are the water rights of a landowner with respect to water that is adjacent to or flows through her property. Under the riparian rights system, someone who owns land beside a stream (a riparian landowner) has the right to use stream water for domestic purposes, such as drinking, bathing, or watering a personal-use produce garden.

The use must be reasonable; for example, upstream riparian owners aren't allowed to use the water in ways that could substantially diminish the stream's flow and deprive downstream owners of its use.

Although "riparian rights" is the general term for this type of water rights, strictly speaking the word **riparian** refers to flowing water: a river, a stream, or a creek. In contrast, **littoral** water is standing water: a pond, a lake, or even an ocean. Under the riparian rights system, someone who owns littoral land (such as lakefront property) has essentially the same water rights as someone who owns land beside a river or stream.

There's an important restriction on riparian (or littoral) rights. The landowner is not permitted to take or divert water from the stream or lake for use on property that does not adjoin that stream or lake.

> **Example:** Brown is a riparian landowner. She owns Parcel C, property that borders Swiftwater River. She also owns Parcel D, property that is about 300 feet inland. She cannot divert water from Swiftwater River to irrigate a vegetable garden on Parcel D, her non-riparian property.

In addition to the right to take water for domestic use, riparian and littoral landowners have the right to use the body of water for activities such as boating, fishing, and swimming. However, if the body of water is **navigable**, the public is generally also entitled to use it for recreation or transportation. A waterway is usually considered navigable if it's large enough to be used by commercial or pleasure watercraft.

A riparian or littoral owner's property may include some land that's underwater. If a stream or lake that serves as the boundary of a property is not navigable, the property owner owns the adjacent submerged land to the midpoint of the streambed or lakebed. But if the stream or lake is navigable, the riparian or littoral landowner's property generally ends at the mean high water mark, and the government owns the submerged land, holding it in trust for the public. This is also the rule for tidal (oceanfront) property.

In Washington, the riparian water rights system was largely replaced with the prior appropriation system (discussed below) in the 1970s.

Appropriative Rights. Riparian and littoral rights are tied to ownership of land beside a body of water. The other major type of water rights, appropriative rights, do not depend on land ownership. Instead, they are based on priority of use (first in time, first in right). This is called the **prior appropriation system**.

To establish an appropriative right, someone who wants to use water from a particular lake or stream applies to the state government (in Washington, the Department of Ecology) for a permit. It isn't necessary for the applicant to own land beside the body of water. Water taken by a permit holder does not have to be used on property adjacent to the water source.

The prior appropriation system is primarily used in the western United States, where water resources are often scarce and therefore carefully controlled.

If someone with an appropriation permit fails to use the water for a certain period of time, he may lose his water rights. The government can then issue a permit to another applicant.

Groundwater. In Washington the prior appropriation system applies to underground water, called "groundwater," as well as surface water; as a general rule, someone who wants to use groundwater must obtain an appropriation permit. However, a landowner may make reasonable use of the groundwater (by drilling a well, for example) without an appropriation permit, provided she takes no more than 5,000 gallons per day.

Solid Mineral Rights

A landowner owns all the solid minerals within the "inverted pyramid" under the surface of her property. These minerals are considered to be real property until they are extracted from the earth, at which point they become personal property.

As was mentioned earlier, a landowner can sell her mineral rights separately from the rest of the property. When the rights to a particular mineral are sold, the purchaser automatically acquires an implied easement—the right to enter the land in order to extract the minerals from it.

Oil and Gas Rights

Ownership of oil and gas is not as straightforward as ownership of solid minerals. In their natural state, oil and gas lie trapped beneath the surface in porous layers of earth. However, once an oil or gas reservoir has been tapped, the oil and gas begin to flow toward the point where the reservoir has been pierced by the well. A well on one parcel of land can attract all the oil and gas from the surrounding properties.

Ownership of oil and gas is governed by the "rule of capture." That is, a landowner owns all of the oil and gas produced from wells on his property. The oil and gas become the personal property of the landowner once they are "captured" and brought to the surface.

The rule of capture has the effect of stimulating oil and gas production, since the only way for a landowner to protect his interest in the underlying gas and oil is to drill his own well to keep the oil and gas from migrating to the neighbor's wells.

Other Appurtenant Rights

In addition to rights concerning air, water, minerals, and oil and gas, there are some other important appurtenant rights.

A piece of land is physically supported by the other land that surrounds it. A landowner has **support rights**—the right to the natural support provided by the land beside and beneath her property. **Lateral support** is support from adjacent land; it may be disturbed by construction or excavation on an adjacent property. **Subjacent support** is support from the underlying earth. Subjacent support may become an issue when a landowner sells her mineral rights.

Easements and restrictive covenants also create appurtenant rights. These are discussed in detail in Chapter 4.

Attachments

You have seen that the land and the appurtenances are part of the real property. The third element of real property is attachments. There are two main categories of attachments:

1. natural, and
2. man-made.

Natural Attachments

Natural attachments are things attached to the earth by roots, such as trees and shrubs. This includes plants that grow spontaneously, without the help of humans, and also plants cultivated by people. As a general rule, natural attachments are part of the real property. In some cases, though, crops to be harvested are treated as personal property. Thus, an orchard of cultivated apple trees would be realty, but the apples growing on the trees could be considered personalty under certain circumstances.

A special rule called the **doctrine of emblements** applies to crops planted by a tenant farmer. If the tenancy is for an indefinite period of time and the tenancy is terminated through no fault of the tenant before the crops are ready for harvest, the tenant has the right to re-enter the land and harvest the first crop that matures after the tenancy is terminated.

Since natural attachments are considered part of the realty, they're usually included in a sale of the land. However, like air rights or mineral rights, the owner can sell natural attachments separately from the land. This is sometimes called **severance** from the real property.

Man-made Attachments: Fixtures

Items that have been attached to land by people are called **fixtures**. For example, a house, a fence, and a cement patio are all fixtures. Like natural attachments, fixtures are considered part of the real property.

Fixtures always start out as personal property. For example, lumber is personal property, but it becomes a fixture when it's used to build a fence. However, it's sometimes difficult to determine whether a particular item has become a fixture or is still personal property. If the item remains personal property, the owner can remove it from the property when the land is sold. But if the item is a fixture, it's transferred to the buyer along with the land unless otherwise agreed.

Distinguishing Fixtures from Personal Property

Buyers and sellers sometimes disagree as to exactly what is being purchased and sold in their transaction. For instance, is the heirloom chandelier in the dining room part of the real property that's being transferred to the buyer, or is it personal property that the seller can remove when he moves out?

The easiest way to avoid this type of controversy is to put the intentions of the parties in writing. If there's a written agreement between a buyer and a seller stipulating how a particular item is going to be treated—as part of the real property or as personal property—then a court would respect and enforce that agreement in a lawsuit. Such a stipulation between buyer and seller would ordinarily be included in the purchase and sale agreement. For example, if the seller plans to dig up certain shrubs in the backyard and take them with her when she moves out, that should be stated in the purchase and sale agreement, since shrubbery is part of the real property unless otherwise agreed.

Similarly, if the seller intends to transfer personal property, such as a couch, to the buyer, that should also be stated in the purchase and sale agreement. In addition to the deed conveying title to the real property, a separate document called a **bill of sale** should be used. A bill of sale conveys title to personal property.

In the absence of a written agreement, courts apply a series of tests to classify the item in dispute. These tests include:

- the method of attachment,
- adaptation of the item to the real property,
- the intention of the annexor, and
- the relationship of the parties.

Method of Attachment. As a general rule, any item that is permanently attached to the land becomes a part of the real estate. A permanent attachment occurs when the item is:

- annexed to the land by roots, like trees or rose bushes;
- embedded in the earth, like sewer lines or septic tanks;
- permanently resting on the land, like a storage shed; or
- attached by any other enduring method, such as cement, plaster, nails, bolts, or screws.

Note that it isn't necessary for an item to be literally attached to the real property in order to be considered a fixture. There may be physical annexation even without actual attachment. The force of gravity alone may be sufficient, as in the case of a building with no foundation. Also, an article enclosed within a building may be considered annexed to the real property if it cannot be removed without dismantling it or tearing down part of the building.

In addition, even easily movable articles may be considered "constructively annexed" to the real property if they are essential parts of other fixtures. For example, the key to the front door of a house is a fixture. Also, fixtures that have been temporarily removed for servicing or repair remain constructively annexed to the real property.

Adaptation to the Property. If an unattached item was designed or specially adapted for use on a particular property, it is probably a fixture. Examples include the pews in a church, or storm windows specifically made for a particular building.

Intention of the Annexor. The method of attachment was once regarded as the most important test in determining whether an item was a fixture, but over time courts decided that test was too rigid.

Fig. 1.2 Fixture Tests

Fixture Tests
• Method of attachment • Adaptation to the property • Intention of the annexor • Relationship of the parties

It did not allow for special situations where something permanently affixed would be more justly classified as personal property. Now the intention of the annexor is considered a more important test. Courts try to determine what the person who annexed the item to the property intended. Did she intend the item to become part of the realty or to remain personal property? Each of the other tests (including method of attachment) is viewed as objective evidence of this intention. For instance, permanently embedding a birdbath in concrete indicates an intention to make the item a permanent fixture, while just setting a freestanding birdbath out in the yard does not.

Relationship of the Parties. Intent is also indicated by the relationship between the parties in the lawsuit: buyer/seller, landlord/tenant, borrower/lender. For example, under this test a tenant who installs an item, such as new lighting, is assumed to be doing so with the intention of removing it at the end of the lease.

On the other hand, it's assumed that an owner making the same alteration is trying to improve the property and does not intend to remove the item. So an item that would be considered personal property if installed by a tenant might be considered a fixture if installed by a seller.

Items installed by a tenant to carry on a trade or business, such as a ceiling hoist in an auto repair shop, are called **trade fixtures.** Trade fixtures may be removed at the end of the tenancy unless the lease includes a provision to the contrary. If a tenant removes trade fixtures that have become an integral part of the building, it is the tenant's responsibility to either restore the property to its original condition or else compensate the landlord for any physical damage resulting from the removal. Trade fixtures that are not removed by the tenant become the property of the landlord.

Manufactured Homes

The distinction between fixtures and personal property has special significance in connection with mobile or manufactured homes. At one time, mobile homes were simply wheeled trailers that could be set up inexpensively in mobile home parks, but the category has expanded to include manufactured homes, which are large structures that can be set permanently on a full-sized lot. Manufactured homes are mostly or entirely assembled in a factory and transported to the property they'll occupy, in contrast to traditional homes that are built on the property (sometimes referred to as site-built or stick-built homes).

Manufactured homes leave the factory as personal property and are initially titled using the same title registration system that's used for motor vehicles. Unless the sale or lease of a manufactured home also involves the sale or lease of associated land, an agent involved in the transaction doesn't need a real estate license. The agent would need a mobile home dealer's license, though.

If the owner of a manufactured home owns the land on which the home is or will be affixed, the owner may go through a procedure called **title elimination.** This eliminates the vehicle title and the home becomes part of the real property where it is located. Lenders generally won't provide financing on the home unless this is done.

Land Description

When ownership of real property is transferred from one party to another, the legal documents for the transaction must specify what parcel of land is being conveyed. The section of a document that identifies the land is referred to as the property description or the **legal description.**

It's essential for the description of the property to be clear and accurate. An ambiguous or erroneous description can make a contract or a deed invalid. Confusion over exactly what parcel of land is being conveyed could cause problems not only for the parties involved in the current transaction, but also for the parties in future transactions.

There are three major methods used to describe land in legal documents:

- metes and bounds,
- government survey, and
- lot and block.

Metes and Bounds

The metes and bounds method describes a parcel of land by specifying the location of its boundaries. The boundaries are described by reference to three things:

- **monuments**, which may be natural objects such as rivers or trees, or man-made objects such as roads or survey markers;
- **courses** (directions) in the form of compass readings; and
- **distances**, measured in any convenient unit of length.

How Metes and Bounds Descriptions Work. A metes and bounds description of a parcel of land first specifies the **point of beginning**, which is a clearly defined point on one of the parcel's boundaries. A monument may be used as the point of beginning (for example, "Beginning at the old oak tree"), or the point of beginning may be described by reference to a monument (for example, "Beginning 206 feet north of the intersection of Front Street and Sutter Road").

After establishing the point of beginning, the description then lists a series of courses and distances to indicate the direction and length of each boundary. For instance, "south 30 degrees east, 137 feet" is a course and distance.

Fig. 1.3 Metes and Bounds Description

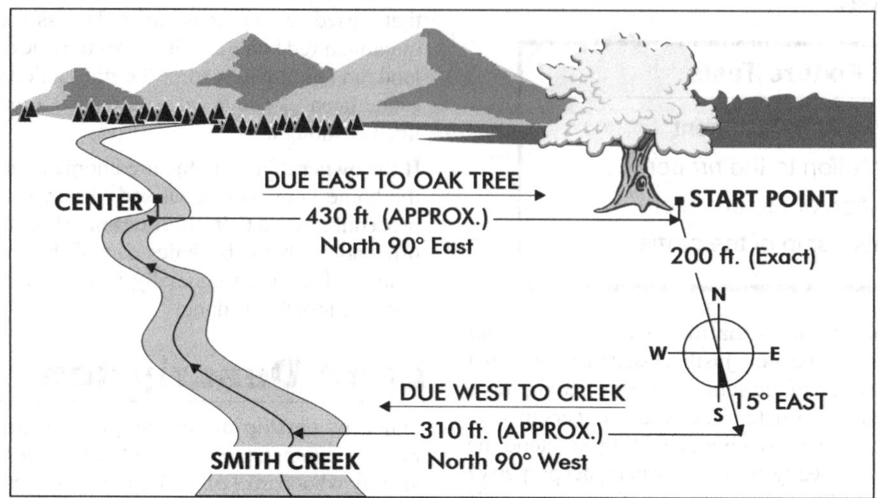

A tract of land located in Spokane County, described as follows: "Beginning at the oak tree, thence south 15° east, 200 feet, thence north 90° west, 310 feet more or less to the centerline of Smith Creek, thence northwesterly along the centerline of Smith Creek to a point directly west of the oak tree, thence north 90° east, 430 feet more or less to the point of beginning."

By starting at the point of beginning and following the courses and distances given in the description, a surveyor could walk along the parcel's boundary lines, all the way around and back to the point of beginning. (A metes and bounds description must end up back at the point of beginning; otherwise it wouldn't describe a completely enclosed parcel of land.)

Fig. 1.4 Compass Bearings

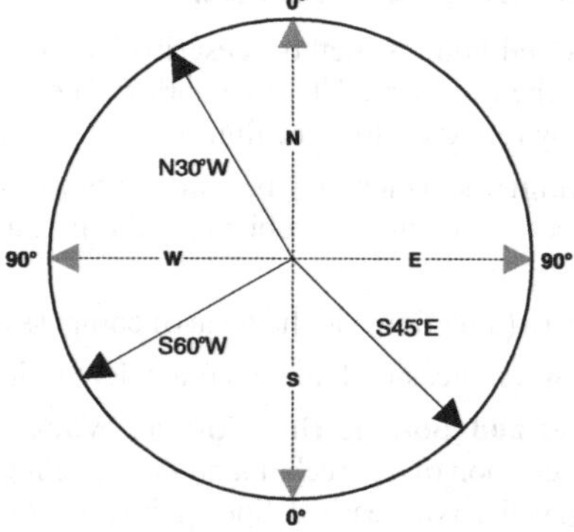

Compass Bearings. The courses in a metes and bounds description are given in a peculiar fashion. A course is described in terms of its deviation from either north or south, whichever is closer. Thus, northwest or 315° is written as north 45° west, since it's a deviation of 45° to the west of north. Similarly, south southeast or 157½° is written as south 22½° east, since it's a deviation of 22½° to the east of south. Due east and due west are both written relative to north: north 90° east and north 90° west, respectively. (There are 360 degrees in a circle.)

Resolving Discrepancies. To specify the direction or length of a boundary, monuments are sometimes used in conjunction with courses or distances, as in "northerly along the eastern edge of Elm Street 115 feet" or "north, 60 feet more or less, to the centerline of Smith Creek."

If there is a discrepancy between a monument and a course or distance, the monument takes precedence. In the examples just given, the first boundary would be along the edge of Elm Street, even if that edge does not run due north, and the second boundary would extend to the center of Smith Creek even if the actual distance to that point is not 60 feet.

Discrepancies may also occur between other elements of a metes and bounds description. To resolve them, the following order of priority is used:

1. natural monuments,
2. man-made monuments,
3. courses,
4. distances,
5. names (such as "Fairfield Ranch"), and
6. areas (such as "40 acres").

In case of a conflict between any two of these elements in a description, the one with higher priority prevails.

Metes and bounds descriptions tend to be lengthy, which makes transcription errors more likely. Furthermore, monuments do not always maintain their exact locations over the years. An actual survey of the property may be necessary when dealing with a metes and bounds description.

Government Survey

In the government survey system, also called the rectangular survey system, land is described by reference to a grid of lines established by survey. (These are imaginary lines, like the lines of latitude and longitude on a globe.) This system of land description was established by the federal government after many eastern states had already been settled. As a result, government survey descriptions are mainly used west of the Mississippi River.

The terminology used in the government survey system may seem confusing at first, so we recommend that you study the accompanying diagrams closely.

The system is made up of a series of large grids covering much of the country. Each of these grids is composed of two sets of lines, one set running north/south, the other east/west. Each grid is identified by a **principal meridian**, which is the original north/south line established in that grid, and by a **base line**, which is the original east/west line. In Washington, the principal meridian is the Willamette Meridian. (See Figure 1.6.)

Grid lines run parallel to the principal meridian and the base line at intervals of six miles. The east/west lines are called **township lines**, and they divide the land into rows or tiers called **township tiers**. The north/south lines, called **range lines**, divide the land into columns called **ranges**. Every fourth range line is a **guide meridian** and every fourth township line is a **correction line**. (See Figure 1.7.)

The area of land that is located at the intersection of a range and a township tier is called a **township**, and it is identified by its position relative to the principal meridian and base line. For example, the township that is located in the fourth tier north of the base line and the third range east of the principal meridian is called "Township 4 North Range 3 East." (See Figure 1.7.) This may be abbreviated as T4N, R3E.

Fig. 1.5 Units of Land Measurement

UNITS OF MEASUREMENT FOR LAND	
UNITS OF AREA	1 Tract = 24 mi. × 24 mi. (576 sq. mi) = 16 town-ships 1 Township = 6 mi. × 6 mi. (36 sq. mi) = 36 sections 1 Section = 1 mi. × 1 mi. (1 sq. mi.) = 640 acres 1 Acre = 43,560 sq. ft. 1 Square Acre = 208.71 ft. × 208.71 feet
UNITS OF LENGTH	1 Mile = 5,280 ft. 1 Yard = 3 ft.
Note: To determine the area of partial sections, simply multiply the fraction of the section by 640. For example: 1 half section = ½ × 640 = 320 acres 1 quarter-section = ¼ × 640 = 160 acres 1 quarter-quarter-section = ¼ × ¼ × 640 = 40 acres	

Grid systems are identical across the country, so a government survey description must include the name of the principal meridian that's being used as a reference. (Since each principal meridian has its own base line, it is not necessary to specify the base line.) It's also a good practice to mention the county and state where the land is situated, to avoid any possible confusion. Thus, for example, a complete description of a township might be T4N, R3E of the Willamette Meridian, Clark County, State of Washington.

Each township measures 36 square miles and contains 36 sections. Each section is one square mile, or 640 acres. These sections are numbered in a special way, starting with the northeast corner and moving west, then down a row and eastward, snaking back and forth and ending with the southeast corner (see Figure 1.8).

Smaller parcels of land can be identified by reference to sections and partial sections, as illustrated in Figure 1.9.

Even in an area where land is described using the government survey method, it may be necessary to use the metes and bounds method in conjunction with it.

This is true, for example, if the parcel to be described is small or non-rectangular. The government survey method is used to identify the general location of the parcel, and then the metes and bounds method is used to specify its precise location and boundaries.

Government Lots. A government lot is a section of land of irregular shape or size that is referred to by a lot number. Because of the curvature of the earth, range lines converge, so it is impossible to keep all sections exactly one mile square. As a result, the sections along the north and west boundaries of each township are irregular in size. The quarter sections along the north and west boundaries of these sections are used to take up the excess or shortage. The quarter-quarter sections, then, along the north and west boundaries of a township are given government lot numbers.

Another situation in which government lots occur is when a body of water or some other obstacle makes it impossible to survey a square-mile section. The irregularly shaped sections are assigned government lot numbers.

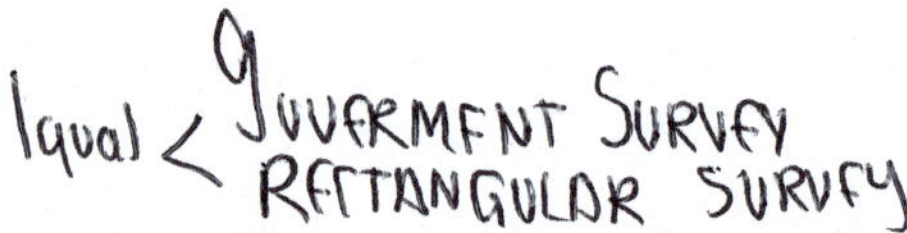

Fig. 1.6 Principal Meridians and Baselines

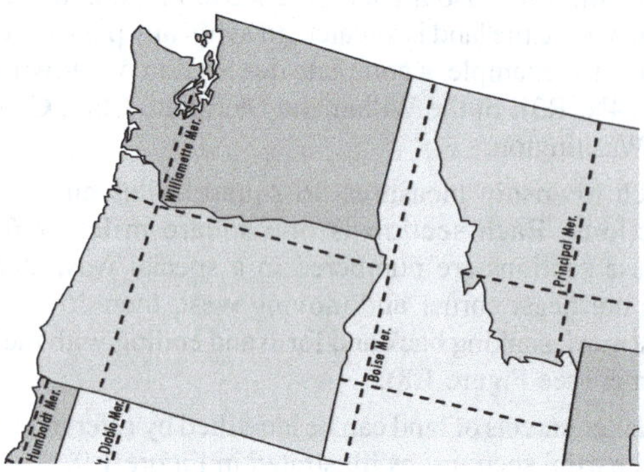

Fig. 1.7 East/west lines are Township Lines, north/south lines are Range Lines

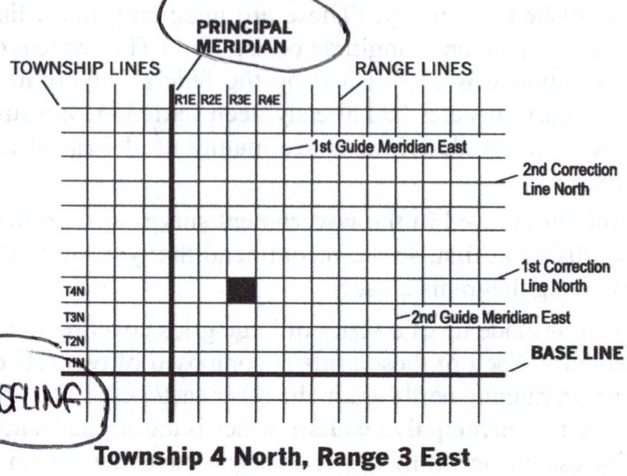

Fig. 1.8 A township Contains 36 Sections

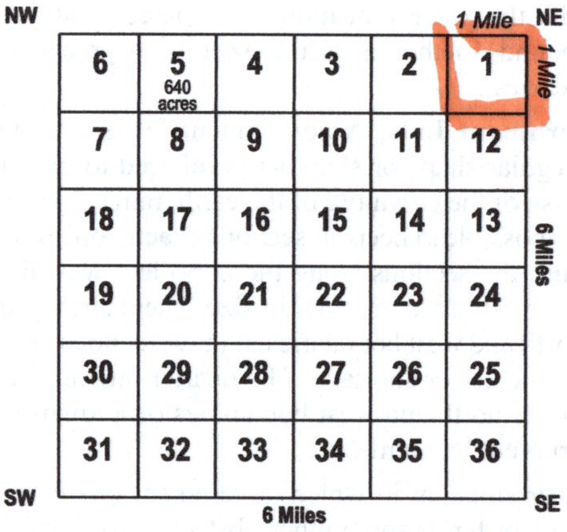

6	5 640 acres	4	3	2	1
7	8	9	10	11	12
18	17	16	15	14	13
19	20	21	22	23	24
30	29	28	27	26	25
31	32	33	34	35	36

Fig. 1.9 A Section can be divided into smaller parcels

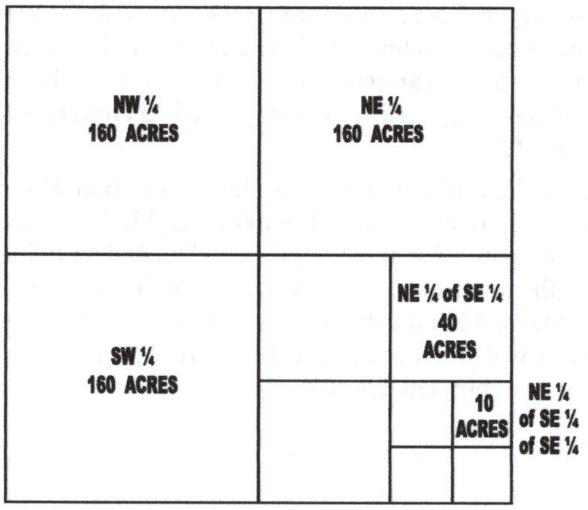

Lot and Block

The lot and block method is sometimes referred to as the platting method or the maps and plats system. It was developed to make legal descriptions of subdivided land more convenient, and it is now used for most property in urban areas.

When land is subdivided, a surveyor uses the metes and bounds method or the government survey method, or both, to map out lots and blocks (groups of lots surrounded by streets) on a subdivision map called a **plat** or a plat map. The plat is then recorded in the county where the land is located.

Once a plat has been recorded, a reference to one of the lot numbers on the plat is a sufficient legal description for that lot. Since a precise description of the lot's location and boundaries is already on file in the county recorder's office, that description may be incorporated into any legal document simply by stating the lot number, the block number (if any), and the name of the subdivision.

Example: The property's legal description reads, "Lot 2, Block 4, Clover Heights Addition, in the City of Vancouver, County of Clark, State of Washington, as per map recorded in Book 25, page 92, of maps, in the office of the recorder of said county." By looking up the plat for this subdivision in the county records, you could learn the precise location and dimensions of Lot 2, Block 4.

Plat maps frequently contain useful information beyond a detailed description of lot boundaries. For example, a plat may include area measurements, the location and dimensions of any easements, the location of survey markers, and a list of use restrictions that apply to the land.

Other Methods of Land Description

There are other ways of describing land besides the three major methods we've discussed. When an adequate description of property is already a matter of public record—contained in a recorded document—then a simple reference to that earlier document serves as an adequate property description in a new document. (For example, "All that land described in the grant deed recorded under recording number 92122401503 in Skagit County, Washington.") Also, generalized descriptions such as "all my lands" or "Smith Farm" can be adequate, as long as they make it possible to determine exactly what property is being described. But it's always best to use the least ambiguous description possible, to prevent future problems. It should be noted that a property's street address is usually not an adequate description for a legal document.

Air Lots. Not every parcel of real property can be described simply in terms of its position on the face of the earth. Descriptions of some forms of real property must also indicate the property's elevation above the ground. For example, a condominium unit on an upper floor occupies a specific parcel of airspace, referred to as an air lot. The underlying description of the unit must specify its elevation.

A position above the ground is described by reference to an established plane of elevation called a **datum**. Most large cities have their own official datum, and frequently subsidiary reference points, called bench marks, are also established. A **bench mark** is a point whose position relative to a datum has been accurately measured. Thereafter, surveyors can use the bench mark as a reference when that's more convenient than using the datum.

Fig. 1.10 Plat Map

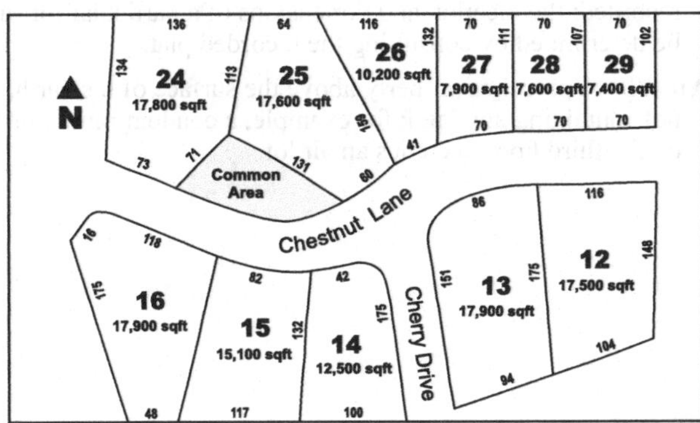

Chapter Summary

1. There are two types of property: real property and personal property. Real property is the land, anything affixed to the land, and anything appurtenant to the land. Movable items, such as furniture, are usually personal property.
2. Appurtenances to land include air rights, water rights, mineral rights, oil and gas rights, and support rights.
3. Attachments may be natural (growing plants) or man-made (fixtures). In the absence of a written agreement, the tests used to distinguish fixtures from personal property include method of attachment, adaptation to the property, intention of the annexor, and relationship of the parties.
4. Before property can be transferred, it must be adequately described. There are three major methods of land description: metes and bounds, government survey, and lot and block.

Key Terms

Real property—Land, attachments, and appurtenances.

Personal property—Anything that is not real property; its main characteristic is movability.

Appurtenance—A right incidental to the land that is transferred with it.

Emblements—Crops, such as wheat, produced annually through the labor of the cultivator.

Trade fixtures—Personal property attached to real property by a tenant for use in a trade or business. Trade fixtures are removable by the tenant.

Riparian rights—The water rights of a landowner whose land borders on a stream, a lake, or other body of water. Riparian rights allow only reasonable use of the water.

Riparian land—Land bordered by flowing water, such as a stream or river.

Littoral land—Land bordered by a stationary body of water, such as a lake or pond.

Appropriative rights—Water rights established by obtaining a government permit, and not based on ownership of land beside a body of water.

Lateral support—The physical support that a piece of land receives from the surrounding land.

Subjacent support—The physical support that a piece of land receives from the underlying earth.

Metes and bounds—A system of land description in which the boundaries of a parcel of land are described by reference to monuments, courses, and distances.

Monument—A visible marker (natural or artificial) used in a survey or a metes and bounds description to establish the boundaries of a piece of property.

Point of beginning—The starting point in a metes and bounds description; a monument or a point described by reference to a monument.

Course—In a metes and bounds description, a direction, stated in terms of a compass bearing.

Distance—In a metes and bounds description, the length of a boundary, measured in any convenient unit of length.

Government survey—A system of land description in which the land is divided into squares called townships, and each township is, in turn, divided up into 36 sections, each one square mile.

Principal meridian—In the government survey system, the main north-south line in a particular grid, used as the starting point in numbering the ranges and township tiers.

Range—In the government survey system, a strip of land six miles wide, running north and south.

Township—The intersection of a range and a township tier in the government survey system. It is a parcel of land that is six miles square and contains 36 sections.

Section—One square mile of land, containing 640 acres. There are 36 sections in a township.

Government lot—In the government survey system, a parcel of land that is not a regular section.

Lot and block—The system of description used for subdivided land. The properties within a subdivision are assigned lot numbers on a plat map, and the plat map is recorded; the location and dimensions of a particular lot can be determined by consulting the recorded plat.

Air lot—A parcel of property above the surface of the earth, not containing any land; for example, a condominium unit on the third floor occupies an air lot.

Chapter Quiz

1. **Real property is equivalent to:**
   a) land
   b) personal property
   c) land, attachments, and appurtenances
   d) land and water

2. **The most important consideration in determining whether an item is a fixture is:**
   a) physical attachment
   b) the annexor's intention
   c) adaptation of the item to the property
   d) intended use of the item

3. **Articles installed in or on realty by tenants for use in a business are called:**
   a) personalty
   b) trade fixtures
   c) emblements
   d) easements

4. **A right that goes with or pertains to real property is called:**
   a) an attachment
   b) an appurtenance
   c) personal property
   d) a fixture

5. **A landowner's rights regarding water in a stream flowing through her land are called:**
   a) riparian rights
   b) littoral rights
   c) appropriative rights
   d) easement rights

6. **Minerals become personal property when they are:**
   a) surveyed
   b) extracted from the land
   c) taken to a refinery
   d) claimed

7. **Rights to oil and gas are determined by:**
   a) the rule of capture
   b) offset wells
   c) the Bureau of Land Management
   d) the Department of the Interior

8. **Whether land borders on a lake or stream is irrelevant under the system of:**
   a) riparian rights
   b) capture rights
   c) littoral rights
   d) appropriative rights

9. **Ted's property is damaged by sinkholes caused by old coal mining tunnels beneath his land. The rights implicated in this situation are:**
   a) riparian rights
   b) subjacent support rights
   c) proximate support rights
   d) lateral support rights

10. **Which of the following is most likely to be considered part of the real property?**
    a) Piano
    b) Dining room table
    c) Mirror
    d) Kitchen sink

11. **Which of the following benefits tenant farmers?**
    a) Doctrine of emblements
    b) Rule of capture
    c) Overlying rights
    d) Method of attachment test

12. **A section of a township contains the following number of acres:**
    a) 360
    b) 580
    c) 640
    d) 1,000

13. **A parcel that measures 1/4 of a mile by 1/4 of a mile is:**
    a) 1/4 of a section
    b) 1/8 of a section
    c) 1/16 of a section
    d) 1/36 of a section

14. **The distance between the east and west boundary lines of a township is:**
    a) one mile
    b) two miles
    c) six miles
    d) ten miles

15. **A township contains 36 sections that are numbered consecutively 1 through 36. The last section in the township is located in the:**
    a) southeast corner
    b) southwest corner
    c) northeast corner
    d) northwest corner

Chapter 2: *Estates in Land and Methods of Holding Title*

I. Estates
   A. Freehold estates
      1. Fee simple estate
      2. Defeasible fee estate
      3. Life estate
   B. Leasehold estates
      1. Estate for years
      2. Periodic estate
      3. Estate at will
      4. Tenancy at sufferance
II. Methods of Holding Title
   A. In severalty
   B. Concurrently
      1. Tenancy in common
      2. Joint tenancy
      3. Community property
   C. Forms of business ownership
      1. Partnerships
      2. Corporations
      3. Limited liability companies
      4. Joint ventures
      5. Trusts
   D. Condominiums and cooperatives

Key Terms

Estate
Freehold Estate
Leasehold Estate
Fee Simple Absolute
Defeasible Fee
Life Estate
Waste
Estate for Years
Periodic Tenancy
Estate at Will
Ownership in Severalty
Tenancyin Common
Joint Tenancy
Right of Survivorship
Community Property
Corporation
Partnership.
Real Estate Investment Trust
Condominium
Cooperative
Timeshare

Real property ownership can take many different forms. An owner typically has full title to the property and full possession of it, but that isn't necessarily the case. An owner may have a more limited interest instead of full title, or may allow someone else (a tenant) to take possession of the property without taking title. In addition, a property may be owned by more than one person at the same time, which is called concurrent ownership. The first part of this chapter explains the various types of ownership interests, and also the types of interests that tenants may have. The second part of this chapter explains concurrent ownership and the different ways co-owners may hold title.

Estates

The word "estate" refers to an interest in land that is or may become possessory. In other words, someone has now, or may have in the future, the right to possess the property—the right to exclusively occupy and use it.

There are several different types of estates, and they are distinguished from one another by differences in duration (how long the estate holder has the right of possession) and time of possession (whether the estate holder has the right to possess the property right now, or not until sometime in the future).

It is important to note that while all estates are interests in land, not every interest in land is an estate. Interests that are not estates are called nonpossessory interests. For example, a mortgage gives a lender a financial interest in the property (a lien), but this interest is not an estate, because it is not a possessory interest. Nonpossessory interests are covered in Chapter 4.

Estates fall into two categories:

1. freehold estates, and
2. leasehold (less-than-freehold) estates.

A **freehold** estate is an interest in real property that has an indeterminable (not fixed or certain) duration. The holder of such an estate is usually referred to as an owner. All other possessory interests are leasehold (less-than-freehold) estates.

Fig. 2.1 Characteristics of Estates

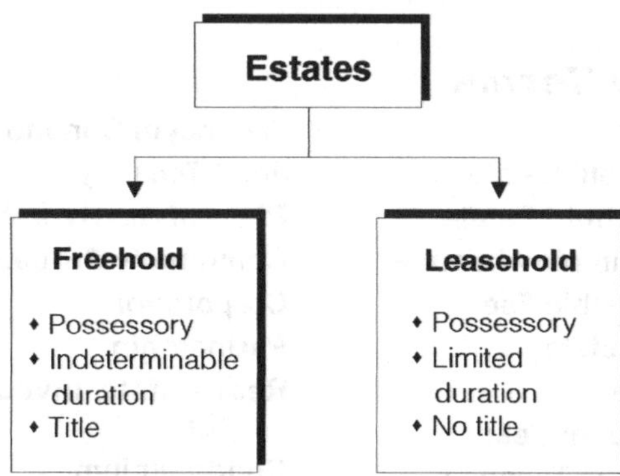

A **leasehold** estate has a limited duration (a one-year lease is an example). The holder of a leasehold estate is referred to as a tenant; a tenant has possession of the property but not title.

Freehold Estates

The freehold estate got its name back in the Middle Ages; it originally referred to the holdings of a freeman under the English feudal system. Freehold estates are subdivided into fee simple estates and life estates.

Fee Simple Estates. The fee simple estate (also called the "fee," the "fee simple," or the "fee simple absolute") is the greatest estate that can exist in land, the highest and most complete form of ownership. It is of potentially infinite duration and represents the whole "bundle of rights."

Fee simple estates are freely transferable and inheritable, so a fee simple is sometimes referred to as an **estate of inheritance**. A fee simple estate has no set termination point, and theoretically can be owned forever by the titleholder and his heirs.

Defeasible Fee Estates. A fee simple estate may be qualified when it is transferred from one owner to another. For example, in a deed, the grantor may specify that the grantee's estate will continue only as long as a certain condition is met, or until a certain event occurs.

> **Example**: Able conveys a parcel of land to his church, "so long as the land is used for church purposes, and if it is no longer used for church purposes it shall revert back to me or my heirs."

This type of qualification creates a **defeasible fee** estate (also known as a qualified fee, base fee, or conditional fee). The owner of a defeasible fee holds the same interest as the owner of a fee simple estate, but the defeasible fee holder's interest is subject to termination.

There are two types of defeasible fees: fee simple determinable, and fee simple subject to a condition subsequent. A **fee simple determinable** ends automatically if the condition is violated; the property reverts back to the grantor without legal action by the grantor. Language in a deed creating a fee simple determinable includes a phrase such as "so long as," "during," or "until." A **fee simple subject to a condition subsequent** doesn't end automatically when the condition is breached.

The grantor must take some action to terminate the estate. This type of estate is created by the words "if" or "on the condition that."

Life Estates. An estate for life, or life estate, is a freehold estate whose duration is limited to the lifetime of a specified person or persons.

> **Example**: Noel gives a parcel of property to Beatrice for her lifetime, calling for a reversion of title to Noel upon Beatrice's death. Beatrice is the life tenant (holder of the life estate), and the duration of the life estate is measured by her lifetime.

The measuring life may be that of the life tenant (as in the example above, where Beatrice's life is the measuring life) or it may be the life of another person. If it is for the life of another person, it may be known as a life estate **pur autre vie** (which is French for "for another life").

Suppose Angie gives a parcel of property to Howard for the life of Charlie. Howard has a life estate that will end when Charlie dies.

The fee simple estate is a perpetual estate; the life estate is a lesser estate because it is limited in duration. In granting a life estate, a fee simple owner transfers only part of what she owns, so there must be something left over after the life estate terminates. What remains is either an estate in reversion or an estate in remainder. These are known as future interests.

Estate in Reversion. If the grantor states that the property will revert back to the grantor at the end of the measuring life, the grantor holds an estate in reversion. The grantor has a future possessory interest in the property. Upon the death of the person whose life the estate is measured by, the property will revert to the grantor (who is sometimes called the **reversioner**) or her heirs.

Estate in Remainder. If the grantor states that the property should go to a person other than the grantor upon the death of the life tenant, that other person has an estate in remainder and is called the **remainderman.** The only difference between reversion and remainder estates is that the former is held by the grantor and the latter by a third party. (If the grantor doesn't name a remainderman, an estate in reversion is created.) The interest that will pass to the designated party on the death of the life tenant is a fee simple estate.

Fig. 2.2 Types of Estates

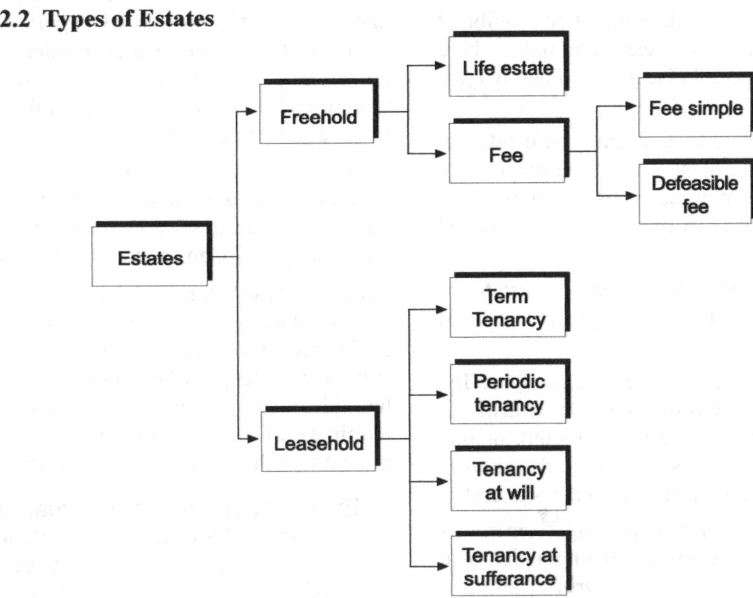

Rights and Duties of Life Tenants. A life tenant has the same rights as a fee simple owner, including the right to profits or rents, and the right to lease or mortgage the property. A life tenant also has the same duties as a fee simple owner: to pay taxes, assessments, and liens. A life tenant has certain additional duties, because someone else has a future interest in the property:

- A life tenant can't commit **waste**, which means that the life tenant must not engage in acts that will permanently damage the property and harm the interests of the reversionary or remainder estate.
- A life tenant must allow reasonable inspection of the property by the remainderman, to check the property for possible waste.

The life tenant may transfer or lease his interest in the property. But it should be noted that the life tenant can give, sell, or lease only that which he owns. In other words, a lease given by a life tenant will terminate upon the death of the person designated as the measuring life. The lease need not be honored by a remainderman. Similarly, a mortgage on a life estate loses its status as a valid lien upon the death of the person named as the measuring life (for this reason, a bank isn't likely to loan very much with only a life estate as security).

Leasehold Estates

Less-than-freehold estates are more commonly called **leasehold estates.** The holder of a leasehold estate is the tenant; the tenant does not own the property, but rather has a right to exclusive possession of the property for a specified period.

The leasehold is created with a **lease.** The parties to a lease are the **landlord (lessor)**, who is the owner of the property, and the **tenant (lessee)**, the party with the right of possession.

The lease creates the relationship of landlord and tenant. It grants the tenant the right of exclusive possession, with a reversion of the possessory rights to the landlord at the end of the tenancy. The lease is a contract, and its provisions are interpreted under contract law as well as landlord-tenant law. Although it creates an interest in real property, the lease itself is classified as personal property.

Landlord-tenant law is covered in Chapter 16. Here we'll just introduce the basic characteristics of the different types of leaseholds. There are four types:

1. the estate for years (term tenancy),
2. the periodic estate (periodic tenancy),
3. the estate at will (tenancy at will), and
4. the tenancy at sufferance.

Estate for Years. An estate for years, also called a term tenancy, is a lease for a fixed term. The name is misleading, because the duration doesn't have to be a year or a period of years; it can be any fixed period, as long as the duration is agreed on in advance.

> **Example:** Gwen rents a cabin in the mountains from Clark for a period from June 1 through September 15. Gwen has an estate for years because the rental term is fixed.

An estate for years can be created only by express agreement. As a general rule, this type of tenancy terminates automatically when the lease term expires; neither party has to give the other notice of termination. In spite of that rule, however, many lease agreements require the terminating party to give notice anyway.

Also, in certain jurisdictions (a few states and various cities around the country), a residential landlord might be prohibited from evicting a tenant at the end of the lease term unless there is "just cause" for the eviction. We'll discuss Washington's just cause law shortly.

A landlord or tenant who wants to terminate an estate for years before the term ends may do so only if the other party has breached the lease agreement or else consents to the early termination. Termination of a lease by mutual consent is called **surrender**.

Unless the lease includes a no-assignment clause, an estate for years is assignable—that is, the tenant can assign her leasehold interest to another person.

Periodic Estate. A periodic estate, more commonly called a periodic tenancy, has no fixed termination date. It lasts for a specific period (for example, one year, one month, or one week) and continues for successive similar periods (another year, month, or week) until one of the parties decides to end it.

Unlike an estate for years, which generally terminates automatically, a periodic tenancy renews itself automatically at the end of each period, unless one party gives written notice of termination to the other before a deadline specified by law or in the lease (for example, a certain number of days before the end of the month). If neither party gives notice by the deadline, the tenancy continues for an additional period.

Like an estate for years, a periodic tenancy is assignable unless assignment is prohibited by the terms of the lease agreement.

Residential Just Cause Requirement. In 2021 the Washington legislature passed a just cause eviction law that largely eliminates a residential landlord's ability to end a periodic tenancy at any time by giving notice to the tenant. Under the statute, a residential month-to-month tenant can stay on indefinitely unless there is just cause (a legitimate reason) for evicting the tenant. **Just cause** for eviction exists if: 1) the tenant has committed a significant breach of the lease; or 2) the unit is being taken off the rental market (because the building is going to be sold, substantially remodeled, or demolished, for example, or because the landlord or a family member plans to occupy the unit).

On the other hand, Washington's just cause requirement may or may not apply to a residential tenancy under a fixed-term lease (an estate for years). These tenancies can still be terminated when the term expires without providing a reason, as long as the landlord has complied with statutory rules about the length of the lease term and notice of termination. (Thus, residential landlords can avoid the just cause requirement by using fixed-term leases instead of month-to-month tenancies.) Otherwise, unless there is just cause for eviction, the tenant must be offered either a new fixed-term lease or else a month-to-month tenancy. (Note that this is only a brief summary of a complicated statute; residential landlords or tenants who need to know whether the just cause requirement applies to their particular situation should consult an attorney.)

Estate at Will. An estate at will is usually created after a periodic tenancy or estate for years has terminated. This estate is created with the agreement of both parties and can be terminated at the will of either.

An estate at will often arises when a lease has expired and the parties are in the process of negotiating the terms of a new lease. The term of the tenancy is indefinite; it will continue until either party gives proper notice of termination. However, as with periodic tenancies, a residential landlord may be required to have just cause to terminate a tenancy at will.

Note, however, that unlike an estate for years or periodic tenancy, which are not affected by the death of the landlord or tenant, an estate at will automatically expires upon the death of either party. Also, an estate at will is not assignable.

Tenancy at Sufferance. The tenancy at sufferance is the lowest type of estate; in fact, though it's sometimes called an "estate at sufferance," technically it isn't an estate at all. In a tenancy at sufferance, a tenant who came into possession of the property lawfully, under a valid lease, holds over after the tenancy has terminated. The tenant continues in possession of the premises, but without the consent of the landlord.

> **Example:** Joe has a one-year lease with Landlord Hassad. At the end of the term, Joe refuses to move out. Joe initially obtained possession of the property legally (under a valid lease), but he is remaining on the property without Hassad's consent.

Tenancy at sufferance is mainly a way to distinguish between someone who entered into possession of the property legally but no longer has a right to possession, and a trespasser, who never had permission to enter the land in the first place. Since a tenant at sufferance does not hold an estate (a possessory interest), the landlord isn't required to give the tenant notice of termination. Even so, the tenant can't simply be forced off the property; the landlord must follow proper legal procedures for eviction.

Methods of Holding Title

Title to real property may be held by one person, which is ownership in severalty, or by two or more persons at the same time, which is concurrent ownership.

Ownership in Severalty

When one person holds title to property individually, the property is owned in severalty. The term is derived from the word "sever," which means to keep separate or apart. A sole owner is free to dispose of the property at will. Real property may be owned in severalty by a natural person (a human being) or an artificial person (such as a corporation, a city, or a state).

Concurrent Ownership

Concurrent ownership (also called co-ownership) exists where two or more people simultaneously share title to a piece of property. There are several forms of concurrent ownership, each with distinctive legal characteristics. Under Washington law, three forms of concurrent ownership are recognized:

- tenancy in common,
- joint tenancy, and
- community property.

Tenancy in Common. Tenancy in common is the most basic form of concurrent ownership. In a tenancy in common, two or more individuals each have an **undivided interest** in a single piece of property. This means that each tenant in common has a right to share possession of the whole property, not just a specified part of it. This is referred to as unity of possession.

Tenants in common may have equal or unequal interests. For example, if three people own property as tenants in common, they might each have a one-third interest in the property, or one of them might have a one-half interest in the property and each of the other two a one-quarter interest. But no matter how small a tenant in common's ownership interest is, he is still entitled to share possession of the whole property.

A tenant in common may deed his interest to someone else without obtaining the consent of the other co-tenants. A tenant in common may also mortgage his interest without the others' consent. At death, a tenant in common's interest is transferred according to the terms of his will, or to his legal heirs.

Termination of Tenancy in Common. Co-tenants who want to terminate a tenancy in common may sell their interests to a single owner. If the co-tenants can't agree to a sale, termination of a tenancy in common may be forced through a **partition suit**, a legal action that divides the interests in the property and destroys the unity of possession. If possible, a court will actually divide the land into separate parcels. If the property cannot be divided fairly, the court will order the property to be sold and the proceeds divided among the tenants based on their fractional interests.

Joint Tenancy. The second form of concurrent ownership is joint tenancy. In a joint tenancy, two or more individuals are joint and equal owners of the property. The key feature that distinguishes joint tenancy from tenancy in common is the **right of survivorship**: on the death of one of the joint tenants, her interest automatically passes by operation of law to the other joint tenant(s). To create a joint tenancy, the "four unities of title" must exist. These unities are:

- unity of interest,
- unity of title,
- unity of time, and
- unity of possession.

Fig. 2.3 Tenancy in Common vs. joint Tenancy: Death of a Co-Owner

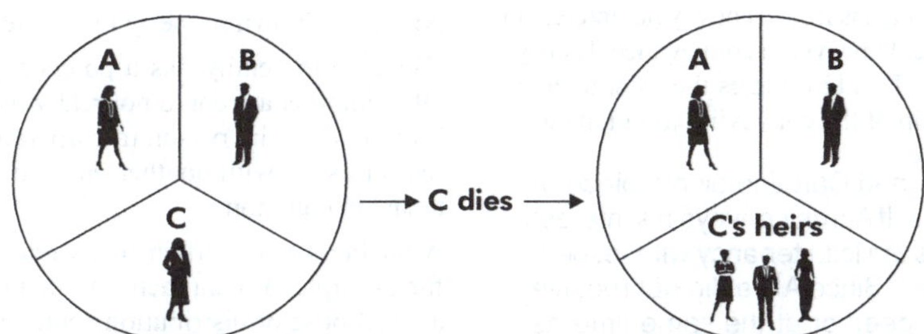

A, B, and C owned property as tenants in common. Then C died, and her heirs inherited her share of the property. Now the property is owned by A, B, and C's heirs as tenants in common.

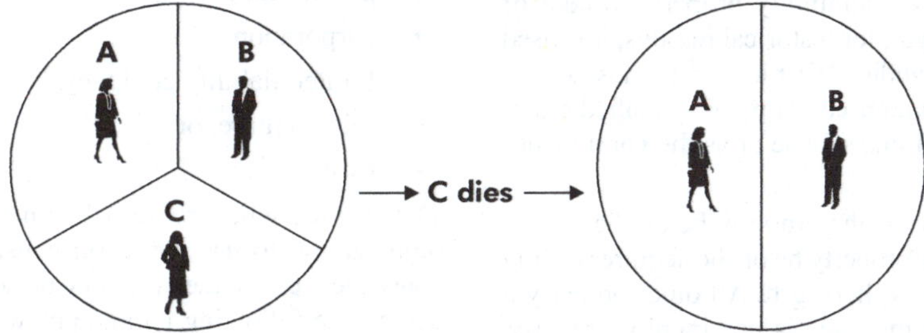

A, B, and C owned property as joint tenants, each with a 1/3 interest. Then C died. Now, by the right of survivorship A and B own the property as joint tenants, each with a 1/2 interest.

These four unities signify that each joint tenant has an equal interest in the property (unity of interest), that each received title through the same deed or will (unity of title), which was executed and delivered at a single time (unity of time), and that each is entitled to undivided possession of the property (unity of possession). If any one of these unities does not exist when the tenancy is created, a joint tenancy is not established.

Since title passes directly to the other joint tenant(s) upon the death of one joint tenant (because of the right of survivorship), property held in joint tenancy can't be willed. The heirs of a deceased joint tenant have no interest in the joint tenancy property.

> **Example:** Jim, Sue, and Bill own property as joint tenants. Jim dies. Sue and Bill now own the entire property fifty-fifty. Jim's heirs cannot make any legal claim to the property. On his death, it ceased to be a part of his estate. Accordingly, the property is not subject to probate and could not have been willed by Jim.

Avoiding the delay and cost of probate proceedings is the primary advantage of joint tenancy. The main disadvantage is that a joint tenant gives up the right to dispose of his interest in the property by will.

Termination of Joint Tenancy. Like a tenancy in common, a joint tenancy can be terminated through a partition suit. But a joint tenancy also terminates automatically if any one of the four unities is destroyed. A joint tenant is free to convey her interest in the property to someone else. However, a conveyance destroys the unities of time and title. This terminates the joint tenancy with respect to the ownership of the conveying joint tenant.

> **Example:** Aaron, Bob, and Caroline own a piece of property as joint tenants. If Aaron conveys his interest to Alice, that terminates the joint tenancy with respect to that one-third interest. Since Alice did not receive title through the same deed or at the same time as Bob and Caroline, Alice can't be a joint tenant. Bob and Caroline are still joint tenants in relation to one another, but Alice holds title as a tenant in common.

Community Property. The community property system of ownership is of Spanish origin; for historical reasons, it is used in several western states, including Washington. In those states, all the property owned by a married couple is classified either as the **separate property** of one spouse or as the **community property** of both spouses.

A spouse's separate property is the property he or she owned before the marriage, and any property he or she acquires during the marriage by inheritance, will, or gift. All other property a spouse acquires during the marriage is community property. For example, property purchased with wages earned by either spouse during the marriage is community property. Each spouse has an undivided one-half interest in the community property.

The separate property of either spouse is free from the interests and claims of the other spouse; it may be transferred or encumbered without the approval or interference of the other spouse. A conveyance or encumbrance of community real property, however, requires the approval of both spouses. (With certain exceptions, such as household furnishings, community personal property can be transferred without spousal consent.)

In some states that do not have a community property system, married couples may hold title to property as tenants by the entirety. A **tenancy by the entirety** is quite similar to a joint tenancy, but there are some differences. A tenancy by the entirety can only be created by a married couple, and (unlike a joint tenant) a tenant by the entirety cannot convey his or her interest without the other tenant's consent. Tenancy by the entirety is not recognized in community property states such as Washington, and it has been abolished in a number of other states as well.

Forms of Business Ownership

The discussion so far has focused on real property ownership by individuals, whether in severalty or concurrently. Real property can also be owned by associations or organizations, such as businesses, nonprofit groups, private clubs, and so on.

The law generally regards this type of entity as an "artificial person" that can enter into contracts, incur debts and liabilities, and own property in much the same way that a natural person can. There are certain differences, however; for instance, an artificial person can't own property in joint tenancy.

Because the entity has a potentially perpetual existence, the other joint tenant could not really have a right of survivorship. So if an artificial person (a corporation, for example) co-owns real property with another entity or person, it holds title as a tenant in common.

A business entity often owns real property for its own use; for example, a manufacturing company might own a factory, a warehouse or distribution center, and an office building that serves as its headquarters. It's also very common for businesses to own real property as an investment.

A business can be organized as a:

- partnership,
- corporation,
- limited liability company,
- joint venture, or
- trust.

The parties who create a business decide which form of organization to use based on considerations such as the tax consequences and the investors' personal liability for the entity's debts. The following paragraphs will compare these different forms of business organization.

Partnerships. A partnership is generally defined as an association of two or more persons, to carry on, as co-owners, a business for profit. There are two types of partnerships: general and limited.

A **general partnership** is formed by contract. The contract does not have to be in writing, although a written agreement is always advisable. Aspects of the partnership that are addressed in the partnership agreement are governed by that agreement. Any aspect not addressed by the agreement is governed by Washington's Uniform Partnership Act.

The partners in a general partnership all share in the profits and management of the partnership. Unless otherwise agreed, each one has an equal share of the profits and losses, and each has an equal voice in management and control of the business. The partners have **unlimited liability**, which means that each partner can be held personally liable for the debts and obligations of the partnership.

Also, each partner is both a principal for and an agent of the general partnership for business purposes. Thus, the authorized acts of one partner (including the execution of legal documents) are binding on the partnership. A partnership is a fiduciary relationship; all the partners have a duty to act with utmost good faith toward one another. (See Chapter 7 for a discussion of agency.)

In general, property acquired for the partnership's business is **partnership property**. Title to partnership property may be held in the partnership's name. Alternatively, it may be held in the name of one or more of the partners, as long as the deed makes reference to the partnership.

Unless otherwise agreed, each partner has an equal right to possess and use all partnership property for partnership purposes. However, a partner is not a co-owner of the partnership property and has no transferable interest in it.

When title to partnership property is held in the partnership's name, it must also be conveyed in the partnership's name. Since each partner is an agent for the partnership, any authorized partner can sign the deed.

A **limited partnership** is a partnership with one or more general partners and one or more limited partners. Limited partnerships must conform to the statutory requirements of the Uniform Limited Partnership Act. To establish a limited partnership, a certificate of limited partnership must be filed with the secretary of state's office.

The general partners in a limited partnership have unlimited liability for the partnership's debts and obligations. By contrast, the limited partners have **limited liability**: they cannot be held personally liable for the partnership's debts and obligations. The Uniform Limited Partnership Act originally allowed only the general partners to manage or control the partnership's business; limited partners would lose their limited liability if they participated in management or control. The act now allows limited partners full participation without affecting their limited liability.

Corporations. A corporation is owned by its shareholders, individuals who purchase shares of stock in the company as an investment. The shareholders have limited liability. A plaintiff with a claim against the corporation can sue only the corporation itself, not the shareholders. Thus, the most that shareholders can lose is the value of their investment in the company.

Corporate property is owned by the corporation in severalty, not by the shareholders; they own only the right to share in the profits of the business. The corporation is governed by a board of directors, which appoints corporate officers to run the business.

Shares in a corporation are **securities**. A security is an investment interest; it gives an investor a financial interest in an enterprise without allowing direct managerial control. (Interests in a limited partnership or limited liability company may also be classified as securities.) Sales of securities are regulated by the federal Securities and Exchange Commission. They may also be subject to state securities regulations, commonly called "blue sky laws." Generally, only licensed securities dealers may sell securities.

The main drawback to the corporate form of organization is the double taxation that applies to all but the smallest corporations. First the corporation must pay income taxes on any profits it generates. Then if the profits are distributed to the shareholders as dividends, the same money is taxed again as the personal income of the shareholders. Business investors can avoid double taxation by choosing a different form of organization, such as a partnership, a limited liability company, or a trust.

Limited Liability Companies. A limited liability company (LLC) combines many of the advantages of a corporation with many of the advantages of a partnership.

To create an LLC, one or more business owners (called members) enter into an LLC agreement and file a certificate of formation with the state. In their agreement, members can specify virtually any manner of allocating income, losses, or appreciation among themselves.

LLC members have the flexibility of a general partnership when it comes to managing the business. Certain members may be appointed to manage the company, or all of the members may manage the company. All managing members can bind the LLC with their actions. However, unlike general partners in a partnership, managing members in an LLC are not personally liable for the company's debts and obligations. LLC members have the same type of limited liability enjoyed by corporate stockholders or limited partners.

As explained above, a major disadvantage of the corporate form of ownership is the double taxation imposed on corporations and their stockholders. In contrast, income earned by an LLC is taxed at only one level—the member level. LLC income is taxed as the personal income of each member, in the same manner as partnership income.

Joint Ventures. A joint venture is similar to a partnership, except that it is created for a single business transaction or for a series of individual transactions. It is not intended to be an ongoing business of indefinite duration. Joint ventures are generally governed by the same rules as partnerships. An example of a joint venture would be a property owner, an architect, and a building contractor joining together to design and construct a particular building.

Trusts. In a trust, one or more trustees manage property for the benefit of one or more **beneficiaries**. A trust instrument vests title to the property in the trustees, who have only the powers expressly granted in the instrument.

Trusts are sometimes used as a form of business ownership. One example is a **real estate investment trust** (REIT). Investors form REITs to finance large real estate projects. REITs are not subject to double taxation if they meet certain requirements set by the IRS. For example, a real estate investment trust must have at least 100 investors and derive at least 75% of its income from real estate-related sources.

As long as a qualifying REIT distributes at least 90% of its income to its investors, the REIT pays income taxes only on the earnings it retains, avoiding double taxation. Yet the investors, like corporate shareholders, are shielded from liability for the REIT's debts. REIT shares are securities, subject to federal regulation.

Condominiums and Cooperatives

Condominiums and cooperatives provide alternatives to ownership of a traditional single-family home. In a sense, they combine aspects of individual ownership with aspects of concurrent ownership.

Condominiums. In Washington, the development and management of condominium properties are governed by state statute. For condominiums created after July 1, 2018, the applicable statute is the Washington Uniform Common Interest Ownership Act. (For condos created before that date, the applicable statute in most circumstances is the Condominium Act, unless the owners association votes to adopt the newer statute.)

Someone who buys a unit in a condominium owns the unit itself in severalty, but shares ownership of the common elements with other unit owners as tenants in common. **Common elements** (also called common areas) are aspects of the condominium property that all of the unit owners have the right to use, such as the driveway or the elevator.

Some features may be designated as **limited common elements**, which are reserved for the owners of certain units. For example, an assigned parking space would be a limited common element. A feature such as a balcony, which is designed for use with a particular unit but is outside of the unit itself, would also be a limited common element.

Each unit owner obtains separate financing to buy her unit, receives an individual property tax bill, and may acquire a title insurance policy for the unit. A lien can attach to a single unit, so that the unit can be foreclosed on separately, without affecting the other units in the condominium. The sale of a unit ordinarily doesn't require the approval of the other unit owners. The seller's interest in the common elements passes to the buyer.

All the unit owners in a condominium automatically belong to a homeowners association (also called a unit owners association or condo association). The association elects a board of directors to manage the condominium, and also votes on other major issues. For example, monthly fees are usually imposed on each unit owner to cover maintenance costs for the common elements. (Note that subdivisions of townhomes or single-family homes may also have homeowners associations.)

A condominium usually involves one or more multifamily residential buildings, but commercial and industrial properties can also be developed as condominiums. To establish a condominium, the developer must record a condominium plan and declaration. A large condominium project may be regulated as a subdivision.

Sometimes the owner of an apartment complex will find it profitable to change the complex into a condominium. This process, called **conversion**, is regulated to protect renters who will be displaced.

Cooperatives. In a cooperative, ownership of the property is vested in a single entity—usually a corporation. The residents of the cooperative building own shares in the corporation, rather than owning the property itself. They are tenants with long-term proprietary leases on their units; they do not hold title to their units.

To establish a cooperative, the corporation gets a mortgage loan to buy or construct the building, and other funds are raised by selling shares in the corporation to prospective tenants. The monthly fee that each tenant pays to the corporation is a pro rata share of the mortgage, taxes, operating expenses, and other debts for the whole property. The cooperative corporation is managed by an elected board of directors.

In many cooperatives, a tenant cannot transfer stock or assign his proprietary lease without the consent of the governing board or a majority of the members. This approval process is used to screen out undesirable tenants; however, discrimination in violation of fair housing laws is not allowed (see Chapter 15).

Differences Between Condominiums and Cooperatives. In a condominium, each unit is owned individually. In a cooperative, a corporation owns the whole project; the tenants own shares in the corporation and have proprietary leases on their units.

In a condominium, each unit owner secures individual financing to buy the unit. In a cooperative, the corporation takes out one blanket loan for the entire project. One advantage of condominiums over cooperatives is that a condominium owner is not responsible for any default on another unit owner's loan. In a cooperative, if one tenant defaults on her share of the mortgage payments, the other tenants must cure the default or risk having the mortgage on the entire project foreclosed. This is also true for tax assessments and other liens.

A condominium owner can usually sell his unit to anyone who can pay for it. In a cooperative, the corporation usually must approve of the proposed tenant.

Timeshares. Sometimes condominium units are offered for sale under a **timeshare** arrangement. Instead of purchasing a unit outright, a timeshare buyer purchases a right to occupy the unit during a particular time slot, or for a certain number of days, each year. Most timeshare condominiums are located in resort areas, where people often want a place to stay for a limited time on a regular basis.

Example: The Garcias like to vacation in Ocean Shores for two weeks every year. Buying a condominium unit there would be expensive and unnecessary, so they decide to buy an interest in a timeshare condominium called the Sea Winds. This entitles them to occupy Unit 6 in the Sea Winds condo every year from July 1 through July 14. Other buyers have the right to occupy Unit 6 during the rest of the year.

The **Washington Timeshare Act** is a consumer protection law that governs the sale of timeshares in this state. It requires timeshare developments to be registered with the Department of Licensing, and also requires people involved in selling timeshares to be registered as **timeshare salespersons.**

Under the Timeshare Act, prospective buyers of timeshare interests must be given a disclosure statement. The law gives buyers a seven-day right of rescission—the right to cancel their purchase and sale agreement within seven days after signing the agreement or receiving the disclosure statement, whichever occurs later.

A real estate licensee is allowed to handle timeshare resales without registering under the Timeshare Act as a timeshare salesperson. The licensee must be acting solely in a brokerage capacity, not selling inventory that she owns herself or that's owned by her firm.

Even though real estate licensees are exempt from the Timeshare Act's registration requirement, they still have to comply with all of the other aspects of the law. For example, they must give buyers a disclosure statement and allow a seven-day right of rescission, just like registered timeshare salespersons.

Chapter Summary

1. An estate is a possessory interest in real property. Someone who has a freehold estate has title to the property and is considered an owner. Someone who has a leasehold (less-than-freehold) estate has possession of the property, but does not have title.
2. Freehold estates include the fee simple absolute, the defeasible fee, and the life estate. A life estate lasts only as long as a specified person is alive; then the property either reverts to the grantor or else passes to the remainderman. Leasehold estates include the estate for years, the periodic estate, and the estate at will. (The tenancy at sufferance, which arises when a tenant holds over without the landlord's permission, is not really an estate.)
3. Title to real property can be held in severalty or concurrently. In Washington, the methods of concurrent ownership are joint tenancy, tenancy in common, and community property. The distinguishing feature of joint tenancy is the right of survivorship.
4. Real property can be owned by a business entity, which may be organized as a general or limited partnership, a corporation, a limited liability company, a joint venture, or a real estate investment trust.
5. In a condominium, each unit is separately owned, and all the unit owners own the common elements as tenants in common. A cooperative is owned by a corporation; a resident owns shares in the corporation, and has a proprietary lease for a particular unit. In a timeshare arrangement, a buyer purchases the right to occupy a condominium unit for a specified period or number of days each year.

Key Terms

Estate—An interest in land that is or may become possessory.

Freehold estate—A possessory interest that has an indeterminable duration.

Leasehold estate—A possessory interest that has a limited duration.

Fee simple absolute—The highest and most complete form of ownership, which is of potentially infinite duration.

Defeasible fee—A fee simple estate that carries a qualification, so that ownership may revert to the grantor if a specified event occurs or a condition is not met. Also called a qualified fee.

Life estate—A freehold estate whose duration is measured by the lifetime of one or more persons.

Waste—Permanent damage to real property caused by the party in possession, harming the interests of other estate holders.

Estate for years—A leasehold estate with a fixed term. Also called a term tenancy.

Periodic tenancy—A leasehold estate that continues from period to period, such as a month-to-month tenancy.

Estate at will—A leasehold estate without a definite termination date that may arise after a periodic tenancy or an estate for years terminates. Also called a tenancy at will.

Ownership in severalty—Sole ownership of property.

Tenancy in common—Joint ownership where there is no right of survivorship.

Joint tenancy—Joint ownership with right of survivorship.

Right of survivorship—The right by which the surviving joint tenant(s) acquire another joint tenant's interest in the property upon her death.

Community property—Property owned jointly by a married couple (in Washington and other community property states).

Corporation—A business entity owned by shareholders, governed by a board of directors, and managed by corporate officers; the shareholders have limited liability.

Partnership—An association of two or more persons to carry on a business for profit as co-owners.

Real estate investment trust—A real estate investment business that qualifies for tax advantages if certain requirements are met.

Condominium—A property that has been developed so that individual unit owners have separate title to their own units, but share ownership of the common elements as tenants in common.

Cooperative—A property that is owned by a corporation and tenanted by shareholders in the corporation who have proprietary leases for their units.

Timeshare—An interest in a condominium unit that entitles the holder to occupy the unit during a specified time slot or number of days every year.

Chapter Quiz

1. **A fee simple title in real estate is of indefinite duration, and can be:**
   a) freely transferred
   b) encumbered
   c) inherited
   d) All of the above

2. **A conveyance of title with the condition that the land shall not be used for the sale of intoxicating beverages creates a:**
   a) less-than-freehold estate
   b) defeasible fee
   c) life estate
   d) reservation

3. **Lewis was given real property for the term of his natural life. Which of the following statements is incorrect?**
   a) Lewis has a freehold estate
   b) Lewis has a fee simple estate
   c) Lewis is the life tenant
   d) If Lewis leases the property to someone else, the lease will terminate if Lewis dies during its term

4. **Baker sold a property to Lane, but reserved a life estate for himself and remained in possession. Later Baker sells his life estate to Clark and surrenders possession to Clark. Lane then demands immediate possession as fee owner. Which of the following is true?**
   a) Lane is entitled to possession
   b) Clark should sue Baker for return of the purchase price
   c) Baker is liable for damages
   d) Clark can retain possession during Baker's lifetime

5. **Cobb owns a property in fee simple; he deeds it to Smith for the life of Jones. Which of the following is true?**
   a) Jones holds a life estate; Smith holds an estate in reversion
   b) Smith holds a life estate; Cobb holds an estate in remainder
   c) Smith holds a fee simple estate; Jones holds a life estate
   d) Smith holds a life estate; Cobb holds an estate in reversion

6. **Johnston, a life tenant, decides to cut down all the trees on the property and sell them for timber. Mendez, the remainderman, can stop Johnston's actions because:**
   a) a life tenant is never permitted to cut down any trees on the property for any reason
   b) a life tenant cannot commit waste
   c) Mendez's interest is superior to Johnston's, since it is a possessory estate
   d) None of the above; Mendez has no legal grounds for stopping Johnston

7. **Jones and Adams signed an agreement for the use and possession of real estate, for a period of 120 days. This is a/an:**
   a) estate for years
   b) estate at sufferance
   c) periodic tenancy
   d) estate at will

8. **The four unities of title, time, interest, and possession are necessary for a:**
   a) tenancy in common
   b) partnership
   c) mortgage
   d) joint tenancy

9. **Which of the following is incorrect? Joint tenants always have:**
   a) equal rights to possession of the property
   b) the right to will good title to heirs
   c) the right of survivorship
   d) equal interests in the property

10. **A, B, and C own property as joint tenants. C dies and B sells her interest in the property to D. The property is now owned:**
    a) as joint tenants by A, D, and C's widow E, his sole heir
    b) by A and D as joint tenants
    c) by A and D as tenants in common
    d) None of the above

11. **Asher and Blake own real property together. Asher has a one-third interest and Blake has a two-thirds interest. How do they hold title?**
    a) Community property
    b) Tenancy at will
    c) Joint tenancy
    d) Tenancy in common

12. All of the following statements about a corporation are true, except:

a) A corporation has a potentially perpetual existence
b) Each shareholder is individually liable for the corporation's acts
c) Corporations are subject to double taxation
d) A corporation can enter into contracts in essentially the same way as an individual person

13. A real estate investment trust must:

a) receive at least 75% of its income from real estate
b) have at least 150 participating investors
c) make sure all investors accept liability for the trust's acts
d) be incorporated in the state in which it does business

14. In a condominium:

a) individual units are owned in severalty, while common elements are owned in joint tenancy
b) individual units are owned in joint tenancy, while common elements are owned in severalty
c) individual units are owned in severalty, while common elements are owned in tenancy in common
d) the entire building is owned in tenancy in common, with residents owning shares

15. A unit in a cooperative is owned:

a) in severalty by the resident of the unit
b) by the corporation that owns the building; the residents own shares in the corporation
c) by all residents of the building as tenants in common
d) by all residents of the building as limited partners

Chapter 3:

Transfer of Real Property

Key Terms

Alienation	**Eminent Domain**
Deed	**Condemnation**
Warranty Deed	**Adverse Possession**
Quitclaim Deed	**Constructive Notice**
Acknowledgment	**Title Search**
Will	**Chain of Title**
Intestate	**Abstract of Title**
Escheat	**Title Insurance**
Dedication	**Title Report**

A property owner may transfer property to someone else by choice, as when an owner deeds property to a buyer or wills it to a friend. Property may also be transferred involuntarily, as in a foreclosure sale or a condemnation. This chapter describes both voluntary and involuntary transfers. It also discusses how and why deeds and other documents are recorded, and how title insurance works.

Title and Alienation

A person who owns property is said to have **title** to it. The process of transferring title to real property (transferring ownership) from one party to another is called **alienation**. Alienation may be either voluntary or involuntary. It's voluntary when a property owner intentionally transfers the property to someone else. It's involuntary when the transfer happens without any action by the owner, which can be the result of rules of law, occupancy (adverse possession), or natural forces.

Voluntary Alienation

Title to a piece of real property can be voluntarily transferred to a new owner by patent, deed, or will.

Patents

Title to all real property originates with the sovereign government. The government holds absolute title to all the land within its boundaries, except what it grants to various other entities or persons. Title to land passes from the government to a private party by a document known as a **patent**. The patent is the ultimate source of title for all the land under private ownership.

Deeds

The most common form of voluntary alienation is transfer by deed. A deed is a legal document that an owner of real property (called the **grantor** in the deed) uses to transfer all or part of his interest in the property to another party, the **grantee**. The process of transferring title to real property by deed is known as conveyance: a grantor conveys real property to a grantee by means of a deed.

A deed (that is, the legal document) should not be referred to as the property's title or the seller's title. The document used to transfer ownership of a motor vehicle is called the title, but in the real estate context "title" is an abstract concept, not a document.

Types of Deeds. There are many different types of deeds. The ones used most often in Washington are the warranty deed, special warranty deed, quitclaim deed, trustee's deed, and deed executed under court order.

Warranty Deed. The warranty deed (also known as the general warranty deed) gives the greatest protection to a real estate buyer. Under a warranty deed, the grantor makes five basic promises, or covenants, to the grantee. These covenants warrant against defects in the title that arose either before or during the grantor's period of ownership (tenure). When a statutory warranty deed form is used, the covenants are implied; they do not have to be expressly stated in the deed.

The first covenant is called the **covenant of seisin**. Seisin means peaceable possession under color of title. Color of title means a good faith belief in ownership. So the covenant of seisin promises that the grantor actually owns the property interest she is transferring to the grantee.

The second covenant is the **covenant of right to convey**. The grantor promises she has the power to make the conveyance. In other words, the grantor either has title to the interest, or is an agent of the owner with the authority to transfer the interest.

The **covenant against encumbrances** warrants that the property is not burdened by any undisclosed easement, lien, or other right of a third party. If such encumbrances do exist, they must be listed in the deed.

The fourth covenant is the **covenant of quiet enjoyment**. This covenant promises that the grantee's possession of the property will not be threatened by any lawful claim made by a third party. It does not protect the grantee from claims that have no legal basis, called spurious claims.

The final covenant in the warranty deed is the **covenant of warranty**. This is a promise that the grantor will defend the grantee's title against claims by third parties that existed when the conveyance was made.

Special Warranty Deed. The special warranty deed contains the same covenants found in the general warranty deed, but the scope of the covenants is limited to defects that arose during the grantor's tenure. The grantor makes no assurances regarding defects that may have existed before he obtained title. This type of deed is often used by fiduciaries who hold land only temporarily and do not want to assume the level of liability imposed by a general warranty deed.

A warranty deed (general or special) conveys the "after-acquired title" of the grantor. This means that if the grantor's title was defective at the time of transfer, but the grantor later acquires a more perfect title, the additional interest passes automatically to the grantee under the original deed.

> **Example:** Warner conveyed her property to Meyers on June 1, by a warranty deed. However, Warner did not have valid title to the property on June 1 because she held title under a forged deed. On August 12, Warner received good title to the property under a properly executed deed. Meyers automatically acquired good title to the property on August 12.

Bargain and Sale Deed. Unlike the types of deeds we've discussed so far, a bargain and sale deed offers a grantee no warranties or covenants. A grantor who executes a bargain and sale deed implies that he owns the property, but doesn't guarantee even that much. This type of deed also will not convey after-acquired title to the grantee. Because of its limitations, bargain and sale deeds are rarely used, usually only in special circumstances.

Quitclaim Deed. The quitclaim deed contains no warranties of any sort, and it does not convey after-acquired title. It conveys only the interest the grantor has when the deed is delivered. It conveys nothing at all if the grantor has no interest at that time. Unlike a bargain and sale deed, it does not even imply that the grantor owns the property. But if the grantor does have an interest in the property, the quitclaim deed will convey it just as well as any other type of deed.

The usual reason for using a quitclaim deed is to cure "clouds" on the title; in such situations, a quitclaim deed may be referred to as a **reformation deed**. A cloud is a title defect, often the result of a technical flaw in an earlier conveyance. Perhaps one of the parties' names was misspelled, or the land was inaccurately described. A quitclaim deed is also used when the grantor is unsure of the validity of her title and wishes to avoid giving any warranties.

> **Example:** Smith holds title by virtue of an inheritance that is being challenged in probate court. If Smith wants to transfer the property, she will probably use a quitclaim deed, because she is not sure that her title is valid.

In a quitclaim deed, words such as "grant" or "convey" should be avoided. The use of these words may imply that the grantor is warranting the title. A quitclaim deed should use only terms such as "release," "remise," or "quitclaim" to describe the transfer.

Fig. 3.1 Warranty Deed

AFTER RECORDING MAIL TO:
Joseph and Hannah Shapiro
3406 N.W. 66th St.
Anytown 99999

Filed for Record at Request of
Acme Escrow Co.
Escrow Number: 001021SHA

Statutory Warranty Deed

Grantor(s): Alan S. Matsumoto
Grantee(s): Joseph R. Shapiro, Hannah L. Shapiro
Abbreviated Legal: Lot 12, Block 8, Jasperson Add., Vol. 10, p. 94
Additional Legal(s) on page: N/A
Assessor's Tax Parcel Number(s): 117600-0720-05

2021031500094

THE GRANTOR Alan S. Matsumoto

for and in consideration of TEN DOLLARS AND OTHER GOOD AND VALUABLE CONSIDERATION

in hand paid, conveys and warrants to Joseph R. Shapiro and Hannah L. Shapiro, a married couple

the following described real estate, situated in the County of Thurston, State of Washington:

LOT 12, BLOCK 8, JASPERSON ADDITION TO THE CITY OF ANYTOWN,
ACCORDING TO THE PLAT THEREOF RECORDED IN VOLUME 10 OF PLATS, PAGE 94,
RECORDS OF THURSTON COUNTY, WASHINGTON.
SITUATE IN THE COUNTY OF THURSTON, STATE OF WASHINGTON.

Dated this 15th day of March, 2021

By *Alan S. Matsumoto* By ________
Alan S. Matsumoto

By ________ By ________

STATE OF WASHINGTON }
County of THURSTON } *SS:*

I certify that I know or have satisfactory evidence that ALAN S. MATSUMOTO

IS the person(s) who appeared before me, and said person(s) acknowledged that HE signed this instrument and acknowledged it to be HIS free and voluntary act for the uses and purposes mentioned in this instrument.

Dated: MARCH 15, 2021

Claire M. Vincent
CLAIRE M. VINCENT
Notary Public in and for the State of WASHINGTON
Residing at FIFE
My appointment expires: 01-16-24

CLAIRE M. VINCENT
STATE OF WASHINGTON
NOTARY --[]-- PUBLIC
MY COMMISSION
EXPIRES 1-16-24

Trustee's Deed. When property is foreclosed under a deed of trust, the trustee conveys the property to the buyer at the foreclosure sale with a trustee's deed. The trustee's deed states that the conveyance is in accordance with the trustee's powers and responsibilities under the deed of trust. (Deeds of trust are discussed in Chapter 10.)

Deeds Executed by Court Order. Court-ordered deeds are used after a court-ordered sale of property. A common example is the sheriff's deed used to transfer property to the highest bidder at a court-ordered foreclosure sale (see Chapter 10). Court-ordered deeds usually state the exact amount of the purchase price approved by the court, and carry no warranties of title.

Requisites of a Valid Deed. A deed will transfer title only if it meets the requirements for validity. To be valid, a deed must:

- be in writing,
- identify the parties,
- be signed by a competent grantor,
- have a living grantee,
- contain words of conveyance (the granting clause), and
- include an adequate description of the property.

In Writing. The **statute of frauds** is a state law that requires certain contracts and other legal transactions to be in writing. With only a few minor exceptions, the statute of frauds applies to any transfer of an interest in real property. An unwritten deed cannot transfer title; it has no legal effect.

Identification of the Parties. Both the grantor and the grantee must be identified in the deed. The name of the grantee is not required, as long as an adequate description is given; for example, "John T. Smith's only sister."

Signed by a Competent Grantor. In addition to requiring a deed to be in writing, the statute of frauds also requires that the deed must be signed by the party who is to be bound by the transfer—the grantor.

A grantor must be legally competent when she signs the deed. This means she must be an adult (generally, at least 18 years old) and of sound mind (not insane or mentally impaired in some other way). If the grantor is not competent, the deed is not valid.

If the grantor can't sign her full name (due to disability or illiteracy), she may sign by making a mark. But a signature by mark must be accompanied by the signatures of witnesses who can attest to the grantor's execution of the deed.

A deed can also be signed by the grantor's **attorney in fact**. The attorney in fact (not necessarily a lawyer) is someone the grantor has appointed to act on her behalf in a document called a **power of attorney**. The power of attorney must specifically authorize the attorney in fact to convey the property.

Deeds from corporations are usually signed by an authorized officer of the corporation.

If there is more than one grantor, all of the grantors must sign the deed. If a prior deed named several grantees, all of them must sign as grantors of a new deed. The signatures of both spouses are required to convey community property (see Chapter 2) or a married person's homestead (see Chapter 4). For this reason, it is a good precaution to state the grantor's marital status in the deed and, if the grantor is married, to have the spouse sign too, even if they believe the spouse does not hold an interest in the property.

Living Grantee. The grantee does not have to be competent in order for the deed to be valid. It is only necessary for the grantee to be alive (or, if the grantee is an entity such as a corporation, legally in existence) and identifiable when the deed is executed. The grantee's signature is not required for a deed to be valid (and, in fact, the grantee rarely signs a deed).

Words of Conveyance. The requirement of words of conveyance, also called a granting clause, is easily satisfied. The single word "grant" or a similar word is sufficient.

Additional technical language should be avoided, since it adds nothing to the validity of the deed and could do more harm than good.

Description of the Property. A deed is not valid unless it contains an adequate description of the property being conveyed. The property's legal description should always be used. (Land description is discussed in Chapter 1.)

Acknowledgment, Delivery, and Acceptance. To successfully convey real property, more than a valid deed is necessary; a proper conveyance also requires acknowledgment, delivery, and acceptance.

Acknowledgment occurs when the grantor swears before a notary public or other official witness that her signature is genuine and voluntary. The witness cannot be a person who has an interest in the transfer. For example, if Grandma deeds her property to Granddaughter, who is a notary public, Granddaughter should not be the one to notarize the deed.

Technically, a deed is valid even if the grantor's signature is not acknowledged. However, an unacknowledged deed cannot be recorded.

To transfer title, a deed must be **delivered** to the grantee. Traditionally, delivery had to occur while the grantor was alive. However, Washington now allows "transfer on death deeds." A transfer on death deed will transfer title to the grantee automatically and without probate when the grantor dies. The grantor can revoke the deed at any time before dying. The deed must state that the transfer will take place on the grantor's death, and it must be recorded.

Acceptance of a valid deed by the grantee completes a property transfer. A grantee may refuse to accept a deed (this occasionally happens because of liability concerns or tax considerations, for example). Note that the grantee may accept delivery through an agent.

> **Example:** Clark deeds his property to Martinez. Clark hands the deed to Martinez's attorney, with the intention of immediately transferring ownership to Martinez. This constitutes delivery to an agent of the grantee, and the title transfer is effective.

Because delivery of a deed involves some complicated legal issues, it's best to consult a real estate lawyer when there is a question concerning delivery.

Non-essential Terms. There are some elements that should be included in a deed, even though they aren't required. A deed should include a **habendum clause** (also called a "to have and to hold" clause), which states the nature of the interest the grantor is conveying. Is the grantor conveying a fee simple absolute or a life estate? Unless otherwise specified, the grantor's entire interest is presumed to pass to the grantee. If there is more than one grantee, the deed should say how they will hold title (for example, whether this is a tenancy in common or a joint tenancy).

Many deeds have an **exclusions and reservations clause**, which is a list of any encumbrances (easements, private restrictions, or liens) that the grantee will be taking title subject to. However, valid encumbrances usually remain in force even if they aren't listed in the deed.

A recital of the purchase price is helpful because it indicates that the transfer is a purchase instead of a gift. (If the transfer were a gift, the grantee might be vulnerable to the claims of the grantor's creditors.) The recital of consideration usually says something like, "for $1.00 and other valuable consideration."

The date of conveyance is standard, but not legally required. Other non-essential items include the grantor's seal, warranties, and technical terminology. "I hereby grant Greenacres Farm to Harry Carter. (signed) Sam Smith" is a valid deed, assuming that Sam Smith is legally competent.

Wills

The will (or testament) is another method of voluntary alienation. In general, a will must be:

1. in writing,
2. signed by the person making it (the testator), and
3. attested to by at least two competent witnesses.

The testator must sign the will in the presence of the witnesses. The witnesses must also sign an acknowledgment that the testator declared the document to be his will.

Although ordinarily a will must be in writing to be valid, under certain circumstances Washington will recognize an oral will, sometimes called a **nuncupative** will. An oral will can be valid if spoken while the testator is on her deathbed with two witnesses present. But if the testator recovers, the will is no longer valid. An oral will can only transfer personal property worth less than $1,000. Real estate can never be transferred by an oral will, since all transfers involving real property must be in writing.

Some states recognize **holographic** wills. A holographic will is an unwitnessed will written entirely in the testator's own handwriting. Washington law does not recognize holographic wills. A holographic will can be valid in Washington only if the testator executes it in a state where holographic wills are valid, then later moves to Washington and does not make out a new will.

Fig. 3.2 Will Terminology

Testator: One who makes a will.

Bequeath: To transfer personal property by will.

Devise: To transfer real property by will.

Executor: Appointed by testator to carry out the instructions in the will.

Administrator: Appointed by the court if no executor was named.

Probate: Procedure to prove a will's validity.

Terminology. The person who makes a will is referred to as the **testator.** A testator **bequeaths** personal property to **legatees** and **devises** real property to **devisees.** An amendment to a will is called a **codicil.** The directions contained in the will are carried out by an **executor** named in the will, under the supervision of the probate court (in Washington, the superior court). **Probate** is the procedure by which a will is proved valid and the testator's directions are carried out. If no executor is named in the will, or there is no will, the court will appoint an **administrator** to manage and distribute the estate.

Probate Procedures. A will does not transfer any interest until the testator has died and the will has been probated. Depending on the procedures followed, the probate court may have to approve all transfers of real property under the will. The court also approves any brokerage commissions pertaining to these transfers.

Involuntary Alienation

We've discussed transferring property voluntarily by patent, deed, and will. Now let's look at the different ways interests in real property can be transferred without any voluntary action on the part of the owner.

Involuntary alienation of real property can be the result of rule of law, adverse possession, or natural forces. Alienation by rule of law includes dedication, intestate succession and escheat, condemnation, and court decisions regarding real property.

Dedication

When a private owner gives real property to the public, it is called dedication. While dedication may be voluntary (for example, a philanthropist might deed land to the city for a park, as a gift), it is usually involuntary. Most often it is required in exchange for a benefit from a public entity.

> **Example:** The county requires a land developer to dedicate land within a new subdivision for public streets. Otherwise, the county will deny permission to subdivide.

This type of involuntary dedication is called **statutory dedication** because it involves compliance with relevant statutory procedures. In the example above, the subdivision statutes require the developer to dedicate land for streets and utilities before a parcel can be subdivided.

A second type of involuntary dedication is called **common law dedication.** The usual requirement for common law dedication is the owner's acquiescence in the public's use of her property for a prolonged period of time. If property has been used by the public for long enough, a government entity can pass an ordinance accepting a common law dedication. The dedication may be treated as a transfer of ownership, or it may only establish a public easement, depending on the circumstances.

> **Example:** Barker owns some lakefront property. For many years, people from town have walked across a corner of the lot to gain access to the lake, and Barker has done nothing to prevent this. Barker's acquiescence to this public use might be considered a common law dedication.

Intestate Succession and Escheat

When someone dies without leaving a will, he is said to have died intestate. The law provides for the division of his property by a process called **intestate succession.** The procedure varies from state to state, but in general the property passes first to the surviving spouse, then to any surviving children, then to various other relatives.

Persons who take property by intestate succession are called **heirs.** Those who receive property by intestate succession are said to have received property by **descent**, rather than by devise or bequest. Intestate succession is supervised by the probate court. The court appoints an administrator, who is responsible for distributing the property in the manner required by the intestate succession statutes.

If a person dies intestate and the probate court can't locate any heirs, then the intestate person's property will pass back to the state according to the law of **escheat.** Since the state is the ultimate source of title to property, it is also the ultimate heir when there are no intervening interested parties. The state may also take ownership of abandoned property through escheat.

Condemnation

The government has the constitutional power to take private property for public use, as long as it pays compensation to the owner of the property. Taking property in this way is called **condemnation.** The government's power to condemn property is called the power of **eminent domain.** Before the power of eminent domain can be exercised, the following requirements must be met:

- The proposed use must be a **public use**—that is, it must benefit the public. For example, taking private property to create a city park or build a freeway would qualify as a public use.
- The condemning entity must pay **just compensation** to the owner. This generally means paying the owner the fair market value of the property.

We'll say more about condemnation in Chapter 5.

Court Decisions

Title to real property can also be transferred by court order in accordance with state statutes and common law precedents. The most common forms of court action affecting title to real property are quiet title actions, suits for partition, and foreclosures.

Quiet Title. A quiet title action is used to remove a cloud on the title when the title cannot be cleared by the more peaceful means of an agreement and a quitclaim deed. In a quiet title action, the court decides questions of property ownership. The result is a binding determination of the various parties' interests in a particular piece of real estate.

> **Example:** A seller has found a potential buyer for his property. However, a title search uncovers a gap in the chain of title: the public record doesn't indicate who owned the property for a certain time period.
>
> The seller brings a quiet title action. The defendants in the action are all persons who have a potential interest in the seller's property. This includes whoever the mystery person was who held title during the gap, even though his or her name is unknown.
>
> The seller asks the court to declare his title valid, thereby "quieting title" to the land. If no defendants appear to challenge the seller's title, the court will grant the seller's request. The buyer can then rely on the court's decision and complete the sale.

Partition. A suit for partition is a means of dividing property owned by more than one person when the co-owners cannot agree on how to divide it. For example, joint tenants may wish to end their joint tenancy but be unable to decide among themselves who gets what portion of the property. The court divides the property for them, and the owners are then bound by the court's decision. In many cases, the court will order the property sold and the proceeds divided among the co-owners.

> **Example:** Green and Black are joint tenants. The joint tenancy property is a vacation home in the mountains. After a serious argument, Green and Black decide they want to terminate their joint tenancy. However, they can't agree on how to divide the property. Green wants to put the property up for sale and divide the proceeds. Black wants to buy out Green's interest and keep the vacation home for himself, but Green says Black isn't offering him enough money.
>
> Finally, Green files a suit for partition. The court orders the vacation home sold and divides the proceeds between Green and Black. Black must abide by this decision, even though he doesn't like it.

Foreclosure. Persons holding liens against real property may force the sale of the property if the debts secured by their liens are not paid. Foreclosure is available for any type of lien that attaches to real property, including mortgages, deeds of trust, construction liens, and judgment liens. (See Chapter 10 for further discussion of foreclosure.)

Adverse Possession

Adverse possession, another form of involuntary alienation, is the process by which the possession and use of property can mature into title. The law of adverse possession encourages the fullest and most productive use of land. It provides that someone who actually uses property may eventually attain a greater interest in that property than the owner who does not use it. The precise requirements for obtaining title by adverse possession vary from state to state.

These requirements are often highly technical, and they must be followed exactly in order to obtain title.

The parties should obtain legal counsel in transactions where title may be affected by adverse possession. Still, a real estate agent needs to know the basics.

Requirements. In Washington, there are five basic requirements for adverse possession. Possession of the land must be:

1. actual,
2. open and notorious,
3. hostile to the owner's interest,
4. exclusive, and
5. continuous and uninterrupted for a specific period of time.

Actual. Actual possession means occupation and use of the property in a manner appropriate to the type of property. It does not require residence on the property unless residence is the appropriate use. Thus, actual possession of farmland may be achieved by fencing the land and planting crops, while actual possession of urban property would usually require a residential or commercial use of the property.

Open and Notorious. The requirement of "open and notorious" possession means that the possession must be obvious enough to put the average owner on notice that her interest in the property is threatened. This requirement overlaps with the actual possession requirement. Actual possession generally constitutes reasonable notice to the world that the adverse possessor is occupying the property.

Hostile. The adverse possessor must intend to claim ownership of the property and defend that claim against all parties. Hostile intent is proven by the adverse possessor's actions. If the adverse possessor uses the property in the same fashion as an owner would use it, then hostile intent exists. Hostile intent can also be proven by color of title. An example of an adverse possessor with color of title is one who takes possession under an invalid deed, with a good faith but mistaken belief that he is the owner of the land. Note that the hostility requirement cannot be satisfied if the possession is with the permission of the actual owner.

Fig. 3.3 Adverse Possession

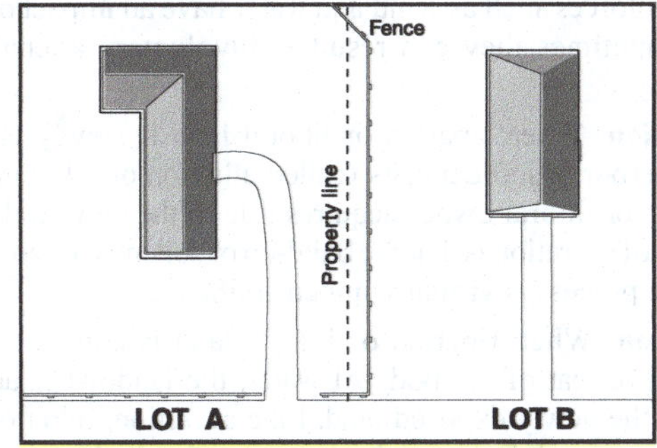

Use of property (here, the strip between Lot A's fence and the true property line) can mature into title by the process of adverse possession.

Exclusive. An adverse possessor must have exclusive possession of the property; in other words, the true owner must be excluded from possession. Someone who is sharing use of the property with the true owner (even without the owner's knowledge) cannot acquire title by adverse possession.

Continuous. An adverse possessor must have continuous and uninterrupted possession of the property for the length of time prescribed by state statute. In Washington, possession generally must be continuous and uninterrupted for ten years. The possession period is only seven years if an adverse possessor has color of title (has taken possession under an invalid deed and with the good faith belief that she owns the property) and pays property taxes on the parcel.

In some cases, intermittent use of the property may be enough to fulfill the continuity requirement. This is true if the property is a type that an owner would ordinarily use only at certain times of year, such as seasonal farmland or summer resort property. However, the continuity requirement is not met if the adverse possessor fails to use the property for a significant period when it would ordinarily be used, or if the true owner interrupts the period of exclusive possession.

Periods of possession by successive adverse possessors can be added together to equal the statutory time period; this is called **tacking.**

> **Example:** Brown adversely possesses property for seven years, then transfers possession to White, who possesses the property for five years. White can claim title because the total period of adverse possession is more than ten years.

Note that title to government property can never be acquired by adverse possession.

Perfecting Title. Since the adverse possessor's interest is not recorded, she must take additional steps to acquire marketable title. Unless the true owner is willing to provide a quitclaim deed, the adverse possessor has to file a quiet title action. Note that once the adverse possessor has title to the property, she is responsible for paying any unpaid property taxes that accrued before she gained title.

Natural Forces

Natural forces such as wind and water have an impact on land, and sometimes they can result in involuntary alienation of property.

Accretion. When riparian or littoral land is slowly enlarged by waterborne soil deposits (called alluvion or alluvium), the riparian or littoral owner acquires title to the new land. A key feature of accretion is that the build-up of soil must be so gradual that the process is virtually imperceptible.

Reliction. When riparian or littoral land is enlarged by the gradual retreat of the body of water, the landowner acquires title to the newly exposed land. Like accretion, reliction must be very gradual. Reliction is also called dereliction.

Avulsion. Accretion and reliction are both gradual processes. By contrast, avulsion occurs suddenly, usually when the main channel of a watercourse shifts due to flooding in a storm. When this happens, property boundaries generally do not change. Land that used to be contiguous but is now on the other side of the river still belongs to the original owner. The original boundaries remain the same even though the river has moved.

It's also called avulsion when land is violently torn away by flowing water or waves and deposited elsewhere. The original owner still has title to that land, if there is some way to claim it. If unclaimed, it eventually becomes part of the property it is now attached to.

Recording

Once an interest in property has been transferred (voluntarily or involuntarily), the new owner protects his interest by recording the document of conveyance with the county clerk. Recording is a way to provide convenient access to information regarding ownership of a property to anyone who's interested.

The Recording Process

Recording is accomplished by filing a deed or other document at the county records office in the county where the property is located. Documents are recorded chronologically, in the order in which they were filed for recording. Each recorded document is assigned a recording number.

County property records are searchable by computer at the records office, and many counties also offer online searches. When someone is considering buying a property, a **title search** is performed to determine the validity of the seller's title and find what other claims there are against the property. By searching the records by grantor or grantee name, or using various other identifiers such as the property's tax parcel number, the prospective buyer or a title company employee can trace the chain of title (the series of recorded deeds that transferred the property from one owner to the next) back in time far enough to establish that the seller is the true owner. The title search can also help the buyer and the lender make sure the seller has not already conveyed the property to another party.

Almost any document affecting title to land may be recorded: a deed, a mortgage, an abstract of judgment, a lis pendens (a notice of pending legal proceedings that may affect property), and so on. As mentioned, a deed or other document of conveyance must be acknowledged before it can be recorded, mainly to protect against forgeries. Also, the federal Fair Housing Act prohibits the recording of any deed that contains a racially restrictive covenant (see Chapter 15).

The Effect of Recording

Recording has two significant consequences. Most importantly, it gives **constructive notice** of recorded interests to "the world." In other words, anyone who later acquires an interest in the property is held to know about all the other recorded interests, even if they do not check the record. (Constructive notice is contrasted with **actual notice**, which occurs when someone actually knows about some fact concerning the property.)

> **Example:** Jones owns Haystack Farm. She sells the farm to Chin, who immediately records his deed. One week later, Jones sells Haystack Farm to Brown. Jones pretends she still owns the farm, and Brown simply takes her word for it; he doesn't do a title search. When Brown tries to record his deed, he discovers that Jones did not have title to Haystack Farm when she sold it to him.
>
> Although Brown didn't actually know about the conveyance from Jones to Chin, he had constructive notice of that conveyance. He could have found out about it by checking the public record. As a result, he has no claim to the property. Chin owns Haystack Farm. Brown could sue Jones to get his money back, but she may be long gone.

A grantee who fails to record her deed can lose title to a subsequent good faith purchaser who did not have notice of the earlier conveyance. In a conflict between two purchasers, the one who records his deed first has good title to the property—even if the other purchaser's deed was executed first.

> **Example:** Jones sells Haystack Farm to Chin, but Chin does not record his deed. One week later, Jones sells the same property to Brown. No one tells Brown about the previous conveyance to Chin.
>
> Since Chin's deed isn't recorded, Brown doesn't have constructive notice of Chin's interest in the property. Even if Brown does a title search, there's nothing in the public record to indicate that Jones no longer owns the property.
>
> Brown qualifies as a subsequent good faith purchaser without notice. If he records his deed before Chin records his, Brown has good title to the property.

In addition to providing constructive notice, recording also creates a presumption that the recorded instrument is valid and effective. Recording will not serve to validate an otherwise invalid deed, however, nor will it protect against interests that arise by operation of law, such as adverse possession.

Possession Provides Notice. A potential purchaser is also held to have constructive notice of the interests of parties in possession of the property, even if those interests aren't recorded. For example, if a tenant has possession under an unrecorded lease, a purchaser would have constructive notice of the lease, even if she never visited the property and is unaware of the tenant.

Title Insurance

Given the complexity of real property law and the high cost of real estate, it's natural that a prospective buyer will want to do everything possible to make sure that he's going to have good title to the property. The warranties carried by a warranty deed offer some assurance about the seller's title, but warranties aren't very useful to the buyer if the seller can't back them up financially.

The buyer could also obtain a complete history of all the recorded interests in the property (called a **chain of title**) or a condensed history of those interests (called an **abstract of title**), and then have the history examined by an attorney who could render an opinion on the condition of the title. But the buyer would still have no protection against latent or undiscovered defects in the title. Therefore, most buyers will protect their interests with a title insurance policy.

In a title insurance policy, the title insurance company agrees to indemnify the policy holder against (in other words, reimburse the policy holder for) losses caused by defects in the title, except for defects specifically excluded from coverage. The title company will also handle the legal defense of any claims covered by the policy.

Obtaining Title Insurance

To obtain title insurance, the buyer (or the seller, on the buyer's behalf) pays a premium to the title company. The premium includes the cost of a **title search**: a review of the public record to confirm that the seller owns the property, and to discover what other recorded interests or claims affect the seller's title. For certain types of coverage, the title company also sends an inspector to the property to look for issues affecting title that don't appear in the public record (see below), and in some cases a survey is performed to check the boundaries. Based on its investigation, the title company issues a **title report** listing the defects and encumbrances that were discovered.

If the title report reveals unexpected problems, the buyer or the buyer's lender might require the seller to clear them up before the transaction proceeds. (For example, the seller might have to obtain a quitclaim deed from her ex-spouse, releasing any possible claim to the property.) If the condition of title is satisfactory to the buyer and/or lender, the title company will issue an insurance policy when the transaction closes.

Any defects or encumbrances discovered by the title company that have not been cleared up will be listed in the policy and excluded from coverage. The policy covers problems that were unknown when the policy was issued, but may come to light at some later time.

The premium for a title insurance policy is paid at closing. A single payment covers the entire life of the policy, which lasts as long as the insured holds an interest in the property.

Title Insurance Coverage

Title insurance coverage is limited in a variety of ways. As we said, known defects and encumbrances are listed in the policy and excluded from coverage. In addition, the liability of the title company cannot exceed the face value of the policy. The extent of protection also varies depending on what type of policy is purchased. There are three main types of policies: standard, extended, and homeowner's.

A **standard coverage** policy protects against problems concerning matters of public record (such as a recorded easement overlooked by the title searcher, or hidden risks like a forged signature on a recorded deed). The title company does not perform a property inspection for a standard coverage policy, so it does not insure against problems that could only be discovered through an inspection.

A property inspection and/or survey is performed for an extended coverage policy. **Extended coverage** insures against all matters covered by the standard policy, plus matters not of public record, such as the rights of parties in possession of the property, unrecorded construction lien claims, and encroachments.

Extended coverage is typically used for the mortgagee's policy, a policy insuring the buyer's lender (as opposed to the owner's policy, the policy insuring the buyer). Lenders require buyers to pay for a mortgagee's policy in virtually all financed transactions.

Finally, title companies offer **homeowner's coverage** for transactions that involve residential property with up to four units. This policy covers most of the same title problems as an extended coverage policy. The key difference between the two types of coverage is that a homeowner's policy protects the buyer, while an extended coverage policy usually protects the lender.

A buyer who wants coverage for a specific item not ordinarily covered by a particular type of policy may be able to purchase an **endorsement** to cover it.

Title insurance coverage is limited to losses resulting from defects in the particular interest covered. Thus, an owner's policy covers only defects in title, a mortgagee's policy only insures the lender's security interest, and a leaseholder's policy only insures the validity of a lease.

Note that title insurance generally does not protect a landowner from losses due to governmental action such as condemnation or zoning changes.

Chapter Summary

1. A transfer of ownership of property from one person to another is called alienation. Alienation may be either voluntary or involuntary.
2. Property may be transferred voluntarily by patent, deed, or will. The deed is the most common way of voluntarily transferring property. To be valid, a deed must be in writing, identify the parties, be signed by a competent grantor, have a living grantee, contain words of conveyance, and include an adequate description of the property. For property to be successfully conveyed, there must be delivery and acceptance as well as a valid deed. Once the deed is delivered and accepted, it should be recorded to protect the new owner's interest.
3. When a person dies, her real property may be transferred to devisees through a will, a trust, or a transfer on death deed, or to heirs by the rules of intestate succession. (A person who dies without a will is said to have died intestate.) Property from an estate is distributed under the jurisdiction of the probate court. If a person dies without a valid will and without heirs, the estate property escheats to the state.
4. In addition to intestate succession and escheat, there are several other methods of involuntary alienation, including dedication, condemnation, court decisions (quiet title, partition, foreclosure), and adverse possession. When someone uses property openly and continuously without the owner's permission for ten years, she may acquire title to it by adverse possession.
5. Documents affecting real property are recorded to provide constructive notice of their contents to anyone interested in the property. Recording also creates a presumption that a document is valid.
6. Under a title insurance policy, the title insurance company will reimburse the insured for losses caused by covered title defects and will defend the title against legal claims. Most transactions involve two title insurance policies: one protecting the buyer (the owner's policy), and one protecting the buyer's lender (the mortgagee's policy).

Key Terms

Alienation—The transfer of title, ownership, or an interest in property from one person to another. Alienation may be voluntary or involuntary.

Deed—A written instrument that, when properly executed, delivered, and accepted, conveys title or ownership of real property from the grantor to the grantee.

Warranty deed—The deed that provides the greatest protection to a purchaser of real property, because it contains five basic covenants against defects in the title.

Quitclaim deed—A deed that conveys and releases any interest in a piece of real property that the grantor may have. It contains no warranties of any kind, but does transfer any right, title, or interest the grantor has at the time the deed is executed.

Acknowledgment—A formal declaration made before an authorized official, such as a notary public or county clerk, by a person who has signed a document; he states that the signature is genuine and voluntary.

Will—The written declaration of an individual that designates how his estate will be disposed of after death.

Intestate—When a person dies without leaving a valid will, she dies intestate.

Escheat—The reversion of property to the state after no one with a legal claim to the property comes forward to claim it. (This may happen, for example, because the owner died without leaving a will and without heirs.)

Dedication—When a private owner voluntarily or involuntarily gives real property to the public.

Eminent domain—The power of the government to take (condemn) private property for public use, upon payment of just compensation to the owner.

Condemnation—The act of taking private property for public use under the power of eminent domain.

Adverse possession—A means by which a person may acquire title to property by using it openly and continuously without the owner's permission for the required statutory period.

Constructive notice—Notice of a fact that a person is held by law to have (as opposed to actual notice); he had the opportunity to discover the fact in question by searching the public record.

Title search—An inspection of the public record to determine all rights to a piece of property.

Chain of title—A complete history of all the recorded interests in a piece of real property.

Abstract of title—A condensed history of the recorded interests in a piece of real property.

Title insurance—An insurance policy that indemnifies a buyer or a lender against losses resulting from title defects that have not been excepted from coverage.

Title report—A report issued after a title search by a title insurance company, listing all defects and encumbrances of record.

Chapter Quiz

1. **The process of transferring real property is called:**
   a) avulsion
   b) quitclaim
   c) alienation
   d) dereliction

2. **The government transfers title to private parties by means of a/an:**
   a) patent
   b) deed
   c) quitclaim
   d) escheat

3. **In a deed, the promise that the grantor owns the property is called the covenant:** PACTO
   a) of quiet enjoyment
   b) against encumbrances
   c) of seisin
   d) of warranty

4. **Clouds on title are usually cleared by:**
   a) a suit for partition
   b) title insurance
   c) adverse possession
   d) a quitclaim deed

5. **A valid deed must refer to a grantee who is:**
   a) competent
   b) over 21 years old
   c) identifiable
   d) intestate

6. **Conveyance requires a valid deed, plus:**
   a) recording
   b) delivery
   c) acceptance
   d) Both b) and c)

7. **A person who makes a will is called a/an:**
   a) grantor
   b) executor
   c) testator
   d) escheat

8. **An unwitnessed, handwritten will is called a:**
   a) witnessed will
   b) holographic will
   c) nuncupative will
   d) None of the above

9. **The process by which possession of property can result in ownership of the property is called:**
   a) fee simple
   b) succession
   c) adverse possession
   d) reliction

10. **A quitclaim deed conveys:**
    a) whatever interest the grantor has
    b) only a portion of the interest held by the grantor
    c) only property acquired by adverse possession
    d) None of the above

11. **A nuncupative will:**
    a) must be entirely handwritten
    b) is invalid in Washington
    c) is an oral will
    d) is only valid for sailors and merchant marines

12. **The five basic promises made by a grantor through a warranty deed include all of the following, except:**
    a) covenant of right to convey
    b) covenant of quiet enjoyment
    c) covenant of habitability
    d) covenant of warranty

13. **When a cloud on the title cannot be cleared with a quitclaim deed, this judicial proceeding decides ownership:**
    a) quiet title action
    b) suit for partition
    c) interpleader action
    d) reformation action

14. **All of the following are requirements for adverse possession, except:**
    a) open and notorious possession
    b) exclusive possession
    c) hostile possession
    d) recorded claim of possession

15. **A standard title insurance policy would protect against:**
    a) adverse possession
    b) encroachments
    c) a forged deed
    d) condemnation

Chapter 4:
Encumbrances

An interest in real property may be held by someone other than the property owner or a tenant; such an interest is called an encumbrance. Nearly every property has encumbrances against it. Some encumbrances represent another person's financial interest in the property. Other encumbrances involve another person's right to make use of the property or to restrict how the owner uses it.

The first part of this chapter explains financial encumbrances, including mortgages and other types of liens. The second part of this chapter covers the nonfinancial encumbrances, including easements and private restrictions, and some related concepts.

Key Terms

Encumbrance
Voluntary Lien
Involuntary Lien
General Lien
Specific Lien
Construction Lien
Judgment Lien
Easement
Easement Appurtenant
Easement in Gross
Easement by Implication
Prescriptive Easement
Merger
Abandonment
Profit
License
Encroachment
Nuisance
CC&Rs

Encumbrances

An encumbrance is a nonpossessory right or interest in real property held by someone other than the property owner. The interest can be financial or nonfinancial in nature. A financial encumbrance only affects title; a nonfinancial encumbrance also affects the use or physical condition of the property.

Financial Encumbrances (Liens)

Financial encumbrances are commonly called **liens**. A lien is a security interest in property; it is held by a creditor of the property owner. If the owner doesn't pay off the debt owed to the creditor, the security interest allows the creditor to force the property to be sold, so that the creditor can collect the debt out of the sale proceeds. This is called **foreclosure**. The most familiar example of a lien is a mortgage.

A creditor who has a lien against (a security interest in) the debtor's property is called a **secured creditor**. The lien does not prevent the debtor from transferring the property, but the new owner takes title subject to the lien. The creditor can still foreclose if the debt is not repaid.

Liens may be voluntary or involuntary. A **voluntary lien** is one the debtor voluntarily gives to the creditor, usually as security for a loan. The two types of voluntary liens that may attach to real property are mortgages and deeds of trust. **Involuntary liens** (sometimes called statutory liens) are given to creditors without the property owner's consent, by operation of law. Examples of involuntary liens are property tax liens and judgment liens.

> **Example:** Dunn sues Bronson for injuries sustained in a car crash and wins a $125,000 judgment. The judgment can become a lien against Bronson's property.

Liens may also be general or specific. A **general lien** attaches to all of the debtor's property. For instance, the judgment lien in the example is a general lien. Any property owned by Bronson could be encumbered by the judgment lien. On the other hand, a **specific lien** attaches only to a particular piece of property. A mortgage is an example of a specific lien. It is a lien against only the particular piece of property offered as security for the loan.

Types of Liens

The most common types of liens against real property include mortgages, deeds of trust, construction liens, judgment liens, attachment liens, and tax and assessment liens.

Mortgages. A mortgage is a specific, voluntary lien created by a contract between the property owner (the **mortgagor**) and the creditor (the **mortgagee**). The mortgagee is usually a lender, who will not loan money unless the borrower gives a lien as security for repayment.

Deeds of Trust. A deed of trust (also called a trust deed) is used for the same purpose as a mortgage. However, there are three parties to a trust deed rather than the two found in a mortgage transaction. The borrower is called the **trustor** (or sometimes the grantor); the lender or creditor is called the **beneficiary**; and there's an independent third party (often an attorney or a title insurance company) called the **trustee**. The most significant difference between mortgages and deeds of trust is in the foreclosure process. Mortgages and deeds of trust are discussed in more detail in Chapter 10.

Construction Liens. A person who provides labor, materials, or professional services for the improvement of real property may be entitled to claim a construction lien against the property. For example, if a plumber who is involved in remodeling a bathroom isn't paid, they can claim a lien against the property for the amount owed. Eventually, if necessary, the plumber could foreclose on the lien, forcing the property to be sold to pay the debt.

A construction lien is a specific, involuntary lien, attaching only to the property where the lien claimant performed work or supplied materials. Construction liens are often called **mechanic's liens**, and a construction lien claimed by someone who provides materials (as opposed to labor) is sometimes called a **materialman's lien.**

Many improvement projects involve a complex hierarchy of contractors, subcontractors, laborers, and materials suppliers, all of whom may be entitled to claim construction liens. In certain cases, a potential construction lien claimant is required to give the property owner a notice of right to claim a lien (also called a "pre-lien notice") within a certain time after they begin providing services or materials. This is not necessary when the claimant has a contract directly with the owner, however.

A claimant must record the claim of lien no later than 90 days after the claimant has stopped working on or providing materials for the project. Potential claimants who miss this deadline lose the right to a construction lien. They are still entitled to be paid for services rendered, but do not have a security interest in the debtor's property.

To foreclose on a construction lien, the lienholder must file a court action within eight months after the claim of lien was recorded.

Judgment Liens. Judgment liens are involuntary, general liens. If a lawsuit results in a money judgment against the loser, the winner (the judgment creditor) may obtain a lien against the loser's (the judgment debtor's) property.

The lien attaches to all the property owned by the debtor in the county where the judgment was entered, and also attaches to any property acquired by the debtor during the lien period (the length of time the judgment creditor has to take action on the lien). If the debtor owns property in other counties, the judgment creditor can make the lien attach to that property by recording an **abstract of judgment** in those counties.

To free property from a judgment lien, the debtor must pay the judgment and then record a document called a **satisfaction of judgment** to provide constructive notice that the lien has been extinguished. If it's not paid, the property can be sold by a designated official to satisfy the judgment. To do this, the court issues a **writ of execution**.

Attachment Liens. When someone files a lawsuit, there is a danger that by the time a judgment is entered, the **defendant** (the party sued) will have sold their property and disappeared, leaving the other party with little more than a piece of paper. To prevent this, the **plaintiff** (the person who started the lawsuit) can ask the court to issue a writ of attachment. A **writ of attachment** directs the sheriff to attach enough of the defendant's property to satisfy the judgment the plaintiff is seeking. When the writ of attachment is recorded, it creates a lien on the defendant's real property.

Also, when a lawsuit that may affect title to real property is pending, the plaintiff may record a document called a **lis pendens**, which is Latin for "action pending." While a lis pendens is not a lien, anyone who purchases the property identified in the lis pendens has constructive notice of the pending lawsuit and therefore is bound by any judgment that results from the suit.

Property Tax Liens. Property is assessed (appraised for tax purposes) and taxed according to its value (ad valorem). When property taxes are levied, a lien attaches to the property until they are paid. Property tax liens are involuntary, specific liens. (Property taxation is discussed in more detail in Chapter 5.)

Special Assessments. Special assessments result from local improvements, such as road paving or sewer lines, that benefit some, but not all, property owners within the county. The properties that benefit from the improvement are assessed for their share of the cost of the improvement. The assessment creates an involuntary, specific lien against the property. (Special assessments are also discussed in Chapter 5.)

Other Tax Liens. Many other taxes, such as federal income taxes, estate or inheritance taxes, and gift taxes, can result in liens against property. These types of tax liens are general liens against all of a taxpayer's properties.

Fig. 4.1 Lien Classifications

	Voluntary	Involuntary
Specific	Mortgages Deeds of trust	Property taxes Special assessments Construction liens
General		Judgment liens IRS liens

Lien Priority

It is not at all unusual for a piece of property to have more than one lien against it. In fact, the dollar amount of all the liens may add up to more than the property will bring at a foreclosure sale. When this happens, the sale proceeds are not allocated among all the lienholders in a "pro rata" fashion (proportionate distribution). Instead, the liens are paid according to their priority. This means that the lien with the highest priority is paid first. If any money is left over, the lien with the second highest priority is paid, and so forth.

As a general rule, lien priority is determined by the date a lien was recorded. The lien that was recorded first will be paid first, even though another lien may have been created first.

> **Example:** Suppose Bakerman borrows money from two banks—$5,000 from National Bank on March 17, and $5,000 from State Bank on May 5 of the same year. Bakerman gives mortgages to both banks when the loan funds are received. If National Bank does not record its mortgage until July 14, but State Bank records its mortgage promptly on May 5, State Bank's lien will be paid before National Bank's in the event of foreclosure.

While "first in time (to record), first in right" is the general rule, there are important exceptions; some types of liens are given special priority. In Washington, special priority is given to property tax and special assessment liens; they have priority over all other liens. Construction liens are another exception. Their priority is determined by the date the claimant began working on the project, even though the claim of lien was recorded later on.

The Homestead Law

Homestead laws are state laws that give homeowners limited protection against lien foreclosure. In Washington, the homestead law offers protection only against general judgment liens. It does not apply to mortgages, deeds of trust, construction liens, liens for child support or spousal maintenance, or liens imposed by a condominium or homeowners association.

A **homestead** is an owner-occupied dwelling, together with any appurtenant buildings and land. Homestead protection is automatic, beginning as soon as the owner starts residing on the property.

An owner can obtain homestead protection in advance, for property they are planning to reside on, by recording a document called a "declaration of homestead" for that property. However, a person may have only one homestead at a time.

In Washington, a married person's homestead can be conveyed or encumbered only if both spouses sign the deed or other instrument.

Exemption. Homestead protection consists of a limited exemption from foreclosure of judgment liens. In Washington, the exemption amount is generally the county median sales price for a single-family home in the preceding calendar year.

A judgment creditor cannot foreclose unless the net value of the property is greater than the exemption amount. The net value is the property's market value, minus all liens that are senior to the lien being foreclosed on.

> **Example:** The Crenshaws own and occupy a home worth $775,000. The liens against the home, in order of priority, are a $6,500 property tax lien, a $430,000 mortgage, and a $15,000 judgment lien. The judgment creditor wants to foreclose on the judgment lien. The county's median sales price last year was $525,000.
>
> The net value of the Crenshaws' home is $338,500 ($775,000 – $436,500 = $338,500). Because the net value is less than the $525,000 exemption amount that currently applies in their county, the judgment creditor can't foreclose.

When the proceeds of the foreclosure sale are distributed, first the exemption amount is paid to the homeowner, then the remaining proceeds are paid to the lienholders in order of priority. The money paid to the former homeowner as a result of the homestead exemption is protected from other creditors (just as it was protected while it was invested in the homestead). The former homeowner can reinvest the funds in a new homestead.

Termination. Homestead protection terminates automatically when the owner sells the property. However, out of the sale proceeds, the exemption amount is still protected from the claims of general creditors for one year following the sale. This allows the owner time in which to reinvest the exempt funds in a new home, which will then become their new homestead.

Fig. 4.2 Types of Encumbrances

Financial Encumbrances	Nonfinancial Encumbrances
• Mortgages • Deeds of trust • Construction liens • Judgment liens • Attachment liens • Property tax liens • Other tax liens	• Easements • Profits • Private restrictions

Nonfinancial Encumbrances

While financial encumbrances affect only title to property, nonfinancial encumbrances affect the physical use or condition of the property itself. Thus, a property owner can find the use of their land limited by a right or interest held by someone else. Nonfinancial encumbrances include easements, profits, and private restrictions. We'll also cover licenses, encroachments, and nuisances in this section; they too involve someone using another's property or affecting the owner's use of it, although they aren't actually interests in real property.

Easements

An easement is a right to use another person's land for a particular purpose. It is a nonpossessory interest in land. That means that the easement holder has a right to use the land, but has no title or right of possession. An easement is not an estate.

> **Example:** A landowner has an easement across their neighbor's lot for access to the public road. They have a right to make reasonable use of that easement to get to and from their property. However, they do not have the right to build a shed on the easement, or to use the easement in any way other than as a driveway.

Types of Easements. There are two main types of easements: easements appurtenant and easements in gross.

Easements Appurtenant. An easement appurtenant burdens one parcel of land for the benefit of another parcel of land. The parcel with the benefit is called the **dominant tenement**; the one with the burden is called the **servient tenement.** The owner of the dominant tenement is called the **dominant tenant**; the owner of the servient tenement is the **servient tenant**. Do not confuse the term "tenement," which is the land, with "tenant," which is the landowner.

One type of easement appurtenant you may encounter is a driveway easement providing access across one parcel of land to another. (A driveway easement is often called an easement for **ingress and egress**, which means entering and exiting.)

In Figure 4.3, Lot B has an easement appurtenant across Lot A. The easement provides access to a public road. Lot B is the dominant tenement. Lot A is the servient tenement.

An easement appurtenant "runs with the land." This means that if either the dominant or servient tenement is transferred to a new owner, the new owner also acquires the benefit or the burden of the easement. Refer to Figure 4.3 again. If Lot B were sold, the new owner would still have an easement across Lot A. If Lot A were sold, the new owner would still bear the burden of allowing the owner of Lot B to use the easement.

An easement that benefits a parcel of land is called an easement appurtenant because it goes along with ownership of the land like other appurtenances (air rights, for example). The easement is appurtenant to the dominant tenement.

Fig. 4.3 Easement Appurtenant

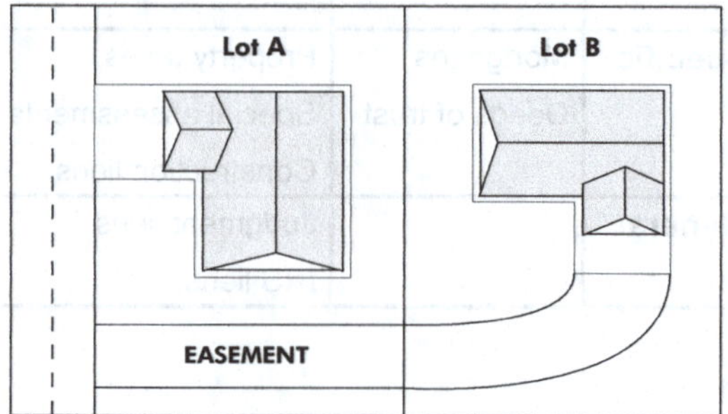

Ordinarily, an easement agreement or a deed creating an easement must be in writing in order for the easement to be valid. To make the easement run with the land, the document usually must also be recorded. In some situations, though, if it would be immediately apparent to a person visiting the property that an easement is in use, the easement could run with the land even though it was never written down or recorded.

Easements in Gross. An easement in gross benefits a person (a dominant tenant) rather than a parcel of land. When someone has an easement in gross, there is no dominant tenement, only a servient tenement.

> **Example:** Wilson has the right to enter Able's land and fish in Able's stream. Wilson is a dominant tenant with an easement in gross over Able's land (the servient tenement). The easement serves Wilson, not a parcel of land.

Since an easement in gross belongs to a person and not a parcel of land, it is a personal right that is extinguished on the death of the dominant tenant. In the example above, when Wilson dies, the easement will disappear. A personal easement in gross may not be assigned by its owner to a third party.

Most easements in gross are commercial easements. Most residential properties are burdened by easements held by a utility company, for instance. This kind of easement allows company employees to enter property to install and service the lines. Because commercial easements in gross are considered more substantial interests than personal easements, they can be assigned from one company to another.

Creating an Easement. Easements (whether appurtenant or in gross) can be created in any of the following ways:

- express grant,
- express reservation,
- implication,
- prescription,
- dedication, or
- condemnation.

Express Grant. An easement is created by express grant when a property owner grants someone else the right to use the property. The grant must be put into writing and comply with all the other requirements for conveyance of an interest in land.

Express Reservation. A landowner who is conveying a portion of their property may reserve an easement in that parcel to benefit the parcel of land that is retained. Like an express grant, an express reservation must be in writing.

> **Example:** Carmichael owns 100 acres bordering on a state highway. She sells 40 acres, including all the highway frontage. In the deed, she reserves to herself an easement across the conveyed land so that she will have access to her remaining 60 acres.

Implication. An easement by implication can be either an implied grant or an implied reservation. This type of easement can arise only when a property is divided into more than one lot, and the grantor neglects to grant or reserve an easement on one lot for the benefit of the other. When this happens, the easement is implied by law.

There are two requirements for an easement to be created by implication:

1. it must be reasonably necessary for the enjoyment of the property, and
2. there must have been apparent prior use.

The second requirement is fulfilled if the use was established before the property was divided, and would have been apparent to prospective purchasers from an inspection of the property. However, different rules apply if one of the parcels would be entirely landlocked without an easement. When an easement for ingress and egress is strictly necessary (not merely reasonably necessary) because there is no other way to reach the landlocked parcel, then a court may declare that there is an easement even though there was no apparent prior use. This subtype of easement by implication is called an **easement by necessity**.

Prescription. An easement by prescription is created through long-term use of land without the permission of the landowner. Acquiring an easement by prescription is similar to acquiring ownership through adverse possession.

Here are the requirements for an easement by prescription:

- the use must be **open and notorious** (apparent to the landowner);
- the use must be **hostile** (without the permission of the landowner); and
- the use must be **reasonably continuous** for a statutory period of time (in Washington, ten years).

Note that although an adverse possessor's use of the property must be exclusive, that isn't a requirement for a prescriptive easement. A prescriptive easement may be created even if the landowner is also using the property.

Dedication. A private landowner may grant an easement to the public to use some portion of their property for a public purpose, such as a sidewalk. The dedication may be expressly stated or implied.

Condemnation. The government may exercise its power of eminent domain and condemn private property to gain an easement for a public purpose, such as a road. This power may also be exercised by private companies that serve the public, such as railroad and power companies.

Terminating an Easement. An easement can be terminated in any of these ways:

- release,
- merger,
- failure of purpose,
- abandonment, or
- prescription.

Release. The holder of an easement may agree to release their rights in the servient tenement. This is done by providing a release document (usually a quitclaim deed) to the owner of the servient tenement, who then records the document.

Merger. Since an easement is, by definition, the right to make some use of another person's land, if the dominant and servient tenements come to be owned by the same person, the easement is no longer necessary and therefore is terminated. This is called merger; ownership of the dominant and servient tenements has merged.

Failure of Purpose. If the purpose for which an easement was created ceases, then the easement terminates. For example, if an easement was created for a railroad, and if the railroad company later discontinued its use and removed the rails, the easement would be terminated through failure of purpose.

Abandonment. An easement is also terminated if the easement holder abandons it. This requires acts by the holder indicating an intent to abandon the easement. Mere non-use is not abandonment.

> **Example:** If the dominant tenant were to build a fence that blocked any further use of an easement that had been used for ingress and egress, it would be reasonable for the servient tenant to conclude that the easement had been abandoned.

Prescription. An easement is extinguished if the servient tenant prevents the dominant tenant from using the easement for the statutory period (ten years).

> **Example:** The servient tenant builds a brick wall around their property. The dominant tenant can no longer use their easement for ingress and egress. If the wall remains undisturbed for ten years, the easement will be terminated.

Profits

A profit is the right to take something from land belonging to someone else. For example, it might be the right to take timber, peat, or gravel from someone else's land. The difference between a profit and an easement is that the easement is just a right to use another's land, but a profit allows the removal of something from the land. A profit must be created in writing or by prescription.

Licenses

Like an easement, a license gives someone the right to make some use of another person's land. However, easements and licenses are different in many ways. An easement is created in writing or through action of law. A license may be merely spoken permission to cross, hunt, fish on, or make some other use of a landowner's property. An easement is irrevocable, but a license can be revoked at the will of the landowner. In general, easements are permanent and licenses are temporary.

A license is a personal right that does not run with the land. It cannot be assigned. Since the license is revocable at the will of the landowner, it is not actually considered an encumbrance or an interest in the property.

Encroachments

An encroachment is a physical object that is wholly or partially on someone else's property, such as a fence or garage built partially over the property line onto the neighbor's land (see Figure 4.4). Most encroachments are unintentional, resulting from a mistake concerning the exact location of the property line.

An encroachment may be a **trespass** if it violates the neighboring owner's right to possession. A court can order the removal of an encroachment through a judicial action called an **ejectment**, or if the cost of the removal would be too high, order the encroacher to pay damages to the neighbor.

Technically, an encroachment is not an encumbrance, because it is not a right or interest held by the encroacher. However, if ignored for the statutory period, the encroachment could ripen into a prescriptive easement or even into title by adverse possession.

Fig. 4.4 Encroachments

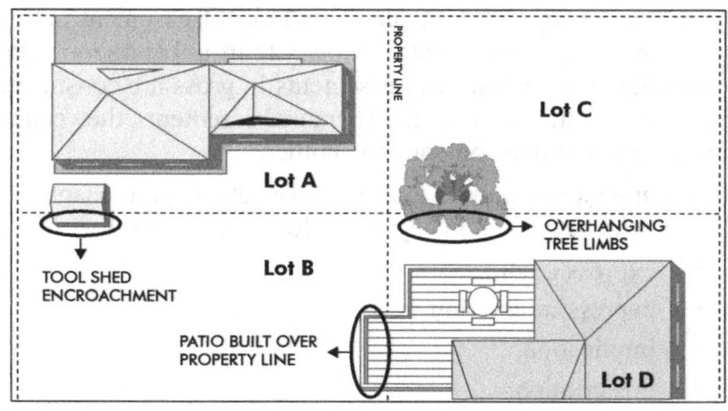

Nuisances

A nuisance is an activity or a condition on neighboring property that interferes with a property owner's reasonable use or enjoyment of their own property, such as odors, noises, fire hazards, or interference with communication signals. Like an encroachment, a nuisance isn't truly an encumbrance, but rather a violation of an owner's possessory rights.

A private nuisance affects only a few surrounding people. For example, rotting garbage in a neighbor's back yard would be a private nuisance. A public nuisance affects a larger community's health or welfare; jet noise and industrial emissions are examples. A property owner may ask a court for an injunction against a private or public nuisance, or may sue for damages.

A related concept is the **attractive nuisance** doctrine. The owner of a property with a feature that is dangerous and attractive to children, such as an unfenced swimming pool or construction site, will be held liable for any harm resulting from failure to keep out trespassing children.

Private Restrictions

Private restrictions (also known as deed restrictions) are restrictions on the use of a property that were imposed by some previous owner. For example, when selling a house long ago, a previous owner might have stated in the deed that the poplar trees in the front yard must not be cut down. Like easements, private restrictions can "run with the land," binding all subsequent owners of the property.

As long as a private restriction isn't unconstitutional, in violation of a law, or contrary to a judicial determination of public policy, it can be enforced in court. (An example of an unenforceable restriction is one prohibiting the sale of property to non-white buyers; see Chapter 15.)

Most subdivision developers impose a list of restrictions on all lots within the subdivision before they begin selling individual lots. This is called a declaration of restrictions, or **CC&Rs**. That stands for covenants, conditions, and restrictions, although all three of those terms mean basically the same thing in this context; they are rules governing how homeowners in the subdivision can use their property. The CC&Rs typically include rules limiting all the lots to single-family residential use, requiring property maintenance, and preventing activities that would bother the neighbors. The rules are intended to ensure that the subdivision will remain a desirable place to live.

Termination of Restrictions. It is up to the property owners within a subdivision (or their homeowners association) to enforce the CC&Rs, which they can do by obtaining an injunction, if necessary. However, if the owners have failed to enforce a particular restriction in the past, they may no longer be able to enforce it.

> **Example:** The subdivision's CC&Rs state that recreational vehicles may not be parked within view of the street. Over the years, however, many homeowners have broken this rule and their neighbors haven't complained. If someone tries to start enforcing the parking restriction now, a court might rule that it has been abandoned and is no longer enforceable.

A private restriction will also terminate if its purpose can no longer be achieved. For example, this might occur because zoning changes and other factors have dramatically altered the character of the neighborhood. If there is a private restriction limiting a property to single-family residential use, but most of the surrounding properties are now used for light industry, the restriction is probably no longer enforceable.

Chapter Summary

1. An encumbrance is a nonpossessory right or interest in real property held by someone other than the property owner. Encumbrances may be financial or nonfinancial.
2. A financial encumbrance (a lien) affects title to property. It gives a creditor the right to foreclose and use the sale proceeds to pay off the debt. A lien is either voluntary or involuntary and either general or specific. The most common types of liens include mortgages, deeds of trust, construction liens, judgment liens, attachment liens, property tax liens, special assessments, and other tax liens.
3. A nonfinancial encumbrance affects the use or condition of the property. Nonfinancial encumbrances include easements, profits, and private restrictions.
4. An easement gives the easement holder the right to use a portion of someone else's property for a specified purpose. An easement runs with the land, affecting the title of subsequent owners of the property or properties in question.
5. An easement appurtenant burdens one parcel of land (the servient tenement) for the benefit of another parcel (the dominant tenement). An easement in gross burdens a parcel of land for the benefit of a person, not another parcel of land.
6. Licenses, encroachments, and nuisances may also affect the use or condition of property. They are not classified as encumbrances, however, because they are not interests in real property.
7. Private restrictions affect how owners may use their own property. Like easements, private restrictions run with the land. A declaration of CC&Rs recorded by a subdivision developer is binding on the future owners of the subdivision lots.

Key Terms

Encumbrance—An interest in real property held by someone other than the property owner.

Voluntary lien—A security interest in property given voluntarily to a creditor by the property owner; in the real estate context, it is either a mortgage or a deed of trust.

Involuntary lien—A security interest given to a creditor by operation of law.

General lien—A lien that attaches to all of a debtor's property.

Specific lien—A lien that attaches only to one particular piece of property.

Construction lien—A lien on property in favor of someone who provided labor or materials to improve it; also called a mechanic's lien or materialman's lien.

Judgment lien—A lien held by someone who has won a judgment in a lawsuit, attaching to property owned by the person who lost the lawsuit.

Easement—The right to use another's land for a particular purpose.

Easement appurtenant—An easement that burdens one parcel of land (the servient tenement) for the benefit of another parcel (the dominant tenement).

Easement in gross—An easement that benefits a person rather than a parcel of land.

Easement by implication—An easement created automatically because it is necessary for the enjoyment of the benefited land.

Prescriptive easement—An easement created by continuous use for the statutory period, without the landowner's permission.

Merger—When both the dominant and servient tenements are acquired by one owner, resulting in termination of the easement.

Abandonment—A way in which an easement may terminate; it requires action by the easement holder, not simply non-use.

Profit—The right to take something (such as timber) from another's land.

License—Revocable permission to enter another's land, which does not create an interest in the property.

Encroachment—A physical object that intrudes onto another's property, such as a tree branch or a fence.

Nuisance—An activity or condition on nearby property that interferes with a property owner's reasonable use and enjoyment of her property.

CC&Rs—Covenants, conditions, and restrictions; private restrictions imposed by a subdivision developer.

Chapter Quiz

1. **Real estate property taxes are:**
   a) general, involuntary liens
   b) general, voluntary liens
   c) specific, voluntary liens
   d) specific, involuntary liens

2. **A lawsuit against Thatcher is pending. The court rules that a lien should be placed on his farm, holding it as security in case of a negative judgment. This is:**
   a) adverse possession
   b) prescription
   c) attachment
   d) appurtenance

3. **A recorded document that informs potential buyers that the property may become subject to a judgment in a lawsuit is a:**
   a) lis pendens
   b) writ of execution
   c) writ of attachment
   d) habendum clause

4. **Which of the following has priority over a mortgage that has already been recorded?**
   a) A deed of trust
   b) A judgment lien
   c) A property tax lien
   d) None of the above

5. **If there were two deeds of trust against the same property and you needed to know which one had higher priority, you could find this information in the county records. The priority is usually established by the:**
   a) printed trust deed forms, which have the words "first deed of trust" and "second deed of trust" on their face
   b) date and time of recording
   c) county auditor's stamp, which says "first trust deed" or "second trust deed"
   d) execution date of each document

6. **When there's an easement appurtenant, the dominant tenement:**
   a) can be used only for purposes of ingress and egress
   b) is burdened by the easement
   c) receives the benefit of the easement
   d) cannot be sold

7. **You have the right to cross another's land to get to your house. You probably own:**
   a) a dominant tenement
   b) a servient tenement
   c) Both of the above
   d) Neither of the above

8. **An easement in gross benefits:**
   a) a dominant tenement
   b) a servient tenement
   c) Both of the above
   d) Neither of the above

9. **Unlike a personal easement in gross, a commercial easement in gross:**
   a) is not an encumbrance
   b) is considered a possessory interest in real property
   c) can be assigned to another party
   d) can be revoked by the owner of the servient tenement

10. **Which of the following is not a method of creating an easement?**
    a) Implication
    b) Express grant in a deed
    c) Dedication
    d) Spoken grant

11. **The creation of an easement by prescription is similar to acquiring ownership of property by:**
    a) adverse possession
    b) escheat
    c) alluvium
    d) intestate succession

12. **A has an easement over B's property. If A buys B's property, the easement:**
    a) goes with the land
    b) is terminated
    c) is unaffected
    d) None of the above

13. **A porch or balcony that hangs over the established boundary line of a parcel of land is called a/an:**
    a) easement in gross
    b) encroachment
    c) easement appurtenant
    d) license

14. **All of the following would be considered nuisances, except:**
    a) fumes from a paper mill
    b) a house with regular drug-dealing activity
    c) radiation from a microwave tower
    d) a garage built on top of the property line

15. **The private restrictions in a subdivision's CC&Rs:**
    a) do not run with the land
    b) were most likely imposed by the developer
    c) can terminate only with the approval of a majority of the lot owners
    d) create a lien against the property

Chapter 5: *Public Restrictions on Land*

I. **Land Use Controls**
   A. Comprehensive planning
   B. Zoning
      1. Nonconforming uses
      2. Variances
      3. Conditional uses
      4. Rezones
   C. Building codes
   D. Subdivision regulations
      1. Physical regulations
      2. Washington Land Development Act
      3. ILSA
   E. Environmental laws
      1. Shoreline Management Act
      2. NEPA
      3. SEPA
      4. CERCLA
      5. Pollution control laws
      6. Environmental hazards

II. **Eminent Domain**

III. **Taxation**
   A. General real estate taxes
   B. Special assessments
   C. Real estate excise tax

Although property owners have many rights in regard to their property, those rights are limited by federal, state, and local governments. This chapter examines the ways in which governmental powers affect real property ownership most directly. It covers planning, zoning, and other public restrictions on land use; the taking of private property for public use; and the taxation of real property.

Key Terms

Police Power
Comprehensive Plan
Zoning
Nonconforming Use
Variance
Conditional Use Permit
Rezone
Building Codes
Eminent Domain
Condemnation
General Real Estate Taxes
Special Assessment
Real Estate Excise Tax

Land Use Controls

In the United States, the powers of government are restricted by the federal and state constitutions. Thus, efforts by the federal, state, and local governments to control the use of private property raise constitutional issues. When a property owner objects to a land use law, the central question is often whether the law is constitutional—whether the federal and state constitutions give the government the power to interfere with private property rights in this way.

The basis for land use control laws is the **police power**. This is the power vested in a state government to adopt and enforce laws and regulations necessary for the protection of the public's health, safety, morals, and general welfare. A state may delegate its police power to local governmental bodies.

It is the police power that allows state and local governments to regulate a private individual's use of their property. The Constitution does not give the federal government a general power to regulate for the public health, safety, morals, and welfare. But the federal government does have authority to use its other powers (such as the power to regulate interstate commerce) to advance police power objectives.

An exercise of the police power must meet constitutional limitations. As a general rule, a land use law or regulation is constitutional if it meets these four criteria:

1. It is reasonably related to the protection of the public health, safety, morals, or general welfare.
2. It applies in the same manner to all property owners who are similarly situated (in other words, it is not discriminatory).
3. It does not reduce a property's value so much that the regulation amounts to a confiscation—an uncompensated taking of property.
4. It benefits the public by preventing harm that would be caused by the prohibited use of the property.

Government land use controls take a variety of forms: comprehensive plans, zoning ordinances, building codes, subdivision regulations, and environmental laws. All of these are intended to protect the public from problems that unrestricted use of private property can cause.

Comprehensive Planning

To alleviate the problems caused by haphazard, unplanned growth, state law generally requires cities and counties to have a planning agency, which is usually called a planning commission.

The planning commission creates a long-term plan for all the development within the city or county. This is often called the "master plan" or "comprehensive plan."

The comprehensive plan outlines the community's development goals and an overall physical layout to achieve those goals. Once the plan has been adopted, all development and all land use regulations (such as zoning laws) must conform to it.

The government uses both its police power and its power of eminent domain (discussed later) to implement the planning commission's comprehensive plan.

In Washington, land use planning and administration are governed by the **Growth Management Act**. The act's goals include:

1. reducing suburban sprawl by concentrating new development in already existing urban growth areas;
2. requiring thorough infrastructure planning, including an emphasis on transportation alternatives;
3. protecting critical areas from environmentally harmful activities, and protecting open space;
4. planning for and accommodating affordable housing; and
5. encouraging economic growth consistent with the act's other goals.

Zoning

Zoning ordinances divide a community into areas (or zones) that are set aside for specific types of uses, such as agricultural, residential, commercial, or industrial use. Each of these basic classifications typically has subcategories. For instance, industrial uses may be divided into light industry and heavy industry; residential uses may be divided into single-family, two- to four-family, and multifamily dwellings.

Fig. 5.1 Setbacks and Side Yards

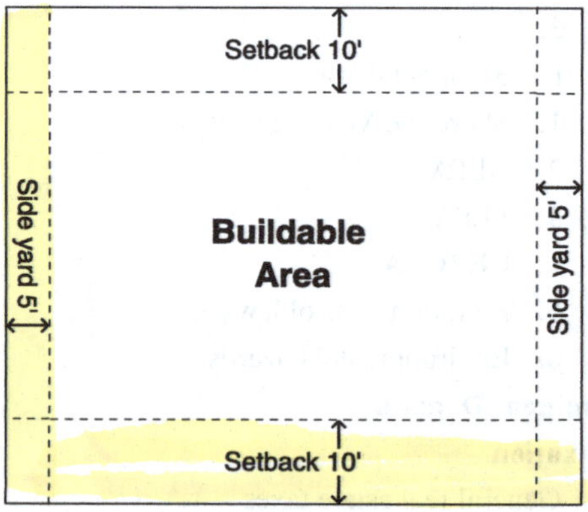

Keeping different types of uses in separate zones helps ensure that only compatible uses are located in the same area. In addition, areas zoned for incompatible uses may be separated by undeveloped areas called **buffers**.

Zoning ordinances regulate the height, size, and shape of buildings, as well as their use. They also usually include setback and side yard requirements, which prescribe the minimum distance between a building and the property lines. These regulations control population density, provide aesthetic guidelines, and help preserve adequate open space and access to air and daylight.

Certain subdivisions, known as planned unit developments, may be zoned with reduced setback and side yard requirements, creating smaller lots in exchange for commonly held green space. (In less urban areas, these subdivisions may be called rural cluster developments.)

Zoning Exceptions and Amendments. Complications inevitably arise when zoning regulations are administered and enforced. So zoning ordinances provide for certain exceptions and changes to their rules, including:

- nonconforming uses,
- variances,
- conditional uses, and
- rezones.

Nonconforming Uses. When an area is zoned for the first time, or when a zoning ordinance is amended, certain established uses that were lawful before may not conform to the new rules. These **nonconforming uses** will usually be permitted to continue.

> **Example:** Smith has been lawfully operating a bakery for seven months when his property is rezoned for single-family residential use. Smith's bakery will be allowed to continue as a nonconforming use.

Even though nonconforming uses are allowed to remain, the local government wants all uses to conform to the current zoning laws at some point. In some cases, an ordinance requires nonconforming uses to be phased out by a certain deadline (for example, ten years after the ordinance is passed).

And even in the absence of such a deadline, the owner of a nonconforming use property is usually prohibited from enlarging the use, rebuilding if the property is destroyed, or resuming the use after abandoning it.

> **Example:** Smith's bakery burns to the ground in a terrible fire. The zoning authority will not allow him to rebuild the bakery in this residential zone. He will have to sell the property and find a suitable property located in a commercial zone.

Variances. In some cases, if a zoning law were strictly enforced, the property owner's injury would far outweigh the benefit of enforcing the zoning requirement. Under these circumstances, a **variance** may be available. A variance is authorization to build or maintain a structure or use that is prohibited by the zoning ordinance.

For example, a variance might authorize construction of a house even though the topography of the lot makes it virtually impossible to comply with normal setback requirements. In most communities, the property owner applies to the local zoning authority for a variance.

A variance usually will not be granted unless the property owner faces severe practical difficulties or undue hardship (not created by the property owner themself) as a result of the zoning. The owner is generally required to prove that the zoning prevents any reasonable use of the land, not merely the most profitable use.

> **Example:** Corelli owns a piece of property that would make a perfect site for a convenience store, but it is in a residential zone. Corelli will not be able to get a variance by claiming that she could make much more money by building a convenience store than she could by building a single-family home.

Most variances authorize only minor deviations from the zoning law. A variance should not change the essential character of the neighborhood or conflict with the community's comprehensive plan.

Conditional Uses. Various special uses, such as schools, hospitals, and churches, don't fit into the ordinary zoning categories. These uses are necessary to the community, yet they may have adverse effects on neighboring properties. So in most communities the zoning authority can issue **conditional use permits** (also called special exception permits), allowing a limited number of these uses to operate in compliance with specified conditions. For example, a property owner might be given a conditional use permit to build a private school in a residential neighborhood, as long as the school meets certain requirements for parking, security, and so on.

Rezones. A property owner who believes that their property has been zoned improperly can petition the local appeals board for a **rezone** (sometimes called a zoning amendment). Usually, notice must be given to surrounding landowners and a hearing must be held before a decision is made on a petition.

When an area is rezoned to a more restrictive use (for example, a change from multifamily dwellings to single-family dwellings), it is referred to as **downzoning**. An **upzone** is the opposite: the zoning becomes less restrictive. For example, an upzone would include raising the building height limits in an urban area to help meet the housing density goals of a comprehensive plan.

Building Codes

The enactment of building codes is another exercise of the police power. Building codes protect the public from unsafe or unworkmanlike construction. They are generally divided into specialized codes, such as a fire code, an electrical code, and a plumbing code.

The codes set standards for construction methods and materials. A structure built before a new, stricter standard is enacted may still be required to meet the new standard. However, if an older structure is protected as a historic landmark, a separate building code usually applies.

Enforcement of building codes is usually accomplished through the building permit system. A property owner must obtain a permit from the city or county before constructing a new building or, with an existing building, making significant repairs or alterations. For example, it is usually necessary to have a building permit in order to add on to a home, to convert a carport into a garage, or even to build a fence over a certain height.

The permit requirement allows officials to inspect the building plans to verify that the plans comply with the building codes and zoning ordinances. A **certificate of occupancy** is issued once the completed building has been inspected and found satisfactory.

Subdivision Regulations

Another way state and local governments control land use is by regulating subdivisions. A subdivision is a division of one parcel of land into two or more parcels.

There are two basic types of subdivision regulations in Washington. The first type establishes requirements concerning the physical aspects of subdivisions, such as access roads, utilities, lot size, and so on. The second type is embodied in the state's Land Development Act. This is actually a consumer protection law rather than a land use control law; it requires subdivision developers to disclose certain information to prospective lot purchasers.

Physical Regulations. Regulations concerning the physical aspects of subdivisions are adopted and administered by each county in Washington. Although the regulations vary from county to county, the procedures for compliance are fairly uniform throughout the state. Someone who wants to subdivide a parcel of land must first notify county officials by submitting a plat map. The plat shows the boundaries of the proposed lots and provides information about arrangements for utilities and other public services. If the property is within city limits or within one mile of a city, the plat map must also be submitted to the proper city officials (usually the planning commission).

The plat must include the legal description of the land to be subdivided. It must also provide for any dedications that the county or city requires, such as dedication of land within the subdivision for public streets. (Dedication is a transfer of property from private to public ownership; see Chapter 3.)

The county or city may approve the plat as submitted, or may require amendments. It is illegal for the subdivider to sell any lots until the plat has been approved.

Washington Land Development Act. The Land Development Act applies to anyone selling or advertising 26 or more unimproved lots to the general public in Washington as part of a common promotional plan. It applies even when the subdivision is located in another state, if it is promoted in this state.

Under the act, a subdivision developer must prepare a **public offering statement**, providing information about the development. The statement includes disclosures concerning liens against the subdivision, the physical condition of the land, compliance with land use laws, and warranties that apply to the purchase of a lot.

The developer should give a public offering statement to each prospective lot buyer at least two days before the buyer signs a purchase contract. Otherwise, the buyer has a right to back out of the transaction (rescind the contract) within two days after receiving the statement. If the developer fails to give the buyer a statement before the transaction closes, the buyer can sue for damages.

The Land Development Act has a number of exemptions. It doesn't apply to a subdivision if fewer than ten lots will be offered for sale in a 12-month period, or if all the subdivision lots:

- are five acres or more,
- have buildings on them (or the developer intends to build within two years),
- are sold to builders for development,
- are sold to one purchaser, or
- lie entirely within city limits.

ILSA. The **Interstate Land Sales Full Disclosure Act** (commonly referred to as ILSA) is a federal consumer protection law concerning subdivisions of vacant land offered for sale or lease in interstate commerce. It has registration requirements (requiring developers to register their projects with a federal agency) and anti-fraud provisions (requiring disclosure of information to buyers and prohibiting misleading sales practices and advertising). The anti-fraud provisions generally apply to subdivisions with 25 or more vacant lots, and the registration requirements generally apply to subdivisions with 100 or more vacant lots, but there are numerous exemptions. The Consumer Financial Protection Bureau enforces ILSA.

Environmental Laws

The federal and state governments have enacted a number of laws aimed at preserving and protecting the physical environment, and some local governments have additional environmental regulations. These laws can have a substantial impact on the ways in which a property owner is allowed to use their land.

Shoreline Management Act. The purpose of this law is to protect Washington's shorelines by regulating development within 200 feet of the high water mark. It applies to coastal shorelines, and to the shores of larger lakes and streams, including wetlands.

National Environmental Policy Act (NEPA). NEPA is a federal law that requires federal agencies to prepare an **environmental impact statement** (EIS) for any governmental action that would have a significant impact on the environment. NEPA also applies to private uses or developments that require the approval of a federal agency.

State Environmental Policy Act (SEPA). Washington's SEPA is similar to NEPA in that it requires preparation of environmental impact statements. Under the state law, an EIS is required in connection with all actions of state and local agencies that may have a significant effect on the environment. The act also applies to private uses and developments that require the approval of the state, county, or city. Thus, SEPA procedures must be followed before a city or county approves rezones, conditional use permits, variances, or building permits.

CERCLA. The Comprehensive Environmental Response, Compensation, and Liability Act, a federal law, concerns liability for environmental cleanup costs. In some cases, the current owners of contaminated property may be required to pay for cleanup, even if they did not cause the contamination. This law is enforced by the federal Environmental Protection Agency (the EPA).

Pollution Control Laws. Federal legislation sets national standards for air and water quality and requires the states to implement these objectives. Permits are required for the discharge of pollutants into the air or water.

Environmental Hazards. Real estate agents should also be aware of the dangers posed by environmental hazards, such as asbestos insulation, lead-based paint, and geologic hazards. Some of these hazards are addressed by federal or state laws.

Asbestos. Asbestos was used for many years in insulation on plumbing pipes and heat ducts, and as general insulation material. It can also be found in floor tile and roofing material. In its original condition, asbestos is considered relatively harmless; but when it gets old and starts to disintegrate into a fine dust, it can cause lung cancer. Asbestos must be enclosed, covered with a permanent seal, or removed by an experienced professional.

Urea Formaldehyde. Adhesives containing urea formaldehyde are found in the pressed wood building materials used in furniture, kitchen cabinets, and some types of paneling. Urea formaldehyde can release formaldehyde gas, which can cause cancer, skin rashes, and breathing problems. However, these materials emit significant amounts of this gas only in the first few years. Older urea formaldehyde materials are not considered dangerous.

Radon. Radon, a colorless, odorless gas, is actually present almost everywhere. It is found wherever uranium is deposited in the earth's crust. As uranium decays, radon gas is formed and seeps from the earth, usually into the atmosphere. However, radon sometimes collects in buildings. For example, radon may enter a house through cracks in the foundation or through floor drains. Exposure to dangerous levels of radon gas may cause lung cancer.

Lead-Based Paint. Lead is extremely toxic to human beings, damaging the brain, the kidneys, and the central nervous system. The most common source of lead in the home is lead-based paint. Although lead is now banned in consumer paint, it is still found in many homes built before 1978. As lead-based paint deteriorates, or if it is sanded or scraped, it forms a lead dust that accumulates inside and outside the home. The dust can be breathed in or ingested, increasing the risk of toxic lead exposure. In some cases, a seller or landlord is required by law to make disclosures concerning lead-based paint to prospective buyers or tenants.

Underground Storage Tanks. Underground storage tanks are found not only on commercial and industrial properties, but also on residential properties. Older homes used underground storage tanks to store fuel oil. A storage tank is considered underground if at least 10% of its volume (including piping) is below the earth's surface. The principal danger from underground storage tanks is that when they grow old, they begin to rust, leaking toxic products into the soil or, even more dangerously, into the groundwater. Removing underground storage tanks and cleaning up the contaminated soil can be time-consuming and expensive. Both federal and state laws regulate the removal of storage tanks and the necessary cleanup.

Water Contamination. Water can be contaminated by a variety of agents, including bacteria, viruses, nitrates, metals such as lead or mercury, fertilizers, pesticides, and radon. These contaminants may come from underground storage tanks, industrial discharge, urban area runoff, malfunctioning septic systems, and runoff from agricultural areas. Drinking contaminated water can cause physical symptoms that range from mild stomach upset to kidney and liver damage, cancer, and death. If a home uses a well as a water source, it should be tested by health authorities or private laboratories at least once a year.

Illegal Drug Manufacturing. If property has been the site of illegal drug manufacturing, there may be substantial health risks for subsequent occupants. The chemicals used to manufacture certain illegal drugs are highly toxic, and the effects of the contamination can linger for a long time. The government can seize any property being used to manufacture illegal drugs. Property should not be listed or sold until any conditions that could subject the property to seizure have been eliminated.

> **Example:** Meyers owns a single-family home that has been used as a rental property for several years. Unknown to Meyers, the current tenants are manufacturing illegal drugs in the basement of the home. The government could seize the property, even though Meyers knows nothing about the drug activity.

Mold. Mold is a commonplace problem in damp parts of houses, such as basements and bathrooms. For most people, the presence of mold does not cause any adverse effects. However, for people who are allergic to mold or who have respiratory problems, the presence of mold may render a house unlivable. Mold can affect residential buildings, commercial buildings, or public buildings such as schools and government offices. Bear in mind that mold may grow out of sight, inside walls or heating ducts, and will not necessarily be discovered in an inspection.

Geologic Hazards. Geologic hazards are a significant concern for many property owners in the coastal regions of the country. Major potential geologic problems include landslides, flooding, subsidence, and earthquakes. When dealing with a property located on or near a steep slope, look for signs of ground movement. Tilting trees, active soil erosion, and cracking, dipping, or slumping ground are all indicators of slide activity. Subsidence is the collapse of ground into underground cavities, which may be natural or man-made. It is wise to consult with a geologist to assess the magnitude of a ground movement problem.

Flooding can also be a serious problem for property owners. Whenever property is located in a flood plain—the low-lying, flat areas immediately adjacent to a river—there is cause for concern. It is prudent to check for signs of previous flood damage to structures, particularly in basements and foundations. In some cases, it may be necessary to obtain flood insurance.

Earthquakes are the least predictable and least controllable of geologic problems. However, steps can be taken to protect buildings against earthquakes. Seismic retrofitting can make a property more desirable and increase its value. Many contractors are able to perform this type of work, and information about seismic retrofitting is widely available from state and local government agencies.

Eminent Domain

As you've seen, the government can regulate the use of private property with a variety of laws—zoning ordinances, building codes, and so on. These laws are based on the police power, the government's power to regulate for the public health, safety, morals, and general welfare. Another governmental power that can be used to control land use is the power of **eminent domain.** For example, to fulfill the open space goals in its comprehensive plan, a local government might use eminent domain to acquire several pieces of property for use as a public park.

As we discussed in Chapter 3, eminent domain is the federal or state government's power to take private property for a public purpose by paying fair market value for the property. A state government may delegate the power of eminent domain to local governments and to private entities that serve the public, such as utility companies and railroads.

Condemnation is the process by which the government exercises its power of eminent domain. When a particular property is needed for a public purpose, the government first offers to buy it from the owner. If the owner refuses to sell for the price offered, the government files a condemnation lawsuit.

The owner's only grounds for objection are that the intended use of the property is not a public use, or that the price offered is not just compensation.

In some cases, others with an interest in a condemned property may be entitled to compensation, as well as the property owner. For example, the government might have to compensate an easement holder, or a commercial tenant who has a long-term lease. While residential tenants in a condemned building are not likely to have a compensable interest in the property, those displaced through the condemnation process may be entitled to advance notice of the termination of their tenancy and assistance with relocation, including payment of moving expenses.

It is important to understand the distinction between eminent domain and the police power. Eminent domain involves a "taking": property is taken away from the owner, and the Constitution requires the government to pay the owner compensation. In an exercise of the police power, private property is regulated, but not taken away from the owner. The government is usually not required to compensate the owner for a proper exercise of the police power, unless the action (such as a new environmental regulation) so significantly reduces the value of the property that a court finds it to be a taking.

Taxation

Real property taxes affect property ownership. The taxes create liens, and if the property owner fails to pay the taxes, the government can sell the property to collect them. Real property taxation has always been a popular method of raising revenue because land has a fixed location, is relatively indestructible, and is essentially impossible to conceal. Thus, there is a high degree of certainty that the taxes will be collected.

In this section, we will discuss these three types of taxes on real property:

- general real estate taxes (also called ad valorem taxes),
- special assessments (also called improvement taxes), and
- the real estate excise tax (also called the transfer tax).

General Real Estate Taxes

General real estate taxes are levied to support the general operation and services of government. Public schools and police and fire protection are examples of government services paid for with general real estate tax revenues. These taxes are levied by a number of governmental agencies, such as cities, counties, school districts, and water districts. Thus, a single property can be situated in five or six taxing districts.

Assessment. General real estate taxes are **ad valorem** taxes. That means the amount of tax owed depends on the value of the property. The valuation of property for purposes of taxation is called **assessment.** In Washington, all real property must be assessed at 100% of its "true and fair value" unless otherwise provided by law. True and fair value means market value: the most probable price that the property would sell for under normal market conditions.

Real property is assessed (revalued) each year on January 1; a physical examination of the property has to be performed at least once every six years. In each county, a Board of Equalization hears appeals of property tax assessments from taxpayers.

Collection of Taxes. Tax bills are mailed to property owners each year in the middle of February. Payment of half the taxes is due on April 30, and the balance is due on October 31.

General real estate taxes become a lien on January 1 of the year in which they are levied. Taxes are levied in October of each year are billed and paid the following year.

The county can foreclose on a property when the taxes have been delinquent for three years. The owner can redeem the property before the sale by paying the amount of delinquent taxes, interest, and any other accumulated costs.

Exemptions. State law exempts numerous types of property from general real estate taxes. For example, the taxes aren't levied against publicly owned property, property used for church purposes, or nonprofit hospitals and schools.

There are also some exemptions available to individual property owners. For example, there is a partial exemption for low-income homeowners who are 61 or older, or retired because of physical disability. In some cases, these owners may also be allowed to defer payment of the partial taxes they owe until their property is sold.

Open Space. Washington has a special rule for taxation of open space (including farm land and timber land), which shows how the power to tax can be used for land use control. Certain land that qualifies as open space is eligible to be assessed not at its market value (which might mean how much it would be worth if developed) but at its value as it is currently being used.

This results in a lower assessment, and therefore in lower taxes, providing an incentive to preserve the property as open space instead of developing it. To have property assessed in this way, the owner must agree that if the property is developed or sold for development, additional taxes will be paid at that point.

Special Assessments

Special assessments, also called local improvement taxes, are levied to pay for improvements that benefit particular properties, such as the installation of streetlights or the widening of a street. Only the properties that benefit from the improvement are taxed, on the theory that the value of those properties is increased by the improvement. A special assessment is usually a one-time tax, although the property owners may be allowed to pay the assessment off in installments.

Like general real estate taxes, special assessments create liens against the taxed properties. If an owner fails to pay the assessment, the government can foreclose on the property.

Here are the distinctions between general real estate taxes and special assessments:

1. General real estate taxes are levied to pay for ongoing government services, such as police protection. A special assessment is levied to pay for a specific improvement, such as adding sidewalks to a section of street.
2. General real estate taxes are levied against all taxable real property within a taxing district, for the benefit of the entire community. A special assessment, on the other hand, is levied against only those properties that benefit from the improvement in question.
3. The amount of general real estate taxes a property owner must pay is based on the property's value. A property owner's share of a special assessment depends on the cost of the project, and it may also vary depending on the benefit the property receives from the project.
4. General real estate taxes are levied every year. A special assessment is a one-time tax, levied only when a property is benefited by a public improvement.

Real Estate Excise Tax

An excise tax is levied on most sales of real property in Washington. The tax is based on the property's selling price, and the tax rate is graduated so that a higher percentage of the price is charged on more costly properties. For example, the excise tax might be 1.6% of the selling price for a relatively inexpensive home, but reach 3.25% for a very expensive home. Most of the tax is paid to the state, but the local government also receives a share, the size of which varies depending on the city or county where the property is located.

The excise tax is ordinarily collected when the buyer's deed is recorded; the recorder's office won't accept a deed for recording unless the tax is paid and a real estate excise tax affidavit is executed. By law, the seller is liable for payment of the excise tax, yet the tax creates a lien against the transferred property (now owned by the buyer). So even though payment is the seller's responsibility, a buyer should always make sure the excise tax is paid, so that the deed can be recorded and lien foreclosure avoided.

Chapter Summary

1. The police power—the government's power to adopt and enforce laws for the protection of the public health, safety, morals, and general welfare—is the basis for land use control laws.
2. Most communities have a comprehensive plan—a long-term plan for development—and many counties and cities are required by law to have one. A local government implements its comprehensive plan with zoning ordinances and other laws.
3. Zoning ordinances provide for certain exceptions to their rules: nonconforming uses, variances, and conditional uses. They also have procedures for rezones.
4. Building codes set standards for construction materials and practices, to protect the public. The codes are enforced through the building permit system.
5. Someone who subdivides land must submit a plat map to the county and comply with local subdivision regulations. In some cases, a developer will also be required to comply with consumer protection laws regulating the sale of subdivision lots.
6. There are a number of important federal and state environmental laws that affect land use, including the Shoreline Management Act, NEPA, SEPA, and CERCLA.
7. Along with environmental laws, real estate agents need to be aware of environmental hazards such as asbestos, urea formaldehyde, radon, lead-based paint, underground storage tanks, water contamination, illegal drug manufacturing, mold, and geologic hazards.
8. A government entity can use the power of eminent domain to implement its comprehensive plan. When property is taken under the power of eminent domain, the government must pay just compensation to the owner. (Compensation is not required when property is merely regulated under the police power.)
9. The government's power to tax also affects property ownership. General real estate taxes are levied each year to pay for ongoing government services. Special assessments are levied to pay for improvements that benefit specific properties. The real estate excise tax must be paid on each sale of real property in Washington.

Key Terms

Police power—The power of state governments to regulate for the protection of the public health, safety, morals, and general welfare.

Comprehensive plan—A long-term plan of development for a community, which is implemented by zoning and other laws.

Zoning—A method of controlling land use by dividing a community into zones for different types of uses.

Nonconforming use—A formerly legal use that does not conform to a new zoning ordinance, but is nonetheless allowed to continue.

Variance—An authorization to deviate from the rules in a zoning ordinance, granted because strict enforcement would cause undue hardship for the property owner.

Conditional use permit—A permit that allows a special use, such as a school or hospital, to operate in a neighborhood where it would otherwise be prohibited by the zoning.

Rezone—An amendment to a zoning ordinance; a property owner who feels her property has been zoned improperly may apply for a rezone.

Building codes—Regulations that set minimum standards for construction methods and materials.

Eminent domain—The government's power to take private property for public use, upon payment of just compensation to the owner.

Condemnation—The process of taking property pursuant to the power of eminent domain.

General real estate taxes—Taxes levied against real property annually to pay for general government services; based on the value of the property taxed (ad valorem).

Special assessment—A tax levied against property that benefits from a local improvement project, to pay for the project.

Real estate excise tax—A tax levied when a piece of real property is sold; based on the selling price of the property.

Chapter Quiz

1. The police power is the government's power to:

a) take private property for public use
b) enact laws for the protection of the public health, safety, morals, and general welfare
c) tax property to pay for police protection
d) None of the above

2. Which of the following is likely to be controlled by a zoning ordinance?

a) Use of the property
b) Building height
c) Placement of a building on a lot
d) All of the above

3. Which of the following is NOT likely to be one of the goals of a land use control law?

a) Ensuring that properties are put to their most profitable use
b) Controlling growth and population density
c) Ensuring that neighboring uses are compatible
d) Preserving access to light and air

4. As a general rule, when a new zoning ordinance goes into effect, nonconforming uses:

a) must comply with the new law within 90 days
b) must shut down within 90 days
c) will be granted conditional use permits
d) are allowed to continue, but not to expand

5. An owner who feels that their property was improperly zoned should apply for a:

a) conditional use permit
b) variance
c) rezone
d) nonconforming use permit

6. A property owner is generally required to show undue hardship in order to obtain a:

a) nonconforming use permit
b) special exception permit
c) rezone
d) variance

7. Which of these is an example of a variance?

a) Authorizing a hospital to be built in a residential zone
b) Authorizing a structure to be built only 12 feet from the lot's boundary, although the zoning ordinance requires 15-foot setbacks
c) Allowing a grocery store to continue in operation after the neighborhood is zoned residential
d) Approving the subdivision of a parcel of land into two or more lots

8. Which of these is NOT an exercise of the police power?

a) Condemnation
b) Building code
c) Zoning ordinance
d) Subdivision regulations

9. Eminent domain differs from the police power in that:

a) the government is required to compensate the property owner
b) it can be exercised only by the state government, not a city or county government
c) it affects only the use of the property, not the title
d) the property must be unimproved

10. Which of the following hazardous substances is a natural product of the decay of radioactive matter?

a) Radon
b) Urea formaldehyde
c) Mold
d) Carbon monoxide

11. A special assessment is the same thing as a/an:

a) general real estate tax
b) improvement tax
c) real estate excise tax
d) ad valorem tax

12. General real estate taxes are:

a) used to support the general operation and services of government
b) levied annually
c) based on the value of the taxed property
d) All of the above

13. Which of these is a federal law concerning liability for environmental cleanup costs?

a) ILSA
b) CERCLA
c) SEPA
d) NEPA

14. The real estate excise tax is based on the property's:

a) selling price
b) fair market value
c) current use
d) highest and best use

15. Under the State Environmental Policy Act (SEPA), an environmental impact statement is required:

a) for every building project
b) only for state or federal projects
c) for all actions of state and local agencies that may have a significant impact on the environment
d) for all actions of state and local agencies on an annual basis

Chapter 6: *Contract Law*

I. Legal Classifications of Contracts
- A. Express vs. implied
- B. Unilateral vs. bilateral
- C. Executory vs. executed

II. Elements of a Valid Contract
- A. Capacity
- B. Mutual consent
- C. Lawful objective
- D. Consideration
- E. Writing requirement

III. Legal Status of Contracts
- A. Void
- B. Voidable
- C. Unenforceable
- D. Valid

IV. Discharging a Contract
- A. Full performance
- B. Agreement between the parties

V. Breach of Contract
- A. Remedies for breach of contract
  1. Rescission
  2. Compensatory damages
  3. Liquidated damages
  4. Specific performance
- B. Tender

VI. Types of Real Estate Contracts
- A. Listing agreements
- B. Buyer representation agreements
- C. Purchase and sale agreements
- D. Land contracts
- E. Leases
- F. Escrow instructions
- G. Option agreements

Contracts are a significant part of the real estate business. Almost everyone has a basic understanding of what a contract is, but real estate agents need more than that. This chapter explains the requirements that must be met in order for a contract to be valid and binding; how a contract can be terminated; what is considered a breach of contract; and what remedies are available when a breach occurs.

Key Terms

Contract	**Voidable**
Capacity	**Unenforceable**
Mutual Consent	**Rescission**
Offer	**Cancellation**
Acceptance	**Assignment**
Counteroffer	**Novation**
Fraud	**Compensatory Damages**
Undue Influence	**Liquidated Damages**
Duress	**Specific Performance**
Consideration	**Tender**
Statute of Frauds	**Option Agreement**
Void	

Introduction

Real estate licensees deal with contracts on a daily basis: listing agreements, purchase and sale agreements, option agreements, and leases are all contracts. Thus, it is essential for a licensee to understand the basic legal requirements and effects of contracts.

Keep in mind, however, that a real estate licensee can't draft contract provisions. Anyone other than a lawyer who drafts a contract for someone else may be charged with the unauthorized practice of law.

Here is a general definition of a **contract**: an agreement between two or more competent persons to do or not do certain things in exchange for consideration. An agreement to sell a car, deliver lumber, or rent an apartment is a contract. If the contract meets minimum legal requirements, it can be enforced in court.

Legal Classifications of Contracts

There are certain basic classifications that apply to any contract, no matter what type it is. Every contract is either express or implied, either unilateral or bilateral, and either executory or executed.

Express vs. Implied

An **express** contract is one that has been put into words. It may be written or oral. Each party to the contract has stated what he or she is willing to do and has been told what to expect from the other party. Most contracts are express. On the other hand, an **implied** contract, or contract by implication, is created by the actions of the parties, not by express agreement.

> **Example:** A written lease agreement expires, but the tenant continues to make payments and the landlord continues to accept them. Both parties have implied their consent to a new lease contract.

Unilateral vs. Bilateral

A contract is **unilateral** if only one of the contracting parties is legally obligated to perform. That party has promised to do a particular thing if the other party does something else; but the other party has not promised to do anything, and is not legally obligated to do anything.

> **Example:** In an open listing agreement, a seller promises to pay a real estate brokerage a commission if the firm finds a buyer for the property. The firm does not promise to try to find a buyer, but if it does, the seller is obligated to pay. An open listing agreement is a unilateral contract.

A **bilateral** contract is formed when each party promises to do something, so that both parties are legally obligated to perform. Most contracts are bilateral.

> **Example:** In a purchase and sale agreement, the seller promises to transfer title to the buyer, and the buyer promises to pay the agreed price to the seller. This is a bilateral contract. Each party has made a promise, and both are obligated to perform.

Executory vs. Executed

An **executory** contract is one that has not yet been performed, or is in the process of being performed. An **executed** contract has been fully performed; the parties have fulfilled the terms of their agreement. In this sense, the terms "executed" and "performed" mean the same thing.

Fig. 6.1 Contract classifications

Express *Written or oral*	OR	**Implied** *Actions of the parties*
Unilateral *One promise*	OR	**Bilateral** *Two promises*
Executory *Not yet fully performed*	OR	**Executed** *Fully performed*

Note, however, that "executed" also has another meaning in connection with contracts. Execution of a contract (or execution of a will, a deed, or some other type of legal document) can simply refer to signing it, not to performing or fulfilling it. The party or parties who execute a document have signed it and taken any other steps needed to make it legally binding (for example, in the case of a will, having it witnessed). Which meaning is intended in a particular case will usually be clear from the context.

Elements of a Valid Contract

To make any type of contract valid and binding, so that a court will enforce it if necessary, four elements are needed:

1. legal capacity to contract,
2. mutual consent,
3. a lawful objective, and
4. consideration.

Capacity

The first requirement for a valid contract is that the parties have the legal capacity to enter into a contract. A person must be at least 18 years old to enter into a valid contract, and they must also be competent.

Age Eighteen. Eighteen years of age is the age of majority in Washington. Minors (those under the age of 18) do not have capacity to contract. If a minor signs a contract, it is voidable by the minor; in other words, it cannot be enforced against them.

> **Example:** A 16-year-old signs a purchase and sale agreement, agreeing to buy a house. The seller cannot enforce the contract against the minor, although the minor could compel the seller to honor the terms of the agreement.

The purpose of this rule is to prevent people from entering into legally binding agreements when they may be too young to understand the consequences.

Competent. A person must also be mentally competent to have capacity to contract. If a court declares a person incompetent, any contract they sign is void. If someone is declared incompetent after signing a contract, the contract may be voidable at the discretion of the court-appointed guardian.

A contract entered into by a person who was temporarily incompetent (for example, under the influence of alcohol or drugs) may be voidable if they take legal action within a reasonable time after regaining mental competency.

Representing Another. Often, one person has the capacity to represent another person or entity in a contract negotiation. For instance, parents or court-appointed guardians handle the affairs of minors and incompetent persons; properly authorized officers represent corporations; individual partners represent partnerships; executors or administrators represent deceased persons; and a competent adult can appoint another competent adult to act on their behalf through a power of attorney. In each of these cases, the authorized representative can enter into a contract on behalf of the person represented.

Mutual Consent

Mutual consent is the second requirement for a valid contract. Each party must consent to the agreement. Consent is presumed once someone signs a contract, so no contract should be signed until its contents are fully understood.

Failure or inability to read an agreement is not an excuse for nonperformance. An illiterate person should have a contract explained thoroughly by someone trustworthy before signing it.

Mutual consent is sometimes called mutual assent, mutuality, or "a meeting of the minds." It is achieved through the process of **offer and acceptance**.

Offer. A contract offer shows the willingness of the person making it (the **offeror**) to enter into a contract on the stated terms. To be valid, an offer must meet two requirements:

1. It must express a willingness to contract. Whatever words make up the offer, they must clearly indicate that the offeror intends to enter into a contract.
2. It must be definite and certain in its terms. An offer that does not clearly state what the offeror is proposing is unenforceable.

Note that an advertisement or listing with a price and details about the property is still not definite enough to constitute a contract offer; it is merely an invitation to negotiate. Items still to be negotiated include the earnest money amount, closing date, and who will serve as escrow agent, for example.

Terminating an Offer. Sometimes circumstances change after an offer is made, or perhaps the offeror has a change of heart. If an offer terminates before it is accepted, no contract is formed. A number of actions or events can terminate an offer before it is accepted, including:

- revocation by the offeror,
- lapse of time,
- death or incompetency of the offeror,
- rejection of the offer, or
- a counteroffer.

The offeror can **revoke** the offer at any time until they are notified that the offer has been accepted. To effect a proper "offer and acceptance," the accepting party must not only accept the offer, but must also communicate that acceptance to the offeror before the offer is revoked. (See the discussion of acceptance, below.)

Many offers include a deadline for acceptance. If a deadline is set and acceptance is not communicated within the time allotted, the offer terminates automatically. If a time limit is not stated in the offer, a reasonable amount of time is allowed. What is reasonable is determined by the court if a dispute arises.

Fig. 6.2 Mutual Consent is achieved through the process of Offer and Acceptance

Offer
- Willingness to contract
- Definite and certain terms

Termination (No Mutual Consent)	Acceptance (Mutual Consent)
• Revocation • Lapse of time • Death or incompetency of the offeror • Rejection of the offer • Counteroffer	• By offeree • Communicated to the offeror • In specified manner • Doesn't vary terms

If the offeror dies or is declared incompetent before the offer is accepted, the offer terminates.

A **rejection** also terminates an offer. Once the **offeree** (the person to whom the offer was made) rejects the offer, they cannot go back later and create a contract by accepting the offer.

> **Example:** Howard offers to purchase Maria's condo for $235,000. Maria rejects the offer the next day. The following week, Maria changes her mind and decides to accept Howard's offer. But her acceptance at this point does not create a contract, because the offer terminated with her rejection.

A **counteroffer** is sometimes called a qualified acceptance. It is actually a rejection of the offer and a tender of a new offer. Instead of either accepting or rejecting the offer outright, the offeree "accepts" with certain modifications. This happens when some, but not all, of the original terms are unacceptable to the offeree. When there is a counteroffer, the roles of the parties are reversed: the original offeror becomes the offeree and can accept or reject the revised offer. If they choose to accept the counteroffer, there is a binding contract. If the counteroffer is rejected, the party making the counteroffer cannot go back and accept the original offer. The counteroffer terminated the original offer.

> **Example:** Martinez offers to buy Harrison's property on the following terms: the purchase price will be $950,000, the downpayment will be $60,000, and the closing date will be January 15. Harrison agrees to all of the terms except the closing date, which she wants to be February 1. By changing one of the terms, Harrison has rejected Martinez's initial offer and made a counteroffer. Now it is up to Martinez to either accept or reject Harrison's counteroffer.

Acceptance. An offer can be revoked at any time until acceptance has been communicated to the offeror. To create a binding contract, the offeree must communicate acceptance to the offeror in the manner and within the time limit stated in the offer (or before the offer is revoked). If no time or manner of acceptance is stated in the offer, a reasonable time and manner is implied.

The offeree's acceptance must also be free of any negative influences, such as fraud, undue influence, or duress. If any of these negative forces influence an offer or acceptance, the contract is voidable by the injured party.

Fraud is misrepresentation of a material fact to another person who relies on the misrepresentation as the truth in deciding whether to enter into a transaction.

- **Actual fraud** occurs when the person making the statement either knows the statement is false and makes it with an intent to deceive, or doesn't know whether or not the statement is true but makes it anyway. For example, a seller who paints over cracks in the basement and then tells the buyer that the foundation is completely sound is committing actual fraud.
- **Constructive fraud** occurs when a person who occupies a position of confidence and trust, or who has superior knowledge of the subject matter, makes a false statement with no intent to deceive. For example, if a seller innocently points out incorrect lot boundaries, it may be constructive fraud.

Undue influence is when someone in a position of trust or authority uses excessive persuasion to overcome another person's free will and pressure them into signing an inequitable contract (or taking some other inadvisable action). Courts consider several factors when deciding whether undue influence existed, including the vulnerability of the victim (due to age, disability, emotional distress, or other issues), the influencer's conduct and level of authority, and the nature and length of the relationship.

Duress is compelling someone to do something—such as enter into a contract—against their will, by using or threatening to use force or constraint.

Lawful Objective

The third requirement for a valid contract is a lawful objective. Both the purpose of the contract and the consideration for the contract (discussed below) must be lawful. Examples of contracts with unlawful objectives are a contract requiring payment of an interest rate above the state's usury limit, or a contract to engage in unlawful gambling (for example, a bet placed with a bookie). A contract that does not have a lawful objective is void.

A contract may contain some lawful provisions and some unlawful provisions. In this situation, it may be possible to sever the unlawful portions of the contract and enforce the lawful portions.

> **Example:** Callahan and Baker enter into a contract for the purchase and sale of an apartment house. A clause in the contract prohibits the buyer from renting the apartments to persons of a certain race. The contract concerning the sale of the property would probably be enforceable, but the racially restrictive clause would be void because it is unlawful.

Consideration

The fourth element of a valid contract is **consideration**. Consideration is something of value exchanged by the contracting parties. It might be money, goods, or services, or a promise to provide money, goods, or services. Whatever form it takes, the consideration must be either a benefit to the party receiving it or a disadvantage to the party offering it. The typical real estate purchase and sale agreement involves a promise by the buyer to pay a certain amount of money to the seller at a certain time, and a promise by the seller to convey title to the buyer when the price has been paid. Both parties have given and received consideration.

While consideration is usually the promise to do a particular act, it can also be a promise to not do a particular act. For example, Aunt Martha might promise to pay her nephew Charles $1,000 if he promises not to smoke.

As a general rule, a contract is enforceable as long as the consideration has value, even though the value of the consideration exchanged is unequal. A contract to sell a piece of property worth $120,000 for $105,000 is enforceable.

In cases where the disparity in value is quite large (for example, a contract to sell a piece of property worth $185,000 for $55,000), a court may refuse to enforce the contract. This would be limited to situations where the parties have unequal bargaining power (for instance, if the buyer is a real estate developer and the seller is elderly, uneducated, and inexperienced in business).

The Writing Requirement

The requirements we've covered so far—capacity, mutual consent, a lawful objective, and consideration—apply to any kind of contract. For most contracts used in real estate transactions, there's a fifth requirement: they must be put into writing, as required by the statute of frauds.

The **statute of frauds** is a state law that requires certain types of contracts to be in writing and signed. Only the types of contracts covered by the statute of frauds have to be in writing; other contracts may be oral.

Each state has its own statute of frauds, and the requirements vary slightly from state to state. As a general rule, however, the statute of frauds applies to almost all contracts typically used in a real estate transaction. In Washington, the statute of frauds applies to:

- any agreement to convey an interest in real property (such as a purchase and sale agreement);
- any agreement that, by its terms, will not be performed within one year after it is made (such as a two-year lease);
- any agreement to assume the debts of another (such as the assumption of a mortgage); and
- any agreement to employ an agent for compensation to sell, buy, lease, or exchange real property (such as a listing agreement).

The "writing" required by the statute of frauds does not have to be in any particular form, nor does it have to be contained entirely in one document. A note or memorandum about the agreement or a series of letters will suffice, as long as the writing:

- identifies the subject matter of the contract,
- indicates an agreement between the parties and its essential terms, and
- is signed by the party or parties to be bound.

If the parties fail to put a contract that falls under the statute of frauds in writing, or if they fail to include all the essential terms of their agreement in the written version that they sign, the contract is usually unenforceable.

However, occasionally a court will enforce such an agreement even though it doesn't fulfill the requirements of the statute of frauds. This might occur if there is evidence that an agreement was reached along with evidence of its terms, and if the party trying to enforce the contract has completely or substantially performed their contractual obligations. This is a relatively rare occurrence; the safest course is to put the complete contract in writing.

Fig. 6.3 Real Estate Contract Requirements

A Valid Real Estate Contract
• Capacity • Mutual consent • Lawful objective • Consideration • In writing

Legal Status of Contracts

Four terms are used to describe the legal status of a contract: a contract is void, voidable, unenforceable, or valid. We've already used these terms in our discussion, and now we'll look more closely at what each one means.

Void

A void contract is no contract at all; it has no legal effect. This most often occurs because one of the essential elements, such as mutual consent or consideration, is absent.

> **Example:** Talbot signed a contract promising to deed some property to Xiao, but Xiao did not offer any consideration in exchange for Talbot's promise. Since the contract is not supported by consideration, it is void.

However, certain required elements can be missing without making the contract void. If an agreement to purchase real estate is not in writing, or fails to include all essential terms of the parties' agreement, the contract is generally unenforceable rather than void. Or if one of the parties to a contract is a minor, then the contract is voidable for the minor and unenforceable for the other party; the minor's lack of full contractual capacity does not automatically make the contract void.

A void contract may be disregarded. Neither party is required to take legal action to withdraw from the agreement.

Voidable

A voidable contract appears on its face to be valid, but has some defect giving one or both of the parties the power to withdraw from the agreement. Contracts entered into by minors or as a result of fraud are normally voidable by the injured party (the minor or the one defrauded).

It is important to note that action must be taken to rescind a voidable contract. Unlike a contract that is void from the outset, a voidable contract cannot simply be ignored. Failure to take action within a reasonable time may result in a court declaring that the contract was ratified.

Alternatively, the injured party may decide to continue with the agreement; in that case, they may expressly ratify it. If a minor wants to void a contract, they can disaffirm it when they turn 18; otherwise, the contract becomes ratified.

Unenforceable

An unenforceable contract is one that cannot be enforced in court. Contracts are unenforceable for various reasons—for example, as we've already said, an oral contract that the statute of frauds requires to be in writing is unenforceable. Here are some other reasons a contract might be unenforceable:

1. its contents cannot be proved,
2. it is voidable by the other party, or
3. the statute of limitations has expired.

Contents Cannot Be Proved. This is most often a problem associated with oral agreements, where it may be impossible to prove who said what. Even if the statute of frauds does not require a certain kind of contract to be written, it is a good idea to put it in writing because it avoids confusion and misunderstanding.

Contract Voidable by Other Party. If a contract is voidable by one of the parties, it is unenforceable by the other party. (Note that the party who has the option of voiding the contract can choose instead to enforce the contract against the other party.)

Statute of Limitations Expired. A statute of limitations is a law that sets a deadline for filing a lawsuit. Unless an injured party files suit before the deadline set by the applicable statute of limitations, their legal claim is lost forever. The purpose of a statute of limitations is to prevent one person from suing another too many years after an event, when memories have faded and evidence has been lost.

Fig. 6.4 Legal Status of Contracts

Type of Contract	Legal Effect	Example
Void	No contract at all	An agreement for which there is no consideration
Voidable	Valid until rescinded by one party	A contract with a minor
Unenforceable	One or both parties cannot sue to enforce	A contract after the limitations period expires
Valid	Binding and enforceable	An agreement that meets all the legal requirements

Every state has a statute of limitations for contracts. If one of the parties to a contract fails to perform their obligations (breaches the contract), the other party has to sue within a certain number of years after the breach. Otherwise, the statute of limitations will run out and the contract will become unenforceable.

In Washington, the statute of limitations generally requires lawsuits concerning written contracts to be filed within six years after their breach, and lawsuits concerning oral contracts to be filed within three years after their breach.

Valid

If an agreement meets all the requirements for contract formation, its contents can be proved, and it is free of any negative influences, it is a valid contract and can be enforced in a court of law.

Discharging a Contract

Once there is a valid, enforceable contract, it may be discharged by:

1. full performance, or
2. agreement between the parties.

Full Performance

Full performance means that the parties have performed all their obligations; the contract is executed. For example, once the deed to the property has been transferred to the buyer, and the seller has received the purchase price, the purchase and sale agreement has been discharged by full performance.

Agreement Between the Parties

The parties to a contract can agree to discharge the contract in any of the following ways:

- rescission,
- cancellation,
- assignment, or
- novation.

Rescission. Sometimes the parties to a contract agree that they would be better off if the contract had never been signed. In such a case, they may decide to rescind the contract.

The buyer and the seller sign an agreement that terminates their previous agreement and puts them as nearly as possible back in the positions they were in before entering into the agreement. If money or other consideration has changed hands, it will be returned.

In certain circumstances, a contract may be rescinded by court order (rather than by agreement). Court-ordered rescission is discussed later in this chapter.

Cancellation. A cancellation does not go as far as a rescission. The parties agree to terminate the contract, but previous acts are unaffected. For example, money that was paid prior to the cancellation is not returned.

When contracting to purchase real property, a buyer generally gives the seller a deposit to show that they are acting in good faith and intend to fulfill the terms of their agreement. This is called an **earnest money deposit**, and the seller is entitled to keep it if the buyer defaults (breaches the contract). If the buyer and seller agree to terminate the contract and the seller refunds the earnest money deposit to the buyer, the contract has been rescinded. If the parties agree that the seller will keep the deposit, the contract has been cancelled.

Assignment. Sometimes one of the parties to a contract wants to withdraw by assigning their interest in the contract to another person. As a general rule, a contract can be assigned to another unless a clause in the contract prohibits assignment. Technically, assignment does not discharge the contract. The new party (the assignee) assumes primary liability for the contractual obligations, but the withdrawing party (the assignor) is still secondarily liable.

> **Example:** A buyer is purchasing a home under a 15-year land contract. In the absence of any prohibitive language in the contract, they can sell the home, accept a cash downpayment, and assign their contract rights and liabilities to the new buyer. The new buyer would assume primary liability for the contract debt, but the original buyer would retain secondary liability.

One exception to the rule that a contract can be assigned unless otherwise agreed: a personal services contract can't be assigned without the other party's consent.

> **Example:** A nightclub has a contract with a singer for several performances. The singer cannot assign their contract to another singer, because it is a personal services contract. The nightclub management has a right to choose who will be singing in their establishment.

Novation. The term "novation" has two generally accepted meanings. One type of novation is the substitution of a new party into an existing contract obligation. If a seller releases the original buyer from a purchase and sale agreement in favor of a new buyer under the same contract, there has been a novation. The first buyer is relieved of all liability connected with the contract.

Novation may also be the substitution of a new obligation for an old one. If a landlord and tenant agree to tear up a three-year lease in favor of a new ten-year lease, it is a novation.

Assignment vs. Novation. The difference between assignment and novation concerns the withdrawing party's liability. When a contract is assigned, there is continuing liability for the assignor. In a novation, on the other hand, the withdrawing party is released from liability, because they were replaced with someone else who was approved by the other original party. Novation, unlike assignment, always requires the other party's consent.

Breach of Contract

A **breach of contract** occurs when one of the parties fails, without legal excuse, to perform any of the promises contained in the agreement. The injured party can seek a remedy in court only if the breach is a **material breach.** A breach is material when the unfulfilled promise is an important part of the contract.

Many contracts, including most real estate purchase and sale agreements, state that **"time is of the essence."** That phrase is used to warn the parties that timely performance is crucial, and failure to meet a deadline would be a material breach. If one party misses a deadline, the other party may choose whether to proceed with the contract or use the "time is of the essence" clause as the basis for ending it.

Remedies for Breach of Contract

There are four possible legal remedies for a breach of contract:

- rescission,
- compensatory damages,
- liquidated damages, or
- specific performance.

Rescission. As previously explained, a rescission is a termination of the contract in which the parties are returned to their original positions. In the case of a purchase and sale agreement, the seller refunds the buyer's earnest money deposit and the buyer gives up their equitable interest in the property. The rescission can be by agreement between the parties, or it can be ordered by a court at the request of one party when the other party has breached the contract.

Compensatory Damages. Financial losses that a party suffers as a result of a breach of contract are referred to as **damages.**

> **Example:** Acme Safes contracts to buy 1,000 hinges from Baker Manufacturing for $12,000, and Baker promises to deliver the hinges by April 22.
>
> As it turns out, Baker fails to deliver the hinges on time, and Acme (in order to fulfill commitments to its customers) must quickly purchase the hinges from another supplier. This other supplier charges Acme $17,000, which is $5,000 more than Baker was charging. Acme has suffered $5,000 in damages as a result of Baker's breach of contract.

The most common remedy for a breach of contract is an award of **compensatory damages.** This is a sum of money that a court orders the breaching party to pay to the other party, to compensate the other party for losses suffered as a result of the breach of contract. Compensatory damages are generally intended to put the nonbreaching party in the financial position they would have been in if the breaching party had fulfilled the terms of the contract.

Example: Continuing with the previous example, suppose Acme Safes sues Baker Manufacturing for breach of contract. The court orders Baker to pay Acme $5,000 in damages. When Baker pays Acme the $5,000, that puts Acme in the financial position it would have been in if Baker had delivered the hinges on time.

Liquidated Damages. The parties to a contract sometimes agree in advance to an amount that will serve as full compensation to be paid in the event that one of the parties breaches the contract. This sum is called **liquidated damages.**

Example: Let's return to the previous example. Now suppose that Acme Safes and Baker Manufacturing included a liquidated damages provision in their contract. The provision states that if Baker breaches the agreement, it will pay Acme $3,000, which will serve as full compensation for the breach.

Baker fails to deliver the hinges to Acme on time, so Acme must purchase them from another supplier, and that costs the company an extra $5,000. But because of the liquidated damages provision in the contract, Acme is only entitled to receive $3,000 from Baker. Acme can't sue for any additional amount, even though the actual damages were greater than $3,000

Although a liquidated damages provision limits the amount of compensation the nonbreaching party will receive, it benefits both parties by making it easier to settle their dispute without going to court. It's sometimes difficult for the nonbreaching party to prove the extent of the actual damages they suffered; a liquidated damages provision makes that unnecessary.

In a real estate transaction, the buyer's earnest money deposit is often treated as liquidated damages. If the buyer breaches the purchase and sale agreement, the seller is entitled to keep the deposit as liquidated damages. The seller usually can't sue the buyer for an additional amount.

On the other hand, a typical purchase and sale agreement doesn't have a liquidated damages provision that applies if it's the seller who breaches instead of the buyer. If the seller breaches the contract, the buyer can sue for compensatory damages.

Specific Performance. Specific performance is a legal remedy for breach of contract that compels a breaching party to perform the contract as agreed. For example, if a seller breaches a purchase and sale agreement, a court could issue an order of specific performance that requires the seller to sign and deliver a deed to the buyer, fulfilling the terms of their contract.

Specific performance is usually available as a remedy only when monetary damages would not be sufficient compensation. For instance, in our example involving failure to deliver hinges as agreed, the court wouldn't order Baker to deliver the hinges to Acme, because hinges could be obtained from another supplier and financial compensation was really all Acme needed.

In contrast, specific performance may be an appropriate remedy for a seller's breach of a purchase and sale agreement, because a piece of real estate is unique; there's no other property that's exactly like the one the seller agreed to sell. Payment of damages would not enable the buyer to purchase another property just like it.

Tender

A tender is an unconditional offer by one of the contract parties to perform their part of the agreement. A tender is usually made when it appears that the other party is going to default; it is necessary before legal action can be taken to remedy the breach of contract.

Example: A seller recently accepted an all-cash offer on his home. The seller now suspects that the buyer does not plan to complete the purchase, and they intends to sue the buyer if this happens. Before they can sue, the seller must attempt to deliver the deed to the buyer as promised in the purchase and sale agreement. When the tender is made, if the buyer refuses to pay the agreed price and accept the deed, the buyer is in default and the seller may then file a lawsuit.

If a buyer believes the seller doesn't plan to complete the sale, the buyer tenders by attempting to deliver to the seller the full payment promised in the purchase and sale agreement. When the seller refuses to accept the money and deliver the deed, they are in default.

Sometimes there is an **anticipatory repudiation** by one of the parties. An anticipatory repudiation is a positive statement by the defaulting party indicating that they will not or cannot fulfill the terms of the agreement. When this happens, no tender is necessary as a basis for a legal action.

Fig. 6.5 Breach of Contract

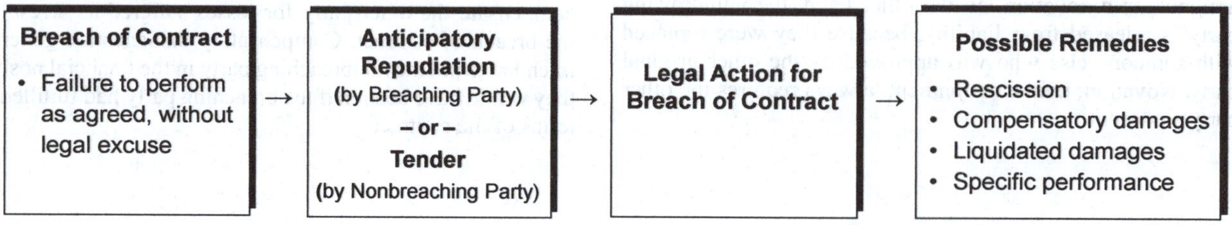

Breach of Contract		Anticipatory Repudiation (by Breaching Party) – or – Tender (by Nonbreaching Party)		Legal Action for Breach of Contract		Possible Remedies
• Failure to perform as agreed, without legal excuse	→		→		→	• Rescission • Compensatory damages • Liquidated damages • Specific performance

Types of Real Estate Contracts

This section provides a brief overview of some of the contracts a real estate agent should be familiar with: listing agreements, buyer representation agreements, purchase and sale agreements, land contracts, leases, escrow instructions, and options. Each of these except the option is discussed in more detail in a later chapter, as noted below.

Listing Agreements

A listing agreement is a written contract between a property owner and a real estate firm. The owner hires the firm to find a buyer or tenant who is ready, willing, and able to buy or lease on the owner's terms.

In Washington and many other states, a firm can't sue to collect a commission unless it has a written listing agreement with the property owner. What the firm must do in order to earn the commission depends on what type of listing has been used—open, exclusive agency, or exclusive right to sell—and on the terms of the contract. Listing agreements are discussed in more detail in Chapter 8.

Buyer Representation Agreements

A buyer representation agreement is a written contract between a prospective property buyer and a real estate firm. The buyer hires the firm to locate a suitable property for the buyer to purchase.

In Washington, the firm can't sue the buyer for compensation unless their agreement is in writing. Buyer agency and buyer representation agreements are discussed in more detail in Chapter 7.

Purchase and Sale Agreements

The purchase and sale agreement is a written contract between a buyer and a seller, stating the terms on which a piece of real property is going to be sold. It should spell out the details of the sale (such as price, closing and possession dates, any liens to be assumed, and any contingencies), and it must be signed by both parties.

In most cases, the prospective buyer is the offeror, and the property seller is the offeree.

- A buyer makes an offer to purchase by filling out a standard purchase and sale agreement form with the terms of their offer. The buyer then signs the form and submits it to the seller or the seller's agent.
- If the seller is willing to sell on the buyer's terms, they sign the purchase and sale agreement form and deliver it to the buyer or the buyer's agent, thus communicating to the buyer their acceptance of the offer.
- If the seller wants to change any of the terms offered, they can make a counteroffer to the buyer. Now the seller is the offeror and the buyer is the offeree.

Once a purchase and sale agreement has been signed by both parties, it is a binding contract, assuming that all of the other requirements for a valid contract have been met. The terms of the agreement cannot be modified unless both parties consent and sign a written amendment to the original contract. Purchase and sale agreements are discussed in more detail in Chapter 9.

Land Contracts

Under a land contract (also called a real estate contract, installment sales contract, or contract for deed), the buyer purchases the seller's property on an installment basis. The parties to the contract are called the **vendor** (the seller) and the **vendee** (the buyer). Periodic payments toward the purchase price are made over a span of years, and during that time the vendor retains legal title to the property. The deed is not delivered to the vendee until the full purchase price has been paid. In the meantime, the vendee has **equitable title** to the property, which is the right to possess and enjoy the property while paying off the purchase price.

> **Example:** Bender agrees to buy Jones's property for $450,000, to be paid at the rate of $45,000 per year, plus 9% interest, for ten years. Jones allows Bender to take possession of the property, and she promises to convey legal title to Bender when he's paid her the full amount owed. Bender and Jones have entered into a land contract.

Land contracts are discussed in more detail in Chapter 10.

Leases

A lease is an agreement that transfers the right of possession and use of real property from the landlord (the property owner) to the tenant. A lease is both a conveyance and a contract. As a conveyance, the lease transfers the right of possession. As a contract, it sets forth the terms of the occupancy: the amount of rent, the rights and responsibilities of the parties, and the duration of the tenancy.

Leases are categorized according to their duration and manner of termination. Many of the terms of a residential lease are governed by Washington's Residential Landlord-Tenant Act. Leases are discussed in more detail in Chapter 16.

Escrow Instructions

Escrow instructions authorize an escrow agent to close a transaction. They set forth the obligations of the parties and the conditions that must be fulfilled before a sale can be finalized. The buyer and the seller generally use joint escrow instructions to avoid giving conflicting directives; however, in some commercial transactions the parties issue separate sets of instructions. Escrow instructions are discussed in more detail in Chapter 13.

Option Agreements

An option agreement is an agreement that gives a party the right to buy, sell, or lease property for a fixed price within a set period of time.

> **Example:** Jensen is offering to sell her property for $400,000. Conners isn't yet sure that he wants to buy the property, but he doesn't want to lose the opportunity to do so. Jensen agrees to give him a three-week option to purchase. They execute a written option agreement, and Conners pays Jensen $1,000 as consideration for the option. The option gives Conners the right to buy the property at the stated price during the next three weeks, but does not in any way obligate him to buy it.

The parties to an option agreement are the **optionor** (the property owner who grants the option) and the **optionee** (the one who has the option right). In an option to purchase, the optionor is the seller and the optionee is the buyer.

The optionor is bound to keep the offer open for the period specified in the option agreement. They can't sell or lease the property to anyone other than the optionee until the option expires.

If the optionee decides to exercise the option (that is, to buy or lease the property on the stated terms), they must give written notice of acceptance to the optionor. If the optionee fails to exercise the option within the specified time, the option expires automatically.

An option agreement may be considered a unilateral contract, because the optionee is not obligated to exercise the option. However, when the option is exercised, the parties have a bilateral contract. (If the option is exercised, but the underlying sale is not yet closed, the parties have an executory bilateral contract.)

Requirements. Because an option is a contract, it must have all the necessary elements of a contract, including consideration. The consideration may be a nominal amount—there's no set minimum. But some consideration must, in fact, pass from the optionee to the optionor; a mere statement of consideration in the agreement is not sufficient. (There is an exception to this rule for lease/option agreements: the provisions of the lease are treated as sufficient consideration to support the option.)

An option contract must be in writing; oral options are unenforceable. Furthermore, since an option to purchase anticipates that a sale may take place, the underlying terms of the sale (such as price and financing) should be spelled out in the option agreement.

Contract Rights. An option agreement gives the optionee a contract right, but does not create an interest in real property. An option is not a lien, and it also cannot be used as security for a mortgage loan.

If the optionor dies during the option period, the optionee may still exercise the right to purchase or lease. The option contract is binding on the heirs and assignees of the optionor.

An option can be assigned, unless the agreement includes a provision prohibiting assignment. One exception is when the consideration paid by the optionee is in the form of an unsecured promissory note. In that case, the optionee must obtain the optionor's written permission before the option may be assigned.

Recording. An option agreement may be recorded to give third parties constructive notice of the option. In that case, if the optionee exercises the option, their interest in the property will relate back to the date the option was recorded and take priority over the rights of intervening third parties.

A recorded option that is not exercised may create a cloud on the optionor's title. The optionor should obtain a release from the optionee and then record the release to remove the cloud.

Right of First Refusal. An option should not be confused with a right of first refusal, which gives a person the first opportunity to purchase or lease real property if it becomes available. For instance, a lease might give the tenant a right of first refusal to purchase the property if the landlord decides to sell it.

Once the property owner offers the property for sale or receives an offer to buy from a third party, the holder of the right of first refusal must be given a chance to match the offer. If the right-holder does not want the property or is unwilling to match the offer, the property may be sold to a third party.

An option also should not be confused with a letter of intent, which merely lays out the parameters for further contract negotiation and isn't binding.

Chapter Summary

1. A contract is an agreement between two or more competent persons to do or not do certain things for consideration. Every contract is either express or implied, either unilateral or bilateral, and either executory or executed.
2. For a contract to be valid and binding, the parties must have the legal capacity to contract, and there must be mutual consent (offer and acceptance), a lawful objective, and consideration. The statute of frauds requires real estate contracts to be in writing.
3. A contract may be void, voidable, unenforceable, or valid.
4. A contract can be discharged by full performance or by agreement between the parties. The parties can agree to terminate the contract by rescission or cancellation, or there can be an assignment or a novation.
5. A breach of contract occurs when a party fails, without legal excuse, to perform any material promise contained in the agreement. When a breach occurs, the four possible remedies are rescission, compensatory damages, liquidated damages, or specific performance.
6. In an option to purchase, the optionee has a right to buy the property at a specified price, but is under no obligation to buy. The optionor can't sell the property to anyone other than the optionee during the option period.

Key Terms

Contract—An agreement between two or more competent persons to do or not do certain things for consideration.

Capacity—A person must be mentally competent and at least 18 years of age to have the capacity to contract.

Mutual consent—The agreement of both parties to the terms of the contract, demonstrated by offer and acceptance.

Offer—A communication that shows the willingness of the person making it (the offeror) to enter into a contract, and that has definite and certain terms.

Acceptance—A communication showing the willingness of the offeree to be bound by the terms of the offer.

Counteroffer—A qualified acceptance; technically a rejection of the offer, with a new offer made on slightly different terms.

Fraud—The misrepresentation of a material fact to someone who relies on the misrepresentation as the truth in deciding whether to enter into a contract.

Undue influence—Pressuring someone or taking advantage of his weakness or distress to induce him to enter into a contract.

Duress—Compelling someone to enter into a contract with the use or threat of force or constraint.

Consideration—Something of value exchanged by the parties to a contract; either a benefit to the party receiving it or a detriment to the party offering it.

Statute of frauds—A state law that requires certain types of contracts (including most contracts related to real estate transactions) to be in writing and signed.

Void—When a contract lacks an essential element, so that it has no legal force or effect.

Voidable—When one of the parties can choose to rescind the contract, because of lack of capacity, fraud, etc.

Unenforceable—When a contract cannot be enforced in a court of law because its contents cannot be proved, or it is voidable by the other party, or the statute of limitations has expired.

Rescission—When a contract is terminated and any consideration given is returned, putting the parties as nearly as possible back into the position they were in prior to entering into the contract.

Cancellation—When a contract is terminated but previous contractual acts are unaffected.

Assignment—When one party transfers her rights and obligations under the contract to another party, but remains secondarily liable.

Novation—When one party is completely replaced with another, or one contract is completely replaced with another, and all liability under the original contract ends.

Compensatory damages—An amount that a court orders one party in a lawsuit to pay to the other party as compensation for a breach of contract or other injury.

Liquidated damages—An amount that the parties agree in advance will serve as full compensation if one of them defaults on the contract.

Specific performance—A remedy for breach of contract in which the court orders the defaulting party to perform as agreed in the contract.

Tender—An unconditional offer by one of the parties to perform his part of the agreement, made when it appears that the other party is going to default.

Option agreement—An agreement that gives one party the right to buy or lease property at a set price within a certain period of time.

Chapter Quiz

1. **A contract can be valid and binding even though:**
   a) it is not supported by consideration
   b) it does not have a lawful objective
   c) it is not put into writing
   d) there was no offer and acceptance

2. **To have legal capacity to contract, a person must have:**
   a) reached the age of majority
   b) been declared competent by a court
   c) a high school diploma or general equivalency certificate
   d) All of the above

3. **An offer to purchase property would be terminated by any of the following, except:**
   a) failure to communicate acceptance of the offer within the prescribed period
   b) revocation after acceptance has been communicated
   c) a qualified acceptance of the offer by the offeree
   d) death or insanity of the offeror

4. **A counteroffer:**
   a) terminates the original offer
   b) will result in a valid contract if accepted by the other party
   c) Both of the above
   d) None of the above

5. **Tucker sends Johnson a letter offering to buy his property for $320,000 in cash, with the transaction to close in 60 days. Johnson sends Tucker a letter that says, "I accept your offer; however, the closing will take place in 90 days." Which of the following is true?**
   a) Johnson's statement is not a valid acceptance
   b) Johnson's statement is a counteroffer
   c) There is no contract unless Tucker accepts the counteroffer
   d) All of the above

6. **Which of these could be consideration for a contract?**
   a) $63,000
   b) A promise to convey title
   c) A promise to not sell property during the next 30 days
   d) All of the above

7. **An executory contract is one that:**
   a) is made by the executor of an estate for the sale of probate property
   b) has not yet been performed
   c) has been completely performed
   d) has been proposed but not accepted by either party

8. **A void contract is one that:**
   a) lacks an essential contract element
   b) needs to be rescinded by the injured party
   c) can be rescinded by agreement
   d) can no longer be enforced because the deadline set by the statute of limitations has passed

9. **A voidable contract is:**
   a) not enforceable by either party
   b) enforceable unless action is taken to rescind it
   c) void unless action is taken to rescind it
   d) None of the above

10. **The statute of frauds is a law that requires:**
    a) all contracts to be supported by consideration
    b) unlawful provisions to be severed from a contract
    c) certain contracts to be unilateral
    d) certain contracts to be in writing and signed

11. **A contract can be discharged by all of the following except:**
    a) novation
    b) performance
    c) cancellation
    d) breach

12. **Brown and Murdock have a five-year contract. After two years, they agree to tear up that contract and replace it with a new ten-year contract. This is an example of:**
    a) novation
    b) rescission
    c) duress
    d) specific performance

13. Graves and Chung are parties to a contract that doesn't prohibit assignment. If Chung assigns his interest in the contract to Stewart:

a) Graves is not required to fulfill the contract
b) Graves can sue for anticipatory repudiation
c) Chung remains secondarily liable to Graves
d) Chung is relieved of all further liability under the contract

14. A clause in the contract provides that if one party breaches, the other will be entitled to $3,500 and cannot sue for more than that. This is a:

a) just compensation provision
b) compensation cap
c) satisfaction clause
d) liquidated damages provision

15. The McClures agreed in writing to sell their house to Jacobsen, but then they refused to go through with the sale. If Jacobsen wants a court order requiring the McClures to convey the house to her as agreed, she should sue for:

a) damages
b) specific performance
c) liquidated damages
d) rescission

Chapter 7:

Real Estate Agency

I. Introduction to Agency
- A. The agency relationship
- B. Agency law

II. Creating an Agency Relationship
- A. Express agreement
- B. Ratification
- C. Estoppel
- D. Implication
- E. Creating a real estate agency

III. Legal Effects of Agency
- A. Scope of authority
- B. Actual vs. apparent authority
- C. Vicarious liability
- D. Imputed knowledge

IV. Duties in an Agency Relationship
- A. Duties to all parties
- B. Duties to the principal
- C. Breach of duty

V. Terminating an Agency
- A. Termination by acts of the parties
- B. Termination by operation of law
- C. Terminating a real estate agency

VI. Real Estate Agency Relationships
- A. Real estate agents in a typical transaction
- B. Types of agency relationships
  1. Seller agency
  2. Buyer agency
  3. Limited dual agency

VII. Agency Disclosure Requirements

VIII. Independent Contractor Status

Agency is a special legal relationship that involves certain duties and liabilities. The law of agency governs many aspects of a real estate agent's relationships with clients and customers. The first part of this chapter explains what an agency relationship is and how one is created, then discusses real estate agency duties and liabilities. The second part of this chapter describes the various types of agency relationships that are possible under Washington's real estate agency statute. Agency disclosure requirements and a broker's status as an independent contractor or an employee are also covered.

Key Terms

Principal	**Confidential Information**
Agent	**Secret Profit**
Third Party	**Multiple Listing Service**
Fiduciary	**Listing Agent**
Ratification	**Buyer's Agent**
Estoppel	**Seller's Agent**
Implication	**Selling Agent**
Actual Authority	**In-House Transaction**
Apparent Authority	**Employee**
Material Facts	**Independent Contractor**

Introduction to Agency

We'll begin our discussion of real estate agency with some basic definitions and some information about the framework of agency law.

The Agency Relationship

An agency relationship arises when one person authorizes another to represent them, subject to their control, in dealings with other people. The parties in an agency relationship are the **agent**, the person authorized to be the other person's representative, and the **principal**, the person who authorizes and controls the actions of the agent. Persons outside the agency relationship who seek to deal with the principal through the agent are called **third parties.**

For example, for a listing agent, the buyer or a potential buyer is a third party. For a buyer's agent, the seller is a third party.

When a seller lists their property with a real estate firm, the firm and the affiliated licensee who took the listing ordinarily become the seller's agents. So do the firm's designated broker and any other managing brokers who are responsible for supervising the licensee. (The designated broker has supervisory responsibility for the entire firm; see Chapter 17.) The seller is the principal, who authorizes the firm and the licensee to act as their agents. The firm and the licensee represent the seller/principal's interests in negotiations with potential buyers/third parties. The seller/principal is the **client**.

A buyer is also likely to have an agency relationship with a real estate firm. As a general rule, when a real estate licensee works with a buyer—for example, by showing the buyer homes, preparing offers to purchase, and negotiating on the buyer's behalf—then the licensee and the firm they work for become the agents of the buyer, and the buyer is the principal and client. The principal is whoever has authorized the firm to act as their representative.

Agency Law

An agency relationship has significant legal implications. For a third party, dealing with the agent can be the legal equivalent of dealing with the principal. For instance, when an agent who is authorized to do so signs a document or makes a promise, it's as if the principal signed or promised. And in some cases, if the agent does something wrong, the principal may be held liable to third parties for harm resulting from the agent's actions.

Those rules are part of general agency law, a body of common law (in other words, law derived from court opinions and not statutes or regulations) that applies to agency relationships in nearly any context. For example, it governs the relationship between lawyer and client, or between trustee and beneficiary. Traditionally, general agency law also governed the relationship between a real estate licensee and their client. In Washington, however, real estate agency relationships are subject to the **Real Estate Brokerage Relationships Act** (REBRA), which went into effect in 1997.

This statute grew out of general agency law, but made important changes to address agency problems that were specific to the real estate field. The statute underwent significant revisions in 2024, including the addition of a requirement for written agreements between all agents and clients.

We will cover both general agency law and Washington's statute, since both are tested on the state licensing examination. General agency law questions are part of the national portion of the exam, while questions concerning REBRA are part of the state portion of the exam.

Creating an Agency Relationship

Under general agency law, no particular formalities are required to create an agency relationship; the only requirement is the consent of both parties. An agency relationship may be formed in four ways: by express agreement, by ratification, by estoppel, or by implication.

Express Agreement

Most agencies are created by express agreement: the principal appoints someone to act as their agent, and the agent accepts the appointment. The agreement does not need to be in writing in order to create a valid agency relationship.

The agency agreement also does not have to be supported by consideration. Agency rights, responsibilities, and liabilities arise even when the principal has no contractual obligation to compensate the agent for the services rendered.

For example, if a licensee doesn't have a written listing agreement with a seller, that licensee cannot sue the seller for compensation. Yet even without a written agreement, the licensee still may be the seller's agent, with all of the duties and liabilities that agency entails.

Ratification

An agency is created by ratification when the principal gives approval after the fact to acts performed by:

- a person who had no authority to act for the principal, or
- an agent whose actions exceeded the authority granted by the principal.

The principal may ratify unauthorized acts either expressly (in words), or else implicitly, by accepting the benefits of the acts. For example, if the principal accepts a contract offer negotiated by someone who wasn't authorized to negotiate on their behalf, the principal has ratified the agency.

Estoppel

Under the legal doctrine of estoppel, a person cannot take a position that contradicts their previous conduct, if someone else has relied on the previous conduct. An agency can be created by estoppel when it would be unfair to a third party to deny the agent's authority, because the principal has allowed the third party to believe there was an agency relationship.

Example: Pam would like to sell some land she owns, though she hasn't listed it yet. She arranges for Carl, an acquaintance who expressed interest in buying the property, to come see it. Pam's chatty, outgoing friend Alan happens to be there when Carl arrives, so the three of them tour the property together. Alan does most of the talking, and Carl gets the mistaken impression that Alan is Pam's real estate agent. Pam doesn't say or do anything that contradicts this misimpression or clarifies the situation for Carl. When Alan points out the property's boundaries to Carl and confidently says it's five acres, Pam stands by silently.

Carl buys Pam's property, making his decision in reliance on the information Alan provided about the boundaries and acreage. It turns out that the information was incorrect and Carl paid substantially more for the land than he should have. He sues Pam, whose main defense is that Alan wasn't her agent.

The court considers the circumstances and rules that an agency relationship between Pam and Alan was created by estoppel. Because of her previous conduct while showing Carl the property, Pam is estopped from denying that Alan was acting as her agent when he gave Carl false information. The court orders Pam to pay damages to Carl.

Implication

An agency may be created by implication when one person behaves toward another in a way that suggests or implies that they are acting as that other person's agent. If the other person reasonably believes that there is an agency relationship, and the supposed agent fails to correct that impression, they may owe the other person agency duties.

Implication vs. Estoppel. Agency by implication and agency by estoppel both involve liability for negligently or deliberately misleading someone about the existence of an agency. In an agency by estoppel, liability is imposed on the "principal" for the actions of someone they allowed to act like their agent, in order to avoid harming a third party (such as the buyer, Carl, in the example above). In contrast, in an agency by implication, liability and agency duties are imposed on the supposed agent, in order to avoid harming the person who believed the agent was representing them.

In real estate transactions, agency by estoppel is uncommon, but agency by implication is not. For example, if a real estate licensee acts as though they are representing the buyer and the buyer believes that to be true, an agency may be created by implication even if they never sign a written representation agreement. Inadvertent dual agency, discussed later in this chapter, involves agency by implication.

Creating a Real Estate Agency

In Washington, under the Real Estate Brokerage Relationships Act, an agency relationship between a real estate firm and a client brokerage services agreement between the firm and the client.

The relationship between a real estate firm and a client (either a seller or buyer) is ordinarily created when one of the firm's brokers and the client sign a brokerage services agreement appointing the firm to represent the client. In common usage, either the firm or the broker (or both) may be referred to as this client's agent.

This written agreement is required regardless of whether the client is a seller or buyer. The client and agent must enter into the agreement before, or as soon as reasonably practical after, the agent begins performing real estate services. The agreement must include the term of the agreement; for a buyer the default term is 60 days, but the parties may opt for a longer term. The agreement must also name the broker appointed as the agent and whether the agency is exclusive or nonexclusive.

The Washington statute does provide that under certain circumstances, a buyer agency relationship may arise even in the absence of a written agreement. It states that if a broker performs real estate brokerage services for a buyer, they are considered to be the buyer's agent. (However, a buyer agency created this way would still need to be confirmed through a written agreement. Otherwise, this would essentially be an agency by implication, and continuing to act as a buyer's agent without a written agreement could be grounds for disciplinary action.)

There's an important exception to this rule concerning buyer agency. A licensee who provides services to a buyer does not automatically become the buyer's agent if the licensee already has a listing agreement with the seller of a particular property the buyer is interested in. In that situation, the broker and the firm are already the seller's agents. In connection with that specific listing, they will continue to represent the seller, unless both the seller and buyer consent in writing to limited dual agency. (We will discuss limited dual agency in more detail later in this chapter.)

Example: Yasmin is a broker who works for Thompson Realty. She agrees to meet up with a prospective buyer, George, to show him three homes listed through the MLS. Although Yasmin intends to ask George to sign a brokerage services agreement when they have a spare moment, they run out of time and no agreement is signed.

Even without a written agreement, under Washington law, Yasmin became George's agent simply by providing real estate services to him. He is her principal and she owes him agency duties such as loyalty and confidentiality. Yasmin's firm, Thompson Realty, and its designated broker are also George's agents in this situation.

On the other hand, suppose Yasmin shows George one of her own listings. In regard to this specific property, Yasmin and her firm are already representing the seller. Because of the existing seller agency relationship, there are two possibilities for Yasmin and her firm. They can continue to represent the seller (and not George). Or alternatively, they can represent both the seller and George if both give written consent to a limited dual agency (and with that consent, Yasmin and her firm would be limited dual agents, representing both the seller and George).

Note that Yasmin's failure to comply with the written services agreement requirement is a violation of Washington's real estate license law (see chapter 17). While it is not likely she would face disciplinary action if she promptly followed up with a written services agreement with George, if she continued to act on his behalf without an agreement, she, her supervising broker, and her firm could face disciplinary action.

There is also an exception for commercial property to the general rule requiring agents to have written brokerage services agreements with clients. A commercial broker representing a buyer may give the buyer a compensation disclosure form instead of a signing a contract with the buyer. The agent needs to disclose in writing the sources and amount of any compensation the broker expects to receive from the transaction.

The Legal Effects of Agency

Once an agency relationship has been established, the principal is bound by acts of the agent that are within the scope of the agent's actual or apparent authority. Under general agency law, the principal may be held liable for harm caused by the agent's negligent or wrongful acts. In addition, the principal may be held to know information that is known to the agent. We will now examine these legal effects of agency.

Scope of Authority

The extent to which the principal can be bound by the agent's actions depends first of all on the scope of authority granted to the agent. There are three basic types of agents:

- universal agents,
- general agents, and
- special agents.

A **universal agent** is authorized to do anything that can be lawfully delegated to a representative. This type of agent has the greatest degree of authority.

A **general agent** is authorized to handle all of the principal's affairs in one or more specified areas. They have the authority to conduct a wide range of activities on an ongoing basis on behalf of the principal.

For example, a business manager who has the authority to handle personnel matters, enter into contracts, and manage the day-to-day operations of the business is considered to be a general agent.

A **special agent** has limited authority to do a specific thing or conduct a specific transaction. For instance, an attorney who is hired to litigate a specific legal matter, such as a person's divorce, is a special agent.

In most cases, a real estate licensee is a special agent, because the licensee has only limited authority. A seller hires a licensee to find a buyer for a particular piece of property, and the licensee is only authorized to negotiate with third parties, not to sign a contract on the seller's behalf. A real estate licensee can be granted broader powers, but usually is not.

Sometimes a seller lists several properties at once under a single listing agreement. Even in that case the listing agent would still be a special agent, because the authority granted by the seller is limited in time and scope.

Actual vs. Apparent Authority

An agent may have actual authority to perform an action on the principal's behalf, or else may have only apparent authority.

Actual authority is authority granted by the principal to the agent, either expressly or by implication. Express actual authority is communicated to the agent in express terms, either orally or in writing. Implied actual authority is the authority to do what is necessary to carry out actions that were expressly authorized.

Example: When a seller lists property with a brokerage firm, the firm and its designated broker are given express actual authority to find a buyer for the property. Based on custom in the real estate industry, the designated broker also has the implied actual authority to delegate certain tasks to an affiliated licensee. (In contrast, the authority granted does not imply the power to enter into a contract or execute a deed on the seller's behalf.)

A person has **apparent authority** when they have no actual authority to act, but the principal negligently or deliberately allows it to appear that the person's actions are authorized.

Fig. 7.1 Types of Agency Authority

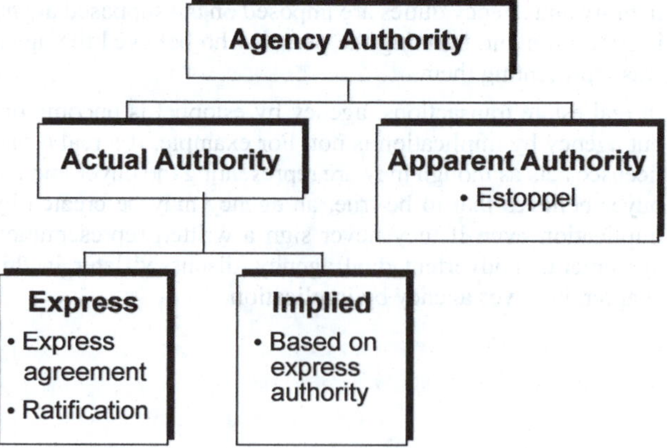

In other words, the principal's words or conduct lead a third party to believe that this person (the **apparent agent** or **ostensible agent**) has authority to act on behalf of the principal. Apparent authority creates an agency by estoppel, which was explained earlier.

A principal is bound by acts performed within the scope of an ostensible agent's apparent authority. However, declarations of the agent alone cannot establish apparent authority; the principal must be aware of the declarations or acts and make no effort to deny that they are authorized.

A third party has a duty, when dealing with an agent, to make a reasonable effort to discover the scope of the agent's authority. The third party will not be able to hold the principal liable when an agent acts beyond the scope of their actual authority and the principal's conduct does not indicate approval of those acts. Especially when a contract between the principal and a third party limits the agent's authority to make representations, the third party is on notice that any representations made by the agent beyond the written terms of the agreement are unauthorized and not binding on the principal.

Vicarious Liability

A **tort** is a negligent or intentional wrongful act involving breach of a duty imposed by law (as opposed to breach of a contractual duty). It is a mistake, accident, or misconduct that results in an injury or financial harm to another person. For example, negligent driving that results in an accident and injures another driver is a tort. Someone who commits a tort may be sued by the injured party and required to compensate them.

Under general agency law, a principal may be held liable for their agent's negligent or wrongful acts. This is referred to as **vicarious liability**. However, Washington's Real Estate Brokerage Relationships Act provides that, as a general rule, there is no vicarious liability between a real estate agent and their principal.

This means that a seller or buyer represented by a firm is ordinarily not liable for any act, error, or omission by the firm's designated broker, by licensees working for the firm.

There are two exceptions to this exclusion from liability. The principal may be liable for their real estate agent's actions if:

1. the principal participated in or authorized the act, error, or omission; or
2. the principal benefited from the act, error, or omission, and a court determines that it is highly probable that the injured party would be unable to enforce a judgment against the agent.

Imputed Knowledge

Under general agency law, a principal is considered to have notice of information that the agent knows, even if the agent never actually tells the principal. In other words, the agent's knowledge is automatically imputed to the principal.

As a result, the principal could be held liable for failing to disclose a problem to a third party, even if the agent never informed the principal of the problem.

Under REBRA, however, the imputed knowledge rule no longer applies in the real estate context in Washington. A principal in a real estate transaction is not automatically held to have notice of facts known by their real estate agent.

Duties in an Agency Relationship

When an agency relationship is established, the principal grants certain powers to the agent. At the same time, the law imposes a number of legal duties on the agent—standards of conduct the agent must meet. We'll begin with background information about general agency law, then focus on the duties that must be fulfilled under Washington's Real Estate Brokerage Relationships Act.

Under general agency law, agency relationships are **fiduciary** relationships. A fiduciary is a person who stands in a special position of trust and confidence in relation to someone else. For example, a trustee is a fiduciary in relation to the beneficiary of the trust and an attorney is a fiduciary in relation to the client. To help prevent exploitation of the other person's trust, the law sets high standards known as fiduciary duties. These include the duty of reasonable skill and care, obedience and utmost good faith, accounting, loyalty, and disclosure of material facts. By contrast, an agent's duties to third parties are much more limited.

Real estate agents in Washington were fiduciaries under general agency law, but REBRA changed that. The statute replaced the fiduciary duties real estate licensees owed to clients with a different—though very similar—set of statutory duties. REBRA also significantly expanded duties licensees owe to third parties in a transaction.

Duties to All Parties

Under REBRA, as we said, a Washington real estate licensee owes duties both to clients and to third parties. Though the set of duties owed to third parties is somewhat smaller than those owed to a principal, many of the duties are the same. In this section we'll discuss the duties that a licensee owes to any party to whom they render services, whether that person is a principal or a third party. These duties are:

- reasonable skill and care,
- honesty and good faith,
- presenting all written communications,
- disclosure of material facts,
- accounting for trust funds,
- providing an agency law pamphlet, and
- making an agency disclosure and a disclosure of compensation.

Reasonable Skill and Care. A licensee has a duty to use reasonable skill and care in the performance of their duties. If a licensee claims to possess certain skills or abilities, they must act as a competent person having those skills and abilities would act. In other words, a person who holds themself out as a real estate licensee must exercise the skill and care that a competent licensee would bring to the transaction. If the licensee causes a party harm due to carelessness or incompetence, the licensee will be liable to that party.

Honesty and Good Faith. A licensee must act toward any party with honesty and good faith. They must avoid inaccuracies in statements to buyers and sellers.

As was explained in Chapter 6, any intentional misrepresentation may constitute actual fraud, and even an unintentional misrepresentation may be considered constructive fraud. In either case, the party to whom the misrepresentation was made would have the right to rescind the transaction and/or sue for damages.

Misrepresentations, which may give rise to a lawsuit, should not be confused with mere opinions, predictions, or puffing. These are nonfactual or exaggerated statements that a party should realize they can't rely on. Since it isn't reasonable to rely on them, opinions, predictions, and puffing generally can't be the basis of a lawsuit.

> **Examples:**
>
> Opinion: "*I think this may be the best buy on the market.*"
>
> Prediction: "*This house is solid—it should still be standing a hundred years from now.*"
>
> Puffing: "*This is a dream house; it has a fabulous view.*"

Present Written Communications. A licensee is obligated to present all types of written communications to or from either party in a timely manner. Written communications include written offers.

A real estate licensee must present all offers and counteroffers to the parties, regardless of how unacceptable a particular one may appear to be. The offeree, not the licensee, decides whether or not to accept a particular offer or counteroffer. Failing to inform a party of an offer (perhaps because its acceptance would mean a smaller commission for the licensee) is a breach of duty.

This duty to present all offers continues even after the property is subject to an existing contract, or when the offeree is already a party to an existing contract.

> **Example:** Seller Howard accepts an offer from Buyer Carmichael. Two days later Trent, Howard's real estate agent, receives another written offer for the same property. Trent has a duty to present this offer to Howard, even though Howard already has a binding contract with Carmichael.

Disclosure of Material Facts. A licensee must disclose any material fact they know to the appropriate party, if the fact is not apparent or readily ascertainable by that party. REBRA defines a **material fact** as information that has a substantial adverse (negative) effect on the value of the property or on a party's ability to perform their contractual duties, or that defeats the purpose of the transaction.

One very important category of material facts is latent property defects. A **latent defect** is a problem that is not discoverable by ordinary inspection. A licensee must disclose any known latent defects to the parties.

A seller also has this duty to prospective buyers. However, in some cases Washington courts apply the principle of "caveat emptor," or "let the buyer beware," to real estate transactions. If buyers see evidence of a possible problem with the property, or if they receive notice of a possible problem in some other way (from a real estate agent or a home inspector, for example), then the buyers are generally expected to protect themselves by investigating further before proceeding with the purchase.

While some states have gone so far as to require real estate licensees to physically inspect the property and report all findings to the buyer, REBRA provides that licensees in Washington do not have the duty to investigate any matters they have not specifically agreed to investigate. They are not required to inspect the property, investigate either party's financial position, or independently verify the seller's statements.

Washington does require sellers of real property to give their buyers a disclosure statement. The purpose of the statement is to disclose the seller's knowledge regarding the condition of the property, including the condition of the buildings and utilities, the existence of any easements and encumbrances, and other material information. Property disclosure statements are discussed in more detail in Chapter 9.

Stigmatized Properties. The seller's property is considered stigmatized if the property (or a neighboring property) was or may have been the site of a violent crime, a suicide or other death, drug- or gang-related activity, political or religious activity, or some other occurrence that could make the property harder to sell.

Generally, past occurrences like these aren't considered material facts unless they adversely affect the property's physical condition or title. So, for example, if the drug-related activity involved methamphetamine production, that would be a material fact that has to be disclosed because making this drug generally leaves harmful residues on a property.

While not strictly an issue of stigmatization, neither a licensee nor a seller has a legal duty to disclose the presence of a sex offender in the neighborhood. In response to a buyer's questions about the possible proximity of sex offenders, an agent's best response is to refer the buyer to online resources where the buyer can investigate further.

Accounting. A licensee must account for any funds or other valuable items received on behalf of a party to a transaction. The licensee is required to report to the party on the status of those funds (called **trust funds**) and avoid mixing (**commingling**) them with their own money.

In most states, a real estate agent must deposit all trust funds in a trust or escrow account in order to help prevent improper use of the funds. Washington's trust fund requirements are discussed in Chapter 17.

Agency Law Pamphlet. A licensee must give an agency law pamphlet to each party to whom they render services. The pamphlet summarizes the provisions of the Real Estate Brokerage Relationships Act. Each party must receive the pamphlet before signing an agency agreement with the licensee, before signing an offer in a transaction handled by the licensee, before consenting to a dual agency, or before waiving any agency rights, whichever of these events comes first.

Agency and Compensation Disclosure. As soon as practical, but in any event before a party that a licensee is helping in a transaction makes or accepts an offer, the licensee must disclose in writing to that party whether the licensee represents the buyer, the seller, both, or neither.

The purpose of this disclosure is to make clear which licensees involved in the transaction are (or are not) representing each of the parties. The specific disclosure requirements are discussed later in this chapter.

Recent revisions to the Real Estate Brokerage Relationships Act have created an additional requirement before the parties reach mutual agreement. If a brokerage firm representing one party is going to receive compensation from the other party, this arrangement needs to be disclosed. Most typically, this would happen if the buyer's broker will be compensated by a commission split paid by the seller.

This compensation disclosure would not be required if each firm was going to receive compensation only from its own client, such as when the seller pays the listing firm and the buyer pays the buyer's agent's firm.

Duties to the Principal

In addition to the general duties owed by licensees to any party they render services to, there are duties that licensees owe only to their clients, the parties they represent as agents. If a licensee represents the seller in a transaction, these duties are owed to the seller.

If a licensee represents the buyer, these duties are owed to the buyer. If a licensee is acting as a dual agent, these duties are owed to both the seller and the buyer.

Loyalty. Loyalty is essential to an agency relationship. The agent must place the principal's interests above the interests of a third party. For instance, the seller's agent must try to negotiate with the buyer to get the highest possible price for the seller, because the agent's loyalty is owed to the seller.

An agent should disclose their opinion of the property's true value to their principal. Misleading a principal as to the value of the property or withholding information that affects its value breaches the agent's duty of loyalty.

The agent must also place the principal's interests above their own interests. This means that the agent must not make any **secret profits** from the agency. A secret profit is a financial benefit that an agent receives without the principal's consent, such as a kickback for referring the principal's business to a contractor.

Conflicts of Interest. A licensee must disclose to the principal any conflicts of interest. For instance, a seller's agent must inform the seller if there is any relationship between the agent and a prospective buyer—before the seller decides whether to accept the buyer's offer. If the buyer is a friend, relative, or business associate of the agent, or a company in which the agent has an interest, there may be a conflict of interest. The seller has the right to have this information when making their decision.

Of course, a seller's agent must also let the seller know if the agent is buying the property themself. It would be a gross breach of duty for a licensee to list a property for less than it is worth, secretly buy it through an intermediary, and then sell it for a profit. This is sometimes called **self-dealing**.

Confidentiality. An agent may not disclose the principal's confidential information to others, even after the termination of the agency relationship. The Real Estate Brokerage Relationships Act defines **confidential information** as information from or concerning a principal that:

1. the licensee acquired during the course of an agency relationship with the principal;
2. the principal reasonably expects to be kept confidential;
3. the principal has not disclosed or authorized to be disclosed to third parties;
4. would, if disclosed, operate to the detriment of the principal; and
5. the principal personally would not be obligated to disclose to the other party.

The last item on this list puts an important limitation on the principal's right to confidentiality. For instance, information about a latent property defect known to the agent must be disclosed to a third party no matter how "confidential" the principal may consider it, because the principal (as well as the agent) is legally obligated to disclose latent defects. On the other hand, the principal's need to sell the property quickly would be considered confidential information that must not be disclosed without the principal's authorization.

Expert Advice. A licensee must advise the principal to seek expert advice on any matters relating to the transaction that are beyond the agent's expertise. For instance, if the principal has questions about the property's structural soundness, the agent should advise the principal to contact a home inspector.

Good Faith and Continuous Effort. In general, real estate licensees have a duty to make a good faith and continuous effort to fulfill the terms of their agency agreement. This means that a seller's agent must make a good faith and continuous effort to find a buyer for the property. A buyer's agent must make a good faith and continuous effort to find a suitable property for the buyer to purchase.

Once a buyer has been found and a purchase and sale agreement has been signed, the seller's agent doesn't have to seek additional offers to purchase, as long as the property remains subject to that contract. (However, any additional offers received still must be presented to the seller.) Similarly, the buyer's agent doesn't have to seek additional properties while the buyer is a party to an existing contract.

Breach of Duty

If a licensee breaches any duties owed to either a principal or a third party, it is considered a tort. (A tort, as explained earlier, is a wrongful act resulting from a breach of a duty imposed by law.) The party injured by the tort, whether it is the principal or a third party, is then entitled to sue for redress.

The most common remedy in a tort suit is compensatory damages. A court will order the licensee to compensate the injured party for the value of the loss that the injured party suffered. This might include repaying any commission collected in a transaction.

Most breaches of duty by a licensee are also violations of the real estate license law. The Department of Licensing may take disciplinary action against the licensee even if the injured party does not pursue a lawsuit. Disciplinary action may include fines as well as suspension or revocation of the licensee's real estate license. (See Chapter 17.)

Terminating an Agency

Once an agency relationship has terminated, the agent is no longer authorized to represent the principal. Under general agency law, an agency may be terminated either by acts of the parties or by operation of law. (Following our discussion of termination under general agency law, we'll address how a real estate agency is terminated under the Real Estate Brokerage Relationships Act.)

Termination by Acts of the Parties

Under general agency law, the ways in which the parties can terminate an agency relationship include:

- mutual agreement,
- revocation by the principal, and
- renunciation by the agent.

Mutual Agreement. The parties may terminate the agency by mutual agreement at any time. If the original agreement was in writing, the termination agreement should also be in writing.

Principal Revokes. The principal may revoke the agency by firing the agent whenever they wish. (Remember that an agency relationship requires the consent of both parties.) However, when revoking an agency breaches a written contract, such as a listing agreement, the principal may be liable to the agent for financial losses resulting from the breach.

An **agency coupled with an interest** cannot be revoked. An agency is coupled with an interest if the agent has a financial interest in the subject matter of the agency. For instance, if a real estate licensee co-owns a property with other people, and they've authorized the licensee to represent them in selling the property, it's an agency coupled with an interest. The co-owners can't revoke it.

Agent Renounces. An agent can renounce the agency at any time. Like revocation, renunciation may be a breach of a written contract, in which case the agent could be liable for the principal's damages resulting from the breach. But since an agency contract is a personal services contract (the agent has agreed to provide personal services to the principal), the principal could not demand specific performance as a remedy. The courts will not force a person to perform personal services, because that would violate the constitutional prohibition against involuntary servitude.

Termination by Operation of Law

Under general agency law, several events terminate an agency relationship automatically, without action by either party. These events include:

- expiration of the agency term;
- fulfillment of the purpose of the agency;
- the death, incapacity, or bankruptcy of either party; and
- extinction of the subject matter.

Expiration of Agency Term. An agency terminates automatically when its term expires. If the agency agreement did not include an expiration date, it is deemed to expire within a reasonable time (which would vary depending on the type of agency in question and other circumstances). If there is no expiration date, either party may terminate the agency without liability for damages, although the other party might be able to demand reimbursement for expenses incurred before the termination.

Fulfillment of Purpose. An agency relationship terminates when its purpose has been fulfilled. For example, if a licensee is hired to sell the principal's property and the licensee does so, the agency is terminated by fulfillment.

Fig. 7.2 Termination Under General Agency Law

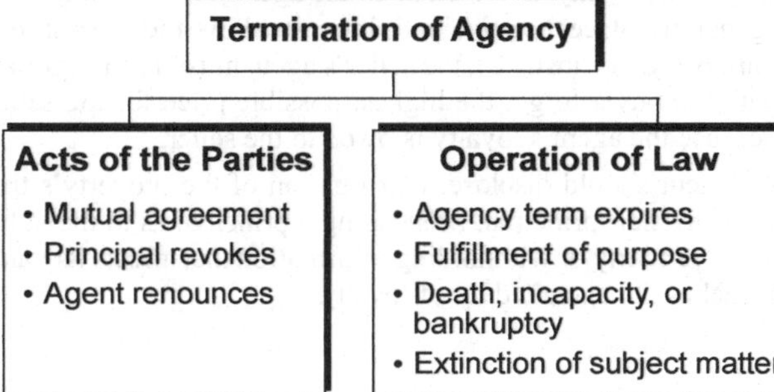

Death, Incapacity, or Bankruptcy. An agency is terminated before it expires if either the agent or the principal dies. Most states provide that the agency also terminates if either party becomes mentally incompetent. Generally, the agent has no authority to act after the death or incompetency of the principal, even if the agent is unaware of the principal's death or incompetency. An agency is also terminated by the bankruptcy of either party.

Extinction of Subject Matter. The subject matter of a real estate agency is the property in question. If the property is in any way extinguished (for example, by being sold or destroyed), the agency automatically terminates.

Terminating a Real Estate Agency

In Washington, under REBRA, a real estate agency relationship begins when the licensee undertakes to provide real estate brokerage services to a principal and continues until the earliest of the following:

1. Completion of performance by the licensee (the terms of the agency agreement are fulfilled).
2. Expiration of the agency term as agreed by the parties. (Note that an exclusive listing agreement should always specify a termination date. That is even a legal requirement in some states, although not in Washington.)
3. Termination of the relationship by mutual consent.
4. Notification from one party to the other that the agency is terminated.

When an agency relationship has terminated, the agent can no longer represent the principal. However, the agent still owes two statutory duties to the principal after the relationship terminates:

1. The agent must account for all money and property received during the relationship.
2. The agent must not disclose confidential information from or concerning the principal that was learned during the agency relationship.

Real Estate Agency Relationships

Washington's Real Estate Brokerage Relationships Act fundamentally changed agency relationships in real estate transactions. Before examining the different types of agency relationships (seller agency, buyer agency, and so on), we're going to describe the way a typical transaction unfolds, in order to compare how real estate agency relationships work under REBRA with how they used to work before REBRA became law in 1997. This historical perspective will help you understand why the law developed as it did.

Real Estate Agents in a Typical Transaction

Prospective buyers looking for a home in a particular area often start their search online, then contact a real estate agent from a brokerage office in the area. (It might be the listing agent for a home they saw online, an agent they already know, or one they learned about from friends or through advertising.) The agent interviews the buyers to find out what kind of a house they want and can afford, discusses current listings with them, and then accompanies them to tour the homes they're interested in.

Residential brokerage firms almost always belong to a **multiple listing service** (MLS). An MLS is a regional or local cooperative made up of real estate firms that agree to exchange information about their exclusive listings to increase exposure of the properties to the public. (Licensees from other firms in the MLS who bring buyers to see a listing are referred to as **cooperating agents.**)

So in our typical transaction, the agent working with the buyers shows them not only homes listed with their own firm, but also homes listed with other firms that are members of the same MLS. If the buyers decide to make an offer on another firm's listing, the agent who's been showing them properties will submit their offer and negotiate with the listing agent. Meanwhile, other cooperating agents are likely to be showing the same home to other buyers, who may make competing offers. On the seller's behalf, the listing agent negotiates with these cooperating agents too.

Now suppose the seller of this home decides to accept the offer submitted by the agent of the buyers we started out with. The transaction enters its next phase, when escrow is opened and the parties and the real estate agents work with the escrow agent to fulfill all requirements that must be completed before the sale can close (see Chapter 13).

The real estate agents directly involved are the listing agent and the agent who submitted the offer that the seller accepted. Also involved, in the background, are each agent's brokerage firm, the firm's designated broker, and any other managing brokers at the firm with supervisory responsibility over that agent.

Residential transactions often unfolded in this way before the Real Estate Brokerage Relationships Act, and they still do. It's the legal relationship between buyers and the licensees who provide services to them that is generally different now.

Before REBRA. Until the 1990s, most residential listing agreements in Washington (and elsewhere in the country) stated that cooperating agents from the MLS were subagents of the seller. This meant that in nearly every sale not only the listing agent but also the agents who showed buyers the seller's house represented the seller, rather than the buyers they were working with. In the typical transaction described above, every one of the licensees we mentioned and their brokerage firms would have been representing the seller; none of the buyers making offers would have had their own agent. Buyers often assumed (mistakenly but understandably) that the real estate licensee who was helping them was representing their interests, not the seller's.

Based on that assumption, buyers often told this licensee confidential information. Yet because this licensee actually represented the seller, they had a duty to pass that information along to the seller.

Buyers sometimes felt betrayed and agents themselves were sometimes confused. All this was hurting the profession. Reform was needed to clear up the confusion over who was representing whom. As one step in this effort, many states (including Washington) passed agency disclosure laws. These laws generally require real estate agents to disclose to the buyer and the seller, in writing, the identity of the party they represent. However, the Washington State Legislature decided that an agency disclosure law was not enough, and so it passed the Real Estate Brokerage Relationships Act.

Under REBRA. As explained earlier in the chapter, under the terms of this legislation a real estate licensee who provides services to a buyer is the buyer's agent, unless there's already a listing agreement with the seller. This rule has two important benefits. First, it turns the buyer's natural assumption—that the licensee they are working with is acting as their agent—into reality. Second, it reduces the danger of inadvertent, undisclosed dual agency (discussed below). Since a licensee usually represents the buyer they are working with, there is no conflict between their agency duties and their desire to help the buyer.

Returning to our typical transaction, under REBRA—that is, under current law—it's likely that only the listing agent (along with the listing brokerage firm and the listing agent's supervisors) is representing the seller. The cooperating agents (and their firms and supervisors) are not representing the seller; instead, they're representing the buyers they've been working with all along.

When the seller accepts a particular buyer's offer, the listing agent continues to represent the seller, and the cooperating agent who prepared and negotiated the accepted offer continues to represent that buyer.

Even under REBRA, though, agency relationships aren't always as straightforward as they are in the transaction we've been using as an example. We'll cover some common complications (such as in-house transactions) in the next section, as we look more closely at the different roles of seller's agents, buyer's agents, and dual agents.

Before we move on, it may be helpful to review how the following terms are used in the context of real estate agency in Washington.

- **Client.** A client is the person who has engaged the services of a real estate licensee. A client may be either a seller or a buyer (or, in a lease transaction, either a landlord or a tenant).
- **Customer.** When an agent is representing a seller or a landlord, third parties are sometimes called customers. A customer may be a buyer or a tenant.
- **Listing agent.** The licensee who takes the listing on a home is called the listing agent or listing broker. The brokerage firm this licensee works for, and/or the firm's designated broker, may also be called the listing agent or listing broker.
- **Buyer's agent.** A licensee who is working with a particular buyer, helping that buyer find and purchase a suitable property, is called the buyer's agent, buyer agent, or buyer broker. The brokerage firm this licensee works for, and/ or the firm's designated broker, may also be called the buyer's agent, buyer agent, or buyer broker.
- **Selling agent.** Especially after a buyer's offer has been accepted, you may hear the buyer's agent (or this agent's brokerage firm) referred to as the "selling agent" or "selling broker," because this agent actually brought the offer to the table. However, this term is confusing because it sounds so similar to "seller's agent," so has largely fallen out of favor. In recent versions of certain forms published by the Northwest Multiple Listing Service, "selling agent" has been replaced with "buyer agent." See the purchase and sale agreement form in Chapter 9 (Figure 9.1), for example.

Types of Agency Relationships

Under the Real Estate Brokerage Relationships Act, there are four types of real estate agency relationships:

- seller agency,
- buyer agency, and
- limited dual agency.

Seller Agency. Whereas traditionally real estate agents nearly always represented the seller, under REBRA the only licensees who represent the seller are the listing firm, the firm's designated broker, the broker who took the listing, and managing brokers at the listing firm who supervise the broker. The listing agreement creates a seller agency relationship.

Under the terms of the listing agreement, the primary task of a seller's agent is to find a buyer for the seller's property at a price that is acceptable to the seller. To accomplish this, the seller's agent advises the seller about preparing the property for sale, helps the seller decide on the listing price, markets the property, and negotiates on the seller's behalf with buyers' agents (or directly with buyers who don't have an agent).

Seller's Agents and Buyers. Throughout a transaction, a seller's agent must use their best efforts to promote the interests of the seller. Yet the seller's agent may also provide some services to prospective buyers.

For example, the seller's agent may help a buyer who doesn't have their own agent fill out a purchase offer form and suggest lenders or mortgage brokers if the buyer hasn't been preapproved. These services are considered to be in the best interests of the seller, and thus do not violate the agent's duties to the seller. Of course, the seller's agent must disclose to the buyer that they are acting as the seller's agent and not the buyer's.

A seller's agent must be very careful to treat the buyer fairly, but the agent must not act as if they are representing the buyer. In other words, the agent must fully disclose all known material facts and answer the buyer's questions honestly. However, the agent should not give the buyer certain kinds of advice, such as how much to offer for the listed property.

> **Example:** Harrison, who works for Yates Real Estate, recently listed Tilden's house. The listing price is $315,000, but Harrison has reason to believe that Tilden would accept an offer of $300,000. Harrison shows the listed house to Markham, who asks Harrison, "How low do you think the seller will go?" Harrison should make it clear to Markham that he is representing Tilden and cannot divulge confidential information to Markham. If Harrison were to do so, Tilden could sue Harrison and Yates Real Estate for breach of agency duties.

In some cases, the seller's agent has had a previous agency relationship with the buyer. In this situation it may be difficult for the agent to represent the seller's interests without feeling some loyalty to the buyer as well.

> **Example:** Suppose Tilden listed her home with Harrison and liked him so well that she wanted Harrison to help her find another home. Harrison shows Tilden one of his own listings.
>
> Under these circumstances, it would be easy for Tilden to think that Harrison is acting as her agent. However, because of the listing agreement, Harrison is the seller's agent, and he should emphasize this fact to Tilden. Tilden should be reminded that Harrison is obligated to disclose any material information Tilden tells him to the seller, and that in all negotiations Harrison will be promoting the seller's best interests. (Alternatively, Harrison could obtain the parties' consent to a dual agency, discussed at the end of this section. Note that a consensual dual agency is distinct from inadvertent dual agency, which we'll talk about next.)
>
> Remember, too, that a real estate agent is not permitted to disclose confidential information about a principal even after the termination of the agency relationship. Thus, Harrison cannot disclose to the seller any confidential information about Tilden that he learned during his earlier agency relationship with Tilden.

In transactions like the one in this example, where the listing agent found the buyer, the licensee risks creating an inadvertent dual agency. **Inadvertent dual agency** occurs if an agent who's representing one party unintentionally leads the other party to believe that the agent is representing them instead, while failing to make the required agency disclosures or obtain both parties' written consent to a dual agency.

> **Example:** Returning to the first part of our example involving Harrison (when he was the listing agent for Tilden's house), let's suppose that Harrison fails to disclose his seller agency to the buyer, Markham. Instead, Harrison behaves as if he's the buyer's agent. He tells Markham that a full-price offer may be necessary, but that the seller is in a hurry to sell and could be willing to accept significantly less.
>
> Markham reasonably believes that Harrison is his agent because of this negotiation advice, and also because there was no agency disclosure stating otherwise.
>
> By his conduct, Harrison has created an inadvertent dual agency. This violates the license law, because he didn't make the proper agency disclosures or obtain written consent to a dual agency. Also, in this particular case, Harrison has violated his duty of loyalty to the seller by disclosing the seller's negotiating position. Potentially either the seller or the buyer, or both, could sue Harrison and his firm for damages.

Buyer Agency. Even before the Real Estate Brokerage Relationships Act became law, some buyers recognized the benefits of having their own agent and were taking the trouble to find a licensee to represent them. Now that buyers are represented by the agent they're working with (unless the agent already has a listing agreement with the seller), the majority of buyers are able to benefit from buyer agency. The advantages of buyer agency include confidentiality and loyalty, objective advice, and help with negotiations.

Confidentiality and Loyalty. A buyer's agent owes agency duties to the buyer, including the duties of confidentiality and loyalty. For many buyers, these two duties make up the most important advantage of buyer agency.

> **Example:** Broker Mendez is helping Buyer Jackson find a home. She shows Jackson many houses, and there are two that interest him. One is a large fixer-upper selling for $350,000. The other is a smaller, newer house in mint condition that's selling for $326,000. Because the duty of loyalty requires Mendez to put Jackson's interests before her own, she advises him to purchase the smaller house because it better suits his needs. She does this even though she would earn a bigger commission if Jackson bought the more expensive house.
>
> Mendez advises Jackson to offer $319,900 for the $326,000 house. Jackson agrees to do that, although he tells Mendez that he's willing to pay the full listing price. Because Mendez is Jackson's agent, she is obligated to keep that confidential. (If she'd been the seller's agent, Mendez would have been required to disclose that information to the seller.)

Objective Advice. A buyer's agent can be relied upon to give the buyer objective advice about the pros and cons of purchasing a particular home. They will point out various issues the buyer should be aware of, such as energy costs, the need for future repairs, and property value trends. By contrast, a seller's agent will present the property in the most positive light and may use expert sales techniques to convince the buyer to sign on the dotted line.

Help with Negotiating. Buyers often feel uncomfortable negotiating for a property, especially one they really want to buy. They may be afraid to make a mistake through ignorance, either offering too little or too much for the property. A buyer's agent can use their negotiating skills and intimate knowledge of the real estate market to help the buyer get the property on the best possible terms.

Creation of Buyer Agency. A buyer and a real estate firm must enter into a written **representation agreement**. (An example is shown in Figure 7.4.) While the provisions in buyer representation agreements vary, they generally include the following:

- the duration of the agency,
- the general characteristics of the property the buyer wants,
- the price range,
- the conditions under which the agent's compensation will be earned,
- who will pay the fee, and
- a description of the agent's duties.

Compensation for Buyer's Agent. A buyer's agent may be compensated in a variety of ways. We'll look at these three forms of compensation:

- a retainer,
- a seller-paid fee, and/or
- a buyer-paid fee.

A **retainer** is a fee paid up front before services are provided. It's not common, but some buyer's agents collect a retainer when they enter into a buyer agency relationship, to ensure that their services won't go entirely uncompensated. The retainer is usually nonrefundable if the buyer fails to buy any property; however, if the buyer does close on a property, the retainer is refunded or credited against any compensation that the buyer owes the agent.

In many cases, a buyer's agent is paid by the seller through a **seller-paid fee**. Traditionally, this would be accomplished through a commission split, where , the brokerage firm of the cooperating agent who procures a buyer is entitled to share the sales commission with the listing brokerage firm, regardless of which party that cooperating agent represents in the transaction. However, listing agreements today often instead ask the seller to say what percentage of the sales price they will pay to the listing agent and then say what percentage of the sales price they will pay to the buyer's agent. (This is to avoid running afoul of antitrust laws, which we will discuss further in Chapter 15.) Listing agreements may also give the seller the option of requesting the buyer to state in the offer how the buyer's agent should be compensated, or simply declining to offer compensation to the buyer's agent.

Note that the source of an agent's commission does not determine who their principal is; a buyer's agent who accepts a seller-paid fee does not then owe agency duties to the seller.

In situations where there will be no seller-paid fee, a buyer representation agreement may provide for a **buyer-paid fee** instead. The buyer-paid fee might be based on an hourly rate, which essentially makes the agent a consultant. Alternatively, a buyer's agent may charge a percentage fee, so that the commission is a percentage of the purchase price of the property. A third possibility is a flat fee—a specified sum that is payable if the buyer purchases a property found by the agent.

A typical arrangement is that the buyer's agent will accept a seller-paid fee if one is available, but otherwise the buyer will pay the agreed fee. Including the alternative of a buyer-paid fee allows the buyer's agent to show the client properties where no commission split is available, such as FSBOs (homes that are for sale by owner) and open listings, or in situations where the seller explicitly states that they will not provide compensation to the buyer's agent.

Limited Dual Agency. As we've said, a dual agency relationship exists whenever a real estate agent represents both the seller and the buyer in the same transaction. Under Washington's Real Estate Brokerage Relationships Act, a legal dual agency is known more formally as a **limited dual agency.** This name was chosen to reflect that what a dual agent can perform for each party is inherently limited, in comparison to what a buyer's agent or a seller's agent can do for their principal.

Because the interests of the buyer and the seller essentially conflict (the buyer wants the lowest possible price, the seller wants the highest), a limited dual agent may face a dilemma about how to serve both clients' interests at the same time.

> **Example:** Davis represents both the buyer and the seller in a transaction. The seller informs Davis she's in a big hurry to sell and will accept any reasonable offer. The buyer tells Davis that he really wants the house and will pay the full listing price if necessary. Should Davis tell the buyer that the seller needs to sell quickly? Should he tell the seller that the buyer is willing to pay the full price?

In fact, it's really impossible for a limited dual agent to fully represent both parties. Thus, instead of the duty of loyalty, Washington law imposes on a limited dual agent the duty to refrain from acting to the detriment of either party. The limited dual agent must do their best to act impartially and treat both clients equally.

Fig. 7.3 Types of Real Estate Agency Relationships

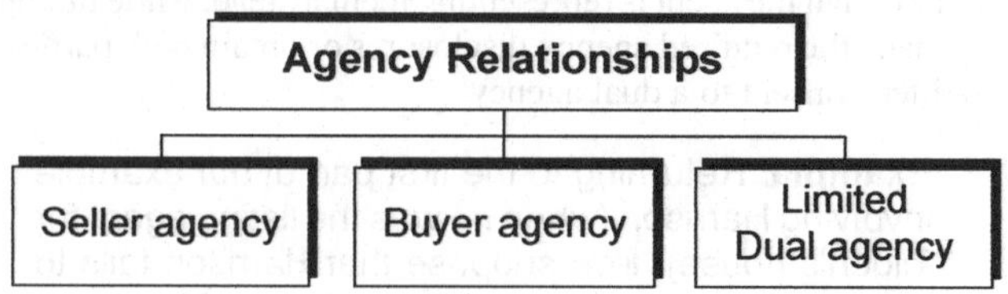

Fig. 7.4 Buyer Representation Agreement

Form 41
Buyer Brokerage Services Agreement
Rev. 8/24
Page 1 of 3

BUYER BROKERAGE SERVICES AGREEMENT

This Buyer Brokerage Services Agreement ("Agreement") is effective upon mutual acceptance ("Effective Date") and is made by and between ______________________________ ("Buyer Brokerage Firm" or "Firm") and ______________________________ ("Buyer") for real property located
Buyer Buyer
in the following areas: ______________________________ (unlimited if not filled in) ("Area").

1. **DEFINITIONS.** "Purchase(s)" includes a contract to purchase, an exchange or contract to exchange, or an option to purchase.

2. **TERM.** This Agreement will expire __________ days (60 days if not filled in) from the Effective Date ("Term"). If this Agreement expires while Buyer is a party to a purchase and sale agreement and represented by Buyer Brokerage Firm as indicated on the purchase and sale agreement, the Term shall automatically extend until the sale is closed or the purchase and sale agreement is terminated.

3. **AGENCY.**
   a. Pamphlet. Buyer acknowledges receipt of the pamphlet entitled "Real Estate Brokerage in Washington."
   b. Buyer Broker. Buyer Brokerage Firm appoints ______________________ ("Buyer Broker") to represent Buyer. This Agreement creates an agency relationship with Buyer Broker and any of Firm's managing brokers who supervise Buyer Broker ("Supervising Broker"). No other brokers affiliated with Firm are agents of Buyer.
   c. Agency Relationship. Buyer Brokerage Firm's representation of Buyer for the purchase of real property in the Area shall be (non-exclusive, if not checked):

      ☐ Exclusive. Buyer may not enter into an agency relationship with another real estate firm during the Term for the purchase of real property in the Area ("Exclusive Agency"); or

      ☐ Non-Exclusive. Buyer may enter into a non-exclusive agency relationship with other real estate firms during the Term ("Non-Exclusive Agency").

4. **LIMITED DUAL AGENCY.**
   a. Buyer Broker as Limited Dual Agent. If initialed below, Buyer consents to Buyer Broker and Supervising Broker acting as limited dual agents in the sale of property that is listed by Buyer Broker. Buyer acknowledges that as a limited dual agent, RCW 18.86.060 prohibits Buyer Broker from advocating terms favorable to Buyer to the detriment of the seller and further limits Buyer Broker's representation of Buyer.

      ______________ Buyer's Initials Date ______________ Buyer's Initials Date

   b. Firm Limited Dual Agency. If Buyer purchases a property listed by one of Firm's brokers other than Buyer Broker ("Listing Broker"), Buyer consents to any Supervising Broker, who also supervises Listing Broker, acting as a limited dual agent.

5. **COMPENSATION.** Buyer acknowledges that there are no standard compensation rates and the compensation in this Agreement is fully negotiable and not set by law. Firm may not receive any compensation for brokerage services provided to Buyer from any source greater than the amount set forth in this Section 5 or any subsequent amendment hereto. The compensation for Buyer Brokerage Firm's services (the "Compensation") shall be:
   a. ________ % of purchase price; $______________; other: ______________________________; or
   b. If Buyer Broker is a limited dual agent and represents both Buyer and the seller, then the Compensation shall be (equal to the amount in subsection 5(a) if not filled in):

      ________ % of purchase price; $______________; other: ______________________________; or
   c. If the seller is not represented by a licensed real estate firm, then the Compensation shall be (equal to the amount in subsection 5(a) if not filled in):

      ________ % of purchase price; $______________; other: ______________________________.

______________ Buyer's Initials Date ______________ Buyer's Initials Date

Form 41
Buyer Brokerage Services Agreement
Rev. 8/24
Page 2 of 3

BUYER BROKERAGE SERVICES AGREEMENT

6. SELLER COMPENSATION OFFER.

A seller may, but is not required to, offer compensation to Firm for representing Buyer in the purchase of seller's real property ("Seller's Offer"). Seller's Offer, if any, shall be stated in the purchase and sale agreement.

Buyer may request that the seller pay the Compensation to Firm as part of Buyer's offer, and Buyer shall pay any amount of the Compensation not paid by seller.

If Seller's Offer is greater than the Compensation, as part of Buyer's offer, Buyer may request that the amount of Seller's Offer that is greater than the Compensation be credited to Buyer (to the extent allowed by Buyer's lender).

7. COMPENSATION TERMS. The Compensation is due (except as otherwise agreed herein) when Buyer purchases real property located in the Area during the Term and:

a. Exclusive Agency. For Exclusive Agency, the purchase closes.

b. Non-Exclusive Agency. For Non-Exclusive Agency, the purchase closes, and Buyer Brokerage Firm represents Buyer in such purchase as indicated on the purchase and sale agreement.

c. Compensation After Expiration. If within _____ days (60 days if not filled in) after the Term:

i. Exclusive Agency. Buyer purchases a property that was brought to the attention of Buyer during the Term by the efforts or actions of Firm, or through information secured directly or indirectly from or through Firm; or a property that Buyer inquired about to Firm during the Term. Compensation is due when the purchase closes.

ii. Non-Exclusive Agency. Buyer purchases a property for which Buyer Brokerage Firm presented a written offer to the seller on behalf of Buyer during the Term. Compensation is due when the purchase closes.

Provided that in either event, if Buyer or the seller pays compensation to another real estate firm representing Buyer in conjunction with such a sale, the amount of compensation payable to Firm shall be reduced by the amount paid to such other firm(s).

d. Additional Consent. Buyer consents to Firm receiving compensation from more than one party, provided that any terms offered to Firm are disclosed as required by RCW 18.86.030 and any amounts paid to Firm reduce Buyer's obligation to Firm.

e. Cancellation Without Legal Cause. For Exclusive Agency, if Buyer cancels this Agreement without legal cause, Buyer may be liable for damages incurred by Firm as a result of such cancellation.

f. Listings. Buyer Broker shall bring listings to the attention of Buyer, regardless of Seller's Offer.

g. VA Financing. If Buyer is obtaining VA financing, VA regulations may require the Compensation be paid by the seller.

8. NO WARRANTIES OR REPRESENTATIONS. Firm makes no warranties or representations regarding the value of or the suitability of any property for Buyer's purposes. Buyer agrees to be responsible for making all inspections and investigations necessary to satisfy Buyer as to the property's suitability and value.

9. INSPECTION RECOMMENDED. Firm recommends that any offer to purchase a property be conditioned on an inspection of the property and its improvements conducted by a licensed inspector. Firm and Buyer Broker have no expertise in these matters and Buyer is solely responsible for interviewing and selecting all inspectors.

10. NO DISTRESSED HOME CONVEYANCE. Firm will not represent or assist Buyer in a transaction that is a "Distressed Home Conveyance" as defined by Chapter 61.34 RCW unless otherwise agreed in writing. A "Distressed Home Conveyance" is a transaction where a buyer purchases property from a "Distressed Homeowner" (defined by Chapter 61.34 RCW), allows the Distressed Homeowner to continue to occupy the property, and promises to convey the property back to the Distressed Homeowner or promises the Distressed Homeowner an interest in, or portion of the proceeds from a resale of the property.

Buyer's Initials ________ Date ________ Buyer's Initials ________ Date ________

Form 41
Buyer Brokerage Services Agreement
Rev. 8/24
Page 3 of 3

BUYER BROKERAGE SERVICES AGREEMENT

11. FAIR HOUSING. Local, state, and federal fair housing laws prohibit discrimination based on sex, marital status, sexual orientation, gender identity, race, creed, color, religion, caste, national origin, citizenship or immigration status, families with children status, familial status, honorably discharged veteran or military status, the presence of any sensory, mental, or physical disability, or the use of a support or service animal by a person with a disability.

12. ATTORNEYS' FEES. In the event either party employs an attorney to enforce any terms of this Agreement and is successful, the other party agrees to pay reasonable attorneys' fees. In the event of trial, the successful party shall be entitled to an award of attorneys' fees and expenses; the amount of the attorneys' fees and expenses shall be fixed by the court. The venue of any suit shall be the county in which the property is located.

13. OTHER.

Buyer's Signature Date	Buyer's Signature Date
Buyer E-mail Address	Buyer Phone Number
Buyer Brokerage Firm	Buyer Broker's Signature Date
Buyer Brokerage Firm License Number	Buyer Broker License Number
Buyer Broker E-mail Address	Buyer Broker Phone Number

The parties to a limited dual agency should be informed that they will not receive full representation. Certain facts must necessarily be withheld from each party; the limited dual agent cannot divulge confidential information about one party to the other party. Returning to the example above, the limited dual agent (Davis) must not tell the buyer the seller's bottom line price, nor tell the seller how much the buyer is willing to pay.

Before acting as a limited dual agent, a licensee must have a buyer agency agreement with the buyer and a seller agency agreement with the seller. Acting as a dual agent without the agency agreements, full disclosure, and written consent to the limited dual agency may give rise to a lawsuit by one or both parties. It's also grounds for disciplinary action by the Department of Licensing (see Chapter 17). Statutory agency disclosure requirements and the consent requirement for limited dual agency are discussed in the next section of this chapter.

In-house Transactions. Under the Real Estate Brokerage Relationships Act, dual agency occurs most often in in-house transactions. It's an **in-house transaction** when the listing agent and the buyer's agent both work for the same brokerage firm. In this situation, the listing agent represents only the seller, the buyer's agent represents only the buyer, and the firm and its designated broker are dual agents, representing both parties. This arrangement is sometimes referred to as a **split agency**, since the brokerage is serving both parties. It may also be called a **designated**, **assigned**, or **appointed agency**, since each of the affiliated licensees is assigned or appointed to represent a different party on behalf of the firm.

Example: Broker Petrov works for Skylark Realty. Petrov has shown a buyer named King several houses over the course of a few weeks. Finally, Petrov shows King a house listed by Broker Vincent, who also works for Skylark Realty. King decides to make an offer on the house. In this transaction, Petrov is the buyer's agent; Vincent is the seller's agent; and Skylark Realty and its designated broker are dual agents. Any Skylark managers who supervise only Vincent, the seller's agent, also represent the seller. Any who supervise only Petrov, the buyer's agent, also represent the buyer. And any who have supervisory responsibility for both Vincent and Petrov (perhaps a branch manager, for example) are dual agents, like the firm's designated broker.

However, a brokerage firm can appoint one licensee to represent both the seller and the buyer. In other words, limited dual agency is not restricted in Washington to in-house transactions; an individual licensee can represent both parties in a limited dual agency as long as both buyer and seller consent to the appointment.

Agency Disclosure Requirements

As we explained earlier, licensees in Washington must give anyone they render services to a pamphlet setting forth the provisions of the Real Estate Brokerage Relationships Act. In addition, they must disclose to anyone they render services to in a transaction which party (or parties) they're representing in the transaction.

A licensee must make the required agency disclosures to a party before that party signs an offer in the transaction. The disclosures must be in writing. They are usually in a paragraph in the purchase and sale agreement entitled "Agency Disclosure"; in that case, the parties' signatures on the agreement indicate their acceptance and understanding of the stated agency relationships (see Chapter 9). Alternatively, a licensee may make the disclosures in a separate disclosure document, which must be signed by the parties as well as the licensee; this is typically used when the parties use a purchase and sale agreement that does not include an agency disclosure section. An example is shown in Figure 7 .5.

Limited Dual Agency Disclosure. Before acting as a limited dual agent, a licensee must obtain the informed written consent of both parties. The limited dual agent must disclose to both parties that they will be acting as a limited dual agent. The terms of the limited dual agent's compensation must also be revealed. The parties will then sign the confirmation of the agency disclosure in the purchase and sale agreement (or the separate disclosure document).

Real estate agents should be extra careful with their disclosures in the context of limited dual agency. Buyers and sellers, eager to get on with the business of buying and selling a home, may agree to a limited dual agency without really understanding what it means. They may accept the agent's explanation at face value and sign a disclosure form without question. Later, one party might feel that the agent was not impartial and had breached their agency duties. This kind of disappointment could lead to legal action..

Independent Contractor Status

To end the chapter, let's examine the legal relationship between a real estate broker and the firm the broker works for. (In this discussion, the term "broker" will generally encompass managing brokers, too.) As we'll discuss in Chapter 17, a broker is not licensed to represent members of the public directly; they can only work as a real estate agent when they are affiliated with a firm.

For certain purposes, a real estate broker is classified either as the firm's **employee** or as an **independent contractor**. An independent contractor is hired to perform a particular job, and they use their own judgment to decide how the job should be completed.

Fig. 7.5 Agency Disclosure Form

Form 42
Agency Disclosure
Rev. 1/24
Page 1 of 1

AGENCY DISCLOSURE

This form is for use when the transaction forms do not otherwise contain an agency disclosure provision.

RCW 18.86.030 requires that a real estate broker disclose to their principal and to all parties in a transaction whether the broker represents the buyer (tenant), the seller (lessor), or both parties as a limited dual agent.

Broker: ______________________________ ("Broker")

Broker's License No. ________________

Real Estate Firm: ______________________________ ("Firm")

Real Estate Firm License No. ________________

Firm, Firm's Designated Broker, Broker's Branch Manager (if any), and Broker's Managing Broker (if any), and Broker represent : ____

______________________________ ________________
Broker's Signature Date

The undersigned Buyer (Tenant) and Seller (Lessor) acknowledge receipt of (i) the pamphlet entitled "Real Estate Brokerage in Washington" and (ii) this Agency Disclosure.

____
Signature Date

____
Signature Date

____
Signature Date

____
Signature Date

In contrast, an employee is hired to perform whatever tasks the employer requires, and is given instructions on how to accomplish each task. An employee is supervised and controlled much more closely than an independent contractor. Various employment and tax laws apply only when someone is hired as an employee, and not when someone is hired as an independent contractor.

Whether a real estate broker is an employee or an independent contractor in relation to the firm they work for depends on the degree of control exercised over the broker by the designated broker, the branch manager, or other managing brokers to whom the designated broker has delegated supervisory responsibilities. If the designated broker or other supervisors closely direct the activities of the broker and control how they carry out their work, the broker may be considered an employee. For example, if a broker is required to work on a set schedule, instructed when to go where, and told what steps to take in marketing each property, then the broker is probably an employee.

However, most firms exercise much less control over their brokers' work than that. They generally focus on the end results—listings, closings, and satisfied clients—and not on the details of how the broker accomplishes those results. A designated broker or other supervisor usually isn't concerned with where the broker is or what they are doing at any given time. The broker is paid on the basis of results (by commission) rather than hours spent on the job. Thus, in most cases, a real estate broker is an independent contractor, not an employee. (An exception: managing brokers who receive salaries for administrative duties may be considered employees.)

If a broker were an employee, the real estate firm would be required to withhold money from the broker's compensation for certain federal and state taxes (income tax, social security, and unemployment insurance) and also contribute a share of some of these taxes. By contrast, an independent contractor is responsible for paying their own social security and income taxes. In Washington, an important exception to this rule is industrial insurance (commonly called workers' compensation), which is insurance to help cover the costs of work-related injuries. A real estate firm must pay industrial insurance premiums to the state Department of Labor and Industries for all of the firm's workers, both employees and independent contractors. However, the firm may require the workers to pay a portion of this cost.

The Internal Revenue Code provides that a real estate agent will be considered an independent contractor for federal income tax purposes if three conditions are met:

1. the individual is a licensed real estate agent;
2. substantially all of their compensation is based on commission rather than hours worked; and
3. the services are performed under a written contract providing that the individual will not be treated as an employee for federal tax purposes.

Bear in mind that even when a real estate broker meets the criteria for independent contractor status, the firm's designated broker and other managing brokers who supervise the broker are still legally responsible for the broker's conduct (see Chapter 17).

Chapter Summary

1. In an agency relationship, the agent represents the principal in dealings with third parties. An agent may be a universal, general, or special agent, depending on the scope of authority granted.
2. Most agency relationships are created by express agreement (oral or written), but they can also be created by ratification, estoppel, or implication. Acts performed by an agent or an ostensible agent are binding on the principal if they fall within the scope of the agent's actual or apparent authority.
3. Agency relationships in Washington cannot exist without a written brokerage services agreement. Typically, this takes the form of a listing agreement for a seller's agent, and a buyer representation agreement for a buyer's agent.
4. A licensee owes a number of statutory duties to any party to whom the licensee renders real estate services, whether or not there is an agency relationship. These duties are reasonable skill and care, honesty and good faith, presenting all written communications, disclosure of material facts, accounting, providing an agency law pamphlet, and making an agency disclosure.
5. A licensee who enters into an agency relationship owes certain additional duties to the principal, including loyalty, disclosure of conflicts of interest, confidentiality, advising the principal to seek expert advice, and a good faith and continuous effort to fulfill the terms of the agency agreement.
6. Under general agency law, an agency relationship may be terminated by mutual agreement; revocation; renunciation; expiration; fulfillment of purpose; the death, incapacity, or bankruptcy of either party; or extinction of the subject matter.
7. Under Washington law, a real estate licensee may act as the seller's agent, the buyer's agent, or a limited dual agent.
8. A seller agency is created with a listing agreement. A seller's agent owes agency duties to the seller and general licensee duties to the buyer. A listing agent must be careful to avoid any actions that might give rise to an agency relationship with the buyer, which would create an inadvertent dual agency.
9. A buyer agency relationship can form when a licensee provides real estate services to a buyer, unless the licensee is already bound by a listing agreement with the seller of the property in question. However, the licensee's firm must enter into a written representation agreement with the buyer. A buyer's agent may be paid by the seller or by the buyer (with a commission, an hourly fee, or a flat rate).
10. A licensee is a limited dual agent when they represent both the seller and the buyer in the same transaction. Limited dual agency is unlawful without the informed written consent of both parties and a written agency agreement with each of them. Limited dual agency most commonly arises in in-house transactions, when the seller and the buyer are brought together by licensees who work for the same real estate firm.
11. A licensee is required to disclose to each party which party they represent in the transaction. The disclosure must be made to each party before that party signs an offer to purchase (a purchase and sale agreement). The disclosure must be in writing; it may take the form of a provision included in the purchase and sale agreement, or it may be a separate document.
12. For the purposes of certain tax and employment laws, a real estate broker is classified either as their brokerage firm's employee or as an independent contractor. In most cases, a broker is an independent contractor, even though the firm and its designated broker have legal responsibility for the broker's conduct.

Key Terms

Principal—The person who authorizes an agent to act on his behalf.

Agent—A person authorized to represent another in dealings with third parties.

Third party—A person seeking to deal with the principal through the agent.

Fiduciary—Someone who holds a special position of trust and confidence in relation to another.

Ratification—When the principal gives approval to unauthorized actions after they are performed, creating an agency relationship after the fact.

Estoppel—When the principal allows a third party to believe an agency relationship exists, so that the principal is legally precluded (estopped) from denying the agency.

Implication—When an agency relationship is created by the actions or conduct of the principal and agent, rather than by a written or spoken agreement.

Actual authority—Authority the principal grants to the agent either expressly or by implication.

Apparent authority—Where no actual authority has been granted, but the principal allows it to appear that the agent is authorized, and therefore is estopped from denying the agency. Also called ostensible authority.

Material facts—Information that has a substantial negative impact on the value of the property or on a party's ability to perform, or that would defeat the purpose of the transaction.

Confidential information—Information from or concerning a principal that was acquired during the course of an agency relationship, that the principal reasonably expects to be kept confidential, that the principal has not disclosed to third parties, that would operate to the detriment of the principal, and that the principal is not legally obligated to disclose to the other party.

Secret profit—Any profit an agent receives as a result of the agency relationship and does not disclose to the principal.

Multiple listing service—A regional or local cooperative of real estate firms and licensees who exchange listing information and help market the listings of other members. When one firm's listing is shown to buyers by licensees from other firms in the MLS, those licensees are called cooperating agents.

Listing agent—The real estate licensee who lists a seller's property for sale with the MLS; also called the listing broker. (The firm that this agent works for may also be called the listing agent or listing broker, or the listing brokerage firm.) The listing agent and firm are the seller's agents, but may act as dual agents with the written consent of the seller and a buyer.

Buyer's agent—A real estate licensee who is representing a buyer in a search for suitable property or in a purchase transaction, or the firm this licensee works for. Also called a buyer agent or buyer broker, or a buyer brokerage firm.

Seller's agent—A real estate licensee who is representing a seller in a real estate transaction, or the firm this licensee works for.

Selling agent—The real estate licensee representing the buyer whose offer has been accepted, or the firm this licensee works for. This term is falling out of favor; instead, the licensee may simply be called the buyer's agent and the firm referred to as the buyer brokerage firm.

In-house transaction—A sale in which the buyer and the seller are brought together by licensees working for the same brokerage firm.

Employee—Someone who works under the direction and control of another (the employer).

Independent contractor—A person who contracts to do a job for another, but retains control over how to carry out the task, rather than following detailed instructions.

Chapter Quiz

1. **An agency relationship can be created in any of the following ways, except:**
   a) written agreement
   b) oral agreement
   c) ratification
   d) verification

2. **After an agency relationship terminates, the agent still owes the principal the duty of:**
   a) loyalty
   b) confidentiality
   c) reasonable skill and care
   d) disclosure of material facts

3. **Garcia acted on behalf of Hilton without her authorization. At a later date, Hilton gave her approval to Garcia's actions. This is an example of:**
   a) express agreement
   b) ratification
   c) estoppel
   d) assumption of authority

4. **A seller lists their home with a brokerage at $290,000; they ask for a quick sale. When the listing broker shows the home to a buyer, they say the seller is financially insolvent and will take $280,000. The buyer offers $280,000 and the seller accepts. The broker:**
   a) did not violate their duties to the seller, because the seller accepted the offer
   b) did not violate their duties to the seller, since they fulfilled the purpose of their agency
   c) violated their duties to the seller by disclosing confidential information to the buyer
   d) was unethical, but did not violate their duties to the seller, since they did not receive a secret profit

5. **Stark lists his property with Agent Bell. Bell shows the property to her cousin, who decides he would like to buy it. Which of the following is true?**
   a) Bell can present her cousin's offer to Stark, as long as she tells Stark that the prospective buyer is one of her relatives
   b) Bell violated her duties to Stark by showing the property to one of her relatives
   c) It was not unethical for Bell to show the property to a relative, but it would be a violation of her duties if she presented her cousin's offer to Stark
   d) It is not necessary for Bell to tell Stark that the buyer is related to her, as long as he is offering the full listing price for the property

6. **A principal can be held liable for harm caused by a real estate licensee if the:**
   a) act resulting in harm was authorized by the principal
   b) licensee has a reputation for unethical practices
   c) licensee has many assets that could be awarded to the injured party
   d) licensee assured the third party that the principal would be liable for any harm caused by the transaction

7. **A real estate agent tells potential buyers: "This is a wonderful house—way better than anything else on the market." This statement would be considered:**
   a) a misrepresentation
   b) actual fraud
   c) self-dealing
   d) puffing

8. **In most cases, a listing agent:**
   a) is authorized to enter into contracts on behalf of the seller
   b) is considered a special agent
   c) Both of the above
   d) Neither of the above

9. **Limited dual agency is:**
   a) no longer legal in Washington State
   b) legal as long as both principals consent to the arrangement in writing
   c) unlawful unless the agent has a written agency agreement with each party
   d) Both b) and c)

10. **Able listed Glover's property. Able:**
    a) cannot give a buyer any information about Glover's property without being considered a dual agent
    b) may give a buyer information about Glover's property without owing agency duties to the buyer
    c) must sign a disclaimer of liability if he presents a buyer's offer to purchase to Glover
    d) is a non-agent

11. **Garza, who works for Granite Homes, is showing Manning a property listed by Lee, who also works for Granite Homes. The designated broker of Granite Homes Is Carter. Who is most likely to be acting as a limited dual agent?**
    a) Garza
    b) Carter
    c) Manning
    d) Lee

12. Broker Kelley works for Forrest Properties. A good friend wants Kelley to try to find a house for her. Kelley shows her a house listed by one of Forrest's other sales agents. Kelley:

a) is in danger of becoming a dual agent
b) is acting as a buyer's agent in this situation
c) should request special approval of the sale from the Real Estate Commission
d) is the seller's agent, no matter how she behaves towards her friend

13. A buyer's agent:

a) may not accept compensation paid by the seller
b) is not required to have a written buyer agency agreement
c) may be paid through a seller-paid fee
d) may not receive compensation that is based on the property's sales price

14. A licensee must disclose which party they representing:

a) to anyone they render services to, before that person signs an offer
b) to anyone they render services to, before the services are rendered
c) to the buyer, before showing the buyer any properties
d) to the seller, before presenting an offer to the seller

15. A limited dual agent must:

a) keep each party's negotiating position confidential
b) disclose all material facts to both parties, no matter how confidential
c) act only as a facilitator, with no agency duties to either party
d) refer all conflicts of interest to the Board of Equalization

Chapter 8:

Listing Agreements

A listing agreement is a written contract between a property owner and a real estate firm. The owner hires the firm to find a buyer who is ready, willing, and able to buy the property on the owner's terms. The listing agreement defines the rights and responsibilities of both the owner and the firm. This chapter explains what a real estate firm is required to do in order to earn a commission, the distinctions between the different types of listings, and the elements of a typical listing agreement.

Key Terms

Open Listing	**Multiple Listing Service**
Procuring Cause	**Net Listing**
Exclusive Agency Listing	**Extender Clause**
Exclusive Right to Sell Listing	**Distressed Home**

Introduction

When a seller hires a real estate firm to help sell a piece of property, they enter into a contract called a **listing agreement**. Even though the listing agreement form is filled out and signed by the listing agent (the individual licensee who is working with the seller), the contract is between the seller and the brokerage firm, not the individual licensee.

The listing agreement creates an agency relationship between the seller and the real estate firm. The individual listing agent also becomes an agent of the seller, as do the designated broker and any other managing brokers who supervise the listing agent. As we said in Chapter 7, agency carries with it a high level of responsibility. The listing firm and the listing agent are required to act in the best interests of the client (the seller/principal) in carrying out the agency.

The agency duties described in Chapter 7 are imposed on the listing firm and its affiliated licensees by law; in addition, the firm and the seller agree to take on certain contractual duties in their listing agreement. The terms of the listing agreement determine what the firm and the listing agent are obligated to do, and under what circumstances the seller must pay the firm a commission.

Earning a Commission

The standard form of payment for a real estate agent is the commission, also called a **brokerage fee**. The commission is usually computed as a percentage of the sales price (the price that the property is sold for), as opposed to the listing price.

A listing brokerage cannot sue a seller for compensation unless three criteria are met. First, there must be a written employment contract; a listing agreement must be in writing (see Chapter 6). Second, the listing firm and the listing agent must have been properly licensed before the agent offered to provide real estate services or procured a promise of compensation (see Chapter 17). Finally, the listing firm must have fulfilled the terms of the listing agreement.

A listing agreement can make payment of the commission depend on any conditions that are mutually acceptable to the listing firm and the seller. For example, the seller could ask to include a "no sale, no commission" provision in the agreement. This would make the commission payable only if the transaction actually closes and the seller receives full payment from the buyer.

Unless otherwise agreed, however, certain standard rules are followed regarding payment of the commission. These include the rules concerning a ready, willing, and able buyer, and those concerning the three types of listings.

Ready, Willing, and Able Buyer

As a general rule, a listing agreement obligates the seller to pay the agent (the listing firm) a commission if a ready, willing, and able buyer is found during the listing period. A buyer is considered "ready and willing" if they make an offer that meets the seller's stated terms. (In the listing agreement, the seller should state the price and any other essential terms—for instance, if the seller requires a specific closing date or downpayment amount.)

A ready and willing buyer is considered "able" if they have the capacity to contract and the financial ability to complete the purchase. The buyer must have enough cash to buy the property on the agreed terms, or be eligible for the necessary financing.

Since the obligation to pay the commission arises when a ready, willing, and able buyer is found, if the seller decides not to accept that buyer's offer, they still owe the commission. Furthermore, if the offer is accepted, the obligation to pay the commission does not terminate just because the sale falls through, at least not if that failure was the seller's fault. For example, if the seller changes their mind about selling or can't deliver marketable title, they still owe the commission. (However, the firm or firms involved may decide against demanding payment.)

Note that if the buyer causes the sale to terminate—for example, because they can't get financing—that might mean the buyer wasn't actually "able," and therefore no commission is owed.

Types of Listing Agreements

Whether a seller owes the agent a commission also depends on the type of listing agreement that they have. The three basic types of listing agreements are the:

- open listing,
- exclusive agency listing, and
- exclusive right to sell listing.

Open Listing. Under an open listing agreement, the seller is obligated to pay the agent a commission only if the agent was the **procuring cause** of the sale. The procuring cause is the person who was primarily responsible for bringing about the agreement between the parties. To be the procuring cause, an agent must have personally obtained the offer from the ready, willing, and able buyer.

An open listing is also called a non-exclusive listing, because a seller is free to give open listings to any number of agents. If a seller signs two open listing agreements with two different agents, and one of the agents sells the property, only the agent who made the sale is entitled to a commission. The other agent is not compensated for their efforts. Or if the seller sells the property directly, without the help of either agent, then the seller does not have to pay any commission at all. The sale of the property terminates all outstanding listings.

Because multiple listing services generally do not accept open listings, they're uncommon for residential properties. Sometimes open listings are used for commercial properties, however.

The open listing arrangement has obvious disadvantages. If two competing agents both negotiate with the person who ends up buying the property, there may be a dispute over which agent was the procuring cause of the sale. Also, because an agent with an open listing agreement is not assured of a commission when the property sells, they may not put as much effort into marketing the property, so it may take longer to sell.

For the most part, open listing agreements are used only when a seller is unwilling to agree to an exclusive listing.

Exclusive Agency Listing. In an exclusive agency listing, the seller agrees to list with only one agent, but retains the right to sell the property themself without being obligated to pay the agent a commission. The agent is entitled to a commission if anyone other than the seller finds a buyer for the property, but not if the seller finds the buyer without the help of an agent. Like open listings, exclusive agency listings can lead to disputes—in this case, over whether the seller truly found the buyer with no help from the agent's marketing efforts.

Exclusive Right to Sell Listing. Under an exclusive right to sell listing, the seller agrees to list with only one agent, and that agent is entitled to a commission if the property sells during the listing term, regardless of who finds the buyer. Even if the seller makes the sale directly, the agent is still entitled to the commission.

In spite of the designation "exclusive right to sell," this type of listing agreement does not actually authorize the agent to sell the property. As with the other types of listings, the agent is authorized only to submit offers to purchase to the seller. (To grant an agent the right to actually sell the property, the seller would have to execute a power of attorney.)

The exclusive right to sell listing is preferred by agents because it gives them the best chance of earning a commission. It's the type of listing that's most commonly used.

Due Diligence. A key distinction between open and exclusive listings concerns the agent's contractual obligations. An open listing is a unilateral contract: the seller promises to pay a commission if the agent finds a buyer, but the agent does not promise to make any effort to do so. If the agent does nothing at all, it is not a breach of contract.

On the other hand, an exclusive listing is a bilateral contract. In exchange for the seller's promise to pay a commission no matter who finds a buyer, the agent (by implication, if not expressly) promises to market the property and make a diligent effort to find a buyer. If the seller can prove that the listing agent did nothing to help sell the property, a court might not require the seller to pay the agent's commission.

Elements of a Listing Agreement

Although an agent and a seller can draw up their listing agreement from scratch, that's rare, at least for residential listings. Most brokerages use one of several available listing agreement forms and make few—if any—modifications to it.

If a firm belongs to a multiple listing service (discussed below), it is usually required to use the listing form provided by the MLS, which generally cannot be modified by the firm.

In this section of the chapter, we will first discuss the basic requirements for any listing agreement, and then look at the provisions of a typical listing agreement form.

Basic Requirements

Washington's statute of frauds requires a listing agreement to be in writing and signed by the seller. The agreement must authorize the brokerage firm to sell (market) the property and provide for the firm's compensation (the commission). It's best to state the commission as a fixed figure, since a court may find an inadequately specific contract to be unenforceable. Therefore, the commission is usually stated as a percentage of the sales price, or occasionally as a set dollar amount.

In a **net listing**, however, the seller states what net amount they will accept as the proceeds from the sale of the property. If the sales price exceeds that net figure, the agent is entitled to keep the excess as their compensation—no matter how much it may turn out to be. Net listings are generally frowned upon; an unscrupulous agent can use them to take advantage of clients. (In some other states, they are entirely illegal.)

The listing agreement must also adequately describe the property to be sold. A complete legal description of the property is not absolutely required by Washington law, as long as the agreement clearly identifies the property in question. Certainly the best practice is to use a legal description.

A slip of paper that says "I will pay Diaz Realty $1,000 for helping me to sell Claraway Farm" could be an enforceable listing agreement in Washington, as long as it is signed by a competent seller. Of course, it is much better to have a formal legal document that sets forth all of the terms of the agreement. All listing agreements should, at a minimum, contain the following:

1. a description of the property;
2. an authorization of the real estate firm to act as the seller's agent;
3. the seller's agreement to pay the firm a commission, along with the commission rate or amount;
4. the terms of sale the seller will accept;
5. the conditions under which the commission will be payable; and
6. the seller's warranties as to the accuracy of the information given to the agent and included in the listing agreement.

In addition, best practice is to include a termination date in an exclusive listing agreement. Since exclusive agency agreements prevent the seller from hiring other agents, a fixed termination date lets the seller know when they can move on if the listing agent isn't satisfactory. That said, Washington doesn't require listing agency agreements to have a termination date. A listing (exclusive or open) with no ending date will terminate after a reasonable time.

Provisions of a Typical Listing Agreement Form

In Washington, as in most other states, there's no single listing agreement form that agents are legally required to use. However, the residential listing agreement published by the Northwest Multiple Listing Service (NWMLS) is used by most of the multiple listing services throughout the state. Various other listing forms (including forms for other types of property) are available through multiple listing services, professional associations, and general publishers of legal forms. Although most listing forms have many common elements, there may also be significant differences between them. A real estate licensee should use only the forms chosen by their brokerage firm, and should become familiar with the provisions of those particular forms. We'll present a general discussion of provisions likely to appear in a typical form, but any given form might omit some of these and include others not discussed here.

Most residential listings are exclusive right to sell agreements with a multiple listing authorization. As an example, the NWMLS listing agreement form is shown in Figure 8.1. An NWMLS listing input form is shown in Figure 8.2.

Fig. 8.1 Exclusive Right to Sell Listing Agreement

Form 1A
Exclusive Sale
Rev. 8/24
Page 1 of 4

EXCLUSIVE SALE AND LISTING AGREEMENT

This Exclusive Sale and Listing Brokerage Services Agreement (the "Agreement") is made by and between ______________ ______________ ("Seller") and
Seller Seller
______________ ("Listing Firm" or "Firm") with regard to the real property commonly known as ______________, City ______________, County ______________, WA, Zip ______________; and legally described on Exhibit A ("the Property").

1. **DEFINITIONS.** (a) "MLS" means the Northwest Multiple Listing Service; and (b) "sell" includes a contract to sell; an exchange or contract to exchange; or an option to purchase. Firm need not submit to Seller any offers to lease, rent, or enter into any agreement other than for sale of the Property.

2. **TERM.** Seller hereby grants to Listing Firm the exclusive right to list and sell the Property from the date of mutual acceptance of this Agreement ("Effective Date") until midnight of ______________ ("Listing Term"). If this Agreement expires while Seller is a party to a purchase and sale agreement for the Property, the Listing Term shall automatically extend until the sale is closed or the purchase and sale agreement is terminated.

3. **AGENCY.**
   a. Pamphlet. Seller acknowledges receipt of the pamphlet entitled "Real Estate Brokerage in Washington."
   b. Listing Broker. Listing Firm appoints ______________ to represent Seller ("Listing Broker"). This Agreement creates an agency relationship with Listing Broker and any of Firm's managing brokers who supervise Listing Broker ("Supervising Broker") during the Listing Term. No other brokers affiliated with Firm are agents of Seller.

4. **LIMITED DUAL AGENCY.**
   a. Listing Broker as Limited Dual Agent. If initialed below, Seller consents to Listing Broker and Supervising Broker acting as limited dual agents in the sale of the Property to a buyer that Listing Broker also represents. Seller acknowledges that as a limited dual agent, RCW 18.86.060 prohibits Listing Broker from advocating terms favorable to Seller to the detriment of the buyer and further limits Listing Broker's representation of Seller.

   ______ Seller's Initials ______ Date ______ Seller's Initials ______ Date

   b. Firm Limited Dual Agency. If the Property is sold to a buyer represented by one of Firm's brokers other than Listing Broker ("Listing Firm's Buyer's Broker"), Seller consents to any Supervising Broker, who also supervises Listing Firm's Buyer's Broker, acting as a limited dual agent.

5. **LIST DATE.** Firm shall submit this listing, including the Property information on the attached Listing Input Sheets and photographs of the Property (collectively "Listing Data"), to be published by MLS on ______________ ("List Date"), which date shall not be more than 90 days from the Effective Date. Seller acknowledges that exposure of the Property to the open market through MLS will increase the likelihood that Seller will receive fair market value for the Property. Accordingly, prior to the List Date, Firm and Seller shall not promote or advertise the Property in any manner whatsoever, including, but not limited to yard or other signs, flyers, websites, e-mails, texts, social media, mailers, magazines, newspapers, open houses, previews, showings, or tours. Seller shall not materially interfere with Listing Firm's marketing of the Property. To address any privacy or similar concerns, Seller may instruct Listing Broker to limit marketing by not displaying the Property address or map location on the internet, by eliminating any and all internet advertising, and by imposing specific showing requirements and other similar restrictions.

6. **FAIR HOUSING.** Seller acknowledges that local, state, and federal fair housing laws prohibit discrimination based on sex, marital status, sexual orientation, gender identity, race, creed, color, religion, caste, national origin, citizenship or immigration status, families with children status, familial status, honorably discharged veteran or military status, the presence of any sensory, mental, or physical disability, or the use of a support or service animal by a person with a disability.

______ Seller's Initials ______ Date ______ Seller's Initials ______ Date

Form 1A
Exclusive Sale
Rev. 8/24
Page 2 of 4

EXCLUSIVE SALE AND LISTING AGREEMENT

7. COMPENSATION. Seller acknowledges that there are no standard compensation rates and the compensation in this Agreement is fully negotiable and not set by law. If during the Listing Term, Seller sells the Property and the sale closes; or the sale fails to close due to Seller's breach of the terms of the purchase and sale agreement, Seller shall pay compensation as follows:

a. Listing Firm Compensation.

i. _____% of the sales price; $ _____________; other: ____; or

ii. If the buyer is not represented by a buyer brokerage firm, the Listing Firm compensation shall be _____% of the sales price; $ ______________; other ______________________________ (equal to the amount in subsection 7(a)(i) above if not filled in).

b. Buyer Brokerage Firm Compensation. Seller acknowledges that offering compensation to a cooperating member of MLS representing the buyer ("Buyer Brokerage Firm") ("Buyer Brokerage Compensation") is not required.

❑ **Seller's Offer of Compensation.** Seller offers Buyer Brokerage Compensation as follows:

i. _____% of the sales price; $ _____________; or other ______________________________ to Buyer Brokerage Firm, which includes another broker affiliated with Listing Firm who represents the buyer; or

ii. If the Listing Broker is a limited dual agent and represents both Seller and the buyer, _____% of the sales price; $ ______________; or other ______________________________ (equal to the amount in subsection 7(b)(i) above if not filled in) to be paid to Listing Firm as Buyer Brokerage Compensation.

iii. Buyer Brokerage Compensation shall be paid as set forth above, unless modified by the buyer in a mutually accepted purchase and sale agreement. The offered amount may not be withdrawn or reduced with respect to a buyer after that buyer or the Buyer Brokerage Firm has notified the Listing Firm or Seller of that buyer's intent to submit an offer (and for three calendar days thereafter). Buyer Brokerage Firm is an intended third-party beneficiary of this Agreement.

iv. If checked, ❑ the offer to pay Buyer Brokerage Compensation shall extend to licensed brokerage firms that are not members of MLS.

❑ **Buyer to Request Compensation in Offer.** In lieu of offering a specific compensation amount, Seller invites the buyer to include in the buyer's offer, the amount that the buyer requests Seller to compensate the Buyer Brokerage Firm, which amount must be agreed to by the parties. "Request in Offer" will be displayed in the compensation section of the listing.

❑ **No Offer of Compensation.** Seller declines to offer and does not intend to pay Buyer Brokerage Compensation. Seller acknowledges that a buyer may still submit an offer that includes an amount that the buyer requests Seller to compensate the Buyer Brokerage Firm. "None" will be displayed in the compensation section of the listing.

c. Expiration of the Listing Term. If Seller shall, within _____ days (180 days if not filled in) after the expiration of the Listing Term, sell the Property to any person to whose attention it was brought through the signs, advertising or other action of the Listing Firm, or on information secured directly or indirectly from or through Firm, during the Listing Term, Seller will pay Firm and Buyer Brokerage Firm the above compensation at closing. Provided, that if Seller pays compensation to other licensed brokerage firms in conjunction with a sale, the amount of compensation payable to Firm shall be reduced by the amount paid to such other listing firm and the compensation payable to Buyer Brokerage Firm shall be reduced by the amount paid to such other buyer brokerage firm.

d. Cancellation Without Legal Cause. If Seller cancels this Agreement without legal cause, Seller may be liable for damages incurred by Firm as a result of such cancellation, regardless of whether Seller pays compensation to another licensed brokerage firm.

e. Additional Consent. Seller consents to Firm receiving compensation from more than one party, provided that any terms offered to Firm are disclosed as required by RCW 18.86.030.

Seller's Initials	Date	Seller's Initials	Date

Form 1A
Exclusive Sale
Rev. 8/24
Page 3 of 4

EXCLUSIVE SALE AND LISTING AGREEMENT

8. PROPERTY ACCESS AND KEYBOX. Listing Firm shall install a keybox on the Property that holds a key to the Property which may be opened by an electronic key held by members of MLS, their brokers, and affiliated appraiser members of MLS. Unless otherwise agreed in writing or as set forth in the attached Listing Input Sheets, Firm and other members of MLS shall be entitled to show the Property at all reasonable times.

a. Property Access for Non-Member Brokers. Listing Firm may be contacted by licensed brokers who are not members of MLS and do not have access to the keybox on the Property. Seller ☐ authorizes; ☐ does not authorize (authorizes if not filled in) Firm to provide access to the Property to licensed brokers who are not members of MLS. If authorized, Listing Firm ☐ shall; ☐ shall not (shall if not filled in) be required to attend any such showing. If authorized, Listing Firm ☐ shall; ☐ shall not (shall if not filled in) require brokers who are not members of MLS to execute an access agreement prior to any showing.

9. MULTIPLE LISTING SERVICE. Seller authorizes Listing Firm and MLS to publish and distribute the Listing Data to other members of MLS and their affiliates and third parties for public display and other purposes, subject to any restrictions imposed by Seller. This authorization shall survive the termination of this Agreement. Firm is authorized to report the sale of the Property (including price and all terms) to MLS and to its members, financial institutions, appraisers, and others related to the sale, provided that any terms reported to MLS before the sale closes shall only be used for aggregated, anonymized reports. Firm may refer this listing to any other cooperating multiple listing service at Firm's discretion or a licensed broker who is not a member of a multiple listing service. Firm shall cooperate with all other members of MLS, members of a multiple listing service to which this listing is referred, and any licensed brokers who are not members of a multiple listing service. MLS is an intended third-party beneficiary of this Agreement and will provide the Listing Data to its members and their affiliates and third parties, without verification and without assuming any responsibility with respect to this Agreement.

10. PROPERTY CONDITION AND INSURANCE. Neither Firm, MLS, nor any members of MLS or of any multiple listing service to which this listing is referred shall be responsible for, and Seller shall indemnify and hold them harmless from, any loss, theft, or damage of any nature or kind whatsoever to the Property, any personal property therein, or any personal injury resulting from the condition of the Property, including entry by the key to the keybox and/or at open houses, except for damage or injury caused by their gross negligence or willful misconduct. Seller is advised to notify Seller's insurance company that the Property is listed for sale and ascertain that the Seller has adequate insurance coverage. If the Property is to be vacant during all or part of the Listing Term, Seller is advised to request that a "vacancy clause" be added to Seller's insurance policy. Seller acknowledges that intercepting or recording conversations of persons in the Property without first obtaining their consent violates RCW 9.73.030 and Seller shall indemnify and hold Firm and other members of MLS harmless from any related claims.

11. SELLER'S WARRANTIES AND REPRESENTATIONS. Seller warrants that Seller has the right to sell the Property on the terms herein. If Seller provides Firm with any photographs, drawings, or sketches of the Property, Seller warrants that Seller has the necessary rights in the photographs, drawings, or sketches to allow Firm to use them as contemplated by this Agreement. Seller shall indemnify and hold Firm and other members of MLS harmless in the event the foregoing warranties are incorrect. Seller represents, to the best of Seller's knowledge, that the Property information on the Listing Input Sheets (attached to and incorporated into this Agreement by this reference) is correct.

12. SHORT SALE / NO DISTRESSED HOME CONVEYANCE. If the proceeds from the sale of the Property are insufficient to cover the Seller's costs at closing, Seller acknowledges that the decision by any beneficiary or mortgagee, or its assignees, to release its interest in the Property, for less than the amount owed, does not automatically relieve Seller of the obligation to pay any debt or costs remaining at closing, including fees such as Firm's compensation. Firm will not represent or assist Seller in a transaction that is a "Distressed Home Conveyance" as defined by Chapter 61.34 RCW unless otherwise agreed in writing. A "Distressed Home Conveyance" is a transaction where a buyer purchases property from a "Distressed Homeowner" (defined by Chapter 61.34 RCW), allows the Distressed Homeowner to continue to occupy the property, and promises to convey the property back to the Distressed Homeowner or promises the Distressed Homeowner an interest in, or portion of, the proceeds from a resale of the property.

13. SELLER DISCLOSURE STATEMENT. Unless Seller is exempt under RCW 64.06, Seller shall provide to Firm as soon as reasonably practicable, a completed "Seller Disclosure Statement" (Form 17 (Residential)), (Form 17C (Unimproved Residential)), or (Form 17 Commercial). Seller shall indemnify, defend, and hold Firm harmless from and against any and all claims that the information Seller provides on Form 17, Form 17C, or Form 17 Commercial is inaccurate.

Seller's Initials Date Seller's Initials Date

Form 1A
Exclusive Sale
Rev. 8/24
Page 4 of 4

EXCLUSIVE SALE AND LISTING AGREEMENT

14. CLOSING. Seller shall furnish and pay for a buyer's policy of title insurance showing marketable title to the Property. Seller shall pay real estate excise tax and one-half of any escrow fees or such portion of escrow fees and any other fees or charges as provided by law in the case of a FHA, USDA, or VA financed sale. Rent, taxes, interest, reserves, assumed encumbrances, homeowner fees and insurance are to be prorated between Seller and the buyer as of the date of closing. Seller shall prepare and execute a certification (NWMLS Form 22E or equivalent) under the Foreign Investment in Real Property Tax Act ("FIRPTA") and Firm may provide a copy of the FIRPTA certification to escrow and the buyer. If Seller is a foreign person or entity, and the sale is not otherwise exempt from FIRPTA, Seller acknowledges that a percentage of the amount realized from the sale will be withheld for payment to the Internal Revenue Service and Seller shall pay any fees, including any fees incurred by the buyer, related to such withholding and payment.

15. DAMAGES IN THE EVENT OF BUYER'S BREACH. In the event Seller retains earnest money as liquidated damages on a buyer's breach, any costs advanced or committed by Firm on Seller's behalf shall be paid therefrom and the balance shall be ❑ retained by Seller; ❑ divided equally between Seller and Firm (retained by Seller if not checked).

16. ATTORNEYS' FEES. In the event either party employs an attorney to enforce any terms of this Agreement and is successful, the other party agrees to pay reasonable attorneys' fees. In the event of trial, the successful party shall be entitled to an award of attorneys' fees and expenses; the amount of the attorneys' fees and expenses shall be fixed by the court. The venue of any suit shall be the county in which the Property is located.

17. OTHER.

Seller's Signature Date	Seller's Signature Date
Seller E-mail Address	Seller Phone Number
Listing Firm	Listing Broker's Signature Date
Listing Firm License Number	Listing Broker License Number
Listing Broker E-mail Address	Listing Broker Phone Number

Fig. 8.2 Listing input sheet

NWMLS Form 1 Rev. 8/24

RESIDENTIAL Exclusive Listing Agreement (page 1 of 5)
LISTING INPUT SHEET

• Indicates Required information ( ) Indicates Maximum Choice *Indicates "Yes" By Default **LISTING #**

ADDRESS

• **State** • **County** • **City**

• **ZIP Code** + 4 • **Area** • **Community/District**

Direction

• **Street #** **Modifier** ❑ N ❑ E ❑ NE ❑ SE ❑ S ❑ W ❑ NW ❑ SW • **Street Name**

Suffix
❑ Avenue ❑ Boulevard ❑ Court Ave ❑ Drive Ct ❑ Lane ❑ Parkway ❑ Street ❑ Street Pl ❑ Way
❑ Avenue Ct ❑ Circle ❑ Court St ❑ Highway ❑ Loop ❑ Place ❑ Street Ct ❑ Terrace
❑ Avenue Pl ❑ Court ❑ Drive ❑ Junction ❑ Park ❑ Road ❑ Street Dr ❑ Trail

Post Direction
❑ N ❑ NE ❑ S ❑ NW ❑ E ❑ SE ❑ W ❑ SW

Unit #

LISTING

$
• **Listing Price** • **Listing Date** • **Expiration Date** • **Tax ID#**

• **Preliminary Title Ordered** ❑ Yes ❑ No

Title Company (60 characters maximum)

• **Offers** (1)
❑ Seller intends to review offers upon receipt
❑ Seller to review offers on Offer Review Date (may review/accept sooner)

Offer Review Date
(required if 2nd "Offers" option is selected)

FIRPTA withholding required? ❑ Yes ❑ No

Equitable Interest ❑ Yes ❑ No

LOCATION

Lot Number **Block** **Plat/Subdivision/Building Name**

PROPERTY INFORMATION

• **Prohibit Blogging** ❑ *Yes ❑ No
• **Allow Automated Valuation** ❑ *Yes ❑ No
• **Show Map Link** ❑ *Yes ❑ No
• **Internet Advertising** ❑ *Yes ❑ No
• **Show Address to Public** ❑ *Yes ❑ No

Buyer Brkg. Comp. (BBC) (25 characters maximum)

Compensation Type ❑ $ ❑ %

Tail Provision (Days)
(required if compensation offered)

Buyer Brkg. Compensation Comments (40 characters maximum)

• **Year Built** **Effective Year Built**

Effective Year Built Source ❑ Public Records ❑ See Remarks

SQFT INFORMATION

Approximate Square Footage = Finished SqFt + Unfinished SqFt (This value is automatically calculated for you)

(Do NOT include SqFt of garage in Finished or Unfinished SqFt fields. Approximate Square Footage should exclude garage.)

Finished SqFt **Unfinished SqFt** • **SqFt Source**

Garage SqFt • **Lot Size (SqFt)** • **Lot Size Source**

VIRTUAL TOURS

Virtual Tour #1 URL (Please include http:// or https://) **Virtual Tour #1 Description**

Virtual Tour #2 URL (Please include http:// or https://) **Virtual Tour #2 Description**

Virtual Tour #3 URL (Please include http:// or https://) **Virtual Tour #3 Description**

INITIALS: Seller Date Seller Date Broker Date

NWMLS Form 1 Rev. 8/24

RESIDENTIAL Exclusive Listing Agreement (page 2 of 5)
LISTING INPUT SHEET

Listing Address: **LAG #**

ADDITIONAL TAX IDs

Additional Tax ID# **Additional Tax ID#** **Additional Tax ID#**
Additional Tax IDs to be listed on attached sheets

BROKER INFORMATION

• **Listing Broker** - ID# | **Broker Name** | **Listing Office** - ID# | **Brokerage Firm Name**

Co-Broker - ID# | **Co-Broker Name** | **Co-Office** - ID# | **Co-Brokerage Firm Name**

LISTING INFORMATION

• **Possession** (3)
❑ Closing
❑ Negotiable
❑ See Remarks
❑ Sub. Tenant's Rights

• **Showing Information** (10)
❑ Appointment
❑ Call Listing Office
❑ Day Sleeper
❑ Gate Code Needed
❑ MLS Keybox
❑ Other Keybox
❑ Owner-Call First
❑ Pet in House
❑ Power Off
❑ Renter-Call First
❑ Security System
❑ See Remarks
❑ ShowingTime
❑ Vacant

• **Potential Terms** (10)
❑ Assumable
❑ Cash Out
❑ Conventional
❑ Farm Home Loan
❑ FHA
❑ Lease/Purchase
❑ Owner Financing
❑ Rehab Loan
❑ See Remarks
❑ State Bond
❑ USDA
❑ VA

Short Term Rental ❑ Yes ❑ No

$ **Monthly Rent ($)** - *if rented*

• **Senior Exemption** ❑ Yes ❑ No

Right of First Refusal ❑ Yes ❑ No

• **Tax Year**

$ • **Annual Taxes**

• **Form 17** (1)
❑ Exempt ❑ Provided
❑ Not Provided

• **Common Interest Cmty** (RCW 64.90) ❑ Yes ❑ No

HOMEOWNER ASSOCIATION INFORMATION

• **Homeowners Association** ❑ Yes ❑ No

$ **HOA Dues**

HOA Dues Freq (1)
❑ Monthly
❑ Quarterly
❑ Annually
❑ Not Applicable

HOA Dues Include (15)
❑ Cable TV
❑ Central Hot Water
❑ Common Area Maintenance
❑ Concierge
❑ Earthquake Ins.
❑ Garbage
❑ Internet
❑ Lawn Service
❑ Natural Gas
❑ Road Maintenance
❑ Security Services
❑ See Remarks
❑ Sewer
❑ Snow Removal
❑ Water

Other Dues/Fees (see remarks) ❑ Yes ❑ No

Association Contact's Name **Association Phone No.**

SCHOOL & OWNER INFORMATION

• **School District** | **Elementary School** | **Junior High/Middle School** | **Senior High School**

• **Owner's Name** | **Owner's Name 2** | **Owner's Phone**

• **Occupant Type** (Owner/Presale/Tenant/Vacant) | • **Phone to Show** | • **Owner's City and State** | • **Occupant's Name**

• **Bank / RE Owned** ❑ Yes ❑ No

• **3rd Party Approval Required** (2)
❑ None ❑ Other - See Remarks
❑ Short Sale

• **Auction** ❑ Yes ❑ No

INITIALS: Seller Date Seller Date Broker Date

RESIDENTIAL Exclusive Listing Agreement (page 3 of 5)
LISTING INPUT SHEET

Listing Address: **LAG #**

SITE INFORMATION

Lot Dimensions

Waterfront Footage (Feet)

Pool (1)
❑ Above Ground ❑ Indoor
❑ Community ❑ In-Ground

Zoning Code

Zoning Jurisdiction (1)
❑ City
❑ County
❑ See Remarks

Lot Topo./Veg. (7)
❑ Brush ❑ Pasture
❑ Dune ❑ Rolling
❑ Equestrian ❑ Sloped
❑ Fruit Trees ❑ Steep Slope
❑ Garden Space ❑ Terraces
❑ Level ❑ Wooded
❑ Partial Slope

View (7)
❑ Bay ❑ Partial
❑ Canal ❑ Pond
❑ City ❑ River
❑ Golf Course ❑ Sea
❑ Jetty ❑ See Remarks
❑ Lake ❑ Sound
❑ Mountain ❑ Strait
❑ Ocean ❑ Territorial

• **Leased Land**
❑ Yes ❑ No

Waterfront (5)
❑ Bank-High ❑ Lake
❑ Bank-Low ❑ No Bank
❑ Bank-Medium ❑ Ocean
❑ Bay ❑ River
❑ Bulkhead ❑ Saltwater
❑ Canal ❑ Sea
❑ Creek ❑ Sound
❑ Jetty ❑ Strait

Site Features (14)
❑ Arena-Indoor ❑ Electric Car Charging ❑ Outbuildings
❑ Arena-Outdoor ❑ Fenced-Fully ❑ Patio
❑ Athletic Court ❑ Fenced-Partially ❑ Propane
❑ Barn ❑ Gas Available ❑ Rooftop Deck
❑ Boat House ❑ Gated Entry ❑ RV Parking
❑ Cabana/Gazebo ❑ Green House ❑ Shop
❑ Cable TV ❑ High Speed Internet ❑ Sprinkler System
❑ Deck ❑ Hot Tub/Spa ❑ Stable
❑ Dock ❑ Irrigation
❑ Dog Run ❑ Moorage

Lot Details (8)
❑ Adjacent to Public Land ❑ High Voltage Line
❑ Alley ❑ Open Space
❑ Corner Lot ❑ Paved Street
❑ Cul-de-sac ❑ Secluded
❑ Curbs ❑ Sidewalk
❑ Dead End Street ❑ Value in Land
❑ Dirt Road
❑ Drought Res Landscape

Water Access (4)
❑ Beach Rights
❑ Community Waterfront/Pvt Beach
❑ Deeded Access
❑ Non-Deeded Access
❑ Tideland Rights

BUILDING INFORMATION

• **Sewer** (2)
❑ Available ❑ Sewer Connected
❑ None ❑ STEP System
❑ Septic

Basement (3)
❑ Daylight ❑ Partially Finished
❑ Fully Finished ❑ Roughed In
❑ None ❑ Unfinished

• **Parking Type** (4)
❑ Carport-Attached ❑ Garage-Detached
❑ Carport-Detached ❑ None
❑ Driveway Parking ❑ Off Street
❑ Garage-Attached

Approved # of Bedrooms (septic)

• **Total Covered Parking**

Builder

• **New Construction**
❑ Yes ❑ No

New Construction State (1)
❑ Completed ❑ Under Construction
❑ Presale

Estimated Completion Date

Architecture (1)
❑ A-Frame/Dome ❑ See Remarks
❑ Cabin ❑ Spanish/SW
❑ Cape Cod ❑ Traditional
❑ Colonial ❑ Tudor
❑ Contemporary ❑ Victorian
❑ Craftsman
❑ Modern
❑ NW Contemporary

Building Condition (1)
❑ Average
❑ Fair
❑ Fixer
❑ Good
❑ Remodeled
❑ Restored
❑ Under Construction
❑ Very Good

• **Style Code** (1)
❑ 10 - 1 Story ❑ 18 - 2 Stories w/Bsmnt
❑ 11 - 1 1/2 Story ❑ 20 - Manuf-Single Wide
❑ 12 - 2 Story ❑ 21 - Manuf-Double Wide
❑ 13 - Tri-Level ❑ 22 - Manuf-Triple Wide
❑ 14 - Split Entry ❑ 24 - Floating Home/ On-Water Res
❑ 15 - Multi Level
❑ 16 - 1 Story w/Bsmnt ❑ 32 - Townhouse
❑ 17 - 1 1/2 Stry w/Bsmnt

Manufactured Home Serial No.

Manufactured Home Manufacturer

Manufactured Home Model Number

• **Exterior** (4)
❑ Brick ❑ See Remarks
❑ Cement Planked ❑ Stone
❑ Cement/Concrete ❑ Stucco
❑ Log ❑ Wood
❑ Metal/Vinyl ❑ Wood Products

Foundation (3)
❑ Concrete Block ❑ See Remarks
❑ Concrete Ribbon ❑ Slab
❑ Post & Block ❑ Tie down
❑ Post & Pillar
❑ Poured Concrete

• **Roof** (3)
❑ Built-up ❑ Metal
❑ Cedar Shake ❑ See Remarks
❑ Composition ❑ Tile
❑ Flat ❑ Torch Down
❑ Green (Living)

Home Faces (1)
❑ East ❑ Southeast
❑ North ❑ Southwest
❑ Northeast ❑ West
❑ Northwest
❑ South

• **Building Information** (3)
❑ Attached/Zero Lot Line
❑ Built on Lot
❑ Detached
❑ Manufactured Home
❑ Modular
❑ Planned Unit Dev

Accessibility Features (12)
❑ Accessible Approach ❑ Accessible Utility
❑ Accessible Entrance ❑ Modifications for Hearing/Vision
❑ Accessible Central Living/Common Area ❑ Accessible Elevator or Lift Installed
❑ Accessible Bedroom ❑ Ceiling Track
❑ Accessible Bath ❑ Smart Technology
❑ Accessible Kitchen ❑ Other

ACCESSORY DWELLING UNIT

Accessory Dwelling Unit (1)
❑ Attached Dwelling
❑ Detached Dwelling

Detached Dwelling (Finished SqFt) **ADU Bedroom(s)** **ADU Bathroom(s)**

INITIALS: Seller Date Seller Date Broker Date

RESIDENTIAL Exclusive Listing Agreement (page 4 of 5)
LISTING INPUT SHEET

Listing Address: **LAG #**

GREEN BUILDING INFORMATION

Green Certification (4)
- ❑ Built Green™
- ❑ LEED™
- ❑ Northwest ENERGY STAR®
- ❑ Other - See Remarks

Built Green™ (1)
- ❑ 1-Star
- ❑ 2-Star
- ❑ 3-Star
- ❑ 4-Star
- ❑ 5-Star

LEED™ (1)
- ❑ Platinum
- ❑ Gold
- ❑ Silver
- ❑ Certified

Northwest ENERGY STAR® (1)
- ❑ NWESH Certified
- ❑ NWESH Presale
- ❑ NWESH Under Construction

Construction Methods (2)
- ❑ Advanced Wall
- ❑ Double Wall
- ❑ Ins. Concrete Form (ICF)
- ❑ Post & Beam
- ❑ Standard Frame
- ❑ Steel & Concrete
- ❑ Strawbale
- ❑ Structural Ins. Panel (SIPs)
- ❑ Tilt-up

EPS Energy Score (0-99,999kWh)

HERS Index Score (0-150)

INTERIOR FEATURES

Lower Fireplaces **Upper Fireplaces** **Main Fireplaces**

Type of Fireplace (5)
- ❑ Electric
- ❑ Gas
- ❑ Other - See Remarks
- ❑ Pellet
- ❑ Wood

Interior Features (17)
- ❑ 2nd Kitchen
- ❑ 2nd Primary BR
- ❑ Bath Off Primary
- ❑ Built-in Vacuum
- ❑ Ceiling Fan(s)
- ❑ Dbl Pane/Storm Windw
- ❑ Dining Room
- ❑ Elevator
- ❑ Fireplace (Primary BR)
- ❑ French Doors
- ❑ High Tech Cabling
- ❑ Hot Tub/Spa
- ❑ Jetted Tub
- ❑ Loft
- ❑ Sauna
- ❑ Security System
- ❑ Skylights
- ❑ SMART Wired
- ❑ Solarium/Atrium
- ❑ Sprinkler System
- ❑ Triple Pane Windows
- ❑ Vaulted Ceilings
- ❑ Walk-in Closet
- ❑ Walk-in Pantry
- ❑ Wet Bar
- ❑ Wine Cellar
- ❑ Wired for Generator

Water Heater Type **Water Heater Location** **Leased Equipment**

• **Energy Source** (6)
- ❑ Electric
- ❑ Geothermal
- ❑ Ground Source
- ❑ Natural Gas
- ❑ Oil
- ❑ Pellet
- ❑ Propane
- ❑ See Remarks
- ❑ Solar (Unspecified)
- ❑ Solar Hot Water
- ❑ Solar PV
- ❑ Wood

• **Heating** (8)
- ❑ 90%+ High Efficiency
- ❑ Baseboard
- ❑ Ductless HP-Mini Split
- ❑ Forced Air
- ❑ Heat Pump
- ❑ High Efficiency (Unspecified)
- ❑ Hot Water Recirc Pump
- ❑ HRV/ERV System
- ❑ Insert
- ❑ None
- ❑ Other - See Remarks
- ❑ Radiant
- ❑ Radiator
- ❑ Stove/Free Standing
- ❑ Tankless Water Heater
- ❑ Wall

• **Cooling** (8)
- ❑ 90%+ High Efficiency
- ❑ Central A/C
- ❑ Ductless HP-Mini Split
- ❑ Forced Air
- ❑ Heat Pump
- ❑ HEPA Air Filtration
- ❑ High Efficiency (Unspecified)
- ❑ Insert
- ❑ None
- ❑ Other - See Remarks
- ❑ Radiant
- ❑ Wall
- ❑ Window Unit A/C

Floor Covering (5)
- ❑ Bamboo/Cork
- ❑ Ceramic Tile
- ❑ Concrete
- ❑ Engineered Hardwood
- ❑ Fir/Softwood
- ❑ Granite
- ❑ Hardwood
- ❑ Laminate
- ❑ Laminate Hardwood
- ❑ Laminate Tile
- ❑ Marble
- ❑ Other Renewable
- ❑ See Remarks
- ❑ Slate
- ❑ Stone
- ❑ Travertine
- ❑ Vinyl
- ❑ Vinyl Plank
- ❑ Wall to Wall Carpet

Appliances That Stay (10)
- ❑ Dishwasher(s)
- ❑ Double Oven
- ❑ Dryer(s)
- ❑ Garbage Disposal
- ❑ Microwave(s)
- ❑ Refrigerator(s)
- ❑ See Remarks
- ❑ Stove(s)/Range(s)
- ❑ Trash Compactor
- ❑ Washer(s)

Excluded Items
❑ Yes ❑ No

UTILITY / COMMUNITY

Community Features (11)
- ❑ Age Restriction
- ❑ Airfield
- ❑ Athletic Court
- ❑ Boat Launch
- ❑ CCRs
- ❑ Clubhouse
- ❑ Gated Entry
- ❑ Golf Course
- ❑ Park
- ❑ Playground
- ❑ Trails

• **Water Source** (3)
- ❑ Community
- ❑ Individual Well
- ❑ Lake
- ❑ Private
- ❑ Public
- ❑ See Remarks
- ❑ Shared Well
- ❑ Shares
- ❑ Water Catchment System
- ❑ Well Needed

Irrigation Comments (Max 40 characters)

Water Company **Power Company** **Sewer Company**

Cable/TV Provider **Internet Service Provider**

Public Transit Nearby
❑ Yes ❑ No

Transit Route

INITIALS: Seller Date Seller Date Broker Date

NWMLS Form 1 Rev. 8/24

RESIDENTIAL Exclusive Listing Agreement (page 5 of 5)
LISTING INPUT SHEET

Listing Address: **LAG #**

ROOM LOCATION

• **Level** (1) M for Main L for Lower S for Split G for Garage U2 for Upper (2nd Floor) U3 for Upper (3rd Floor) U4 for Upper (4th Floor)

Approved Accessory	______	**Extra Fin Room**	______	**Living Room**	______
Bonus Room	______	**Family Room**	______	**Primary Bedroom**	______
Den/Office	______	**Great Room**	______	**Rec Room**	______
Dining Room	______	**Kitchen with Eating Space**	______	**Studio**	______
Entry	______	**Kitchen w/o Eating Space**	______	**Utility Room**	______

No. of Bedrooms M____ L ____ U2____ U3____ U4____
(Excluding Primary Bedroom)

No. of Full Baths M____ L ____ U2____ U3____ U4____

No. of ½ Baths M____ L ____ U2____ U3____ U4____

No. of Bathtubs ________ **No. of Showers** ________

No. of ¾ Baths M____ L ____ U2____ U3____ U4____

REMARKS

Marketing Remarks. CAUTION! The comments you make in the following lines are limited to descriptions of the land and improvements only. These remarks will appear in the client handouts and websites. (750)

Confidential Broker-Only Remarks. Comments in this category are for broker's use only. (500)

• **Driving Directions to Property** (200)

INITIALS: ______ Seller ______ Date ______ Seller ______ Date ______ Broker ______ Date

Brokerage's Authority, Listing Period, and Property Description. The first lines in a listing agreement form usually identify the real estate firm and establish the firm's agency authority. In an exclusive right to sell agreement, the clause that establishes agency authority usually says something like, "The agent shall have the sole and exclusive right to submit offers to purchase and to receive deposits."

Also in this opening section there are usually blanks to specify a termination date for the listing agreement and give the property's address (with a reference to an attached legal description).

Agency Relationships. Listing agreement forms commonly include a provision concerning the agency relationships created by the agreement. In this provision, the seller authorizes the brokerage to appoint the listing licensee to act as the seller's agent. By law, that means the listing firm and the managing brokers who supervise the listing licensee are also the seller's agents. The agency provision typically also states that other licensees affiliated with the firm do not represent the seller, and may represent the buyer.

This provision may also contain an acknowledgement by the seller that the seller has received the pamphlet on Washington's Real Estate Brokerage Relationships Act that the agent is legally obligated to provide (again, see Chapter 7).

List Date. In addition to stating the date the listing period will terminate, the listing agreement may have a "list date" provision. The **list date** the parties agree to is the deadline for submitting the listing to the multiple listing service. The list date provision prohibits the listing agent or the seller from advertising the property during the period between signing the listing agreement and the list date, when all MLS members will have access to the listing information.

If another affiliated licensee finds the buyer, the firm will be a dual agent (see the discussion of in-house transactions in Chapter 7).

Commission. The listing agreement form has a blank for specifying the brokerage commission percentage or amount.

It may also contain a provision regarding how the buyer's agent will be compensated. For example, the NWMLS form allows the seller to choose between stating what percentage of the sales price will be used to compensate the buyer's agent, requesting the buyer to describe in the offer how the buyer's agent expects to be compensated, or stating that the seller does not intend to compensate the buyer's broker.

The listing agreement should also spell out how and when the listing agent will earn the commission. An exclusive right to sell listing form typically provides that the listing agent will earn a commission if any of the following events occur:

1. During the listing period, the listing agent (or a cooperating agent from the MLS) secures a buyer who is willing and able to buy on the exact terms specified by the seller in the listing agreement or on other terms acceptable to the seller (in other words, a ready, willing, and able buyer).
2. The seller sells, exchanges, or enters into a contract to sell or exchange the property during the term of the listing agreement.
3. The seller sells the property within a certain period (for example, six months) after the expiration date of the listing agreement, to anyone who first became aware of the property through any advertising or other marketing activities of the listing agent (or other agents in the MLS).

Extender Clause. The third condition listed above is an example of an **extender clause** (sometimes called a "safety," "protection," or "carryover" clause). It is intended to prevent the seller from delaying acceptance of a buyer's offer until after the listing expires in order to avoid paying a commission.

Most listing agreements contain an extender clause, but the specific terms differ. For example, sometimes the obligation to pay a commission after the listing has expired is only triggered when the property is sold to a buyer that the agent actually negotiated with during the listing period.

Or the clause may be broader, obligating the seller to pay a commission if the property is sold within the extension period to anyone who first learned about it in any way that could be traced to the listing agent or another MLS agent. Under such a broad provision, the seller could become liable for a commission unwittingly, since it can be very difficult for a seller to know the names of all potential buyers who viewed the property during the listing period.

Sometimes if a property fails to sell during the listing period, the seller then lists it with another brokerage. In that case, it's possible for the seller to become liable for a commission to two different firms.

If the sale occurs during the first listing's extension period and the buyer was introduced to the property during the first listing period, the first firm is entitled to a commission under the extender clause, and the second firm is entitled to a commission under the terms of the second listing. If both firms are members of the same MLS, they could agree to split one commission rather than make the seller pay twice.

Often extender clauses include safeguards for the seller. The listing brokerage may be required to give the seller a list of the potential buyers they negotiated with during the listing period. Or the extender clause might state that a commission will not be due if the property is listed with another real estate firm during the extension period, protecting the seller from becoming liable for two commissions.

Short Sales and Distressed Homes. In a short sale, the proceeds from a property's sale aren't enough to repay the debt secured by the property; nevertheless, the lender agrees to accept the sale proceeds and release the borrower from the debt. (Short sales are also discussed in Chapter 10.) When a potential short sale is being listed, the listing agent should give the seller a written disclosure explaining that the lender's approval of a short sale won't necessarily relieve the seller of liability for costs owed at closing, including the brokerage commission. This disclosure may be included in the listing form itself.

Because of Washington's Distressed Property Law, which concerns foreclosure rescue scams, a residential listing form may state that the real estate firm will not represent the seller in a distressed home conveyance.

Or the form might include a provision in which the seller warrants that their home is not in foreclosure or in imminent danger of foreclosure. (The Distressed Property Law is discussed at the end of this chapter.)

Access and Keyboxes. A listing form typically provides that the agent will have access to the property at reasonable times, so that they can show it to prospective buyers.

MLS listing forms usually include a provision authorizing the installation of a keybox on the property and permitting MLS agents to enter and show the home when the seller isn't there. A **keybox** is a device that holds a copy of the house key, which the seller can padlock to a porch railing or some other appropriate place outside; cooperating agents open the keybox with a master key or a combination from the MLS. The listing agreement form may provide that affiliated third parties, such as appraisers or inspectors, are also authorized to use the keybox to gain access to the home. The listing form will typically have a disclaimer of liability on the part of the MLS or the agents for any loss or damage to the seller's property—the listed home itself and personal property on the premises—absent gross negligence or intentional misconduct.

Seller's Warranties. Most listing forms include some warranties by the seller, which allow the listing agent to rely on certain information the seller provides. Most fundamentally, the seller warrants that they have the right to sell the property on the stated terms. The seller also warrants the accuracy of the property information that is made part of the listing agreement (see the discussion of the listing input sheet, below).

There may be additional warranties; for example, the seller may warrant that there are no encroachments, or that the property conforms to applicable zoning regulations.

The form usually states that the seller takes responsibility for the information given and will indemnify the listing agent against any losses caused by errors or omissions. This statement is called a "hold harmless agreement."

Fair Housing. Recently, the NWMLS form added a reminder to sellers that fair housing laws prohibit discrimination based on sexual orientation, race, disability, family status, and many other categories. See Chapter 15 for a full list of protected classes and related information.

Closing Costs. Most listing agreement forms provide that the seller will pay for the buyer's title insurance policy and certain other closing costs, such as the excise tax and half of the escrow fee. Keep in mind that these provisions in the listing agreement do not create any obligation toward potential buyers. These are promises that the seller makes to their listing agent, and failure to fulfill them can lead only to liability for the commission, not to liability toward a buyer.

Multiple Listing Provision. As we said in Chapter 7, a multiple listing service is a regional or local cooperative of real estate firms (and their licensees) that exchange information about their exclusive listings to increase exposure of the properties to the public. Any member may try to secure buyers for any of the listed properties. The listing agreement forms used by an MLS include a provision authorizing the agent to submit the listing to the MLS for publication.

Other members of the listing firm's multiple listing service are called cooperating agents. As a general rule, cooperating agents represent the buyer they're working with, but they may instead act as an agent of the seller (along with the listing agent), or in some other capacity as agreed to by the parties. The MLS provision in a listing agreement form typically includes a clause to make this clear. The brokerage firm of the cooperating agent who finds the buyer (the buyer brokerage firm, also called the selling brokerage) is ordinarily entitled to receive a share of the listing brokerage's commission, regardless of which party the cooperating agent is representing. (See Chapter 7 for further discussion of cooperating agents.)

MLS forms include a disclaimer provision stating that the information given in the listing is not confidential and will be available to third parties, and that the MLS is not a party to the listing contract. An MLS assumes no responsibility with respect to particular transactions beyond gathering and circulating information about the properties. It assumes no responsibility for verifying that the information is accurate.

Property Condition and Insurance. Most listing forms contain a provision limiting liability of the agent and the MLS for any theft or damage to the property (both to the house and the possessions within), as well as for personal injury, unless the loss is due to gross negligence or willful misconduct. The seller is advised to check that they have adequate insurance coverage. Some sellers are tempted to place a "nanny cam" to record visits by potential buyers; the NWMLS form contains a reminder that recording others without consent violates Washington law.

Firm's Right to Market the Property. Under the terms of many listing forms, the seller agrees not to lease the property, grant an option, or enter into any other agreement that might interfere with the marketing or sale of the property. If the seller breaches this agreement, they will be liable to the brokerage for the full commission.

The form may also state that the listing agent is not obligated to submit any offers to the seller other than offers for immediate purchase, so that offers to lease the property or requests for an option to purchase need not be relayed to the seller.

Seller Disclosure Statement. A listing form may include a provision concerning the disclosure statement that Washington law requires a seller in a real estate transaction to give to the buyer upon the signing of a purchase and sale agreement (see Chapter 9). Such a provision in the listing usually states that the seller will give the listing agent a completed and signed disclosure statement, unless the transaction is exempt from the disclosure law.

Although the law doesn't require the seller to give the buyer a disclosure statement until a purchase and sale agreement is signed, this provision in the listing agreement obligates the seller to fill out a disclosure statement and give it to the listing agent as soon as possible. It's better for the listing agent to learn about any problems with the property early on in the selling process.

The listing provision typically also states that the seller takes full responsibility for the information given in the disclosure statement. The seller agrees to defend the listing agent against any claims based on inaccuracies in the statement.

Damages in the Event of Buyer's Breach. Listing agreement forms often provide that the listing agent is entitled to half of any damages that the seller receives as a result of the buyer's default. In practical terms, this usually means that the listing agent will get half of the forfeited earnest money (see Chapter 9).

Attorneys' Fees. Most listing agreement forms provide that if either party has to employ an attorney to enforce the contract, the attorneys' fees of the winning party must be paid by the losing party.

Signatures. The listing agreement is signed by both parties, the listing agent and the seller. When filling out the form, the listing agent should write in the name of the brokerage firm and then sign their own name on the "By" line underneath the firm's name.

If the property is owned by more than one person, all co-owners should sign the listing agreement. If a seller is married, the spouse should also sign the agreement.

Listing Information. The listing forms used by multiple listing services include one or more pages for information about the property and the listing, such as the NWMLS "Listing Input Sheet" shown in Figure 8.2. The purpose of a listing input sheet is to generate detailed information for distribution by the MLS. The form is completed online and submitted to the MLS.

All of the following information is generally required on a listing input sheet:

- property address,
- location on a coded official map,
- architectural style of the home,
- listing price,
- identity of the listing agent,
- expiration date of the listing,
- age of the home,
- number of bedrooms and bathrooms,
- county tax ID number,
- buyer brokerage commission share,
- name of the occupant, and
- name, address, and phone number of the owner.

The rest of the input sheet has spaces to fill in or boxes to check to describe a wide variety of property features and amenities. There is also a place for information about encumbrances and property taxes.

Distressed Property Listings

Washington's Distressed Property Law helps protect homeowners from foreclosure rescue scams by strictly regulating distressed home consultants. Real estate licensees providing routine brokerage services to clients are excluded from the definition of a distressed home consultant, though. That said, a licensee who's involved in a distressed home conveyance is subject to the requirements of this law.

A distressed home is a personal residence that's in danger of foreclosure or already in foreclosure. A **distressed home conveyance** is one where a buyer purchases a distressed home from its owner, allows the (former) owner to continue to occupy the home for more than 20 days after closing, and promises to convey the home back to the owner, or promises the owner a portion of the proceeds from the resale of the home.

In a distressed home conveyance, the buyer and/or any licensees involved may be considered distressed home consultants. A consultant owes fiduciary duties to the seller and must enter into a written contract with the seller called a distressed home consultant agreement. The contract must disclose the services that will be provided, as well as the consultant's compensation.

Note that a distressed home can be listed or sold without triggering this requirement. For example, if a seller who's facing foreclosure sells their home and will relinquish possession upon closing or within 20 days after closing, the transaction doesn't meet the definition of a distressed home conveyance; therefore a licensee involved isn't required to have a distressed home consultant agreement with the seller.

Chapter Summary

1. The listing agreement is an employment contract between the seller and the real estate firm. The seller agrees to pay the firm a stated commission if a ready, willing, and able buyer is found during the listing period.
2. The three basic types of listing agreements are the open listing, the exclusive agency listing, and the exclusive right to sell listing. The type of listing determines the circumstances under which the firm is entitled to be paid a commission.
3. A written listing agreement is an enforceable contract if it adequately identifies the property to be sold, includes a promise to pay compensation to the listing agent, and is signed by the seller.
4. The listing agreement should also state the terms of sale the seller will accept, the conditions under which the commission would be paid, the duration of the contract, and the seller's warranties regarding the accuracy of the information provided about the property.
5. A multiple listing service is a cooperative association of licensed firms and agents who exchange information about their exclusive listings and help sell property listed by other members.
6. An extender clause provides that the seller will be liable for the listing agent's commission if the property is sold during a certain period after the listing expires to a buyer the listing firm dealt with during the listing period.
7. Washington's Distressed Property Law applies to certain transactions involving homes that are in foreclosure or in danger of foreclosure. Real estate licensees providing routine brokerage services are generally exempt from the requirements of this law, however.

Key Terms

Open listing—A non-exclusive listing under which the real estate firm earns a commission only if it is the procuring cause of the sale.

Procuring cause—The person who directly or indirectly brings about a sale.

Exclusive agency listing—A listing under which the real estate firm is entitled to a commission if any agent sells the property, but the owner may sell the property directly without being obligated to pay a commission.

Exclusive right to sell listing—A listing under which the owner must pay the brokerage a commission on the sale of the property, no matter who was the procuring cause.

Multiple listing service—A regional or local cooperative of real estate firms and licensees who exchange listing information and help market the listings of other members. When one firm's listing is shown to buyers by licensees from other firms in the MLS, those licensees are called cooperating agents.

Net listing—A listing in which the commission is any amount received from the sale over and above the "net" required by the seller.

Extender clause—A provision in a listing agreement that obligates the seller to pay a commission if the property is sold within a certain period after the listing expires to someone the agent introduced to the property during the listing period. Also called a safety clause or carryover clause.

Distressed home—A personal residence that is being foreclosed on, or that is in imminent danger of foreclosure.

Chapter Quiz

1. **The type of listing that provides for payment of a commission to the listing firm regardless of who sells the property is a/an:**
   a) open listing
   b) exclusive agency listing
   c) exclusive right to sell listing
   d) net listing

2. **The type of listing that provides for the payment of a commission to the listing firm only if it was the procuring cause of the sale is a/an:**
   a) open listing
   b) exclusive agency listing
   c) exclusive right to sell listing
   d) net listing

3. **The type of listing that provides for the payment of a commission that consists of any proceeds from the sale over a specified amount is a/an:**
   a) open listing
   b) exclusive agency listing
   c) exclusive right to sell listing
   d) net listing

4. **A listing agreement must contain all of the following, except:**
   a) a specific dollar amount for compensation
   b) the signature of the seller
   c) an adequate description of the property
   d) an authorization to sell the property in exchange for compensation

5. **The type of listing that provides for the payment of a commission to the listing firm if anyone other than the seller finds the buyer is a/an:**
   a) open listing
   b) exclusive agency listing
   c) exclusive right to sell listing
   d) net listing

6. **The listing agent has negotiated an offer from a ready, willing, and able buyer that matches the seller's terms of sale set forth in the listing agreement. Which of the following is true?**
   a) The seller is required to accept the offer and pay the listing agent a commission
   b) The seller is required to accept the offer, but not required to pay the listing agent a commission
   c) The listing agent has earned the commission, whether or not the seller accepts the offer
   d) The listing agent has not earned the commission unless this is an exclusive agency listing

7. **Which of these is a basic requirement for an enforceable listing agreement in Washington?**
   a) Adequate description of the property
   b) Multiple listing provision
   c) Extender clause
   d) Warranty that the seller owns the property

8. **An extender clause provides that:**
   a) the listing agent is entitled to a commission whether or not they are the procuring cause
   b) the buyer must pay part of the listing agent's commission
   c) the seller warrants the safety of the premises
   d) the listing agent may be entitled to a commission if the property is sold after the listing expires

9. **Matthews, a property owner, entered into an exclusive right to sell listing agreement with Ferris Realty. Ferris negotiated a sale between Matthews and Buyer Swanson. Both Matthews and Swanson signed a purchase and sale agreement. Two weeks later, Matthews and Swanson mutually agreed to cancel their agreement. Under the circumstances:**
   a) Matthews is still obligated to pay Ferris Realty the full sales commission
   b) Matthews owes Ferris Realty half of the sales commission
   c) Swanson owes Ferris Realty the full sales commission
   d) Ferris Realty is not entitled to a commission, because the sale did not close

10. **Under an exclusive right to sell listing, the listing agent:**
   a) has the authority to accept an offer on the seller's behalf
   b) is authorized to reject offers that do not meet the seller's stated terms
   c) will earn the sales commission only if someone other than the owner procures a buyer
   d) has the exclusive right to submit offers to purchase to the seller

11. **A multiple listing provision in a listing agreement generally:**
   a) makes other members of the MLS cooperating agents
   b) authorizes the listing agent to submit the listing to the MLS for publication
   c) includes a disclaimer provision that states that the MLS is not a party to the listing agreement
   d) All of the above

12. Which of these types of listings is considered to be a unilateral contract?

a) Open listing
b) Exclusive agency listing
c) Exclusive right to sell listing
d) Net listing

13. Under the terms of most listings, the seller will owe the listing agent the commission even if the:

a) seller turns down a reasonable offer for less than the listing price
b) prospective buyer is not ready, willing, and able
c) sale fails to close because the seller's title is not marketable
d) listing agent terminates the agreement

14. Under the terms of an exclusive listing agreement, the listing agent is:

a) under no obligation to make an effort to find a buyer
b) required to find at least three ready, willing, and able buyers during the listing period
c) obligated to market the property and make a diligent effort to find a buyer
d) None of the above

15. In the listing agreement, the seller agrees to pay certain closing costs. This creates a legal obligation to:

a) the buyer only
b) the listing agent only
c) both the buyer and the listing agent
d) neither the buyer nor the listing agent

Chapter 9:

Purchase and Sale Agreements

Most real estate sales are initiated by a written contract between the buyer and the seller, who agree on a price and the other terms of sale. The contract between the buyer and the seller of real property is the purchase and sale agreement, which may also be called an earnest money agreement. This chapter will describe the purpose and effect of a purchase and sale agreement, preparation of the agreement, the elements required to make it a binding contract, and the operation of contingency clauses. The final section of the chapter covers laws requiring certain information to be disclosed when property is sold, including Washington's seller disclosure law and the federal law concerning lead-based paint.

Key Terms

Purchase and Sale Agreement	**Contingency Clause**
Earnest Money	**Bump Clause**
Time is of the Essence Clause	**Home Warranty Plan**
Closing	

Purpose and Effect of a Purchase and Sale Agreement

The contract between a buyer and a seller to purchase and sell real property is more than a preliminary agreement. If it contains the necessary elements and is properly executed, the parties are legally bound by all of the terms of the agreement. Neither party may change nor add any terms without the written consent of the other, and neither may withdraw from the transaction without legal consequences. In fact, the whole purpose of a purchase and sale agreement is to hold the buyer and the seller to the original terms of their agreement until the transaction is ready to close.

To be a valid and enforceable contract, the purchase and sale agreement must be created by offer and acceptance and supported by consideration (see Chapter 6).

In most cases, the buyer is the offeror, offering to buy the seller's property on specific terms. The buyer usually provides an **earnest money deposit**, to show the seller that they are serious about the purchase.

The buyer's written offer is set forth in a purchase and sale agreement form, which the buyer signs before it is presented to the seller. If the seller decides to accept the buyer's offer, they also sign the form, and it becomes a binding contract. The mutual promises of the parties (the promise to buy and the promise to sell) are the consideration supporting the contract.

The basic requirements for a valid purchase and sale agreement are relatively simple. The agreement must identify the parties and the property, state the price and the method of payment, and state the time for delivery of title and possession. Despite this basic simplicity, most purchase and sale agreements are quite detailed. It is important that the agreement between the parties be stated clearly and accurately; anything that isn't made absolutely clear at the outset can give rise to a dispute later on, and may prevent the transaction from closing.

In practical terms, the buyer and the seller need a document that preserves their agreement while other matters are attended to that will enable the sale to close. For instance, most buyers do not have the cash necessary to close the sale, so they have to arrange to borrow all or part of the money for the purchase. The buyer also needs to make sure that the seller actually owns the property (through a title search), and may want to arrange for a physical inspection of the property. There might be liens or other encumbrances that need to be dealt with, and the seller may be required to repair the property to satisfy the requirements of the buyer's lender.

All of these things cost time and money. Neither party wants to spend time or money without the assurance that the original agreement is still in effect. As long as the purchase and sale agreement is a valid contract, it protects both parties by providing legal recourse if one fails to perform. Either party could file a lawsuit against the other for breach of contract.

The court could order the breaching party to pay the other party damages as compensation for losses resulting from the breach, or even issue an order of specific performance, requiring the seller to fulfill his side of the bargain (see Chapter 6). Because a court could order the seller to deed the property to the buyer, the buyer is considered to have equitable title to the property as soon as the purchase and sale agreement is executed, even though they won't acquire legal title until closing.

Who May Prepare a Purchase and Sale Agreement

It is legal—though often unwise—for the parties to an agreement to write their own contract. But if someone who is not a party draws up a contract on behalf of the parties, that is considered to be the practice of law. As a general rule, only a licensed attorney at law is allowed to write a contract for others.

However, a limited exception to that rule applies to certain real estate agreements. A real estate agent can prepare routine real estate agreements using standard printed forms. This is allowed because the provisions of these contract forms were originally written and approved by attorneys with expertise in real estate law.

In the typical residential real estate transaction, the real estate agent fills in the blanks of a standard purchase and sale agreement form and obtains the signatures of the parties. In filling out the form, the agent is held to the same standard of care that is demanded of an attorney. An agent who prepares a purchase and sale agreement improperly could be held liable for any damages caused to either party.

Real estate agents run into trouble when they go beyond merely filling in the blanks. Sometimes an agent writes a special clause to insert into the pre-printed form to meet an unusual situation. Or an agent might give the parties his opinion of the meaning or effect of provisions in the document. Actions like these go beyond what the law generally allows real estate agents to do and may constitute the unauthorized practice of law. The unauthorized practice of law is a criminal offense, and a real estate agent can be prosecuted even if they gave accurate legal advice. It is also grounds for suspension or revocation of the agent's real estate license (see Chapter 17).

A real estate agent may only fill out forms in connection with a transaction actually being handled by that agent. And an agent is not allowed to charge a separate fee (in addition to the brokerage commission) for completing the forms.

> **Example:** Suppose Agent Dahl is involved in a complicated commercial real estate transaction. He is confused by some of the paperwork, so he gets Agent Merrick (a friend of his) to fill out the purchase and sale agreement. Merrick charges the client a separate fee for her work. This is the unauthorized practice of law, because Merrick filled out forms for a transaction that she was not handling and accepted separate compensation for her work.

Available Forms and Guidance

In Washington and most other states, there is no single purchase and sale agreement form that all real estate agents use. A variety of forms are available from multiple listing services, other professional organizations, and legal form publishers.

A residential purchase and sale agreement form from the Northwest Multiple Listing Service (NWMLS) is shown in Figure 9.1 as an example.

The organizations that provide forms sometimes offer line-by-line guidance for filling in each provision. A real estate agent should read any explanatory materials provided and obtain advice for any aspects of the form that they do not understand. Relying on advice from professional sources helps ensure that the agent will meet the required standard of care.

Here are two basic precautions to take when filling out a purchase and sale agreement:

- A form must be used only for the purpose intended. For instance, the NWMLS purchase and sale agreement form in Figure 9.1 is intended for residential sales only. It shouldn't be used for anything else.
- Forms should always be filled in completely. If an entry isn't applicable to a given transaction, the agent should write in "N/A," rather than leaving the space blank. All boxes should be checked where appropriate.

Elements of a Purchase and Sale Agreement

As explained in Chapter 6, the statute of frauds requires every real estate purchase and sale agreement to be in writing. An enforceable purchase and sale agreement generally must contain all of the following elements:

- identification of the parties,
- an adequate description of the property,
- the total price and the method of payment,
- the closing date,
- the date of possession,
- the type of deed and the condition of title,
- liens or other encumbrances the buyer will take title subject to, and
- any conditions or contingencies (such as a financing contingency).

We will look at several of these elements more closely, and then discuss contingency clauses in detail, since they play a crucial role in many real estate transactions.

The Parties

Of course, the parties to the purchase and sale agreement are the buyer and the seller. When preparing a purchase and sale agreement, there are two key questions to ask about the parties. First, does everyone who is signing the form have the capacity to contract?

If any of the parties is underage or mentally incompetent, the purchase and sale agreement—like any contract—will be voidable or void. (See Chapter 6.)

Second, is everyone with an ownership interest in the property signing the contract? If not, the buyer may only be able to force the sale of a partial interest in the property. In some cases, the buyer would not be able to enforce the contract at all.

Particular care should be taken with married parties. In Washington and other community property states, the law requires both spouses to join in any sale, encumbrance, or purchase of community real property. Since it can be difficult to know for certain whether a particular piece of property is community property or separate property, it's advisable to obtain the signature of the spouse in every transaction involving a married person, just in case.

Also, a married person's homestead cannot be sold without the signature of both spouses. (Community property is covered in Chapter 2, and homestead property in Chapter 4.)

Business Entities. When a partnership is a party to a purchase and sale agreement, the names of all general partners (and their spouses) and the name of the partnership itself should be listed in the contract. For all types of business entities (partnerships, corporations, and LLCs), the company's address and the state in which it is organized or incorporated should also be shown.

A business entity's legal authority to enter into the transaction must be established. Before closing, the escrow agent (or other closing agent) will require documentation proving that the partner, corporate officer, or other representative who is signing on behalf of the entity has the authority to do so. The documentation could take the form of a power of attorney or a resolution of the board of directors.

Note that even if the closing agent is specific about what documentation and signatures are required to close the transaction, that doesn't necessarily mean that those will, in fact, make the transaction legally valid. A closing agent does not give legal advice. So if there is doubt about who needs to sign the documents, it's necessary to consult a lawyer.

Property Description

A purchase and sale agreement is not enforceable unless it includes an adequate description of the property, one that would be sufficient in a deed (see Chapter 1). A complete legal description should be used whenever possible. The NWMLS form states that the legal description will be attached to the agreement as "Exhibit A." Like any attachment to a contract, it should be signed or initialed by the parties.

Price and Method of Payment

The full purchase price should be stated in the agreement. The amount of the earnest money should be noted as well. If the buyer will obtain a bank loan or other third-party financing for the purchase, a financing addendum should be attached to the purchase and sale agreement. If the buyer is going to assume the seller's existing mortgage or if seller financing is involved, a seller financing addendum should be attached to the agreement. These addenda set forth specific information about how the purchase price will be paid.

If the seller will be financing all or part of the purchase, the interest rate and payment terms for the seller financing must be stated, and a copy of the financing documents that the parties will be executing must be attached to the purchase and sale agreement.

If the parties later agree to financing terms that differ from those specified in the attachments, the buyer and seller must have their agreement reviewed by an attorney and must provide notice of their attorney's approval. (For more information about financing arrangements, see Chapters 10 and 11.)

Fig. 9.1 Purchase and Sale Agreement

Form 21
Residential PSA
Rev. 8/24
Page 1 of 6

RESIDENTIAL PURCHASE AND SALE AGREEMENT
Specific Terms

1. **Date:** ____________ **MLS No.:** ____________ **Offer Expiration Date:** ____________
2. **Buyer:** ____________ Buyer ____________ Buyer ____________ Status
3. **Seller:** ____________ Seller ____________ Seller
4. **Property:** Legal Description attached as Exhibit A. Tax Parcel No(s).: ________, ________, ________,
   ____________ Address ____________ City ____________ County ____________ State ____________ Zip
5. **Included Items:** ❑ stove(s)/range(s); ❑ refrigerator(s); ❑ washer(s); ❑ dryer(s); ❑ dishwasher(s); ❑ microwave(s); ❑ fireplace insert(s); ❑ wood stove(s); ❑ satellite dish; ❑ security system; ❑ hot tub; ❑ attached camera(s); ❑ attached speaker(s); ❑ attached TV(s); ❑ generator; ❑ ____________
6. **Purchase Price:** $ ____________ U.S. Dollars
7. **Earnest Money:** $ ________ U.S. Dollars; Delivery Date _____ days after mutual acceptance
   To be held by ❑ Buyer Brokerage Firm; ❑ Closing Agent; ❑ In the form of a Promissory Note (included as an Addendum)
8. **Default:** (check only one) ❑ Forfeiture of Earnest Money; ❑ Seller's Election of Remedies
9. **Title Insurance Company:** ____________
10. **Closing Agent:** ____________ Company ____________ Individual (optional)
11. **Closing Date:** ____________; **Possession Date:** ❑ on Closing; ❑ Other ____________
12. **Services of Closing Agent for Payment of Utilities:** ❑ Requested (attach NWMLS Form 22K); ❑ Waived
13. **Charges/Assessments Levied Before but Due After Closing:** ❑ assumed by Buyer; ❑ prepaid in full by Seller at Closing
14. **Seller Citizenship (FIRPTA):** Seller ❑ is; ❑ is not a foreign person for purposes of U.S. income taxation
15. **Information Verification Period:** ❑ Expires ______ days after mutual acceptance; ❑ Satisfied/Waived
16. **Agency Disclosure:** Buyer represented by: ❑ Buyer Broker; ❑ Buyer/Listing Broker (limited dual agent); ❑ unrepresented
    Seller represented by: ❑ Listing Broker; ❑ Listing/Buyer Broker (limited dual agent); ❑ unrepresented
17. **Buyer Brokerage Compensation:** ____________ (a) Seller's Offer (if any); ____________ (b) Amount to be Paid by Seller ❑ Addendum for Buyer Credit
18. **Addenda:** ____________

Buyer Signature / Date	Seller Signature / Date
Buyer Signature / Date	Seller Signature / Date
Buyer Address	Seller Address
City, State, Zip	City, State, Zip
Buyer Phone No. / Fax No.	Seller Phone No. / Fax No.
Buyer E-mail Address	Seller E-mail Address
Buyer Brokerage Firm / MLS Office No.	Listing Brokerage Firm / MLS Office No.
Buyer Broker (Print) / MLS LAG No.	Listing Broker (Print) / MLS LAG No.
Firm Phone No. / Broker Phone No. / Firm Fax No.	Firm Phone No. / Broker Phone No. / Firm Fax No.
Firm Document E-mail Address	Firm Document E-mail Address
Buyer Broker E-mail Address	Listing Broker E-mail Address
Buyer Broker DOL License No. / Firm DOL License No.	Listing Broker DOL License No. / Firm DOL License No.

Form 21
Residential PSA
Rev. 8/24
Page 2 of 6

RESIDENTIAL PURCHASE AND SALE AGREEMENT
General Terms

a. Purchase Price. Buyer shall pay to Seller the Purchase Price, including the Earnest Money, in cash at Closing, unless otherwise specified in this Agreement. Buyer represents that Buyer has sufficient funds to close this sale in accordance with this Agreement and is not relying on any contingent source of funds, including funds from loans, the sale of other property, gifts, retirement, or future earnings, except to the extent otherwise specified in this Agreement. The parties shall use caution when wiring funds to avoid potential wire fraud. Before wiring funds, the party wiring funds shall take steps to confirm any wire instructions via an independently verified phone number and other appropriate measures.

b. Earnest Money. Buyer shall deliver the Earnest Money by the Delivery Date listed in Specific Term No. 7 (2 days after mutual acceptance if not filled in) to the party holding the Earnest Money (Buyer Brokerage Firm or Closing Agent). If sent by mail, the Earnest Money must arrive at Buyer Brokerage Firm or Closing Agent by the Delivery Date. If the Earnest Money is held by Buyer Brokerage Firm and is over $10,000.00 it shall be deposited into an interest bearing trust account in Buyer Brokerage Firm's name provided that Buyer completes an IRS Form W-9. Interest, if any, after deduction of bank charges and fees, will be paid to Buyer. Buyer shall reimburse Buyer Brokerage Firm for bank charges and fees in excess of the interest earned, if any. If the Earnest Money held by Buyer Brokerage Firm is over $10,000.00 Buyer has the option to require Buyer Brokerage Firm to deposit the Earnest Money into the Housing Trust Fund Account, with the interest paid to the State Treasurer, if both Seller and Buyer so agree in writing. If the Buyer does not complete an IRS Form W-9 before Buyer Brokerage Firm must deposit the Earnest Money or the Earnest Money is $10,000.00 or less, the Earnest Money shall be deposited into the Housing Trust Fund Account. Buyer Brokerage Firm may transfer the Earnest Money to Closing Agent at Closing. If all or part of the Earnest Money is to be refunded to Buyer and any such costs remain unpaid, the Buyer Brokerage Firm or Closing Agent may deduct and pay them therefrom. The parties instruct Closing Agent to provide written verification of receipt of the Earnest Money and notice of dishonor of any check to the parties and Brokers at the addresses and/or fax numbers provided herein.

Upon termination of this Agreement, a party or the Closing Agent may deliver a form authorizing the release of Earnest Money to the other party or the parties. The party(s) shall execute such form and deliver the same to the Closing Agent. If either party fails to execute the release form, a party may make a written demand to the Closing Agent for the Earnest Money. Pursuant to RCW 64.04.220, Closing Agent shall deliver notice of the demand to the other party within 15 days. If the other party does not object to the demand within 20 days of Closing Agent's notice, Closing Agent shall disburse the Earnest Money to the party making the demand within 10 days of the expiration of the 20 day period. If Closing Agent timely receives an objection or an inconsistent demand from the other party, Closing Agent shall commence an interpleader action within 60 days of such objection or inconsistent demand, unless the parties provide subsequent consistent instructions to Closing Agent to disburse the earnest money or refrain from commencing an interpleader action for a specified period of time. Pursuant to RCW 4.28.080, the parties consent to service of the summons and complaint for an interpleader action by first class mail, postage prepaid at the party's usual mailing address or the address identified in this Agreement. If the Closing Agent complies with the preceding process, each party shall be deemed to have released Closing Agent from any and all claims or liability related to the disbursal of the Earnest Money. If either party fails to authorize the release of the Earnest Money to the other party when required to do so under this Agreement, that party shall be in breach of this Agreement. For the purposes of this section, the term Closing Agent includes a Buyer Brokerage Firm holding the Earnest Money. The parties authorize the party commencing an interpleader action to deduct up to $750.00 for the costs thereof. The parties acknowledge that RCW 64.04.220 requires the court to award the Closing Agent its reasonable attorneys' fees and costs associated with an interpleader action.

c. Included Items. Any of the following items, including items identified in Specific Term No. 5 if the corresponding box is checked, located in or on the Property are included in the sale: built-in appliances; wall-to-wall carpeting; curtains, drapes and all other window treatments; window and door screens; awnings; storm doors and windows; installed television antennas; ventilating, air conditioning and heating fixtures; trash compactor; garbage disposal; fireplace doors, gas logs and gas log lighters; irrigation fixtures; electric garage door openers; water heaters; installed electrical fixtures; lighting fixtures; shrubs, plants and trees planted in the ground; and other fixtures; and all associated operating remote controls and access permissions. Unless otherwise agreed, if any of the above items are leased or encumbered, Seller shall acquire clear title before Closing.

d. Condition of Title. Unless otherwise specified in this Agreement, title to the Property shall be marketable at Closing. The following shall not cause the title to be unmarketable: rights, reservations, covenants, conditions and restrictions, presently of record and general to the area; easements and encroachments, not materially affecting the value of or unduly interfering with Buyer's reasonable use of the Property; and reserved oil and/or mining rights. Seller shall not convey or reserve any oil and/or mineral rights after mutual acceptance without Buyer's written consent. Monetary encumbrances or liens not assumed by Buyer, shall be paid or discharged by Seller on or before Closing. Title shall be conveyed by a Statutory Warranty Deed. If this Agreement is for conveyance of a buyer's interest in a Real Estate Contract, the Statutory Warranty Deed shall include a buyer's assignment of the contract sufficient to convey after acquired title.

Buyer's Initials	Date	Buyer's Initials	Date	Seller's Initials	Date	Seller's Initials	Date

Form 21
Residential PSA
Rev. 8/24
Page 3 of 6

RESIDENTIAL PURCHASE AND SALE AGREEMENT
General Terms

e. Title Insurance. Seller authorizes Buyer's lender or Closing Agent, at Seller's expense, to apply for the then-current ALTA form of Homeowner's Policy of Title Insurance for One-to-Four Family Residence, from the Title Insurance Company. If Seller previously received a preliminary commitment from a Title Insurance Company that Buyer declines to use, Buyer shall pay any cancellation fees owing to the original Title Insurance Company. Otherwise, the party applying for title insurance shall pay any title cancellation fee, in the event such a fee is assessed. If the Title Insurance Company selected by the parties will not issue a Homeowner's Policy for the Property, the parties agree that the Title Insurance Company shall instead issue the then-current ALTA standard form Owner's Policy, together with homeowner's additional protection and inflation protection endorsements, if available. The Title Insurance Company shall send a copy of the preliminary commitment to Seller, Listing Broker, Buyer and Buyer Broker. The preliminary commitment, and the title policy to be issued, shall contain no exceptions other than the General Exclusions and Exceptions in the Policy and Special Exceptions consistent with the Condition of Title herein provided. If title cannot be made so insurable prior to the Closing Date, then as Buyer's sole and exclusive remedy, the Earnest Money shall, unless Buyer elects to waive such defects or encumbrances, be refunded to the Buyer, less any unpaid costs described in this Agreement, and this Agreement shall thereupon be terminated. Buyer shall have no right to specific performance or damages as a consequence of Seller's inability to provide insurable title.

f. Closing and Possession. This sale shall be closed by the Closing Agent on the Closing Date. If the Closing Date falls on a Saturday, Sunday, legal holiday as defined in RCW 1.16.050, or day when the county recording office is closed, the Closing Agent shall close the transaction on the next day that is not a Saturday, Sunday, legal holiday, or day when the county recording office is closed. "Closing" means the date on which all documents are recorded and the sale proceeds are available to Seller. Seller shall deliver keys, garage door remotes, and access codes to Buyer on the Closing Date or on the Possession Date, whichever occurs first. Buyer shall be entitled to possession at 9:00 p.m. on the Possession Date. Seller shall maintain the Property in its present condition, normal wear and tear excepted, until the Buyer is provided possession. Seller shall either repair or replace any system or appliance (including, but not limited to plumbing, heat, electrical, and all Included Items) that becomes inoperative or malfunctions prior to Closing with a system or appliance of at least equal quality. Buyer reserves the right to walk through the Property within 5 days of Closing to verify that Seller has maintained the Property and systems/appliances as required by this paragraph. Seller shall not enter into or modify existing leases or rental agreements, service contracts, or other agreements affecting the Property which have terms extending beyond Closing without first obtaining Buyer's consent, which shall not be unreasonably withheld. If possession transfers at a time other than Closing, the parties shall execute NWMLS Form 65A (Rental Agreement/Occupancy Prior to Closing) or NWMLS Form 65B (Rental Agreement/Seller Occupancy After Closing) (or alternative rental agreements) and are advised of the need to contact their respective insurance companies to assure appropriate hazard and liability insurance policies are in place, as applicable.

RCW 19.27.530 requires the seller of any owner-occupied single-family residence to equip the residence with a carbon monoxide alarm(s) in accordance with the state building code before a buyer or any other person may legally occupy the residence following the sale. RCW 43.44.110 requires the seller of a dwelling unit, that does not have at least one smoke detection device, to provide at least one smoke detection device in the unit before the buyer or any other person occupies the unit following a sale. The parties acknowledge that the Brokers are not responsible for ensuring that Seller complies with RCW 19.27.530 or RCW 43.44.110. Buyer and Seller shall hold the Brokers and their Firms harmless from any claim resulting from Seller's failure to install a carbon monoxide alarm(s) or smoke detector(s) in the Property.

g. Section 1031 Like-Kind Exchange. If either Buyer or Seller intends for this transaction to be a part of a Section 1031 like-kind exchange, then the other party shall cooperate in the completion of the like-kind exchange so long as the cooperating party incurs no additional liability in doing so, and so long as any expenses (including attorneys' fees and costs) incurred by the cooperating party that are related only to the exchange are paid or reimbursed to the cooperating party at or prior to Closing. Notwithstanding the Assignment paragraph of this Agreement, any party completing a Section 1031 like-kind exchange may assign this Agreement to its qualified intermediary or any entity set up for the purposes of completing a reverse exchange.

h. Closing Costs and Prorations and Charges and Assessments. Seller and Buyer shall each pay one-half of the escrow fee unless otherwise required by applicable FHA or VA regulations. Taxes for the current year, rent, interest, and lienable homeowner's association dues shall be prorated as of Closing. Buyer shall pay Buyer's loan costs, including credit report, appraisal charge and lender's title insurance, unless provided otherwise in this Agreement. If any payments are delinquent on encumbrances which will remain after Closing, Closing Agent is instructed to pay such delinquencies at Closing from money due, or to be paid by, Seller. Buyer shall pay for remaining fuel in the fuel tank if, prior to Closing, Seller obtains a written statement from the supplier as to the quantity and current price and provides such statement to the Closing Agent. Seller shall pay all utility and internet charges, including unbilled charges. Unless waived in Specific Term No. 12, Seller and Buyer request the services of Closing Agent in disbursing funds necessary to satisfy unpaid utility charges in accordance with RCW 60.80 and Seller shall provide the names and addresses of all utilities providing service to the Property and having lien rights (attach NWMLS Form 22K Identification of Utilities or equivalent).

Buyer's Initials	Date	Buyer's Initials	Date	Seller's Initials	Date	Seller's Initials	Date

Form 21
Residential PSA
Rev. 8/24
Page 4 of 6

RESIDENTIAL PURCHASE AND SALE AGREEMENT
General Terms

Buyer is advised to verify the existence and amount of any local improvement district, capacity or impact charges or other assessments that may be charged against the Property before or after Closing. Seller will pay such charges that are or become due on or before Closing. Charges levied before Closing, but becoming due after Closing shall be paid as agreed in Specific Term No. 13.

i. **Sale Information**. Listing Broker and Buyer Broker are authorized to report this Agreement (including price and all terms) to the Multiple Listing Service that published it and to its members, financing institutions, appraisers, and anyone else related to this sale. Buyer and Seller expressly authorize all Closing Agents, appraisers, title insurance companies, and others related to this Sale, to furnish the Listing Broker and/or Buyer Broker, on request, any and all information and copies of documents concerning this sale.

j. **Seller Citizenship and FIRPTA**. Seller warrants that the identification of Seller's citizenship status for purposes of U.S. income taxation in Specific Term No. 14 is correct. Seller shall execute a certification (NWMLS Form 22E or equivalent) under the Foreign Investment in Real Property Tax Act ("FIRPTA") and provide the certification to the Closing Agent within 10 days of mutual acceptance. If Seller is a foreign person for purposes of U.S. income taxation, and this transaction is not otherwise exempt from FIRPTA, Closing Agent is instructed to withhold and pay the required amount to the Internal Revenue Service. Seller shall pay any fees incurred by Buyer related to such withholding and payment.

If Seller fails to provide the FIRPTA certification to the Closing Agent within 10 days of mutual acceptance, Buyer may give notice that Buyer may terminate the Agreement at any time 3 days thereafter (the "Right to Terminate Notice"). If Seller has not earlier provided the FIRPTA certification to the Closing Agent, Buyer may give notice of termination of this Agreement (the "Termination Notice") any time following 3 days after delivery of the Right to Terminate Notice. If Buyer gives the Termination Notice before Seller provides the FIRPTA certification to the Closing Agent, this Agreement is terminated and the Earnest Money shall be refunded to Buyer.

k. **Notices and Delivery of Documents**. Any notice related to this Agreement (including revocations of offers or counteroffers) must be in writing. Notices to Seller must be signed by at least one Buyer and shall be deemed delivered only when the notice is received by Seller, by Listing Broker, or at the licensed office of Listing Broker. Notices to Buyer must be signed by at least one Seller and shall be deemed delivered only when the notice is received by Buyer, by Buyer Broker, or at the licensed office of Buyer Broker. Documents related to this Agreement, such as NWMLS Form 17, Information on Lead-Based Paint and Lead-Based Paint Hazards, Public Offering Statement or Resale Certificate, and all other documents shall be delivered pursuant to this paragraph. Buyer and Seller must keep Buyer Broker and Listing Broker advised of their whereabouts in order to receive prompt notification of receipt of a notice.

Facsimile transmission of any notice or document shall constitute delivery. E-mail transmission of any notice or document (or a direct link to such notice or document) shall constitute delivery when: (i) the e-mail is sent to both Buyer Broker and Buyer Brokerage Firm or both Listing Broker and Listing Brokerage Firm at the e-mail addresses specified on page one of this Agreement; (ii) Buyer Broker or Listing Broker provide written acknowledgment of receipt of the e-mail (an automatic e-mail reply does not constitute written acknowledgment); or (iii) if a party is unrepresented, the e-mail is sent directly to the party's e-mail address specified on page one of this Agreement. At the request of either party, or the Closing Agent, the parties will confirm facsimile or e-mail transmitted signatures by signing an original document.

l. **Computation of Time**. Unless otherwise specified in this Agreement, any period of time measured in days and stated in this Agreement shall start on the day following the event commencing the period and shall expire at 9:00 p.m. of the last calendar day of the specified period of time. Except for the Possession Date, if the last day is a Saturday, Sunday or legal holiday as defined in RCW 1.16.050, the specified period of time shall expire on the next day that is not a Saturday, Sunday or legal holiday. Any specified period of 5 days or less, except for any time period relating to the Possession Date, shall not include Saturdays, Sundays or legal holidays. If the parties agree that an event will occur on a specific calendar date, the event shall occur on that date, except for the Closing Date, which, if it falls on a Saturday, Sunday, legal holiday as defined in RCW 1.16.050, or day when the county recording office is closed, shall occur on the next day that is not a Saturday, Sunday, legal holiday, or day when the county recording office is closed. When counting backwards from Closing, any period of time measured in days shall start on the day prior to Closing and if the last day is a Saturday, Sunday or legal holiday as defined in RCW 1.16.050, the specified period of time shall expire on the next day, moving forward, that is not a Saturday, Sunday or legal holiday (e.g. Monday or Tuesday). If the parties agree upon and attach a legal description after this Agreement is signed by the offeree and delivered to the offeror, then for the purposes of computing time, mutual acceptance shall be deemed to be on the date of delivery of an accepted offer or counteroffer to the offeror, rather than on the date the legal description is attached. Time is of the essence of this Agreement.

m. **Integration and Electronic Signatures**. This Agreement constitutes the entire understanding between the parties and supersedes all prior or contemporaneous understandings and representations. No modification of this Agreement shall be effective unless agreed in writing and signed by Buyer and Seller. The parties acknowledge that a signature in electronic form has the same legal effect and validity as a handwritten signature.

Buyer's Initials	Date	Buyer's Initials	Date	Seller's Initials	Date	Seller's Initials	Date

Form 21
Residential PSA
Rev. 8/24
Page 5 of 6

RESIDENTIAL PURCHASE AND SALE AGREEMENT
General Terms

n. Assignment. Buyer may not assign this Agreement, or Buyer's rights hereunder, without Seller's prior written consent, unless the parties indicate that assignment is permitted by the addition of "and/or assigns" on the line identifying the Buyer on the first page of this Agreement.

o. Default. In the event Buyer fails, without legal excuse, to complete the purchase of the Property, then the following provision, as identified in Specific Term No. 8, shall apply:

- **i. Forfeiture of Earnest Money**. That portion of the Earnest Money that does not exceed five percent (5%) of the Purchase Price shall be forfeited to the Seller as the sole and exclusive remedy available to Seller for such failure.
- **ii. Seller's Election of Remedies**. Seller may, at Seller's option, (a) keep the Earnest Money as liquidated damages as the sole and exclusive remedy available to Seller for such failure, (b) bring suit against Buyer for Seller's actual damages, (c) bring suit to specifically enforce this Agreement and recover any incidental damages, or (d) pursue any other rights or remedies available at law or equity.

p. Professional Advice and Attorneys' Fees. Buyer and Seller are advised to seek the counsel of an attorney and a certified public accountant to review the terms of this Agreement. Buyer and Seller shall pay their own fees incurred for such review. However, if Buyer or Seller institutes suit against the other concerning this Agreement, or if the party holding the Earnest Money commences an interpleader action, the prevailing party is entitled to reasonable attorneys' fees and expenses.

q. Offer. This offer must be accepted by 9:00 p.m. on the Offer Expiration Date, unless sooner withdrawn. Acceptance shall not be effective until a signed copy is received by the other party, by the other party's broker, or at the licensed office of the other party's broker pursuant to General Term k. If this offer is not so accepted, it shall lapse and any Earnest Money shall be refunded to Buyer.

r. Counteroffer. Any change in the terms presented in an offer or counteroffer, other than the insertion of or change to Seller's name and Seller's warranty of citizenship status, shall be considered a counteroffer. If a party makes a counteroffer, then the other party shall have until 9:00 p.m. on the counteroffer expiration date to accept that counteroffer, unless sooner withdrawn. Acceptance shall not be effective until a signed copy is received by the other party, the other party's broker, or at the licensed office of the other party's broker pursuant to General Term k. If the counteroffer is not so accepted, it shall lapse and any Earnest Money shall be refunded to Buyer.

s. Offer and Counteroffer Expiration Date. If no expiration date is specified for an offer/counteroffer, the offer/counteroffer shall expire 2 days after the offer/counteroffer is delivered by the party making the offer/counteroffer, unless sooner withdrawn.

t. Agency Disclosure. Buyer Brokerage Firm, Buyer Brokerage Firm's Designated Broker, Buyer Broker's Branch Manager (if any) and Buyer Broker's Managing Broker (if any) represent the same party that Buyer Broker represents. Listing Brokerage Firm, Listing Brokerage Firm's Designated Broker, Listing Broker's Branch Manager (if any), and Listing Broker's Managing Broker (if any) represent the same party that the Listing Broker represents. All parties acknowledge receipt of the pamphlet entitled "Real Estate Brokerage in Washington."

u. Brokerage Firm Compensation. Seller and Buyer shall pay compensation in accordance with any listing or compensation agreement to which they are a party. The Listing Brokerage Firm's compensation shall be paid as specified in the listing agreement. The compensation offered by Seller to the Buyer Brokerage Firm, if any, is set forth in Specific Term No. 17(a), and if there is any inconsistency between the Buyer Brokerage Firm's compensation offered and the description of the offered compensation stated in Specific Term No. 17(a), the terms shall be as set forth in the published offer. Seller shall pay the Buyer Brokerage Firm compensation set forth in Specific Term No. 17(b). Seller and Buyer hereby consent to Listing Brokerage Firm or Buyer Brokerage Firm receiving compensation from more than one party. Seller and Buyer hereby assign to Listing Brokerage Firm and Buyer Brokerage Firm, as applicable, a portion of their funds in escrow equal to such compensation and irrevocably instruct the Closing Agent to disburse the compensation directly to the Firm(s). In any action by Listing or Buyer Brokerage Firm to enforce this paragraph, the prevailing party is entitled to court costs and reasonable attorneys' fees. Seller and Buyer agree that the Firms are intended third-party beneficiaries under this Agreement.

v. Cancellation Rights/Lead-Based Paint. If a residential dwelling was built on the Property prior to 1978, and Buyer receives a Disclosure of Information on Lead-Based Paint and Lead-Based Paint Hazards (NWMLS Form 22J) after mutual acceptance, Buyer may rescind this Agreement at any time up to 3 days thereafter.

w. Information Verification Period. Unless satisfied/waived, Buyer shall have the time period set forth in Specific Term No. 15 (10 days after mutual acceptance if not filled in) to verify all information provided from Seller or Listing Brokerage Firm related to the Property. This contingency shall be deemed satisfied unless Buyer gives notice identifying the materially inaccurate information within the time period set forth in Specific Term No. 15. If Buyer gives timely notice under this section, then this Agreement shall terminate and the Earnest Money shall be refunded to Buyer.

Buyer's Initials	Date	Buyer's Initials	Date	Seller's Initials	Date	Seller's Initials	Date

Form 21
Residential PSA
Rev. 8/24
Page 6 of 6

RESIDENTIAL PURCHASE AND SALE AGREEMENT
General Terms

x. Property Condition Disclaimer. Buyer and Seller agree, that except as provided in this Agreement, all representations and information regarding the Property and the transaction are solely from the Seller or Buyer, and not from any Broker. The parties acknowledge that the Brokers are not responsible for assuring that the parties perform their obligations under this Agreement and that none of the Brokers has agreed to independently investigate or confirm any matter related to this transaction except as stated in this Agreement, or in a separate writing signed by such Broker. In addition, Brokers do not guarantee the value, quality or condition of the Property and some properties may contain building materials, including siding, roofing, ceiling, insulation, electrical, and plumbing, that have been the subject of lawsuits and/or governmental inquiry because of possible defects or health hazards. Some properties may have other defects arising after construction, such as drainage, leakage, pest, rot and mold problems. In addition, some properties may contain soil or other contamination that is not readily apparent and may be hazardous. Brokers do not have the expertise to identify or assess defective or hazardous products, materials, or conditions. Buyer is urged to use due diligence to inspect the Property to Buyer's satisfaction and to retain inspectors qualified to identify the presence of defective or hazardous materials and conditions and evaluate the Property as there may be defects and hazards that may only be revealed by careful inspection. Buyer is advised to investigate whether the Property is suitable for Buyer's intended use and to ensure the water supply is sufficient to meet Buyer's needs. Buyer is advised to investigate the cost of insurance for the Property, including, but not limited to homeowner's, fire, flood, earthquake, landslide, and other available coverage. Buyer acknowledges that local ordinances may restrict short term rentals of the Property. Buyer and Seller acknowledge that home protection plans may be available which may provide additional protection and benefit to Buyer and Seller. Brokers may assist the parties with locating and selecting third-party service providers, such as inspectors or contractors, but Brokers cannot guarantee or be responsible for the services provided by those third parties. The parties shall exercise their own judgment and due diligence regarding third-party service providers.

y. Fair Housing. Seller and Buyer acknowledge that local, state, and federal fair housing laws prohibit discrimination based on sex, marital status, sexual orientation, gender identity, race, creed, color, religion, caste, national origin, citizenship or immigration status, families with children status, familial status, honorably discharged veteran or military status, the presence of any sensory, mental, or physical disability, or the use of a support or service animal by a person with a disability.

Buyer's Initials Date | Buyer's Initials Date | Seller's Initials Date | Seller's Initials Date

Included Items

An "Included Items" paragraph states that certain items are included in the sale unless otherwise noted in the agreement. The list usually includes appliances, attached electronic equipment, hot tubs, fireplace inserts, and so forth. Even without this provision in the agreement, many of the items listed would be considered fixtures or attachments and included in the sale (see Chapter 1), but the provision prevents disputes over this issue.

If there is an item on the list that the seller does not want to include in the sale, the real estate agent should be sure to attach an addendum to the agreement stating that the item is excluded. Similarly, if items that do not appear on the list will be included in the sale, those should be specified in an addendum.

Closing Date

The closing date is the date when the proceeds of the sale are disbursed to the seller, the deed is delivered to the buyer, and all the appropriate documents are recorded.

The purchase and sale agreement must provide a specific date for closing. The lender should be consulted as to when the funds will be available to close the transaction. In setting a closing date, it is also important to consider how long it will take to meet any conditions that have been set. The buyer may have to obtain a loan and sell his current home. The seller will have to obtain title insurance, clear any liens, and perhaps make some repairs. (These conditions are discussed in more detail later in this chapter.) The chosen closing date must allow the parties sufficient time to meet all these obligations and conditions.

> **Example:** The purchase and sale agreement is going to be conditioned on the buyer obtaining a VA-guaranteed loan. A lender tells the real estate agent that it currently takes about two weeks to obtain VA loan approval, and the agent knows it normally takes four or five business days after loan approval and the satisfaction of any other conditions for the closing officer to finish the necessary work and close the transaction. So the agent suggests that the parties choose a closing date at least 20 days after the date the purchase and sale agreement is signed.

If the closing date is approaching and an inspection report is not yet available, or it looks like some other contingency will not be satisfied in time, the parties may want to change the closing date by executing a written extension agreement. The purchase and sale agreement will terminate on the date set for closing, so it is important to get an extension agreement signed as soon as possible. Failure to extend the closing date by amending the agreement may result in a contract that cannot be enforced.

Closing Agent and Closing Costs

It's a good idea to appoint an escrow agent or other closing agent in the purchase and sale agreement. Closing agents perform a wide variety of tasks connected with closing a real estate transaction, such as ordering inspections and title insurance, arranging for liens to be paid off and released, and preparing and recording documents on behalf of both the buyer and the seller. They may also hold funds and documents in escrow for the parties, distributing them only when specified conditions have been fulfilled. (Escrow and the closing process are discussed in more detail in Chapter 13.)

The purchase and sale agreement should also state which party is responsible for paying the closing agent's fees (typically, they are split between the parties) and various other closing costs (such as costs connected with the buyer's loan). In addition, the agreement should set forth how certain property expenses (such as taxes and homeowners association dues) and any property income (rent from tenants, for example) will be shared. These are ordinarily prorated as of the closing date, unless otherwise agreed (see Chapter 13).

The purchase and sale agreement may include a provision concerning compliance with the Foreign Investment in Real Property Tax Act (FIRPTA), a federal law that applies to some transactions in which the seller is a "foreign person"—in other words, not a U.S. citizen or resident alien. FIRPTA is discussed in greater detail in Chapter 13.

Possession

Unless the parties make other arrangements, possession of the property is usually transferred to the buyer when the transaction closes. If the buyer wants to take possession earlier, or if the seller wants a few extra days to vacate the property, that should be provided for in the purchase and sale agreement; the parties should also execute a separate rental agreement.

The seller usually agrees that the property will be maintained in its present condition until the buyer takes possession.

Casualty Loss

Another issue that may be addressed in the purchase and sale agreement is casualty loss. For instance, what happens if the house burns down after the agreement is executed, but before closing? Unless the buyer has already taken possession of the property, the seller ordinarily bears the risk of loss until closing.

So if the property is destroyed or substantially damaged before the transaction closes, the buyer is generally not required to go through with the purchase. (However, the purchase and sale agreement may allocate the risk of loss in some other fashion.)

Conveyance and Title

Almost every purchase and sale agreement includes provisions pertaining to the conveyance of the property and the condition of title. The type of deed that the seller will execute in favor of the buyer (ordinarily a warranty deed) is specified. There is usually a clause in which the seller agrees to provide marketable title, free of undisclosed encumbrances, with a homeowner's title insurance policy. The seller also agrees to pay off (at or before closing) any liens that the buyer is not assuming. Any unusual encumbrances that will remain after closing must be disclosed in the purchase and sale agreement.

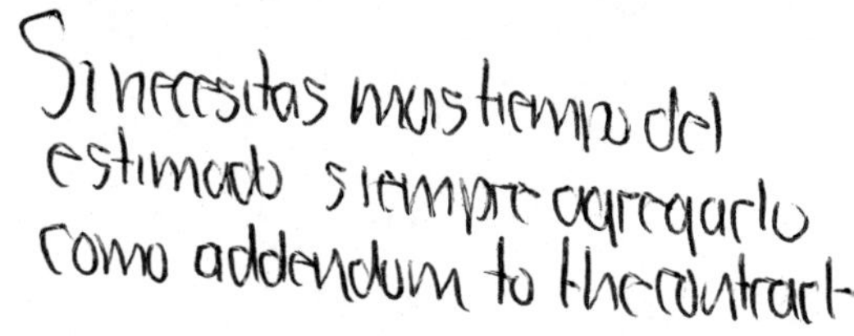

Many agreements go into more detail about what will be considered marketable title. For example, an agreement might say that CC&Rs that apply to the entire neighborhood or subdivision will not make the title unmarketable, nor will easements that do not significantly interfere with the buyer's use of the property (an easement for underground wiring, for instance). There will be no problem if encumbrances of that type show up as exceptions on the preliminary title report. However, if the report reveals other undisclosed encumbrances (such as an access easement that would interfere with the buyer's use of the property) and the seller cannot remove them before closing, then the title will be considered unmarketable, and the buyer can refuse to go through with the purchase.

Time is of the Essence

A purchase and sale agreement usually states that "time is of the essence of this agreement." This phrase means more than simply that the parties hope the sale progresses as quickly as possible; it means they are legally required to meet all deadlines set in the agreement.

A contract in which time is of the essence is one in which performance on or before the exact dates specified (not just within a reasonable time thereafter) is considered one of the essential terms of the agreement. Failure to meet any of the deadlines is a breach of contract.

Since time is of the essence in a purchase and sale agreement, the closing must take place on the date stated in the agreement. It's possible for either party to waive this clause, allowing the other party to perform after the deadline. But as a general rule, meeting all deadlines is an essential part of fulfilling a purchase and sale agreement.

Default

Another issue addressed in a purchase and sale agreement is the seller's remedies in the event that the buyer defaults, or breaches the contract. (The buyer's remedies in case the seller defaults usually aren't specifically listed; they include the right to sue for damages or specific performance, as explained in Chapter 6.)

A purchase and sale agreement form typically allows the parties to specify either that the earnest money will be treated as liquidated damages if the buyer defaults, or that the seller will be permitted an election of remedies.

An election of remedies means that after the buyer has defaulted, the seller can decide whether to simply keep the buyer's earnest money deposit, sue for actual damages, sue for specific performance, or pursue some other legal remedy.

In most cases, however, the parties agree in advance that instead of allowing the seller an election of remedies, the earnest money will serve as liquidated damages.

In that case, the seller will be entitled to keep the earnest money without having to prove that they suffered a financial loss as a result of the buyer's default. But the seller also gives up the right to sue the buyer for any additional damages or for specific performance. Keeping the earnest money will be the seller's only remedy.

Under Washington law, no more than 5% of the property's purchase price can be treated as liquidated damages in a purchase and sale agreement. So if the buyer's earnest money deposit was more than 5% of the price, the seller is required to return the excess to the buyer.

A purchase and sale agreement also typically includes an attorneys' fees provision. If one of the parties must resort to a lawsuit to enforce the contract and wins the lawsuit, then the losing party is obligated to pay the winning party's attorneys' fees.

Agency Disclosure

In Washington, a purchase and sale agreement usually includes an agency disclosure provision. In this provision, the real estate agents involved in the transaction specify which party each of them is representing. Washington law requires this information to be disclosed in writing to each party before they sign an offer (see Chapter 7), and the provision in the purchase and sale agreement fulfills this requirement. The parties' signatures on the agreement indicate their acceptance and understanding of the stated agency relationships.

Addenda

A paragraph that may be labeled "Addenda" or "Additional Provisions" indicates whether there are attachments to the agreement that contain additional contract provisions. There might be addenda concerning payment terms, fixtures to be excluded from the sale, FHA/VA financing, inspections, and so on. In order to incorporate additional provisions into the agreement, the attachments should be listed in the space provided, and the parties must initial and date each page of the attachments.

Earnest Money

A purchase and sale agreement form will provide space to fill in the amount of the buyer's earnest money deposit. It should also have a place to indicate what form the deposit takes (personal check, promissory note, wire transfer, or some other form) and explain how the deposit will be held while the transaction is pending.

Sometimes the buyer gives his agent a check for the deposit when the purchase and sale agreement form is filled out, before the agent submits the buyer's offer to the listing agent. In this situation, the purchase and sale agreement usually provides that the buyer's agent will hold the buyer's check undeposited until the seller has accepted the buyer's offer (or, if the seller makes a counteroffer, until a final agreement is reached).

That makes it easy to return the deposit to the buyer if the seller rejects the offer outright, or if the parties never reach a final agreement. Once the parties have a binding contract, the buyer's agent will either turn the check over to the closing agent for deposit into escrow, or else deposit the check into one of their real estate firm's trust accounts, if appropriate.

More commonly, however, the purchase and sale agreement form provides that the buyer has a certain number of days after mutual acceptance to deliver the earnest money, either to the buyer brokerage firm or to the closing agent.

The rules concerning real estate firm trust accounts are explained in Chapter 17. Briefly, if a deposit is for $10,000 or less, it has to be kept in the firm's housing trust fund account (a pooled trust account), with the interest paid to the state. If the deposit is for more than $10,000, the parties may choose instead to have it deposited in a separate trust account, with the interest paid either to the buyer or to the seller, as agreed. (The NWMLS residential purchase and sale agreement provides that the interest will be paid to the buyer.)

The appropriate amount for an earnest money deposit varies according to local custom; it can be any amount that both parties agree on. (Remember, however, that the seller can keep no more than 5% of the purchase price as liquidated damages if the buyer defaults.) Naturally, the buyer wants to make a small deposit, while the seller wants to receive a large deposit. The deposit is supposed to express the buyer's commitment to the purchase, and it should not be so small that forfeiting it would be painless. If the buyer goes through with the transaction, the deposit is ordinarily applied to the purchase price.

If a transaction falls through after the earnest money has been deposited into escrow or into a trust account, there may be a dispute over the earnest money; the buyer and the seller may each feel entitled to it. In a residential transaction, if one of the parties submits a written demand for release of all or part of the earnest money, the deposit holder (the escrow agent or the real estate firm holding the funds in trust) is generally required to notify the other party or parties in writing and give them a chance to submit written objections. If there are no objections, the deposit holder must release the funds as demanded. But if another party submits an objection or a conflicting demand for the funds, the deposit holder must file an **interpleader** action, turning the matter over to a court. In an interpleader action, the court decides which party is the rightful owner of the funds. The law sets specific deadlines for notifying the parties, for submission of objections, and for releasing or interpleading the funds.

Brokerage Fee

A purchase and sale agreement form often includes a clause in which the buyer and seller agree to pay the real estate commission, as stated in any representation or commission agreement they entered into earlier.

Signatures

Of course, space is provided on the form for the signatures of the parties. In general, the buyer's signature turns the form into an offer to purchase, and the seller's signature turns it into a binding contract.

Offer and Acceptance. The purchase and sale agreement form has a provision in which to set a deadline for acceptance of the offer. The manner in which the seller is required to communicate acceptance may also be specified. For example, it might say the seller's acceptance is not effective until a copy of the agreement signed by the seller has been returned to the buyer's agent.

If the seller fails to accept in the prescribed manner by the deadline, the offer terminates and the earnest money is returned to the buyer. (Note that in addition to meeting any other requirements specified by the buyer, the seller's acceptance must be in writing to satisfy the statute of frauds.)

Counteroffers

The purchase and sale agreement form may include a provision concerning counteroffers, in case the seller wants to modify the buyer's offer instead of accepting it outright. The provision may set a deadline for the buyer's acceptance of the counteroffer. Remember that a counteroffer is not an acceptance; the buyer isn't bound unless they accept the seller's counteroffer.

When a seller wants to make a counteroffer, it's best to write it on another form or a separate attachment, rather than crossing out or writing over the terms on the original form. Printed counteroffer forms are available for this purpose.

Amendments

After the buyer and the seller have signed the purchase and sale agreement, the terms of the contract can only be modified in writing. All parties who signed the original agreement must also sign the amendment for it to be binding.

Don't confuse an amendment with an addendum. An amendment is a written modification that occurs after the parties have signed the purchase and sale agreement, while an addendum is an attachment added to the agreement prior to signature.

Backup Offers

A prospective buyer may be so enthusiastic about a property that they decide to submit an offer even though the seller has already accepted an offer from another buyer. The second offer, known as a **backup offer**, would be contingent on the failure of the existing sales contract. If the seller accepts the backup offer, the parties will have a deal in place should the original sale fail to close.

Contingency Clauses

Most of the time, the agreement between a buyer and a seller is conditional; in other words, it is legally binding only if certain conditions are fulfilled. These conditions are called "contingency clauses," or simply "contingencies." The contract is contingent on fulfillment of the conditions.

The most common type of contingency clause is a financing contingency, which makes the contract dependent on whether the buyer is able to obtain financing. Other common contingencies concern the sale of the buyer's present home, or the satisfactory completion of some type of inspection (for example, a structural, pest, or septic tank inspection).

If a contract contains a contingency clause, the contract will be enforceable if—and only if—that contingent event occurs. If it does not occur, the contract is terminated. When a purchase and sale agreement terminates because a contingent event does not occur, the buyer is usually entitled to a refund of the earnest money deposit.

The parties are obligated to make a reasonable effort to fulfill the condition set forth in a contingency clause. For instance, the buyer must apply for financing, or the seller must order the required inspections. As with every contract, the parties to a purchase and sale agreement have an obligation to act in good faith; each must cooperate so that both can benefit from the contract. It is best to make this obligation of good faith explicit in the contingency clause.

The party who benefits from the contingency clause usually has the right to waive it. For example, a buyer could waive a pest inspection contingency. In that case the parties would be bound by the agreement whether or not the results of the pest inspection were satisfactory, or even if no pest inspection were performed.

In some purchase and sale agreement forms, the closing date is expressly tied to fulfillment of a contingency. If a real estate agent believes that fulfillment of a condition in a purchase and sale agreement may affect the closing date, the agent should point that out to the parties.

All contingencies must be spelled out in the purchase and sale agreement or in attached addenda that are incorporated into the agreement. If a printed form contains boxes to be checked for each of the different kinds of contingencies, the agent filling out the form must be sure that all appropriate boxes are checked.

Any contingency clause should include these four things:

1. exactly what the condition is and what has to be done to meet it;
2. the procedure for notifying the other party of either satisfaction or waiver of the condition;
3. a date by which the condition must be satisfied or waived; and
4. the rights of the parties in the event the condition is not satisfied or waived by the specified date.

As with the purchase and sale agreement itself, there are attorney-approved contingency addendum forms that can be attached to the agreement. A real estate agent should use one of those forms instead of writing a complicated provision.

Financing Contingencies

Many residential transactions are contingent on whether the buyer is able to obtain financing. That's why it's particularly important to describe the financing arrangements in the purchase and sale agreement. The buyer is required to make a diligent, good faith effort to obtain financing on the terms stated in the agreement. But if, despite the buyer's best efforts, no lenders are willing to make a loan on those terms, then the buyer can terminate the agreement without forfeiting the deposit.

A financing contingency should contain enough information to clearly identify the type of loan that the buyer wants. It isn't possible to include the details of all loan programs a buyer might qualify for, but the contingency clause should include the following basic information:

1. the type of the loan;
2. the amount of the downpayment;
3. the deadline by which the buyer must apply for a loan, and the consequences for missing that deadline;
4. the deadline for obtaining a loan commitment, and the consequences of a failure to obtain a loan commitment; and
5. the party who is to pay the costs and fees associated with the loan application (normally the buyer).

FHA, VA, and RD Financing. A financing contingency often includes special provisions concerning FHA, VA, and RD (rural development) financing. The regulations that govern these financing programs prohibit the buyer from paying certain loan and closing costs, and so the financing contingency provides that the seller agrees to pay these costs if the buyer is applying for an FHA, VA, or RD loan.

Note that if there is a low appraisal in an FHA, VA, or RD transaction, the buyer can't be required to go through with the purchase, even if the seller is willing to reduce the price (although the buyer may choose to buy the property at the reduced price). There is an exception to this rule, however: if the seller can get a reappraisal that indicates the property is worth the originally agreed-on price, the buyer must proceed with the transaction. This reappraisal has to be made by the same appraiser who initially submitted the low appraisal.

Contract Conditioned on Sale of Buyer's Home

Purchase and sale agreements are often contingent on the buyer's ability to sell their current home. In fact, even when this is not an express condition, it may be a hidden one. Most buyers are planning to use part of the proceeds from the sale of the current home for a downpayment on the new home, and won't be able to qualify for the loan described in the financing contingency clause without selling the current home.

Under those circumstances, the sale of the current home should be an express condition in the purchase and sale agreement. Otherwise the seller may be misled into believing that the buyer has a much better chance of being able to complete the purchase than they actually have. It's generally a waste of time for the seller to accept a contingent offer from a buyer who is unlikely to fulfill the condition.

The contract clause should specify what will fulfill a condition concerning sale of the current home. Is it fulfilled when the buyer accepts an offer on the current home? Or is it fulfilled only when the sale of the current home actually closes? The parties and the agent should carefully consider how much time is allowed for this contingency. There's a natural conflict between the desires of the buyer and the seller. The buyer wants as much time as possible in order to get the highest possible price for their current home. The seller wants the present transaction to close as soon as possible.

Bump Clauses. To deal with these conflicting interests, the **bump clause** has evolved. A bump clause enables the seller to keep the property on the market pending fulfillment of a contingency. It's now common to include one in the purchase and sale agreement when the transaction depends on the sale of the buyer's current home.

If the seller receives another offer before the buyer's home is sold, the seller can demand that the buyer waive the condition or rescind the contract. A bump clause can be used with any type of contingency, and one is most likely to be used when there is a good chance that the contingency will not be fulfilled on time.

Fig. 9.2 Sample Contingency Clause Concerning Sale of Buyer's Home

Sale of Buyer's Home. This agreement is contingent upon Buyer's accepting an offer to sell Buyer's present residence, located at ________________. Buyer must notify Seller, in writing, within ____ days after the date of the Seller's signature on this agreement that Buyer has accepted a written offer to sell Buyer's home. The price and terms of that sale agreement must be such that Buyer will receive sufficient net proceeds to make completion of this transaction possible. If Buyer fails to provide Seller with such notice within said ___-day period, then this purchase and sale agreement shall terminate and the earnest money shall be refunded to Buyer.

If the sale of Buyer's home fails to close through no fault of Buyer after expiration of the contingency period, then, unless Buyer waives this contingency, this purchase and sale agreement shall terminate and the earnest money shall be refunded to Buyer.

Time Frame. Although it's difficult, if not impossible, to predict how long it will take a buyer to sell their home, there is one practical detail to keep in mind. The agent must make sure that there isn't a conflict in the terms of the purchase and sale agreement. For example, the buyer should not be given 60 days to find a buyer for their home if the original sale is supposed to close in 45 days.

Inspection Contingencies

Another kind of contingency clause concerns an expert inspection of the property. For example, a purchase and sale agreement might include provisions making the contract contingent upon a structural inspection, a geological inspection, or a pest control inspection. In fact, if an appraiser notes that pests might be a problem, then the buyer's lender may require a pest control inspection to be performed before the buyer's loan is approved.

Contingency clauses dealing with inspections sometimes simply state that they can be met only with "satisfactory" test results, leaving what is satisfactory to the buyer's discretion. In other cases, an inspection contingency includes some objective standard, such as a determination that no immediate repairs are needed, or that necessary repairs can't exceed a set cost, such as $1,000.

Any objective standards set in an inspection contingency clause should be ones that will satisfy the buyer's personal standards. For example, a particular buyer might not want to buy a house that has ever had a termite infestation. Even if there's no immediate need for repairs, or if the damage is negligible, that buyer simply doesn't want a house that is susceptible to termite infestation. In that case, the clause should allow the buyer to withdraw from the transaction if the inspection reveals any past or present infestation.

An inspection contingency clause is often a separate page attached to the purchase and sale agreement as an addendum. It should establish:

- who is responsible for ordering and paying for the inspection;
- when and how the buyer must give the seller notice of disapproval of the inspection report;
- the seller's option to either perform repairs or terminate the purchase and sale agreement, refunding the buyer's earnest money; and
- a time limit for re-inspection by the buyer if the seller performs repairs.

The seller should be aware that if an inspection reveals building code violations or certain other problems, public authorities could order the seller to correct the violations, whether or not the transaction proceeds.

Second Buyer Contingencies

When it appears that a transaction might fail because a condition is not met, the seller may want to accept an offer from a second buyer. To allow this, a provision is usually included in the second purchase and sale agreement making it contingent on the failure of the first transaction, and on the first buyer's release of all claims.

The best way to accomplish this is by asking the first buyer to execute a rescission agreement in which the parties agree to rescind the first contract.

Property Disclosure Laws

In many transactions, sellers are required by law to make certain disclosures to buyers about the property being transferred. In this section, we'll explain Washington's seller disclosure law and a federal law requiring disclosures concerning lead-based paint.

Seller Disclosure Law

Washington law requires a seller of real property to give the buyer a **seller disclosure statement.** This requirement generally applies to the sale of any type of real property except agricultural or timber land.

However, certain types of transactions are exempt from this law. For example, a seller disclosure statement is not required:

- in a foreclosure sale or when a borrower gives a lender a deed in lieu of foreclosure;
- when property is transferred as a gift to a family member; or
- when property is transferred pursuant to bankruptcy proceedings or the settlement of an estate.

A transaction may also be exempt because another disclosure requirement applies instead. That's true for sales that are subject to disclosure requirements under the Common Interest Ownership Act or the Timeshare Act, for example.

Disclosures. The questions that must be answered in a seller disclosure statement are set forth in the state statute. Different disclosures are required for unimproved residential property, improved residential property, and commercial property. A seller disclosure form for improved residential property is shown in Figure 9.3.

The purpose of the disclosure statement is to disclose the seller's knowledge about the condition of the property, including the condition of the buildings, the availability of utilities, the existence of any easements and encumbrances, and other material information. The statement is for disclosure purposes only; it is not a part of the purchase and sale agreement.

The seller disclosure form specifically states that the disclosures are made by the seller and may not be regarded as representations made by any of the real estate licensees involved in the transaction. Furthermore, the law provides that the statement is not a warranty from either the seller or the real estate agents. Neither the seller nor the agents will be liable for any inaccuracies in the statement unless they had personal knowledge of the inaccuracies.

Deadlines and Right of Rescission. The seller must give the buyer the disclosure statement within **five business days** after a purchase and sale agreement is signed, unless the parties agree in writing to another time frame, or the buyer signs a written waiver of the right to receive the statement. However, a waiver is not allowed for the Environmental section of the form, if any of the questions in that section would be answered "Yes."

Within **three business days** after receiving the statement (or another time frame agreed to in writing), the buyer can either "approve and accept" the disclosure statement or rescind the purchase and sale agreement. The choice between acceptance and rescission is at the complete discretion of the buyer. There are no objective standards that can be applied to the disclosure statement to measure its adequacy. If the buyer doesn't like something revealed in the disclosure statement, however trivial, the buyer can rescind the agreement. In fact, the buyer can rescind the agreement simply because they decided they don't want the property after all, even if the decision isn't actually based on information disclosed by the seller.

If the buyer decides to rescind the agreement, they must deliver a written notice of rescission to the seller or the seller's agent before the three-day period expires. The buyer will then be entitled to a refund of the earnest money deposit.

After delivery of the disclosure statement, information may later come to light that makes the disclosure statement inaccurate.

> **Example:** The seller filled out the seller disclosure statement and gave it to the buyer within the five-day time frame. The buyer examined the statement, was satisfied with it, and waived the right to rescind the agreement. Two weeks later, the seller realizes that there's an encroachment on the property. The disclosure statement given to the buyer is no longer accurate.

When this happens, the seller must either give the buyer an amended disclosure statement or else take corrective action so that the original disclosure statement is accurate again. If the seller provides an amended statement, the buyer has three business days to either accept the amended statement or rescind the purchase and sale agreement.

> **Example:** The seller in the previous example gives the buyer an amended disclosure statement. The buyer, who has had second thoughts about buying the property anyway, decides to rescind the purchase and sale agreement.

If the seller neither provides an amended statement nor takes corrective action—or if the seller never provided a disclosure statement in the first place—the buyer can rescind the contract at any time before closing. Once the sale closes, however, the buyer's right of rescission ends. Even if new information comes to light after closing, the buyer doesn't have the right to rescind the transaction.

Lead-Based Paint Disclosure Law

In transactions involving housing built before 1978, federal law requires a seller to disclose information concerning lead-based paint to potential buyers. A landlord is also required to make these disclosures to potential tenants. Many of the homes built before 1978 contain some lead-based paint. The paint is usually not dangerous if properly maintained, but if it deteriorates, it may cause brain damage and organ damage in young children.

The law requires the seller or landlord of a dwelling built before 1978 to do all of the following:

- disclose the location of any lead-based paint that they are aware of in the home (in both the dwelling unit and the common areas, if applicable);
- provide a copy of any report concerning lead-based paint in the home, if it has been inspected; and
- give buyers or tenants a copy of a pamphlet on lead-based paint prepared by the U.S. Environmental Protection Agency.

In addition, buyers (but not tenants) must be offered at least a ten-day period in which to have the home tested for lead-based paint.

Fig. 9.3 Seller disclosure statement for improved residential property

Form 17
Seller Disclosure Statement
Rev. 7/19
Page 1 of 6

SELLER DISCLOSURE STATEMENT
IMPROVED PROPERTY

SELLER: ______________________________ ______________________________
Seller Seller

To be used in transfers of improved residential real property, including residential dwellings up to four units, new construction, condominiums not subject to a public offering statement, certain timeshares, and manufactured and mobile homes. See RCW Chapter 64.06 for further information.

INSTRUCTIONS TO THE SELLER

Please complete the following form. Do not leave any spaces blank. If the question clearly does not apply to the property check "NA." If the answer is "yes" to any asterisked (*) item(s), please explain on attached sheets. Please refer to the line number(s) of the question(s) when you provide your explanation(s). For your protection you must date and initial each page of this disclosure statement and each attachment. Delivery of the disclosure statement must occur not later than five (5) business days, unless otherwise agreed, after mutual acceptance of a written purchase and sale agreement between Buyer and Seller.

NOTICE TO THE BUYER

THE FOLLOWING DISCLOSURES ARE MADE BY THE SELLER ABOUT THE CONDITION OF THE PROPERTY LOCATED AT ______________________________, CITY ______________________________, STATE _______, ZIP ______________, COUNTY______________________________ ("THE PROPERTY") OR AS LEGALLY DESCRIBED ON THE ATTACHED EXHIBIT A.

SELLER MAKES THE FOLLOWING DISCLOSURES OF EXISTING MATERIAL FACTS OR MATERIAL DEFECTS TO BUYER BASED ON SELLER'S ACTUAL KNOWLEDGE OF THE PROPERTY AT THE TIME SELLER COMPLETES THIS DISCLOSURE STATEMENT. UNLESS YOU AND SELLER OTHERWISE AGREE IN WRITING, YOU HAVE THREE (3) BUSINESS DAYS FROM THE DAY SELLER OR SELLER'S AGENT DELIVERS THIS DISCLOSURE STATEMENT TO YOU TO RESCIND THE AGREEMENT BY DELIVERING A SEPARATELY SIGNED WRITTEN STATEMENT OF RESCISSION TO SELLER OR SELLER'S AGENT. IF THE SELLER DOES NOT GIVE YOU A COMPLETED DISCLOSURE STATEMENT, THEN YOU MAY WAIVE THE RIGHT TO RESCIND PRIOR TO OR AFTER THE TIME YOU ENTER INTO A PURCHASE AND SALE AGREEMENT.

THE FOLLOWING ARE DISCLOSURES MADE BY SELLER AND ARE NOT THE REPRESENTATIONS OF ANY REAL ESTATE LICENSEE OR OTHER PARTY. THIS INFORMATION IS FOR DISCLOSURE ONLY AND IS NOT INTENDED TO BE A PART OF ANY WRITTEN AGREEMENT BETWEEN BUYER AND SELLER.

FOR A MORE COMPREHENSIVE EXAMINATION OF THE SPECIFIC CONDITION OF THIS PROPERTY YOU ARE ADVISED TO OBTAIN AND PAY FOR THE SERVICES OF QUALIFIED EXPERTS TO INSPECT THE PROPERTY, WHICH MAY INCLUDE, WITHOUT LIMITATION, ARCHITECTS, ENGINEERS, LAND SURVEYORS, PLUMBERS, ELECTRICIANS, ROOFERS, BUILDING INSPECTORS, ON-SITE WASTEWATER TREATMENT INSPECTORS, OR STRUCTURAL PEST INSPECTORS. THE PROSPECTIVE BUYER AND SELLER MAY WISH TO OBTAIN PROFESSIONAL ADVICE OR INSPECTIONS OF THE PROPERTY OR TO PROVIDE APPROPRIATE PROVISIONS IN A CONTRACT BETWEEN THEM WITH RESPECT TO ANY ADVICE, INSPECTION, DEFECTS OR WARRANTIES.

SELLER ❑ IS/ ❑ IS NOT OCCUPYING THE PROPERTY.

I. SELLER'S DISCLOSURES:

*If you answer "Yes" to a question with an asterisk (*), please explain your answer and attach documents, if available and not otherwise publicly recorded. If necessary, use an attached sheet.

1. TITLE	**YES**	**NO**	**DON'T KNOW**	**N/A**
A. Do you have legal authority to sell the property? If no, please explain.	❑	❑	❑	❑
*B. Is title to the property subject to any of the following?				
(1) First right of refusal	❑	❑	❑	❑
(2) Option	❑	❑	❑	❑
(3) Lease or rental agreement	❑	❑	❑	❑
(4) Life estate?	❑	❑	❑	❑
*C. Are there any encroachments, boundary agreements, or boundary disputes?	❑	❑	❑	❑
*D. Is there a private road or easement agreement for access to the property?	❑	❑	❑	❑
*E. Are there any rights-of-way, easements, or access limitations that may affect the Buyer's use of the property?	❑	❑	❑	❑
*F. Are there any written agreements for joint maintenance of an easement or right-of-way?	❑	❑	❑	❑
*G. Is there any study, survey project, or notice that would adversely affect the property?	❑	❑	❑	❑
*H. Are there any pending or existing assessments against the property?	❑	❑	❑	❑

SELLER'S INITIALS ______ Date ______ SELLER'S INITIALS ______ Date ______

Form 17
Seller Disclosure Statement
Rev. 7/19
Page 2 of 6

SELLER DISCLOSURE STATEMENT
IMPROVED PROPERTY
(Continued)

	YES	NO	DON'T KNOW	N/A
*I. Are there any zoning violations, nonconforming uses, or any unusual restrictions on the property that would affect future construction or remodeling?	☐	☐	☐	☐
*J. Is there a boundary survey for the property?	☐	☐	☐	☐
*K. Are there any covenants, conditions, or restrictions recorded against the property?	☐	☐	☐	☐

PLEASE NOTE: Covenants, conditions, and restrictions which purport to forbid or restrict the conveyance, encumbrance, occupancy, or lease of real property to individuals based on race, creed, color, sex, national origin, familial status, or disability are void, unenforceable, and illegal. RCW 49.60.224.

2. WATER

A. Household Water

(1) The source of water for the property is: ☐ Private or publicly owned water system ☐ Private well serving only the subject property *☐ Other water system

	YES	NO	DON'T KNOW	N/A
*If shared, are there any written agreements?	☐	☐	☐	☐
*(2) Is there an easement (recorded or unrecorded) for access to and/or maintenance of the water source?	☐	☐	☐	☐
*(3) Are there any problems or repairs needed?	☐	☐	☐	☐
(4) During your ownership, has the source provided an adequate year-round supply of potable water?	☐	☐	☐	☐

If no, please explain: ______________________________

	YES	NO	DON'T KNOW	N/A
*(5) Are there any water treatment systems for the property?	☐	☐	☐	☐

If yes, are they: ☐ Leased ☐ Owned

	YES	NO	DON'T KNOW	N/A
*(6) Are there any water rights for the property associated with its domestic water supply, such as a water right permit, certificate, or claim?	☐	☐	☐	☐
(a) If yes, has the water right permit, certificate, or claim been assigned, transferred, or changed?	☐	☐	☐	☐
*(b) If yes, has all or any portion of the water right not been used for five or more successive years?	☐	☐	☐	☐
*(7) Are there any defects in the operation of the water system (e.g. pipes, tank, pump, etc.)?	☐	☐	☐	☐

B. Irrigation Water

	YES	NO	DON'T KNOW	N/A
(1) Are there any irrigation water rights for the property, such as a water right permit, certificate, or claim?	☐	☐	☐	☐
*(a) If yes, has all or any portion of the water right not been used for five or more successive years?	☐	☐	☐	☐
*(b) If so, is the certificate available? (If yes, please attach a copy.)	☐	☐	☐	☐
*(c) If so, has the water right permit, certificate, or claim been assigned, transferred, or changed?	☐	☐	☐	☐
*(2) Does the property receive irrigation water from a ditch company, irrigation district, or other entity?	☐	☐	☐	☐

If so, please identify the entity that supplies water to the property:

____

C. Outdoor Sprinkler System

	YES	NO	DON'T KNOW	N/A
(1) Is there an outdoor sprinkler system for the property?	☐	☐	☐	☐
*(2) If yes, are there any defects in the system?	☐	☐	☐	☐
*(3) If yes, is the sprinkler system connected to irrigation water?	☐	☐	☐	☐

3. SEWER/ON-SITE SEWAGE SYSTEM

A. The property is served by:
☐ Public sewer system ☐ On-site sewage system (including pipes, tanks, drainfields, and all other component parts)
☐ Other disposal system
Please describe: ______________________________

SELLER'S INITIALS Date SELLER'S INITIALS Date

Form 17
Seller Disclosure Statement
Rev. 7/19
Page 3 of 6

SELLER DISCLOSURE STATEMENT
IMPROVED PROPERTY
(Continued)

	YES	NO	DON'T KNOW	N/A
B. If public sewer system service is available to the property, is the house connected to the sewer main?	☐	☐	☐	☐
If no, please explain: ____				
*C. Is the property subject to any sewage system fees or charges in addition to those covered in your regularly billed sewer or on-site sewage system maintenance service?	☐	☐	☐	☐
D. If the property is connected to an on-site sewage system:				
*(1) Was a permit issued for its construction, and was it approved by the local health department or district following its construction?	☐	☐	☐	☐
(2) When was it last pumped? ____				
*(3) Are there any defects in the operation of the on-site sewage system?	☐	☐	☐	☐
(4) When was it last inspected? ____			☐	☐
By whom: ____				
(5) For how many bedrooms was the on-site sewage system approved? ____ bedrooms			☐	☐
E. Are all plumbing fixtures, including laundry drain, connected to the sewer/on-site sewage system?	☐	☐	☐	☐
If no, please explain: ____				
*F. Have there been any changes or repairs to the on-site sewage system?	☐	☐	☐	☐
G. Is the on-site sewage system, including the drainfield, located entirely within the boundaries of the property?	☐	☐	☐	☐
If no, please explain: ____				
*H. Does the on-site sewage system require monitoring and maintenance services more frequently than once a year?	☐	☐	☐	☐

NOTICE: IF THIS RESIDENTIAL REAL PROPERTY DISCLOSURE IS BEING COMPLETED FOR NEW CONSTRUCTION WHICH HAS NEVER BEEN OCCUPIED, SELLER IS NOT REQUIRED TO COMPLETE THE QUESTIONS LISTED IN ITEM 4 (STRUCTURAL) OR ITEM 5 (SYSTEMS AND FIXTURES).

4. STRUCTURAL

	YES	NO	DON'T KNOW	N/A
*A. Has the roof leaked within the last 5 years?	☐	☐	☐	☐
*B. Has the basement flooded or leaked?	☐	☐	☐	☐
*C. Have there been any conversions, additions or remodeling?	☐	☐	☐	☐
*(1) If yes, were all building permits obtained?	☐	☐	☐	☐
*(2) If yes, were all final inspections obtained?	☐	☐	☐	☐
D. Do you know the age of the house?	☐	☐	☐	☐
If yes, year of original construction: ____				
*E. Has there been any settling, slippage, or sliding of the property or its improvements?	☐	☐	☐	☐
*F. Are there any defects with the following: (If yes, please check applicable items and explain)	☐	☐	☐	☐

☐ Foundations	☐ Decks	☐ Exterior Walls
☐ Chimneys	☐ Interior Walls	☐ Fire Alarms
☐ Doors	☐ Windows	☐ Patio
☐ Ceilings	☐ Slab Floors	☐ Driveways
☐ Pools	☐ Hot Tub	☐ Sauna
☐ Sidewalks	☐ Outbuildings	☐ Fireplaces
☐ Garage Floors	☐ Walkways	☐ Siding
☐ Wood Stoves	☐ Elevators	☐ Incline Elevators
☐ Stairway Chair Lifts	☐ Wheelchair Lifts	☐ Other ____

	YES	NO	DON'T KNOW	N/A
*G. Was a structural pest or "whole house" inspection done?	☐	☐	☐	☐
If yes, when and by whom was the inspection completed? ____				
H. During your ownership, has the property had any wood destroying organism or pest infestation?	☐	☐	☐	☐
I. Is the attic insulated?	☐	☐	☐	☐
J. Is the basement insulated?	☐	☐	☐	☐

SELLER'S INITIALS ____ Date ____ SELLER'S INITIALS ____ Date ____

Form 17
Seller Disclosure Statement
Rev. 7/19
Page 4 of 6

SELLER DISCLOSURE STATEMENT
IMPROVED PROPERTY
(Continued)

	YES	NO	DON'T KNOW	N/A
5. SYSTEMS AND FIXTURES				
*A. If any of the following systems or fixtures are included with the transfer, are there any defects?				
If yes, please explain: ______________________				
Electrical system, including wiring, switches, outlets, and service	❑	❑	❑	❑
Plumbing system, including pipes, faucets, fixtures, and toilets	❑	❑	❑	❑
Hot water tank	❑	❑	❑	❑
Garbage disposal	❑	❑	❑	❑
Appliances	❑	❑	❑	❑
Sump pump	❑	❑	❑	❑
Heating and cooling systems	❑	❑	❑	❑
Security system: ❑ Owned ❑ Leased	❑	❑	❑	❑
Other ______________________	❑	❑	❑	❑
*B. If any of the following fixtures or property is included with the transfer, are they leased? (If yes, please attach copy of lease.)				
Security System: ______________________	❑	❑	❑	❑
Tanks (type): ______________________	❑	❑	❑	❑
Satellite dish: ______________________	❑	❑	❑	❑
Other: ______________________	❑	❑	❑	❑
*C. Are any of the following kinds of wood burning appliances present at the property?				
(1) Woodstove?	❑	❑	❑	❑
(2) Fireplace insert?	❑	❑	❑	❑
(3) Pellet stove?	❑	❑	❑	❑
(4) Fireplace?	❑	❑	❑	❑
If yes, are all of the (1) woodstoves or (2) fireplace inserts certified by the U.S. Environmental Protection Agency as clean burning appliances to improve air quality and public health?	❑	❑	❑	❑
D. Is the property located within a city, county, or district or within a department of natural resources fire protection zone that provides fire protection services?	❑	❑	❑	❑
E. Is the property equipped with carbon monoxide alarms? (Note: Pursuant to RCW 19.27.530, Seller must equip the residence with carbon monoxide alarms as required by the state building code.)	❑	❑	❑	❑
F. Is the property equipped with smoke detection devices? (Note: Pursuant to RCW 43.44.110, if the property is not equipped with at least one smoke detection device, at least one must be provided by the seller.)	❑	❑	❑	❑
6. HOMEOWNERS' ASSOCIATION/COMMON INTERESTS				
A. Is there a Homeowners' Association? Name of Association and contact information for an officer, director, employee, or other authorized agent, if any, who may provide the association's financial statements, minutes, bylaws, fining policy, and other information that is not publicly available: ______________________	❑	❑	❑	❑
B. Are there regular periodic assessments?	❑	❑	❑	❑
$__________ per ❑ month ❑ year				
❑ Other: ______________________				
*C. Are there any pending special assessments?	❑	❑	❑	❑
*D. Are there any shared "common areas" or any joint maintenance agreements (facilities such as walls, fences, landscaping, pools, tennis courts, walkways, or other areas co-owned in undivided interest with others)?	❑	❑	❑	❑
7. ENVIRONMENTAL				
*A. Have there been any flooding, standing water, or drainage problems on the property that affect the property or access to the property?	❑	❑	❑	❑
*B. Does any part of the property contain fill dirt, waste, or other fill material?	❑	❑	❑	❑
*C. Is there any material damage to the property from fire, wind, floods, beach movements, earthquake, expansive soils, or landslides?	❑	❑	❑	❑
D. Are there any shorelines, wetlands, floodplains, or critical areas on the property?	❑	❑	❑	❑
*E. Are there any substances, materials, or products in or on the property that may be environmental concerns, such as asbestos, formaldehyde, radon gas, lead-based paint, fuel or chemical storage tanks, or contaminated soil or water?	❑	❑	❑	❑
*F. Has the property been used for commercial or industrial purposes?	❑	❑	❑	❑

______________________ ______________________
SELLER'S INITIALS Date SELLER'S INITIALS Date

Form 17
Seller Disclosure Statement
Rev. 7/19
Page 5 of 6

SELLER DISCLOSURE STATEMENT
IMPROVED PROPERTY

(Continued)

	YES	NO	DON'T KNOW	N/A
*G. Is there any soil or groundwater contamination?	☐	☐	☐	☐
*H. Are there transmission poles or other electrical utility equipment installed, maintained, or buried on the property that do not provide utility service to the structures on the property?	☐	☐	☐	☐
*I. Has the property been used as a legal or illegal dumping site?	☐	☐	☐	☐
*J. Has the property been used as an illegal drug manufacturing site?	☐	☐	☐	☐
*K. Are there any radio towers in the area that cause interference with cellular telephone reception?	☐	☐	☐	☐

8. LEAD BASED PAINT (Applicable if the house was built before 1978).

A. Presence of lead-based paint and/or lead-based paint hazards (check one below):

☐ Known lead-based paint and/or lead-based paint hazards are present in the housing (explain). ______________________

☐ Seller has no knowledge of lead-based paint and/or lead-based paint hazards in the housing.

B. Records and reports available to the Seller (check one below):

☐ Seller has provided the purchaser with all available records and reports pertaining to lead-based paint and/or lead-based paint hazards in the housing (list documents below).

____

☐ Seller has no reports or records pertaining to lead-based paint and/or lead-based paint hazards in the housing.

9. MANUFACTURED AND MOBILE HOMES

If the property includes a manufactured or mobile home,

	YES	NO	DON'T KNOW	N/A
*A. Did you make any alterations to the home? If yes, please describe the alterations: ______________________	☐	☐	☐	☐
*B. Did any previous owner make any alterations to the home?	☐	☐	☐	☐
*C. If alterations were made, were permits or variances for these alterations obtained?	☐	☐	☐	☐

10. FULL DISCLOSURE BY SELLERS

A. Other conditions or defects:

	YES	NO	DON'T KNOW	N/A
*Are there any other existing material defects affecting the property that a prospective buyer should know about?	☐	☐	☐	☐

B. Verification

The foregoing answers and attached explanations (if any) are complete and correct to the best of Seller's knowledge and Seller has received a copy hereof. Seller agrees to defend, indemnify and hold real estate licensees harmless from and against any and all claims that the above information is inaccurate. Seller authorizes real estate licensees, if any, to deliver a copy of this disclosure statement to other real estate licensees and all prospective buyers of the property.

______________________ ______________________
Seller Date Seller Date

If the answer is "Yes" to any asterisked (*) items, please explain below (use additional sheets if necessary). Please refer to the line number(s) of the question(s).

Form 17
Seller Disclosure Statement
Rev. 7/19
Page 6 of 6

SELLER DISCLOSURE STATEMENT
IMPROVED PROPERTY
(Continued)

II. NOTICES TO THE BUYER

1. **SEX OFFENDER REGISTRATION**
INFORMATION REGARDING REGISTERED SEX OFFENDERS MAY BE OBTAINED FROM LOCAL LAW ENFORCEMENT AGENCIES. THIS NOTICE IS INTENDED ONLY TO INFORM YOU OF WHERE TO OBTAIN THIS INFORMATION AND IS NOT AN INDICATION OF THE PRESENCE OF REGISTERED SEX OFFENDERS.

2. **PROXIMITY TO FARMING/WORKING FOREST**
THIS NOTICE IS TO INFORM YOU THAT THE REAL PROPERTY YOU ARE CONSIDERING FOR PURCHASE MAY LIE IN CLOSE PROXIMITY TO A FARM OR WORKING FOREST. THE OPERATION OF A FARM OR WORKING FOREST INVOLVES USUAL AND CUSTOMARY AGRICULTURAL PRACTICES OR FOREST PRACTICES, WHICH ARE PROTECTED UNDER RCW 7.48.305, THE WASHINGTON RIGHT TO FARM ACT.

3. **OIL TANK INSURANCE**
THIS NOTICE IS TO INFORM YOU THAT IF THE REAL PROPERTY YOU ARE CONSIDERING FOR PURCHASE UTILIZES AN OIL TANK FOR HEATING PURPOSES, NO COST INSURANCE MAY BE AVAILABLE FROM THE POLLUTION LIABILITY INSURANCE AGENCY.

III. BUYER'S ACKNOWLEDGEMENT

1. **BUYER HEREBY ACKNOWLEDGES THAT:**

   A. Buyer has a duty to pay diligent attention to any material defects that are known to Buyer or can be known to Buyer by utilizing diligent attention and observation.

   B. The disclosures set forth in this statement and in any amendments to this statement are made only by the Seller and not by any real estate licensee or other party.

   C. Buyer acknowledges that, pursuant to RCW 64.06.050(2), real estate licensees are not liable for inaccurate information provided by Seller, except to the extent that real estate licensees know of such inaccurate information.

   D. This information is for disclosure only and is not intended to be a part of the written agreement between the Buyer and Seller.

   E. Buyer (which term includes all persons signing the "Buyer's acceptance" portion of this disclosure statement below) has received a copy of this Disclosure Statement (including attachments, if any) bearing Seller's signature(s).

   F. If the house was built prior to 1978, Buyer acknowledges receipt of the pamphlet *Protect Your Family From Lead in Your Home.*

   DISCLOSURES CONTAINED IN THIS DISCLOSURE STATEMENT ARE PROVIDED BY SELLER BASED ON SELLER'S ACTUAL KNOWLEDGE OF THE PROPERTY AT THE TIME SELLER COMPLETES THIS DISCLOSURE. UNLESS BUYER AND SELLER OTHERWISE AGREE IN WRITING, BUYER SHALL HAVE THREE (3) BUSINESS DAYS FROM THE DAY SELLER OR SELLER'S AGENT DELIVERS THIS DISCLOSURE STATEMENT TO RESCIND THE AGREEMENT BY DELIVERING A SEPARATELY SIGNED WRITTEN STATEMENT OF RESCISSION TO SELLER OR SELLER'S AGENT. YOU MAY WAIVE THE RIGHT TO RESCIND PRIOR TO OR AFTER THE TIME YOU ENTER INTO A SALE AGREEMENT.

   BUYER HEREBY ACKNOWLEDGES RECEIPT OF A COPY OF THIS DISCLOSURE STATEMENT AND ACKNOWLEDGES THAT THE DISCLOSURES MADE HEREIN ARE THOSE OF THE SELLER ONLY, AND NOT OF ANY REAL ESTATE LICENSEE OR OTHER PARTY.

   Buyer ____________ Date ______ Buyer ____________ Date ______

2. **BUYER'S WAIVER OF RIGHT TO REVOKE OFFER**
Buyer has read and reviewed the Seller's responses to this Seller Disclosure Statement. Buyer approves this statement and waives Buyer's right to revoke Buyer's offer based on this disclosure.

   Buyer ____________ Date ______ Buyer ____________ Date ______

3. **BUYER'S WAIVER OF RIGHT TO RECEIVE COMPLETED SELLER DISCLOSURE STATEMENT**
Buyer has been advised of Buyer's right to receive a completed Seller Disclosure Statement. Buyer waives that right. However, if the answer to any of the questions in the section entitled "Environmental" would be "yes," Buyer may not waive the receipt of the "Environmental" section of the Seller Disclosure Statement.

   Buyer ____________ Date ______ Buyer ____________ Date ______

SELLER'S INITIALS ______ Date ______ SELLER'S INITIALS ______ Date ______

Specific warnings must be included in the purchase agreement or lease, along with signed statements from the parties acknowledging that the requirements of this law have been fulfilled. The signed acknowledgments must be kept for at least three years as proof of compliance.

Agent's Responsibilities. The law also imposes responsibilities on real estate agents in transactions involving pre-1978 housing. An agent is required to ensure that the seller or landlord knows his obligations under the disclosure law and fulfills those obligations. It is also the agent's responsibility to make sure that the purchase agreement or lease contains the required warnings, disclosures, and signatures.

Penalties. Sellers, landlords, or real estate agents who fail to fulfill their obligations under this law may be ordered to pay the buyer or tenant treble damages (three times the amount of any actual damages suffered by the buyer or tenant). Civil and criminal penalties may also be imposed. Although a real estate agent may be held liable for a seller or landlord's failure to provide the documents required by the law, the agent isn't responsible for information withheld by the seller or landlord.

Exemptions. Some transactions are exempt from the provisions of the lead-based paint disclosure law. This includes transactions involving zero-bedroom units (such as efficiency or studio apartments, dormitories, and room rentals); leases for less than 100 days; housing for the elderly or disabled (unless young children live there); rental housing that has been inspected by a certified inspector and found to be free of lead-based paint; and foreclosure sales.

Home Warranty Plans

Regardless of what information is disclosed in the seller disclosure statement, home buyers may choose to protect themselves against the risk of unexpected and potentially expensive repairs by purchasing a home warranty plan (also called a home protection plan). This is a short-term insurance policy, usually in effect only for the first few years of home ownership, that will reimburse the owner for the cost of repairing or replacing covered systems, components, or appliances, such as the heating or electrical system or the dishwasher. Sometimes a seller or a real estate agent offers to purchase home warranty coverage for prospective buyers to help sell the home.

Chapter Summary

1. A properly executed purchase and sale agreement is a binding contract that holds the parties to the terms of their agreement until all conditions have been fulfilled and the transaction is ready to close.
2. A real estate agent may prepare a purchase and sale agreement form if the agent is representing one of the parties in the transaction. The agent is limited to filling in the blanks on standard forms that have been drafted by attorneys. No separate fee for completing the documents may be charged. The agent preparing the purchase and sale agreement will be held to the same standard of care as an attorney.
3. The parties to a purchase and sale agreement are the buyer(s) and the seller(s); all parties must have capacity to contract. Everyone with an interest in the property must sign the agreement. Signatures of both spouses should be obtained in a transaction involving married parties.
4. Every purchase and sale agreement must have an adequate description of the property, specify the total purchase price and method of payment, set a closing date and date of possession, and state by what type of deed and in what condition title will be conveyed.
5. Because a purchase and sale agreement typically contains a "time is of the essence" clause, the closing date is a material term of the contract. Closing must take place on the date stated in the agreement, unless the parties agree in writing to an extension.
6. The purchase and sale agreement will include provisions concerning the earnest money deposit, including the amount and form of the deposit, and how it will be handled while the transaction is pending. In the event that the buyer defaults, the earnest money usually serves as liquidated damages.
7. A purchase and sale agreement often has a provision that makes it contingent on whether one or more events occur. It's common for a transaction to be contingent on financing, inspections, and/or the sale of the buyer's current home. Contingency clauses must clearly state the condition to be fulfilled, notification procedures, time limits, and the rights of the parties if the conditions are not met.
8. In Washington, a real property seller is required to give the buyer a disclosure statement providing information about the property based on the seller's own knowledge. The buyer can rescind the purchase and sale agreement within three business days after receiving the statement.

Key Terms

Purchase and sale agreement—A binding contract between a buyer and a seller of real property, setting forth the terms of the sale.

Earnest money—A sum the buyer gives to the seller when making an offer to purchase, as a sign of good faith; it is applied to the purchase price if the buyer goes through with the transaction, and forfeited to the seller if the buyer defaults.

Time is of the essence clause—A contract provision that imposes a legal duty to meet all of the deadlines in the contract.

Closing—When the transaction documents are recorded, the deed is delivered to the buyer, and the sale proceeds are made available for disbursement to the seller.

Contingency clause—A contract clause which provides that unless some specified event occurs, the contract is not binding.

Bump clause—A clause that allows the seller to demand that the buyer waive the "sale of the buyer's home" contingency or rescind the contract, if the seller receives another offer.

Home warranty plan—An insurance policy that reimburses a homeowner for expenses related to the failure of covered systems, components, or appliances on the property. Also called a home protection plan.

Chapter Quiz

1. **In most transactions, a purchase and sale agreement form is initially filled out as a/an:**
    a) option to purchase offered by a seller to a potential buyer
    b) buyer's offer to purchase, for submission to the property seller
    c) agent's preliminary proposal to a seller
    d) property owner's offer to sell on specified terms

2. **Which of the following may NOT fill out a purchase and sale agreement form?**
    a) An attorney at law
    b) A real estate agent representing one of the parties
    c) A real estate agent who is not a party and is not representing either party
    d) The seller

3. **A purchase and sale agreement should state:**
    a) only the essential terms of the sale, leaving other details to be worked out in the final contract
    b) the listing price as well as the purchase price
    c) the total purchase price, the method of payment, and the basic financing terms
    d) the seller's reasons for selling the property

4. **The purchase and sale agreement states that it will not be binding unless the buyer can obtain financing. This is a:**
    a) contingency clause
    b) defeasibility clause
    c) bump clause
    d) lender's clause

5. **An earnest money deposit is:**
    a) 10% of the purchase price, unless otherwise agreed
    b) usually treated as liquidated damages if the buyer defaults
    c) not applied to the purchase price if the transaction closes
    d) always returned if the sale falls through

6. **In a purchase and sale agreement, the phrase "time is of the essence" means that the:**
    a) contract provisions must be performed on or before the specified date(s)
    b) seller is in a hurry to sell the property
    c) buyer must obtain the necessary financing within 30 days
    d) closing must take place as soon as possible

7. **The closing date specified in the purchase and sale agreement:**
    a) is just an estimate, without real significance
    b) should allow time for all contingencies to be satisfied
    c) can be changed (if necessary) by the real estate agent without the parties' consent
    d) should be the same as the closing date set forth in the listing agreement

8. **A bump clause:**
    a) allows the closing to be delayed for 30 days at either party's option
    b) increases the purchase price at closing to reflect the inflation rate
    c) prevents the buyer from waiving any contingencies
    d) allows the seller to keep the property on the market after accepting the buyer's offer

9. **The purchase and sale agreement includes a financing contingency. If the buyer applies to lenders but cannot obtain financing on the specified terms:**
    a) the seller is required to finance the purchase
    b) the buyer is required to accept less favorable terms
    c) the buyer may terminate the transaction, and the seller will return the buyer's earnest money
    d) the transaction is terminated, and the seller is allowed to keep the earnest money

10. **When a contract includes a contingency clause:**
    a) the parties are required to make a good faith effort to fulfill the condition
    b) the contingency can be waived by the party for whose benefit it was included
    c) Both of the above
    d) Neither of the above

11. **If the seller is going to finance the purchase:**
    a) the financing section of the purchase and sale agreement can be left blank
    b) a copy of the financing documents the parties will be using should be attached to the purchase and sale agreement
    c) the real estate agent should oversee the finance arrangements
    d) the purchase and sale agreement should include a bump clause

12. Sam is purchasing a home from Hal, a married man. Hal assures Sam that title to the property is in Hal's name alone, and that Hal's wife, Rita, does not need to sign the purchase and sale agreement. Which of the following is true?

a) Sam should insist that both Hal and Rita sign the purchase and sale agreement
b) Sam should insist that both Hal and the listing agent sign the purchase and sale agreement
c) Only Hal can sign the purchase and sale agreement, not Rita
d) If only Hal signs the purchase and sale agreement, Sam should purchase additional title insurance

13. If the seller rejects the buyer's offer and presents the buyer with a counteroffer, the agent's best course of action would be to:

a) cross out the old terms on the purchase and sale agreement, fill in the new terms, and have the buyer initial the changes
b) cross out the old terms on the purchase and sale agreement, fill in the new terms, and have the seller initial the changes
c) use a counteroffer form, signed by the seller, to present the seller's counteroffer to the buyer
d) relay the counteroffer to the buyer by phone

14. An inspection contingency clause should include all of the following, except:

a) who is responsible for paying for the inspection
b) the method for notifying the seller of disapproval of the inspection report
c) the amount of the penalty the buyer must pay for rejecting the inspection report
d) the seller's option to perform the repairs or terminate the contract

15. The seller just accepted the buyer's offer to purchase their house. At this point, the buyer's interest in the property is called:

a) legal title
b) indivisible title
c) chattel title
d) equitable title

Chapter 10: *Principles of Real Estate Financing*

Financing—lending and borrowing money—is essential to the real estate industry. If financing weren't available, buyers would have to pay cash for their property, and far fewer people could afford to buy a home. Real estate agents sometimes help their clients and customers with the financing process, so they need a good understanding of the subject. This chapter starts with background information about real estate cycles, how the government influences real estate finance, and the secondary market. The chapter then goes on to explain how mortgages and other financing instruments work, the foreclosure process, and various types of mortgage loans. The process of applying for a mortgage loan is covered in Chapter 11.

Key Terms

Federal Reserve Board
Reserve Requirements
Discount Rate and Federal Funds Rate
Open Market Operations
Primary Market
Secondary Market
Promissory Note
Mortgage
Deed of Trust
Acceleration Clause
Alienation Clause
Assumption
Defeasance Clause
Satisfaction of Mortgage
Deed of Reconveyance
Land Contract

The Economics of Real Estate Finance

Most buyers need to borrow money in order to purchase real estate. Whether a particular buyer will be able to obtain a loan depends in part on their personal financial circumstances, and in part on national and local economic conditions. In this section, we're going to discuss real estate cycles and the government's role in the economy to help you understand the economic factors that affect real estate lending.

Real Estate Cycles

From a lender's point of view, a loan is an investment. A lender loans money in the expectation of a return on the investment. The borrower will repay the money borrowed, plus interest; the interest is the lender's return.

As a general rule, investors demand a higher return on risky investments than they do on comparatively safe ones. That holds true for loan transactions: the greater the risk that the borrower won't repay the loan, the higher the interest rate charged. But the interest rate a lender charges on a particular loan also depends on market forces and real estate cycles.

The real estate market is cyclical: it goes through active periods followed by slumps. These periodic shifts in the level of activity in the real estate market are called **real estate cycles**. Residential real estate cycles can be dramatic or moderate, and they can be local or regional. At any given time and place, there may be a buyer's market, where few people are buying and homes sit on the market for a long time, or there may be a seller's market, where many people are buying and homes sell rapidly.

These cycles obey the **law of supply and demand**. When demand for a product exceeds the supply (a seller's market), the price charged for the product tends to rise, and the price increase stimulates more production (provided the resources are available). As production increases, more of the demand is satisfied, until eventually the supply outstrips demand and a buyer's market is created. At that point, prices fall and production tapers off until demand catches up with supply, and the cycle begins again.

Real estate cycles are caused in part by changes in the supply of and demand for mortgage loan funds. The supply of mortgage funds depends on how much money investors have available and choose to invest in real estate loans. The demand for mortgage funds depends on how many people want to purchase real estate and can afford to borrow enough money to do so.

Interest rates represent the price of mortgage funds. They affect supply and demand, and they also fluctuate in response to changes in supply and demand. Interest is sometimes called "the cost of money."

In an ideal economy, supply and demand are more or less in balance. In reality, the forces affecting supply and demand often change, and so does the balance between them. But as long as supply and demand are reasonably close, the economy functions well. When supply far exceeds demand, or vice versa, the economy can suffer.

Real estate cycles can be moderated, though not eliminated, by factors that either help keep interest rates under control or directly affect the supply of mortgage funds. Federal economic policy plays a key role in moderating real estate cycles.

Interest Rates and Federal Policy

Economic stability is directly tied to the supply of and demand for money. If money is plentiful and can be borrowed cheaply (that is, interest rates are low), increased economic activity is often the result. On the other hand, if funds are scarce or expensive to borrow, an economic slowdown will result.

Thus, manipulation of the availability and cost of money can help achieve economic balance. The federal government influences real estate finance, as well as the rest of the U.S. economy, through its **fiscal policy** and its **monetary policy**.

Fiscal Policy. Fiscal policy refers to how the federal government manages its money. Congress and the president determine fiscal policy through tax legislation and the federal budget. The U.S. Treasury implements fiscal policy by managing tax revenues, expenditures, and the national debt.

When the federal government spends more money than it takes in, a shortfall called the **federal deficit** results. It is the Treasury's responsibility to borrow enough money to cover the deficit. It does this by issuing interest-bearing securities that are backed by the U.S. government and purchased by private investors. These securities include Treasury bills, notes, and bonds. Investors often choose these government securities over other possible investments because they are comparatively low-risk.

When the government borrows money, it competes with private industry for available investment funds. Economists and politicians debate what impact this has on the economy. According to some, by draining the number of dollars in circulation, heavy government borrowing increases interest rates and may lead to an economic slowdown; the greater the federal deficit, the more money the government needs to borrow, and the greater the effect on the economy. Others argue that the federal deficit has little effect on interest rates and economic growth.

The government's taxation policies also affect the supply of and demand for money. As with the deficit, the effect of taxation on the economy is controversial. Basically, when taxes are low, taxpayers have more money to lend and invest. When taxes are high, taxpayers not only have less money to lend or invest, they also may be more likely to invest what money they do have in tax-exempt securities instead of taxable investments. Since rental real estate and real estate mortgages are taxable investments, this may have a significant impact on the real estate finance industry.

Monetary Policy. Monetary policy refers to the direct control the federal government exerts over the money supply and interest rates. The main goal of monetary policy is to keep the U.S. economy healthy.

Monetary policy is determined by the **Federal Reserve**, commonly called "the Fed." The Federal Reserve System, established in 1913, is the nation's central banking system. It is governed by the Federal Reserve Board and the board's chairman. It has 12 districts nationwide, with a Federal Reserve Bank in each district. Thousands of commercial banks across the country are members of the Federal Reserve.

The Fed regulates commercial banks and provides financial services to member banks. But setting and implementing the government's monetary policy is perhaps the Fed's most important function.

The major objectives of monetary policy are high employment, economic growth, price stability, interest rate stability, and stability in financial and foreign exchange markets. Although these goals are interrelated, we are most concerned with the Federal Reserve policies that affect the availability and cost of borrowed money (interest rates), since those have the most direct impact on the real estate industry.

The Fed uses three tools to implement its monetary policy and influence the economy:

- key interest rates,
- reserve requirements, and
- open market operations.

Key Interest Rates. The Fed has considerable influence over two interest rates, the federal funds rate and the discount rate. These are the interest rates charged when a bank borrows money, either from another bank or from a Federal Reserve Bank. When the Fed works to raise or lower the interest rates that its member banks have to pay, the banks will typically raise or lower the interest rates they charge their customers. Lower interest rates tend to stimulate the economy, and higher rates tend to slow it down. (The Fed may increase rates if it decides that a slower pace is desirable to keep price inflation in check.)

Reserve Requirements. Commercial banks are required to maintain a certain percentage of their customers' funds on deposit at the Federal Reserve Bank. These reserve requirements help prevent financial panics (a "run on the bank") by assuring depositors that their funds are safe and accessible; the bank will always have enough money available to meet unusual customer demand.

Reserve requirements also give the Fed some control over economic growth. By increasing reserve requirements, the Fed reduces the amount of money banks have available to lend, which tends to push interest rates up, making borrowing expensive and putting a brake on growth. On the other hand, a reduction in reserve requirements frees up more money for lending, leading to lower interest rates and promoting business growth.

Open Market Operations. The Fed also buys and sells government securities; these transactions are called open market operations. They are the Fed's chief method of controlling the money supply, and, indirectly, controlling inflation and interest rates. Only money in circulation is considered part of the money supply, so actions by the Fed that put money into circulation increase the money supply, and actions that take money out of circulation decrease it.

When the Fed buys government securities from an investor, it increases the money supply, because the money that the Fed uses to pay for the securities goes into circulation. When the Fed sells government securities to an investor, the money that the buyer uses to pay for the securities is taken out of circulation, decreasing the money supply. Interest rates tend to fall with increases in the money supply, and to rise with decreases in the money supply.

Other Agencies that Affect Finance. Aside from the Federal Reserve, there are a number of other federal agencies and programs that have an impact on real estate finance.

Federal Home Loan Bank System. The Federal Home Loan Bank System (FHLB) is made up of twelve regional, privately owned wholesale banks. The banks loan funds to FHLB members—local community lenders—and accept their mortgages and other loans as collateral. The FHLB, which is overseen by the Federal Housing Finance Agency, is active in promoting affordable housing.

Federal Deposit Insurance Corporation. The FDIC was created in 1933 to insure bank deposits against bank insolvency. If a bank or other lending institution fails, the FDIC will step in to protect the institution's customers against the loss of their deposited funds, up to specified limits.

HUD. The Department of Housing and Urban Development (HUD) is a federal cabinet-level department. Among many other things, HUD's responsibilities include urban renewal projects, public housing, FHA-insured loan programs, and enforcement of the federal Fair Housing Act (see Chapter 15). Ginnie Mae (discussed later in this chapter) and the Federal Housing Administration (discussed in Chapter 11) are both part of HUD.

Rural Housing Service. The Rural Housing Service is an agency within the Department of Agriculture. To help people living in rural areas build, purchase, or improve their homes, the Rural Housing Service makes loans and grants; it also guarantees loans made by lending institutions. In addition, it finances the construction of affordable housing in rural areas.

Real Estate Finance Markets

There are two "markets" that supply the funds available for real estate loans: the primary market and the secondary market. In addition to using monetary policy to control the money supply and interest rates, another way in which the federal government has helped moderate the severity and duration of real estate cycles is by establishing a strong, nationwide secondary market. The secondary market limits the adverse effects of local economic circumstances on real estate lending. We'll look first at the primary market, then at the secondary market.

Primary Market

The **primary market** is the market in which mortgage lenders make loans to home buyers. When buyers apply for a loan to finance their purchase, they're seeking a loan in the primary market.

Originally, the primary market was entirely local. It was made up of the various lending institutions in a community—the local banks and savings and loan associations. (Today the primary market is considerably more complicated, since there are interstate lenders, online lenders, nationwide mortgage companies, and so on.) The traditional source of funds for the primary market was the savings of individuals and businesses in the local area. A bank or savings and loan would use the savings deposits of members of the local community to make mortgage loans to members of that same community.

The local economy has a significant effect on the amount of deposited funds available to a lender, and on the local demand for them. When employment is high, consumers are more likely to borrow money for cars, vacations, or homes. Businesses expand and borrow to finance their growth. At the same time, fewer people are saving. This decrease in deposits means that less local money is available for lending, making it difficult to meet the increased demand for loans. On the other hand, when an area is in an economic slump, consumers are more inclined to save than to borrow. Businesses suspend plans for growth. The result is a drop in the demand for money, and the local lending institutions' deposits grow.

From a lender's point of view, either too little or too much money on deposit is cause for concern. In the first case, with little money to lend, a lender's primary source of income is affected. In the second case, the lender is paying interest to its depositors, and if it is unable to reinvest the deposited funds quickly, it will lose money.

The solution to these problems has been for lenders to look beyond their local area. When local savings deposits are low, a lender needs to get funds from other parts of the country to lend locally.

When local demand for loans is low, a lender needs to send funds to other parts of the country where demand is higher. This is where the secondary market comes in. The secondary market makes it easy for lenders to transfer funds around the country.

Secondary Market

The **secondary market** is a national market. In the secondary market, private investors, government agencies, and government-sponsored enterprises buy and sell mortgages secured by real estate in all parts of the United States.

Buying and Selling Loans. Mortgage loans can be bought and sold just like other investments—stocks or bonds, for example. The value of a loan is influenced by the rate of return on the loan compared to the market rate of return, as well as the degree of risk associated with the loan (the likelihood of default). Investors generally buy mortgage loans at a discount. For example, a loan with $100,000 in remaining payments might sell for $80,000.

The availability of funds in the primary market (a local lender's ability to lend money to prospective borrowers) now depends a great deal on the existence of the national secondary market. As explained above, a particular lender may have either too much or too little money to lend, depending on conditions in the local economy. It's the secondary market that provides balance by transferring funds from areas where there is an excess to areas where there is a shortage. When local demand for funds is high, lenders can take loans they've already made, sell them on the secondary market, and use the proceeds of those sales to make more loans. When local demand for loan funds is low, lenders can use their excess funds to purchase loans on the secondary market.

The secondary market has a stabilizing effect on local mortgage markets. Lenders are willing to commit themselves to long-term real estate loans even when local funds are scarce, because they can raise more funds by liquidating their loans on the secondary market.

Fannie Mae and Freddie Mac. The federal government has played a central role in developing the secondary market for residential mortgage loans, primarily by establishing two large-scale loan buyers, the Federal National Mortgage Association (FNMA) and the Federal Home Loan Mortgage Corporation (FHLMC). You're more likely to hear them referred to as Fannie Mae and Freddie Mac. They are **government-sponsored enterprises** (GSEs) regulated by the Federal Housing Finance Agency.

Congress created Fannie Mae as a federal agency in 1938, at the end of the Great Depression, in order to provide a secondary market for FHA-insured loans. It was eventually reorganized as a private enterprise, but it is still chartered by the federal government.

Congress created Freddie Mac in 1970. Its original purpose was to assist savings and loan associations (which had been hit particularly hard by a recession) by buying their conventional loans.

Both Fannie Mae and Freddie Mac now buy large numbers of conventional, FHA, and VA mortgage loans from primary market lenders, and then issue securities using the loans as collateral ("securitizing" the loans). They sell these **mortgage-backed securities** to investors. As the underlying loans are repaid by the borrowers, the GSEs pass the payments through to the investors, providing a return on their investment.

Fig. 10.1 By selling the loans they make, lenders obtain money to make more loans

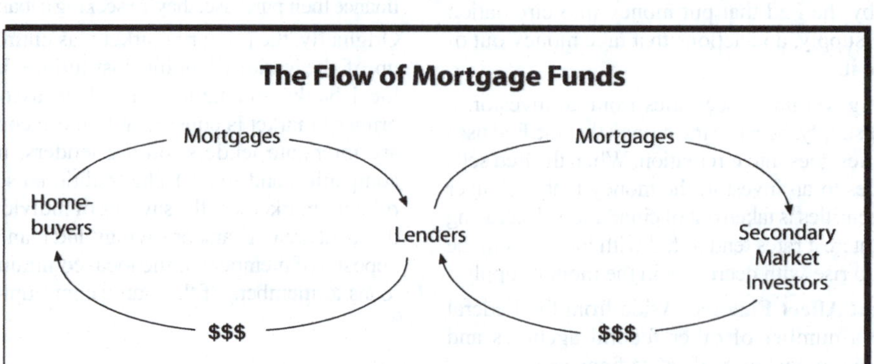

Of course, Fannie Mae and Freddie Mac don't want to buy loans that carry a high risk of default. To prevent that, the enterprises have established their own underwriting standards. **Underwriting standards** are the criteria used to evaluate a loan applicant and the property offered as security, to determine if the loan would be a good investment or would involve too much risk. Lenders may apply their own underwriting standards when they make loans, but they generally can't sell the loans to Fannie Mae or Freddie Mac unless the loans conform to the GSE underwriting standards. Because most lenders want to have the option of selling their loans on the secondary market, the majority of conventional mortgage loans in the U.S. are now made in accordance with the GSE standards. (Underwriting standards are discussed in more detail in Chapter 11.)

Another entity involved in the secondary market for residential mortgages is the Government National Mortgage Association (GNMA, or **Ginnie Mae**). In addition to various other functions, Ginnie Mae guarantees mortgage-backed securities secured by FHA or VA loans. It's a federal agency, part of HUD, not a government-sponsored enterprise.

Real Estate Finance Documents

Now let's turn to the legal aspects of real estate financing. Once a buyer has found a lender willing to finance their purchase on acceptable terms, the buyer must sign the finance documents. The legal documents used in conjunction with most real estate loans are a promissory note and a security instrument, which is either a mortgage or a deed of trust.

We'll look first at promissory notes, then at security instruments and foreclosure procedures, and then at the land contract, a document used in some seller-financed transactions.

Promissory Notes

A **promissory note** is a written promise to repay a debt. One person loans another money, and the other signs a promissory note, promising to repay the loan (plus interest, in most cases). The borrower who signs the note is called the **maker**, and the lender is called the **payee**.

Basic Provisions. A promissory note states the loan amount (the **principal**), the amount of the payments, when and how the payments are to be made, and the maturity date—when the loan is to be repaid in full. The note also states the interest rate, and whether it is fixed or variable. (In some situations, the state **usury** law may prohibit the interest rate charged from exceeding a specified maximum.)

A promissory note used in a real estate transaction does not need to contain a legal description of the property, because the note concerns only the debt, not the property. The legal description is instead included in the security instrument.

The note usually explains the consequences of a failure to repay the loan as agreed. Real estate lenders often protect themselves with late charges, acceleration clauses, and similar provisions; these will be discussed later in this chapter.

Types of Notes. There are various types of promissory notes, classified according to the way the principal and interest is paid off. With a **straight note** (also called a **term note**), the periodic payments are interest only, and the full amount of the principal is due in a lump sum (called a **balloon payment**) when the loan term ends.

With an **installment note**, the periodic payments include part of the principal as well as interest. If the installment note is **fully amortized**, the periodic payments are enough to pay off the entire loan, both principal and interest, by the end of the term. (Amortization is discussed in Chapter 11.)

Fig. 10.2 Promissory Note

Promissory Note

FOR VALUE RECEIVED, Maker promises to pay to the order of
______________________________, or to Bearer,

THE SUM OF $__________________, paid as follows:
$_________ OR MORE per month starting ____________,
including interest at the fixed rate of ______% per annum, with the final payment due on ___________.

ACCELERATION: In the event of default, Payee or Bearer can declare all sums due and payable at once.

____
Maker/Borrower

Date: _________________

Whether the payments are interest-only or amortized, the interest paid on a real estate loan is virtually always **simple interest**. This means it is computed on the remaining principal balance.

Negotiable Instrument. A promissory note is usually a **negotiable instrument**, which means that the payee (the lender) has the option of assigning the debt to someone else by endorsing the note. (The person to whom the note is assigned may be referred to as an **assignee**.)

A note is endorsed to transfer the right to payment to another party in the same way that a check is endorsed. A check is another example of a negotiable instrument.

Security Instruments

When someone borrows money to buy real estate, in addition to signing a promissory note in favor of the lender, they are also required to sign a **security instrument**. As we said earlier, the security instrument is either a mortgage or a deed of trust.

Relationship Between Note and Security Instrument. It's important to understand the relationship between the promissory note and the security instrument.

The promissory note is the borrower's binding promise to repay the loan. The security instrument is a contract that makes the real property collateral for the loan; it secures the loan by creating a lien on the property. If the borrower doesn't repay the loan as agreed, the security instrument gives the lender the right to foreclose on the property.

A promissory note can be enforced even if it is not accompanied by a security instrument. If the borrower does not repay as agreed, then the lender can file a lawsuit and obtain a judgment against the defaulting borrower. But without a security instrument, the lender might have no way of collecting the judgment. For example, the borrower may have already sold all of their property, leaving nothing for the lender (now the judgment creditor) to obtain a lien against.

Title Theory vs. Lien Theory. Historically, when real property was used as security for a loan, the lender required the borrower to transfer title to the lender until the loan was repaid, although the borrower remained in possession of the property. When title is transferred only as collateral, unaccompanied by possessory rights, it is called **legal title**, bare title, or naked title. The property rights the borrower retains (without legal title) are referred to as **equitable title** or equitable rights.

Fig. 10.3 Purpose of a security instrument

Security Instrument
Mortgage or Deed of Trust

- Makes the borrower's property collateral for the loan
- Gives the lender the power to foreclose if the debt is not repaid

Today, a handful of states (called "title theory" states) classify the signing of a mortgage or a deed of trust as a transfer of legal title to the lender or trustee. Most states (including Washington) follow "lien theory" instead. In these states, a mortgage or a deed of trust only creates a lien against the property; it doesn't transfer title. The borrower retains full title to the property throughout the term of the loan, and the lender simply has the right to foreclose on the lien if the borrower defaults.

Note that while the license exam might include a question that involves title theory and lien theory, the distinction between them has lost practical importance. Whichever theory applies, the borrower will lose the property if the loan isn't repaid.

Mortgage vs. Deed of Trust. Now let's consider the two types of real property security instruments, mortgages and deeds of trust. Both are contracts in which a property owner gives someone else a security interest in the property, usually as collateral for a loan. The most important difference between a mortgage and a deed of trust concerns the procedures for foreclosure if the borrower defaults. We will discuss the foreclosure process later in this chapter.

There are two parties to a mortgage: the **mortgagor** and the **mortgagee.** The mortgagor is the property owner and borrower. The mortgagee is the lender.

A deed of trust (sometimes called a trust deed) has three parties: the **trustor** or **grantor** (the borrower), the **beneficiary** (the lender), and the **trustee.** The trustee is a neutral third party who will handle the foreclosure process, if necessary.

Foreclosure can be considerably easier with a deed of trust than with a mortgage, which makes deeds of trust popular with lenders. In Washington and a number of other states, deeds of trust are now much more widely used than mortgages.

Note that the terms "mortgage" and "mortgage loan" are often used to refer to any type of loan secured by real property, whether the security instrument actually used in the transaction is a mortgage or a deed of trust.

Recording. Whether it's a mortgage or a deed of trust, the lender should have the security instrument recorded immediately after the loan is made. It doesn't have to be recorded to create a valid lien on the property, but without recording the public won't have constructive notice of the lien. Other parties who acquire an interest in the property without notice of the lender's security interest won't be subject to it, and subsequent liens will have priority over the lender's lien.

Provisions in Finance Documents

There is no standard mortgage or deed of trust form, but any security instrument must contain certain provisions and should contain certain others. Many of the following provisions will be found in nearly every mortgage or deed of trust; some of them may also appear in the promissory note. In a few cases (noted below), there is a distinction between the type of provision found in a mortgage and the type found in a deed of trust.

Mortgaging or Granting Clause. Every security instrument must state that the borrower is mortgaging or (in a deed of trust) granting the property to the lender as security for the loan. This is the fundamental purpose of the security instrument, and the borrower must agree to it in the document.

Property Description. Like a deed or any other document that transfers an interest in real estate, the security instrument must contain a complete and unambiguous description of the collateral property.

Taxes and Insurance. Security instruments invariably require the borrower to pay general real estate taxes, special assessments, and hazard insurance premiums when due. If the borrower allows the taxes to become delinquent or the insurance to lapse, the value of the lender's security interest could be severely diminished—by tax lien foreclosure or by a fire, for example.

Acceleration Clause. An **acceleration clause** states that if the borrower defaults, the lender has the option of declaring the entire loan balance (all the principal still owed) due and payable immediately. Sometimes this is referred to as "calling the note." If the borrower fails to pay the balance as demanded, the lender can sue to enforce the promissory note or foreclose on the lien.

An acceleration clause is likely to appear in both the promissory note and the security instrument. Acceleration can be triggered by failing to make the loan payments as agreed, or by some other breach, such as failing to keep the property insured.

Alienation Clause. An **alienation clause** is also called a **due-on-sale clause**. This provision gives the lender the right to accelerate the loan—to demand immediate payment of the entire loan balance, as described above—if the borrower sells the property or otherwise alienates an interest in it. (Alienation refers to any transfer of an interest in real estate. See Chapter 3.) An alienation clause does not prohibit the sale of the property, but allows the lender to force the borrower to pay off the loan if the property is sold without the lender's approval. Unlike an acceleration clause, an alienation clause kicks in even though no violation of the security agreement has occurred (selling the property doesn't constitute a breach).

Whether or not there's an alienation clause in the security instrument, a sale of the property doesn't extinguish the lender's lien. If the loan isn't paid off at closing, the buyer will take title subject to the lien. In some cases, the buyer may assume the loan, taking over the payments; but in any case, the lien remains.

In an **assumption**, the borrower sells the security property to a buyer who agrees to take legal responsibility for the loan and pay it off according to its terms. The buyer becomes primarily liable to the lender for repayment of the loan, but the seller (the original borrower) retains secondary liability in case the buyer defaults.

By contrast, when a buyer takes title subject to an existing mortgage or deed of trust without assuming it, the original borrower remains fully liable for the debt. The buyer is not personally liable to the lender, although in case of default the lender can still foreclose.

Even though the sale of the property doesn't extinguish the mortgage or deed of trust lien, lenders prefer to have the opportunity to approve or reject a prospective buyer. Thus, most mortgages and deeds of trust include an alienation clause. When a lender evaluates a buyer and concludes that they are creditworthy, the lender may agree to an assumption of the loan. The lender will usually charge an assumption fee, and may also raise the interest rate on the loan. In most cases, the lender will release the original borrower from any further liability. (When the original borrower is released from liability, it's technically a novation—see Chapter 6—but it's still usually called an assumption.)

A buyer assuming a loan should ask the lender to provide a **certificate of reduction**, which states the principal balance as of the assumption date.

Late Payment Penalty. If the lender wants to impose a penalty for late payment, the amount and conditions under which the penalty can be imposed must be clearly stated. In most cases, the borrower is allowed a grace period; in other words, a late payment penalty is charged only after the payment is a certain number of days overdue.

Prepayment Penalty. Many lenders do not impose any restrictions on prepayment. This is usually addressed in the promissory note; for example, a note might call for a payment of "$500.00 or more." The words "or more" indicate that prepayment is allowed.

Some notes may contain a provision that allows prepayment of a certain percentage of the principal each year, but imposes a penalty if the borrower prepays more than that percentage. For example, a note might state, "The borrower may prepay up to 20% of the original loan amount during any 12-month period without penalty. If the borrower prepays more than 20%, a prepayment fee equal to six months' interest on the excess will be charged."

Notes that contain prepayment penalties usually only impose them for a certain period of time, such as the first three years of the loan term.

Prepayment penalties are prohibited in FHA and VA loans, and in loans that will be sold to Fannie Mae or Freddie Mac. They are also prohibited by federal law in adjustable-rate mortgages and high-cost loans. Washington law limits prepayment penalties too, but only for adjustable-rate mortgages.

Most mortgages don't have prepayment penalty provisions, although some subprime loans contain them. A mortgage loan without a prepayment penalty is an **open mortgage**.

Subordination Clause. Occasionally a security instrument includes a **subordination clause**, which states that the instrument will have lower lien priority than another mortgage or deed of trust to be executed in the future. The clause makes it possible for a later security instrument to have a higher priority position—usually first lien position—even though this earlier security instrument was executed and recorded first.

Subordination clauses are common in mortgages and deeds of trust that secure purchase loans for unimproved land, when the borrower is planning to get a construction loan later on.

Deed in Lieu

Fig. 10.4 Comparison of Mortgages and Deeds of Trust

Security Instruments	
Mortgage	**Deed of Trust**
• Mortgagor and mortgagee • Judicial foreclosure • Equitable redemption before decree of foreclosure • Statutory redemption after sheriff's sale • Deficiency judgment allowed (subject to limitations)	• Trustor, beneficiary, and trustee • Nonjudicial foreclosure • Reinstatement before trustee's sale • No post-sale redemption • No deficiency judgment

The construction lender will demand first lien position for its loan because of the risk of loss associated with uncompleted work. Lien priority is ordinarily determined by recording date ("first in time is first in right"), but the subordination clause in the earlier land loan allows the later construction loan to have first lien position.

Defeasance Clause. A **defeasance clause** states that the borrower will regain title and the security instrument will be canceled when the debt has been paid.

When a debt secured by a mortgage has been paid in full, a document called a **satisfaction of mortgage** is used to release the mortgage lien.

The lender must deliver the satisfaction of mortgage to the borrower after the final loan payment has been made. The mortgage will be a cloud on the borrower's title until they have the satisfaction recorded.

When a debt secured by a deed of trust has been paid in full, removing the lien is handled a little differently: the lender directs the trustee to give the borrower a **deed of reconveyance**, also called a reconveyance deed. Like a satisfaction of mortgage, the deed of reconveyance is recorded to clear the borrower's title. Either a satisfaction of mortgage or a deed of reconveyance may be referred to as a **lien release.**

Foreclosure Procedures

If the borrower doesn't repay a secured loan as agreed, the lender may foreclose on the property and collect the debt from the proceeds of a forced sale. Establishing the lender's right to foreclose is the basic purpose of a security instrument. There are two main forms of foreclosure: judicial and nonjudicial. As a general rule, mortgages are foreclosed judicially, and deeds of trust are foreclosed nonjudicially.

Judicial Foreclosure. As the term suggests, a judicial foreclosure is carried out through the court system. Upon default, the lender files a lawsuit against the borrower in a court in the county where the collateral property is located. If there are **junior lienholders** (creditors whose liens have lower priority than the mortgage being foreclosed on), the foreclosing lender should make sure they are notified of the lawsuit.

Junior liens are ordinarily extinguished by the foreclosure of a senior lien, but only if the lienholder received notice of the foreclosure action.

When the complaint is heard in court, in the absence of unusual circumstances the judge will issue a **decree of foreclosure**, ordering the property to be sold to satisfy the debt. The sale takes the form of an auction, and since it is usually the county sheriff's office that conducts the auction, it is referred to as a **sheriff's sale.** The property is sold to the highest bidder, who is given a **certificate of sale.**

Between the time the lawsuit is filed and the actual sale of the property, the borrower is entitled to redeem the property by paying off the mortgage debt in full, plus any costs incurred. This is referred to as the **equitable redemption** period. After the sale, the borrower is given an additional period to redeem the property, which is called the **statutory redemption** period. In Washington, the statutory redemption period is one year, unless the lender has waived their rights to a deficiency judgment.

In that case, the statutory redemption period is eight months. A **deficiency judgment** is a judgment against the borrower for the difference between the debt and the proceeds of the sheriff's sale, if the proceeds weren't sufficient to pay off the debt in full.

In some cases, either by law or by the terms of the loan agreement, the lender cannot seek a deficiency judgment even if the foreclosure sale proceeds do not completely pay off the debt. This is called a **non-recourse mortgage.**

During the statutory redemption period, the holder of the certificate of sale does not have title to the property. If the borrower doesn't redeem the property, a **sheriff's deed** is provided to the holder of the certificate of sale when the redemption period expires. At that point, the borrower has no further claim to the property.

The redemption period makes bidding at a judicial foreclosure sale unappealing to many investors; they don't want to wait so long to gain title to the property. For this reason, there are often no outside bidders at a judicial foreclosure sale, and the lender acquires the property by bidding the amount the borrower owes.

When there are outside bidders at the auction and if real estate prices are rising, the proceeds from the sale might exceed the amount necessary to satisfy all valid liens against the property.

If so, the surplus belongs to the foreclosed owner (the borrower).

Nonjudicial Foreclosure. Every deed of trust has a **power of sale clause.** If the trustor (the borrower) defaults, this provision authorizes the trustee to sell the property through a process known as nonjudicial foreclosure. Without having to obtain a decree of foreclosure from a court, the trustee can conduct an auction called a trustee's sale and use the sale proceeds to pay off the debt owed to the beneficiary. As with a sheriff's sale, if the trustee's sale results in a surplus, the excess amount belongs to the foreclosed owner.

State law spells out the procedures for nonjudicial foreclosure. These procedures give the borrower an opportunity to **cure** the default and **reinstate** the loan. First, the trustee must give a **notice of default** to the borrower. Generally, 30 days after the notice of default, the trustee issues a **notice of sale** to the borrower and also records a notice of sale in the county where the property is located. The notice of sale must also be sent to junior lienholders and to anyone who recorded a request for notice.

Until shortly before the sale, if the borrower pays the lender the delinquent amount plus late charges and costs incurred, the default is cured. The foreclosure is terminated and the loan is reinstated. This is very different from the right of equitable redemption in a judicial foreclosure, where the borrower has to pay off the entire debt (not just the delinquent amount) in order to prevent foreclosure.

Many lenders prefer a deed of trust to a mortgage because it enables them to bypass court proceedings, which are often slow. Also, the trustee's sale is final; there is no statutory redemption period afterward. The successful bidder at a trustee's sale is given a **trustee's deed.** The disadvantage of a deed of trust from the lender's point of view is that after nonjudicial foreclosure there is no right to a deficiency judgment. If the proceeds of the trustee's sale are insufficient to satisfy the debt, the lender takes a loss; the lender can't sue the borrower to make up the deficiency.

Alternatives to Foreclosure

There are three alternatives to foreclosure for a defaulting homeowner: loan workouts, deeds in lieu of foreclosure, and short sales. A lender might agree to one of these alternatives to save time, money, and aggravation.

Loan Workouts. A loan workout from the lender can sometimes be the simplest way to avoid a foreclosure. Some workouts involve a repayment plan—an adjustment in the repayment schedule, often referred to as a forbearance. The borrower gets extra time to make up a missed payment or is allowed to skip a few payments. (The skipped payments are added on to the repayment period.)

If a forbearance wouldn't solve the problem (for instance, if the payment amount is about to increase dramatically, far beyond the borrower's means), the lender may agree to modify the terms of the loan. A **loan modification** might involve changing an ARM to a fixed-rate mortgage (to prevent it from resetting to a higher rate), reducing the interest rate, or reducing the amount of principal owed.

Deed in Lieu of Foreclosure. A defaulting borrower who can't negotiate a loan workout might offer to give the lender a deed in lieu of foreclosure, sometimes called a **deed in lieu.** The deed in lieu transfers title from the borrower to the lender; this satisfies the debt and stops foreclosure proceedings. The borrower should make sure that the lender won't have the right to sue for a deficiency judgment if the eventual sale of the property (by the lender) does not cover the full amount owed.

The lender takes title subject to any other liens that encumber the property. Thus, before accepting a deed in lieu, the lender will determine what other liens have attached to the property since the original loan was made.

Short Sales. Another alternative to foreclosure is a short sale. In a short sale, the owner sells the house for whatever it will bring (something "short" of the amount owed because the home's market value has decreased). The lender receives the sale proceeds and, in return, releases the borrower from the debt. As when arranging a deed in lieu, the borrower will want to avoid the possibility of a deficiency judgment. State law requires the lender to send a notice informing the borrower whether it waives or reserves the right to collect a deficiency judgment.

The existence of secondary liens won't necessarily prevent a lender from approving a short sale. This is because—unlike with a deed in lieu—the lender isn't taking responsibility for the property or its liens. However, the presence of multiple liens will complicate matters, since all of the lienholders must consent to the sale. The junior lienholders (or creditors) aren't likely to get much, if anything, from a short sale and may not be willing to approve the transaction. In this situation, a foreclosure may be inevitable.

A potential drawback to a short sale is that the loan amount forgiven by the lender may be treated as taxable income (although Congress has temporarily suspended this rule for mortgage loans secured by the taxpayer's principal residence). The written-off amount is reported on a 1099 form.

Land Contracts

Most real estate buyers finance their purchases with a loan from an institutional lender. But some transactions are financed by the seller; the seller extends credit to the buyer, accepting a downpayment and arranging to be paid over time, instead of requiring full payment at closing.

In certain cases a seller offers more favorable terms than institutional lenders are offering (such as an exceptionally low interest rate), in order to attract a wider range of potential buyers and obtain a higher price for the property.

In a seller-financed transaction, the seller may ask the buyer to execute a mortgage or a deed of trust, just like an institutional lender. Sellers also have the option of using a third type of security instrument: the **land contract**, also called a contract for deed, installment sales contract, real estate contract, or contract of sale.

The parties to a land contract are the **vendor** (the seller) and the **vendee** (the buyer). The vendee agrees to pay the purchase price (plus interest) in installments over a specified number of years.

The vendee takes possession of the property right away, but the vendor retains legal title until the full price has been paid. In the meantime, the vendee has equitable title to the property. When the contract is finally paid off, the vendor delivers the deed to the vendee.

The vendee should have the contract recorded promptly after signing it, to protect their equitable interest. While the contract is being paid off, the vendee is usually required to pay the property taxes and keep the property insured. The vendor may use the legal title to the property for any purpose that does not impair the vendee's interest. The vendor is not allowed to encumber the property in any way that would prevent the transfer of clear title to the vendee as agreed.

Forfeiture. If a vendee defaults on a land contract, the vendor can foreclose judicially. Alternatively, the vendor may choose to declare a **forfeiture**, which is a remedy available only in connection with a land contract. In a forfeiture, the vendor terminates the contract without having to go to court, and without having to refund the payments the vendee has made. The vendor ends up with full ownership of the property (free of the vendee's equitable interest) and the vendee has nothing. However, Washington law allows this only if there is a forfeiture clause in the contract (nearly all land contracts have one) and the contract is recorded. The law also gives a vendee who has substantial equity in the property some protection against forfeiture.

Types of Mortgage Loans

You will often hear "mortgage" or "deed of trust" coupled with an adjective that serves to describe the particular function of the security instrument or the circumstances in which it is used. For example, a "construction mortgage" is a mortgage used to secure a construction loan; a "blanket mortgage" is one that secures a loan with two or more parcels of property as collateral. Below are explanations of some of the most common of these terms. For the most part, we will use the term "mortgage" here, rather than the cumbersome phrase "mortgage or deed of trust." In each case, however, a deed of trust could be (and in Washington, usually is) used instead of a mortgage.

First Mortgage. A first mortgage is simply the security instrument that holds first lien position; it has the highest lien priority of any security instrument. A second mortgage is one that holds second lien position, and so on.

Senior and Junior Mortgages. Any mortgage that has a higher lien position than another is called a senior mortgage in relation to that other one, which is called a junior mortgage. A first mortgage is senior to a second mortgage; a second mortgage is junior to a first mortgage, but senior to a third.

As was explained in Chapter 4, lien priority is important in the event of a foreclosure, because the sale proceeds are used to pay off the first lien first. If any money remains, the second lien is paid; then the third is paid, and so on, until the money is exhausted. Obviously, it is much better to be in first lien position than in third.

Purchase Loan. A purchase loan is a mortgage loan that finances the purchase of the property that is the collateral for the loan. A buyer borrows money to buy property and gives the lender a mortgage on that same property to secure the loan. (Home equity loans and refinancing, described later in the chapter, are examples of mortgage loans that are not purchase loans.)

Purchase Money Mortgage. This term is used in two ways. Occasionally it's used interchangeably with "purchase loan," to mean a loan used to finance the purchase of the property that's the collateral for the loan. Usually, though, "purchase money mortgage" is used more narrowly, to mean a mortgage that a buyer gives to a seller in a seller-financed transaction. Instead of paying the full price in cash at closing, the buyer gives the seller a mortgage on the property and pays the price off in installments. In such a situation, the seller is said to "take back" or "carry back" the mortgage.

> **Example:** The sellers have agreed to finance the sale of their house by carrying back a mortgage. The sales price is $460,000. The buyers make a $50,000 downpayment and sign a mortgage document and a promissory note in favor of the sellers for the remaining $410,000. The buyers will pay the sellers in monthly installments at 5% interest over the next 15 years, and the sellers will have a lien against the house until the financing is paid off. This is a purchase money mortgage.

In this narrower sense, a purchase money mortgage is sometimes called a **soft money mortgage**, because the borrower receives credit from the seller instead of actual cash. (In contrast, when private investors lend a buyer cash to buy or develop a commercial property, it may be called a **hard money mortgage**.)

Budget Mortgage. The monthly payment on a budget mortgage includes not just principal and interest on the loan, but one-twelfth of the year's property taxes and hazard insurance premiums as well. The lender holds the tax and insurance payments in a reserve account (impound account) until they're due. Most residential loans are secured by budget mortgages. This is the safest and most practical way for lenders to make sure the property taxes and insurance premiums are paid on time.

Package Mortgage. When personal property is included in a sale of real estate and financed along with the real estate with one loan, the security instrument is called a package mortgage. For example, if a buyer bought ovens, freezers, and other equipment along with a restaurant building, the purchase might be financed with a package mortgage.

Construction Loan. A construction loan (sometimes called an **interim loan**) is a temporary loan used to finance the construction of improvements on the land. When the construction is completed, the construction loan is replaced by permanent financing, which is called a **take-out loan**.

Construction loans are risky. There is always a danger that the borrower will overspend on a construction project and exhaust the loan proceeds before construction is completed. If the borrower cannot afford to finish, the lender is left with a security interest in a partially completed project.

Accordingly, lenders charge high interest rates and loan fees on construction loans, and they supervise the progress of the construction.

Lenders have devised a variety of plans for disbursement of construction loan proceeds that guard against overspending by the borrower. Perhaps the most common is the **fixed disbursement plan**. This calls for a series of predetermined disbursements, called obligatory advances, at various stages of construction. Interest begins to accrue with the first disbursement.

> **Example:** The construction loan agreement stipulates that the lender will release 10% of the proceeds when the project is 20% complete, and thereafter 20% draws will be available whenever construction has progressed another 20% toward completion.

The lender will often hold back 10% or more of the loan proceeds until the period for claiming construction liens has expired, to protect against unpaid subcontractor and supplier liens that could affect the marketability of the property. The construction loan agreement usually states that if a valid construction lien is recorded, the lender may use the undisbursed portion of the loan to pay it off.

Blanket Mortgage. Sometimes a borrower mortgages several pieces of property as security for one loan. For example, a ten-acre parcel subdivided into twenty lots might be used to secure one loan made to the subdivider. Blanket mortgages usually have a **partial release clause** (also called a partial satisfaction clause, or in a blanket deed of trust, a partial reconveyance clause). This provision requires the lender to release certain parcels from the blanket lien when specified portions of the overall debt have been paid off.

> **Example:** A ten-acre parcel subdivided into twenty lots secures a $1,000,000 loan. After selling one lot for $100,000, the subdivider pays the lender $90,000 and receives a release for the lot that is being sold. The blanket mortgage is no longer a lien against that lot, so the subdivider can convey clear title to the lot buyer.

Participation Mortgage. A participation mortgage allows the lender to participate in the earnings generated by the mortgaged property, usually in addition to collecting interest payments on the principal. In some cases the lender participates by becoming a part-owner of the property. Participation loans are most common on large commercial projects where the lender is an insurance company or other large investor.

Shared Appreciation Mortgage. Real property usually appreciates (increases in value) over time. Appreciation usually benefits only the property owner, by adding to their equity. (**Equity** is the difference between a property's market value and the liens against it.) With a shared appreciation mortgage, however, the lender is entitled to a specified share of the increase in the property's value. Thus, a shared appreciation mortgage is actually a variation on the participation mortgage discussed above.

Wraparound Mortgage. A wraparound mortgage is a new mortgage that includes or "wraps around" an existing first mortgage on the property. Wraparounds are generally used only in seller-financed transactions.

> **Example:** A home is being sold for $600,000; there is an existing $440,000 mortgage on the property. Instead of assuming that mortgage, the buyer merely takes title subject to it. The buyer gives the seller a $120,000 downpayment and a second mortgage for the remaining $480,000 of the purchase price. The $480,000 second mortgage is a wraparound mortgage. Each month, the buyer makes a payment on the wraparound to the seller, and the seller uses part of that payment to make the monthly payment on the underlying $440,000 mortgage.

Wraparound financing works only if the underlying loan does not contain an alienation clause (see the discussion earlier in this chapter). Otherwise the lender would require the seller to pay off the underlying loan at the time of sale. A wraparound arrangement should always be designed so that the underlying loan will be paid off before the wraparound, to ensure that the buyer's title will not still be encumbered with the seller's debt after the buyer has paid the full purchase price.

Open-end Mortgage. An open-end mortgage sets a borrowing limit, but allows the borrower to reborrow, when needed, any part of the debt that has been repaid without having to negotiate a new mortgage. The interest rate on the loan is usually a variable rate that rises and falls with market interest rates. The open-end mortgage is often used as a business tool by builders and farmers.

Graduated Payment Mortgage. A graduated payment mortgage allows the borrower to make smaller payments at first and gradually step up to larger payments. For example, the payments might increase annually for the first three to five years of the loan, and then remain level for the rest of the loan term. This arrangement can benefit borrowers who expect their earnings to increase during the next few years.

Swing Loan. It often happens that a buyer is ready to purchase a new home before they've succeeded in selling their current home. The buyer needs funds for the downpayment and closing costs right away, without waiting for the proceeds from the eventual sale of their current home. In this situation, the buyer may be able to obtain a swing loan.

A swing loan is usually secured by equity in the property that is for sale, and it will be paid off when that sale closes. A swing loan is also called a **gap loan** or **bridge loan**.

Home Equity Loan. A borrower can obtain a mortgage loan using the equity in property they already own as collateral. This is called an **equity loan**; when the property is the borrower's residence, it's called a **home equity loan**.

As mentioned earlier, equity is the difference between a property's market value and the liens against it. In other words, it's the portion of the property's current value that the owner owns free and clear, which is therefore available to serve as collateral for another loan.

With an equity loan, the lender agrees to loan a sum of money to the property owner in exchange for a mortgage against the property. (This is likely to be a second mortgage; the existing first mortgage is the loan the owner used to purchase the property.)

Sometimes a home equity loan is used to finance remodeling or other improvements to the property. In other cases, it's used for expenses unrelated to the property, such as a major purchase, college tuition, medical bills, or paying off credit cards.

Instead of having to apply for a home equity loan when they need money for a particular purpose, some homeowners have a **home equity line of credit** (or HELOC) that they can draw on when the need arises. This works in much the same way as a credit card—with a credit limit and minimum monthly payments—except that the debt is automatically secured by the borrower's home. A HELOC is a revolving credit account, in contrast to a home equity loan, which has a fixed loan amount with regular payments made over a certain term.

Reverse Mortgage. Reverse mortgages, sometimes called reverse annuity mortgages or reverse equity mortgages, are designed to provide income to older homeowners. The owner borrows against the home's equity but will receive a monthly check from the lender, rather than making monthly payments. Typically, a reverse mortgage borrower must be over a certain age (generally 62) and must own the home with little or no outstanding mortgage balance. The home usually must be sold when the owner dies in order to pay back the mortgage.

Subprime Mortgage. A subprime mortgage is a loan made to a borrower who wouldn't qualify for an ordinary mortgage loan, perhaps because their credit history or debt-to-income ratio doesn't meet the usual standards, or because they are unable or unwilling to provide the documentation usually required. A subprime lender typically charges higher interest rates and fees to offset the extra risk the loan entails. Subprime lending is discussed in more detail in Chapter 11.

Refinancing. Borrowers who refinance their mortgage are obtaining an entirely new mortgage loan to replace the existing one. The funds from the refinancing loan are used to pay off the existing loan. The refinancing might be from the same lender that made the existing loan, or from a different lender.

Borrowers often choose to refinance when market interest rates drop; refinancing at a lower interest rate can result in substantial savings over the long run. Another situation in which borrowers are likely to refinance is when the payoff date of the existing mortgage is approaching and a large balloon payment will be required.

In some cases, borrowers get a refinance loan for more than the amount needed to pay off their existing loan, which means that they also receive cash from the transaction. This is called **cash-out refinancing**. Depending on the terms of the refinance loan, the additional funds might be used for property improvements, debt consolidation, or other purposes.

Chapter Summary

1. The federal government influences real estate finance directly and indirectly through its fiscal and monetary policy. The federal deficit may affect the availability of investment funds. The Federal Reserve Board uses reserve requirements, the discount rate, and open market operations to implement monetary policy, influencing the pace of economic growth and market interest rates.
2. The primary market is the finance market in which lenders make mortgage loans to borrowers. In the secondary market, mortgages are bought and sold by investors. The federal government created the government-sponsored enterprises Fannie Mae and Freddie Mac to help moderate local real estate cycles.
3. A promissory note is a written promise to repay a debt. For a real estate loan, the borrower is required to sign a negotiable promissory note along with a security instrument, which makes the borrower's property collateral for the loan.
4. The two main types of security instruments are mortgages and deeds of trust. The central difference between the two types is that a deed of trust always includes a power of sale clause, which allows the trustee to foreclose nonjudicially in the event of default.
5. Most security instruments include an acceleration clause and an alienation clause; some also have a prepayment provision or a subordination clause. If there is no alienation clause, the loan can be assumed without the lender's consent.
6. A mortgage is foreclosed judicially. The borrower has an equitable right of redemption before the sheriff's sale and a statutory right of redemption for a certain period afterwards. The lender may be entitled to a deficiency judgment.
7. A deed of trust can be foreclosed nonjudicially, by the trustee, which is usually much faster and less expensive than judicial foreclosure. Until shortly before the trustee's sale, the borrower has the right to cure the default and reinstate the loan. After the sale, the borrower has no right of redemption. The lender cannot obtain a deficiency judgment.
8. With a land contract, the buyer (vendee) takes possession of the property and makes installment payments to the seller (vendor). The seller retains legal title until the contract is paid off. If the buyer breaches the contract, the seller may declare a forfeiture.
9. There are many different types of mortgage loans, including purchase money, budget, package, construction, blanket, participation, shared appreciation, wraparound, open-end, graduated payment, swing, home equity, reverse mortgages, subprime, and refinance loans.

Key Terms

Federal Reserve Board—The body that regulates commercial banks and sets and implements the federal government's monetary policy; commonly called "the Fed."

Reserve requirements—The percentages of customer deposits commercial banks must keep on reserve with a Federal Reserve Bank.

Discount rate and federal funds rate—Two interest rates controlled by the Fed that have an effect on market interest rates.

Open market operations—The Fed's activities in buying and selling government securities.

Primary market—The local finance market, where individuals obtain loans from banks, savings and loans, and other types of mortgage lenders.

Secondary market—The national finance market, where mortgages are bought and sold as investments.

Promissory note—A written promise to repay a debt.

Mortgage—A two-party security instrument that gives the lender (mortgagee) the right to foreclose on the security property by judicial process if the borrower (mortgagor) defaults.

Deed of trust—A three-party security instrument that includes a power of sale clause, allowing the trustee to foreclose nonjudicially if the borrower (trustor) fails to pay the lender (beneficiary) or otherwise defaults.

Acceleration clause—A provision in loan documents that gives the lender the right to demand immediate payment in full if the borrower defaults.

Alienation clause—A provision in a security instrument that gives the lender the right to accelerate the loan if the borrower transfers the property; also called a due-on-sale clause.

Assumption—When a borrower sells the security property to a buyer who agrees to take on personal liability for repayment of the existing mortgage or deed of trust.

Defeasance clause—A provision giving the borrower the right to regain title to the security property when the debt is repaid.

Satisfaction of mortgage—The document a mortgagee gives to the mortgagor when the mortgage debt is paid off, releasing the property from the lien.

Deed of reconveyance—The document the trustee gives the trustor when the debt secured by a deed of trust is paid off, releasing the property from the lien.

Land contract—A contract between a seller (vendor) and a buyer (vendee) of real estate, in which the seller retains legal title to the property while the buyer pays off the purchase price in installments.

Chapter Quiz

1. **In a tight money market, when business is slow, a reduction in interest rates would be expected to cause:**
   a) an increase in real estate sales
   b) more bank lending activity
   c) increased business activity
   d) All of the above

2. **Which of the following actions by the Federal Reserve Board would tend to increase the money supply?**
   a) Selling government securities on the open market
   b) Buying government securities on the open market
   c) Increasing the federal discount rate
   d) Increasing reserve requirements

3. **Funds for single-family mortgage loans are supplied by:**
   a) Fannie Mae
   b) savings and loan associations
   c) Both a) and b)
   d) Neither a) nor b)

4. **With an installment note, the periodic payments:**
   a) include both principal and interest
   b) are interest only
   c) are principal only
   d) are called balloon payments

5. **A mortgage loan provision that permits the lender to declare the entire loan balance due upon default by the borrower is a/an:**
   a) acceleration clause
   b) escalator clause
   c) forfeiture clause
   d) subordination clause

6. **A mortgage loan provision that permits the lender to declare the entire loan balance due if the property is sold is a/an:**
   a) escalator clause
   b) subordination clause
   c) alienation clause
   d) prepayment provision

7. **After a sheriff's sale, the mortgagor has a certain period in which to redeem the property. This period is called the:**
   a) lien period
   b) equitable redemption period
   c) statutory redemption period
   d) reinstatement period

8. **After a trustee's sale, if there are any sale proceeds left over after paying off liens and foreclosure expenses, the money belongs to the:**
   a) sheriff
   b) beneficiary
   c) trustee
   d) foreclosed owner

9. **The document that a mortgagee gives a mortgagor after the debt has been completely paid off is called a:**
   a) partial release
   b) satisfaction of mortgage
   c) deed of reconveyance
   d) sheriff's deed

10. **In a nonjudicial foreclosure, the borrower is entitled to:**
    a) a statutory redemption period following the sheriff's sale
    b) a deficiency judgment
    c) a deed in lieu of foreclosure
    d) cure the default and reinstate the loan before the trustee's sale

11. **When a buyer gives a mortgage to the seller instead of an institutional lender, it may be referred to as a:**
    a) purchase money mortgage
    b) land contract
    c) shared appreciation mortgage
    d) reverse mortgage

12. **A budget mortgage:**
    a) is a loan made to a low-income borrower
    b) is a construction loan with a fixed disbursement plan
    c) is secured by personal property as well as real property
    d) has monthly payments that include taxes and insurance as well as principal and interest

13. **The owner of five parcels of real property wants a loan. they offer all five parcels as security. They will be required to execute a:**
    a) soft money mortgage
    b) participation mortgage
    c) package mortgage
    d) blanket mortgage

14. Victor is borrowing money to buy some land, and he plans to build a home on the property later on. To ensure that he will be able to get a construction loan when the time comes, Victor should make sure the mortgage he executes for the land loan includes a/an:

a) lien waiver
b) subordination clause
c) acceleration clause
d) wraparound clause

15. Under a fixed disbursement plan for a construction loan, the contractor is entitled to their final draw when:

a) the project has been satisfactorily completed
b) 80% of the work has been completed
c) the building department issues a certificate of occupancy
d) the period for claiming construction liens expires

Chapter 11: *Applying for a Residential Loan*

- **I. Choosing a Lender**
  - A. Types of mortgage lenders
  - B. Loan costs
    1. Origination fees
    2. Discount points
    3. Interest rate lock-ins
    4. Truth in Lending Act
    5. Mortgage Acts and Practices Rule
- **II. Loan Application Process**
  - A. Preapproval
  - B. Application form
  - C. Underwriting the loan
- **III. Basic Loan Features**
  - A. Loan term
  - B. Amortization
  - C. Loan-to-value ratios
  - D. Secondary financing
  - E. Fixed and adjustable interest rates
- **IV. Residential Financing Programs**
  - A. Conventional loans
  - B. FHA-insured loans
  - C. VA-guaranteed loans
- **V. Predatory Lending**

When it's time to arrange financing, a home buyer must shop for a loan and choose a lender. Next, the buyer fills out a loan application and supplies supporting documentation. Then the lender evaluates the application and decides whether or not to approve the loan. The first part of this chapter describes the different types of lenders in the primary market, explains loan fees, and discusses the Truth in Lending Act, a law that helps prospective borrowers compare loans. The second part of the chapter covers the loan application form and the underwriting process. The next part of the chapter explains various features of a home purchase loan, and provides an overview of the major residential finance programs. The chapter ends with a discussion of predatory lending.

Key Terms

Mortgage Company
Mortgage Broker
Point
Origination Fee
Discount Points
Truth In Lending Act (Tila)
Loan Estimate
Annual Percentage Rate (Apr)
Total Interest Percentage (Tip)
Loan Underwriting
Stable Monthly Income
Income Ratios
Housing Expense to Income Ratio
Debt to Income Ratio
Net Worth
Credit Score
Automated Underwriting (AU)
Fully Amortized Loan
Loan-to-Value Ratio
Secondary Financing
Fixed-Rate Loan
Adjustable-Rate Mortgage
Index
Margin
Negative Amortization
Conventional Loan
Nonconforming Loan
PMI
MIP.
Certificate of Eligibility
Notice of Value (NOV)
Residual Income
Predatory Lending

Choosing a Lender

Many home buyers look to their real estate agent for guidance in choosing a lender. Agents should be familiar with the lenders in their area and know how to help buyers compare the loans that different lenders are offering. We're going to discuss the various types of lenders that make home purchase loans, the fees that lenders charge, and the Truth in Lending Act.

Types of Mortgage Lenders

There are several major sources of residential financing in the primary market. Residential mortgage lenders include:

- commercial banks,
- thrift institutions,
- credit unions, and
- mortgage companies.

Commercial Banks. A commercial bank is either a national bank, chartered (authorized to do business) by the federal government, or a state bank, chartered by a state government. Commercial banks are the largest source of investment funds in the United States. As their name implies, they were traditionally oriented toward commercial lending activities, supplying capital for business ventures and construction activities on a comparatively short-term basis.

In the past, residential mortgages weren't a major part of the business of commercial banks. That was partly because most of their deposits were demand deposits (checking accounts), and the government limited the amount of long-term investments they could make. But eventually commercial banks began accepting more long-term deposits, and demand deposits now represent a considerably smaller share of banks' total deposits than they once did.

While commercial banks have continued to emphasize commercial loans, they have also diversified their lending, with a substantial increase in personal loans and home mortgages. They now have a significant share of the residential finance market.

Thrift Institutions. Savings and loan associations and savings banks are often grouped together and referred to as **thrift institutions** (or thrifts).

Savings and Loans. Savings and loan associations (S&Ls) are chartered by either the federal government or a state government.

Savings and loans started out in the nineteenth century strictly as residential real estate lenders. Over the years they carried on their original function, investing the majority of their assets in purchase loans for single-family homes. By the mid-1950s, they dominated local residential mortgage markets, becoming the nation's largest single source of funds for financing homes.

Many factors contributed to the dominance of savings and loans; one of the most important was that home purchase loans had become long-term loans (often with 30-year terms). Since most of the funds held by S&Ls were long-term deposits, S&Ls were comfortable making long-term home loans.

While savings and loans have branched out into different types of lending, they continue to focus on home mortgage loans. Yet S&Ls no longer dominate the residential finance market, because other types of lenders have become more involved in it.

Savings Banks. Savings banks started out in the nineteenth century offering financial services to small depositors, especially immigrants and members of the working class. They were called mutual savings banks (MSBs) because they were organized as mutual companies, owned by and operated for the benefit of their depositors (as opposed to stockholders).

Traditionally, MSBs were similar to savings and loans. They served their local communities. Their customers were individuals rather than businesses, and most of their deposits were savings deposits. Although the MSBs made many residential mortgage loans, they did not concentrate on them to the extent that S&Ls did. The MSBs were also involved in other types of lending, such as personal loans.

Today, savings banks can be organized as mutual companies or stock companies. Residential mortgages continue to be an important part of their business.

Credit Unions. Credit unions are depository institutions, like banks and S&Ls; however, they are set up as member-owned, not-for-profit financial cooperatives. Credit unions were originally intended to serve only members of a particular group, such as the members of a labor union or a professional association, or the employees of a large company. Today, many credit unions allow anyone in their geographic area to join.

Credit unions traditionally provided small personal loans to their members. Many now emphasize home equity loans, which tend to be short-term, and most also make home purchase loans.

Mortgage Companies. Unlike banks, S&Ls, and credit unions, mortgage companies are not depository institutions, so they don't lend out depositors' funds. Instead, they often act as **loan correspondents**, intermediaries between large investors and home buyers applying for financing.

A loan correspondent lends an investor's money to buyers and then **services** the loans (collecting and processing the loan payments on behalf of the investor) in exchange for servicing fees. In some cases a bank or an S&L will act as a loan correspondent, but mortgage companies have specialized in this role.

Mortgage companies frequently act on behalf of large investors, such as life insurance companies and pension funds. These investors control vast amounts of capital in the form of insurance premiums and employer contributions to employee pensions. That money generally isn't subject to sudden withdrawal, so it's well suited to investment in long-term mortgages. Since these large investors typically operate on a national scale, they have neither the time nor the resources to understand the particular risks of local real estate markets or to deal with the day-to-day management of their loans. So they work with local loan correspondents instead.

Mortgage companies also borrow money from banks on a short-term basis and use the money to make (or **originate**) loans, which they then sell to the secondary market agencies and other private investors. Using short-term financing to originate loans before selling them to permanent investors is referred to as **warehousing**.

Banks and S&Ls generally keep some of the loans they make "in portfolio," instead of selling them to investors. In contrast, mortgage companies don't keep any of the loans they make. The loans are either made on behalf of an investor or else sold to an investor. In many cases, insurance companies, pension funds, and other large investors now simply buy loans from mortgage companies instead of using them as loan correspondents. The mortgage companies often continue to service the loans on behalf of the investors, in exchange for servicing fees.

Mortgage companies that make loans (using an investor's funds or borrowed funds, as described above) are sometimes called **mortgage bankers**. Other mortgage companies merely act as mortgage brokers and don't actually make loans. A **mortgage broker** negotiates loans, bringing borrowers together with lenders in exchange for a commission. Once a loan is arranged, the mortgage broker's involvement ends.

Private Lenders. Real estate limited partnerships, real estate investment trusts (see Chapter 2), and other types of private investment groups put a great deal of money into real estate. They often finance large residential developments and commercial ventures, such as shopping centers and office buildings. They don't offer loans to individual home buyers, however.

From the home buyer's point of view, the most important type of private lender is the home seller. Sellers can provide all the financing for the purchase of their homes or merely supplement the financing their buyers obtain from an institutional lender. Sellers are an especially important source of financing when institutional loans are hard to come by or market interest rates are high.

Comparing Types of Lenders. At one time, financial institutions in the United States were quite specialized. It was almost as if each type of institution had its own function—its own types of deposits, its own types of services, and its own types of loans.

That is no longer true. In general, all of the major depository institutions can now be regarded as "financial supermarkets," offering a wide range of services and loans.

There still are differences between the types of institutions, in terms of lending habits and government regulations, but these generally won't affect a loan applicant who wants to finance the purchase of a home.

Loan Costs

For most buyers, the primary consideration in choosing a lender is how much the loan they need is going to cost. While the interest rate has the greatest impact, lenders impose other charges that can greatly affect the cost of a loan. Most important among these are origination fees and discount points. These are often grouped together and referred to as **points**. The term "point" is short for "percentage point." A point is one percentage point (one percent) of the loan amount. For example, on a $100,000 loan, one point would be $1,000; six points would be $6,000.

Origination Fees. Processing loan applications and making loans is called loan origination. A **loan origination fee** is designed to pay administrative costs the lender incurs in processing a loan; it is sometimes called a service fee, an administrative charge, or simply a loan fee. An origination fee is charged in most residential loan transactions (except for "no fee loans," where the lender compensates by charging a higher interest rate). The origination fee is ordinarily paid by the buyer.

> **Example:** The buyer is borrowing $200,000, and the lender is charging 1.5 points (1.5% of the loan amount, or $3,000) as an origination fee. The buyer will pay this $3,000 fee to the lender at closing.

Discount Points. Lenders charge **discount points** to increase their upfront yield (their return) on a loan. With discount points, a lender not only receives interest payments throughout the loan term, but also collects an additional sum of money up front, when the loan is funded. As a result, the lender is willing to make the loan at a lower interest rate than it would without the discount points—thus reducing the borrower's monthly payment amount. The lender is paid a lump sum at closing so the borrower can avoid paying more interest later.

Discount points aren't charged in all residential loan transactions, but they are quite common. The number of discount points charged usually depends on how the loan's interest rate compares to market interest rates; typically, a lender that offers an especially low rate charges more points to make up for it.

The number of discount points required to increase the lender's yield by one percentage point on a 30-year loan varies. One lender offering an interest rate one percentage point below market rates might charge six points to make up the difference, while another lender might charge four points.

In some cases, a seller is willing to pay the discount points on the buyer's loan in order to help the buyer qualify for financing. Even if the lender's rate quote doesn't include discount points, the seller may offer to pay points to make the loan more affordable. This type of arrangement is called a **buydown**: the seller pays the lender points to "buy down" the interest rate on the buyer's loan.

Rate Lock-ins. A prospective borrower may want to have the interest rate quoted by the lender "locked in" for a specified period. Unless the interest rate is locked in, the lender can change it at any time until the transaction closes. If market interest rates are rising, the lender is likely to increase the interest rate on the loan. That could cost the borrower a lot of money over the long term, or else actually price the borrower out of the transaction altogether.

Locking in the interest rate doesn't make sense if interest rates are expected to go down. Lenders typically charge the borrower the locked-in rate even if market rates drop in the period before closing.

Though it's not common, some lenders charge the borrower a fee to lock in the interest rate. The fee is typically applied to the borrower's closing costs if the transaction closes. If the lender rejects the borrower's application, the fee is refunded; it will be forfeited to the lender, though, if the borrower withdraws from the transaction.

Truth in Lending Act. An origination fee, discount points, and other charges may increase the cost of a mortgage loan significantly. They also make it more difficult to compare the costs of loans offered by different lenders. For example, suppose one lender charges 7% interest, a 1% origination fee, and no discount points, while another charges 6.75% interest, a 1% origination fee, and two discount points. It isn't easy to tell at a glance which of these loans will cost the borrower more in the long term. (The second loan is just slightly less expensive.)

The **Truth in Lending Act** (TILA) is a federal consumer protection law that addresses this problem of comparing loan costs. The act requires lenders to disclose the complete cost of credit to consumer loan applicants, and it also regulates the advertisement of consumer loans. The Truth in Lending Act is implemented by a set of rules known as **Regulation Z.**

Loans Covered by TILA. A loan is a **consumer loan** if it's used for personal, family, or household purposes. A consumer loan is covered by the Truth in Lending Act if it is to be repaid in more than four installments, or is subject to finance charges, and is either:

- for $58,300 or less (in 2021; the dollar figure is subject to annual adjustment based on the Consumer Price Index), or
- secured by real property.

Thus, any mortgage loan is covered by the Truth in Lending Act as long as the proceeds are used for personal, family, or household purposes (such as buying a home or sending children to college).

Loans Exempt from TILA. The Truth in Lending Act applies only to loans made to natural persons, so loans made to corporations or organizations aren't covered. Loans for business, commercial, or agricultural purposes are also exempt. So are loans in excess of the maximum dollar amount shown above, unless they are secured by real property. (Real estate loans for personal, family, or household purposes are covered regardless of the loan amount.)

TILA only applies to loans from lenders who regularly extend consumer credit. Most seller financing is exempt, because extending credit isn't in the seller's ordinary course of business.

Disclosure Requirements. Both TILA and the Real Estate Settlement Procedures Act (RESPA, discussed in Chapter 13) impose loan cost disclosure requirements that apply to most home purchase, home equity, and refinance loans. Exempt transactions include home equity lines of credit, reverse mortgages, mortgages secured by any dwelling not attached to land, and loans made by creditors who make five or fewer mortgage loans per year.

The two essential disclosure documents prescribed by TILA and RESPA are the **loan estimate form** (see Figure 11.1) and the **closing disclosure form.** (The closing disclosure form, which must be provided to the borrower at least three days before the loan transaction closes, will be discussed in Chapter 13.) The disclosures in the loan estimate are intended to help applicants understand the features, risks, and cost of the mortgage loan for which they're applying. Applicants can use the information to compare credit costs and shop around for the best terms.

The loan estimate also helps the applicant make sure that the lender doesn't change the loan costs or terms once it's too late for the applicant to change lenders. The lender is generally held to the amounts set forth in the original loan estimate, unless a change in circumstances requires a change in the disclosed figures. If that happens, the lender must provide a revised loan estimate.

The information that must be disclosed on the loan estimate form will vary depending on the specifics of the loan and may also be affected by state law. The disclosures must include information such as the loan's interest rate and the payment amount, whether the loan is assumable, the estimated closing costs, any late payment fees, and the total amount of cash that the buyer will need to close the loan. In addition, the loan estimate must disclose the annual percentage rate and the total interest percentage.

The **annual percentage rate** (APR) expresses the total cost of the loan as an annual percentage of the loan amount. This key figure enables a prospective borrower to compare loans more accurately than the interest rate alone.

The APR is sometimes referred to as the effective rate of interest, as opposed to the nominal rate (the interest rate stated on the face of the promissory note). In addition to interest, the loan-related charges taken into account in calculating the APR include any of the following that will be paid by the borrower: an origination fee, discount points, a mortgage broker's fee, a finder's fee, or mortgage insurance premiums. Loan-related charges paid to third parties (instead of to the lender), such as the credit report fee, the appraiser's fee, and title insurance costs, are not reflected in the APR. Neither are charges paid by someone other than the borrower (such as seller-paid discount points).

The **total interest percentage** (TIP) expresses the total amount of interest that the borrower will pay over the loan term as a percentage of the loan amount. It includes only interest, with none of the other fees and costs that are reflected in the APR. The TIP gives the prospective borrower a clearer picture of how interest impacts the total amount paid over the life of the loan.

The charges stated in the loan estimate must be estimated in good faith using the best information available at the time. If the transaction proceeds to closing and an actual charge exceeds the estimated charge, the lender may be required to refund the difference to the borrower.

Certain charges are subject to a zero tolerance limitation, which means that the borrower cannot be charged more than the amount originally disclosed. This includes all charges imposed directly by the lender (such as the origination fee) or paid to a service provider affiliated with the lender. Most third-party charges, such as the appraisal fee and title insurance costs, are subject to a 10% cumulative tolerance limitation; the total of the actual charges in this category cannot be more than 10% over the estimated charges. However, the 10% limitation won't apply to a particular charge if the borrower chose the service provider, rather than using a service provider required or suggested by the lender.

To help home loan applicants understand loan costs and other closing costs, lenders must give applicants an information booklet called "Your Home Loan Toolkit," published by the Consumer Financial Protection Bureau.

240,00 Sale price
211,000 loan amount

2,100 x 4

Fig. 11.1 Loan Estimate Form

FICUS BANK
4321 Random Boulevard • Somecity, ST 12340

Save this Loan Estimate to compare with your Closing Disclosure.

Loan Estimate

DATE ISSUED	2/15/20XX
APPLICANTS	Michael Jones and Mary Stone 123 Anywhere Street Anytown, ST 12345
PROPERTY	456 Somewhere Avenue Anytown, ST 12345
SALE PRICE	$240,000

LOAN TERM	30 years
PURPOSE	Purchase
PRODUCT	5 Year Interest Only, 5/3 Adjustable Rate
LOAN TYPE	☒ Conventional ☐ FHA ☐ VA ☐ ____________
LOAN ID #	123456789
RATE LOCK	☐ NO ☒ YES, until 4/16/20XX at 5:00 p.m. EDT *Before closing, your interest rate, points, and lender credits can change unless you lock the interest rate. All other estimated closing costs expire on* ***3/4/20XX*** *at 5:00 p.m. EDT*

Loan Terms

Loan Terms		Can this amount increase after closing?
Loan Amount	$211,000	**NO**
Interest Rate	4%	**YES** • Adjusts **every 3 years** starting in year 6 • Can go **as high as 12%** in year 15 • See **AIR Table on page 2** for details
Monthly Principal & Interest *See Projected Payments below for your Estimated Total Monthly Payment*	$703.33 211,000 x .04 ÷ 12	**YES** • Adjusts **every 3 years** starting in year 6 • Can go **as high as $2,068** in year 15 • Includes **only interest** and **no principal** until year 6 • See **AP Table on page 2** for details
		Does the loan have these features?
Prepayment Penalty		**NO**
Balloon Payment		**NO**

Projected Payments

Payment Calculation	**Years 1-5**	**Years 6-8**	**Years 9-11**	**Years 12-30**
Principal & Interest	$703.33 *only interest*	$1,028 min $1,359 max	$1,028 min $1,604 max	$1,028 min $2,068 max
Mortgage Insurance	+ 109	+ 109	+ 109	+ —
Estimated Escrow *Amount can increase over time*	+ 0	+ 0	+ 0	+ 0
Estimated Total Monthly Payment	$812	$1,137–$1,468	$1,137–$1,713	$1,028–$2,068

Estimated Taxes, Insurance & Assessments *Amount can increase over time*	$533 a month	**This estimate includes** ☒ Property Taxes ☒ Homeowner's Insurance ☐ Other: *See Section G on page 2 for escrowed property costs. You must pay for other property costs separately.*	**In escrow?** NO NO

Costs at Closing

Estimated Closing Costs	$8,791	Includes $5,851 in Loan Costs + $2,940 in Other Costs – $0 in Lender Credits. *See page 2 for details.*
Estimated Cash to Close	$27,791	Includes Closing Costs. *See Calculating Cash to Close on page 2 for details.*

Visit **www.consumerfinance.gov/mortgage-estimate** for general information and tools.

LOAN ESTIMATE

PAGE 1 OF 3 • LOAN ID # 123456789

Source: Consumer Financial Protection Bureau

Closing Cost Details

Loan Costs

A. Origination Charges	$3,110
1 % of Loan Amount (Points)	$2,110
Application Fee	$500
Processing Fee	$500

B. Services You Cannot Shop For	$820
Appraisal Fee	$305
Credit Report Fee	$30
Flood Determination Fee	$35
Lender's Attorney Fee	$400
Tax Status Research Fee	$50

C. Services You Can Shop For	$1,921
Pest Inspection Fee	$125
Survey Fee	$150
Title – Courier Fee	$32
Title – Lender's Title Policy	$665
Title – Settlement Agent Fee	$325
Title – Title Search	$624

D. TOTAL LOAN COSTS (A + B + C)	$5,851

Other Costs

E. Taxes and Other Government Fees	$152
Recording Fees and Other Taxes	$152
Transfer Taxes	

F. Prepaids	$1,352
Homeowner's Insurance Premium (12 months)	$1,000
Mortgage Insurance Premium (months)	
Prepaid Interest ($23.44 per day for 15 days @ 4.00%)	$352
Property Taxes (months)	

G. Initial Escrow Payment at Closing		
Homeowner's Insurance	per month for	mo.
Mortgage Insurance	per month for	mo.
Property Taxes	per month for	mo.

H. Other	$1,436
Title – Owner's Title Policy (optional)	$1,436

I. TOTAL OTHER COSTS (E + F + G + H)	$2,940

J. TOTAL CLOSING COSTS	$8,791
D + I	$8,791
Lender Credits	

Calculating Cash to Close

Total Closing Costs (J)	$8,791
Closing Costs Financed (Paid from your Loan Amount)	$0
Down Payment/Funds from Borrower	$29,000
Deposit	– $10,000
Funds for Borrower	$0
Seller Credits	$0
Adjustments and Other Credits	$0
Estimated Cash to Close	$27,791

Adjustable Payment (AP) Table

Interest Only Payments?	YES for your first 60 payments
Optional Payments?	NO
Step Payments?	NO
Seasonal Payments?	NO
Monthly Principal and Interest Payments	
First Change/Amount	$1,028 – $1,359 at 61st payment
Subsequent Changes	Every three years
Maximum Payment	$2,068 starting at 169th payment

Adjustable Interest Rate (AIR) Table

Index + Margin	MTA + 4%
Initial Interest Rate	4%
Minimum/Maximum Interest Rate	3.25%/12%
Change Frequency	
First Change	Beginning of 61st month
Subsequent Changes	Every 36th month after first change
Limits on Interest Rate Changes	
First Change	2%
Subsequent Changes	2%

LOAN ESTIMATE PAGE 2 OF 3 • LOAN ID # 123456789

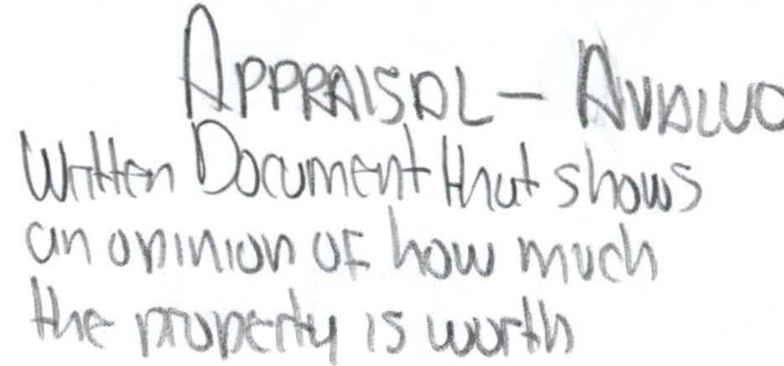

Additional Information About This Loan

LENDER	Ficus Bank	**MORTGAGE BROKER**	
NMLS/__ LICENSE ID		**NMLS/__ LICENSE ID**	
LOAN OFFICER	Joe Smith	**LOAN OFFICER**	
NMLS/__ LICENSE ID	12345	**NMLS/__ LICENSE ID**	
EMAIL	joesmith@ficusbank.com	**EMAIL**	
PHONE	123-456-7890	**PHONE**	

Comparisons	**Use these measures to compare this loan with other loans.**	
In 5 Years	$54,944	Total you will have paid in principal, interest, mortgage insurance, and loan costs.
	$0	Principal you will have paid off.
Annual Percentage Rate (APR)	4.617%	Your costs over the loan term expressed as a rate. This is not your interest rate.
Total Interest Percentage (TIP)	81.18%	The total amount of interest that you will pay over the loan term as a percentage of your loan amount.

Other Considerations

Appraisal	We may order an appraisal to determine the property's value and charge you for this appraisal. We will promptly give you a copy of any appraisal, even if your loan does not close. You can pay for an additional appraisal for your own use at your own cost.
Assumption	If you sell or transfer this property to another person, we ☐ will allow, under certain conditions, this person to assume this loan on the original terms. ☒ will not allow assumption of this loan on the original terms.
Homeowner's Insurance	This loan requires homeowner's insurance on the property, which you may obtain from a company of your choice that we find acceptable.
Late Payment	If your payment is more than *15* days late, we will charge a late fee of *5% of the monthly principal and interest payment*.
Refinance	Refinancing this loan will depend on your future financial situation, the property value, and market conditions. You may not be able to refinance this loan.
Servicing	We intend ☐ to service your loan. If so, you will make your payments to us. ☒ to transfer servicing of your loan.

Confirm Receipt

By signing, you are only confirming that you have received this form. You do not have to accept this loan because you have signed or received this form.

Applicant Signature	Date	Co-Applicant Signature	Date

LOAN ESTIMATE — PAGE 3 OF 3 • LOAN ID #123456789

Timing of Disclosures. A lender must give a loan applicant the loan estimate form and the information booklet within three business days after receiving the application.

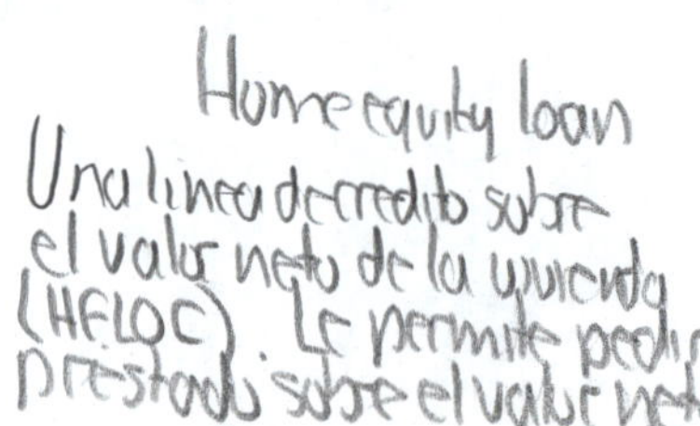

The lender can't require the applicant to pay any fees (such as an application fee, an appraisal fee, or an underwriting fee) until the loan estimate has been provided and the applicant has indicated an intent to proceed with the loan transaction. (One exception is the credit report fee, which may be collected beforehand.)

Right of Rescission. The Truth in Lending Act provides for a right of rescission in connection with certain types of nonpurchase mortgage loans (see below), if the security property is the borrower's principal residence. In these transactions, the borrower may rescind the loan agreement up until three days after signing it, receiving the disclosure statement, or receiving notice of the right of rescission, whichever comes latest. If the borrower never receives the statement or the notice, the right of rescission doesn't expire for three years.

The right of rescission generally applies only to home equity loans and to refinancing with a new lender. There's no right of rescission for a loan financing the purchase or construction of the borrower's residence. Nor is there a right of rescission for refinancing when the same lender that made the original loan is making the new loan, unless that lender is advancing additional funds (beyond the original loan amount). In that case, the right of rescission applies only to the additional amount.

Advertising Under TILA. The Truth in Lending Act strictly controls advertising of credit terms. Its advertising rules apply to anyone who advertises consumer credit, not just lenders. For example, a real estate agent advertising financing terms for a listed home has to comply with TILA and Regulation Z.

It's always legal to state the cash price or the annual percentage rate in an ad. If the APR is stated, the interest rate may also be given, as long as it isn't more prominent than the APR. But if the ad contains other specific loan terms known as **triggering terms** (the downpayment amount or percentage, the repayment period or number of payments, the amount of any payment, or the amount of any finance charge), then other information must also be disclosed. For example, if an ad says, "Assume seller's payments—only $1,525 a month," it will violate the Truth in Lending Act if it does not go on to reveal the APR, any required downpayment, and the repayment schedule, with the number and timing of the payments and all payment amounts, including any balloon payment. However, general statements such as "low monthly payment," "easy terms," or "affordable interest rate" do not trigger the full disclosure requirement.

Mortgage Acts and Practices Rule. The Mortgage Acts and Practices Rule is a federal regulation that's intended to limit deceptive mortgage advertising. The rule, also known as Regulation N, applies to all entities who advertise residential mortgage financing to consumers, except for banks and similar supervised financial institutions. For instance, the rule applies to independent mortgage companies and mortgage brokers, and it also applies to real estate agents if they advertise home financing.

The rule prohibits misrepresentations concerning loan features or the lender, and the deceptive use of certain terminology. In addition to avoiding these practices, advertisers must comply with recordkeeping requirements.

Marketing materials, training materials, sales scripts, and other communications that describe mortgage products must be retained for at least two years.

The Loan Application Process

Once a buyer has compared loan costs and selected a lender, the next step is applying for the loan. The buyer fills out a loan application form and provides the lender with supporting documentation. The application is then submitted to the lender's underwriting department, which evaluates the application and ultimately approves or rejects the proposed loan.

Preapproval

Almost all buyers get **preapproved** for a loan before house-hunting in earnest. A prospective buyer submits a loan application to a lender, and if the lender approves the application, the buyer is preapproved for a specified maximum loan amount.

Preapproval lets the buyer know in advance, before shopping, just how expensive a house she can afford. If a house meets the lender's standards and is in the established price range, the buyer will be able to buy it. This spares the buyer the disappointment of initially choosing a house that turns out to be too expensive and having the loan request turned down.

Preapproval is especially important in an active market, where sellers rarely even consider offers from buyers who aren't preapproved. Even in a slower market, an offer may not get serious consideration unless the buyer has been preapproved.

Preapproval also helps streamline the closing process once the buyer has found the right house.

Loan Application Form

A mortgage loan application form asks the prospective borrower for detailed information about their finances. The information helps the lender identify and turn down applicants who are likely to create collection problems.

Most mortgage lenders use a standard residential loan application form developed by Fannie Mae and Freddie Mac. The form requires all of the following information:

1. **Personal information**, such as the applicant's social security number, age, education, marital status, and number of dependents.
2. **Current housing expense** (monthly rent or house payment).
3. **Employment information** (such as job title, type of business, and duration of employment) concerning the applicant's current position and, if he's been with the current employer for less than two years, concerning previous jobs.
4. **Income** from all sources, including employment (salary, wages, bonuses, and/or commissions), investments (dividends and interest), and pensions.
5. **Assets**, which may include money in bank accounts, stocks and bonds, real estate, life insurance, retirement funds, cars, jewelry, and other personal property.
6. **Liabilities**, including credit card debts, car loans, real estate loans, alimony or child support payments, and unpaid taxes.

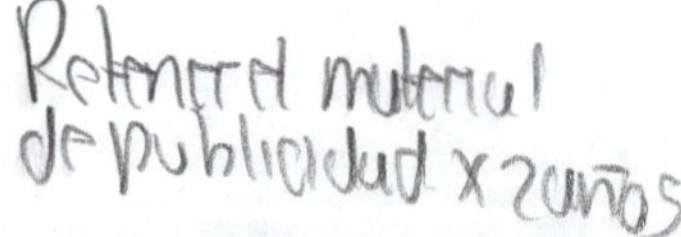

The lender will verify the applicant's information concerning income, assets, and liabilities (for example, by sending verification forms to the applicant's employer and bank).

Underwriting the Loan

Once a loan application has been submitted and the information has been verified, the next step in the loan process is loan underwriting. **Loan underwriting** is the process of evaluating both the applicant and the property she wants to buy to determine whether they meet the lender's minimum standards. The person who conducts the evaluation is called a loan underwriter or credit underwriter (though software handles much of the analytical work in a typical residential transaction). The guidelines used to decide whether a proposed loan would be an acceptable risk (in other words, whether the applicant qualifies for the loan) are called **underwriting standards** or **qualifying standards**.

A lender is generally free to set its own underwriting standards. In practice, however, most lenders apply underwriting standards set by Fannie Mae and Freddie Mac. And for FHA and VA loans, standards set by HUD or the VA must be used.

Qualifying the Buyer. In evaluating a loan applicant's financial situation, an underwriter must consider many factors. These factors fall into three main groups: credit history, income, and net worth.

Credit History. The first major component of creditworthiness is an applicant's credit history, or credit reputation. In most cases the loan underwriter analyzes the applicant's credit history using credit reports and credit scores obtained from three national consumer credit reporting agencies.

The information in a **credit report** indicates how reliably a consumer has paid bills and other debts, and whether there have been any severe problems such as bankruptcy or foreclosure. Using the credit report and a statistical model that correlates different types of credit information with actual loan defaults, a credit reporting agency calculates a consumer's **credit score.** Generally, loan applicants with high credit scores are much less likely to default on their mortgage than those with low scores.

Credit problems can indicate financial irresponsibility, but in some cases they result from a personal crisis such as loss of a job, divorce, or hospitalization. A loan applicant with a poor credit history should explain any extenuating circumstances to the lender.

Incorrect information sometimes becomes part of a consumer's credit report, which can pose serious problems for a person trying to get a loan. Under the Equal Credit Opportunity Act (ECOA), iIf a lender takes an adverse action (such as denying a loan application) because of information in a credit report, the lender must give the applicant written notice about the action and disclose which credit reporting agency provided the report.if a lender takes an adverse action (such as denying a loan application) because of information in a credit report, the lender must give the applicant written notice about the action and disclose which credit reporting agency provided the report.

The federal **Fair Credit Reporting Act** (FCRA) helps protect consumers against erroneous credit reporting. The FCRA entitles consumers to one free credit report per year, to enable them to check for errors. Creditors and credit reporting agencies must investigate disputed information and correct any errors. The act also sets limits on how long negative information may remain on credit reports; the limit is seven years for most information, but it's ten years for bankruptcies.

Income. Another primary consideration for the underwriter is whether the loan applicant's monthly income is enough to cover the proposed monthly mortgage payment in addition to all of the applicant's other expenses. So the underwriter needs to determine how much income the applicant has.

Not all income is equal in an underwriter's eyes, however. To be taken into account in deciding whether the applicant qualifies for the loan, income must meet standards of quality and durability. In other words, it must be from a dependable source, such as an established business, and it must be likely to continue for some time. Income that meets the tests of quality and durability is generally referred to as the loan applicant's **stable monthly income**. (Note that stable monthly income is a pre-tax figure. In other words, it's the applicant's gross income, as opposed to the net income after social security, income tax, or other taxes have been subtracted.)

Once the underwriter has calculated the loan applicant's stable monthly income, the next step is to measure its adequacy: Is the stable monthly income enough so that the applicant can afford the proposed monthly mortgage payment? To answer this question, underwriters use **income ratios**. The rationale behind the ratios is that if a borrower's expenses exceed a certain percentage of their monthly income, the borrower may have a difficult time making the payments on the loan.

There are two main types of income ratios:

- A **housing expense to income ratio** measures the proposed monthly mortgage payment against the applicant's pretax stable monthly income.
- A **debt to income ratio** (also called a **debt service ratio**) measures all of the applicant's monthly obligations (the proposed mortgage payment, plus car payments, child support payments, etc.) against the stable monthly income.

For these calculations, the monthly mortgage payment includes principal, interest, taxes, insurance, and any homeowners association dues (often abbreviated as PITI or PITIA). Each ratio is expressed as a percentage; for example, a loan applicant's housing expense to income ratio would be 29% if their proposed mortgage payment represented 29% of their stable monthly income. Whether that ratio would be considered too high would depend on the lender and on the type of loan applied for. Each of the major residential loan programs (conventional, FHA-insured, or VA-guaranteed) has its own income ratio limits.

Net Worth. The third prong of the underwriting process is evaluating the borrower's net worth. An individual's net worth is determined by subtracting their total personal liabilities from their total personal assets.

If a loan applicant has built up a significant net worth from earnings and investments, that indicates creditworthiness. The applicant apparently knows how to manage their financial affairs.

Net worth also matters because the applicant needs to have sufficient funds (cash or other liquid assets) to cover the downpayment, the closing costs, and other expenses incidental to the purchase of the property.

In addition, it's desirable for a loan applicant to have cash reserves left over after closing. Reserves provide some assurance that she would be able to handle a financial emergency, such as unexpected bills or a temporary interruption of income, without defaulting on the mortgage. Some lenders require an applicant to have sufficient reserves to cover a certain number of mortgage payments. Even when reserves aren't specifically required, they strengthen the loan application.

Qualifying the Property. In addition to deciding whether the buyer is a good risk, underwriting involves determining whether the property that the buyer wants to purchase is a good risk. Is the property worth enough to serve as collateral for the loan amount in question? In other words, if foreclosure became necessary, would the property sell for enough money to pay off the loan? To answer these questions, the underwriter relies on an appraisal report commissioned by the lender. The appraisal provides an expert's estimate of the property's value. (Appraisal is covered in Chapter 12.)

Automated Underwriting. Mortgage lenders use automated underwriting (AU) to handle much of the underwriting process. In automated underwriting, computer software performs an analysis of the loan application and the applicant's credit report and makes a recommendation for or against approval. A human underwriter then evaluates the application in light of the AU recommendation.

AU systems are based on statistics regarding the performance of millions of loans—whether the borrowers made the payments on time or defaulted. Analysis of these statistics provides strong evidence of which factors in a loan application make default more or less likely.

Loan Commitment. Once the underwriting analysis has been completed, a report summarizing the characteristics of the prospective borrower, the property, and the proposed loan is prepared. This summary, sometimes called a **mortgage evaluation**, is submitted to a loan committee, which will make the final decision on whether to approve the loan. If the committee's decision is favorable, the lender issues a loan commitment, agreeing to make the loan on specified terms.

Subprime Lending. What happens to home buyers whose credit history doesn't meet standard underwriting requirements? Some of them may be able to obtain a loan by applying to a **subprime** lender. Subprime lending involves making riskier loans than prime (or standard) lending.

Although many of the buyers who obtain subprime mortgages have blemished credit histories and mediocre credit scores, that's not always the case.

For example, subprime financing may also be necessary for buyers with good credit who:

- can't (or would rather not have to) meet the income and asset documentation requirements of prime lenders;
- have more debt than prime lenders consider acceptable; or
- want to make a smaller downpayment than prime lenders would allow.

Subprime lenders apply more flexible underwriting standards and, in exchange, typically charge much higher interest rates and fees than prime lenders. In addition to having high interest rates and fees, subprime loans are more likely than prime loans to have features such as prepayment penalties, balloon payments, and negative amortization. These features help subprime lenders counterbalance some of the extra risks involved in their loans, although they can also cause trouble for the borrowers. (See the discussion of predatory lending later in this chapter.)

A boom in subprime lending began in the late 1990s and continued into the new century. However, a significant number of these subprime loans turned out to be poor risks, and many of the borrowers defaulted on their loans. The resulting foreclosure epidemic in 2008 and 2009 affected not just the mortgage industry but the economy as a whole. As a result, it is now more difficult to get subprime loans.

Mortgage Fraud. Mortgage fraud causes many millions of dollars in losses each year. Common types of mortgage fraud include borrowers lying on loan applications and loan professionals misleading secondary market investors. For instance, loan applicants may lie about their employment, assets, or liabilities in order to secure loans that they wouldn't otherwise qualify for.

Investors may falsely claim to be purchasing property as their principal residence in order to qualify for lower interest rates and fees. Lenders may misrepresent the quality of poor loans when selling them to investors in the secondary market.

Both federal and state law prohibit mortgage fraud. In 2009, in response to the mortgage crisis, Congress passed the Fraud Enforcement and Recovery Act, which toughened up existing federal antifraud provisions and took particular aim at mortgage fraud. At about the same time, the state of Washington enacted the Mortgage Lending and Homeownership statute, which contains various provisions concerning mortgage fraud. Both the federal and state laws provide for significant jail time and fines for violations.

Basic Loan Features

In this section, we'll look at the basic features of a home mortgage loan. These include the loan term; the amortization; the loan-to-value ratio; a secondary financing arrangement (in some cases); and a fixed or adjustable interest rate. A lender is likely to present a home buyer with a number of options concerning these various loan features. Each of them affects how large a loan the buyer will qualify for, and ultimately how expensive a home the buyer can purchase.

Loan Term

A mortgage loan's **term** (also known as the **repayment period**) has a significant impact on both the monthly mortgage payment and the total amount of interest paid over the life of the loan. The longer the term, the lower the monthly payment, and the more interest paid. Since the 1930s, the standard term for a mortgage loan has been 30 years.

Although 30-year loans continue to predominate, 15-year loans have also become popular. A 15-year loan has higher monthly payments than a comparable 30-year loan, but the 15-year loan offers substantial interest savings for the borrower.

Lenders frequently offer lower interest rates on 15-year loans, because the shorter term means less risk for the lender. And since the money is borrowed for a much shorter period, the total amount of interest paid is sharply reduced. In many cases the borrower will save hundreds of thousands of dollars in interest charges over the life of the loan (see Figure 11.2). A 15-year loan also offers free and clear ownership of the property in half the time.

However, the monthly payments are significantly higher for a 15-year loan, and in some cases a much larger downpayment would be necessary to reduce the monthly payments to a level the borrower can afford.

Fig. 11.2 A 15-year loan offers substantial savings over a 30-year loan

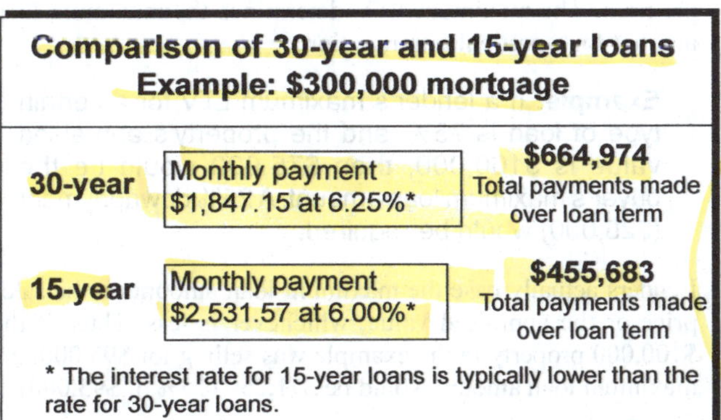

Comparison of 30-year and 15-year loans
Example: $300,000 mortgage

30-year	Monthly payment $1,847.15 at 6.25%*	**$664,974** Total payments made over loan term
15-year	Monthly payment $2,531.57 at 6.00%*	**$455,683** Total payments made over loan term

* The interest rate for 15-year loans is typically lower than the rate for 30-year loans.

Example: Bob has a choice between a 30-year loan at 6.5% and a 15-year loan at 6.25%. Based on his stable monthly income, he can afford to make monthly principal and interest payments of about $2,000. This is enough to amortize a $316,000 loan at 6.5% over 30 years, but it will amortize only about $233,000 at 6.25% over 15 years. In other words, Bob could qualify for a $316,000 loan under the 30-year plan, but will be able to borrow only $233,000 if he chooses the 15-year option.

There are alternatives to 15- and 30-year loans. For some borrowers, a 20-year loan is a good compromise between the two, with some of the advantages of each. And while 30 years is the maximum repayment period in many loan programs, some programs allow borrowers to choose a 40-year term, to maximize their purchasing power.

Amortization

Most mortgage loans are **fully amortized.** A fully amortized loan is repaid within a certain period of time by means of regular payments that include a portion for principal and a portion for interest. As each payment is made, the appropriate amount of principal is deducted from the debt and the remainder of the payment, which represents the interest, is retained by the lender as earnings or profit.

With each payment, the amount of the debt is reduced and the interest due with the next payment is recalculated based on the lower balance. The total payment remains the same throughout the term of the loan, but every month the interest portion of the payment is reduced and the principal portion is increased. (See Figure 11.3.) The final payment pays off the loan completely; the principal balance is zero and no further interest is owed.

Example: A $190,000 loan at 6% interest can be fully amortized over a 30-year term with monthly principal and interest payments of $1,139.15. If the borrower pays $1,139.15 each month, then the loan will be fully repaid (with interest) after 30 years.

There are two alternatives to fully amortized loans: partially amortized loans and interest-only loans. A **partially amortized** loan requires regular payments of both interest and principal, but those payments are not enough to repay all of the principal; the borrower is required to make a large balloon payment (the remaining principal balance) at the end of the loan term.

Example: A $190,000 partially amortized mortgage at 6% interest calls for regular monthly payments of $1,296.13 for principal and interest, with a loan term of five years. Because the monthly payments are more than enough to cover the interest on the loan, some of the principal will be repaid during the five-year term. But since it would take 30 years to fully repay the loan at this rate, a substantial amount of principal (roughly $167,000) will still be unpaid after five years. This amount will be due as a balloon payment. To pay it, the borrower will have to refinance the property or come up with the funds from some other source.

With an **interest-only** loan (also called a **term mortgage**), the borrower's regular payments during the loan term cover the interest accruing on the loan, without paying any of the principal off. The entire principal amount—the amount originally borrowed—is due at the end of the term.

The term "interest-only loan" is also used to refer to a loan that's structured to allow interest-only payments during a specified period at the beginning of the loan term. At the end of the initial period, the borrower must begin making amortized payments that will pay off all of the principal and interest by the end of the term.

Fig. 11.3 Payments for a Fully Amortized Loan

Example: $190,000 loan @ 6.00%, 30-year term, monthly payments

Payment No.	Beginning Balance	Total Payment	Interest Portion	Principal Portion	Ending Balance
1	$190,000.00	$1,139.15	$950.00	$189.15	$189,810.85
2	$189,810.85	$1,139.15	$949.05	$190.09	$189,620.76
3	$189,620.76	$1,139.15	$948.10	$191.04	$189,429.72
4	$189,429.72	$1,139.15	$947.15	$192.00	$189,237.72
5	$189,237.72	$1,139.15	$946.19	$192.96	$189,044.74

This type of interest-only loan was very popular during the subprime boom, since the low initial payments enabled buyers to purchase a more expensive home than they otherwise could have. For many buyers, however, these loans eventually backfire. When the interest-only period ends, they can't afford the amortized payments, and the payment shock ultimately results in foreclosure. These loans are now rarely used.

Loan-to-Value Ratios

The loan-to-value ratio (LTV) for a particular transaction expresses the relationship between the loan amount and the value of the property. The lower the LTV, the smaller the loan amount and the bigger the downpayment.

> **Example:** If a lender makes an $80,000 loan secured by a home appraised at $100,000, the loan-to-value ratio is 80%. The loan amount is 80% of the property's value, and the buyer makes a 20% downpayment. If the lender loaned $75,000 secured by the same property, the LTV would be 75% and the downpayment would be 25%.

The downpayment represents the borrower's initial investment or equity in the property. A property owner's equity is the difference between the property's market value and the amount of the liens against it. The lower the loan-to-value ratio, the greater the borrower's equity. (Repayment of the loan principal increases the borrower's equity over time; so does future appreciation, an increase in the property's value due to market forces. If the property depreciates—loses value—that decreases the borrower's equity.)

The loan-to-value ratio affects the degree of risk involved in the loan—both the risk of default and the risk of loss in the event of default. A borrower who has a substantial investment in the property will try harder to avoid foreclosure; and when foreclosure is necessary, the lender is more likely to recover the entire debt if the LTV is relatively low.

The higher the LTV, the greater the lender's risk. Because of this, lenders tend to apply stricter underwriting standards to high-LTV loans and charge the borrowers higher rates.

Lenders also establish a maximum loan-to-value ratio for a given type of loan, or apply the maximum LTV for a given loan program. The maximum LTV determines the maximum loan amount for a particular transaction.

> **Example:** If a lender's maximum LTV for a certain type of loan is 75%, and the property's appraised value is $100,000, then $75,000 would be the buyer's maximum loan amount. A 25% downpayment ($25,000) would be required.

Lenders actually base the maximum loan amount on the sales price or the appraised value, whichever is less. Thus, if the $100,000 property in the example was selling for $95,000, the maximum loan amount would be $71,250 (75% of $95,000).

Secondary Financing

Sometimes a buyer obtains two mortgage loans at once: a primary loan to pay for most of the purchase price, and a second loan to pay part of the downpayment or closing costs required for the first loan. This supplementary second loan is called **secondary financing.** Secondary financing may come from an institutional lender, the seller, or a private third party.

In most cases, the primary lender will allow secondary financing only if it complies with certain requirements. For example, the borrower must be able to qualify for the combined payment on the first and second loans. The borrower is usually required to make a minimum downpayment out of their own funds. And the second loan must be payable at any time, without a prepayment penalty.

Fixed and Adjustable Interest Rates

A fixed-rate loan is repaid over its term at an unchanging rate of interest. For example, the interest rate is set at 3.25% when the loan is made, and the borrower pays 3.25% interest on the unpaid principal throughout the loan term.

When market interest rates are relatively low and stable, fixed-rate loans work well for borrowers and lenders. But in periods when market rates are high and volatile, neither borrowers nor lenders are comfortable with fixed-rate loans. High interest rates price many borrowers out of the market. And if market rates are fluctuating rapidly, lenders prefer not to tie up their funds for long periods at a set interest rate.

A type of loan that addresses both of these issues is the **adjustable-rate mortgage** (ARM). An ARM permits the lender to periodically adjust the loan's interest rate so that it accurately reflects changes in the cost of money. With an ARM, it's the borrower who is affected by interest rate fluctuations. If rates climb, the borrower's monthly payment goes up; if they decline, the payment goes down.

Depending on economic conditions and other factors, lenders may offer ARMs at a lower initial interest rate (sometimes much lower) than they are charging for fixed-rate loans in that market.

How an ARM Works. With an adjustable-rate mortgage, the borrower's interest rate is determined initially by the cost of money at the time the loan is made. Once the rate has been set, it's tied to one of several widely recognized indexes, and future interest adjustments are based on the upward and downward movements of the index.

Index and Margin. An **index** is a published statistical rate that is a reliable indicator of changes in the cost of money. Examples include the one-year Treasury bill index and the Eleventh District cost of funds index. At the time a loan is made, the lender selects the index it prefers, and thereafter the loan's interest rate will rise and fall with the rates reported for the index.

Since the index is a reflection of the lender's cost of money, it is necessary to add a **margin** to the index to ensure sufficient income for administrative expenses and profit. The lender's margin is usually 2% or 3%, or somewhere in between. The index plus the margin equals the interest rate charged to the borrower.

Example:

5.25%	Current index value
+ 2.00%	Margin
7.25%	Borrower's interest rate

It is the index that fluctuates during the loan term and causes the borrower's interest rate to increase and decrease; the lender's margin remains constant.

Adjustment Periods. The borrower's interest rate is not adjusted every time the index changes. Each ARM has a **rate adjustment period**, which determines how often its interest rate is adjusted. A rate adjustment period of one year is the most common.

An ARM also has a **payment adjustment period**, which determines how often the borrower's monthly mortgage payment is increased or decreased (reflecting changes in the interest rate). For most ARMs, payment adjustments are made at the same intervals as rate adjustments.

Caps. If market interest rates rise rapidly, so will an ARM's index, which could lead to a sharp increase in the interest rate the lender charges the borrower. Of course, a higher interest rate translates into a higher monthly payment. This creates the potential for "payment shock." In other words, the monthly payments on an ARM might increase so dramatically that the borrower can't afford to pay them.

To help protect borrowers from payment shock and lenders from default, ARMs have interest rate and payment caps. An **interest rate cap** limits how much the lender can raise the interest rate on the loan, even if the index goes way up. A **mortgage payment cap** limits how much the lender can increase the monthly payment.

Negative Amortization. If an ARM has certain features, payment increases may not keep up with increases in the loan's interest rate, so that the monthly payments don't cover all the interest owed. The lender usually handles this by adding the unpaid interest to the loan's principal balance; this is called **negative amortization**.

Ordinarily, a loan's principal balance declines steadily, although gradually. But negative amortization causes the principal balance to go up instead of down. The borrower may owe the lender more money than he originally borrowed. Today, lenders usually structure their ARMs to avoid negative amortization, which lessens the chance of ultimate default and foreclosure.

Hybrid ARMs. Most ARMs in today's market have a two-tiered rate adjustment structure. These are called hybrid ARMs, because they're like a combination of an ARM and a fixed-rate loan. With a **hybrid ARM**, the interest rate is fixed for a specified number of years at the start of the loan term, and then the rate becomes adjustable.

For example, a 3/1 hybrid ARM has a fixed rate during the first three years, with annual rate adjustments after that. A 5/1 ARM has a five-year fixed-rate period, and so on. As a general rule, the longer the initial fixed-rate period, the higher the initial interest rate.

Residential Financing Programs

Residential financing programs can be divided into two main groups: conventional loans and government-sponsored loans. In this section, we'll look first at conventional loans, and then at the most important loan programs sponsored by the federal government: the FHA-insured loan program and the VA-guaranteed loan program. (Another federal program, the Rural Housing Service loan program, offers additional possibilities for low-income buyers in rural areas; information about RHS loans may be found online.) As you'll see, each program has its own qualifying standards and its own rules concerning the downpayment and other aspects of the loan.

Conventional Loans

A conventional loan is simply any institutional loan that is not insured or guaranteed by a government agency. For example, FHA-insured and VA-guaranteed loans are not conventional loans, because they are backed by a government agency.

The rules for conventional loans presented here reflect the criteria established by the government-sponsored enterprises that purchase conventional loans, Fannie Mae and Freddie Mac (see Chapter 10). When a loan does not meet secondary market criteria it is considered **nonconforming** and cannot be sold to the major secondary market entities. Most lenders want to be able to sell their loans on the secondary market, so they tailor their standards for conventional loans to match those set by Fannie Mae or Freddie Mac.

Conforming Loan Limits. Fannie Mae or Freddie Mac generally won't purchase a loan if the loan amount exceeds the applicable conforming loan limit. (There are different maximums for properties with one, two, three, or four dwelling units.) The conforming loan limits are based on median housing prices nationwide, and they may be adjusted annually to reflect changes in median prices.

Conventional loans that exceed the conforming loan limits are known as jumbo loans. Lenders typically apply stricter underwriting standards when making a jumbo loan, and they sometimes also charge a higher interest rate.

Conventional LTVs. Traditionally, the standard loan-to-value ratio for a conventional loan has been 80% of the appraised value or sales price of the home, whichever is less. Lenders feel confident that a borrower who makes a 20% downpayment with their own funds is unlikely to default; the borrower has too much to lose. And even if the borrower were to default, a foreclosure sale would be fairly likely to generate at least 80% of the purchase price.

While an 80% LTV may still be regarded as the standard, today many conventional loans have higher loan-to-value ratios; 90% is very common. Many lenders allow LTVs up to 95%, and loans with a 97% LTV may be available through special programs.

Because the lender's risk is greater when the borrower's downpayment is smaller, lenders require borrowers to obtain private mortgage insurance for any conventional loan with an LTV over 80%. (Private mortgage insurance is discussed below.) Some lenders also charge higher interest rates and larger loan fees for conventional loans with higher LTVs. The rules for loans with LTVs over 90% tend to be especially strict.

Owner-Occupancy. Residential lenders make a distinction between owner-occupied homes and investment properties. An owner-occupied home, as the term suggests, is one that the owner (the borrower) plans to live in themself, either as their principal residence or a second home. An investment property is a house that the owner/investor intends to rent out to tenants. Owner-occupants are considered less likely to default than non-occupant borrowers.

Owner-occupancy isn't a requirement for conventional loans, except for loans made through certain special programs (affordable housing programs, for example). Usually, however, a lender will apply stricter rules to investors than to owner-occupants. For instance, a lender might set 95% as its maximum LTV for owner-occupants, but limit investors to a 90% LTV.

Private Mortgage Insurance. Private mortgage insurance (PMI) is designed to protect lenders from the greater risk of high-LTV loans; PMI makes up for the reduced borrower equity. PMI is usually required on all conventional loans that have an LTV over 80% (in other words, whenever the borrower is making a downpayment of less than 20%).

When insuring a loan, the mortgage insurance company assumes only a portion of the risk of default. It typically covers the upper 20% or 25% of the loan amount, not the entire loan amount. The higher the LTV, the higher the coverage requirements and the premiums, since the risk of default is greater. For example, a 95% loan will have a higher coverage requirement and higher premiums than a 90% loan.

In the event of default and foreclosure, the lender, at the insurer's option, will either sell the property or relinquish it to the insurer, then make a claim for reimbursement of actual losses (if any) up to the policy limit. Losses incurred by the lender may take the form of unpaid interest, property taxes and hazard insurance, attorney's fees, and the cost of preserving the property during the period of foreclosure and resale, as well as the expense of selling the property itself.

As the borrower pays off the loan, and as the value of the security property increases, the loan-to-value ratio decreases. With a lower LTV, the risk of default and foreclosure loss is reduced, and eventually the private mortgage insurance has fulfilled its purpose. Under the federal Homeowners Protection Act, lenders are required to cancel a loan's PMI once the loan has been paid down to 80% of the property's original value, if the borrower formally requests the cancellation. And once the loan balance reaches 78% of the original value, cancellation is automatically required, even if the borrower doesn't request it.

Conventional Qualifying Standards. Fannie Mae and Freddie Mac's underwriting standards include detailed guidelines for evaluation of a loan applicant's income, net worth, and credit history. To determine whether the applicant's stable monthly income is sufficient, an underwriter may calculate both a housing expense to income ratio and a debt to income ratio.

> **Example:** Suppose the lender's maximum housing expense to income ratio is 28% and maximum debt to income ratio is 36%. If a loan applicant's housing expense to income ratio is 26% (under the lender's limit), but her debt to income ratio is 41% (over the lender's limit), then the lender probably would not approve the loan unless there were special considerations.

In some cases, the underwriter will consider only the debt to income ratio. Because the debt to income ratio takes all of the applicant's monthly obligations into account, it is considered a more reliable indicator of creditworthiness than the housing expense to income ratio.

Many lenders require applicants for a conventional loan to have the equivalent of two months of mortgage payments in reserve after making the downpayment and paying all their closing costs. For riskier loans, a lender might require enough in reserve to cover three months of payments, or even more. Additional reserves beyond the minimum requirement generally strengthen a loan application.

Assumption. Most conventional loan agreements include an alienation clause, which means the borrower can't sell the property and arrange for the buyer to assume the loan without the lender's permission. Typically, the lender will evaluate the buyer with the same qualifying standards that it applies in a new loan transaction. If the lender approves the assumption, it will charge an assumption fee, and it may also adjust the interest rate to the current market rate.

FHA-Insured Loans

The Federal Housing Administration (FHA) was created by Congress in 1934 in the National Housing Act. The purpose of the act, and of the FHA, was to generate new jobs through increased construction activity, to exert a stabilizing influence on the mortgage market, and to promote the financing, repair, improvement, and sale of real estate nationwide.

Today the FHA is part of the Department of Housing and Urban Development (HUD). Its primary function is insuring mortgage loans; the FHA compensates lenders who make loans through its programs for losses that result from borrower default. The FHA does not build homes or make loans.

In effect, the FHA serves as a giant mortgage insurance agency. Its insurance program, known as the Mutual Mortgage Insurance Plan, is funded with premiums paid by FHA borrowers.

Under the plan, lenders who have been approved by the FHA to make insured loans either submit applications from prospective borrowers to the local FHA office for approval or, if authorized by the FHA to do so, perform the underwriting functions themselves.

Note that the FHA does not accept applications directly from borrowers; borrowers must begin by applying to a lender such as a bank or a mortgage company.

As the insurer, the FHA is liable to the lender for the full amount of any losses resulting from default and foreclosure. In exchange for insuring a loan, the FHA regulates many of the terms and conditions on which the loan is made.

Characteristics of FHA Loans. The typical FHA-insured loan has a 30-year term, although the borrower may have the option of a shorter term. The property purchased with the most common type of FHA loan, a **203(b)** loan, may have up to four dwelling units, and it must be the borrower's primary residence. The FHA requires all the loans it insures to have first lien position.

The downpayment required for an FHA loan is often considerably less than it would be for a conventional loan financing the same purchase (see below). Regardless of the size of the downpayment, mortgage insurance is required on all FHA loans.

Prepayment penalties are not allowed. An FHA loan can be paid off at any time without penalty.

FHA Loan Amounts. FHA programs are primarily intended to help low- and middle-income home buyers. So HUD sets maximum loan amounts, limiting the size of the loans that can be insured under a particular program. FHA maximum loan amounts vary from one place to another because they are based on median housing costs in each area. An area where housing is expensive has a higher maximum loan amount than a low-cost area does.

However, there's also a "ceiling" for FHA loan amounts that applies nationwide; no matter how high prices are in a particular area, FHA loans can't exceed that ceiling. As a result, FHA financing tends to be less useful in areas where housing is exceptionally expensive. The FHA ceiling is tied to Fannie Mae and Freddie Mac's loan amount limits for conforming loans, and it is subject to annual adjustment.

Loan-to-Value Ratios. The loan amount for a particular transaction is determined not just by the FHA loan ceiling for the local area, but also by the FHA's rules concerning loan-to-value ratios.

The maximum loan-to-value ratio for an FHA loan depends on the borrower's credit score. If the borrower's credit score is 580 or above, the maximum LTV is 96.5%. If their score is 500 to 579, the maximum LTV is 90%. Someone with a score below 500 isn't eligible for an FHA loan.

In transactions with FHA financing, the required downpayment (the difference between the maximum loan amount and the appraised value or sales price, whichever is less) is called the borrower's **minimum cash investment**. In an FHA transaction with maximum financing (a 96.5% LTV), the borrower must make a minimum cash investment of 3.5%.

FHA Qualifying Standards. As with any institutional loan, the underwriting for an FHA-insured loan involves the analysis of the applicant's income, net worth, and credit history. But the FHA's underwriting standards are not as strict as the Fannie Mae/Freddie Mac standards used for conventional loans. The FHA standards make it easier for low- and middle-income home buyers to qualify for a mortgage.

Income. Just as with a conventional loan, an underwriter evaluating an application for an FHA loan will apply two ratios to determine the adequacy of the applicant's income. However, the FHA's maximum income ratios are higher than the ones typically set for conventional loans. This means that an FHA borrower's mortgage payment and other monthly obligations can be a larger percentage of their income than a conventional borrower's.

Although FHA programs are targeted toward low- and middle-income buyers, there is no maximum income level. A person with a high income could qualify for an FHA loan, as long as the requested loan didn't exceed the maximum loan amount for the area.

Funds for Closing. At closing, an FHA borrower must have sufficient funds to cover the minimum cash investment, any discount points she has agreed to pay, and certain other closing costs. (Note that secondary financing generally can't be used for the minimum cash investment, unless the source of the second loan is a nonprofit or governmental agency, or a family member.) An FHA borrower is usually not required to have reserves after closing.

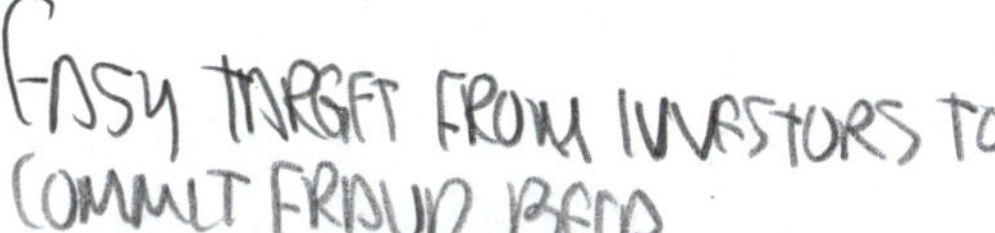

FHA Insurance Premiums. Mortgage insurance premiums for FHA loans are sometimes referred to as the **MIP**. In most cases an FHA borrower pays both a one-time premium and annual premiums. The one-time premium may be paid at closing, or else financed along with the loan amount and paid off over the loan term.

For loans issued since 2013 with an original loan-to-value ratio over 90%, the annual MIP must be paid for the entire loan term. For loans with an original LTV of 90% or less, the annual MIP will be canceled after 11 years.

Assumption of FHA Loans. Any creditworthy buyer can assume an FHA loan. The loan's interest rate is not increased upon assumption, so assumability can be a real selling point to a buyer if the loan has a below-market rate. The buyer must intend to occupy the home as their primary residence.

VA-Guaranteed Loans

The VA-guaranteed home loan program was established to help veterans finance the purchase of their homes with affordable loans. VA financing offers many advantages over conventional financing and has few disadvantages. The program is administered by the U.S. Department of Veterans Affairs (the VA).

Eligibility for VA Loans. Eligibility for a VA home loan is based on length of continuous active duty service in the U.S. armed forces. The minimum requirement varies from 90 days to 24 months, depending on when the veteran served. (Longer periods are required for peacetime service.) Eligibility may also be based on longtime service in the National Guard or reserves. Military personnel who receive a dishonorable discharge are not eligible for VA loans.

A veteran's surviving spouse may be eligible for a VA loan if he or she has not remarried and the veteran was killed in action or died of service-related injuries. A veteran's spouse may also be eligible if the veteran is listed as missing in action or is a prisoner of war.

Application Process. To apply for a VA-guaranteed loan, a veteran must apply to an institutional lender and provide a Certificate of Eligibility issued by the VA. The lender will process the veteran's loan application and forward it to the VA. Note that the Certificate of Eligibility isn't a guarantee that the veteran will qualify for a loan.

The property that the veteran wants to purchase must be appraised in accordance with VA guidelines. The appraised value is set forth in a document called a **Notice of Value**, or NOV (also referred to as a Certificate of Reasonable Value, or CRV).

When a lender approves a VA loan, the loan is guaranteed by the federal government. If the borrower defaults, the VA will reimburse the lender for part or all of any resulting loss. The loan guaranty works essentially like mortgage insurance; it protects the lender against a large loss if the borrower fails to repay the loan.

Characteristics of VA Loans. A VA loan can be used to finance the purchase or construction of a single-family residence or a multifamily residence with up to four units. The veteran must intend to occupy the home. (In the case of a multifamily property, the veteran must occupy one of the units.)

VA-guaranteed loans are attractive to borrowers for a number of reasons, including the following:

- Unlike most home loans, a VA loan does not require a downpayment. The loan amount can be as large as the sales price or appraised value, whichever is less. In other words, the loan-to-value ratio can be 100%. (VA borrowers who have the funds for a downpayment may choose to make one, in order to reduce the amount they're borrowing and their monthly payment.)
- The VA doesn't set a maximum loan amount or maximum income limits. (In other words, VA loans aren't restricted to low- or middle-income buyers.)
- VA underwriting standards are less stringent than conventional underwriting standards.
- VA loans don't require the extra expense of mortgage insurance.

The interest rate for a VA loan is negotiated between the lender and the borrower in the usual way. The lender may charge discount points, and the points may be paid by the borrower, the seller, or a third party. The lender cannot charge a prepayment penalty.

A VA borrower must pay a funding fee, which the lender will remit to the VA. The fee is generally about 2% of the loan amount, but it decreases if the borrower makes a downpayment.

VA Guaranty. Like private mortgage insurance, the VA guaranty covers only part of the loan amount. The guaranty amount has been increased periodically over the history of the program. Currently, the guaranty is 25% of the loan amount for most VA loans.

Restoration of Entitlement. The amount of the guaranty available to a particular veteran is sometimes called the vet's "entitlement." If a veteran sells property that was financed with a VA loan and repays the loan in full from the proceeds of the sale, the veteran receives a full restoration of guaranty rights for future use. There is also a one-time restoration of entitlement available for borrowers who pay off their VA loan without selling the property and then want to use another VA loan to purchase another property.

Because of the owner-occupancy requirement, the new property would need to become the borrower's primary residence. (Restoration of entitlement is also referred to as reinstatement.)

Substitution of Entitlement. If a home purchased with a VA loan is sold and the loan is assumed instead of repaid, the veteran's entitlement can be restored under certain circumstances. The buyer who assumes the loan must be an eligible veteran and must agree to substitute their entitlement for the seller's. The loan payments must be current, and the buyer must be an acceptable credit risk. If these conditions are met, the veteran can formally request a substitution of entitlement from the VA.

Note that a VA loan can be assumed by a non-veteran who meets the VA's standards of creditworthiness. But the entitlement of the veteran seller will not be restored if the buyer assuming the loan is not a veteran.

Default. If a VA borrower defaults and the foreclosure sale results in a loss, the borrower may be liable to the VA for the amount the VA pays the lender based on the guaranty. Also, the borrower's guaranty entitlement won't be restored (and he won't be eligible for another VA loan) until he reimburses the VA for the full amount paid out.

Qualifying Standards. Lenders must follow guidelines established by the VA to evaluate a VA loan applicant's creditworthiness. The applicant's income is analyzed using two methods, and it must qualify under both tests. The first one is the income ratio method; the VA sets a maximum debt to income ratio. In many cases the maximum ratio allowed for a VA loan is considerably higher than the maximum debt to income ratio that would be acceptable if the veteran applied for a conventional loan.

The second method used to qualify a VA loan applicant is the residual income method. Residual income is calculated by subtracting the proposed mortgage payment, estimated property maintenance and utility costs, payroll taxes, and all other recurring obligations from the veteran's gross monthly income. The veteran's residual income must meet the VA's minimum requirements, which vary based on the region of the country where the veteran lives, family size, and the size of the proposed loan.

Predatory Lending

Predatory lending refers to practices that unscrupulous mortgage lenders and mortgage brokers use to take advantage of (prey upon) unsophisticated borrowers for their own profit. Real estate agents and appraisers sometimes participate in predatory lending schemes, and in some cases a buyer or seller may play a role in deceiving the other party.

Predatory lending is especially likely to occur in the subprime market. It tends to be more common in refinancing and home equity lending, but home purchase loans are also affected.

Here are some examples of predatory lending practices:

- **Predatory steering:** Steering a buyer toward a more expensive loan when the buyer could qualify for a less expensive one.
- **Fee packing:** Charging interest rates, points, or processing fees that far exceed the norm and aren't justified by the cost of the services provided.
- **Loan flipping:** Encouraging a home owner to refinance repeatedly in a short period, when there's no real benefit to the borrower for doing so (but the lender collects loan fees on each new loan).
- **Predatory property flipping:** Buying property at a discount (because the seller needs a quick sale) and then rapidly reselling it to an unsophisticated buyer for an inflated price. (This is illegal when a real estate agent, an appraiser, and/or a lender commit fraud to deceive the seller and/or the buyer about the true value of the property.)
- **Disregarding borrower's ability to pay:** Making a loan based on the property's value, without using appropriate qualifying standards to determine the borrower's ability to afford the loan payments.
- **Balloon payment abuses:** Making a partially amortized or interest-only loan with low monthly payments, without disclosing to the borrower that a large balloon payment will be required after a short period.
- **Fraud:** Misrepresenting or concealing unfavorable loan terms or excessive fees, falsifying documents, or using other fraudulent means to induce a prospective borrower to enter into a loan agreement.
- **Excessive or unfair prepayment penalties:** Imposing an unusually large penalty, and/or failing to limit the penalty period to the first few years of the loan term.

Predatory lenders and mortgage brokers deliberately target borrowers who aren't able to understand the transaction they're entering into, or don't know that better alternatives are available to them. Potential borrowers are especially likely to be targeted if they're elderly, have a limited income, are poorly educated, or speak limited English.

As public awareness of predatory lending has grown, laws intended to prevent it have been implemented, but it remains a genuine problem.

Chapter Summary

1. Real estate lenders in the primary market include savings and loan associations, commercial banks, savings banks, mortgage companies, credit unions, and private lenders.
2. Lenders charge an origination fee to cover their administrative costs, and sometimes charge discount points to increase the yield on the loan. One point is 1% of the loan amount.
3. The Truth in Lending Act applies to any consumer loan that is secured by real property. It requires lenders and credit arrangers to give loan applicants a disclosure statement about loan costs. It also regulates how financing information is presented in advertising.
4. In qualifying a buyer for a real estate loan, an underwriter examines the buyer's income, net worth, and credit history to determine if he can be expected to make the proposed monthly mortgage payments. Income ratios measure the adequacy of the buyer's stable monthly income.
5. The traditional loan term for a mortgage loan is 30 years, but loans with terms of 15, 20, and 40 years are also available. A 15-year loan requires higher payments than a comparable 30-year loan, but the borrower will pay substantially less in interest over the loan term.
6. A fully amortized loan has equal payments that pay off all of the principal and interest by the end of the loan term. Most mortgage loans are fully amortized, but partially amortized loans and interest-only loans are also available in some cases.
7. The loan-to-value ratio for a particular transaction expresses the relationship between the loan amount and the property's appraised value or sales price, whichever is less. The higher the loan-to-value ratio, the greater the lender's risk.
8. Secondary financing may be used to cover part of the downpayment and closing costs required for the primary loan. A secondary financing arrangement must comply with rules set by the primary lender.
9. The interest rate on a mortgage loan may be either fixed or adjustable. An ARM's interest rate is tied to an index, and it is adjusted at specified intervals to reflect changes in the index.
10. A conventional loan is an institutional loan that is not insured or guaranteed by the government. Private mortgage insurance is required for loans with LTVs over 80%.
11. FHA-insured loans are distinguished from conventional loans by less stringent qualifying standards, lower downpayments, and less cash needed for closing. The maximum loan amount available for an FHA loan depends on housing costs in the area where the property is located. FHA mortgage insurance is required on all FHA loans.
12. Eligible veterans may obtain a VA-guaranteed home loan. No downpayment is required for a VA loan. The VA sets a maximum guaranty amount, but does not set a maximum loan amount. The qualifying standards for a VA loan are considerably less stringent than the standards for conventional loans.
13. Predatory lending refers to lending practices used by lenders and other parties to take advantage of unsophisticated borrowers. Examples of predatory lending practices include predatory steering, fee packing, loan flipping, and disregarding the borrower's ability to afford the payments.

Key Terms

Mortgage company—A type of lender that is not a depository institution and that makes loans on behalf of large investors or using borrowed funds. Sometimes called a mortgage banker.

Mortgage broker—An individual or company that arranges loans between borrowers and investors, but does not make or service the loans.

Point—One percent of the amount of a loan.

Origination fee—A fee that a lender charges to cover the administrative costs of processing a loan.

Discount points—A fee that a lender may charge to increase the yield on the loan, over and above the interest rate.

Truth in Lending Act (TILA)—A federal consumer protection law that requires lenders to give borrowers information about loan costs.

Loan estimate—A form that TILA and RESPA require a lender to give to a loan applicant, providing detailed information about the loan and estimates of the closing costs.

Annual percentage rate (APR)—The relationship of the total cost of a loan to the loan amount, expressed as an annual percentage.

Total interest percentage (TIP)—The total amount of interest that the borrower will pay over the loan term, expressed as a percentage of the loan amount.

Loan underwriting—Evaluating the creditworthiness of the buyer and the value of the property to determine if a loan should be approved.

Stable monthly income—Income that satisfies the lender's standards of quality and durability.

Income ratios—Percentages used to determine whether a loan applicant's stable monthly income is sufficient.

Housing expense to income ratio—A percentage that measures a loan applicant's proposed monthly mortgage payment against the applicant's stable monthly income.

Debt to income ratio—A percentage that measures all of a loan applicant's monthly obligations (including the proposed mortgage payment) against the applicant's stable monthly income.

Net worth—An individual's total personal assets minus her total personal liabilities.

Credit score—A number that is calculated by applying a statistical model to a loan applicant's credit report, used as an indication of how likely the applicant is to default on the proposed loan.

Automated underwriting (AU)—Analysis of a loan application with computer software that makes a preliminary recommendation for or against approval.

Fully amortized loan—A loan that is fully paid off by the end of its term by means of regular principal and interest payments.

Loan-to-value ratio—The relationship between the loan amount and the property's appraised value or sales price, whichever is less.

Secondary financing—A second loan to help pay the downpayment or closing costs associated with the primary loan.

Fixed-rate loan—A loan repaid over its term at an unchanging rate of interest.

Adjustable-rate mortgage—A loan that allows the lender to periodically adjust the loan's interest rate to reflect changes in market interest rates.

Index—A published rate that is a reliable indicator of the current cost of money.

Margin—The difference between the index value on an ARM and the interest rate the borrower is charged.

Negative amortization—When unpaid interest is added to a loan's principal balance.

Conventional loan—An institutional loan that is not insured or guaranteed by a government agency.

Nonconforming loan—A loan that does not meet the underwriting standards of the major secondary market entities.

PMI—Private mortgage insurance; insurance designed to protect lenders from the greater risks of high-LTV conventional loans.

MIP—The mortgage insurance premiums required for FHA-insured loans.

Certificate of Eligibility—The document that establishes a veteran's eligibility to apply for a VA home loan.

Notice of Value (NOV)—The document issued when a home is appraised in connection with the underwriting of a VA loan.

Residual income—The amount of monthly income a VA borrower has left over after deducting monthly expenses and taxes.

Predatory lending—Lending practices used by unscrupulous lenders and mortgage brokers to take advantage of unsophisticated borrowers.

Chapter Quiz

1. **Which one of the following bodies would be most likely to make a 90% conventional loan for the purchase of a residence?**
   a) Federal Housing Administration
   b) Federal National Mortgage Association
   c) Farm Home Loan Administration
   d) Acme Mortgage Bankers

2. **To increase its yield on the loan, the lender is charging 2% of the loan amount, to be paid at closing. This charge is called:**
   a) the origination fee
   b) PMI
   c) the index
   d) discount points

3. **The Truth in Lending Act and Regulation Z:**
   a) place restrictions on how much a lender can charge for a consumer loan
   b) require lenders to give loan applicants a disclosure statement concerning loan costs
   c) prohibit lenders from advertising specific financing terms
   d) All of the above

4. **A loan's APR expresses the relationship between:**
   a) the total cost of the loan and the loan amount
   b) the interest rate on the loan and the discount rate
   c) the downpayment and the total cost of the loan
   d) the monthly payment and the interest rate

5. **After determining the quantity of the loan applicant's stable monthly income, the underwriter measures the adequacy of the income using:**
   a) the consumer price index
   b) income ratios
   c) credit scoring
   d) federal income tax tables

6. **Fifteen-year mortgages typically have all of the following disadvantages, except:**
   a) a higher interest rate
   b) higher monthly payments
   c) a larger downpayment
   d) All of these are disadvantages of a 15-year mortgage

7. **The house was appraised for $293,000 and the sales price is $290,000. If the loan-to-value ratio is 90%, how much is the loan amount?**
   a) $254,400
   b) $261,000
   c) $263,700
   d) $283,000

8. **With an adjustable-rate mortgage, the interest rate:**
   a) is adjusted at specified intervals, and so is the payment amount
   b) is adjusted monthly, and so is the payment amount
   c) increases and decreases, but the payment amount remains the same
   d) may increase periodically, but does not decrease

9. **Unpaid interest added to the loan balance is referred to as:**
   a) payment shock
   b) partial amortization
   c) negative amortization
   d) participation interest

10. **For conventional loans, private mortgage insurance is required when the loan-to-value ratio is:**
    a) 75% or higher
    b) 90% or higher
    c) over 95%
    d) over 80%

11. **The FHA:**
    a) makes loans
    b) insures loans
    c) buys and sells loans
    d) All of the above

12. **All of the following statements about FHA loans are true, except:**
    a) no downpayment is required
    b) the borrower is usually not required to have reserves after closing
    c) mortgage insurance is required on all loans
    d) the borrower must occupy the property as their primary residence

13. **A VA loan can be assumed:**
    a) only by an eligible veteran
    b) only by an eligible veteran who agrees to a substitution of entitlement
    c) by any buyer who passes the credit check
    d) by any buyer, without regard to creditworthiness

14. A veteran may obtain a VA-guaranteed loan on a:

a) single-family residence only
b) four-plex, as long as all of the units are rented out to tenants
c) residence with up to two units, as long as the veteran occupies one unit
d) residence with up to four units, as long as the veteran occupies one unit

15. Which of the following statements about predatory lending is true?

a) Predatory lending only affects subprime borrowers
b) Predatory lending does not occur in connection with home purchase loans
c) Predatory lenders are especially likely to target the elderly and people who speak only limited English
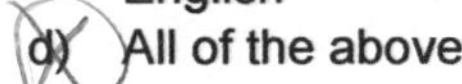
d) All of the above

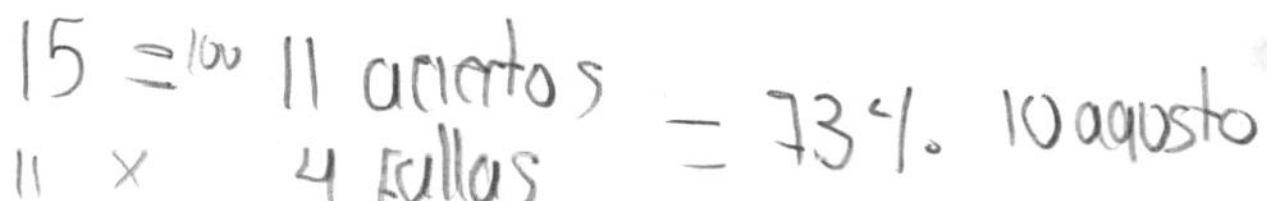

Chapter 12:

Real Estate Appraisal

- **I. Introduction to Appraisal**
- **II. Value**
  - A. Market value
  - B. Principles of value
- **III. The Appraisal Process**
- **IV. Gathering Data**
  - A. General data
    1. Economic trends
    2. Neighborhood analysis
  - B. Specific data
    1. Site analysis
    2. Building analysis
- **V. Approaches to Value**
  - A. Sales comparison approach to value
    1. Elements of comparison
    2. Adjustments
    3. Use of listings
  - B. Cost approach to value
    1. Estimating replacement cost
    2. Estimating depreciation
    3. Adding land value
  - C. Income approach to value
    1. Gross income
    2. Operating expenses
    3. Capitalization
    4. Gross income multipliers
- **VI. Reconciliation and Final Estimate of Value**

The foundation of every real estate transaction is the value placed on the property in question. The value of a home affects its selling price, financing terms, rental rate, property tax assessment, and insurance coverage, and the income tax consequences of owning it. The parties to a transaction need to know what the property is worth aside from any emotional or other subjective considerations, and for this they rely on an appraisal. This chapter examines the concept of value and explains the various methods appraisers use to estimate value.

Key Terms

Market Value	**Physical Deterioration**
Highest and Best Use	**Functional Obsolescence**
Principle of Change	**External Obsolescence**
Principle of Substitution	**Income Approach**
Sales Comparison Approach	**Effective Gross Income**
Arm's Length Transaction	**Net Operating Income**
Cost Approach	**Capitalization Rate**
Depreciation	**Economic Rent**

Introduction to Appraisal

An **appraisal** is an estimate or an opinion of value. It usually takes the form of a written **appraisal report**, which sets forth the appraiser's opinion of the value of a piece of property as of a given date. An appraisal is sometimes called a **valuation.**

An appraiser may be asked to help a seller decide on a fair asking price, or a buyer may seek an opinion as to how much to pay for the property. Most often, an appraisal is requested by a mortgage lender, when a buyer has applied for a loan. The lender uses the appraisal to decide whether the property the buyer has chosen is suitable security for a loan, and if so, what the maximum loan amount should be.

Most appraisals are performed by **fee appraisers**—independent appraisers hired to value a particular property in exchange for a fee. Fee appraisers are either self-employed or work for an appraisal firm. (Other appraisers are employed by government agencies, financial institutions, insurance companies, or other businesses.)

In addition to helping to determine a fair price or a maximum loan amount, an appraiser's services are regularly required in order to:

- assess whether planned improvements are the most cost-effective use of the land;
- estimate a property's value for purposes of taxation (assessment);
- establish rental rates;
- estimate the relative values of properties being exchanged;
- determine the amount of hazard insurance coverage necessary;
- estimate remodeling costs or their contribution to value;
- help establish just compensation in a condemnation proceeding; or
- estimate the value of properties involved in the liquidation of estates, corporate mergers and acquisitions, or bankruptcies.

Regardless of the situation, the person who hires the appraiser is the client. The appraiser is the client's agent. A principal/agent relationship exists and the rules of agency law apply (see Chapter 7).

An appraiser's fee is determined in advance, based on the expected difficulty of the appraisal and the amount of time it is likely to take. The fee cannot be calculated as a percentage of the appraised value of the property, nor can it be based on the client's satisfaction with the appraiser's findings.

To help ensure their independence and impartiality, appraisers in home loan transactions are subject to special rules. For example, if a loan will be secured by the borrower's home, federal law prohibits the appraiser from having any financial interest in the property. If a loan will be sold to Fannie Mae or Freddie Mac, the appraiser can't have any substantive communication with the mortgage loan originator (the loan officer or mortgage broker); the appraisal must be arranged through an independent appraisal management company or through a separate department within the lender's organization. In addition, a real estate agent can't select or compensate the appraiser.

Under both federal and state law, it's illegal for an appraiser's client or anyone else with an interest in a transaction to attempt to improperly influence the appraisal through coercion, extortion, or bribery. However, it is permissible to ask the appraiser to consider additional property information, explain the basis for their value estimate more fully, or correct errors in the appraisal report.

The state of Washington licenses and certifies appraisers, and state law requires anyone who appraises real estate located in Washington to be licensed or certified, or registered as an appraiser trainee. (That requirement does not apply to a real estate licensee preparing a price opinion for a client, however. A broker price opinion or competitive market analysis is not considered an appraisal.)

Under federal law, only appraisals prepared by state-licensed or state-certified appraisers in accordance with the **Uniform Standards of Professional Appraisal Practice** (USPAP) can be used in federally related loan transactions. The USPAP are guidelines adopted by the Appraisal Foundation, a nonprofit organization. The majority of residential real estate loans are federally related, since the category includes loans made by any financial institution regulated or insured by the federal government and loans sold to the federal secondary market entities. (Certain transactions, including residential transactions for $400,000 or less, are exempt from the licensed or certified appraiser requirement.) However, regardless of the loan amount, all transactions involving FHA financing require the services of a state-certified appraiser; state licensure is not adequate for FHA loans.

Value

Value is a term with many meanings. One common definition is "the present worth of future benefits." Value is usually measured in terms of money. For appraisal purposes, value falls into two general classifications: value in use and value in exchange. **Value in use** is the subjective value that a particular person places on a property, while **value in exchange** is the objective value of a property as viewed by any disinterested person. A property's value in use and value in exchange may be quite different, depending on the circumstances.

> **Example:** A large, expensive, one-bedroom home, designed, built, and occupied by its owner, would undoubtedly be worth more to the owner than to the average buyer. Most buyers would look at the property objectively and expect more than one bedroom for the price.

Value in exchange is the more significant of the two types of value. Value in exchange is better known as **market value**. Estimating a property's market value is the purpose of most appraisals.

Market Value

For something to have market value, four elements are required: utility, scarcity, transferability, and demand. In other words, the item must render a service or fill a need; it must not be universally available; it must be possible to transfer it from one owner to another; and there must be a desire to own it. This holds true for real property as well as other commodities.

Here is the most widely accepted definition of market value, the one used by the federal financial institution regulatory agencies:

> *The most probable price which a property should bring in a competitive and open market under all conditions requisite to a fair sale, the buyer and seller each acting prudently and knowledgeably, and assuming the price is not affected by undue stimulus.*

Notice that according to this definition, market value is the *most probable* price (not "the highest price") that the property *should bring* (not "will bring"). Appraisal is a matter of estimation and likelihood, not certainty.

Market Value vs. Market Price. There's an important distinction between market value and market price. Market price is the price actually paid for a property, regardless of whether the parties to the transaction were informed and acting free of unusual pressure. Market value is what should be paid if a property is purchased and sold under all the conditions requisite to a fair sale. These conditions include an open and competitive market, prudent and informed parties, and no undue stimulus (that is, no unusual pressure to sell or buy immediately).

Principles of Value

Of the major forces that influence our attitudes and behavior, there are three categories of forces that interact to create, support, or erode property values:

- social ideals and standards,
- economic fluctuations, and
- government regulations.

A change in attitudes regarding family size and the emergence of the two-car family are examples of social forces that affect the value of homes (in this case, homes with too many bedrooms or with one-car garages). Economic forces include employment levels, interest rates, and any other factors that affect the community's purchasing power. Government regulations, such as zoning ordinances, serve to promote, stabilize, or discourage the demand for property.

Over the years, appraisers have developed a reliable body of principles, referred to as the **principles of value**, that take these factors into account and guide appraisers in making decisions in the valuation process. Let's take a look at each of these principles.

Principle of Highest and Best Use. A property's **highest and best use** is the most profitable use that is legally permissible, physically possible, and financially feasible; in other words, it is the use that will provide the greatest net return to the owner over a period of time. **Net return** usually refers to net income, but it can't always be measured in terms of money. With residential properties, for example, net return might manifest itself in the form of amenities—the pleasure and satisfaction derived from living on the property.

Fig. 12.1 Evaluating highest and best use

Highest and Best Use (Alternative Use Considerations)		
	Annual Income	**Estimated Value**
Present Use: Warehouse	$30,250 (actual)	$275,000
Alternative Use 1: Parking lot	$29,500 (estimated)	$268,000
Alternative Use 2: Gas station	$31,500 (estimated)	$285,000
Alternative Use 3: Triplex	$34,200 (estimated)	$310,000

Determining a property's highest and best use may simply be a matter of confirming that deed restrictions or an existing zoning ordinance limit the property to its present use. It's often true that the present use of a property is its highest and best use. But change is constant, and a warehouse site that was once profitable might now generate a greater net return as a parking lot. Figure 12.1 presents an example of alternative use considerations for a warehouse.

Principle of Change. The principle of change holds that real estate values are constantly in flux, moving up and down in response to changes in the various social, economic, and governmental forces that affect value. A property's value also changes as the property itself improves or deteriorates. A property that was worth $300,000 last year may be worth $325,000 today, and its value is likely to change in the coming year as well. Because value is always subject to change, an estimate of value must be tied to a specific point in time, which is called the **effective date** of the appraisal.

Related to the principle of change is the idea that property has a four-phase life cycle: **integration, equilibrium, disintegration**, and **rejuvenation**. Integration (also called development) is the early stage, when the property is being developed. Equilibrium is a period of stability, when the property undergoes little, if any, change. Disintegration is a period of decline, when the property's economic usefulness is near an end and constant upkeep is necessary.

And rejuvenation (also known as revitalization) is a period of renewal, when the property is reborn, perhaps with a different highest and best use.

Every property has both a physical life cycle and an economic life cycle. It's typically the property's **economic life**—the period when the land and its improvements are profitable—that ends first. An appraiser must take these life cycle stages into account when estimating a property's present worth.

Principle of Anticipation. It's the future, not the past, that's important to appraisers. Knowing that property values change, an appraiser asks: What is happening to this property? What is its future? How do prospective buyers view its potential? The appraiser must be aware of the social, economic, and governmental factors that will affect the future value of the property.

Value is created by the anticipated future benefits of owning a property. It is future benefits, not past benefits, that arouse a desire to own.

Anticipation can help or hurt value, depending on what informed buyers and sellers expect to happen to the property in the future. They usually expect property values to increase, but in certain situations they anticipate that values will decline, as when the community is experiencing a severe recession.

Principle of Supply and Demand. The principle of supply and demand affects almost every commodity, including real estate. Values tend to rise as demand increases and supply decreases, and to diminish when the reverse is true. It's not so much the demand for or supply of real estate in general that affects values, but the demand for or supply of a particular type of property.

For instance, a generally depressed community may have one or two very attractive, sought-after neighborhoods. The value of homes in those neighborhoods remains high, no matter what the general trend is for the rest of the community.

Principle of Substitution. The principle of substitution states that no one will pay more for a property than they would have to pay for an equally desirable substitute property, provided that there would be no unreasonable delay in acquiring the substitute property. Explained another way, the principle of substitution holds that if two properties for sale are alike in every respect, the least expensive will be in greater demand.

Principle of Conformity. The maximum value of land is achieved when there is an acceptable degree of social and economic conformity (similarity) in the area. Conformity should be reasonable, not carried to an extreme.

In a residential appraisal, aspects of conformity that the appraiser considers are similarities in the age, size, style, and quality of the homes in the neighborhood. Nonconformity can work either to the benefit or to the detriment of the nonconforming home. The value of a home of much lower quality than those around it is increased by its association with the higher-quality homes; this is the principle of **progression**.

> **Example:** A small, unkempt home surrounded by large, attractive homes will be worth more in this neighborhood than it would be if it were situated in a neighborhood of other small homes in poor condition.

Conversely, the value of a large, expensive home in a neighborhood of small, inexpensive homes will suffer because of its surroundings; this is the principle of **regression**.

Principle of Contribution. The principle of contribution concerns the value that an improvement contributes to the overall value of the property. Most improvements contribute less to value than they cost to make. For example, a remodeled basement can increase the value of a home, but usually doesn't increase the home's value by as much as it cost to carry out the remodeling.

Principle of Competition. Competition can have a dramatic impact on the value of property, especially income property. For example, if one convenience store in a neighborhood is extremely profitable, its success is likely to bring a competing convenience store into the area. This competition will probably mean lower profits for the first store (as some of its customers begin doing business with the second store), and lower profits will reduce the property's value.

The Appraisal Process

Properly done, the appraisal process is orderly and systematic. While there's no official procedure, appraisers generally carry out the appraisal process using the following eight steps.

1. **Define the problem.** Each client wants an appraiser to solve a specific problem: to estimate the value of a particular property as of a particular date and for a particular purpose. The first step in the appraisal process is to define the problem to be solved. This involves identifying the **subject property**—what property and which aspect(s) of it are to be appraised—and establishing the purpose of the appraisal and how the client intends to use it. Unless instructed to do otherwise, the appraiser will estimate the property's value as of the date the appraisal is performed.
2. **Determine the scope of work.** Determining the scope of work refers to figuring out what work is needed to solve the appraisal problem: in other words, the type and extent of research and analyses required by the assignment. Together, defining the appraisal problem and determining the scope of work are sometimes called the appraiser's preliminary analysis.
3. **Collect and verify the data.** The data on which the value estimate is based is divided into two categories: general and specific.

   General data concerns matters outside the subject property that affect its value. It includes population trends, prevailing economic circumstances, zoning, and proximity of amenities (such as shopping, schools, and transportation), as well as the condition and quality of the neighborhood.

   Specific data concerns the subject property itself. The appraiser will gather information about the title, the buildings, and the site. (General and specific data will be discussed in more detail in the next section of the chapter.)
4. **Analyze the data.** Data analysis actually occurs throughout the appraisal process. As data is collected, the appraiser analyzes its relevance as an indicator of the subject property's value.
5. **Determine site value.** A site valuation is an estimate of the value of the land, excluding the value of any existing or proposed improvements. In the case of unimproved property, site valuation is the same as appraising the property as is. For improved property, site valuation means appraising the property as if vacant. Site valuation is necessary to determine the highest and best use of the property, but it's also important in tax assessment appraisal and other situations.
6. **Apply the approaches to value.** In some cases, the appraiser will approach the problem of estimating value three different ways: with the sales comparison approach, the cost approach, and the income approach. In other cases, they will use only the method that seems most appropriate for the problem to be solved. Whether one, two, or three approaches are used is a matter of judgment.

Sometimes a particular method cannot be used. Raw land, for example, cannot be appraised using the cost approach. A public library, on the other hand, must be appraised by the cost approach because it does not generate income and no market exists for it.

7. **Reconcile value indicators for the final value estimate.** The figures yielded by each of the three approaches are called **value indicators**; they give indications of what the property is worth, but are not final estimates themselves. The appraiser will take into consideration the purpose of the appraisal, the type of property being appraised, and the reliability of the data gathered for each of the three approaches. they will place the greatest emphasis on the approach that seems to be the most reliable indication of value.
8. **Issue appraisal report.** The appraisal report contains the formal presentation of the value estimate and an explanation of what went into its determination.

Fig. 12.2 The Appraisal Process

Steps in the Appraisal Process
1. Define the problem
2. Determine scope of work
3. Collect and verify data
4. Analyze data
5. Determine site value
6. Apply the approaches to value
7. Reconcile value indicators
8. Issue appraisal report

Gathering Data

Once the appraiser knows what property they are to appraise, what the purpose of the appraisal is, and what work will be needed to produce the opinion of value, they begin to gather the necessary data. As mentioned above, data is broken down into general data (about the neighborhood and other external influences) and specific data (about the subject property itself).

General Data

General data includes both general economic data about the community and information about the subject property's neighborhood.

Economic Trends. The appraiser examines economic trends for hints as to the direction the property's value might take in the future. Economic trends can take shape at the local, regional, national, or international level, although local trends have the most significant impact on a property's value. Generally, prosperous conditions tend to have a positive effect on property values; economic declines have the opposite effect.

Economic forces include population growth shifts, employment and wage levels (purchasing power), price levels, building cycles, personal tax and property tax rates, building costs, and interest rates.

An appraiser might project future economic growth by looking at economic activity in basic industries, which are the local economy's foundation, as well as non-basic (service) industries, which support the basic industries. This type of projection is known as **economic-base analysis.**

Neighborhood Analysis. A property's value is inevitably tied to its surrounding neighborhood. A neighborhood is a residential, commercial, industrial, or agricultural area that contains similar types of properties. Its boundaries are determined by physical barriers (such as highways and bodies of water), land use patterns, the age or value of homes or other buildings, and the economic status of the residents.

Neighborhoods are continually changing and, like the individual properties that make them up, they have a four-phase life cycle of integration, equilibrium, disintegration, and rejuvenation.

When evaluating the future of a neighborhood, the appraiser must consider its physical, social, and economic characteristics, and also governmental influences.

Here are some of the specific factors appraisers look at when gathering data about a residential neighborhood:

1. **Percentage of home ownership.** Is there a high degree of owner-occupancy, or do rental properties predominate? Owner-occupied neighborhoods are generally better maintained and less susceptible to deterioration.
2. **Vacant homes and lots.** An unusual number of vacant homes or lots suggests a low level of interest in the area, which has a negative effect on property values. On the other hand, significant construction activity in a neighborhood signals strong interest in the area.
3. **Conformity.** The homes in a neighborhood should be reasonably similar to one another in style, age, size, and quality. Strictly enforced zoning and private restrictions promote conformity and protect property values.
4. **Changing land use.** Is the neighborhood in the midst of a transition from residential use to some other type of use? If so, the properties may be losing their value.
5. **Contour of the land.** Mildly rolling topography is preferred to terrain that is either monotonously flat or excessively hilly.
6. **Streets.** Wide, gently curving streets are more appealing than narrow or straight ones. Streets should be hard-surfaced and well maintained.
7. **Utilities.** Is the neighborhood adequately serviced by electricity, water, gas, sewers, telephones, Internet, and cable TV?
8. **Nuisances.** Nuisances in or near a neighborhood (odors, eyesores, industrial noises or pollutants, or exposure to unusual winds, smog, or fog) hurt property values.
9. **Prestige.** Is the neighborhood considered prestigious, in comparison to others in the community? If so, that will increase property values.

Fig. 12.3 Neighborhood Data Form

NEIGHBORHOOD DATA FORM

Property adjacent to:
NORTH *Plum Boulevard, garden apartments*
SOUTH *Cherry Boulevard, single-family residences*
EAST *14th Avenue, single-family residences*
WEST *12th Avenue, single-family residences*

Population: ☐ increasing ☐ decreasing ☑ stable

Stage of Life Cycle: ☐ integration ☑ equilibrium ☐ disintegration ☐ rebirth

Tax Rate: ☐ higher ☐ lower ☑ same as competing areas

Services: ☑ police ☑ fire ☑ garbage ☐ other

Average family size: *3.5*

Predominant occupations: *white collar, skilled tradesman*

Distance from:
Commercial areas *3 miles*
Primary schools *6 blocks*
Secondary schools *1 mile*
Recreational areas *2 miles*
Cultural areas *3 miles*
Places of worship *Methodist, Catholic, Baptist*
Public transportation *Bus stops nearby, excellent service*
Freeways/highways *10 blocks*

Typical Properties	%	Age	Price Range	% Owner-Occupied
vacant lots	0			
single-family residences	80%	10 years	$275,000-$280,000	93%
2- to 4-unit apartments	15%	15 years		
over 4-unit apartments	5%	5 years		
non-residential	0			

Nuisances in neighborhood (odors, noise, etc.) *none*
Hazards in neighborhood (chemical storage, pollution, etc.) *none*

10. **Proximity.** How far is it to traffic arterials and to important points such as downtown, employment centers, and shopping centers?
11. **Schools.** What schools serve the neighborhood? Are they highly regarded? Are they within walking distance? The quality of a school or school district can make a major difference in property values in a residential neighborhood.
12. **Public services.** Is the neighborhood properly serviced by public transportation, police, and fire units?
13. **Government influences.** Does zoning in and around the neighborhood promote residential use and insulate the property owner from nuisances? How do the property tax rates compare with those of other neighborhoods nearby?

Specific Data

Specific data has to do with the property itself. Often the appraiser will evaluate the site (the land and utilities) and the improvements (the buildings) separately. For example, when a property is being assessed for tax purposes, most states require the assessment to show the distribution of value between the land and the improvements. Another reason for appraising the land separately is to see if it is worth too much or too little compared to the value of the improvements. When an imbalance exists, the land is not serving its highest and best use. The primary purpose of site analysis is to determine highest and best use.

Site Analysis. A thorough site analysis calls for accumulation of a good deal of data concerning the property's physical characteristics, as well as factors that affect its use or the title.

A site's physical characteristics include all of the following:

1. **Width.** This refers to the lot's measurements from one side boundary to the other. Width can vary from front to back, as in the case of a pie-shaped lot on a cul-de-sac.
2. **Frontage.** Frontage is the length of the front boundary of the lot, the boundary that abuts a street or a body of water. The amount of frontage is often a more important consideration than width because it measures the property's accessibility, or its access to something desirable.
3. **Area.** Area is the size of the site, usually measured in square feet or acres. Comparisons between lots often focus on the features of frontage and area. Commercial land is usually valued in terms of frontage; that is, it is worth a certain number of dollars per front foot. Industrial land, on the other hand, tends to be valued in terms of square feet or acreage. Residential lots are measured both ways: by square feet or by acreage in most instances, but by front foot when the property abuts a lake or a river, or some other desirable feature.
4. **Depth.** Depth is the distance between the site's front boundary and its rear boundary. Greater depth (more than the norm) can mean greater value, but it doesn't always. For example, suppose Lot 1 and Lot 2 have the same amount of frontage along a lake, but Lot 2 is deeper; Lot 2 is not necessarily more valuable than Lot 1. Under certain circumstances, combining two or more adjoining lots to achieve greater width, depth, or area will make the larger parcel more valuable than the sum of the values of its component parcels. The increment of value that results when two or more lots are combined to produce greater value is called **plottage**. The process of assembling lots to increase their total value is most frequently part of industrial or commercial land development.
5. **Shape.** Lots with uniform width and depth (such as rectangular lots) are almost always more useful than irregularly shaped lots. This is true for any kind of lot—residential, commercial, or industrial.
6. **Topography.** A site is generally more valuable if it is aesthetically appealing. Rolling terrain is preferable to flat, monotonous land. On the other hand, if the site would be costly to develop because it sits well above or below the street or is excessively hilly, then that lessens its value.
7. **Utilities.** Site analysis includes an investigation into the availability and cost of utility connections. Remote parcels lose value because the cost of bringing utility lines to the site is high or even prohibitive. The site must also be evaluated for adding utilities. For instance, in areas not served by sewers, a **percolation test** might be required to measure how quickly water dissipates through the soil. The results of the test will determine whether a septic system can be added to the property.
8. **Site in relation to area.** How a lot is situated in relation to the surrounding area influences its value. For instance, a retail store is often worth more if it is located on a corner, because it enjoys more exposure and its customers have access from two different streets. The effect the corner location has on the value of a business site is called **corner influence**.

   By contrast, a corner location may have a negative effect on the value of a residential property. Although corner lots are often larger than lots located in the middle of the block, they are more exposed to traffic and noise.

Building Analysis. The improvements to the site must also be analyzed. Here are some of the primary considerations in a residential appraisal:

1. **Construction quality.** Is the quality of the materials and workmanship good, average, or poor?
2. **Age/condition.** How old is the home? (If the age is not known, it can be determined by consulting the county assessor's records.) Is its overall condition good, average, or poor?
3. **Size of house (square footage).** Square footage generally refers to the improved living area, excluding the garage, basement, and porches. (Note that an appraiser will exclude the square footage of any addition that was built without a permit.)
4. **Basement.** A functional basement, especially a finished basement, contributes to value. (As we mentioned earlier, however, the amount a finished basement contributes to value is often not enough to recover the cost of the finish work.)
5. **Interior layout.** Is the floor plan functional and convenient? It should not be necessary to pass through a public room (such as the living room) to reach other rooms, or to pass through one of the bedrooms to reach another.
6. **Number of rooms.** The appraiser will add up the total number of rooms in the house, excluding bathrooms and (usually) basement rooms.
7. **Number of bedrooms.** The number of bedrooms has a major impact on value. For instance, if all else is equal, a two-bedroom home is worth considerably less than a three-bedroom home.
8. **Number of bathrooms.** A full bath is a sink, toilet, bathtub, and shower; a three-quarters bath is a sink, toilet, and tub or shower; a half bath is a sink and toilet only. The number of bathrooms can have a noticeable effect on value.
9. **Air conditioning.** The presence or absence of an air conditioning system is important in hot regions.
10. **Energy efficiency.** An energy-efficient home is more valuable than a comparable one that is not. Energy-efficient features such as double-paned windows, good insulation, and weather stripping increase value.
11. **Garage/carport.** As a general rule, an enclosed garage is considered better than a carport. How many cars can the garage accommodate? Is there work or storage space in addition to parking space? Is it possible to enter the home directly from the garage or carport, protected from the weather?

Fig. 12.4 Site Data Form

SITE DATA FORM

Address: *10157 - 13th Avenue*
Legal Description: *see attached description*
Size *50′ x 200′* Shape *Rectangular*
Square Feet *10,000* Street Paving *Asphal*
Landscaping *professional* Topsoil *good*
Drainage *good* Frontage *good*
☐ corner lot ☑ ins

Utilities: ☑ water ☑ telephone ☑ gas ☑ sewers ☑ electricity ☑ storm drains

Improvements: ☑ side ☑ curb ☑ alleys ☑ dri

Fig. 12.5 Building Data Form

BUILDING DATA FORM

Address: *10157 - 13th Avenue*
Age: *7 yrs.* Square feet: *1,350*
Number of rooms: *7* Quality of construction: *excellent*
Style: *ranch*

	Good	Bad	Fair
Exterior (general condition)	✓		
Foundation(slab/bsmt./crawl sp.) (circled: crawl sp.)	✓		
Exterior (brick/frame/veneer/stucco/aluminum) (circled: frame)	✓		
Garage (attached/detached/single/double) (circled: attached)	✓		
Patio/porch/shed/other (circled: Patio)	✓		
Interior (general condition)	✓		
Walls (drywall/wood/plaster) (circled: drywall)	✓		
Ceilings	✓		
Floor (wood/tile/carpet/concrete) (circled: tile, carpet)	✓		
Electrical wiring	✓		
Heating (electrical/gas/oil/other) (circled: electrical)	✓		
Air conditioning	✓		
Fireplace(s) *one*	✓		
Kitchen	✓		
Bathroom(s) *two*	✓		
Bedroom(s) *three*	✓		

Additional amenities *none*
Design advantages *convenient, sunny kitchen*
Design flaws *none*
Energy efficiency *insulation, weather-stripping, storm windows, heat pump*

	Living Rm.	Dining Rm.	Ktchn.	Bdrm.	Bath	Family Rm.
Basement						
1st Floor	✓	✓	✓	✓	✓	
2nd Floor						
Attic						

Depreciation:
Deferred Maintenance *normal wear*
Functional Obsolescence *none*
External Obsolescence *none*

Approaches to Value

Once the appraiser has accumulated the necessary general and specific data, they will begin applying one or more of the three methods of appraising property:

- the sales comparison approach,
- the cost approach, and
- the income approach.

Different types of properties lend themselves to different appraisal methods. For example, appraisers rely most on the sales comparison approach in valuing older residential properties. Churches and public buildings, such as libraries or courthouses, aren't sold on the open market, nor do they generate income, so the cost approach is invariably used. On the other hand, the income approach is usually the most reliable method for appraising an apartment complex, and also for office and retail properties.

Sales Comparison Approach to Value

The **sales comparison approach** (also known as the market data approach) is the best method for appraising residential property, and the most reliable method for appraising raw land. It involves comparing the subject property to similar properties that have recently sold, referred to as **comparable sales** or **comparables.**

The appraiser gathers pertinent information about comparables and makes feature-by-feature comparisons with the subject property. The appraiser then translates their findings into an estimate of the market value of the subject property. Appraisers use this method whenever possible because the sales prices of comparables—which reflect the actions of informed buyers and sellers in the marketplace—are excellent indicators of market value.

For residential property, an appraiser needs at least three reliable comparable sales to have enough data for the sales comparison approach. It's usually possible to find three good comparable homes, but when it isn't, the appraiser will use one or both of the alternative appraisal methods—the cost approach and, in some cases, the income approach.

Elements of Comparison. To determine whether a particular sale can legitimately be used as a comparable, the appraiser checks the following aspects of the transaction, sometimes called the primary elements of comparison.

Date of Comparable Sale. The sale should be recent, within the past six months if possible. Recent sales give a more accurate indication of what is happening in the marketplace today. If the market has been inactive and there are not three legitimate comparable sales from the past six months, the appraiser can go back further, as long as they provide justification in the appraisal report for doing so. When the market is going through a major shift, such as a rapid downswing during a recession, comparable sales should be no more than three months old.

When using an older comparable, the appraiser must adjust the sales price for inflationary or deflationary trends or any other forces that have affected prices in the area. It is not advisable to use a comparable that is more than one year old, even with adjustments.

Example: A comparable residential property sold ten months ago for $380,000. Local property values have risen by 5% over the past ten months. The comparable property, then, should be worth approximately 5% more than it was ten months ago.

$380,000	Value ten months ago
× 105%	Inflation factor
$399,000	Approximate present value

Location of Comparable Sale. Whenever possible, the appraiser should select comparables from the same neighborhood as the subject property. Absent any legitimate comparables in the neighborhood, the appraiser can look elsewhere, but the properties selected should at least come from very similar neighborhoods.

If a comparable selected from an inferior neighborhood is structurally identical to the subject property, it is probably less valuable; conversely, a structurally identical comparable in a superior neighborhood is probably more valuable than the subject property.

Location generally contributes more to the value of real estate than any other characteristic. A high-quality property cannot overcome the adverse effects on value that a low-quality neighborhood causes. On the other hand, the value of a relatively weak property is enhanced by a stable and desirable neighborhood.

Physical Characteristics. To qualify as a comparable, a property should have physical characteristics (such as construction quality, design, and amenities) that are similar to those of the subject property. When a comparable has a feature that the subject property lacks, or lacks a feature that the subject property has, the appraiser will adjust the comparable's price. The goal is to make the comparable seem as similar as possible to the subject property; an appraiser never makes adjustments to the subject property.

Example: One of the comparables the appraiser is using is quite similar to the subject property overall, but there are several significant differences. The subject property has a two-car garage, while the comparable has only a one-car garage. Based on experience, the appraiser estimates that space for a second car adds approximately $5,000 to the value of a home in this area. The comparable actually sold for $322,500. The appraiser will add $5,000 to the comparable's price, to estimate what the comparable would have been worth with a two-car garage.

On the other hand, the comparable has a fireplace and the subject property does not. The appraiser estimates that a fireplace adds approximately $1,400 to the value of a home. They will subtract $1,400 from the comparable's price, to estimate what the comparable would have sold for without a fireplace.

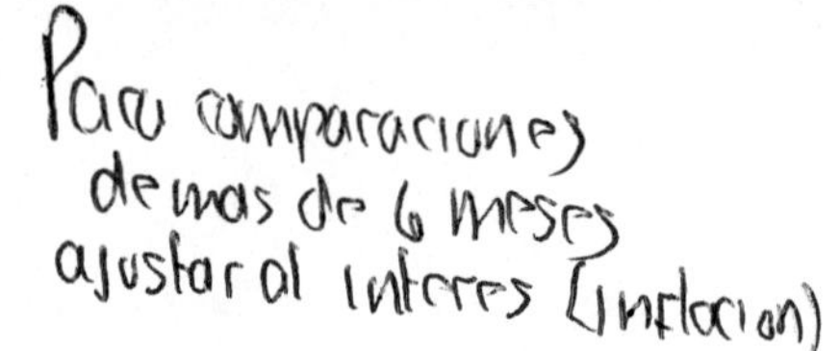

After adjusting the comparable's price up or down for each difference in this way, the appraiser can identify what the comparable would have sold for if it had been identical to the subject property. When the appraiser repeats this process for each comparable, the value of the subject property becomes evident.

Terms of Sale. The terms of sale can affect the price a buyer will pay for a property. Attractive financing concessions (such as seller-paid discount points or seller financing with an especially low interest rate) can make a buyer willing to pay a higher price than they would otherwise be willing to pay.

An appraiser has to take into account the influence the terms of sale may have had on the price paid for a comparable property. If the seller offered the property on very favorable terms, there's an excellent chance the sales price did not represent the true market value of the comparable.

Under the Uniform Standards of Professional Appraisal Practice, an appraiser giving an estimate of market value must state whether it's the most probable price:

1. in terms of cash,
2. in terms of financial arrangements equivalent to cash, or
3. in other precisely defined terms.

If the estimate is based on financing with special conditions or incentives, those terms must be clearly set forth, and the appraiser must estimate their effect on the property's value. Market data supporting the value estimate (comparable sales) must be explained in the same way.

Fig. 12.6 Comparable Sales Comparison Chart

Comparable Sales Comparison Chart

	Subject Property	Comparables			
		1	2	3	4
Sales price		*$391,750*	*$396,500*	*$387,000*	*$388,500*
Location	*quiet street*				
Age	*7 yrs.*				
Lot size	*50'x200'*				
Construction	*frame*			*+6,000*	
Style	*ranch*				
Number of Rooms	*7*		*–5,000*		
Number of Bedrooms	*3*				
Number of Baths	*2*	*+3,500*			*+3,500*
Square feet	*1,350*				
Exterior	*good*				
Interior	*good*				
Garage	*1 car attached*				
Other improvements		*–4,000*			
Financing					
Date of sale		*–3,000*	*–3,000*		
Net Adjustments		*–3,500*	*–8,000*	*+6,000*	*+3,500*
Adjusted Price		*$388,250*	*$388,500*	*$393,000*	*$392,000*

Conditions of Sale. Last but not least, a comparable sale can be relied on as an indication of what the subject property is worth only if it occurred under normal conditions. That is, the sale was between unrelated parties (an "arm's length transaction"); both the buyer and the seller were informed of the property's attributes and deficiencies; both were acting free of unusual pressure; and the property was offered for sale on the open market for a reasonable length of time.

Thus, the appraiser must investigate the circumstances of each comparable sale to determine whether the price paid was influenced by a condition that would render it unreliable as an indication of value.

For example, if the property sold only days before a scheduled foreclosure sale, the sales price probably reflects the pressure under which the seller was acting. Or if the buyer and seller were relatives, it's possible that the price was less than it would have been between two strangers. Or if the property sold the same day it was listed, it may have been underpriced. In each of these cases, there's reason to suspect that the sales price did not reflect the property's true value, so the appraiser would not use the transaction as a comparable sale.

Comparing Properties and Making Adjustments. A proper comparison between the subject property and each comparable is essential to an accurate estimate of value. The more similar the properties, the easier the comparison. A comparable property that is the same design and in the same condition as the subject property, on a very similar site in the same neighborhood, which sold under typical financing terms the previous month, will give an excellent indication of the market value of the subject property.

However, except perhaps in a new subdivision where the houses are nearly identical, the appraiser usually cannot find such ideal comparables. There are likely to be at least some significant differences between the comparables and the subject property.

So, as you've seen, the appraiser has to make adjustments, taking into account differences in time, location, physical characteristics, and terms of sale, in order to arrive at an **adjusted selling price** for each comparable.

It stands to reason that the more adjustments an appraiser has to make, the less reliable the resulting estimate of value will be. These adjustments are an inevitable part of the sales comparison approach, but appraisers try to keep them to a minimum by selecting the best comparables available.

Although the appraiser bases their estimate of the subject property's value on the adjusted prices of the comparables, it's important to understand that the value estimate is never merely an average of those prices; careful analysis is required. Also note that the original cost of the subject property (how much the current owners paid for it) is irrelevant to the appraisal process.

Use of Listings. When comparable sales are scarce (as when the market is just emerging from a dormant period), the appraiser may compare the subject property to properties that are presently listed for sale. The appraiser must keep in mind, however, that listing prices often represent the ceiling of the market value range.

The appraiser might also use prices offered by buyers, though these can be difficult to confirm, since records of offers aren't always kept. Offers are usually at the low end of the market value range. Actual market value is typically somewhere between offers and listing prices.

Cost Approach to Value

The second method of appraisal, the **cost approach**, is based on the premise that the value of a property is limited by the cost of replacing it. (This follows from the principle of substitution: if the asking price for a home was more than it would cost to build a new one just like it, no one would buy it.)

The cost approach involves estimating how much it would cost to replace the subject property's existing buildings, and then adding to that the estimated value of the site. Because the cost approach involves estimating the value of land and buildings separately, then adding the estimates together, it is sometimes called the **summation method.**

There are three steps to the cost approach:

1. Estimate the cost of replacing the improvements.
2. Estimate and deduct any accrued depreciation.
3. Add the value of the lot to the depreciated value of the improvements.

We'll look at each of these steps. First, however, it's important to distinguish between replacement cost and reproduction cost. **Reproduction cost** is the cost of constructing an exact duplicate—a replica—of the subject building, at current prices. **Replacement cost**, on the other hand, is the current cost of constructing a building with a utility equivalent to the subject's—that is, a building that can be used in the same way as the subject. Reproduction cost and replacement cost may be the same if the subject property is a new home. But if the structure is older, and was built with the detailed workmanship and expensive materials of earlier times, then the reproduction cost and the replacement cost will be quite different. So the appraiser must base their estimate of value on the replacement cost. The reproduction cost would be much higher, and it would not represent the current market value of the improvements.

Estimating Replacement Cost. The replacement cost of a building can be estimated in three different ways:

1. the square foot method,
2. the unit-in-place method, and
3. the quantity survey method.

Fig. 12.7 Calculating Value with the Cost Approach

Cost Approach
Replacement cost of improvements
– Depreciation
+ Value of land
Value of subject property

Square Foot. The simplest way to estimate replacement cost is the **square foot method** (also known as the comparative cost or comparative unit method). By analyzing the average cost per square foot of construction for recently built comparable homes, the appraiser can calculate what the square foot cost of replacing the subject home would be. The number of square feet in a home is determined by measuring the outside dimensions of each floor of the structure.

To calculate the cost of replacing the subject property's improvements, the appraiser multiplies the estimated cost per square foot by the number of square feet in the subject.

> **Example:** The subject property is a ranch-style house with a wood exterior, containing 1,600 square feet. Based on an analysis of the construction costs of three recently built homes of comparable size and quality, the appraiser estimates that it would cost $115.38 per square foot to replace the home.
>
> | | |
> |---:|---|
> | 1,600 | Square feet |
> | × 115.38 | Cost per square foot |
> | $184,608 | Estimated cost of replacing improvements |

Of course, a comparable structure (or "benchmark" building) is unlikely to be exactly the same as the subject property. Variations in design, shape, and grade of construction will affect the square-foot cost, either moderately or substantially. When recently built comparable homes aren't available, then the appraiser relies on current cost manuals to estimate the basic construction costs.

Unit-in-Place. The **unit-in-place method** involves estimating the cost of replacing specific components of the building, such as the floors, roof, plumbing, and foundation, as determined from cost manuals. For example, one of the estimates might be a certain number of dollars per one hundred square feet of roofing. Another component estimate would be a certain amount per cubic yard of concrete for an installed foundation. Then the appraiser adds all the estimates together to determine the replacement cost of the structure itself.

Quantity Survey. The **quantity survey method** involves a detailed estimate of the quantities and prices of construction materials and labor, which are added to the indirect costs (building permit, survey, etc.) to arrive at what is generally regarded as the most accurate replacement cost estimate. Because it's complex and time consuming, this method is generally used only by experienced contractors and price estimators.

Estimating Depreciation. When the property being appraised is a used home, the presumption is that it is not as valuable as a comparable new home; it has depreciated in value. So, after estimating replacement cost—which indicates what the improvements would be worth if they were new—the appraiser's next step is to estimate the depreciation.

Depreciation is a loss in value due to any cause. Value can be lost as a result of physical deterioration, functional obsolescence, or external obsolescence.

- **Physical deterioration** is a loss in value due to wear and tear or damage. It's easier to spot this type of depreciation than the other types, and easier to estimate its impact on value.

  Physical deterioration may be curable or incurable. Depreciation is considered **curable** if the cost of correcting it could be recovered in the sales price when the property is sold. Depreciation is **incurable** if it is impossible to correct, or if it would cost so much to correct that it would be impractical to do so. Curable physical deterioration is often referred to as **deferred maintenance.**
- **Functional obsolescence** is a loss in value due to functional inadequacies, often caused by age or by poor design. Examples include a poor floor plan, an unappealing design, outdated fixtures, or too few bathrooms in relation to the number of bedrooms. Like physical deterioration, functional obsolescence may be curable or incurable.
- **External obsolescence** is caused by conditions outside the property itself, such as adverse zoning changes, neighborhood deterioration, traffic problems, or exposure to nuisances, like noise from airport flight patterns. If it relates to factors such as neighborhood deterioration or poor access to downtown or other employment centers, it may also be referred to as economic obsolescence. Identifying external obsolescence is the primary purpose of an appraiser's neighborhood analysis. External obsolescence is beyond a property owner's control, so it's virtually always incurable.

Estimating depreciation accurately is the most difficult phase of the replacement cost method of appraisal. Depreciation estimates are often highly subjective, and they are never any more reliable than the judgment and skill of the appraiser who is making them.

Fig. 12.8 A house with four bedrooms and just one bath loses value due to functional obsolescence

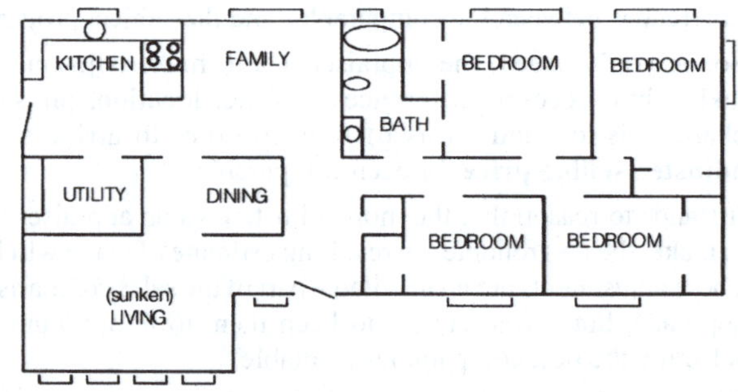

Adding Land Value. The last step in the replacement cost process is to add the value of the land to the depreciated value of the improvements. The value of the land is estimated by the sales comparison method. Prices recently paid for lots similar to the subject lot are compared and used as indications of what the subject lot is worth.

Keep in mind that the value of the land is not depreciated. An appraiser regards land as indestructible; it does not lose value.

Income Approach to Value

The **income approach** (also known as the capitalization method) is based on the idea that there is a relationship between the income a property generates and its market value to an investor. In effect, the income approach seeks to determine the present value of a property's future income.

Gross Income. When using the income approach, the appraiser first finds the property's gross income. They do this by estimating the rent the property would command if it were presently available for lease on the open market. What it would earn on the open market is called the **economic rent**, as distinguished from what it is actually earning now, which is called the **contract rent** or **scheduled rent**. Contract rent can be used to gauge the property's earnings potential. A pattern of rent increases or decreases is a strong indication of whether the contract rent is above or below the economic rent.

The economic rent is the property's **potential gross income**, what it could earn if it were fully occupied and all rents owed were collected. But it is unrealistic to expect a rental property to be fully occupied throughout its productive life; vacancies must be expected. Also, there are going to be tenants who do not pay their rent. So the appraiser must make a deduction from potential gross income to allow for occasional vacancies and unpaid rents. Called a **vacancy factor**, this deduction is expressed as a percentage of the potential gross income. For example, the appraiser might deduct 5% from potential gross income as a vacancy factor. Once the vacancy factor is deducted, the appraiser is left with a more reliable income figure, called **effective gross income.**

Operating Expenses. From the effective gross income, the appraiser deducts the expenses connected with operating the building. They fall into three classifications: fixed expenses, variable expenses, and reserves for replacement.

- **Fixed expenses:** Expenses that occur at regular intervals and remain the same regardless of the building's occupancy rate, such as property taxes, salaries, and hazard insurance.
- **Variable expenses:** Expenses that may increase or decrease depending on changes in the occupancy rate or the extent of services provided, including utilities, supplies, cleaning, repairs, services for tenants, and administrative costs.
- **Reserves for replacement:** Regular allowances set aside to replace structures and equipment that are expected to wear out, such as roofs, heating equipment, air conditioners, and (in a residential building) kitchen appliances.

The income that is left when operating expenses are deducted from effective gross income is called **net operating income** (NOI). It is net operating income that is capitalized to determine the property's value (see the next section).

Some expenses connected with ownership of an income property, such as the owner's income tax and the mortgage payments (called **debt service**), are not deducted from the effective gross income to arrive at the net income. These are not considered operating expenses from an appraisal standpoint.

Capitalization. The process of converting net operating income into a meaningful value is called **capitalization.** The mathematical procedure is expressed in this formula:

Annual Net Operating Income ÷ Capitalization Rate = Value

> **Example:** The property's annual net operating income is $55,700 and the capitalization rate is 11%. According to the capitalization formula, the property's value is $506,364.
>
> $55,700 ÷ 0.11 = $506,364

The **capitalization rate** is the rate of return an investor (a potential purchaser) would want to receive on the money they invest in the property (the purchase price). When the investor chooses the rate of return, it is plugged into the formula shown above. By dividing the net operating income by the desired rate of return, the investor can determine how much they can pay for the property and still realize that desired return.

> **Example:** The property's annual net operating income is $45,000 and the investor's desired return is 12%.
>
> $45,000 ÷ 0.12 = $375,000
>
> The investor can pay up to $375,000 for a property earning $45,000 in net income and realize their desired yield of 12%.

Selecting a Capitalization Rate. To appraise property using the income approach, the appraiser must be familiar with the rate of return that investors generally demand for similar properties.

There are a number of ways for an appraiser to determine a property's capitalization rate. For instance, the appraiser could analyze recent sales of comparable income properties and assume that the subject property would have a capitalization rate similar to theirs. This is known as the **direct comparison method.**

Regardless of the method used for selecting the capitalization rate, two very important considerations are the quality and the durability of the investment property's income. Quality (how reliable the tenants are) and durability (how long the income can be expected to last) influence the risk factor. The greater the risk, the higher the capitalization rate and the lower the property's value. On the other hand, the smaller the risk, the lower the capitalization rate and the higher the value.

Gross Income Multipliers. Single-family residences generally aren't thought of as income-producing properties, so traditional income analysis techniques do not apply. If a residential appraiser uses an income method at all, they will use a simplified version called the **gross income multiplier method.** As a rule, this method is applied only when appraising small rental properties. It's sometimes called the **gross rent multiplier method,** since rents are typically the only form of income generated by residential rental properties.

In the gross income multiplier method, the appraiser looks at the relationship between a rental property's gross income and the price paid for the property.

Example:

Sales price:	$275,000
Monthly rent:	$1,675
Conclusion:	The monthly rent is equal to 0.61% of the sales price; the sales price is approximately 165 times the monthly rent.

Monthly rents may run about 1% of selling prices in one market, and more or less in another. A market exists where specific rental properties compete with each other for tenants. For competitive reasons, rents charged for similar properties tend to be much alike within the same market. As a result, if one rental property has a monthly income that is 1% of its sales price, comparable properties will have similar income-to-price ratios.

A monthly multiplier is established by dividing the sales price by the gross monthly rental income. An annual multiplier is calculated by dividing the sales price by the gross annual rental income.

Example:

Sales Price		Monthly Rent		Monthly Multiplier
$240,000	÷	$1,475	=	162.71
Sales Price		**Annual Rent**		**Annual Multiplier**
$240,000	÷	$17,700	=	13.56

After locating at least four comparable residential rental properties, the appraiser can determine their monthly or annual gross income multipliers (either is acceptable—it's a matter of the appraiser's preference) by dividing the rents into their respective selling prices.

Example:

Comp No.	Sales Price	Monthly Rent	Monthly Multiplier
1	$235,000	$1,450	162.07
2	$237,500	$1,460	162.67
3	$242,000	$1,500	161.33
4	$245,000	$1,525	160.66

The appraiser uses the multipliers of the comparables to determine an appropriate multiplier for the subject property, taking into account the similarities and differences between the properties. Then the appraiser multiplies the rent that the subject property generates by the chosen multiplier for a rough estimate of its value as income-producing property.

The principal weakness of the gross income multiplier method is that it is based on gross income figures and does not take into account vacancies or operating expenses. If two rental homes have the same rental income, the gross income multiplier method would indicate they are worth the same amount; but if one is older and has higher maintenance costs, the net return to the owner would be less, and so would the value of the property.

Unless the appraiser knows the comparables are truly similar (having similar vacancy rates and operating expenses), the appraiser must take into account the rough nature of the value indicated by this method.

If possible, the appraiser should use the subject property's economic rent, as opposed to the contract rent (the rent the owner is actually receiving), in calculating the gross income multiplier.

Example: The owner leased the home two years ago for $1,600 a month, and the lease contract has another year to go. Market rents have risen sharply over the past two years, so that the property could now command a much higher rent—probably about $1,875 a month. If the appraiser were to use the $1,600 contract rent in the gross income multiplier method instead of the $1,875 economic rent, it would distort the estimate of value.

Reconciliation and Final Estimate of Value

Throughout the appraisal process, the appraiser is gathering facts on which they will base the ultimate conclusion, the final estimate of the property's value. In many cases, the facts require nothing beyond simple verification; their meaning is self-evident. In other cases, they require expert interpretation. Nowhere in the appraisal process does the appraiser's experience and judgment play a more critical role. For example, with a single-family residence, an appraiser is likely to give more weight to the result reached by the sales comparison approach, treating the result of the cost approach mainly as an upper limit on value.

The final value estimate is not simply the average of the results yielded by the three approaches to value—sales comparison, cost, and income. Rather, it is the figure that represents the appraiser's expert opinion of the subject property's value after all the data has been assembled and analyzed. Usually the values indicated by the different approaches vary at least somewhat. The process of deriving a single estimate of value from the differing indicators is called **reconciliation.**

Once the appraiser has determined the final estimate of value, they present it to the client in an appraisal report. The two most common types of reports are the narrative report and the form report. A **narrative report** is a thorough, detailed, written presentation of the facts and reasoning behind the appraiser's estimate of value. A **form report** is a brief, standard form used by lending institutions and government agencies (for example, the FHA and VA), presenting only the key data and the appraiser's conclusions. This is the most common type of appraisal report. The Uniform Residential Appraisal Report form, used in most residential transactions, is shown in Figure 12.9.

Fig. 12.9 Uniform Residential Appraisal Report

Uniform Residential Appraisal Report

File #

The purpose of this summary appraisal report is to provide the lender/client with an accurate, and adequately supported, opinion of the market value of the subject property.

SUBJECT

Property Address | City | State | Zip Code

Borrower | Owner of Public Record | County

Legal Description

Assessor's Parcel # | Tax Year | R.E. Taxes $

Neighborhood Name | Map Reference | Census Tract

Occupant ☐ Owner ☐ Tenant ☐ Vacant | Special Assessments $ | ☐ PUD | HOA $ | ☐ per year ☐ per month

Property Rights Appraised ☐ Fee Simple ☐ Leasehold ☐ Other (describe)

Assignment Type ☐ Purchase Transaction ☐ Refinance Transaction ☐ Other (describe)

Lender/Client | Address

Is the subject property currently offered for sale or has it been offered for sale in the twelve months prior to the effective date of this appraisal? ☐ Yes ☐ No

Report data source(s) used, offering price(s), and date(s).

CONTRACT

I ☐ did ☐ did not analyze the contract for sale for the subject purchase transaction. Explain the results of the analysis of the contract for sale or why the analysis was not performed.

Contract Price $ | Date of Contract | Is the property seller the owner of public record? ☐ Yes ☐ No | Data Source(s)

Is there any financial assistance (loan charges, sale concessions, gift or downpayment assistance, etc.) to be paid by any party on behalf of the borrower? ☐ Yes ☐ No

If Yes, report the total dollar amount and describe the items to be paid.

NEIGHBORHOOD

Note: Race and the racial composition of the neighborhood are not appraisal factors.

Neighborhood Characteristics	One-Unit Housing Trends	One-Unit Housing		Present Land Use %	
Location ☐ Urban ☐ Suburban ☐ Rural	Property Values ☐ Increasing ☐ Stable ☐ Declining	PRICE	AGE	One-Unit	%
Built-Up ☐ Over 75% ☐ 25–75% ☐ Under 25%	Demand/Supply ☐ Shortage ☐ In Balance ☐ Over Supply	$ (000)	(yrs)	2-4 Unit	%
Growth ☐ Rapid ☐ Stable ☐ Slow	Marketing Time ☐ Under 3 mths ☐ 3–6 mths ☐ Over 6 mths	Low		Multi-Family	%
Neighborhood Boundaries		High		Commercial	%
		Pred.		Other	%

Neighborhood Description

Market Conditions (including support for the above conclusions)

SITE

Dimensions | Area | Shape | View

Specific Zoning Classification | Zoning Description

Zoning Compliance ☐ Legal ☐ Legal Nonconforming (Grandfathered Use) ☐ No Zoning ☐ Illegal (describe)

Is the highest and best use of the subject property as improved (or as proposed per plans and specifications) the present use? ☐ Yes ☐ No If No, describe

Utilities	Public	Other (describe)		Public	Other (describe)	Off-site Improvements—Type	Public	Private
Electricity	☐	☐	Water	☐	☐	Street	☐	☐
Gas	☐	☐	Sanitary Sewer	☐	☐	Alley	☐	☐

FEMA Special Flood Hazard Area ☐ Yes ☐ No | FEMA Flood Zone | FEMA Map # | FEMA Map Date

Are the utilities and off-site improvements typical for the market area? ☐ Yes ☐ No If No, describe

Are there any adverse site conditions or external factors (easements, encroachments, environmental conditions, land uses, etc.)? ☐ Yes ☐ No If Yes, describe

IMPROVEMENTS

General Description	Foundation	Exterior Description materials/condition	Interior materials/condition
Units ☐ One ☐ One with Accessory Unit	☐ Concrete Slab ☐ Crawl Space	Foundation Walls	Floors
# of Stories	☐ Full Basement ☐ Partial Basement	Exterior Walls	Walls
Type ☐ Det. ☐ Att. ☐ S-Det./End Unit	Basement Area sq. ft.	Roof Surface	Trim/Finish
☐ Existing ☐ Proposed ☐ Under Const.	Basement Finish %	Gutters & Downspouts	Bath Floor
Design (Style)	☐ Outside Entry/Exit ☐ Sump Pump	Window Type	Bath Wainscot
Year Built	Evidence of ☐ Infestation	Storm Sash/Insulated	Car Storage ☐ None
Effective Age (Yrs)	☐ Dampness ☐ Settlement	Screens	☐ Driveway # of Cars
Attic ☐ None	Heating ☐ FWA ☐ HWBB ☐ Radiant	Amenities ☐ Woodstove(s) #	Driveway Surface
☐ Drop Stair ☐ Stairs	☐ Other Fuel	☐ Fireplace(s) # ☐ Fence	☐ Garage # of Cars
☐ Floor ☐ Scuttle	Cooling ☐ Central Air Conditioning	☐ Patio/Deck ☐ Porch	☐ Carport # of Cars
☐ Finished ☐ Heated	☐ Individual ☐ Other	☐ Pool ☐ Other	☐ Att. ☐ Det. ☐ Built-in

Appliances ☐ Refrigerator ☐ Range/Oven ☐ Dishwasher ☐ Disposal ☐ Microwave ☐ Washer/Dryer ☐ Other (describe)

Finished area **above** grade contains: | Rooms | Bedrooms | Bath(s) | Square Feet of Gross Living Area Above Grade

Additional features (special energy efficient items, etc.)

Describe the condition of the property (including needed repairs, deterioration, renovations, remodeling, etc.).

Are there any physical deficiencies or adverse conditions that affect the livability, soundness, or structural integrity of the property? ☐ Yes ☐ No If Yes, describe

Does the property generally conform to the neighborhood (functional utility, style, condition, use, construction, etc.)? ☐ Yes ☐ No If No, describe

Freddie Mac Form 70 March 2005 | Page 1 of 6 | Fannie Mae Form 1004 March 2005

Uniform Residential Appraisal Report

File #

There are comparable properties currently offered for sale in the subject neighborhood ranging in price from $ to $.

There are comparable sales in the subject neighborhood within the past twelve months ranging in sale price from $ to $.

SALES COMPARISON APPROACH

FEATURE	SUBJECT	COMPARABLE SALE # 1		COMPARABLE SALE # 2		COMPARABLE SALE # 3	
Address							
Proximity to Subject							
Sale Price	$		$		$		$
Sale Price/Gross Liv. Area	$ sq. ft.	$ sq. ft.		$ sq. ft.		$ sq. ft.	
Data Source(s)							
Verification Source(s)							
VALUE ADJUSTMENTS	DESCRIPTION	DESCRIPTION	+(-) $ Adjustment	DESCRIPTION	+(-) $ Adjustment	DESCRIPTION	+(-) $ Adjustment
Sale or Financing Concessions							
Date of Sale/Time							
Location							
Leasehold/Fee Simple							
Site							
View							
Design (Style)							
Quality of Construction							
Actual Age							
Condition							
Above Grade Room Count	Total Bdrms. Baths	Total Bdrms. Baths		Total Bdrms. Baths		Total Bdrms. Baths	
Gross Living Area	sq. ft.	sq. ft.		sq. ft.		sq. ft.	
Basement & Finished Rooms Below Grade							
Functional Utility							
Heating/Cooling							
Energy Efficient Items							
Garage/Carport							
Porch/Patio/Deck							
Net Adjustment (Total)		☐ + ☐ -	$	☐ + ☐ -	$	☐ + ☐ -	$
Adjusted Sale Price of Comparables		Net Adj. % Gross Adj. %	$	Net Adj. % Gross Adj. %	$	Net Adj. % Gross Adj. %	$

I ☐ did ☐ did not research the sale or transfer history of the subject property and comparable sales. If not, explain

My research ☐ did ☐ did not reveal any prior sales or transfers of the subject property for the three years prior to the effective date of this appraisal.

Data source(s)

My research ☐ did ☐ did not reveal any prior sales or transfers of the comparable sales for the year prior to the date of sale of the comparable sale.

Data source(s)

Report the results of the research and analysis of the prior sale or transfer history of the subject property and comparable sales (report additional prior sales on page 3).

ITEM	SUBJECT	COMPARABLE SALE # 1	COMPARABLE SALE # 2	COMPARABLE SALE # 3
Date of Prior Sale/Transfer				
Price of Prior Sale/Transfer				
Data Source(s)				
Effective Date of Data Source(s)				

Analysis of prior sale or transfer history of the subject property and comparable sales

Summary of Sales Comparison Approach

Indicated Value by Sales Comparison Approach $

RECONCILIATION

Indicated Value by: Sales Comparison Approach $ Cost Approach (if developed) $ Income Approach (if developed) $

This appraisal is made ☐ "as is", ☐ subject to completion per plans and specifications on the basis of a hypothetical condition that the improvements have been completed, ☐ subject to the following repairs or alterations on the basis of a hypothetical condition that the repairs or alterations have been completed, or ☐ subject to the following required inspection based on the extraordinary assumption that the condition or deficiency does not require alteration or repair:

Based on a complete visual inspection of the interior and exterior areas of the subject property, defined scope of work, statement of assumptions and limiting conditions, and appraiser's certification, my (our) opinion of the market value, as defined, of the real property that is the subject of this report is $, as of , which is the date of inspection and the effective date of this appraisal.

Freddie Mac Form 70 March 2005 Page 2 of 6 Fannie Mae Form 1004 March 2005

Uniform Residential Appraisal Report

File #

ADDITIONAL COMMENTS

COST APPROACH TO VALUE (not required by Fannie Mae)

Provide adequate information for the lender/client to replicate the below cost figures and calculations.

Support for the opinion of site value (summary of comparable land sales or other methods for estimating site value)

ESTIMATED ☐ REPRODUCTION OR ☐ REPLACEMENT COST NEW	OPINION OF SITE VALUE .... = $
Source of cost data	Dwelling Sq. Ft. @ $ .... =$
Quality rating from cost service Effective date of cost data	Sq. Ft. @ $ .... =$
Comments on Cost Approach (gross living area calculations, depreciation, etc.)	
	Garage/Carport Sq. Ft. @ $ .... =$
	Total Estimate of Cost-New .... = $
	Less Physical | Functional | External
	Depreciation =$( )
	Depreciated Cost of Improvements........ =$
	"As-is" Value of Site Improvements........ =$
Estimated Remaining Economic Life (HUD and VA only) Years	Indicated Value By Cost Approach .... =$

INCOME APPROACH TO VALUE (not required by Fannie Mae)

Estimated Monthly Market Rent $ X Gross Rent Multiplier = $ Indicated Value by Income Approach

Summary of Income Approach (including support for market rent and GRM)

PROJECT INFORMATION FOR PUDs (if applicable)

Is the developer/builder in control of the Homeowners' Association (HOA)? ☐ Yes ☐ No Unit type(s) ☐ Detached ☐ Attached

Provide the following information for PUDs ONLY if the developer/builder is in control of the HOA and the subject property is an attached dwelling unit.

Legal name of project

Total number of phases Total number of units Total number of units sold

Total number of units rented Total number of units for sale Data source(s)

Was the project created by the conversion of an existing building(s) into a PUD? ☐ Yes ☐ No If Yes, date of conversion

Does the project contain any multi-dwelling units? ☐ Yes ☐ No Data source(s)

Are the units, common elements, and recreation facilities complete? ☐ Yes ☐ No If No, describe the status of completion.

Are the common elements leased to or by the Homeowners' Association? ☐ Yes ☐ No If Yes, describe the rental terms and options.

Describe common elements and recreational facilities

Freddie Mac Form 70 March 2005 Page 3 of 6 Fannie Mae Form 1004 March 2005

Uniform Residential Appraisal Report

File #

This report form is designed to report an appraisal of a one-unit property or a one-unit property with an accessory unit; including a unit in a planned unit development (PUD). This report form is not designed to report an appraisal of a manufactured home or a unit in a condominium or cooperative project.

This appraisal report is subject to the following scope of work, intended use, intended user, definition of market value, statement of assumptions and limiting conditions, and certifications. Modifications, additions, or deletions to the intended use, intended user, definition of market value, or assumptions and limiting conditions are not permitted. The appraiser may expand the scope of work to include any additional research or analysis necessary based on the complexity of this appraisal assignment. Modifications or deletions to the certifications are also not permitted. However, additional certifications that do not constitute material alterations to this appraisal report, such as those required by law or those related to the appraiser's continuing education or membership in an appraisal organization, are permitted.

SCOPE OF WORK: The scope of work for this appraisal is defined by the complexity of this appraisal assignment and the reporting requirements of this appraisal report form, including the following definition of market value, statement of assumptions and limiting conditions, and certifications. The appraiser must, at a minimum: (1) perform a complete visual inspection of the interior and exterior areas of the subject property, (2) inspect the neighborhood, (3) inspect each of the comparable sales from at least the street, (4) research, verify, and analyze data from reliable public and/or private sources, and (5) report his or her analysis, opinions, and conclusions in this appraisal report.

INTENDED USE: The intended use of this appraisal report is for the lender/client to evaluate the property that is the subject of this appraisal for a mortgage finance transaction.

INTENDED USER: The intended user of this appraisal report is the lender/client.

DEFINITION OF MARKET VALUE: The most probable price which a property should bring in a competitive and open market under all conditions requisite to a fair sale, the buyer and seller, each acting prudently, knowledgeably and assuming the price is not affected by undue stimulus. Implicit in this definition is the consummation of a sale as of a specified date and the passing of title from seller to buyer under conditions whereby: (1) buyer and seller are typically motivated; (2) both parties are well informed or well advised, and each acting in what he or she considers his or her own best interest; (3) a reasonable time is allowed for exposure in the open market; (4) payment is made in terms of cash in U. S. dollars or in terms of financial arrangements comparable thereto; and (5) the price represents the normal consideration for the property sold unaffected by special or creative financing or sales concessions* granted by anyone associated with the sale.

*Adjustments to the comparables must be made for special or creative financing or sales concessions. No adjustments are necessary for those costs which are normally paid by sellers as a result of tradition or law in a market area; these costs are readily identifiable since the seller pays these costs in virtually all sales transactions. Special or creative financing adjustments can be made to the comparable property by comparisons to financing terms offered by a third party institutional lender that is not already involved in the property or transaction. Any adjustment should not be calculated on a mechanical dollar for dollar cost of the financing or concession but the dollar amount of any adjustment should approximate the market's reaction to the financing or concessions based on the appraiser's judgment.

STATEMENT OF ASSUMPTIONS AND LIMITING CONDITIONS: The appraiser's certification in this report is subject to the following assumptions and limiting conditions:

1. The appraiser will not be responsible for matters of a legal nature that affect either the property being appraised or the title to it, except for information that he or she became aware of during the research involved in performing this appraisal. The appraiser assumes that the title is good and marketable and will not render any opinions about the title.

2. The appraiser has provided a sketch in this appraisal report to show the approximate dimensions of the improvements. The sketch is included only to assist the reader in visualizing the property and understanding the appraiser's determination of its size.

3. The appraiser has examined the available flood maps that are provided by the Federal Emergency Management Agency (or other data sources) and has noted in this appraisal report whether any portion of the subject site is located in an identified Special Flood Hazard Area. Because the appraiser is not a surveyor, he or she makes no guarantees, express or implied, regarding this determination.

4. The appraiser will not give testimony or appear in court because he or she made an appraisal of the property in question, unless specific arrangements to do so have been made beforehand, or as otherwise required by law.

5. The appraiser has noted in this appraisal report any adverse conditions (such as needed repairs, deterioration, the presence of hazardous wastes, toxic substances, etc.) observed during the inspection of the subject property or that he or she became aware of during the research involved in performing this appraisal. Unless otherwise stated in this appraisal report, the appraiser has no knowledge of any hidden or unapparent physical deficiencies or adverse conditions of the property (such as, but not limited to, needed repairs, deterioration, the presence of hazardous wastes, toxic substances, adverse environmental conditions, etc.) that would make the property less valuable, and has assumed that there are no such conditions and makes no guarantees or warranties, express or implied. The appraiser will not be responsible for any such conditions that do exist or for any engineering or testing that might be required to discover whether such conditions exist. Because the appraiser is not an expert in the field of environmental hazards, this appraisal report must not be considered as an environmental assessment of the property.

6. The appraiser has based his or her appraisal report and valuation conclusion for an appraisal that is subject to satisfactory completion, repairs, or alterations on the assumption that the completion, repairs, or alterations of the subject property will be performed in a professional manner.

Freddie Mac Form 70 March 2005 Page 4 of 6 Fannie Mae Form 1004 March 2005

Uniform Residential Appraisal Report

File #

APPRAISER'S CERTIFICATION: The Appraiser certifies and agrees that:

1. I have, at a minimum, developed and reported this appraisal in accordance with the scope of work requirements stated in this appraisal report.

2. I performed a complete visual inspection of the interior and exterior areas of the subject property. I reported the condition of the improvements in factual, specific terms. I identified and reported the physical deficiencies that could affect the livability, soundness, or structural integrity of the property.

3. I performed this appraisal in accordance with the requirements of the Uniform Standards of Professional Appraisal Practice that were adopted and promulgated by the Appraisal Standards Board of The Appraisal Foundation and that were in place at the time this appraisal report was prepared.

4. I developed my opinion of the market value of the real property that is the subject of this report based on the sales comparison approach to value. I have adequate comparable market data to develop a reliable sales comparison approach for this appraisal assignment. I further certify that I considered the cost and income approaches to value but did not develop them, unless otherwise indicated in this report.

5. I researched, verified, analyzed, and reported on any current agreement for sale for the subject property, any offering for sale of the subject property in the twelve months prior to the effective date of this appraisal, and the prior sales of the subject property for a minimum of three years prior to the effective date of this appraisal, unless otherwise indicated in this report.

6. I researched, verified, analyzed, and reported on the prior sales of the comparable sales for a minimum of one year prior to the date of sale of the comparable sale, unless otherwise indicated in this report.

7. I selected and used comparable sales that are locationally, physically, and functionally the most similar to the subject property.

8. I have not used comparable sales that were the result of combining a land sale with the contract purchase price of a home that has been built or will be built on the land.

9. I have reported adjustments to the comparable sales that reflect the market's reaction to the differences between the subject property and the comparable sales.

10. I verified, from a disinterested source, all information in this report that was provided by parties who have a financial interest in the sale or financing of the subject property.

11. I have knowledge and experience in appraising this type of property in this market area.

12. I am aware of, and have access to, the necessary and appropriate public and private data sources, such as multiple listing services, tax assessment records, public land records and other such data sources for the area in which the property is located.

13. I obtained the information, estimates, and opinions furnished by other parties and expressed in this appraisal report from reliable sources that I believe to be true and correct.

14. I have taken into consideration the factors that have an impact on value with respect to the subject neighborhood, subject property, and the proximity of the subject property to adverse influences in the development of my opinion of market value. I have noted in this appraisal report any adverse conditions (such as, but not limited to, needed repairs, deterioration, the presence of hazardous wastes, toxic substances, adverse environmental conditions, etc.) observed during the inspection of the subject property or that I became aware of during the research involved in performing this appraisal. I have considered these adverse conditions in my analysis of the property value, and have reported on the effect of the conditions on the value and marketability of the subject property.

15. I have not knowingly withheld any significant information from this appraisal report and, to the best of my knowledge, all statements and information in this appraisal report are true and correct.

16. I stated in this appraisal report my own personal, unbiased, and professional analysis, opinions, and conclusions, which are subject only to the assumptions and limiting conditions in this appraisal report.

17. I have no present or prospective interest in the property that is the subject of this report, and I have no present or prospective personal interest or bias with respect to the participants in the transaction. I did not base, either partially or completely, my analysis and/or opinion of market value in this appraisal report on the race, color, religion, sex, age, marital status, handicap, familial status, or national origin of either the prospective owners or occupants of the subject property or of the present owners or occupants of the properties in the vicinity of the subject property or on any other basis prohibited by law.

18. My employment and/or compensation for performing this appraisal or any future or anticipated appraisals was not conditioned on any agreement or understanding, written or otherwise, that I would report (or present analysis supporting) a predetermined specific value, a predetermined minimum value, a range or direction in value, a value that favors the cause of any party, or the attainment of a specific result or occurrence of a specific subsequent event (such as approval of a pending mortgage loan application).

19. I personally prepared all conclusions and opinions about the real estate that were set forth in this appraisal report. If I relied on significant real property appraisal assistance from any individual or individuals in the performance of this appraisal or the preparation of this appraisal report, I have named such individual(s) and disclosed the specific tasks performed in this appraisal report. I certify that any individual so named is qualified to perform the tasks. I have not authorized anyone to make a change to any item in this appraisal report, therefore, any change made to this appraisal is unauthorized and I will take no responsibility for it.

20. I identified the lender/client in this appraisal report who is the individual, organization, or agent for the organization that ordered and will receive this appraisal report.

Freddie Mac Form 70 March 2005 | Page 5 of 6 | Fannie Mae Form 1004 March 2005

Uniform Residential Appraisal Report File

21. The lender/client may disclose or distribute this appraisal report to: the borrower; another lender at the request of the borrower; the mortgagee or its successors and assigns; mortgage insurers; government sponsored enterprises; other secondary market participants; data collection or reporting services; professional appraisal organizations; any department, agency, or instrumentality of the United States; and any state, the District of Columbia, or other jurisdictions; without having to obtain the appraiser's or supervisory appraiser's (if applicable) consent. Such consent must be obtained before this appraisal report may be disclosed or distributed to any other party (including, but not limited to, the public through advertising, public relations, news, sales, or other media).

22. I am aware that any disclosure or distribution of this appraisal report by me or the lender/client may be subject to certain laws and regulations. Further, I am also subject to the provisions of the Uniform Standards of Professional Appraisal Practice that pertain to disclosure or distribution by me.

23. The borrower, another lender at the request of the borrower, the mortgagee or its successors and assigns, mortgage insurers, government sponsored enterprises, and other secondary market participants may rely on this appraisal report as part of any mortgage finance transaction that involves any one or more of these parties.

24. If this appraisal report was transmitted as an "electronic record" containing my "electronic signature," as those terms are defined in applicable federal and/or state laws (excluding audio and video recordings), or a facsimile transmission of this appraisal report containing a copy or representation of my signature, the appraisal report shall be as effective, enforceable and valid as if a paper version of this appraisal report were delivered containing my original hand written signature.

25. Any intentional or negligent misrepresentation(s) contained in this appraisal report may result in civil liability and/or criminal penalties including, but not limited to, fine or imprisonment or both under the provisions of Title 18, United States Code, Section 1001, et seq., or similar state laws.

SUPERVISORY APPRAISER'S CERTIFICATION: The Supervisory Appraiser certifies and agrees that:

1. I directly supervised the appraiser for this appraisal assignment, have read the appraisal report, and agree with the appraiser's analysis, opinions, statements, conclusions, and the appraiser's certification.

2. I accept full responsibility for the contents of this appraisal report including, but not limited to, the appraiser's analysis, opinions, statements, conclusions, and the appraiser's certification.

3. The appraiser identified in this appraisal report is either a sub-contractor or an employee of the supervisory appraiser (or the appraisal firm), is qualified to perform this appraisal, and is acceptable to perform this appraisal under the applicable state law.

4. This appraisal report complies with the Uniform Standards of Professional Appraisal Practice that were adopted and promulgated by the Appraisal Standards Board of The Appraisal Foundation and that were in place at the time this appraisal report was prepared.

5. If this appraisal report was transmitted as an "electronic record" containing my "electronic signature," as those terms are defined in applicable federal and/or state laws (excluding audio and video recordings), or a facsimile transmission of this appraisal report containing a copy or representation of my signature, the appraisal report shall be as effective, enforceable and valid as if a paper version of this appraisal report were delivered containing my original hand written signature.

APPRAISER

Signature ____________________
Name ____________________
Company Name ____________________
Company Address ____________________
____
Telephone Number ____________________
Email Address ____________________
Date of Signature and Report ____________________
Effective Date of Appraisal ____________________
State Certification # ____________________
or State License # ____________________
or Other (describe) ____________ State # ____________
State ____________________
Expiration Date of Certification or License ____________

ADDRESS OF PROPERTY APPRAISED
____
____

APPRAISED VALUE OF SUBJECT PROPERTY $ ____________

LENDER/CLIENT
Name ____________________
Company Name ____________________
Company Address ____________________
____
Email Address ____________________

SUPERVISORY APPRAISER (ONLY IF REQUIRED)

Signature ____________________
Name ____________________
Company Name ____________________
Company Address ____________________
____
Telephone Number ____________________
Email Address ____________________
Date of Signature ____________________
State Certification # ____________________
or State License # ____________________
State ____________________
Expiration Date of Certification or License ____________

SUBJECT PROPERTY

☐ Did not inspect subject property
☐ Did inspect exterior of subject property from street
Date of Inspection ____________________
☐ Did inspect interior and exterior of subject property
Date of Inspection ____________________

COMPARABLE SALES

☐ Did not inspect exterior of comparable sales from street
☐ Did inspect exterior of comparable sales from street
Date of Inspection ____________________

Freddie Mac Form 70 March 2005 Page 6 of 6 Fannie Mae Form 1004 March 2005

Chapter Summary

1. An appraisal is an estimate or an opinion of value. Most real estate appraisals concern the property's market value, the price it is likely to bring on the open market in a sale under normal conditions.
2. Appraisers have developed many "principles of value" that guide them in the valuation process. These include the principles of highest and best use, change, supply and demand, substitution, conformity, contribution, anticipation, and competition.
3. The steps in the appraisal process include defining the problem, determining the scope of work, collecting and verifying the data, analyzing the data, valuing the site, applying the approaches to value, reconciling the value indicators, and issuing the appraisal report.
4. General data concerns factors outside the subject property itself that influence the property's value; the appraiser gathers general data by evaluating economic and social trends and by performing a neighborhood analysis. Specific data (about the subject property itself) is gathered through site analysis and building analysis.
5. In the sales comparison approach to value (which is the most important method of appraisal for residential properties), the appraiser compares the subject property to comparable properties that were sold recently, and uses the adjusted selling prices of the comparables to estimate the value of the subject property.
6. In the cost approach to value, the appraiser estimates the cost of replacing the improvements, deducts any depreciation, and adds the estimated value of the land to arrive at an estimate of the value of the whole property. The three types of depreciation are physical deterioration, functional obsolescence, and external obsolescence. Depreciation is curable if the cost of correcting it could be recovered in the sales price when the property is sold. Curable physical deterioration is also called deferred maintenance.
7. In the income approach to value, the appraiser divides the property's net income by a capitalization rate to estimate its value to an investor. The appraiser first estimates the property's potential gross income (economic rent), then deducts a vacancy factor to determine the effective gross income, then deducts operating expenses to determine net operating income, and finally divides net operating income by a capitalization rate to find the property's value. The gross income multiplier method is a simplified version of the income approach that is sometimes used in appraising residential rental properties.

Key Terms

Market value—The most probable price that a property should bring in a competitive and open market under all conditions requisite to a fair sale, the buyer and seller each acting prudently and knowledgeably, and assuming the price is not affected by undue stimulus.

Highest and best use—The most profitable use of the property; the one that provides the greatest net return over time.

Principle of change—Real property is in a constant state of change; it goes through a four-phase life cycle of integration, equilibrium, disintegration, and rejuvenation.

Principle of substitution—No one will pay more for a piece of property than they would have to pay for an equally desirable substitute.

Sales comparison approach—The method of appraisal in which the appraiser compares the subject property to recently sold comparable properties.

Arm's length transaction—A transaction in which there is no pre-existing family or business relationship between the parties.

Cost approach—The method of appraisal in which the appraiser estimates the replacement cost of the building, deducts depreciation, and adds the value of the site.

Depreciation—Loss in value due to any cause. Depreciation is curable if the cost of correcting it could be recovered in the sales price when the property is sold.

Physical deterioration—Depreciation caused by wear and tear, damage, or structural defects. Curable physical deterioration is called deferred maintenance.

Functional obsolescence—Depreciation caused by functional inadequacies or outmoded design.

External obsolescence—Depreciation caused by forces outside the property, such as neighborhood decline or proximity to nuisances; also called economic obsolescence.

Income approach—The method of appraising property in which net income is converted into value using a capitalization rate.

Effective gross income—A property's potential gross income, minus a vacancy factor.

Net operating income—A property's effective gross income, minus operating expenses. Also called net income.

Capitalization rate—The rate of return an investor wants on her investment in the property.

Economic rent—The rent that a property would earn on the open market if it were currently available for rent, as distinguished from the rent it is actually earning now (the contract rent).

Chapter Quiz

1. An appraisal is a/an:

a) scientific determination of a property's value
b) property's average value, as indicated by general and specific data
c) estimate of a property's value as of a specific date
d) mathematical analysis of a property's value

2. The focus of most appraisals is the subject property's:

a) market value
b) market price
c) sales price
d) value in use

3. A property's highest and best use is the use that:

a) will generate the greatest net return
b) will generate the highest gross return
c) best promotes the public health, safety, and welfare
d) is best suited to the present owner's plans

4. The earliest phase of a property's life cycle, when it is being developed, is called:

a) substitution
b) regression
c) integration
d) disintegration

5. Developers have announced plans to build a multimillion dollar shopping center next door to a vacant commercial lot you own. Property values in the area will tend to increase as a result of this announcement. This is an example of the principle of:

a) highest and best use
b) supply and demand
c) substitution
d) anticipation

6. The owner of an apartment building has asked an appraiser to determine if it would make financial sense to put in a swimming pool for the tenants' use. The appraiser will be most concerned with the principle of:

a) regression
b) substitution
c) conformity
d) contribution

7. If someone were to build a high-quality home costing $450,000 in a neighborhood where all of the other homes were valued at around $175,000, the expensive home would suffer a loss in value. This illustrates the principle of:

a) regression
b) supply and demand
c) progression
d) aversion

8. An appraiser gathers general data in a:

a) site analysis
b) building analysis
c) neighborhood analysis
d) None of the above

9. The sales comparison approach would be much more important than the other two methods (the cost approach and the income approach) in the appraisal of a/an:

a) six-unit apartment building
b) industrial building
c) shopping center
d) single-family home

10. A residential appraiser looking for good comparables is most likely to consider homes that:

a) have not changed hands within the past three years
b) are currently listed for sale
c) were sold within the past six months
d) were listed for less than they eventually sold for

11. In which of the following situations would the sales comparison method of appraisal be least reliable?

a) When all the comparables are in the same price range
b) When the real estate market has been inactive for quite a while
c) When some of the comparables are located in another neighborhood
d) When the subject property is in better condition than the comparables

12. When applying the sales comparison method to appraise a single-family home, an appraiser would never use as a comparable a similar home that:

a) sold over six months ago
b) sold recently but is located in another neighborhood
c) was sold by owners who were forced to sell because of financial difficulties
d) is situated on a corner lot

13. When using the replacement cost approach, which of the following would be least important?

a) Current construction cost per square foot
b) Rental cost per square foot
c) Depreciation
d) Estimated land value

14. An appraiser is applying the cost approach in valuing an elegant building that was built in 1894. Which of the following is most likely to be true?

a) The building's replacement cost is the same as its reproduction cost
b) The building's replacement cost is a better indicator of its market value than its reproduction cost
c) The building's reproduction cost is a better indicator of its market value than its replacement cost
d) The building's replacement cost is much greater than its reproduction cost

15. In the income approach to value, which of the following is not considered to be one of the property's operating expenses?

a) General real estate taxes
b) Maintenance expenses
c) Reserves for replacement
d) Mortgage payments

Chapter 13:
Closing Real Estate Transactions

I. Escrow

II. Closing Costs and Settlement Statements
   A. Preparing a settlement statement
   B. Guide to settlement statements
      1. Settlement charges
      2. Prorations
      3. Payment amounts at closing

III. Income Tax Aspects of Closing
   A. Form 1099-S reporting
   B. Form 8300 reporting
   C. FIRPTA

IV. Real Estate Settlement Procedures Act
   A. Transactions covered by RESPA
   B. RESPA requirements
   C. Closing disclosures

The real estate agent's job doesn't end when the parties sign the purchase and sale agreement. Many matters must be taken care of before the sale can be finalized, and the service provided by the real estate agent during the closing process is just as important as the agent's marketing efforts before the sale. Guiding the parties through closing prevents unnecessary delays and earns the agent a reputation for professionalism. This chapter explains the purpose of escrow, the steps involved in closing, and Washington's Escrow Agent Registration Act. It also discusses how settlement statements work, how closing costs are allocated and prorated, income tax aspects of closing, and the requirements of the federal Real Estate Settlement Procedures Act.

Key Terms

Closing	**Credit**
Escrow	**Reserve Account**
Escrow Agent	**Prorate**
Licensed Escrow Agent	**Prepaid Interest**
Licensed Escrow Officer	**Respa**
Escrow Instructions	**Settlement Service Provider**
Settlement Statement	**Loan Estimate**
Debit	**Closing Disclosure**

Introduction

Once a buyer and a seller have signed a purchase agreement, the parties and their agents begin making preparations to finalize the transaction. Finalizing a real estate transaction is called **closing** or **settlement.**

The closing process varies considerably from one state to another. In some states, all of the parties involved in the transaction get together to sign and exchange documents and transfer funds. In many other states (including Washington), the closing process is handled by a third party through the creation of an escrow.

Escrow

Escrow is an arrangement in which money and documents are held by a third party (the **escrow agent**) on behalf of the buyer and the seller. The parties usually give the escrow agent written **escrow instructions**, which determine under what conditions and at what time the agent will distribute the money and documents to the proper parties. The escrow agent is a dual agent, representing both the buyer and the seller, with fiduciary duties to both parties (see Chapter 7).

The purpose of escrow is to ensure that the seller receives the purchase price, the buyer receives clear title to the property, and the lender's security interest in the property is perfected. Escrow protects each party from the other's change of mind. For example, if the seller suddenly doesn't want to sell the property as agreed, they can't just refuse to deliver the deed to the buyer. Once a deed has been given to an escrow agent, if the buyer fulfills all the conditions specified in the escrow instructions and deposits the purchase price into escrow, the escrow agent is required to deliver the deed to the buyer. An added advantage of escrow is convenience: the parties do not have to be present to close the transaction.

Escrow agents perform a wide variety of services to prepare a transaction for closing. An escrow closing may involve the following steps:

- obtaining a title report from the title insurance company;
- paying off existing loans secured by the property;
- preparing the deed and other documents;
- depositing funds from the buyer (and the seller if necessary);
- requesting the funding of the buyer's loan;
- prorating expenses and allocating closing costs;
- preparing a settlement statement or closing disclosure form;
- obtaining title insurance policies;
- arranging to have documents recorded; and
- disbursing funds and delivering documents.

However, the escrow agent's services are usually quite limited in nature. For example, while an escrow agent will order a title report in accordance with the escrow instructions, the escrow agent won't go over the report with the parties and discuss any unexpected problems that the report might reveal. Reviewing the report and deciding whether to proceed with the transaction is up to the parties.

Escrow Agent Registration Act

Washington's Escrow Agent Registration Act requires escrow agents to be licensed and registered with the Department of Financial Institutions. A company that is licensed to engage in the escrow business under the Registration Act is called a **licensed escrow agent**. The individuals that a licensed escrow agent employs to handle transactions must be **licensed escrow officers**, and they must be supervised by the company's **designated escrow officer**. The designated escrow officer must be a licensed escrow officer, and also must be a partner, a corporate officer, or the sole proprietor of the company, depending on how the company is organized.

To become a licensed escrow agent, a company must comply with bonding requirements and have errors and omissions insurance. The company's owners and managers must submit their business history, fingerprints, and personal credit reports.

To become a licensed escrow officer, an individual must pass a state exam and submit proof of good character, fingerprints, and a personal credit report.

A licensed escrow agent is responsible for keeping adequate transaction records and maintaining a trust account for clients' funds in a recognized Washington depository. The director of the Department of Financial Institutions may investigate the actions of licensed escrow agents and escrow officers and suspend or revoke their licenses if they have committed dishonest or prohibited acts.

Exemptions. There are several significant exemptions from the Escrow Agent Registration Act's licensing requirements. Attorneys, title insurance companies, other insurance companies, and lending institutions are allowed to perform escrow services without being licensed or registered under the act; so are those acting under the supervision of a court, such as receivers, trustees in bankruptcy, guardians, executors, and probate administrators. A real estate licensee handling the escrow for their own transaction (one for which they are providing brokerage services) is also exempt, provided that there is no additional charge for the escrow services.

Throughout this chapter, we refer to the person who handles the closing process for a transaction as the escrow agent, in accordance with common usage. Keep in mind, however, that the closing agent is not necessarily a licensed escrow agent or a licensed escrow officer. In many transactions, the closing agent is someone acting under one of the exemptions from the Registration Act, such as an attorney, an employee of the buyer's lender or the title company, or a real estate agent.

Closing Costs and Settlement Statements

Most real estate transactions involve a wide variety of costs in addition to the purchase price: inspection fees, title insurance charges, loan fees, and so on. These are known as **closing costs**. Some of these closing costs are paid by the buyer, and some are paid by the seller. Some are paid by one party to the other; for example, the buyer may have to reimburse the seller for property taxes the seller already paid. Other closing costs are paid by one of the parties to a third party; the purchase and sale agreement may require the seller to pay a pest inspector's fee, for instance.

There are also other payments to be made in connection with closing. For example, the seller often has to pay off an existing mortgage or other liens. Determining who is required to pay how much to whom at closing can be a complicated matter.

So for each transaction, the escrow agent prepares a **settlement statement**. A settlement statement (also known as a closing statement) sets forth all of the financial details of the transaction. It shows exactly how much the buyer will have to pay at closing, and exactly how much the seller will take away from closing. A simplified example of a settlement statement is shown in Figure 13.1.

Fig. 13.1 Simplified Settlement Statement

	Buyer		Seller	
	Debits	**Credits**	**Debits**	**Credits**
Purchase price	175,000.00			175,000.00
Deposit		8,750.00		
Excise tax			2,240.00	
Sales commission			12,250.00	
Payoff of seller's loan			92,950.00	
Assumption of seller's loan				
New loan		140,000.00		
Seller financing				
Owner's title insurance			120.00	
Lender's title insurance	456.00			
Origination/assumption fee	2,100.00			
Discount points				
Property taxes				
In arrears				
Paid in advance	684.50			684.50
Hazard insurance				
Assumption of policy				
New policy	260.00			
Interest				
Payoff of seller's loan			382.86	
Assumption				
New loan (prepaid)	161.08			
Reserve account				
Payoff of seller's loan				286.05
Assumption				
Credit report	40.00			
Appraisal	275.00			
Survey				
Pest inspection and repairs			150.00	
Personal property				
Recording fees	50.00		25.00	
Escrow fee	147.00		147.00	
Balance due from buyer		30,423.58		
Balance due to seller			67,705.69	
TOTALS	179,173.58	179,173.58	175,970.55	175,970.55

In most residential transactions, the settlement statement is part of the closing disclosure form required under the Real Estate Settlement Procedures Act (discussed at the end of this chapter). The buyer's lender is responsible for providing closing disclosure forms to the parties; the escrow agent may assist the lender in preparing these.

Preparing a Settlement Statement

The items listed on a settlement statement are either **debits** or **credits**. A debit is a charge payable by a party; the purchase price is a debit for the buyer, for example, and the sales commission is a debit for the seller. Credits are items payable to a party; the buyer is credited for their new loan, and the seller for the purchase price.

Preparing a settlement statement involves determining what charges and credits apply to a given transaction and making sure each one is allocated to the right party. When allocating expenses, the person preparing the statement uses the terms of the purchase and sale agreement or the escrow instructions as a guide. The allocation can also be determined by custom (local or general), provided the custom doesn't conflict with the terms of the parties' contract. For example, in most places the buyer usually pays the cost of an appraisal, so that cost would ordinarily be charged to the buyer.

But if the seller agreed in the purchase agreement to pay the appraisal fee, the agreement would take precedence over custom and the expense would be a debit for the seller on the settlement statement.

Of course, neither custom nor the agreement between the parties will be honored if they are contrary to local, state, or federal law.

Although a real estate agent typically won't ever be called upon to prepare a formal settlement statement, every agent should know what closing costs are likely to be involved in a transaction and how they are customarily allocated. The buyer and the seller may want to negotiate the allocation of particular costs, and in any case they should have a good idea of their costs before signing a contract. Brokerage software can help the agent prepare a preliminary estimate of closing costs for each party.

Guide to Settlement Statements

The simplified settlement statement in Figure 13.1 uses the double entry accounting method, so each party has a credit column and a debit column. The sum of the buyer's credits must equal the sum of the buyer's debits. The sum of the seller's credits must equal the sum of the seller's debits. Think of the settlement statement as a check register for a bank account. Debits are like checks written against the account, and credits are the equivalent of deposits into the account. When the transaction closes, the balance in each party's account should be zero.

When an item is to be paid by one party to the other, it will appear on the settlement statement as a debit for the paying party and as a credit for the party paid. An obvious example is the purchase price, which is debited to the buyer and credited to the seller.

If an item is paid by one of the parties to a third party, it appears on the settlement statement in the paying party's debit column, and it does not appear in the other party's columns at all. For example, the seller is customarily charged for the state excise tax, which is paid to the county treasurer. The tax is a debit for the seller, but it is not a credit for the buyer.

Similarly, certain items are shown as a credit for one party, but not as a debit for the other. The seller's reserve balance is a case in point. If the sale calls for the payoff of the seller's existing mortgage, any reserves held by the seller's lender (to cover recurring expenses such as property taxes or insurance premiums) are refunded. They are a credit for the seller, but not a debit for the buyer.

Settlement Charges. Here is a list of items that will or may appear on a typical settlement statement. (As mentioned, in most residential transactions the settlement statement is a section of the closing disclosure form.)

Purchase Price. Paid by the buyer to the seller, the purchase price is listed as a debit for the buyer and a credit for the seller.

Earnest Money Deposit. In most transactions, the buyer provides an earnest money deposit. If the transaction closes, the earnest money is applied to the purchase price. Since the buyer has already paid the earnest money, it appears on the settlement statement as a credit for the buyer. And since the full purchase price has already been debited to the buyer and credited to the seller, no entry for the earnest money is made on the seller's side of the statement. (The earnest money deposit is the only entry on the settlement statement that is handled in this manner.)

Sales Commission. The real estate sales commission is normally paid by the seller, so it is entered as a debit for the seller.

New Loan. If the buyer secures a new loan to finance part or all of the sale, the loan amount is listed as a credit for the buyer. Like the deposit, the buyer's loan is part of the purchase price already credited to the seller, so no entry is made on the seller's side of the statement.

Assumed Loan. If the buyer assumes the seller's existing loan, it is part of the money used to finance the transaction, so (like a new loan) it is credited to the buyer. The assumed loan balance is a debit for the seller.

Seller Financing. If the seller accepts a mortgage or deed of trust from the buyer for part of the purchase price, that shows up in the buyer's credit column, just like an institutional loan. At the same time, a seller financing arrangement reduces the amount of money the seller will receive at closing, so it is listed as a debit for the seller.

If the property is sold under a land contract, the contract price (less the downpayment) is credit extended by the seller. It reduces the seller's net at closing and is used by the buyer to finance the purchase, so it's a debit for the seller and a credit for the buyer.

Payoff of Seller's Loan. If the seller pays off an existing mortgage loan, their net is reduced by that amount. The payoff is a debit for the seller. No entry is made on the buyer's side of the statement.

Prepayment Penalty. A prepayment penalty is a charge the seller's lender may impose on the seller for paying the loan off before the end of its term. It would be a debit for the seller on the settlement statement.

Seller's Reserve Account. As was mentioned earlier, the seller often has reserves on deposit with their lender to cover recurring expenses such as property taxes, insurance premiums, and homeowners association dues. The lender uses the funds in the reserve account (also called an **impound account** or **escrow account**) to pay these expenses when they come due.

When the seller's loan is paid off, the unused balance in the reserve account is refunded to the seller. If this is handled through escrow, the refunded amount appears as a credit on the seller's side of the settlement statement. If the buyer is assuming the loan and the reserve account, the reserves would appear as a credit for the seller and a debit for the buyer. (Alternatively, the seller's lender may refund the reserve account balance directly to the seller after closing.)

Appraisal Fee. The appraisal is usually required by the buyer's lender, so the fee is ordinarily a debit for the buyer.

Credit Report. The buyer's lender charges the buyer for the credit investigation, so this is also a debit for the buyer.

Survey. Sometimes a lender requires a survey as a condition for making the loan. Unless otherwise agreed, the cost of the survey is a debit for the buyer.

Origination Fee. This is the lender's one-time charge to the borrower for setting up the loan (see Chapter 11). It's a debit for the buyer.

Discount Points. The discount points are a debit for the buyer, unless the seller has agreed to pay for a buydown (see Chapter 11). In that case, the points are a debit for the seller.

Assumption Fee. A lender charges an assumption fee when the buyer is assuming the seller's existing loan. The assumption fee is a debit for the buyer.

Owner's Title Insurance Premium. The premium for the owner's title insurance policy (which protects the buyer) is customarily paid by the seller. So this is a debit for the seller, unless otherwise agreed.

Lender's Title Insurance Premium. The lender requires the buyer to provide an extended coverage policy to protect the lender's lien priority. The premium for this policy is a debit for the buyer, unless otherwise agreed.

Sale of Personal Property. If the seller is selling the buyer some personal property along with the real property, the price of these items should be credited to the seller and debited to the buyer. (The seller should sign a bill of sale to be delivered to the buyer at closing along with the deed.)

Inspection Fees. The cost of an inspection is allocated by agreement between the parties. For example, the buyer might agree to pay for the cost of a pest inspection, while the seller agrees to pay for repairs if the inspection shows that any are necessary.

Hazard Insurance Policy. The lender generally requires the buyer to pay for one to three years of hazard insurance coverage in advance. This is a debit for the buyer.

Excise Tax. This is a tax imposed on most sales of real property in Washington (see Chapter 5). It is customarily paid by the seller, so it would usually be listed in the seller's debit column.

Attorney's Fees. A buyer or seller who is represented by an attorney in the transaction is responsible for their own attorney's fees. On the settlement statement, the fees will show up as a debit for the appropriate party.

Recording Fees. The fees for recording the various documents involved in the transaction are usually charged to the party who benefits from the recording. For example, the fees for recording the deed and the new mortgage or deed of trust are debits for the buyer; the fee for recording a satisfaction of the old mortgage is a debit for the seller.

Escrow Fee. Also called a settlement fee or closing fee, the escrow fee is the escrow agent's charge for their services. The buyer and the seller commonly agree to split the escrow fee; in that case, half the fee will be debited to each party.

Prorations. There are, of course, certain recurring expenses connected with ownership of real estate, such as property taxes and mortgage interest payments. As a general rule, the seller is responsible for these expenses during their period of ownership, but not beyond. So the person preparing a settlement statement checks to see what the status of each of these expenses will be on the closing date: current, paid in advance, or in arrears. An expense paid in advance or in arrears must be prorated to determine what portion is the seller's responsibility. To **prorate** an expense is to divide and allocate it proportionately, according to time, interest, or benefit.

If the seller has paid a particular expense in advance, they are entitled to a partial refund, which appears as a credit for the seller on the settlement statement. On the other hand, if the seller will be in arrears at closing, the amount that they owe is entered as a debit on the statement. (Note that in this context, "in arrears" does not necessarily mean that payment of the bill for the expense is already overdue. It means that as of the closing date the seller will owe a portion or share of the expense, which will be deducted from the proceeds of the sale.)

If the expense is one that will continue after closing, as in the case of property taxes, the buyer is responsible for it once their period of ownership begins. This type of expense will be prorated between seller and buyer. If the seller has not paid their share of the bill yet, it will show up on the settlement statement as a debit for the seller. It will also be a credit for the buyer. That's because the buyer will have to pay the seller's share, along with their own share, when the bill becomes due at some point after closing. In contrast, if the seller has paid the bill in advance, the buyer's share will be a debit for the buyer and a credit for the seller (reimbursing the seller for the buyer's share of the bill already paid).

The first step in prorating an expense is to divide it by the number of days it covers to determine the **per diem** (daily) rate. So an annual expense would be divided by 365 days (366 in a leap year); the per diem rate would be $^1/_{365}$ of the annual amount. A monthly expense would be divided by the number of days in the month in question (28, 29, 30, or 31).

The next step is to determine the number of days during which a particular party is responsible for the expense. The final step is to multiply that number of days by the per diem rate, to arrive at the share of the expense that party is responsible for. Examples appear below. (See Chapter 18 for further discussion of proration calculations.)

Property Taxes. The seller is responsible for property taxes up to the day of closing; the buyer is responsible for them thereafter. The parties will agree on (or rely on local custom to settle) which party pays the taxes for the closing date itself; more often than not, the buyer is responsible. If the seller has already paid the property taxes for the year, they are entitled to a prorated refund at closing. On the settlement statement, this will appear as a credit for the seller and a debit for the buyer.

If the property taxes covering the final part of the seller's period of ownership have not yet been paid, the amount that the seller owes at closing will be a debit for the seller and a credit for the buyer on the settlement statement.

Interest on Seller's Loan. Interest on a real estate loan is almost always paid in arrears, after it accrues. In other words, the interest accruing on the loan during a given month is paid as part of the next month's payment. For instance, a loan payment due on September 1 includes the interest that accrued during August. If a transaction closes in the middle of the payment period, the seller owes the lender some interest.

> **Example:** The closing date is August 15. Although the seller made a payment on their loan on August 1, that payment did not include any of the interest that is accruing during August. At closing, the seller will owe the lender interest for the period from August 1 through August 15. The escrow agent prorates the interest, charging the seller only for those days, rather than the whole month's interest. The prorated amount is entered on the settlement statement as a debit for the seller.
>
> If the buyer assumes the loan, their first payment will be due on September 1, and it will pay all of the interest for August. The seller will be debited for the interest owed up to August 15, and the buyer will be credited for the same amount.

Prepaid Interest on Buyer's Loan. Another expense that the escrow agent prorates (one that does not concern the seller) is the interest on the buyer's new mortgage loan. Just as the interest on the seller's loan does not affect the buyer, the prepaid interest on the buyer's loan does not affect the seller. As a general rule, the first payment date of a new loan is not the first day of the month immediately following closing, but rather the first day of the next month after that.

> **Example:** A buyer is financing the purchase of a home with a new bank loan. Closing takes place on January 23. The buyer is not required to make a payment on the new loan on February 1. Instead, the first payment isn't due until March 1.

Even though the first payment isn't due for an extra month, interest begins accruing on the loan on the closing date. As explained above, the first regular payment will cover the interest for the preceding month. So if the transaction closes on January 23, the first payment will be due on March 1, and that payment will cover the interest accrued in February. However, it will not cover the interest accrued between January 23 and January 31. Instead, the lender requires the buyer to pay the interest for those nine days in January at closing. This is called **prepaid interest** or **interim interest**. It will appear as a debit for the buyer on the settlement statement.

> **Example:** The buyer is borrowing $418,500 at 7% interest to finance the purchase. The annual interest on the loan during the first year will be $29,295 ($418,500 × 7% = $29,295). The escrow agent divides that annual figure by 365 to determine the per diem interest rate.
>
> $29,295 ÷ 365 = $80.26 per diem
>
> There are nine days between the closing date (January 23) and the first day of the following month, so the lender will expect the buyer to prepay nine days' worth of interest at closing.
>
> $80.26 × 9 days = $722.34 prepaid interest
>
> The escrow agent will enter $722.34 as a debit for the buyer on the settlement statement.

Thus, in most transactions, the seller and the buyer each must pay some mortgage interest that accrues on the closing date. That's because there are usually two entirely different loans involved: the seller's existing loan, which ends on the closing date, and the buyer's new loan, which begins on the closing date. (If the buyer is assuming the seller's loan instead, the parties need to agree on which of them will be responsible for the interest that accrues on the closing date.)

Rent. So far we've only discussed prorated expenses. In some transactions, there is also income to be prorated at closing. If the property generates rental income and the tenants have paid for some period beyond the closing date, the seller is debited and the buyer credited for the rent paid in advance. If the rent is paid in arrears, the seller will be credited for the amount due up to closing, and the buyer will be debited for the same amount.

Note that tenants' security deposits are not prorated. The seller must transfer all of the deposits to the buyer, since the leases will continue after closing.

Payment Amounts at Closing. As we said earlier, on a settlement statement the sum of one party's credits should equal the sum of that party's debits, so that the final balance in each party's "account" is zero. In order for the statement to work this way, it must list the amount of money that the buyer will have to bring to closing, and also the amount of money the seller will take away from closing.

Amount Due from Buyer. Add up all of the buyer's credits, then add up all of the buyer's debits. Subtract the buyer's credits from the buyer's debits to find the balance due, which is the amount of money the buyer will have to deposit into escrow in order to close the transaction.

Enter this amount as a credit for the buyer. Now the buyer's credits column should add up to exactly the same amount as the buyer's debits column.

Amount Due to Seller. Add up all of the seller's credits, then add up all of the seller's debits. Subtract the seller's debits from the seller's credits. The result is the amount of money (if any) the seller will receive from the sale at closing. Enter this amount as a debit if credits exceed debits, but as a credit if debits exceed credits. Now the seller's credits column should add up to exactly the same amount as the seller's debits column.

Note that the buyer's two column totals must match each other, and the seller's two column totals must match each other. However, the buyer's column totals don't have to match the seller's column totals.

Income Tax Aspects of Closing

Nearly all real estate transactions have tax implications (see Chapter 14), and it's up to each party to fulfill their own tax obligations. However, there are certain requirements related to income taxes that must be met when a transaction closes.

Form 1099-S Reporting

The Internal Revenue Service generally requires an escrow agent to report real property sales on Form 1099-S. The form is used to report the seller's name and social security number and the gross proceeds from the sale. However, the form doesn't have to be filed for the sale of a principal residence if: 1) the seller certifies in writing that the property was their principal residence and none of the gain is taxable; and 2) the property sold for $250,000 or less ($500,000 or less if the seller is married). Certain other types of transactions are also exempt from the requirement.

An escrow agent may not charge the parties an extra fee for complying with 1099-S reporting requirements.

Form 8300 Reporting

The IRS requires an escrow agent who receives more than $10,000 in cash to report the cash payment on Form 8300, in order to help detect money laundering and tax evasion. This rule applies whether the agent received the cash in a single payment or in a series of related payments.

> **Example:** ABC Escrow is handling the closing for Sam's real estate purchase. As part of the process, Sam is required to deposit $12,000 into escrow. He gives this amount to ABC in two cash payments: $8,000 on Thursday, and the other $4,000 on Friday. Although the individual amounts are less than $10,000, ABC will need to submit Form 8300 to the IRS because the payments relate to the same transaction.

The escrow agent must file Form 8300 within 15 days of receiving the cash. A copy of the form should be kept on file for five years.

FIRPTA

The Foreign Investment in Real Property Tax Act (FIRPTA) is a federal law designed to help prevent foreign investors from evading their tax liability on income generated from the sale of real estate they owned in the United States. FIRPTA requires the property buyer to determine whether the seller is a "foreign person," defined as someone who is not a U.S. citizen or resident alien. If the seller is a foreign person, the buyer generally must withhold 15% of the amount realized from the sale and forward those funds to the IRS. (In most cases, the amount realized is simply the sales price.) Payment must be made within 20 days after the transfer date. The escrow agent usually handles these requirements on behalf of the buyer.

Note that many residential transactions are exempt from FIRPTA. If the amount realized on the sale of a property that the buyer will use as a principal residence is $300,000 or less, no withholding is required. If the amount realized is between $300,000 and $1 million, only 10% needs to be withheld.

Real Estate Settlement Procedures Act

The Real Estate Settlement Procedures Act (**RESPA**) applies to any professional involved in the settlement process, including not just escrow agents but also real estate agents, title company employees, and mortgage loan originators. The law affects how closing is handled in most residential transactions financed with institutional loans. It has two main goals:

- to provide borrowers with information about their closing costs; and
- to eliminate kickbacks (referral fees) that unnecessarily increase the cost of settlement.

Transactions Covered by RESPA

RESPA applies to "federally related" loan transactions. A loan is federally related if:

1. it will be secured by a mortgage or deed of trust against:
    - property on which there is (or on which the loan proceeds will be used to build) a dwelling with four or fewer units;
    - a condominium unit or a cooperative apartment; or
    - a lot with (or on which the loan proceeds will be used to place) a mobile home; and
2. the lender is federally regulated, has federally insured accounts, is assisted by the federal government, makes loans in connection with a federal program, sells loans to Fannie Mae or Freddie Mac, or makes residential real estate loans totaling more than $1,000,000 per year.

In short, the act applies to most institutional lenders and to most residential loans.

Exemptions. RESPA does not apply to the following loan transactions:

- a loan used to purchase 25 acres or more;
- a loan used primarily for a business, commercial, or agricultural purpose;
- a loan used to purchase vacant land, unless there will be a one- to four-unit dwelling built on it or a mobile home placed on it;
- temporary financing, such as a construction loan; or
- an assumption for which the lender's approval is neither required nor obtained.

Note that RESPA also does not apply to seller-financed transactions, since those are not federally regulated.

RESPA Requirements

RESPA imposes these requirements on federally related loan transactions:

1. If the lender or another settlement service provider requires the borrower to use a particular appraiser, title company, or other service provider, that requirement must be disclosed to the borrower when the loan application or service agreement is signed.
2. If a settlement service provider refers a borrower to an affiliated provider, that business relationship must be fully disclosed, along with the fact that the referral is optional. Fee estimates for the services in question must also be given.
3. If the borrower will have to make deposits into a reserve account (impound account) to cover taxes, insurance, and other recurring costs, the lender cannot require excessive deposits (more than necessary to cover the expenses when they come due, plus a two-month cushion).
4. A lender, a loan originator, a title company, a real estate agent, or any other settlement service provider may not:
   - pay or receive a **kickback** (a payment from one settlement service provider to another for referring customers, often called a referral fee);
   - pay or receive an **unearned fee** (a charge that one settlement service provider shares with another provider who hasn't actually performed any services in exchange for the payment); or
   - charge a fee for the preparation of an impound account statement or any of the required disclosure forms.

   Note that RESPA's prohibition against kickbacks does not apply to referral fees that one real estate licensee or firm pays to another licensee or firm for referring potential customers or clients.
5. A seller may not require a buyer to use a specific title insurance company.

The law also requires the lender in a federally related loan transaction to provide two key disclosure forms, the loan estimate and the closing disclosure. The loan estimate is discussed in Chapter 11; we'll briefly describe the closing disclosure form next.

Closing Disclosures

As we explained in Chapter 11, RESPA and the Truth in Lending Act (TILA) require lenders to give most home mortgage applicants a loan estimate form, which provides estimates of the charges that they would have to pay in connection with the loan. If the loan application is approved and the transaction proceeds, the lender must give the borrower a closing disclosure at least three business days before the closing date. The property seller is also entitled to receive a closing disclosure no later than the closing date. An example of a completed closing disclosure form is shown in Figure 13.2. This example includes the borrower's costs and the seller's costs on the same form, but a separate form may be prepared for each party instead, to protect their privacy.

The closing disclosure reiterates much of the information from the loan estimate form, replacing estimates with the actual charges. (The lender's own charges, such as the origination fee and discount points, may not be more than the figures given on the loan estimate form, and there are limits on how much certain other charges can increase over the estimated figures. See Chapter 11.) The "Closing Cost Details" section of the form serves as a settlement statement, listing all of the debits and credits and the exact amount that each party must pay or will receive at closing.

If the amounts listed in the closing disclosure change, the lender generally must provide the borrower with a revised closing disclosure form at or before closing. If the borrower requests it, the lender must make the revised form available for inspection one business day before closing.

Fig. 13.2 Closing Disclosure Form

Closing Disclosure

This form is a statement of final loan terms and closing costs. Compare this document with your Loan Estimate.

Closing Information		Transaction Information		Loan Information	
Date Issued	4/15/20XX	**Borrower**	Michael Jones and Mary Stone	**Loan Term**	30 years
Closing Date	4/15/20XX		123 Anywhere Street	**Purpose**	Purchase
Disbursement Date	4/15/20XX		Anytown, ST 12345	**Product**	Fixed Rate
Settlement Agent	Epsilon Title Co.	**Seller**	Steve Cole and Amy Doe		
File #	12-3456		321 Somewhere Drive	**Loan Type**	☒ Conventional ☐ FHA
Property	456 Somewhere Ave		Anytown, ST 12345		☐ VA ☐ ___________
	Anytown, ST 12345	**Lender**	Ficus Bank	**Loan ID #**	123456789
Sale Price	$180,000			**MIC #**	000654321

Loan Terms		Can this amount increase after closing?
Loan Amount	$162,000	**NO**
Interest Rate	3.875%	**NO**
Monthly Principal & Interest *See Projected Payments below for your Estimated Total Monthly Payment*	$761.78	**NO**
		Does the loan have these features?
Prepayment Penalty		**YES** • **As high as $3,240** if you pay off the loan during the first 2 years
Balloon Payment		**NO**

Projected Payments		
Payment Calculation	**Years 1-7**	**Years 8-30**
Principal & Interest	$761.78	$761.78
Mortgage Insurance	+ 82.35	+ —
Estimated Escrow *Amount can increase over time*	+ 206.13	+ 206.13
Estimated Total Monthly Payment	$1,050.26	$967.91

		This estimate includes	In escrow?
Estimated Taxes, Insurance & Assessments *Amount can increase over time* *See page 4 for details*	$356.13 a month	☒ Property Taxes	**YES**
		☒ Homeowner's Insurance	**YES**
		☒ Other: Homeowner's Association Dues	**NO**
		See Escrow Account on page 4 for details. You must pay for other property costs separately.	

Costs at Closing		
Closing Costs	$9,712.10	Includes $4,694.05 in Loan Costs + $5,018.05 in Other Costs – $0 in Lender Credits. *See page 2 for details.*
Cash to Close	$14,147.26	Includes Closing Costs. *See Calculating Cash to Close on page 3 for details.*

CLOSING DISCLOSURE — PAGE 1 OF 5 • LOAN ID # 123456789

Source: Consumer Financial Protection Bureau

Closing Cost Details

Loan Costs	Borrower-Paid		Seller-Paid		Paid by Others
	At Closing	Before Closing	At Closing	Before Closing	
A. Origination Charges	**$1,802.00**				
01 0.25 % of Loan Amount (Points)	$405.00				
02 Application Fee	$300.00				
03 Underwriting Fee	$1,097.00				
04					
05					
06					
07					
08					
B. Services Borrower Did Not Shop For	**$236.55**				
01 Appraisal Fee to John Smith Appraisers Inc.					$405.00
02 Credit Report Fee to Information Inc.		$29.80			
03 Flood Determination Fee to Info Co.	$20.00				
04 Flood Monitoring Fee to Info Co.	$31.75				
05 Tax Monitoring Fee to Info Co.	$75.00				
06 Tax Status Research Fee to Info Co.	$80.00				
07					
08					
09					
10					
C. Services Borrower Did Shop For	**$2,655.50**				
01 Pest Inspection Fee to Pests Co.	$120.50				
02 Survey Fee to Surveys Co.	$85.00				
03 Title – Insurance Binder to Epsilon Title Co.	$650.00				
04 Title – Lender's Title Insurance to Epsilon Title Co.	$500.00				
05 Title – Settlement Agent Fee to Epsilon Title Co.	$500.00				
06 Title – Title Search to Epsilon Title Co.	$800.00				
07					
08					
D. TOTAL LOAN COSTS (Borrower-Paid)	**$4,694.05**				
Loan Costs Subtotals (A + B + C)	$4,664.25	$29.80			

Other Costs	Borrower-Paid At Closing	Borrower-Paid Before Closing	Seller-Paid At Closing	Seller-Paid Before Closing	Paid by Others
E. Taxes and Other Government Fees	**$85.00**				
01 Recording Fees Deed: $40.00 Mortgage: $45.00	$85.00				
02 Transfer Tax to Any State			$950.00		
F. Prepaids	**$2,120.80**				
01 Homeowner's Insurance Premium (12 mo.) to Insurance Co.	$1,209.96				
02 Mortgage Insurance Premium (mo.)					
03 Prepaid Interest ($17.44 per day from 4/15/13 to 5/1/13)	$279.04				
04 Property Taxes (6 mo.) to Any County USA	$631.80				
05					
G. Initial Escrow Payment at Closing	**$412.25**				
01 Homeowner's Insurance $100.83 per month for 2 mo.	$201.66				
02 Mortgage Insurance per month for mo.					
03 Property Taxes $105.30 per month for 2 mo.	$210.60				
04					
05					
06					
07					
08 Aggregate Adjustment	– 0.01				
H. Other	**$2,400.00**				
01 HOA Capital Contribution to HOA Acre Inc.	$500.00				
02 HOA Processing Fee to HOA Acre Inc.	$150.00				
03 Home Inspection Fee to Engineers Inc.	$750.00			$750.00	
04 Home Warranty Fee to XYZ Warranty Inc.			$450.00		
05 Real Estate Commission to Alpha Real Estate Broker			$5,700.00		
06 Real Estate Commission to Omega Real Estate Broker			$5,700.00		
07 Title – Owner's Title Insurance (optional) to Epsilon Title Co.	$1,000.00				
08					
I. TOTAL OTHER COSTS (Borrower-Paid)	**$5,018.05**				
Other Costs Subtotals (E + F + G + H)	$5,018.05				
J. TOTAL CLOSING COSTS (Borrower-Paid)	**$9,712.10**				
Closing Costs Subtotals (D + I)	$9,682.30	$29.80	$12,800.00	$750.00	$405.00
Lender Credits					

CLOSING DISCLOSURE PAGE 2 OF 5 • LOAN ID # 123456789

Calculating Cash to Close

Use this table to see what has changed from your Loan Estimate.

	Loan Estimate	Final	Did this change?
Total Closing Costs (J)	$8,054.00	$9,712.10	**YES** • See **Total Loan Costs (D)** and **Total Other Costs (I)**
Closing Costs Paid Before Closing	$0	– $29.80	**YES** • You paid these Closing Costs **before closing**
Closing Costs Financed (Paid from your Loan Amount)	$0	$0	**NO**
Down Payment/Funds from Borrower	$18,000.00	$18,000.00	**NO**
Deposit	– $10,000.00	– $10,000.00	**NO**
Funds for Borrower	$0	$0	**NO**
Seller Credits	$0	– $2,500.00	**YES** • See Seller Credits in **Section L**
Adjustments and Other Credits	$0	– $1,035.04	**YES** • See details in **Sections K and L**
Cash to Close	$16,054.00	$14,147.26	

Summaries of Transactions

Use this table to see a summary of your transaction.

BORROWER'S TRANSACTION

K. Due from Borrower at Closing		**$189,762.30**
01	Sale Price of Property	$180,000.00
02	Sale Price of Any Personal Property Included in Sale	
03	Closing Costs Paid at Closing (J)	$9,682.30
04		
Adjustments		
05		
06		
07		
Adjustments for Items Paid by Seller in Advance		
08	City/Town Taxes to	
09	County Taxes to	
10	Assessments to	
11	HOA Dues 4/15/13 to 4/30/13	$80.00
12		
13		
14		
15		
L. Paid Already by or on Behalf of Borrower at Closing		**$175,615.04**
01	Deposit	$10,000.00
02	Loan Amount	$162,000.00
03	Existing Loan(s) Assumed or Taken Subject to	
04		
05	Seller Credit	$2,500.00
Other Credits		
06	Rebate from Epsilon Title Co.	$750.00
07		
Adjustments		
08		
09		
10		
11		
Adjustments for Items Unpaid by Seller		
12	City/Town Taxes 1/1/13 to 4/14/13	$365.04
13	County Taxes to	
14	Assessments to	
15		
16		
17		
CALCULATION		
Total Due from Borrower at Closing (K)		$189,762.30
Total Paid Already by or on Behalf of Borrower at Closing (L)		– $175,615.04
Cash to Close ☒ From ☐ To Borrower		**$14,147.26**

SELLER'S TRANSACTION

M. Due to Seller at Closing		**$180,080.00**
01	Sale Price of Property	$180,000.00
02	Sale Price of Any Personal Property Included in Sale	
03		
04		
05		
06		
07		
08		
Adjustments for Items Paid by Seller in Advance		
09	City/Town Taxes to	
10	County Taxes to	
11	Assessments to	
12	HOA Dues 4/15/13 to 4/30/13	$80.00
13		
14		
15		
16		
N. Due from Seller at Closing		**$115,665.04**
01	Excess Deposit	
02	Closing Costs Paid at Closing (J)	$12,800.00
03	Existing Loan(s) Assumed or Taken Subject to	
04	Payoff of First Mortgage Loan	$100,000.00
05	Payoff of Second Mortgage Loan	
06		
07		
08	Seller Credit	$2,500.00
09		
10		
11		
12		
13		
Adjustments for Items Unpaid by Seller		
14	City/Town Taxes 1/1/13 to 4/14/13	$365.04
15	County Taxes to	
16	Assessments to	
17		
18		
19		
CALCULATION		
Total Due to Seller at Closing (M)		$180,080.00
Total Due from Seller at Closing (N)		– $115,665.04
Cash ☐ From ☒ To Seller		**$64,414.96**

CLOSING DISCLOSURE

PAGE 3 OF 5 • LOAN ID # 123456789

Additional Information About This Loan

Loan Disclosures

Assumption
If you sell or transfer this property to another person, your lender
☐ will allow, under certain conditions, this person to assume this loan on the original terms.
☒ will not allow assumption of this loan on the original terms.

Demand Feature
Your loan
☐ has a demand feature, which permits your lender to require early repayment of the loan. You should review your note for details.
☒ does not have a demand feature.

Late Payment
If your payment is more than *15* days late, your lender will charge a late fee of *5% of the monthly principal and interest payment.*

Negative Amortization (Increase in Loan Amount)
Under your loan terms, you
☐ are scheduled to make monthly payments that do not pay all of the interest due that month. As a result, your loan amount will increase (negatively amortize), and your loan amount will likely become larger than your original loan amount. Increases in your loan amount lower the equity you have in this property.
☐ may have monthly payments that do not pay all of the interest due that month. If you do, your loan amount will increase (negatively amortize), and, as a result, your loan amount may become larger than your original loan amount. Increases in your loan amount lower the equity you have in this property.
☒ do not have a negative amortization feature.

Partial Payments
Your lender
☒ may accept payments that are less than the full amount due (partial payments) and apply them to your loan.
☐ may hold them in a separate account until you pay the rest of the payment, and then apply the full payment to your loan.
☐ does not accept any partial payments.
If this loan is sold, your new lender may have a different policy.

Security Interest
You are granting a security interest in
456 Somewhere Ave., Anytown, ST 12345

You may lose this property if you do not make your payments or satisfy other obligations for this loan.

Escrow Account
For now, your loan
☒ will have an escrow account (also called an "impound" or "trust" account) to pay the property costs listed below. Without an escrow account, you would pay them directly, possibly in one or two large payments a year. Your lender may be liable for penalties and interest for failing to make a payment.

Escrow		
Escrowed Property Costs over Year 1	$2,473.56	Estimated total amount over year 1 for your escrowed property costs: *Homeowner's Insurance* *Property Taxes*
Non-Escrowed Property Costs over Year 1	$1,800.00	Estimated total amount over year 1 for your non-escrowed property costs: *Homeowner's Association Dues* You may have other property costs.
Initial Escrow Payment	$412.25	A cushion for the escrow account you pay at closing. See Section G on page 2.
Monthly Escrow Payment	$206.13	The amount included in your total monthly payment.

☐ will not have an escrow account because ☐ you declined it ☐ your lender does not offer one. You must directly pay your property costs, such as taxes and homeowner's insurance. Contact your lender to ask if your loan can have an escrow account.

No Escrow		
Estimated Property Costs over Year 1		Estimated total amount over year 1. You must pay these costs directly, possibly in one or two large payments a year.
Escrow Waiver Fee		

In the future,
Your property costs may change and, as a result, your escrow payment may change. You may be able to cancel your escrow account, but if you do, you must pay your property costs directly. If you fail to pay your property taxes, your state or local government may (1) impose fines and penalties or (2) place a tax lien on this property. If you fail to pay any of your property costs, your lender may (1) add the amounts to your loan balance, (2) add an escrow account to your loan, or (3) require you to pay for property insurance that the lender buys on your behalf, which likely would cost more and provide fewer benefits than what you could buy on your own.

CLOSING DISCLOSURE PAGE 4 OF 5 • LOAN ID # 123456789

Loan Calculations

Total of Payments. Total you will have paid after you make all payments of principal, interest, mortgage insurance, and loan costs, as scheduled.	$285,803.36
Finance Charge. The dollar amount the loan will cost you.	$118,830.27
Amount Financed. The loan amount available after paying your upfront finance charge.	$162,000.00
Annual Percentage Rate (APR). Your costs over the loan term expressed as a rate. This is not your interest rate.	4.174%
Total Interest Percentage (TIP). The total amount of interest that you will pay over the loan term as a percentage of your loan amount.	69.46%

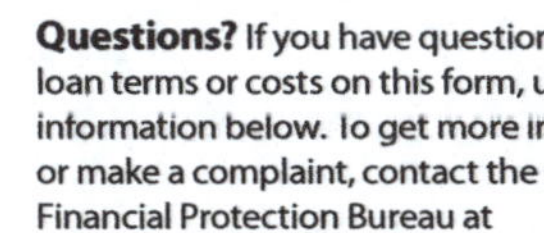

Questions? If you have questions about the loan terms or costs on this form, use the contact information below. To get more information or make a complaint, contact the Consumer Financial Protection Bureau at **www.consumerfinance.gov/mortgage-closing**

Other Disclosures

Appraisal
If the property was appraised for your loan, your lender is required to give you a copy at no additional cost at least 3 days before closing. If you have not yet received it, please contact your lender at the information listed below.

Contract Details
See your note and security instrument for information about
- what happens if you fail to make your payments,
- what is a default on the loan,
- situations in which your lender can require early repayment of the loan, and
- the rules for making payments before they are due.

Liability after Foreclosure
If your lender forecloses on this property and the foreclosure does not cover the amount of unpaid balance on this loan,

☒ state law may protect you from liability for the unpaid balance. If you refinance or take on any additional debt on this property, you may lose this protection and have to pay any debt remaining even after foreclosure. You may want to consult a lawyer for more information.

☐ state law does not protect you from liability for the unpaid balance.

Refinance
Refinancing this loan will depend on your future financial situation, the property value, and market conditions. You may not be able to refinance this loan.

Tax Deductions
If you borrow more than this property is worth, the interest on the loan amount above this property's fair market value is not deductible from your federal income taxes. You should consult a tax advisor for more information.

Contact Information

	Lender	Mortgage Broker	Real Estate Broker (B)	Real Estate Broker (S)	Settlement Agent
Name	Ficus Bank		Omega Real Estate Broker Inc.	Alpha Real Estate Broker Co.	Epsilon Title Co.
Address	4321 Random Blvd. Somecity, ST 12340		789 Local Lane Sometown, ST 12345	987 Suburb Ct. Someplace, ST 12340	123 Commerce Pl. Somecity, ST 12344
NMLS ID					
ST License ID			Z765416	Z61456	Z61616
Contact	Joe Smith		Samuel Green	Joseph Cain	Sarah Arnold
Contact NMLS ID	12345				
Contact ST License ID			P16415	P51461	PT1234
Email	joesmith@ficusbank.com		sam@omegare.biz	joe@alphare.biz	sarah@epsilontitle.com
Phone	123-456-7890		123-555-1717	321-555-7171	987-555-4321

Confirm Receipt

By signing, you are only confirming that you have received this form. You do not have to accept this loan because you have signed or received this form.

Applicant Signature　　Date　　Co-Applicant Signature　　Date

CLOSING DISCLOSURE　　PAGE 5 OF 5 • LOAN ID # 123456789

Chapter Summary

1. After a purchase and sale agreement has been signed, the next stage of the transaction is the closing process. Closing is often handled through escrow, an arrangement in which money and documents are held by a third party (the escrow agent) on behalf of the buyer and the seller, and distributed when all of the conditions in the escrow instructions have been fulfilled.
2. In Washington, escrow agents and escrow officers must be licensed, but many groups (including lawyers, title companies, and lenders) are exempt from those requirements. A real estate licensee is exempt while handling escrow for a transaction in which they are also providing brokerage services, as long as no special fee is charged.
3. A settlement statement details all the charges payable by (debits) and payable to (credits) each of the parties at closing. Who pays which closing costs may be determined by agreement or by local custom. Certain expenses must be prorated as of the closing date.
4. Certain requirements related to income taxes must be fulfilled when a real estate transaction closes. These include the 1099-S and 8300 reporting requirements and the FIRPTA tax withholding requirement.
5. RESPA applies to almost all residential loan transactions involving institutional lenders. It requires lenders to give borrowers information about closing costs and prohibits kickbacks (referral fees) between settlement service providers.
6. In conjunction with the Truth in Lending Act, RESPA requires lenders to give loan applicants a loan estimate form. If the application is approved, the lender (or the escrow agent, on the lender's behalf) must prepare closing disclosures for both the borrower and the property seller. One section of the closing disclosure form serves as a settlement statement.

Key Terms

Closing—The final stage of a real estate transaction, in which documents are signed and delivered and funds are transferred. Also called settlement.

Escrow—An arrangement in which money and documents are held by a third party on behalf of the buyer and the seller.

Escrow agent—A third party who holds money and documents in trust and carries out the closing process. Also called a closing agent.

Licensed escrow agent—A business that is licensed to provide escrow services under Washington's Escrow Agent Registration Act.

Licensed escrow officer—An individual who is licensed under the Escrow Agent Registration Act to perform escrow services as an employee of a licensed escrow agent.

Escrow instructions—A written document that tells the escrow agent how to proceed and states the conditions each party must fulfill before the transaction can close.

Settlement statement—A statement that sets forth all the financial aspects of a real estate transaction in detail and indicates how much money each party will be required to pay or will receive at closing.

Debit—An amount payable by a party.

Credit—An amount payable to a party.

Reserve account—Funds on deposit with a lender to pay the property taxes, insurance premiums, and other recurring expenses when due. Also called an impound account or an escrow account.

Prorate—To divide and allocate an expense proportionately, according to time, interest, or benefit, determining what share of it a particular party is responsible for.

Prepaid interest—Interest on the buyer's new mortgage loan that the lender requires to be paid at closing, covering the period from the closing date through the last day of the month.

RESPA—The Real Estate Settlement Procedures Act, a federal law that requires disclosure of closing costs to loan applicants and prohibits kickbacks (referral fees) between settlement service providers.

Settlement service provider—Under RESPA, an individual or business that provides services in connection with the closing of a transaction, such as a lender, a mortgage broker, a title company, an escrow agent, or a real estate agent.

Loan estimate—In a residential transaction subject to RESPA and/or the Truth in Lending Act, a form that the lender must give to the buyer (the loan applicant), providing detailed information about the loan and estimates of the closing costs.

Closing disclosure—In a residential transaction subject to RESPA and/or the Truth in Lending Act, a form that the lender must give to the parties before closing, listing the actual closing costs.

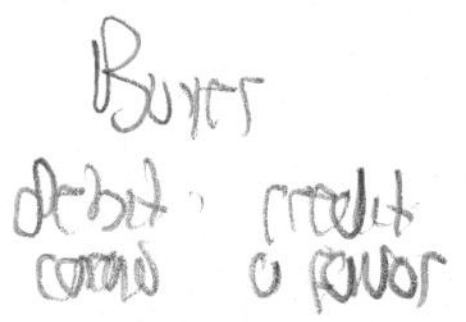

Chapter Quiz

1. **The Henrys listed their home with Louise, a licensed real estate agent, who found them a buyer. Now Louise is handling the closing for this transaction. She's exempt from the licensing requirements of the Washington Escrow Agent Registration Act only if:**
   a) this is a residential transaction
   b) the sales price is $100,000 or less
   c) she doesn't charge a separate fee for her escrow services
   d) the escrow fee she charges doesn't exceed the limits set by the Registration Act

2. **Every debit on the buyer's side of the settlement statement is a charge that:**
   a) will be paid to the buyer at closing
   b) must be paid by the buyer at closing
   c) the buyer must pay to the seller at closing
   d) the seller must pay to the buyer at closing

3. **On a settlement statement, the purchase price will be listed as:**
   a) a debit for the buyer
   b) a debit for the seller
   c) Both of the above
   d) Neither of the above

4. **An escrow agent who receives more than $10,000 in cash from one of the parties must:**
   a) refuse to accept the cash payment and require a cashier's check instead
   b) prepare a revised loan estimate
   c) withhold 15% and forward it to the IRS
   d) report the cash payment to the IRS

5. **How does the buyer's earnest money deposit show up on a settlement statement?**
   a) It's listed as a debit on the buyer's side of the statement, and as a credit on the seller's side of the statement
   b) It's listed as a credit on the buyer's side of the statement, but it isn't listed on the seller's side because it's included in the purchase price
   c) It's listed as a credit on the seller's side of the statement, but it isn't listed on the buyer's side because it will be refunded at closing
   d) It's listed as a debit on both the buyer's side and the seller's side of the statement

6. **When a buyer assumes a mortgage, how does the mortgage balance appear on the settlement statement?**
   a) Only as a credit for the seller
   b) Only as a debit on the seller's side of the statement
   c) As a credit for the buyer and a debit for the seller
   d) As a credit for the seller and a debit for the buyer

7. **Which of the following is ordinarily one of the seller's closing costs?**
   a) Sales commission
   b) Credit report fee
   c) Appraisal fee
   d) Origination fee

8. **Which of the following is ordinarily one of the buyer's closing costs?**
   a) Sales commission
   b) Lender's title insurance premium
   c) Excise tax
   d) None of the above

9. **On a settlement statement, prepaid interest would usually appear as a:**
   a) seller's debit
   b) buyer's credit
   c) seller's credit
   d) buyer's debit

10. **The Matsons are selling their home. They are current on their mortgage payments, having made their most recent payment on May 1. They will be paying off their mortgage when the sale closes on May 17. At closing, the Matsons will probably be:**
    a) entitled to a refund of the mortgage interest accruing in May
    b) required to pay the mortgage interest accruing in May
    c) entitled to a refund of the prepayment penalty
    d) required to pay part of the mortgage interest that accrued in April

11. **A settlement statement:**
    a) is given to the buyer but not the seller
    b) sets out the charges to be paid by each party or to each party at closing
    c) is given only to the buyer's lender
    d) is required only in transactions closed by licensed escrow agents

12. **When an item is prorated, it means that:**
    a) it is deleted from the cost of the sale
    b) it is calculated on the basis of a particular time period
    c) it is not paid until closing
    d) the escrow agent must pay the fee

13. **Under RESPA, a loan is considered federally related if:**
    a) it will be used to finance the purchase of real property
    b) the property has up to four dwelling units
    c) the lender is federally regulated
    d) All of the above

14. **Under FIRPTA:**
    a) a foreign investor can never buy or sell property without special authorization
    b) if a seller is not a U.S. citizen or resident alien, the escrow agent generally has to deduct 15% of the amount realized and send it to the IRS
    c) the escrow agent must notify the real estate agent if the buyer is a foreign investor
    d) a foreign investor purchasing property in the U.S. must pay an additional 15% over and above the purchase price and submit it to the IRS

15. **Tim, a real estate agent, has a friend who is purchasing a property through another agent. The purchase price is $95,000. Tim offers to act as escrow agent for the transaction for a small fee. Tim:**
    a) is exempt from the Escrow Agent Registration Act because he is a real estate agent
    b) is violating the Escrow Agent Registration Act, because he isn't acting as a real estate agent in the transaction and he's charging a fee for escrow services
    c) is exempt from the Escrow Agent Registration Act because he is acting for a personal acquaintance
    d) is exempt from the Escrow Agent Registration Act because the sales price is less than $100,000

Chapter 14:

Federal Income Taxation and Real Estate

Almost every business transaction has tax consequences, and real estate transactions are no exception. Not only is there a tax that arises at the time of sale (the real estate excise tax discussed in Chapter 5), but in many cases the transaction also generates income tax liability. This chapter provides an overview of how federal income taxation affects the transfer and ownership of real estate. It explains some income tax terminology, discusses certain types of transactions that receive special tax treatment, and also covers tax deductions available to real estate owners.

Key Terms

Income	**Involuntary conversion**
Deduction	**Depreciation deductions**
Initial basis	**Repair expenses**
Adjusted basis	**Capital expenditures**
Realization	**"Tax-free" exchange**
Recognition	**Like-kind property**
Installment sale	**Boot**

Basic Taxation Concepts

As you no doubt know, in the United States the federal government taxes the income of individuals and businesses on an annual basis. Before discussing how the transfer or acquisition of real estate can affect the federal income taxes a seller or a buyer is required to pay, we need to explain some basic terms and concepts.

Progressive Tax

A tax may be "proportional," "regressive," or "progressive," depending on how its burden is distributed among taxpayers. A tax is proportional if the same tax rate is applied to all levels of income. A tax is regressive if the rate applied to higher levels of income is lower than the rate applied to lower levels.

Our federal income tax is a **progressive** tax; this means that, as a general rule, the more a taxpayer earns in a given tax year, the higher their tax rate will be. In other words, someone who earns a large income usually pays a greater percentage of their income in taxes (not simply a greater tax amount) than someone who earns a small income.

Tax rates increase in uneven steps called **tax brackets**. An additional dollar earned by a given taxpayer may be taxed at a higher rate than the dollar earned just before it, because it crosses the line into a higher bracket. But the additional dollar earned will not increase the tax this taxpayer is required to pay on dollars previously earned. The term **marginal tax rate** refers to the rate that will apply to the last dollar a taxpayer earns.

Income

When asked about their income, many people tend to think only in terms of the wages or salary they earn at a job. The Internal Revenue Service (IRS) takes a much broader view of income, however. It regards any economic benefit realized by a taxpayer as part of their income, unless it is a type of benefit specifically excluded from income by the tax code. (The concept of realization is discussed below.)

For certain purposes, the IRS classifies investment income from an enterprise in which the investor/taxpayer doesn't materially participate (such as a limited partnership) as **passive income** instead of ordinary income. This is covered later in the chapter.

Deductions and Tax Credits

The federal tax code authorizes certain expenses to be deducted from income. For example, if a business loses money in a particular tax year, the owner may be allowed to deduct the loss. A taxpayer who's entitled to a **deduction** can subtract a specified amount from their income before it is taxed. By reducing the amount of income that's taxed, the deduction also reduces the amount of tax the taxpayer owes.

In contrast to deductions, **tax credits** are subtracted directly from the amount of tax owed. The taxpayer's income is added up, the tax rate is applied, and then any applicable tax credits are subtracted to determine how much the taxpayer will actually have to pay.

The government often uses deductions and tax credits to implement social and economic policy. For example, allowing homeowners to deduct mortgage interest from their taxable income helps make homeownership more affordable. (The mortgage interest deduction is explained later in this chapter.)

Classifications of Real Property

The tax rules that apply to a particular piece of real estate often depend on what type of property it is. For income tax purposes, real property can be divided into the following classes:

1. principal residence property,
2. personal use property,
3. unimproved investment property,
4. property held for the production of income,
5. property used in a trade or business, and
6. dealer property.

Principal Residence Property. A principal residence (also called a main home) is the home the taxpayer owns and occupies as their primary dwelling. It might be a single-family home, a duplex, a condominium unit, a cooperative apartment, or a mobile home. If the taxpayer owns two homes and lives in both of them, the one in which they live most of the time is the principal residence. A taxpayer cannot have two principal residences at the same time.

Personal Use Property. Real property that a taxpayer owns for personal use, other than the principal residence, is classified as personal use property. A second home or a vacation cabin belongs in this category.

Unimproved Investment Property. Unimproved investment property is vacant land that produces no rental income. The land is held simply as an investment, in the expectation that it will appreciate (increase in value over time).

Property Held for Production of Income. Property held for the production of income includes residential, commercial, and industrial property that is used to generate rental income for the owner.

Property Used in a Trade or Business. This category (also called business property) includes land and buildings that the taxpayer owns and uses in their trade or business, such as a factory owned by the manufacturer, or a small building the owner uses for their own retail business.

Dealer Property. This is property held primarily for sale to customers rather than for long-term investment. If a developer subdivides land for sale to the public, the lots will usually be included in this classification until they are sold.

Gains and Losses

The sale or exchange of an asset (such as real estate) nearly always results in either a **gain** or a **loss**. Gains are treated as income, so any gain is taxable unless a provision in the tax code says it is exempt from taxation. A loss can be deducted from income only if a provision in the tax code authorizes the deduction.

Certain types of assets—including real estate that an individual taxpayer owns for personal use or as an investment—are categorized as capital assets. A gain or loss on the sale of a capital asset is called a **capital gain** or a **capital loss**.

A taxpayer's capital gains and losses are netted against each other on an annual basis. If the taxpayer has a net gain, it is taxed as a capital gain. (This benefits the taxpayer, because the maximum tax rate applied to most capital gains is considerably lower than the rate for wages and other earned income.) If there is a net loss, the taxpayer may be entitled to deduct the loss, but there is a $3,000 annual limit on how much may be deducted. Losses in excess of the limit can be carried forward and deducted in future years. (However, losses on a principal residence or other real property owned for personal use are not deductible, so they aren't netted against capital gains.)

Investments that allow a taxpayer to reduce their taxes by deducting losses from income from another source are referred to as **tax shelters**.

Business and Rental Property. Gains and losses on the sale of real property used in a business or held for the production of income (rental property) are treated somewhat differently from gains and losses on the sale of personal use and investment property. If business property or rental property is owned for more than one year and then sold, a gain on the sale is treated as a capital gain. But a loss on the sale is deductible as an ordinary loss rather than a capital loss. This is an advantage, because the $3,000 annual limit on the deduction of capital losses doesn't apply. The full amount of the loss can be deducted in the year it's incurred.

Losses resulting from the operation of a rental property (as opposed to its sale) are also deductible as ordinary losses in some cases. We'll discuss deduction of operating losses at the end of the chapter.

Basis

For income tax purposes, a property owner's **basis** in the property is their investment in it. If a taxpayer sells an asset, the basis is the maximum amount that they can receive in payment for the asset without realizing a gain. To determine gains and losses, it's necessary to know the taxpayer's basis in the property in question.

Initial Basis. In most cases, a taxpayer's **initial basis** (also called cost basis, unadjusted basis, or **book value**) is equal to the actual amount of their investment—that is, how much it cost to acquire the property. For instance, if they paid $280,000 for a rental house plus $12,000 in closing costs, they have an initial basis of $292,000 in the property.

If a taxpayer sells an asset, their gain on the sale is the amount by which the sale proceeds exceed their basis. To determine the amount of a gain or a loss, it's necessary to know the taxpayer's basis in the property. In our example, the seller could turn around and sell the house for $292,000 without having to report a gain to the IRS. If they sold the house for $300,000, though, they would have to report a gain of $8,000.

Adjusted Basis. A taxpayer's initial basis in a property may be increased or decreased to arrive at an **adjusted basis**, which reflects capital expenditures and, in some cases, depreciation deductions. (We'll discuss depreciation deductions later in this chapter.)

Capital expenditures are expenditures made to improve the property, such as money a homeowner spends on adding a new room or remodeling the kitchen. Capital expenditures increase the value of the property or significantly extend its useful life. They are added to the initial basis in calculating the adjusted basis.

> **Example:** Greene buys an investment property for $345,000 plus $11,000 in closing costs. Four years later, she spends $45,000 on improvements to the property, remodeling the bathrooms and the kitchen in both units. Her adjusted basis in the property is now $401,000.

Maintenance expenses, such as repainting or replacing a broken window, are not capital expenditures. Maintenance expenses do not affect basis. (However, the owner of rental or business real estate can deduct maintenance expenses, as we'll discuss shortly.)

With rental or business real estate, a taxpayer's initial basis is also adjusted to take into account depreciation deductions (again, discussed in more detail later in this chapter). These deductions are subtracted from the initial basis in calculating the adjusted basis.

  Initial basis
\+ Capital expenditures
– Depreciation deductions
  Adjusted basis

Realization

A gain is not considered taxable until it is **realized.** Although ownership of an asset involves gain if the asset is appreciating in value, for income tax purposes, a gain is realized only when the asset is sold or exchanged. At that point, the gain is separated from the asset and becomes subject to taxation.

> **Example:** Referring back to the example given above, suppose that during Greene's six years of ownership property values have been increasing steadily. Her improved property (which she bought for $356,000 and invested another $45,000 in) now has a market value of $489,000. She has enjoyed an economic gain or benefit: she now owns property that is worth $88,000 more than what she put into it. However, that $88,000 won't be realized—and therefore won't be treated as income subject to taxation—until she sells the property.

The gain or loss realized on a transaction is the difference between the net sales price (referred to as the **amount realized**) and the adjusted basis of the property:

  Amount realized (net sales price)
– Adjusted basis
  Gain or loss

In calculating the amount realized, the sales price includes money or other property received in exchange for the property, plus the amount of any mortgage debt that is eliminated. This means that if the buyer takes the property subject to the seller's mortgage or assumes it, the amount of that debt is treated as part of the sales price for tax purposes.

The sales price is reduced by selling expenses (such as the brokerage commission and the seller's other closing costs) to arrive at the amount realized.

Recognition and Deferral

There is a further complication: not all gains are taxed in the same year they are realized. It's true that a gain is usually recognized by the IRS (and therefore taxed) in the year it is realized. But with certain types of transactions, the tax code allows a taxpayer to defer recognition of a gain (and payment of income tax on the gain) until some later time. These exceptions in the tax code are called "nonrecognition provisions," and we'll discuss them next.

Nonrecognition Transactions

When a nonrecognition provision in the tax code applies to a particular transaction, the taxpayer isn't required to pay taxes on a gain in the year it is realized. The following types of real estate transactions are covered by nonrecognition provisions:

- installment sales,
- involuntary conversions, and
- "tax-free" exchanges.

Keep in mind that nonrecognition provisions do not completely exclude the gain from taxation, but merely postpone the tax consequences to a later year. These are not really "tax-free" transactions. The realized gain is simply recognized and taxed in a subsequent year.

Installment Sales

The tax code considers a sale to be an **installment sale** if less than 100% of the sales price is received in the year of sale. Nearly all seller-financed transactions are installment sales. Installment sale reporting allows the taxpayer/seller to defer recognition of part of the gain to the year(s) in which it is actually received. In effect, taxes are paid only on the portion of the profit received each year. Installment sale reporting is permitted for all classes of property, except that dealer property is eligible only under special circumstances.

Involuntary Conversions

An involuntary conversion occurs when an asset is turned into cash without the voluntary action of the owner, as when an asset is condemned, destroyed, stolen, or lost, and the owner receives a condemnation award or insurance proceeds. Since the award or proceeds usually represent the property's replacement cost or market value, the owner often realizes a gain on an involuntary conversion.

However, recognition of a gain on an involuntary conversion can be deferred if the taxpayer uses the money received to replace the property within the replacement period set by the IRS. Generally, the replacement period lasts for two years after the date the property was destroyed, lost, or condemned. Recognition of the gain is deferred only to the extent that the condemnation award or insurance proceeds are reinvested in the replacement property. Any part of the gain used for purposes other than purchase of replacement property will be taxed as income.

"Tax-Free" Exchanges

Section 1031 of the tax code concerns real property exchanges. Although 1031 exchanges are commonly called "tax-free" exchanges, they're really just tax-deferred exchanges. When unimproved investment property, income-producing property, or property used in a trade or business is exchanged for **like-kind property**, recognition of any realized gain can be deferred. Principal residence property, personal use property, and dealer property are not eligible for this type of tax deferral.

The property the taxpayer receives in the exchange must be like-kind—that is, the same kind as the property given. This rule refers to the general nature of the properties rather than their quality. Most real estate is considered to be of like kind for the purposes of a 1031 exchange, without regard to whether it's improved, unimproved, residential, commercial, or industrial. For example, if a taxpayer exchanges a strip shopping center for an apartment complex, the transaction can qualify as a tax-free exchange.

If nothing other than like-kind property is received in the exchange, no gain or loss is recognized in the year of the exchange. However, anything other than like-kind property that the taxpayer receives is called **boot** and recognized in the year of the exchange. In a real estate exchange, boot might be cash, stock, other types of personal property, or the difference between mortgage balances.

> **Example:** A taxpayer trades a property with a mortgage debt of $120,000 for a property with a mortgage debt of $100,000. The taxpayer has received $20,000 in boot because of the reduction in debt (regardless of whether or not there has been a formal assumption of the loan). The taxpayer will have to pay taxes on a gain of $20,000, just as if she had received $20,000 in cash along with the real property.

Originally, 1031 exchanges were limited to simultaneous transfers of ownership (direct trades of property). Now 1031 tax deferral benefits are also available when a taxpayer sells a property to one party and then buys a like-kind property from another party, in two separate transactions. Time limits apply: after selling the original (relinquished) property, the taxpayer has 45 days to identify a replacement property, and the purchase of the replacement property must close within 180 days of the sale of the relinquished property.

Note that if a real estate licensee arranges a transaction between two parties that qualifies as a 1031 exchange, they may receive compensation from both parties.

Fig. 14.1 Eligibility for Tax-Free Exchanges

"Tax-Free" Exchanges
1. Only property held for production of income, property used in a trade or business, or unimproved investment property is eligible.
2. Must be exchanged for like-kind property.
3. Any boot is taxed in the year it is received.

Exclusion of Gain from the Sale of a Principal Residence

We will discuss only one exclusion from capital gains taxation, the one of the greatest interest to most homeowners: the exclusion of gain on the sale of a principal residence.

A taxpayer may exclude the entire gain on the sale of their principal residence, up to $250,000 if the taxpayer is filing a single return, or $500,000 if the taxpayer is married and filing a joint return.

Example:

$275,000	Amount realized (after selling costs)
– 80,000	Seller's basis in home
$195,000	Gain realized

Whether filing singly or jointly, the seller can exclude the entire amount of the gain—$195,000—from taxation.

If the amount of the gain on the sale of the home exceeds the $250,000 or $500,000 limit, the amount in excess of the limit will be taxed at the capital gains rate.

Eligibility. To qualify for this exclusion, the seller must have both owned and used the property as a principal residence for at least two years during the five-year period ending on the date of sale. Because of this rule, this exclusion is available only once every two years.

If the sellers are married and filing a joint return, only one spouse has to meet the ownership test, but both spouses must meet the use test. If only one spouse meets both the ownership test and the use test, the maximum exclusion the married couple can claim is $250,000, even if they file a joint return.

If the seller owned and used the property as a principal residence for less than two years because of special circumstances (for example, if they sold the home after only a year because of a change in health or employment), they may be able to claim a reduced exclusion.

Deductions Available to Property Owners

As we explained at the beginning of the chapter, a deduction is subtracted from a taxpayer's income before the tax rate is applied. Homeowners generally can deduct property taxes, mortgage interest, points paid to a lender, and, in limited cases, casualty or theft losses.

Owners of certain other kinds of real estate (such as rental property) can also take those deductions, along with deductions for depreciation, repairs, and operating losses.

Property Tax Deductions

General real estate taxes are deductible for any type of property up to a certain dollar limit. Special assessments for repairs or maintenance are deductible, but those for improvements (such as new sidewalks) are not.

Mortgage Interest Deductions

For most property, interest paid on a mortgage or deed of trust is usually completely deductible. However, there are limitations on interest deductions for personal residences (principal residences or second homes).

A taxpayer may deduct interest payments on mortgage or home equity loan debt of up to $750,000 ($375,000 for a married taxpayer filing separately) that is used to buy, build, or improve a first or second residence.

(The limit is $1,000,000 for loans originated before 2018.) When the loan amount exceeds the applicable limit, the interest on the excess isn't deductible.

Homeowners with relatively modest mortgages are often better off simply taking the standard deduction and not using this or other itemized deductions.

Occasionally a condominium project borrows money by mortgaging the common areas, and the unit owners are required to pay a share of the mortgage payment. In that case, a unit owner may deduct the interest portion of their share from taxable income.

Deductibility of Points

The IRS considers points paid to a lender in connection with a new loan (including discount points and the origination fee) to be prepaid interest, and the borrower is generally allowed to deduct them. This is true even if the points were paid by the seller on the borrower's behalf. (The borrower's basis in the property must be reduced by the amount of the seller-paid points.)

Note that fees a lender charges to cover specific services aren't deductible, even if the lender refers to them as points. This includes, for example, appraisal fees, document preparation fees, and mortgage insurance premiums.

If a seller paying off a loan is required to pay a prepayment penalty, the amount of the penalty is usually deductible. For income tax purposes, a prepayment penalty is treated as a form of interest.

Uninsured Casualty or Theft Loss Deductions

When property is destroyed, damaged, or stolen and the loss isn't covered or is only partially covered by insurance, the property owner generally can deduct the uninsured loss from taxable income. However, uninsured losses involving a taxpayer's principal residence or other personal use property are deductible only if they resulted from a federally declared disaster.

To calculate the amount of the deductible loss, the value of the property after the loss is subtracted from its value before the loss. This reduction in value is compared to the owner's adjusted basis in the property. Any insurance reimbursement that the owner has received or will receive is subtracted from the lower of those two figures; for most types of property, the result is the amount of the deductible loss.

Fig. 14.2 Favorable Tax Treatment for Real Property

Eligibility for Favorable Income Tax Treatment			
	Installment Sale	"Tax-Free" Exchange	Depreciation Deductions
Principal Residence	Yes	No	No
Personal Use	Yes	No	No
Unimproved Investment	Yes	Yes	No
Trade or Business	Yes	Yes	Yes
Income	Yes	Yes	Yes
Dealer	No	No	No

Depreciation Deductions

Depreciation deductions (sometimes called cost recovery deductions) permit a taxpayer to recover the cost of an asset over a period of years. Only property used for the production of income or used in a trade or business is eligible for depreciation deductions. They can't be taken in connection with a principal residence or other personal use property, unimproved investment property, or dealer property.

Depreciable Property. In general, only property that wears out and will eventually have to be replaced is **depreciable**—that is, eligible for depreciation deductions. For example, apartment buildings, business or factory equipment, and the trees in commercial fruit orchards all have to be replaced, so they are depreciable. But land doesn't wear out, so it's not depreciable.

Time Frame. The entire expense of acquiring a depreciable asset cannot be deducted in the year it's incurred (although that's permitted with many other business expenses, such as wages, supplies, and utilities). However, the expense can be deducted over a number of years; for most real estate, the recovery period is between 27½ and 39 years. The length of the recovery period is a reflection of legislative policy and has little, if any, relationship to the actual length of time that the property will be economically useful. The whole field of depreciation deductions has been subject to frequent modification by Congress.

Effect on Basis. As we said in the discussion of basis at the beginning of the chapter, depreciation deductions reduce the taxpayer's adjusted basis in the property. Note that this reduction occurs whether or not the taxpayer actually takes the deduction. If the deduction was allowable—that is, the taxpayer was entitled to take it—the basis will be reduced. By reducing the basis, these deductions affect the taxpayer's eventual gain or loss on resale of the property.

Repair Deductions

A repair expense is an expenditure incurred to keep the property in ordinary, efficient operating condition. For most types of real property, expenditures for repairs are deductible in the year paid. However, repair expenses are not deductible for principal residences or other personal use property. This includes expenditures for maintenance, upkeep, and ordinary wear and tear, and it also includes condominium assessments.

For any type of real property, repair expenses shouldn't be confused with capital expenditures. Repairs are made to maintain value. As explained earlier, capital expenditures add to the value of the property and frequently prolong its economic life. Capital expenditures aren't deductible in the year made, but rather are added to the taxpayer's basis. The resulting increase in the basis will affect the gain or loss on the eventual sale of the property. It will also increase the allowable depreciation deductions if the property is eligible for those.

Deducting Rental Property Operating Losses

A taxpayer who owns and actively manages a rental property may deduct up to $25,000 of operating losses from their ordinary income. (The deduction is reduced or eliminated for higher-income taxpayers.) To understand this rule, you need to understand the distinction between ordinary income and passive income.

Passive Income. Generally, **passive income** is income a taxpayer earns from an enterprise (such as a limited partnership) in which they are a passive investor, with little or no role in managing the business.

Rental income is a special case, however: the IRS regards rental income as passive income even if the taxpayer participates in the management of the rental property. (We'll explain an important exception at the end of this section.)

Treatment of Passive Losses. In most cases, passive losses—losses from passive activities—can only be deducted from passive income, not from ordinary income.

> **Example:** Woodruff, a high school teacher, earned $70,000 last year at his job, but his small ownership interest in a real estate investment trust lost $11,000. He can't deduct the $11,000 loss (a passive loss) from his teaching salary (which is ordinary income), because passive losses can only be deducted from passive income.

However, losses from the operation of rental property receive special treatment, as long as the taxpayer actively participates in the property's management and meets certain other requirements. (For example, an owner who makes decisions about tenants and repairs, instead of having a property manager do that, is actively participating in management.) Unlike other passive losses, up to $25,000 in operating losses from rental property can be deducted from ordinary income.

> **Example:** Now suppose that Woodruff (the high school teacher in the previous example) owns and actively manages a rental duplex. Last year, due to higher taxes and a lot of repairs, the property's annual operating expenses added up to $50,000 and the rental income was only $48,000. This $2,000 passive loss is deductible from ordinary income. So Woodruff can take a $2,000 deduction against the $70,000 salary he earned from his teaching job.

Not every rental property owner who actively participates in management of the property can take advantage of this rule. There are several significant restrictions. For example, the taxpayer can't be involved in any other passive activities, and their adjusted gross income can't exceed a certain limit.

Operating Losses vs. Other Losses. Don't confuse an operating loss with lost income due to rental property vacancies. If a rental property sits vacant for all or part of the year, that lost income isn't deductible. The only figure that can be deducted is the overall difference between a rental property's annual income and annual operating expenses—an operating loss.

Also, don't confuse an operating loss with a loss from the sale of a rental property. Losses from the sale of a rental property are subject to different rules, which we discussed at the beginning of this chapter.

Exception for Real Estate Professionals. Finally, as we mentioned, there's an important exception to these passive loss rules. For taxpayers who fulfill the IRS definition of a "real estate professional," income from rental activities isn't passive income. That means those taxpayers aren't subject to the $25,000 limit on deducting operating losses from rentals from their ordinary income. This can result in significant tax savings. A real estate professional must meet a higher standard than mere active participation in management; but the rules are complicated, so we'll simplify them somewhat. To qualify as a real estate professional, a taxpayer must:

- materially participate in a real estate business (such as owning and managing income properties);
- spend more than half their yearly working time in that business; and
- work at least 750 hours in that business during the year.

Chapter Summary

1. Any economic benefit realized by a taxpayer is treated as part of their income, unless there is a specific provision of the tax code that excludes it from income. The tax code provides for certain deductions from income before the tax rate is applied, and also for tax credits, which are subtracted from the amount of tax owed.
2. A gain or a loss is realized when an asset is sold. A gain is recognized (taxed) in the year it is realized, unless a nonrecognition or exclusion provision in the tax code applies.
3. A taxpayer's initial basis in property is the amount they originally invested in it. To determine the adjusted basis, capital expenditures are added to the initial basis, and allowable depreciation deductions are subtracted from it. The taxpayer's gain or loss is the difference between the amount realized and the adjusted basis.
4. Classifications of real property include principal residence property, personal use property, unimproved investment property, property held for the production of income, property used in a trade or business, or dealer property.
5. The tax code's nonrecognition provisions for real property transactions allow taxation of gain to be deferred in installment sales, involuntary conversions, and "tax-free" (Section 1031) exchanges. There is also an exclusion of up to $250,000 (or $500,000 if filing jointly) of gain allowed on the sale of a principal residence.
6. Taxpayers are allowed to deduct various expenses related to real property from their taxable income. There are deductions for property taxes; mortgage interest; points paid to a lender; uninsured casualty or theft losses; depreciation (only for income property and property used in a trade or business); repair expenses (not for principal residences or other personal use property); and operating losses from rental property.

Key Terms

Income—Any economic benefit realized by a taxpayer that is not excluded from income by the tax code.

Deduction—An expense that can be used to reduce taxable income.

Initial basis—The amount of the taxpayer's original investment in the property; what it cost to acquire the property.

Adjusted basis—The initial basis plus capital expenditures and minus allowable depreciation deductions.

Realization—A gain or a loss is realized when it is separated from the asset; this separation generally occurs when the asset is sold.

Recognition—A gain is said to be recognized when it is taxable; it is recognized in the year it is realized unless recognition is deferred by the tax code.

Installment sale—A sale in which less than 100% of the sales price is received in the year of sale.

Involuntary conversion—When property is converted to cash without the voluntary action of the owner, as when it is condemned, destroyed, stolen, or lost.

Depreciation deductions—Deductions from the taxpayer's income to allow the cost of an asset to be recovered over a period of years; allowed only for depreciable property that is held for the production of income or used in a trade or business. Also called cost recovery deductions.

Repair expenses—Money spent on repairs to keep property in ordinary, efficient operating condition.

Capital expenditures—Money spent on improvements to property, which add to its value or prolong its economic life.

"Tax-free" exchange—When like-kind property is exchanged, allowing taxation of the gain to be deferred; also called a 1031 exchange.

Like-kind property—In a tax-free exchange, property received that is of the same kind as the property transferred; any two pieces of real estate are considered to be of like kind.

Boot—Something given or received in a tax-free exchange that is not like-kind property, such as cash.

Chapter Quiz

1. **The basis of a principal residence would be adjusted to reflect:**
   a) depreciation deductions
   b) expenses incurred to keep the property in good repair
   c) mortgage interest paid
   d) the cost of installing a deck

2. **A married couple bought a home for $250,000. After living in the home for three years, they sold it for only $246,000. How much of this loss can they deduct on their federal income tax return?**
   a) The full $4,000 loss
   b) Only $3,000
   c) Only $2,000
   d) None of it

3. **Which of the following might the owner of unimproved investment property deduct on this year's federal income tax return?**
   a) A loss on the sale of the property
   b) The depreciation of the land
   c) The entire amount of any capital expenditures
   d) Any of the above

4. **Which of the following exchanges could not qualify as a "tax-free" exchange?**
   a) An office building for a hotel
   b) An apartment house for a warehouse
   c) Timber land for farm equipment
   d) A city lot for a ranch

5. **Under the federal income tax code, gain is usually taxed in the year it is:**
   a) audited
   b) realized
   c) recovered
   d) deferred

6. **Munson just sold his principal residence. After deducting his selling costs, the amount of gain realized was $163,000. Munson will be allowed to exclude the entire amount of the gain from taxation only if:**
   a) he is married and is filing a joint return
   b) he has never claimed this exclusion before, since it can only be used once in a lifetime
   c) the gain is not considered a capital gain
   d) he owned and occupied the property as his principal residence for two of the previous five years

7. **Torino owns a triplex as an investment property. She paid $450,000 for it, including her closing costs. The allowable depreciation deductions for the property have amounted to $20,000, Torino has spent $50,000 on capital improvements, and the market value of the property has risen by 15%. What is Torino's adjusted basis?**
   a) $537,500
   b) $500,000
   c) $480,000
   d) $430,000

8. **Gillespie is buying a home that will be his principal residence. He is financing the purchase with a $200,000 mortgage loan. How much of the interest that he pays on the loan can he deduct from his income?**
   a) All of it
   b) Up to $100,000 in interest
   c) 50%
   d) None of it

9. **Tom renovates four units in his apartment building. The cost is:**
   a) deductible
   b) added to basis
   c) depreciable
   d) Both b) and c)

10. **Sherrick is selling a lot for $72,000. Her adjusted basis in the property is $56,000. In addition to the 6% sales commission she'll be paying, she will also have to pay $2,500 in closing costs. For federal income tax purposes, what is the gain Sherrick will realize in this transaction?**
    a) $6,820
    b) $9,180
    c) $16,000
    d) $22,820

Chapter 15: *Antidiscrimination Laws and Other Marketing Regulations*

- **I. Racism and Housing Discrimination in the U.S. and Washington**
  - A. Understanding structural racism
  - B. Consequences of housing discrimination and segregation
- **II. Federal Antidiscrimination Legislation**
  - A. Civil Rights Act of 1866
  - B. Civil Rights Act of 1964
  - C. Federal Fair Housing Act
    1. Exemptions
    2. Display of poster
    3. Prohibited acts
    4. Disability and familial status
    5. Enforcement
  - D. Federal fair lending laws
  - E. Americans with Disabilities Act
- **III. Washington Antidiscrimination Legislation**
  - A. Washington Law Against Discrimination
    1. Prohibited practices
    2. Exemptions
    3. Enforcement
  - B. Washington Fairness in Lending Act
  - C. Washington Real Estate License Law
- **IV. Other Marketing Regulations**
  - A. Antitrust laws
  - B. Restrictions on telephone and electronic marketing

Antidiscrimination laws are intended to promote fairness. In the real estate context, one of the main goals of these laws is equal housing opportunity. Anyone with the necessary financial resources should be able to choose a home or apartment in any neighborhood, regardless of race, religion, national origin, gender, or other characteristics that have historically been used as a basis for discrimination. There are also antidiscrimination laws that affect nonresidential real estate.

Real estate agents need to be familiar with the laws that prohibit discrimination in real estate transactions and related business activities. These laws directly affect how agents can market properties. Complying with these laws—and encouraging others to comply with them—is an essential part of a real estate agent's professional duties.

This chapter begins with historical information about racism and housing discrimination in the United States and in Washington, along with a discussion of structural racism and the consequences of residential segregation. After that, we'll look at the federal antidiscrimination laws that affect real estate, and then at the Washington laws.

Besides antidiscrimination laws, there are other laws that have an impact on how real estate agents market properties. We'll end the chapter with information about antitrust laws and laws that limit telephone and electronic marketing.

Key Terms

Blockbusting	**Public Accommodation**
Steering	**Price Fixing**
Redlining	**Group Boycott**
Familial Status	**Tie-In Arrangement**
Disability	**Market Allocation**

Racism and Housing Discrimination in the United States and in Washington

One of the most serious and persistent problems throughout American history has been racism and its harmful effects on millions of citizens—not just on individuals, but across generations. Openly discriminatory policies and actions by the government and by private parties are less common now than in the past, but unjust acts continue to happen. Moreover, the legacies of earlier discriminatory systems remain. In particular, they still cast a shadow over property ownership today.

A fundamental chapter in this history was the enslavement of Black people, especially but not exclusively in the South. Against their will, hundreds of thousands of Africans were brought to what eventually became the United States, where for centuries they and their descendants were denied their liberty, forced to perform unpaid labor, and bought and sold. Treated as property themselves, enslaved people were prohibited from owning property or receiving education, among many other restrictions.

In 1865, the North's victory in the Civil War put an end to this system. During the Reconstruction era immediately following the war, constitutional and legislative changes—the Thirteenth Amendment (which prohibited slavery), Fourteenth Amendment (which promoted equal protection under the law), and Fifteenth Amendment (which prohibited discrimination in voting rights), along with the Civil Rights Act of 1866—attempted to put formerly enslaved people on a more equal footing.

However, backsliding at the end of the Reconstruction era quickly undid much of this initial progress. Government programs to distribute land and supplies to former slaves—such as the "40 acres and a mule" initiative and the Freedmen's Bureau—were defunded and disbanded. This gave rise to the sharecropping system, where former slaves worked as tenant farmers on other people's land, in predatory arrangements.

Southern states also enacted "Jim Crow" laws, which legally enforced racial segregation practices and restricted the ability of Black citizens to vote, serve in public office, or even patronize local businesses. The U.S. Supreme Court upheld such laws in the 1896 case *Plessy v. Ferguson*, establishing the doctrine of "separate but equal" as a principle of constitutional law. In other words, a law segregating the use of facilities based on race (segregated train cars, for example) was constitutional as long as the accommodations for Black people were equal to those for white people.

One response to the Jim Crow era was the Great Migration, when many Black people simply left the South, moving to northern cities to work in factories. Some cities reacted to this influx with their own overtly discriminatory laws, such as exclusionary zoning to segregate the new arrivals in certain neighborhoods.

Explicitly racist zoning ordinances were prohibited in 1917; in *Buchanan v. Warley,* the Supreme Court struck down a Louisville ordinance that prohibited Black residents from living in majority white neighborhoods. As a result of that decision, though, there was an increased use of restrictive covenants—language in deeds restricting who properties could be sold to, imposed by private property owners rather than by law—which still had the same discriminatory effect.

During the Great Depression in the 1930s, the Federal Housing Administration was created to promote homeownership. By insuring residential mortgage loans (protecting lenders against financial losses from foreclosures), the FHA made it easier for people who wanted to buy a home to obtain the necessary financing. Unfortunately, the FHA wound up also promoting racial discrimination in housing, by refusing to insure loans in neighborhoods with large non-white populations, based on a presumption that the rates of default and foreclosure would be unacceptably high. This practice became known as "redlining," because the FHA issued maps showing those neighborhoods colored in red. (Redlining is discussed in more detail later in the chapter.)

Another Depression-era innovation that helped Americans to build wealth also systematically excluded Black Americans in its early form: Social Security initially excluded agricultural and domestic workers from its benefits, which disproportionately affected Black workers. After World War II, the GI Bill helped veterans become homeowners through the VA-guaranteed loan program, which spurred a post-war housing boom. However, this program did little to help Black veterans; they were eligible for VA loans, but the loans were issued through private lenders that continued to engage in redlining and other forms of lending discrimination.

Even so, there was considerable progress in the decades following World War II, starting in the court system. In the 1948 case *Shelley v. Kraemer*, the Supreme Court ruled that discriminatory restrictive covenants were no longer legally enforceable. More broadly, in the 1956 case *Brown v. Board of Education,* the Supreme Court ruled against its earlier "separate but equal" doctrine, holding that segregated facilities were inherently unequal and therefore unconstitutional. While the *Brown* decision was specifically about public schools, its rationale came to be applied to all areas of civic life.

In the following decade, Congress passed the Civil Rights Act of 1964 and the Voting Rights Act of 1965, bringing about the end of Jim Crow segregation laws and guaranteeing access to voting, education, and public spaces to everyone regardless of race. However, these federal statutes did not specifically address the issue of housing discrimination. Although discriminatory restrictive covenants were illegal, enforcing that prohibition was difficult, and banks continued to redline, perpetuating racial segregation in the nation's cities. Congress finally took action against racial discrimination in housing (as well as discrimination based on national origin, religion, and other protected classes) with the Civil Rights Act of 1968, which we'll cover in the next section of the chapter.

Racism in Washington. The history of racism in America is commonly associated with the South, where slavery was particularly entrenched in the economy and culture and, in the twentieth century, where many notorious acts of anti-Black violence and many notable civil rights protests took place. But racism was also widespread in the rest of the country, including the state of Washington. One difference is that much of Washington's history centers on anti-Asian racism. Workers who came from Asia provided a significant share of the labor that helped in the nation's expansion to the West Coast, and were then subject to considerable violence and exclusion, especially once they began acquiring property and starting businesses.

Prominent examples include the expulsion of Chinese residents from Tacoma in 1885 and from Seattle in 1886. Residents were forcibly driven from town, sometimes placed onto ships or trains to transport them elsewhere. In Tacoma, the then-empty Chinese neighborhood was razed. Another event with an impact in Washington was the federal government's internment of Japanese residents of the West Coast during World War II. Many of those interned people (the majority of whom were American citizens) lost property that they owned before internment, which they were unable to regain after the war.

Anti-Black racism was also not unusual in Washington. In the 1950s and 1960s this included redlining and other discriminatory lending practices by local banks, which effectively limited Black residents to a few neighborhoods such as Seattle's Central District, while also making it more difficult to maintain and renovate homes there. These economic harms were compounded by preferential hiring for factory jobs, as well as police enforcement of "sundown zones" (areas where Black people were not allowed after sunset) in suburban cities and in north Seattle, which was mostly white.

This reached a climax in 1964, when Seattle voters were faced with a citywide referendum on whether to prohibit discrimination in rentals and home sales. Local real estate agents advocated against the referendum, with one advertisement asking, "Your Rights are at stake! Would you like a criminal record because you sold your home or rented an apartment to a person of your choice?" In the end, the citizens of Seattle opposed the antidiscrimination referendum by a nearly 2-to-1 margin. Seattle didn't successfully enact an ordinance against housing discrimination until 1968, and that was put in place by the city council rather than by public vote.

Understanding Structural Racism

Unspoken assumptions, handed down for generations and deeply internalized, that certain groups of people are unlikely to succeed, are likely to cause problems, or are naturally inferior or subordinate—these consciously or unconsciously influence millions of interpersonal interactions and small decisions every day. The cumulative result of all these individual actions is a system of largely invisible but enduring social barriers that perpetuate inequality and make it more difficult for those groups of people to thrive and prosper.

This phenomenon is what is sometimes referred to as **structural racism** (also known as systemic racism), where racism has become woven into the fabric of society, across a variety of institutions as well as cultural and media environments. **Interpersonal racism**—where prejudices and biases directly affect how people interact with people of other races—is only the most visible component of structural racism.

Structural racism also involves **institutional racism**, where governmental or private-sector systems work better for members of certain races than other races. That doesn't necessarily involve systems overtly designed to favor or exclude certain people; often, it's about allocating finite resources inequitably, or taking an attitude of "well, that's how it's always been done," without further consideration of who that might benefit or harm.

The difference between interpersonal racism and institutional racism can also be thought as of the distinction between direct and indirect discrimination. **Direct discrimination** occurs, for instance, when an employer refuses to hire a job applicant or a landlord rejects a rental applicant based on race (or another protected class).

Indirect discrimination, by contrast, occurs when an institution or entity has a rule or policy that in theory applies equally to all people, but establishes requirements that may be more difficult for people of a certain race or other protected class to meet. In other words, there may not be a discriminatory intent, but there is nevertheless a discriminatory impact.

> **Example:** As a blanket policy, a landlord refuses to rent to anyone who has ever been arrested, without regard to the nature or severity of the crime. On its face, the landlord's policy is racially neutral, but people in certain racial groups are statistically more likely to have been arrested, as a result of the same social forces we're discussing. Thus, the landlord's policy has a disproportionate impact on those groups (and would in fact be illegal, as you'll see later on).

There is one additional component of structural racism, and it may be the subtlest one of all. This component is **internalized racism**: the web of assumptions, stereotypes, and values that everyone absorbs from the culture that surrounds them. In addition to assumptions of racial superiority and expected privileges for the favored group, this can also involve an internalized sense of inferiority among members of other groups, which might shape their expectations of what they can hope to achieve or how they respond to adversity.

Consequences of Housing Discrimination and Segregation

While the examples of racism that get the most attention in history books and in the news are usually acts or threats of physical violence, the more pervasive effects tend to be less overt and more related to institutional racism, taking the form of lost opportunities. This can mean, for example, lost employment opportunities, lost educational opportunities, or lost housing opportunities.

These opportunities, in fact, can all be interrelated. Living in the neighborhood of your choice can mean access to better schools, which down the line can mean better employment prospects. Similarly, living in a particular neighborhood may put you within commuting distance of better employment opportunities. It may even lead to better health, because the neighborhood is located away from sources of pollution like freeways or heavy industry, for example, or offers better access to supermarkets, not just convenience stores and fast food.

The problem of lost housing opportunities also has a very large impact on generational wealth. Home ownership is one of the primary ways that middle-class families in the U.S. have traditionally built wealth and passed it along to following generations, either through direct inheritance of property or through the inheritance of wealth that grew out of the proceeds of a home sale, or a series of them over a lifetime.

When you hear discussion of a "wealth gap" between the races in the U.S.—and recent estimates have found that the median white family has a net worth of at least ten times that of the median Black family—much of that is rooted in the disparity of opportunities to build and transfer housing wealth. When someone is prevented by institutional obstacles from buying a house in neighborhoods where property is likely to appreciate faster, or prevented from buying property at all, that makes it much more difficult to build up personal wealth.

It also makes it more difficult to deploy that wealth—by selling property or borrowing against it—to create additional opportunities, such as paying for advanced education or starting a business.

This wealth gap, and the residential segregation that contributed to it, didn't occur simply through millions of unrelated transactions and individual consumer choices. Instead, it happened partly through specific federal, state, and local laws or regulations that required segregation. (This is called *de jure* segregation, segregation by law.)

For example, in the early twentieth century many municipalities had zoning ordinances that specifically prohibited non-white people from living in certain neighborhoods. During the Great Depression, federal agencies such as the Federal Housing Administration and the Home Owners' Loan Corporation would not insure or refinance loans in racially integrated areas. During World War II, federal housing on military bases excluded Black civilians.

In addition, segregation occurred through the actions of private entities and individuals, which is called *de facto* segregation, segregation in fact. For instance, many banks would not issue loans for the purchase or rehabilitation of homes in non-white neighborhoods, or make loans to people of color intending to purchase in white neighborhoods; this was common even before the FHA more formally established the practice of redlining. Commercial loans to subdivision developers were often conditioned on the developer having racially restrictive covenants in place to prevent homeowners from selling their property to people of color.

Real estate boards, both nationally and locally, frequently had codes of ethics that encouraged segregation. It was very common for real estate agents to engage in "steering": dissuading minority buyers from purchasing homes in white neighborhoods, or deliberately showing them homes only in non-white neighborhoods. Some agents engaged in "blockbusting," using fear tactics about the possibility of minority residents moving into a neighborhood to get white residents to list their homes for sale; this helped spur "white flight" from cities to suburbs. These practices contributed to the residential segregation that persists in much of the country. (Steering and blockbusting will be covered in more detail later in the chapter.)

Federal Antidiscrimination Legislation

Now we'll turn to the federal and state laws that prohibit discrimination in real estate transactions and related activities. Through that prohibition, these laws attempt to reverse patterns of residential segregation and eliminate other barriers to buying or renting property. We'll start with the federal laws, which include these statutes:

- the Civil Rights Act of 1866,
- the Civil Rights Act of 1964,
- the federal Fair Housing Act,
- federal fair lending laws, and
- the Americans with Disabilities Act.

Civil Rights Act of 1866

The Civil Rights Act of 1866 states that "all citizens of the United States shall have the same right, in every state and territory as is enjoyed by white citizens thereof to inherit, purchase, lease, sell, hold and convey real and personal property." In regard to property ownership and property transactions, the act prohibits any discrimination based on race or color.

The law was enacted immediately after the Civil War, but largely ignored for almost a century. In the 1960s, during the civil rights movement, the act was challenged as an unconstitutional interference with private property rights. But the U.S. Supreme Court upheld the act in the landmark case of *Jones v. Mayer*, decided in 1968. The court ruled that the 1866 Act "prohibits all racial discrimination, private or public, in the sale and rental of property," and that it is constitutional based on the Thirteenth Amendment to the U.S. Constitution, the amendment that prohibits slavery.

Someone who has been discriminated against in violation of the Civil Rights Act of 1866 can sue in federal court. The court could issue an injunction ordering the defendant to stop discriminating. The court could also order the defendant to pay the plaintiff both **compensatory damages** (to compensate for losses and suffering caused by the discrimination) and **punitive damages** (an additional sum to punish the defendant for wrongdoing).

Civil Rights Act of 1964

The Civil Rights Act of 1964 was one of the first attempts made by the federal government to promote equal opportunity in housing. The act prohibited discrimination based on race, color, religion, or national origin in many programs and activities for which the federal government offered financial assistance. Unfortunately, the effect of the act was extremely limited, because most FHA and VA loans weren't covered. In fact, it's estimated that less than 1% of all houses purchased were covered by the act. It wasn't until the Civil Rights Act of 1968 that major progress was made toward fair housing goals.

Federal Fair Housing Act

The federal Fair Housing Act is also known as Title VIII of the Civil Rights Act of 1968. It goes further than either the 1866 Civil Rights Act or the 1964 Civil Rights Act, making it illegal to discriminate on the basis of **race**, **color**, **religion**, **sex**, **national origin**, **disability**, or **familial status** in the sale or lease of residential property or in the sale or lease of vacant land for the construction of residential buildings. The law's prohibition against sex discrimination covers discrimination based on gender identity or sexual orientation as well.

The Fair Housing Act also limits discrimination based on a person's criminal history. It prohibits a landlord from refusing to rent to a person simply based on the existence of an arrest or conviction record. Instead, a landlord must consider prospective tenants on a case-by-case basis, taking into account individual circumstances such as the severity of the crime and the amount of time that has passed since the conviction.

If an applicant's criminal record indicates a demonstrable danger to residents or their property, a landlord may deny the application.

In addition to residential sales and leasing, the Fair Housing Act applies to discrimination in advertising, lending, real estate brokerage, and other services in connection with residential real estate transactions. However, unlike the 1866 Civil Rights Act, the Fair Housing Act does not apply to nonresidential transactions, such as those involving commercial or industrial properties. For example, the Fair Housing Act does not apply to hotels or bed and breakfasts, because they are commercial properties where guests stay for only a short period of time.

Exemptions. While the Fair Housing Act applies to the majority of residential real estate transactions, three categories of transactions are exempt from it.

1. **Sale or Rental by Private Owner.** The law doesn't apply to the sale or rental of a single-family home by its owner, provided that:
    - the seller or landlord doesn't own more than three such homes;
    - no real estate agent is employed in the transaction; and
    - no discriminatory advertising is used.

    If the owner isn't the most recent occupant of the home, they may use this exemption only once every 24 months.
2. **Rental in an Owner-Occupied Dwelling.** The law doesn't apply to the rental of a unit or a room in a dwelling with up to four units, provided that:
    - the owner occupies one of the units as their residence;
    - no real estate agent is employed; and
    - no discriminatory advertising is used.

    (This is sometimes called the **Mrs. Murphy exemption.**)
3. **Religious Organization or Private Club Accommodations.** In dealing with their own property in noncommercial transactions, religious organizations or societies or affiliated nonprofit organizations may limit occupancy to or give preference to their own members, provided that membership isn't restricted on the basis of race, color, or national origin.

These limited exemptions apply very rarely. Remember, the 1866 Civil Rights Act prohibits discrimination based on race or color in any property transaction, regardless of any exemptions available under the Fair Housing Act. In addition, there is no exemption for any transaction involving a real estate licensee. And for Washington residents, these federal exemptions don't really matter, because the exemptions in the Washington law governing discrimination in real estate transactions are narrower; these will be discussed later in the chapter.

Display of Poster. Regulations implementing the Fair Housing Act require a fair housing poster such as the one in Figure 15.1 to be prominently displayed at any place of business involved in the sale, rental, or financing of dwellings. This includes real estate offices, lenders' offices, apartment buildings, condominiums, and model homes in subdivisions.

If a fair housing complaint is filed against a business, failure to display the poster may be treated as evidence of discriminatory practices.

Prohibited Acts. The Fair Housing Act prohibits any of the following acts if they are done on the basis of race, color, religion, sex, national origin, disability, or familial status:

- refusing to rent or sell residential property after receiving a bona fide offer;
- refusing to negotiate for the sale or rental of residential property, or otherwise making it unavailable;
- changing the terms of sale or lease for different potential buyers or tenants;
- using advertising that indicates a preference or intent to discriminate;
- representing that property is not available for inspection, sale, or rent when it is in fact available;
- using discriminatory criteria when making a housing loan;
- limiting participation in a multiple listing service or similar service; or
- coercing, intimidating, threatening, or interfering with anyone on account of their enjoyment, attempt to enjoy, or encouragement or assistance to others in enjoying the rights granted by the Fair Housing Act.

Fig. 15.1 Fair Housing Poster

U. S. Department of Housing and Urban Development

EQUAL HOUSING OPPORTUNITY

We Do Business in Accordance With the Federal Fair Housing Law

(The Fair Housing Amendments Act of 1988)

It is illegal to Discriminate Against Any Person Because of Race, Color, Religion, Sex, Handicap, Familial Status, or National Origin

- In the sale or rental of housing or residential lots
- In advertising the sale or rental of housing
- In the financing of housing
- In the provision of real estate brokerage services
- In the appraisal of housing
- Blockbusting is also illegal

Anyone who feels he or she has been discriminated against may file a complaint of housing discrimination:
1-800-669-9777 (Toll Free)
1-800-927-9275 (TTY)
www.hud.gov/fairhousing

U.S. Department of Housing and Urban Development
Assistant Secretary for Fair Housing and Equal Opportunity
Washington, D.C. 20410

Previous editions are obsolete

form HUD-928.1 (6/2011)

Also prohibited by the Fair Housing Act are the discriminatory practices known as blockbusting, steering, and redlining, which were introduced in the first section of the chapter.

- **Blockbusting** occurs when someone tries to induce homeowners to list or sell their properties by predicting that members of another race (or people with disabilities, people of a particular ethnic background, etc.) will be moving into the neighborhood, and that this will have undesirable consequences, such as lower property values. The blockbuster then profits by purchasing the homes at reduced prices or (in the case of a real estate agent) by collecting commissions on the induced sales. Blockbusting is also known as **panic selling**.

  Example: Immediately after a Black family moves into an all-white neighborhood, agents working for XYZ Realty start calling all the other homeowners in the neighborhood. The agents warn that several other Black families are planning on buying homes in the neighborhood, and they claim that police have predicted a significant increase in crime, property values are expected to drop dramatically, and within months the owners will find it difficult to sell their homes at any price. Because of these "facts" made up by XYZ agents, several homeowners immediately list their homes with XYZ Realty. XYZ Realty is guilty of blockbusting.

- **Steering** refers to channeling prospective buyers or tenants toward or away from specific neighborhoods based on their race (or religion, national origin, etc.) in order to maintain or change the character of those neighborhoods.

  Example: The sales agents at PQR Realty are "encouraged" to show Latino buyers only properties in the city's predominantly Latino neighborhood. Non-Latino buyers aren't shown properties there, except by specific request. This is done on the principle that Latino buyers would be "more comfortable" living in the Latino neighborhood and non-Latino buyers would be "uncomfortable" there. PQR Realty is guilty of steering.

  A buyer may, on occasion, ask an agent about the demographics of a neighborhood that they are considering. The agent may truthfully answer such a question, even if that results in the buyer deciding not to look at properties in the neighborhood because of the race or ethnicity of its residents. However, the agent should not disparage the neighborhood or otherwise discourage the buyer from looking there; that would be considered steering. In fact, the best practice would simply be to tell the buyer where to look up information about neighborhood demographics (for instance, on the Census Bureau website or by contacting the local Chamber of Commerce), rather than saying anything that might create even an inference of steering.

  In addition, a real estate agent should never make reference to a neighborhood's demographics in an advertisement or any other online or printed description of the property and its surrounding community. This goes beyond the obvious prohibition against explicitly saying something like "Latino neighborhood" in an ad, to describing nearby features such as landmarks or businesses that are commonly associated with a particular race or nationality.

  This also applies to features associated with a particular religion; an advertisement should not state, for example, "Catholic school nearby" or "walking distance to synagogue," even though those might seem like innocent selling points rather than evidence of intent to discriminate on the basis of religion.

  Similarly, the duty to avoid the appearance of steering extends to the property itself. When staging a property for an open house or other showings, keep the decoration as neutral as possible. Avoid decorating with objects plainly associated with a particular race, religion, or other protected class, because that could create an impression of an intent to discriminate.

- **Redlining** is the refusal to make a loan because of the racial or ethnic composition of the neighborhood in which the security property is located.

  Example: A buyer applies to Community Savings for a loan to purchase a home located in the Cherrywood neighborhood. Cherrywood is a predominantly minority neighborhood. Community Savings rejects the loan, because it fears that property values in Cherrywood may decline in the future because of recent racial tensions in the area. Community Savings is guilty of redlining.

The prohibition against redlining is enforced through the Home Mortgage Disclosure Act, which will be discussed later in the chapter.

Buyer Love Letters. A practice that became common in recent decades, as many buyers found themselves competing against other buyers in bidding wars, is sending introductory letters to sellers. In these letters, often called "buyer love letters," buyers attempt to humanize themselves to a home seller, hoping to gain a competitive advantage over other buyers who have submitted offers for the same property.

Buyers typically state what they find appealing about the seller's house (and tend to gush about it—hence the nickname "love letters") and describe their plans for the property. The buyers might also describe themselves, their family, and their careers and even include photos, essentially marketing themselves to the seller. While such a letter isn't likely to help a buyer win out over a substantially larger offer from someone else, it might tip the balance between two otherwise similar offers if one of the buyers can form some sort of emotional connection with the seller.

The problem with this practice is that the letter is likely to reveal details about what protected classes a buyer belongs to, especially if pictures are included. The letter or a photo might suggest or plainly show the buyer's race, national origin, religion, or sexual orientation, and that could create a problematic situation. Suppose a buyer sends a personally revealing letter with a photo, then loses out in a bidding war. That unsuccessful buyer might wonder whether the seller refused their offer based on their race or another protected characteristic they revealed. Or suppose an unsuccessful buyer who didn't submit a letter learns that the successful buyer did do so. This could lead them to wonder whether the seller preferred the other offer based on personal information revealed in the successful buyer's letter. Either situation could lead to a claim of discrimination, with the letter presented as evidence.

This creates a potential conflict for both buyers' and sellers' agents. On one hand, agency law obligates them to act diligently to find the optimal property for a buyer or the best possible offer for a seller. On the other hand, they are also obligated by federal and state antidiscrimination laws to not take actions that could lead to discrimination. As a result, "love letters" have become disfavored, and some states have even sought to ban the practice. While they remain legal in Washington, they're not advisable in most situations.

Sellers' agents should discourage sellers from accepting these letters and (if the sellers agree) tell buyers' agents not to submit them along with offers. Buyers' agents should not recommend that their clients send letters to sellers. When working with buyers who want to send a letter, an agent should recommend that it be limited to a description of what they like about the property. Descriptions or photos of the buyers should not be included.

Loan Programs. Certain home loan programs are associated with particular protected classes. Sellers should not disfavor an offer because it's contingent on this type of financing, even if some programs have the reputation of requiring more paperwork or longer closing times. Similarly, agents should not refuse to work with buyers who want to use this type of loan program.

One example is the Department of Housing and Urban Development's Section 184 Indian Home Loan Guarantee Program, which is designed to help Native Americans buy homes. Another example is the VA-guaranteed loan program; although veteran or military status is not a protected class under the federal Fair Housing Act, it is under Washington law, as we'll discuss in the next section of the chapter. Rejecting an offer because it involves financing through this type of loan program could give the buyer a foothold to allege discrimination.

Downpayment assistance programs and other affordable housing programs targeted at low- or moderate-income home buyers also should not be disfavored, if there is any potential relationship between the program's targeted buyers and a particular protected class.

Disability and Familial Status. Originally, the Fair Housing Act did not prohibit discrimination based on disability or familial status; these classifications were added to the law in 1988.

Disability. Under the Fair Housing Act, it's illegal to discriminate against someone because they have a disability (referred to as a "handicap" in the statute). A **disability** is defined as a physical or mental impairment that substantially limits one or more major life activities. This includes people with addiction or mental health issues. But the act does not protect those who are a direct threat to the health or safety of others, or who are illegally using controlled substances.

A residential landlord must allow a disabled tenant to make reasonable modifications to the property at the tenant's expense, so long as the modifications are necessary for the tenant's full use and enjoyment of the premises. (The tenant can be required to restore the premises to their original condition at the end of the tenancy, however.)

Landlords must also make reasonable exceptions to their rules to accommodate disabled tenants. For example, even if they don't allow pets, they can't refuse to rent to someone with a guide dog or other service animal. In addition, landlords may not charge a pet deposit for a service animal.

New residential construction with four or more units is required to comply with wheelchair accessibility rules under the Fair Housing Act. (This requirement has been in effect since 1991.) Doorways, bathrooms, and kitchens should be designed to accommodate wheelchairs.

Wheelchair accessibility requirements do not apply to the upper stories of multi-story buildings, unless there is an elevator that would allow wheelchair users to reach those units.

Familial Status. Discrimination on the basis of familial status refers to discriminating against someone because a child (a person under 18 years old) is or will be living with them. Parents, legal guardians, pregnant women, and those in the process of obtaining custody of a child are protected against discrimination on the basis of their familial status.

It's unlawful for anyone to discriminate in selling, renting, or lending money to buy residential property because the applicant is pregnant or lives with a child. "Adults only" apartment or condominium complexes are prohibited, and so are complexes divided into "adult" and "family" areas. State and local laws may limit the number of occupants allowed per unit based on the square footage, but property managers may not unreasonably restrict the number of tenants per unit beyond this requirement.

However, under a separate statute called the Housing for Older Persons Act, the law includes an exemption for properties that qualify as "housing for older persons." Children can be excluded from properties that fit into one of the following categories:

1. properties developed under a government program to assist the elderly;
2. properties intended for and solely occupied by persons 62 or older; or
3. properties that adhere to policies that demonstrate an intent to house persons 55 or older, if at least 80% of the units are occupied by at least one person who is 55 years old or older.

Enforcement. The Fair Housing Act is enforced by the Department of Housing and Urban Development (HUD), through its Office of Fair Housing and Equal Opportunity. An aggrieved person may file a lawsuit in federal or state court or file a complaint with HUD.

Anyone who has been harmed by housing discrimination can file a complaint (or a lawsuit). Naturally this would include a residential tenant or buyer whose rental application or offer to purchase was rejected for a discriminatory reason. However, there is a wider range of possible complainants.

For example, someone who believes a discriminatory act is about to occur can file a complaint before it actually does occur. And a "tester" (a person working with a fair housing advocacy group who poses as an apartment-seeker to investigate discrimination) may file a complaint if they were discriminated against, even though they did not actually want to rent a unit.

Any employee (minority or non-minority) of a landlord or real estate firm who was disciplined for objecting to a discriminatory act could file a complaint. So could any tenant who experiences housing discrimination related to a third party—for example, a white tenant whose lease is terminated over visits by her Latino boyfriend. Even a real estate agent who loses out on a commission because of a seller's discriminatory acts could pursue a complaint.

Similarly, a variety of persons and entities could have complaints filed against them. This includes not just property owners, real estate agents, and brokerages, but also property managers, lenders, developers, homeowner's associations, insurance companies, and other service providers who affect housing opportunities.

A complaint must be filed with HUD within one year after the discriminatory act occurred. The agency will investigate the complaint and attempt to confer with the parties in order to reconcile their differences and persuade the violator to abide by the law. If this doesn't resolve the dispute and the complainant's claims appear valid, an administrative hearing is held (unless either party chooses federal court instead). In an administrative hearing, HUD attorneys litigate the case on behalf of the complainant. If a case involves a "pattern or practice" of discrimination, the U.S. Attorney General can file suit in federal court.

When someone is held to have violated the Fair Housing Act, the administrative law judge or the court may issue an injunction ordering the violator to stop the discriminatory conduct, or to take affirmative steps to correct a violation. The violator may also be ordered to pay compensatory damages and attorney's fees to the complainant. In addition, a federal court can order the violator to pay punitive damages to the complainant. An administrative law judge can't award punitive damages, but can impose a civil penalty, to be paid to the government. The civil penalty amounts are significant, ranging from a maximum of over $20,000 for a first offense to over $100,000 for a third offense.

If the case is brought by the U.S. Attorney General (based on an allegation of a "pattern or practice" of discrimination), the court may issue injunctive relief or other court orders as necessary, and court-awarded civil penalties over $200,000 are possible.

In states such as Washington, where the state fair housing laws are very similar to the federal law, HUD may refer complaints to the equivalent state agency. (The state agency here is the Washington Human Rights Commission.)

In addition, Washington's Department of Financial Institutions (DFI) accepts complaints against lenders such as banks or credit unions. A complaint involving redlining or other loan-related housing discrimination could be referred to DFI. The agency also accepts discrimination complaints related to other entities and individuals that it regulates, including mortgage brokers, escrow agents, and payday lenders.

Federal Fair Lending Laws

As we discussed earlier, the Fair Housing Act prohibits discrimination in residential mortgage lending. It doesn't apply to other types of credit transactions, however.

The **Equal Credit Opportunity Act** (ECOA) applies to all credit transactions, including residential real estate loans. The act prohibits lenders, loan brokers, and others involved in financing from discriminating based on race, color, religion, national origin, sex, marital status, age (as long as the applicant has reached the age of majority), sexual orientation, gender identity, or because the applicant's income is derived partly or wholly from public assistance.

The **Home Mortgage Disclosure Act** provides a way to evaluate whether lenders are fulfilling their obligation to serve the housing needs of the communities where they're located. The act facilitates the enforcement of federal laws against redlining.

Under the Home Mortgage Disclosure Act, large institutional lenders in metropolitan areas must file annual reports on the residential mortgage loans (both purchase and improvement loans) they originated or purchased during the fiscal year. The information is categorized by number and dollar amount, type of loan (FHA, VA, other), and geographic location by census tract or county. The reports may reveal areas where few or no home loans have been made, alerting investigators to possible redlining.

Americans with Disabilities Act

Although the Fair Housing Act prohibits discrimination on the basis of disability, that law applies only to housing. Another federal law, the **Americans with Disabilities Act** (ADA), which went into effect in 1992, is intended to ensure that people with disabilities have equal access to public facilities. The ADA requires any business or nonresidential facility open to the public to be accessible to people with disabilities.

Under the ADA, it's illegal to discriminate against anyone on the basis of disability in any place of public accommodation or other commercial facility. A disability is defined as a physical or mental impairment that substantially limits one or more of an individual's major life activities (the same definition used for the Fair Housing Act).

The definition of **public accommodation** in the ADA includes any nonresidential place that is owned, operated, or leased by a private entity and open to the public, if operation of the facility affects commerce.

This definition encompasses a wide variety of facilities open to the public, such as hotels, restaurants, retail stores, banks, schools, and professional offices. For instance, the office of a real estate brokerage is open to the public and therefore must be accessible to people with disabilities. (Also, offices and workplaces that aren't regularly visited by members of the public may fall within the broader category of commercial facilities and need to be made accessible.)

To ensure the accessibility of places of public accommodation, the ADA requires each of the following to be accomplished, as long as it is "readily achievable":

- Architectural barriers and communication barriers must be removed so that goods and services are accessible to people with disabilities.
- Auxiliary aids and services must be provided so that no one with a disability is excluded, denied services, segregated, or otherwise treated differently from other individuals.
- New commercial construction must be accessible to people with disabilities, unless that would be structurally impractical.

For example, the owner of a commercial building with no elevator may have to install automatic entry doors and a buzzer at street level so that customers of a second-floor business can ask for assistance. The law might also require the owner of a commercial building to alter the height of some amenities to make them accessible to someone in a wheelchair, add grab bars to restroom stalls, and take a variety of other steps to make the building's facilities accessible.

Washington Antidiscrimination Legislation

Real estate agents, sellers, landlords, and others involved in real estate activities must comply not only with the federal laws we've covered so far, but also with state laws that prohibit discrimination. The Washington Law Against Discrimination, the Washington Fair Lending Act, and the real estate license law all include provisions designed to promote fairness in real estate transactions.

Washington Law Against Discrimination

The Washington Law Against Discrimination declares that discrimination is a matter of state concern because it threatens the rights and privileges of state inhabitants and the foundations of a free democratic society. Compared to the federal antidiscrimination laws we've just discussed, this state law covers more types of activities and extends protection from discrimination to more classes of people.

In real estate transactions, the Washington law prohibits discrimination based on **race, creed, color, national origin, sex, sexual orientation, gender identity, marital status, or familial status; sensory, physical, or mental disability; use of a trained guide dog or service animal; honorably discharged veteran or military status; and citizenship or immigration status.**

To further the purposes of the Washington Law Against Discrimination, the Human Rights Commission was created and given the mission of eliminating and preventing discrimination in this state.

Prohibited Practices. The Washington Law Against Discrimination isn't just a fair housing law. It prohibits a wide range of discriminatory practices in employment, insurance, and credit transactions; in places of public accommodation and amusement (such as restaurants, movie theaters, hotels, stores, and most other commercial enterprises); and in regard to all types of real property.

Discrimination is prohibited in any real estate transaction. This includes the sale, appraisal, brokering, exchange, purchase, rental, or lease of real property; transacting or applying for a real estate loan; and the provision of brokerage services.

If based on discrimination against one of the protected classes we listed above (race, creed, color, national origin, etc.), it is against the law to do or attempt to do any of the following:

- refuse to engage in a real estate transaction;
- discriminate in the terms or conditions of a transaction;
- discriminate in providing services or facilities in connection with a real estate transaction;
- refuse to receive or fail to transmit a bona fide offer;
- refuse to negotiate;
- represent that property is not available for inspection, sale, rental, or lease when it is in fact available;
- fail to advise a prospect about a property listing, or refuse to allow the prospect to inspect the property;
- discriminate in the sale or rental of a dwelling, or otherwise make unavailable or deny a dwelling to anyone;
- make, print, circulate, or publish any advertisement, notice, or sign which indicates, directly or indirectly, an intent to discriminate;
- use any application form or make any record or inquiry which indicates, directly or indirectly, an intent to discriminate;
- offer, solicit, accept, use, or retain a listing with the understanding that a person may be discriminated against;
- expel a person from occupancy;
- discriminate in negotiating, executing, or financing a real estate transaction;
- discriminate in negotiating or executing any service or item in connection with a real estate transaction (such as title insurance or mortgage insurance);
- refuse to allow a disabled person to make reasonable modifications to a dwelling;

Washington laws antidiscrimation is more strict by federal

- refuse to make reasonable accommodations in rules or policies that would enable a disabled person to use a dwelling;
- fail to construct new multifamily dwellings in compliance with accessibility requirements imposed by the federal Fair Housing Act;
- induce, for profit, anyone to sell or rent by making representations regarding entry into the neighborhood of a person of a protected class (blockbusting);
- insert in a written instrument relating to real property any condition, restriction, or prohibition based on a protected class, or honor or attempt to honor such a provision (any such provision in a deed or any other conveyance or instrument relating to real property is void); or
- discriminate in any credit transaction (whether or not it is related to real estate) in denying credit, increasing fees, requiring collateral, or in any other terms or conditions.

In short, just about every form of discrimination in real estate transactions or any services associated with real estate transactions is unlawful if it is based on a person's status as a member of any of the protected classes.

Fig. 15.2 Antidiscrimination Legislation

Legislation	Prohibits Discrimination
Civil Rights Act of 1866	Based on race, in real estate transactions
Federal Fair Housing Act	In sale, lease, or financing of housing
Americans with Disabilities Act	Based on disability, in public accommodations
Washington Law Against Discrimination	In sale, lease, or financing of any real estate

Exemptions. The Washington Law Against Discrimination has few exemptions. Educational institutions may discriminate based on sex, marital status, or familial status in student housing. Private clubs and certain cemeteries and mausoleums operated by religious or sectarian institutions may discriminate based on religion. Discrimination based on familial status is allowed in connection with property that qualifies as housing for older persons under the federal Fair Housing Act.

The Washington law has no general exemptions for sellers or landlords in ordinary transactions. However, it does exempt transactions that involve sharing an owner-occupied dwelling unit, or the sublease of a portion of a dwelling unit occupied by the sublessor. In other words, a homeowner who rents rooms in their own house does not have to comply with this law when choosing lodgers; and a tenant does not have to comply when choosing a roommate to share an apartment unit or rental house.

Of course, the Washington Law Against Discrimination has no exemptions for real estate licensees engaged in professional activities.

Enforcement. For claims alleging an unfair practice in a real estate transaction, an injured party may file a written complaint with the Human Rights Commission within one year after the alleged discrimination took place. The Commission will then conduct an investigation. If the investigation reveals a reasonable basis for a belief that discrimination occurred, the Commission will act on the complaint.

First, the Commission will try to eliminate the unlawful discrimination by conference, conciliation, and persuasion. If that's unsuccessful, the Commission may schedule a hearing before an administrative law judge. If the judge finds unlawful discrimination, a cease and desist order may be issued. The judge may also require affirmative relief, payment of actual damages to the victim, and payment of a civil penalty to the government.

Either party may appeal the outcome of the administrative hearing to the superior court by filing an appeal within 30 days after being served with the final order.

As an alternative to an administrative hearing, the injured party may choose to have the attorney general enforce the law by bringing a civil action against the alleged discriminator.

Washington Fairness in Lending Act

The Washington Fairness in Lending Act prohibits redlining. Under this act, financial institutions may not deny single-family home loan applications solely because the home is located in a particular geographic area. They also may not vary the terms of the loan (such as by requiring a higher downpayment, higher interest rate, or shorter amortization term, or by deliberately undervaluing the property in an appraisal).

The act doesn't prevent a lending institution from using sound underwriting practices (including considering the borrower's creditworthiness and the market value of the property), but it outlaws the use of lending standards that have no economic basis.

Washington Real Estate License Law

Under the real estate license law, a licensee's violation of any federal or state antidiscrimination law is also a violation of the license law and grounds for disciplinary action (see Chapter 17). If a real estate licensee discriminates in sales or hiring activity, their license could be suspended or revoked. In addition, the licensee could face a substantial fine for each offense, and/or be required to complete an educational course in civil rights laws and nondiscriminatory real estate practices. Violations of the license law are also punishable as gross misdemeanors.

Other Marketing Regulations

As you've seen, antidiscrimination laws affect how a real estate agent may market property. Other laws that have an impact on marketing practices include antitrust laws, which prohibit real estate agents from joining together to engage in anticompetitive behavior, and laws that place restrictions on communications with prospective clients or customers.

Antitrust Laws

Federal and state antitrust laws prohibit business practices that are considered "anticompetitive" because they unfairly limit competition between companies and ultimately harm consumers.

Antitrust laws are based on the idea that business competition is good for both the economy and society as a whole. Although these laws aren't specifically targeted at real estate agents, they impose certain restrictions on how a real estate agent may behave toward clients, customers, and other agents.

Antitrust laws are not new. The first U.S. antitrust law was the **Sherman Act**, a federal law passed in 1890. The Sherman Act prohibits any agreement that has the effect of unreasonably restraining trade, including conspiracies. A **conspiracy** occurs when two or more business entities participate in a common scheme, the effect of which is the unreasonable restraint of trade.

The most famous antitrust cases involved giant companies such as Standard Oil or American Telephone & Telegraph, monopolies that dominated or completely controlled a market. But in 1950 antitrust laws were held to apply to the real estate industry. In a landmark case, *U.S. v. National Association of Real Estate Boards*, the Supreme Court held that mandatory fee schedules, established and enforced by a real estate board, violated the Sherman Act.

If a real estate agent violates antitrust laws, they (and the firm they works for) will be subject to both civil and criminal actions. If an individual is found guilty of violating the Sherman Act, they can be fined up to one million dollars and/or sentenced to ten years' imprisonment. If a corporation is found guilty of violating the Sherman Act, it can be fined up to one hundred million dollars.

Activities prohibited by antitrust laws can be grouped into four main categories:

- price fixing,
- group boycotts,
- tie-in arrangements, and
- market allocation.

Price Fixing. Price fixing is defined as the cooperative setting of prices or price ranges by competing companies. In the real estate context, the prices in question are commission rates. To avoid even the appearance of price fixing, agents from two different brokerage firms should not discuss their commission rates. (Note that it's a discussion between agents from competing firms that is dangerous; agents working for the same firm can discuss commission rates with one another.)

One exception to this general prohibition is that agents from two competing firms may discuss the commission split between the listing agent and the buyer's agent in a cooperative sale.

Even a casual announcement that a real estate firm is planning on raising its commission rates could lead to antitrust problems.

> **Example:** Wood, the designated broker of XYZ Realty, goes to a dinner given by her local MLS. She's called on to discuss current market conditions and, in the middle of her speech, she announces that she's going to raise her firm's commission rates, no matter what anyone else does. This statement could be viewed as an invitation to conspire to fix prices. If any other MLS members raise their rates in response to this announcement, they could be held to have accepted Wood's invitation to conspire.

As this example suggests, competing agents don't have to actually consult with each other to be charged with conspiring to fix commission rates. The kind of scenario described above could be enough to lead to an antitrust lawsuit.

Publications that appear to fix prices are prohibited as well. Any MLS or other association that tries to publish "recommended" or "going" rates for commissions could be sued.

Real estate firms should not use listing agreement forms that have the commission rate pre-printed as part of the form, and real estate agents should never imply to potential clients that the rate their firm is charging is nonnegotiable because it is fixed by law or by MLS policy.

Group Boycotts. A group boycott is an agreement between two or more business competitors (for example, real estate agents from different firms, or an association of competing firms such as a multiple listing service) to exclude another competitor from fair participation in business activities. The purpose of a group boycott is to hurt or destroy a competitor's business, and it is an antitrust violation.

> **Example:** The local multiple listing service refuses an application for membership from a new firm because the firm charges clients a flat fee instead of a percentage of the sales price as a commission—a practice current MLS members fiercely oppose. This action by the MLS, which severely impairs the new firm's ability to participate in the local market, is an illegal group boycott.

Tie-in Arrangements. A tie-in arrangement is defined as an agreement "to sell one product only on condition that the buyer also purchases a different (or tied) product."

> **Example:** Fisher is a subdivision developer. Tyson, a builder, wants to buy a lot. Fisher tells Tyson that he will sell him a lot only if Tyson agrees that after Tyson builds a house on the lot, he will list the improved property with Fisher. (This is called a "list-back" agreement.)

The developer's requirement in the example is an illegal tie-in arrangement. Note, however, that list-back agreements aren't necessarily illegal. A list-back agreement violates antitrust laws only if signing it is a required condition of the sale. Two parties may mutually agree on a list-back agreement without violating antitrust laws.

Market Allocation. Market allocation occurs when business competitors agree not to sell certain products or services in specified areas or to certain customers in specified areas. This is illegal because it limits competition.

As with group boycotts, it's the collective action that makes market allocation illegal. An individual real estate firm is free to determine the market areas in which it wants to specialize (if any); similarly, the firm can allocate territory to particular licensees affiliated with the firm. Allocation of territory between competing firms, however, is a violation of antitrust law.

> **Example:** ABC Realty assigns Agent Ava to handle all new customers in the luxury home market, and assigns Agent Paxton to all new customers in the vacant land market. This practice does not violate antitrust law.
>
> However, if ABC Realty and XYZ Realty agreed to allocate customers so that ABC Realty will handle all luxury homes and XYZ Realty will handle all vacant land, this would violate antitrust law.

Restrictions on Telephone and Electronic Marketing

Federal and state "do not call" and "anti-spam" laws regulate telephone, fax, email, and text message marketing. They have an impact on the methods real estate agents can use to advertise their services and their clients' properties.

For example, one sales technique that real estate agents sometimes use is **cold calling**, telephoning potential sellers or buyers who have not contacted them first. Real estate agents may not cold call individuals who have registered with the Do Not Call Registry maintained by the Federal Trade Commission (commonly called the Do Not Call list). Violators of this law are subject to substantial fines for each incident.

Even if they're on the Do Not Call list, it's not illegal to call current clients, or to call someone who asked to be contacted by the agent or the real estate firm within the last three months. An agent also doesn't have to check the Do Not Call list before calling a former client within the 18-month period following their last transaction.

Some real estate agents may want to send marketing materials to potential clients by fax. The federal Telephone Consumer Protection Act prohibits sending unsolicited faxes. If an agent already has an established business relationship with a client, the agent may send faxes, but they must include instructions on how to opt out of receiving further faxed communications.

The federal law that restricts commercial electronic messages (email and text messages) is known as the CAN-SPAM Act, which is short for the Controlling the Assault of Non-Solicited Pornography and Marketing Act. Under this law, all commercial emails and texts (not just unsolicited ones) must contain instructions on how to opt out of receiving future messages from the sender.

Chapter Summary

1. Housing discrimination has been a significant part of the nation's history of structural racism. Discriminatory practices in selling and lending created geographic patterns of racial segregation that persist today and make it more difficult for people of color to build and transfer generational wealth.
2. Discrimination in real estate transactions is prohibited by the Civil Rights Act of 1866, the federal Fair Housing Act, the Washington Law Against Discrimination, and the real estate license law.
3. The Civil Rights Act of 1866 prohibits discrimination based on race or color in real estate transactions. The Civil Rights Act of 1964 prohibits discrimination based on race, color, religion, or national origin in programs and activities for which the federal government provided financial assistance.
4. The federal Fair Housing Act prohibits discrimination based on race, color, religion, sex, national origin, disability, or familial status. Unlike the Civil Rights Act of 1866, it applies only to transactions involving residential property.
5. The forms of discrimination prohibited under the federal Fair Housing Act include blockbusting, steering, and redlining. Blockbusting is attempting to obtain listings or encourage sales by predicting the entry of minorities into the neighborhood and implying that this will cause a decline in the neighborhood. Steering is the channeling of buyers or renters to specific neighborhoods based on race or other protected characteristics. Redlining is the refusal to make loans on properties located in a particular area based on the racial or ethnic composition of the area.
6. Federal laws that address discrimination in credit transactions include the Fair Housing Act, the Equal Credit Opportunity Act, and the Home Mortgage Disclosure Act.
7. The Americans with Disabilities Act guarantees people with physical or mental disabilities equal access to public accommodations.
8. The Washington Law Against Discrimination prohibits discrimination based on race, creed, color, national origin, sex, sexual orientation or gender identity, marital status, or familial status; use of a trained guide dog or service animal; honorably discharged veteran or military status, or citizenship and immigration status. It applies not just to housing, but also to employment, insurance, and credit transactions; places of public accommodation; and all types of real property transactions.
9. Antitrust laws prohibit price fixing, group boycotts, tie-in arrangements, and market allocation. Real estate agents should be especially careful to avoid discussing commission rates with competing agents.
10. Real estate agents making cold calls must avoid calling households that have registered with the Do Not Call Registry. Agents must also comply with laws regulating unsolicited faxes (the Telephone Consumer Protection Act) and all commercial emails and text messages (the CAN-SPAM Act).

Key Terms

Blockbusting—Attempting to induce homeowners to list or sell their homes by predicting that members of another race or ethnic group, or people with some type of disability, will be moving into the neighborhood.

Steering—Channeling prospective buyers or tenants toward or away from particular neighborhoods based on their race, religion, or national origin, in order to maintain or change the character of the neighborhoods.

Redlining—Refusing to make a loan because of the racial or ethnic composition of the neighborhood in which the security property is located.

Familial status—Refers to those who have children (persons under 18 years old) living with them. It also includes someone who is pregnant or is in the process of securing custody of a child.

Disability—A physical or mental impairment that substantially limits one or more major life activities.

Public accommodation—A nonresidential place that is owned, operated, or leased by a private entity and is open to the public, such as a real estate office, a doctor's office, a retail store, a restaurant, a hotel, or a theater.

Price fixing—The cooperative setting of prices by competing firms.

Group boycott—An agreement between two or more business competitors to exclude another competitor from fair participation in business activities.

Tie-in arrangement—An agreement in which a seller agrees to sell one product only on the condition that the buyer also purchases a different product.

Market allocation—An agreement between competitors to divide up a market, in which the parties agree that one or both won't sell certain products or services in specified areas, or won't sell to certain customers in specified areas.

Chapter Quiz

1. When a real estate agent channels prospective buyers away from a particular neighborhood because of their race, it is called:

a) blockbusting
b) steering
c) redlining
d) clipping

2. A real estate licensee is helping the Jacksons sell their single-family home. Can this transaction be exempt from the federal Fair Housing Act?

a) Yes, as long as the Jacksons own no more than three single-family homes
b) Yes, as long as no discriminatory advertising is used
c) No, because a real estate agent is involved
d) No, the act applies to all residential sales transactions, without exception

3. The Gardenia Village condominium has a "No Kids" rule. This is not a violation of the federal Fair Housing Act:

a) if the condo qualifies as "housing for older persons" under the terms of the law
b) if no discriminatory advertising is used
c) because age discrimination is not prohibited by the Fair Housing Act
d) because condominiums aren't covered by the Fair Housing Act

4. Title VIII of the Civil Rights Act of 1968 prohibits:

a) discrimination in housing
b) discrimination in residential lending
c) Both a) and b)
d) Neither a) nor b)

5. Blockbusting is an acceptable practice:

a) only under the supervision of real estate licensees
b) only when approved by either HUD or the Justice Department
c) only if the seller and buyer mutually agree
d) under no circumstances

6. For violations of the Washington Law Against Discrimination, complaints should be filed with the:

a) Department of Fair Employment and Housing
b) Washington Human Rights Commission
c) Washington Housing Council
d) Washington Association of REALTORS®

7. The Home Mortgage Disclosure Act helps to enforce the prohibition against:

a) redlining
b) steering
c) blockbusting
d) flipping

8. A landlord who is subject to the provisions of the federal Fair Housing Act must:

a) permit a disabled tenant to make reasonable modifications to the property at the tenant's expense
b) make reasonable exceptions to the landlord's rules to accommodate disabled tenants
c) Both a) and b)
d) Neither a) nor b)

9. Under Washington law, it would be permissible for a landlord to refuse to rent to a prospective tenant because the tenant:

a) has a child
b) was born in Germany
c) has a low income
d) None of the above

10. In comparison to the federal Fair Housing Act, the Washington Law Against Discrimination:

a) protects more classes of people
b) is narrower in scope
c) provides exactly the same coverage
d) has many more exemptions

11. The owners of a single-family home are selling the property without the involvement of a real estate agent and without using discriminatory advertising. The sellers refuse a full-price offer from a married couple, and they make it completely clear that their refusal is based on the couple's sexual orientation. This refusal is:

a) illegal under the federal Fair Housing Act
b) illegal under the Washington Law Against Discrimination
c) legal under both laws
d) illegal under both laws

12. Which of the following is not covered by the federal Fair Housing Act?

a) A commercial property
b) An eight-unit multifamily dwelling
c) A triplex listed for sale with a real estate licensee
d) A vacant lot intended for residential construction

13. A developer who intended to rent housing in a particular development only to persons 45 years of age or over would be in violation of the:

a) Civil Rights Act of 1866
b) Civil Rights Act of 1964
c) Fair Housing Act
d) Americans with Disabilities Act

14. A real estate agent is taking a listing. In their discussion with the seller, which of the following statements would suggest a violation of the Sherman Antitrust Act?

a) "My office typically charges a 6% commission for this type of transaction"
b) "I cannot charge less than the commission rate established by the local MLS"
c) "You'll owe me a commission if the property sells, even if another agent finds the buyer"
d) "My firm's commission rates are lower than those charged by many other firms"

15. Federal antitrust laws apply:

a) only to franchised real estate firms, because of their ability to conspire to restrain trade
b) only to real estate firms large enough to actually affect the real estate market
c) only to individual agents, not to real estate companies
d) to the real estate industry as a whole

Chapter 16:

Property Management

Many real estate firms engage in property management to some degree, so all real estate agents should have a basic knowledge of property management principles. This chapter provides an overview of the property management profession. Since property managers primarily manage investment property, the first section of the chapter discusses the basics of investing in real estate.

The next section describes some of the differences between types of managed properties. After that, we discuss the management agreement, the management plan, and the various functions of a property manager. The final section of the chapter looks at the laws that govern landlord-tenant relationships.

Key Terms

Property Management	**Lease**
Investment	**Automatic Renewal Clause**
Portfolio	**Statement of Operations**
Liquidity	**Rent Roll**
Yield	**Statement of Disbursements**
Appreciation	**Preventive Maintenance**
Equity	**Corrective Maintenance**
Leverage	**Assignment**
Cash Flow	**Sublease**
Rental Schedule	**Novation**
Fixed Expense	**Eviction**
Variable Expense	**Unlawful Detainer**

Property Management as a Profession

While most real estate agents focus primarily on sales transactions, many licensees spend some or all of their time acting as property managers. In this chapter, we'll use the term property manager to refer to someone other than the property owner who supervises the operation of income property in exchange for a fee. Until the 1930s, most real estate investors in the U.S. managed their own properties, perhaps hiring an assistant to collect rents. Then, during the Great Depression, countless borrowers defaulted on their mortgages, and many properties ended up in the hands of lenders. The lenders were saddled with management responsibilities for extensive property holdings, but they had little property management experience. Of necessity, some formed their own property management departments, and others came to depend on the real estate industry to provide the necessary expertise.

Although the lenders eventually resold the properties they acquired during the Depression, the value of efficient property management had been discovered, and increasing numbers of property owners began to use the services of property managers.

Property management became even more important as construction and business practices changed. Better elevators and steel framing allowed the construction of taller structures, so apartment and office buildings became larger. Shopping centers replaced the corner store, and flourishing commercial activity led to the creation of industrial parks. It became increasingly difficult for property owners to manage all of their holdings, and professional, efficient, and effective outside management often became a necessity rather than a luxury.

Investing in Real Estate

A property manager's job typically begins after someone has decided to invest in income-producing property, such as an apartment building, an office building, or a shopping center. As we'll discuss later, the primary function of a property manager is to help the property owner achieve their investment goals. So before we go into the nuts and bolts of property management, let's take a brief look at general investment principles and at real estate as an investment. (A word of caution: real estate agents should not act as investment counselors; they should recommend that clients consult an accountant or an investment specialist for investment advice.)

An investment is an asset that is expected to generate a **return** (a profit). A return on an investment can take various forms, including interest, dividends, rent, or appreciation. An asset appreciates (increases in value) because of inflation (a general increase in prices in the overall economy), and may also appreciate because of a rising demand for the asset. For example, a parcel of prime vacant land appreciates as land suitable for development becomes increasingly scarce.

Different real estate investors might have different investment goals; some might be interested in a steady income stream and would be most focused on maximizing rent, while others might be more interested in wealth building and most focused on the appreciation of their properties. These differences might necessitate different management approaches.

Types of Investments

Investments can be divided into two general categories: ownership investments and debt investments. With **ownership investments**, the investor takes an ownership interest in the asset. Real estate and stocks are examples of ownership investments. The return on ownership investments usually takes the form of dividends, rent, and/or appreciation.

A **debt investment** is essentially a loan that an investor makes to an individual or entity. For example, a bond is a debt owed to an investor by a government entity or corporation. The investor lends the entity money for a set period of time, and in return the entity promises to repay the money on a specific date (the maturity date), along with a certain amount of interest. An ordinary mortgage loan is another example of a debt investment, from the lender's point of view.

Investors often choose to **diversify** their investments—that is, they invest in a variety of different types of investments, instead of putting all their eggs in one basket. The mix of investments that an investor owns is referred to as their **portfolio**.

Investment Characteristics

An investor evaluates any investment opportunity in terms of **safety**, **liquidity**, and **yield** (which is the total return on the investment, or **ROI**). These three characteristics are interrelated. Safety and liquidity tend to go together. On the other hand, for a high return an investor often sacrifices safety or liquidity, or both.

Safety. An investment is considered safe if there's little risk that the investor will actually lose money on it. Even if the investment doesn't generate the return they hopes for, the investor will at least be able to recover the money they originally invested.

Some types of investments are very safe, because they carry a guarantee. The federal deposit insurance that protects funds (up to $250,000) in a bank account is a simple example; it's highly unlikely that a depositor will lose any of the money they put in the bank. On the other hand, some types of investments are inherently risky. For instance, an investor who puts their money into an uncertain venture such as a brand-new company is likely to lose their investment if the company isn't a success.

Liquidity. A **liquid asset** is one that can be converted into cash (liquidated) quickly. Money in a bank account is extremely liquid: to convert it into cash, the investor has only to present the bank with a withdrawal slip or check. Mutual funds, stocks, and bonds are less liquid—they may take a little longer (perhaps a few days) to convert into cash. Other items, such as jewelry or coin collections, aren't considered liquid at all, because an investor might have to wait months to find a buyer and exchange those assets for cash. Similarly, real estate isn't a liquid asset.

As a general rule, the more liquid the asset, the lower the return. For example, the money in an ordinary savings account is very liquid, but it offers only a modest return, in the form of a low rate of interest. If you make a commitment to keep the funds deposited for a specified period (with a certificate of deposit), you'll get a slightly higher rate. A longer period generally means a higher rate of return.

Liquidity is an advantage because the investor can cash in the investment immediately if the funds are needed for an unexpected expense, or if a better investment opportunity arises. Money in a nonliquid investment is effectively "locked up" and unavailable for other purposes. Real estate and other nonliquid assets can be excellent investments, but their lack of liquidity has consequences that a prospective investor should take into account.

Yield. Investments that are both safe and liquid tend to offer the lowest returns. In a sense, investors "pay" for safety and liquidity with a low return. To get a high return, an investor usually must take the risk of losing some or even all of the money originally invested. The investor may also have to sacrifice liquidity, allowing the money to be tied up for a while.

Of course, except with the very safest investments, the yield isn't fixed at the time the investment is made. The yield can change with market conditions, such as an increase or decrease in market interest rates.

As a general rule, the greater the risk, the higher the potential yield needs to be; otherwise investors won't be willing to make the investment. Investors also expect higher yields from long-term investments, as compensation for keeping their money tied up for longer periods of time.

With some types of investments, the return on investment will be much greater if the investor can afford to keep the investment for a long period of time and take advantage of healthy market conditions. This is true of real estate.

Example: Separately, Jeanne and Harold each invested $400,000 in a rental home around the same time and in the same area. One year later, Jeanne desperately needs some cash and is forced to sell her rental home for somewhat less than she paid. After selling expenses, she ends up with only $350,000 out of her original $400,000 investment.

Harold, on the other hand, keeps his rental home for 12 years. He's in no hurry to sell his property, so he can wait for optimal market conditions. He sells at the peak of a real estate cycle, when property values are high. Because Harold could choose when to sell his property, he walks away from the transaction with a net gain of $90,000, a healthy return on his original $400,000 investment.

Advantages of Investing in Real Estate

People invest in real estate for many reasons. The advantages of investing in real estate can be broken down into three general categories:

- appreciation,
- leverage, and
- cash flow.

Appreciation. When property **appreciates**, that means it is increasing in value due to changes in the economy or other outside factors. Although real estate values fluctuate, over a period of several years real estate tends to appreciate at a rate equal to or higher than the rate of inflation. And when buildable property becomes scarce, the value of properties in prime locations may increase more rapidly.

Appreciation causes a property owner's equity to increase. **Equity** is the difference between the value of the property and the liens against it, so an increase in the property's value increases the owner's equity in the property. Also, each monthly mortgage payment typically increases the owner's equity, by reducing the loan's remaining principal balance. Equity adds to the investor's net worth and can also be used to secure an equity loan. So even though real estate isn't considered a liquid asset, equity in real estate can be used to generate cash funds.

Leverage. Real estate investors can take advantage of **leverage**, which means using borrowed money to invest in an asset. If the asset appreciates, then the investor earns money on the money borrowed as well as the money they invested.

Fig. 16.1 Investing in Real Estate

Advantages of Real Estate Investment
• Appreciation • Leverage • Cash flow

Example: Martha buys a rental home for $215,000. She makes a 25% downpayment ($53,750) and borrows the rest of the price. The rent the property generates covers all operating expenses, plus the mortgage payment and income taxes. The property appreciates at almost 3% per year for five years, and then Martha sells it for $249,000, clearing $86,750 after paying off her mortgage.

Over five years, she's made a $33,000 profit ($86,750 – $53,750 = $33,000). This represents a 61% return on her investment ($33,000 ÷ $53,750 = 0.61), which averages out to a 12.2% annual return over the five-year period. The property appreciated at 3% per year, but because she only invested 25% of the purchase price, Martha was able to generate a much more substantial return on the investment than 3%.

Cash Flow. Many real estate investments generate a positive cash flow, in addition to appreciating in value. **Cash flow** is spendable income. For income-producing properties, it's the amount of money left after all the property's expenses have been paid, including operating costs, mortgage payments, and taxes. When a real estate investment generates a positive cash flow, the investor's monthly income increases. Thus, a real estate investment can increase both the investor's net worth (through appreciation) and their income (through positive cash flow).

Investors sometimes use the term "cash on cash," which refers to a property's annual cash flow divided by the initial investment; that's one way for an investor to calculate their rate of return. Rental income is the main way a property can generate cash flow.

Another way a property can generate cash is through a **sale-leaseback** arrangement. In a sale-leaseback, the owner of a building used in the owner's business sells the building to an investor, but then leases it back from the investor and continues to use it. The money generated by the sale can be used for expansion, acquiring inventory, or investment elsewhere. At the same time, the seller can deduct the rent paid to lease the property from their income taxes as a business expense. Sometimes a sale-leaseback arrangement also includes a **buyback agreement**, in which it's agreed that the seller will buy the property back for its fair market value after a certain number of years.

Types of Managed Properties

Now let's turn to our discussion of property management. We'll start with the different types of properties that a property manager may be called upon to manage. There are four basic types of income-producing property:

1. residential,
2. office,
3. retail, and
4. industrial.

Each type of property has unique characteristics and demands a different kind of management expertise, so property managers often specialize in one particular type of property. In the following paragraphs, we'll discuss some of the differences between property types.

Apartment buildings, the most common kind of residential rental property, typically offer month-to-month or one-year leases. That means they have a much higher turnover rate than industrial property, where leases often run for 20 years or more. As a result, residential property managers tend to spend more of their time on marketing and leasing. Residential property managers also must fulfill the legal responsibilities imposed by Washington's Residential Landlord-Tenant Act, which is designed to protect residential tenants.

Office buildings have very different housekeeping requirements from residential buildings. Office buildings endure much heavier foot traffic; they have facilities that get continuous use (such as washrooms and elevators) and thus need frequent cleaning; and management is often responsible for cleaning the tenants' spaces as well as the common areas. Lease negotiations are also very different for office space than for residential space. Office tenants generally have more clout than residential tenants, and almost any aspect of an office lease might involve back-and-forth bargaining. Landlords commonly offer major concessions to attract office tenants, such as free rent for a limited period or a large allowance for extensive remodeling.

Leasing space to an appropriate tenant is a concern with any type of property, but it's especially important for property managers who specialize in retail property, particularly shopping centers. The success of each tenant in a shopping center depends in part on the customers that each of the other tenants attract, so it's vital to lease to strong, compatible tenants. Also, a portion of the rent is usually based on the store's income, so the owner has a vested interest in the financial success of each tenant. The tenant mix must appeal to the widest variety of potential shoppers, while avoiding too much direct competition within the shopping center itself.

These are only some of the ways in which property types differ. But even from these few examples, it's easy to see that the different types of properties require very different management plans. Most property managers specialize in one or two property types for this reason.

However, there are general management principles that apply to any type of income property. Our discussion will focus mainly on managing residential properties, but most of the principles and practices we'll be describing apply to the other types of property as well.

Fig. 16.2 Income-Producing Properties

Types of Income Properties
Residential (rental homes and apartments) **Office** (office buildings and office parks) **Retail** (stores and shopping centers) **Industrial** (industrial parks)

The Management Agreement

The first step in the management process is for the property owner and the property manager to enter into a **management agreement.** This contract establishes and defines their working relationship. In the same way that a listing agreement creates an agency relationship between a seller and a real estate firm offering brokerage services, the management agreement creates an agency relationship between a property owner and a firm offering property management services. And in the same way a firm designates an affiliated licensee to work with a seller, a firm will also designate one or more of its affiliated licensees to provide management services for the property owner. For purposes of this discussion we'll use the term "property manager" to refer to the individual licensee who performs duties for the property owner on behalf of the real estate firm.

The management agreement must be in writing and signed by both parties, and the document should set forth all of the terms of their agreement. It's especially important for the exact duties and powers of the manager to be explicitly stated. What kinds of decisions can the manager freely make, and what kinds must be referred to the owner? For example, suppose several units in an apartment building need new carpets.

Can the manager replace the carpets without consulting the owner, or is this a decision that the owner wants to make? Other areas in which questions might arise include the authority to execute leases, make major repairs, choose an insurance company and policy for the property, or embark on a major advertising campaign.

At a minimum, the management agreement should include:

- the term of the agreement;
- the manager's compensation (a percentage of gross income, a commission on new rentals, a fixed fee, or a combination of all of these);
- the type of property and its legal description;
- the number of units or square footage;
- the manager's duties;
- the scope of the manager's authority; and
- how frequent and how detailed the manager's reports to the owner will be.

In most cases, the management agreement authorizes the property manager to collect rents and to hold and refund tenants' security deposits. It usually also authorizes them to pay expenses related to the management of the property, so that they can purchase supplies, pay contractors for routine repairs, and so forth.

The property manager must bear in mind that after the management agreement is signed, an agency relationship exists between the manager and the owner, and thus the manager is bound by all the duties of an agent (see Chapter 7). Also note that, as with listing and buyer agency agreements, it is the firm who "owns" the management agreement, not the affiliated licensee.

The Management Plan

Once a manager has entered into a management agreement, the actual business of managing begins. The first (and often most important) step in managing a property is drawing up a **management plan**. A management plan outlines the manager's strategy for financial management and physical upkeep, and focuses on achieving the owner's goals.

It's important to remember that there are many different reasons for investing in income property—different property owners have different management goals. For instance, one property owner may simply want a steady, reliable stream of income. Another owner may want to address some of the property's cosmetic problems, to get it ready for a quick sale. Another may want to increase the property's long-term value in order to reap a bigger profit in later years. An owner's goals can also change over the period of ownership.

Example: When he's in his early 40s, Greg decides to buy a small apartment building. He has other sources of income, so he regards the building as a long-term investment and is willing to spend money on major improvements. However, as the years pass, Greg's needs change. When he retires, he is suddenly more interested in maximizing his cash flow from the apartment building. The management plan for the property needs to be revised to reflect Greg's new goals.

Preliminary Study

A management plan can be created only after a comprehensive study of all of the facets of the property, including its location, its physical characteristics, its financial status, and its policies of operation. This preliminary study includes a regional analysis, a neighborhood analysis, a property analysis, and a market analysis.

Regional Analysis. Preparing a management plan begins with a study of the region (the city or metropolitan area) in which the property is located. The manager analyzes the general economic conditions, physical attributes, and population growth and distribution. Among the most significant considerations are trends in occupancy rates, market rental rates, employment levels, and (for residential property) family size and lifestyle.

Occupancy Rates. According to the law of supply and demand, when the demand for an item is greater than the supply, the price or value of the item increases. And when the supply exceeds the demand, the price or value of the item decreases. This basic rule applies to rental properties just as it applies to other commodities.

From a property manager's point of view, the supply of rental units is the total number of units available for occupancy in the area where the managed property is located. The demand for rental units is the total number of potential tenants in that area who are able to pay the rent for those units. When demand exceeds supply, rental rates go up; when supply exceeds demand, rental rates go down.

To set rental rates for a managed property, a property manager must determine the occupancy trend for the area. If the trend is toward higher occupancy levels, the value of the units will increase as space grows more scarce. It is during these times that managers raise rents and reduce services. On the other hand, if there is a trend toward higher vacancy rates, a unit's value will decrease. In periods of high vacancy, tenants are likely to resist rent increases or make more demands for services or repairs when leases are renewed.

Occupancy levels fluctuate constantly based on a mixture of national, regional, and local factors. The direction and speed of the changes have a significant impact on the property manager's operating and marketing policies.

Market Rental Rates. In addition to evaluating occupancy trends, a property manager should keep track of market rental rates, the rates currently charged for comparable rental units. The manager should set rental rates for the managed units at a level that will make them competitive.

Various published reports provide information about rental rates; for example, the Bureau of Labor Statistics publishes data on rents paid for residential units. A property manager may also collect data on local rental rates from rental advertising and from other online resources. This research can give the manager a basic picture of market trends.

Labor Force. A property manager should be aware of local employment trends, since employment levels and the size of the labor force affect how many potential tenants can afford to rent. The manager should also know whether earnings are increasing or decreasing. Falling wages place downward pressure on rents.

Family Size and Lifestyle. Family size has a great deal to do with the value of particular residential units. If the average family size were three (two parents and one child), five-bedroom units would have less appeal and two-bedroom units would be very attractive. Thus, the two-bedroom units would command a higher price per square foot than the five-bedroom units. A property manager needs to be aware of the national trend toward smaller and even single-person households, and also any local trends in family size and lifestyle.

Neighborhood Analysis. After the regional analysis, the next step in the preliminary study is to analyze the neighborhood where the property is located. The definition of a neighborhood varies considerably from one place to another. In rural areas, a neighborhood may consist of many square miles. In an urban area, a neighborhood may be only a few blocks.

The qualities of the neighborhood have a significant bearing on the property's value and use. Important neighborhood characteristics include:

- the level of maintenance (whether buildings and grounds are well cared for);
- an increasing or decreasing population; and
- the economic status of the residents.

A property manager should discover the reasons behind any neighborhood trends. Is the population density increasing because of new multifamily developments, or because large old single-family homes are being divided into apartments? The construction of new apartments is a sign of economic prosperity; the division of houses into apartments is not.

A neighborhood analysis helps a property manager factor location into the management plan. No matter how effectively a property is operated, its location has a strong impact on its profitability. Realistic management goals must take location into account.

Property Analysis. Of course, to develop a management plan, the manager must become very familiar with the physical characteristics of the property itself. They will inspect the property, noting its architectural design, physical condition, facilities, and general layout.

The following characteristics are particularly important:

- the number and size of the living units, or the number of rentable square feet;
- the appearance of the property and the rental spaces (age, architectural style, layout, view, fixtures);
- the physical condition of the building (roof, elevators, windows);
- the physical condition of the rental spaces (floor coverings, stairways, shades or blinds, walls, entryways);
- the amenities provided (exercise facilities, storage units);
- the services provided (janitorial services, repair services, security);
- the relationship of the land to the building (Is the land used efficiently? Is there adequate parking?);
- the occupancy rate and tenant composition; and
- the size and efficiency of the staff.

Market Analysis. The last step in the preliminary study for a management plan is the market analysis, which provides information on competing properties. To do a market analysis, the manager must first define the pertinent market. The major divisions of the real estate market are residential, office, retail, and industrial. Each of these can be broken down into subcategories. For instance, the residential market can be divided into single-family rental homes, duplexes, townhouses, walk-up apartments, small multistory apartments, and large apartment complexes.

Once the manager has identified the market that the managed property competes in, several characteristics must be examined:

- the number of units available in the area;
- the average age and character of the buildings in which the units are located;
- the quality of the average unit in the market (size, condition, layout, facilities);
- the number of potential tenants in the area;
- the current price for the average unit; and
- the average occupancy rate.

The property manager compares the managed property to comparable properties in the neighborhood to derive an understanding of the managed property's advantages and disadvantages. Armed with this information, the manager can establish an effective management strategy.

The Management Proposal

After completing the preliminary study, the property manager develops a management proposal and submits it to the property owner for approval. The manager's proposal includes a rental schedule, income and expense projections, a schedule of day-to-day operations, and perhaps suggestions for physical changes to the property itself.

Rental Schedule. A rental schedule lists all the various types of units and their rental rates. For example, an apartment building may consist of studio apartments, one-bedroom apartments, and two-bedroom apartments. Some apartments may have views, others may not. Rental rates will vary accordingly.

Rental schedules are based on all the data collected during the regional, neighborhood, property, and market analyses. This information helps the manager determine the highest rent that can be charged while maintaining the optimum occupancy level. To set the rate for a particular type of unit, the manager can adjust the market rental rate for the average comparable unit up or down to reflect the differences between the comparable and the type of unit in question. Because this method of setting rates depends on market conditions, the rental schedule should be reexamined periodically to see if it's still current. Either an unusually high vacancy rate or an unusually low vacancy rate indicates that the property's rental rates are out of line with the community. If the vacancy rate is high, the rent may be too expensive; if the vacancy rate is unusually low, the rent may be below the norm.

Budgets. The property manager also sets up a budget of income and operating expenses (see Figure 16.3). The manager lists the total value of all rentable space at the scheduled rental rates, then subtracts a figure for projected delinquent rental payments and vacancies (sometimes called a vacancy factor). Any other income sources, such as laundry facilities, vending machines, or parking, should also be listed.

Next, the estimated operating expenses—both fixed expenses and variable expenses—are listed. **Fixed expenses** include such items as property taxes, insurance premiums, and employee salaries. **Variable expenses** include utilities, maintenance, and repairs.

Finally, the manager deducts projected operating expenses from projected revenues to arrive at a cash flow figure.

Day-to-Day Operations. In addition to long-range financial planning, the management proposal should include the manager's plans for the property's day-to-day operations. The manager has to decide how much (if any) staffing will be required and what the employment policies and procedures will be.

Physical Alterations. In some cases, the property manager's proposal will include recommendations for remodeling, rehabilitation, or other physical alterations to the property. For instance, after a thorough examination of the property, the customer base, and the market, a manager might decide that the property would be worth much more if the building were altered to match current lifestyles in the area.

Example: In a medium-density urban neighborhood where most of the residents own cars but street parking is at a premium, an older building lacks a parking lot. There is a large lawn on one side of the building, however. If the lawn were replaced with parking spaces, that could attract more potential tenants, and also, if monthly parking fees are charged, provide a new revenue stream for the building owner.

Owner's Approval. Once completed, the management proposal is presented to the property owner. When the proposal is approved, it becomes the management plan: the blueprint for managing the property.

Management Functions

Property managers carry out a wide variety of management duties. They have to market the property, negotiate leases, and handle tenant relations. They must keep detailed financial records and prepare regular reports for the property owner. Finally, they need to arrange for the maintenance and repairs that will preserve the value of the property.

Leasing and Tenant Relations

The tasks involved in leasing and tenant relations include marketing the rental spaces, negotiating leases, addressing tenants' complaints, and collecting rents.

Marketing. Property managers generally use advertising to bring potential tenants to their properties. The more people who view a rental space, the more likely it is to be leased, and leased to a good tenant.

Different types of properties require different types and amounts of advertising. For some properties, advertising is necessary only when there's a vacancy to fill. In fact, if the property is attractive and in a prominent location, advertising may not be necessary at all. On the other hand, if the property is in an isolated location, continuous advertising of a general nature may be required to generate enough interest to fill vacancies when they occur.

Successful advertising brings in a good number of potential tenants in the least amount of time for the lowest cost. Property managers often evaluate the effectiveness of their advertising in terms of the number of potential tenants for the advertising dollars spent. For example, based on experience, a property manager might have a general rule of thumb that the cost of advertising shouldn't exceed $30 per prospect. Thus, newspaper advertising that costs $300 should bring at least ten prospective tenants to the property.

To reach the greatest number of potential tenants for the lowest possible cost, the property manager must be familiar with the various types of advertising and know which will be most effective for the property in question. The manager may consider using signs, online ads and websites, newspaper ads, direct mail, or some combination of these tools.

Signs. Small, tasteful signs on the property are often used, whether there is a vacancy or not, to inform passersby of the name of the management firm and how to acquire rental information. The use of signs is most successful for office buildings, large apartment complexes, and shopping centers.

Online Advertising. Almost all properties are advertised online using sites such as Zillow and Craigslist. At little or no cost, the ads can include photographs of the property, maps, and other information that would be too costly to include in print advertising.

Fig. 16.3 Operating Budget

	Jan	Feb	Mar	Apr	May	June	July	Aug	Sept	Oct	Nov	Dec	Annual
Income													
Scheduled Rents													
Less:													
Vacancies													
Rent Loss													
Effective Rent													
Miscellaneous Income													
Total Income													
Expenses													
Administrative													
Management Costs													
Other Adm. Costs													
Operating													
Payroll													
Supplies													
Heating													
Electricity													
Water and Sewer													
Gas													
Maintenance													
Grounds													
Maint. and Repairs													
Painting, Decorating													
Taxes and Insurance													
Real Estate Taxes													
Other Taxes, Fees													
Insurance													
Contract Service													
Total Expenses													
Net Operating Income													
Less Reserves													
Net Income													
Less Debt Service													
Cash Flow													

Most property managers maintain a website to advertise the properties that they manage. Also, in many cases a website dedicated to a particular apartment complex, office building, or other property makes sense.

Newspaper Advertising. Newspaper advertising includes classified ads and display ads. **Classified ads** (relatively inexpensive line-type advertising that appears in the "classified" section of the newspaper) are the traditional way to advertise residential rental space, although in many cases newspaper advertising has given way to online advertising.

Display ads are larger and more expensive than classified ads. A display ad often includes a photograph of the property, and it may appear in any section of the newspaper. Display advertising might be used to advertise space in a new office building, industrial park, or shopping center.

Direct Mail. To be effective, direct mail advertising must be sent to potential tenants, not just to the general public. So a property manager who wants to use direct mail must compile or purchase a mailing list. With a good mailing list and a brochure designed to appeal to prospective tenants, direct mail can be an effective advertising method. Also, the same brochure can be handed out to those who visit the property.

Leasing. A prospect has seen an advertisement and comes to look at the available rental space. Now it's the property manager's job to convince the prospect that the rental space is desirable. They will usually tour the property together, and during the tour the manager will emphasize the property's positive qualities and amenities. The manager will point out traffic patterns and access to public transportation, the characteristics of the other tenants, the exterior and interior condition of the property, and its overall cleanliness. If it's commercial property, the manager and the prospect may discuss how the space could be altered to suit the prospect's needs, and how additional space could be incorporated if the tenant needs to expand.

After the tour, if the prospect is still interested in the property, it's the property manager's responsibility to make sure that the prospect is qualified to lease it. Although financial stability is a key consideration, it's not the only one. The manager must also decide whether the prospect is likely to be a responsible and cooperative tenant.

At a minimum, this involves checking the prospect's references and contacting the previous landlord. The manager can also use their own judgment, but must be very careful to avoid violating antidiscrimination laws (see Chapter 15).

If the manager (and/or the owner, depending on how authority is allocated in the management agreement) decides in favor of the prospect, the next step is to sign a rental agreement or lease. The requirements for a valid lease are explained later in this chapter, in the discussion of landlord-tenant law.

Lease Renewal. Unless the tenant has caused problems, a property manager would much rather renew an existing lease than find a new tenant. Renewal avoids a vacancy between the time one tenant moves out and another moves in. A rental property has greater stability with long-term tenants, and it's usually easier and less expensive to satisfy the requirements of an existing tenant than to improve the space for a new tenant.

A property manager should always be aware of which tenants are nearing the end of their lease term and notify them that their lease is about to expire. With commercial properties, the manager should follow up on the notice, by phone or in person, to ask if the tenants want to renew. If so, the terms of the new lease must be negotiated.

Some leases contain an **automatic renewal clause**, which provides that the lease will be automatically renewed on the same terms unless one party notifies the other of their intent to terminate the lease. Absent a renewal of the lease, residential tenancies sometimes continue on a month-to-month basis.

Tenant Complaints. Of course, keeping tenants happy is a crucial part of the property manager's job. Making sure that the property is kept clean and in good repair is essential, and so is responding promptly and professionally to requests and complaints.

Rent Collection. Rental property can't be profitable unless the rents are collected when due. Careful selection of tenants in the first place is the most effective way to avoid delinquent rents. A high occupancy rate doesn't benefit the property owner unless the tenants meet their financial obligations.

The amount of the rent, the time and place of rent payment, and any penalties imposed for late payment should be clearly stated in the lease. The manager should consistently follow a collection plan that includes adequate recordkeeping and immediate notification of late payments. When all collection attempts fail, the manager must be prepared to take legal action to evict the tenant in accordance with the owner's policies.

Recordkeeping and Manager/Owner Relations

A property manager must account to the owner for all money received and disbursed. It's up to the owner to decide how frequent and detailed operating reports should be. This often depends on how involved the owner wants to be in the management of the property.

For example, an owner with extensive property holdings who is also engaged in another full-time occupation may not want to be bothered with detailed, time-consuming reports. But a retired person with only one or two income-producing properties may want to be very involved in their management, and will therefore want a lot of information.

Statement of Operations. In many cases, the property manager's report to the owner takes the form of a monthly statement of operations. A statement of operations typically includes the following sections: a summary of operations, the rent roll, a statement of disbursements, and a narrative report of operations.

The **summary of operations** is a brief description of the property's income and expenses that makes it easier for the owner to evaluate the property's monthly financial performance. The summary is supported by the accompanying information in the rest of the statement of operations.

The **rent roll** is a report on rent collection (see Figure 16.4). Both occupied and vacant units are listed in the rent roll, as well as the total rental income, both collected and uncollected. The rent roll breaks down rental figures into the previous balance, current rent, total amount received, and balance due.

The information in the rent roll is obtained from the individual ledger sheets kept on each tenant and rental space. A ledger sheet typically shows the tenant's name, unit, email address and phone number, regular rent, other recurring charges, security deposit information, move-in date, lease term, payments made, and balances owed. Property management software makes it easy to maintain all this information.

Fig. 16.4 Rent Roll

Rent Roll

Property *Magnolia Heights* **Period** *April*

Owner *S.T. Jones* **Prepared by** *M. Smith*

Unit Number	Occupant	Previous Balance	Current Rent	Date Received	Other Amounts	Description	Total Received	Balance Due
101	G. Tsui	0	900	4/1			900	0
102	F. Brown	700	700	4/9			1400	0
103	K. Plane	0	700	4/2	100	Parking	800	0
104	C. Flynn	0	850	4/1			850	0
105	P. Sneed	850	850	4/15			850	850
106	L. Hurt	0	850	4/1	100	Parking	950	0
107	E. Winn	0	700	4/2			700	0

The **statement of disbursements** lists all of the expenses paid during the pertinent time period. A written order should be prepared for every purchase so that an accurate accounting can be made of all expenditures and the purpose of each one. Disbursements are usually classified according to type, which makes analysis easier. For example, maintenance expenses, tax and insurance expenses, and administrative expenses are each grouped separately.

In addition to the numerical accounts given to the owner, it's often helpful to include a **narrative report of operations** in the statement of operations. This is simply a letter explaining the information set forth in the other sections of the statement. The narrative report can add a personal touch, and it's especially important if the income was lower or the expenses were higher than expected. If there is a deviation from the normal cash flow, the owner will want a clear explanation. If the reason for a drop in cash flow is not explained, the owner may doubt the competence or integrity of the property manager.

Keeping in Touch. In addition to sending various reports and statements to the owner, the manager should contact the owner in person from time to time. A telephone call or an appointment to explain a particular proposal or problem or to ask a question is often much more effective than an email or a letter. A formal meeting is a good idea if the monthly report is especially unusual.

Maintenance

In addition to leasing, tenant relations, recordkeeping, and reporting to the owner, a property manager also supervises property maintenance. There are four basic categories of maintenance:

1. **Preventive maintenance:** This preserves the physical integrity of the property and reduces corrective maintenance costs. (Cleaning the gutters is an example of preventive maintenance.)
2. **Corrective maintenance:** Actual repairs that keep equipment, utilities, and amenities functioning properly. (Fixing a leaking faucet is an example of corrective maintenance.)
3. **Housekeeping:** Cleaning the common areas and grounds on a regular basis (for example, vacuuming hallways and cleaning elevators).
4. **New construction:** This includes tenant alterations made at the beginning of the tenancy and when the lease is renewed, as well as cosmetic changes designed to make the building more attractive (for example, remodeling the lobby).

Most maintenance activities are handled by building maintenance employees or by outside maintenance services. However, a property manager must be able to recognize the maintenance needs of the property and see that they are fulfilled.

The property manager should direct the activities of the maintenance staff or independent contractors by giving them an inspection and maintenance schedule. First, the manager should inventory the building's equipment and physical elements (such as the plumbing, furnace, roof, and walls). Then they should set a schedule of regular inspections, cleaning, and repairs.

For instance, walls and roofs should be scheduled for periodic inspection, painting, and repairs. Elevators and fire control systems should be serviced on a regular basis.

The property manager should keep accurate records of when the various elements were inspected, serviced, replaced, or repaired (see Figure 16.5). These routine inspections and maintenance activities will help preserve the value of the building and prevent major repair expenses, and records concerning them can also be important evidence in a lawsuit.

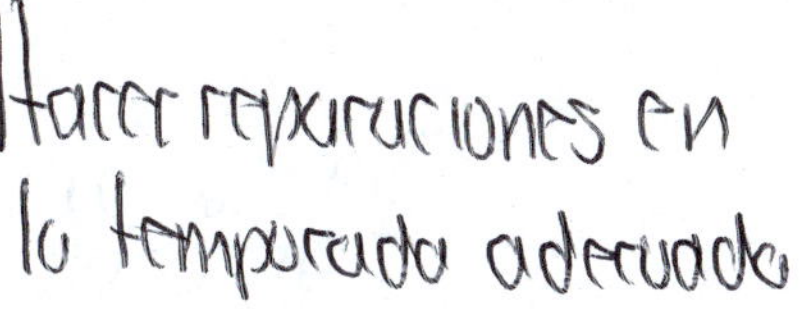

Fig. 16.5 Property Maintenance Record

Property Maintenance Record

Property *Magnolia Heights*

Date	Action	Location	by Whom	Time	Cost
4/12	inspect elevator	lobby	Elevator Express	1.5 hr.	contract
4/22	clean roof	roof	Johnson	5 hr.	contract
4/23	fix drain	Unit 104	Top Plumbing	1 hr.	$125

When managing commercial property, a property manager often has to alter the interior of the building to meet the needs of a new tenant. These alterations can range from a simple repainting job to completely redesigning or rebuilding the space. (If the property is new construction, the interior is often left incomplete so that it can be built out to fit the needs of particular tenants.) Property managers dealing with remodeling or new construction must be aware that federal law requires places of public accommodation and other commercial facilities to be accessible to the disabled. (See the discussion of the Americans with Disabilities Act in Chapter 15.)

Landlord-Tenant Law

Property managers need to understand the rules that govern the relationship between landlord and tenant. Both the lease and the law define this relationship. In this final section, we'll look at the requirements for a valid lease, the various issues a lease typically addresses, and the impact of landlord-tenant law on leasing.

Requirements for a Valid Lease

A **lease** is a contract between a property owner (the landlord) and a tenant that gives the tenant possession of the property for a period of time, in exchange for rent. The lease must meet all of the requirements for a valid contract (see Chapter 6), and it must include an unambiguous description of the property. Leases are also called **rental agreements**; that's especially common in residential tenancies.

In Washington, a lease for any fixed term must be in writing and signed by the property owner. If the term is over one year, the owner's signature must be acknowledged (notarized).

A rental agreement for a periodic tenancy, such as a month-to-month tenancy, does not have to be put in writing unless the rental period is more than one year or the property is managed by a real estate firm. (All leases or rental agreements for properties managed by a real estate firm must be in writing.) Of course, even when a written lease isn't legally required, it's preferable to have one.

A lease that should be in writing, but is not, creates a periodic tenancy instead of a lease for a fixed term. (See Chapter 2 for a discussion of the different types of leasehold estates.)

A written lease may be valid even if the tenant doesn't sign it; the tenant's acceptance of the lease is implied by occupancy and payment of rent. Even so, to protect both parties, it's better to have both property owner and tenant sign the lease.

In many cases, the management agreement authorizes the property manager to sign leases as the landlord's agent. Without such a specific authorization, the property manager's signature may not create a valid lease.

Lease Provisions

Now let's discuss some key lease provisions. Note that provisions in residential leases must comply with Washington's Residential Landlord-Tenant Act, and also with any similar local laws that may apply.

Payment of Rent. The consideration that the tenant gives the landlord for the lease is the promise to pay rent. Most leases require payment at the beginning of the rental period. If a lease does not specify when the rent is to be paid, it's due at the end of the rental period.

Use of Premises. Unless a lease includes use restrictions, the tenant may use the property for any legal purpose. Many leases do impose use restrictions, however; for example, a lease for a space in a mall might have a provision restricting the space to a particular kind of retail use, in order to preserve the tenant mix.

The restricting language must be clear, and it should state that the leased premises are to be used only for the specified purpose and for no other.

Security Deposit. Most leases require the tenant to provide a **security deposit** at the beginning of the tenancy. When the tenancy ends, the landlord or property manager may use the deposit to cover unpaid rent, or to pay for cleaning or repairing the premises. But no portion of the deposit may be kept to pay for the cleaning or repair to mitigate normal wear and tear resulting from ordinary use of the property.

In Washington, a residential landlord or property manager can require a security deposit only if there's a written lease or rental agreement. The tenant must be given a written checklist describing the condition and cleanliness of the unit at the beginning of the tenancy. Both the landlord (or manager) and the tenant must sign the checklist, indicating that they agree about the unit's initial condition.

The landlord or manager must place the tenant's security deposit in a trust account and give the tenant a receipt for the funds. At the end of the tenancy, the landlord or manager must return the entire security deposit to the tenant within 30 days after the lease terminates, or else provide a written explanation of the specific reasons why all or part of the deposit is being retained. Receipts or invoices must be presented to provide evidence of the specific costs that are withheld.

Any nonrefundable fee (such as a nonrefundable cleaning fee) must be designated "nonrefundable" in the lease. It may not be referred to as a deposit.

Entry and Inspection. A lease typically provides for inspection of the leased premises by the landlord or property manager under specified conditions. In Washington, a residential tenant may not unreasonably refuse legitimate requests to enter the unit to inspect it, perform repairs, provide other agreed-upon services, or show the unit to prospective buyers or tenants. Except in an emergency, the landlord or manager must give the tenant notice before entering the unit. Two days' notice is usually required, but only one day's notice is necessary if the unit is going to be shown.

Option to Renew. A lease may contain a provision that gives the tenant an option to renew the lease at the end of its term. Most options require the tenant to give notice of their intention to exercise the option on or before a specific date.

Maintenance. The tenant must return the premises to the landlord in the same condition they were in at the beginning of the tenancy, except for normal wear and tear. If the tenant is responsible for damage beyond normal wear and tear, they can be required to pay for the repair of that damage. The landlord is usually responsible for maintaining the building common areas, such as the stairs, hallways, or elevators.

Transferring Leasehold Estates

A landlord can sell the leased property during the term of the lease, but the buyer takes title subject to the lease. This means the buyer must honor the lease for the remainder of its term.

A tenant can also transfer their leasehold estate to another party, through assignment, subleasing, or novation.

The tenant has the right to assign or sublease without the landlord's consent, unless the lease says otherwise (most leases do require the landlord's consent). A novation always requires the landlord's consent.

In an **assignment**, the tenant transfers the leasehold estate to another party for the entire remainder of the lease term.

> **Example:** Landlord leases office space to Tenant for a five-year period. A year after the leasehold begins, Tenant transfers possession of the leased space to XYZ Corporation for the remaining four years. The agreement between Tenant and XYZ is an assignment, because the transfer is for the balance of the unexpired term.

The assignee (the new tenant) becomes liable to the landlord for the rent, and the original tenant becomes secondarily liable for the rent. The assignee has the primary responsibility for paying the rent, but the original tenant is not fully released from the duty to pay it.

In a **sublease**, the original tenant transfers only part of their remaining interest. They may be giving the subtenant (the new tenant) the right to share possession with them, or the right to possess only part of the leased property. Or they may be giving the subtenant the right to possess the whole property, but for only part of the unexpired term.

> **Example:** Landlord leases office space to Tenant for a five-year period. A year after the leasehold begins, Tenant transfers possession of the leased space to XYZ Corporation, but reserves the last year for themself. This agreement is a sublease, because Tenant has transferred less than the full balance of the leasehold.

The subtenant (also called the sublessee) is liable for the rent to the original tenant, rather than to the landlord, and the original tenant is still liable to the landlord. This arrangement is sometimes referred to as a **sandwich lease**, since the original tenant is in the middle, sandwiched between the landlord and the subtenant.

A **novation** is an alternative to an assignment or a sublease. In a novation, a new contract is created and the old contract is extinguished. A landlord might agree to accept a new tenant in place of the original tenant, creating a new lease. The purpose of a novation is to terminate the liability of the tenant under the terms of the original lease.

Terminating a Leasehold Interest

As was discussed in Chapter 2, how a lease terminates depends on the type of tenancy in question. A month-to-month tenancy or other periodic tenancy ordinarily ends when either party gives the other party proper notice of termination. A lease for a fixed term ordinarily terminates automatically at the end of its term. (Note that for residential tenancies,

Washington's just cause eviction law has significantly modified these traditional rules. See Chapter 2.) A fixed-term lease may also terminate before the end of its term in any of the following ways.

Surrender. A landlord and a tenant may mutually agree to terminate a lease. This is known as surrender.

Breach of Covenant of Quiet Enjoyment. Every lease carries an **implied covenant of quiet enjoyment**. This covenant is the landlord's promise that the tenant's possession of the property will not be disturbed, either by the landlord or by a third party with a lawful claim to the property. The tenant is guaranteed exclusive possession and quiet enjoyment of their leasehold estate. The covenant may be expressly stated in the lease, but it applies whether it appears in the lease or not. (That's why it's referred to as an implied covenant.)

The covenant of quiet enjoyment is breached when the tenant is wrongfully evicted from the leased property. There are two types of eviction: actual and constructive.

Actual eviction occurs when the landlord actually expels the tenant from the property. **Constructive eviction** occurs when the landlord causes or permits a substantial interference with the tenant's possession of the property. For example, a landlord's failure to provide running water to a residence is a constructive eviction.

Breach of Warranty of Habitability. By law, all residential leases carry an **implied warranty of habitability**. This is the landlord's implied guarantee that the premises meet all building and housing code regulations that affect health and safety. If the premises do not meet these criteria, then the tenant must notify the landlord of the defective condition and the landlord must correct it within a certain time period prescribed by statute. If the landlord takes legal action to evict the tenant for nonpayment of rent, the tenant can use the poor condition of the premises as a defense in court.

Failure to Pay Rent. The tenant has a duty to pay rent as required by the terms of the lease. However, if the tenant fails to pay the rent, that doesn't automatically terminate the leasehold. The landlord is required by statute to give notice to the tenant of the nonpayment. After receiving notice, if the tenant still fails to pay, the landlord may file an **unlawful detainer action**, asking the court to evict the tenant.

If the court finds the tenant in default, it may issue a **writ of restitution** (or writ of possession), which requires the tenant to move out peaceably or be forcibly removed by the county sheriff.

Although unlawful detainer actions are given priority on the court's docket, the legal process of eviction may seem slow to a landlord or property manager. However, landlords and property managers should not take matters into their own hands.

Someone who tries "self-help" eviction (forcing a tenant out with threats, or by changing the locks or cutting off the utilities) instead of using the legal process could end up facing a costly lawsuit.

Illegal or Unauthorized Use. If a tenant uses the leased premises in an illegal manner (for example, in violation of the zoning code), the landlord may demand that the tenant cease the illegal activity or leave the premises. Even if a tenant uses the premises in a legal manner, if that particular use isn't authorized by the lease, then the tenant has violated the lease and the landlord can terminate the tenancy.

Destruction of the Premises. Destruction of the leased premises by a fire or other natural disaster generally terminates a lease. If the lease is for only a part of a building, such as an office, apartment, or retail space, the destruction of the building frustrates the entire purpose of the lease, so the tenant will be released from their duty to pay the rent. On the other hand, if the lease agreement is for the use of a building and the land it rests on (as is the case with a farm, for example), the destruction of the building may not terminate the lease, because the purpose of the lease is not entirely frustrated. The tenant isn't relieved from the duty to pay the rent through the end of the rental period.

Condemnation. Condemnation of property by a government entity can also result in the premature termination of a lease. (See Chapter 5 for a discussion of condemnation.)

Types of Leases

There are five major types of leases: gross leases, graduated leases, net leases, percentage leases, and ground leases.

Sometimes called a flat, straight, or fixed lease, a **gross lease** provides for a fixed rental amount. The tenant is obligated to pay a fixed sum of money and the landlord pays the property's operating expenses (such as property taxes and insurance). The tenant may still be billed directly for certain utilities, especially electricity. Most apartment rentals are gross leases.

A **graduated lease** is similar to a gross lease, but it provides for periodic increases in the rent, usually set at specific future dates and often based on the Consumer Price Index or some other measure of inflation. These increases are made possible by the inclusion of an **escalation clause**. A graduated lease is also called a step-up lease or an index lease.

A **net lease** requires the tenant to pay a fixed rent, plus some or all of the operating expenses for the leased premises—maintenance costs, property taxes, and insurance. (If the tenant is responsible for all three of those categories of operating expenses, the lease may be referred to as a **triple net lease.**) The tenant commonly also pays all of the utilities—for instance, not just electricity, but also water and garbage pickup. Commercial leases are often net leases.

Many retail businesses have **percentage leases**, especially in shopping centers. The rent is based on a percentage of the gross or net income from the tenant's business. Typically, the lease provides for a minimum rent plus a percentage of the tenant's business income above the stated minimum.

When a tenant leases land and agrees to construct a building on that land, it's called a **ground lease**. Ground leases are common in metropolitan areas; they are usually long-term, in order to make the construction of the building worth the tenant's while.

Chapter Summary

1. An investment is an asset that is expected to generate a return for the investor. Three basic characteristics of an investment are its liquidity, safety, and yield. The advantages of real estate investment include appreciation, leverage, and cash flow.
2. There are four main types of income-producing property: residential, office, retail, and industrial. Property managers often specialize in one or two types of property.
3. A property manager must have a written management agreement with the property owner. The agreement should include all of the terms of the management arrangement, including compensation, the manager's duties, the scope of the manager's authority, and provisions for reporting to the owner.
4. Before preparing a management plan, the manager should conduct a regional analysis, a neighborhood analysis, a property analysis, and a market analysis. The information gathered during this preliminary study will help the manager set a rental schedule, prepare a budget, and plan the day-to-day operations.
5. The functions of a property manager include marketing the property, leasing, handling tenant complaints, rent collection, recordkeeping, preparing reports for the owner, and arranging for the maintenance of the property.
6. A landlord-tenant relationship is governed by the terms of the lease and by landlord-tenant law. Unless otherwise agreed in the lease, assignment and subleasing are allowed without the landlord's consent, although the original tenant will not be released from liability.
7. A lease may terminate before the end of its term as a result of surrender, breach of the implied covenant of quiet enjoyment, breach of the implied warranty of habitability, failure to pay rent, illegal or unauthorized use of the premises, or the destruction or condemnation of the property.
8. The various types of leases include the gross (or fixed) lease, graduated lease, net lease, percentage lease, and ground lease.

Key Terms

Property management—When someone other than the property owner supervises the operation of an income-producing property.

Investment—An asset that is expected to generate a return (a profit).

Portfolio—The mix of investments owned by an individual or company.

Liquidity—An asset's ability to be converted into cash quickly.

Yield—The return on investment (ROI) to an investor, stated as a percentage of the amount invested.

Appreciation—An increase in the value of an asset; generally due either to inflation or to an increasing scarcity of or demand for the asset.

Equity—The difference between a property's value and the liens against it.

Leverage—Using borrowed money to invest in an asset. If the asset appreciates, the investor earns money on the money borrowed as well as the money invested.

Cash flow—Spendable income; the amount of money left after all of the property's expenses (operating costs, mortgage payments, and taxes) have been paid.

Rental schedule—A list of the rental rates for units in a particular building.

Fixed expense—A property management expense that doesn't vary depending on rental income or current management needs (for example, property taxes).

Variable expense—A property management expense that varies depending on current management needs (for example, repair expenses).

Lease—A contract for possession of real estate in exchange for payment of rent.

Automatic renewal clause—A lease provision that ensures automatic renewal of the lease unless the tenant or the landlord gives the other party notice of termination.

Statement of operations—A periodic report showing the total money received and disbursed and the overall condition of the property during a given period.

Rent roll—A report on rent collections; a list of a property's total rental income, both collected and uncollected.

Statement of disbursements—A list of all of a property's expenses incurred during a specific operating period.

Preventive maintenance—A program of regular inspection and care to prevent problems.

Corrective maintenance—Ongoing repairs that are made to a building and its equipment to restore it to good operating condition.

Assignment—When a tenant transfers the entire remainder of her leasehold estate to another person (the assignee).

Sublease—When a tenant transfers less than her entire leasehold estate to another person (the subtenant); the subtenant might share possession with the tenant, or have the right to possess only a portion of the leased premises, or have the right to possess the entire premises for only a portion of the remainder of the lease term.

Novation—The substitution of a new lease obligation for an old one, or a new party for one of the original parties.

Eviction—The actual or constructive expulsion of a person (usually a tenant) from real property.

Unlawful detainer—A lawsuit filed by a landlord to evict a defaulting tenant.

Chapter Quiz

1. **The main disadvantage of investing in real estate is:**
   a) the use of leverage to increase returns
   b) lack of liquidity
   c) uniformly low returns
   d) a constantly increasing supply, which decreases values

2. **The difference between the value of real property and the liens against it is called:**
   a) equity
   b) leverage
   c) portfolio
   d) cash flow

3. **"Yield" is another term for an investment's rate of:**
   a) return
   b) depreciation
   c) occupancy
   d) tenant turnover

4. **A property manager's main purpose must be to fulfill:**
   a) their career goals
   b) the owner's objectives
   c) the government's affordable housing goals
   d) the cash flow goals of their office

5. **If a regional analysis shows that the typical family size is four, with two parents and two children, which of the following apartment units would be the most marketable?**
   a) Studio
   b) Five-bedroom
   c) Three-bedroom
   d) It is unlikely that one type of unit would be preferred over any another

6. **The type of property that ordinarily demands the most marketing is:**
   a) residential
   b) office
   c) retail
   d) industrial

7. **A property management agreement should always include the:**
   a) manager's regional analysis
   b) manager's compensation
   c) owner's future plans for the property
   d) statement of operations

8. **By completing a market analysis, a property manager discovers that the average rental rate for comparable residential units is $1,950. For the subject property, the property manager should set a rental rate of:**
   a) $1,850 per unit, to undercut the competition
   b) $2,025 per unit, because tenants aren't very well informed and will probably pay a higher-than-average price
   c) $1,950 per unit, to remain competitive
   d) None of the above; a fixed rental rate should not be set, so the property manager can maintain flexibility when renting units

9. **If it becomes necessary to evict a tenant, the landlord or property manager should:**
   a) file an unlawful detainer action
   b) take legal action only after trying self-help methods, such as shutting off utilities
   c) breach the implied warranty of habitability
   d) use either leverage or a form of constructive eviction

10. **Insurance premiums would be considered a:**
    a) variable expense
    b) per diem expense
    c) fixed expense
    d) pro rata expense

11. **A brief description of the property's income and expenses is called a:**
    a) statement of operations
    b) summary of operations
    c) statement of disbursements
    d) rent roll

12. **If a property owner wants to know which tenants are behind in their rent, they should examine the:**
    a) rent schedule
    b) statement of disbursements
    c) narrative report of operations
    d) rent roll

13. **The most effective way to reduce expensive repair bills is to:**
    a) emphasize preventive maintenance
    b) put off repairs for as long as possible
    c) institute a policy of tenant-paid repairs
    d) find cheap repair companies

14. Repairs that return equipment to a functional condition are called:

a) preventive maintenance
b) corrective maintenance
c) general housekeeping
d) remodeling

15. A property manager is about to begin managing a new building. All of the following should be accomplished before they start the actual management of the property, except:

a) execution of a property management agreement
b) preparation of a property management proposal
c) preparation of a statement of operations
d) completion of a market analysis

Chapter 17: *Real Estate Careers and the Real Estate License Law*

I. **Real Estate as a Career**
   - A. Working as a real estate agent
   - B. Real estate firms
   - C. Professional associations and codes of ethics
   - **D. Related careers**

II. **Administration of the License Law**

III. **Real Estate Licenses**
   - A. When a license is required
   - B. Exemptions from licensing requirements
   - C. Types of licenses
   - D. Licensing qualifications and the application process
   - E. License expiration and renewal

IV. **Regulation of Business Practices**
   - A. Agency relationships
     1. Creating agency relationships
     2. Duties owed by licensee
     3. Terminating agency relationships
     4. Vicarious liability
     5. Imputed knowledge
   - B. Supervision and licensee responsibilities
   - C. Affiliations and termination
   - D. Office requirements
   - E. Advertising
   - F. Trust accounts
   - G. Records
   - H. Commissions
   - I. Referral fees
   - J. Handling transactions

V. **Disciplinary Action**
   - A. Grounds for disciplinary action
   - B. Disciplinary procedures
   - C. Sanctions for license law violations

A successful real estate career requires not just hard work but also a certain set of strengths and skills. We'll begin this chapter with a brief overview of what working as a real estate agent is like and the skills and qualities that agents need. We'll then talk about the types of real estate firms that agents can work for, and also professional associations that can help them learn the skills necessary for success.

Real estate careers in Washington are controlled by the provisions of the state's real estate license law, and we'll spend the bulk of this chapter discussing that law. We'll explain the administration of the law, when a real estate license is required, and the qualifications for licensure. Next, we'll discuss how the license law regulates the business practices of real estate firms—governing how firms form agency relationships, run their offices, supervise their sales agents, and handle client funds. Finally, we'll cover license law violations and disciplinary procedures.

Key Terms

License Law	**Interim License**
Real Estate Commission	**Inactive License**
Real Estate Firm	**Fee Broker**
Managing Broker	**Blind Ad**
Broker	**Trust Account**
Affiliated Licensee	**Commingling**
Designated Broker	**Transaction Folder**
Business Opportunity	**Cease and Desist Order**

Real Estate as a Career

Before discussing the real estate license law and how it affects real estate agents—both new and experienced—we're going to briefly discuss real estate careers. Real estate is a flexible, lucrative, and enjoyable career for many people, but it's not for everyone. In this section, we'll discuss what it's like to work (and succeed) as a real estate agent, the different types of real estate firms an agent can work for, and the professional associations agents can join.

Working as a Real Estate Agent

Practically speaking (although not legally speaking), real estate agents work for themselves. Even though an agent must be affiliated with a brokerage firm and supervised by a designated broker, most firms expect their affiliated licensees to generate their own business. To a great extent, it's up to the individual agent to get new listings and find prospective buyers. An agent must therefore be self-motivated and disciplined to earn a good living.

Brokerages usually don't require their agents to work on a fixed schedule, so agents have a lot of freedom. Experienced agents can generally choose how much to work based on their financial needs, temperament, and ambition. However, a part-time effort generally isn't enough to get a new agent off the ground. It takes a big investment of time and energy to build a clientele.

Also, even though agents don't have a fixed schedule, that doesn't mean their time is their own. Since most home buyers and sellers hold down full-time jobs, a lot of real estate activity takes place outside of ordinary business hours. Agents often have to work evenings, weekends, and holidays, making themselves available when buyers and sellers want them.

In addition, real estate agents have to get along with all kinds of people. It may be necessary to spend a lot of time with certain clients or customers, some of them likable, some of them not. And because a real estate transaction is a very big deal for most people, it's not uncommon for buyers and sellers to be anxious, short-tempered, or demanding. Someone who doesn't honestly enjoy meeting and working closely with people will probably be miserable in a real estate career.

Real estate agents also must be able to tolerate uncertainty and rejection. There are a lot of ups and downs in the real estate business. Sometimes a listed property fails to sell. Sometimes a transaction falls through because of an unresolvable conflict. Sometimes an agent has to hear "no" dozens of times before getting to hear one "yes." A real estate agent must be able to handle all of this calmly or even cheerfully. An agent with the stamina and determination to keep going in spite of setbacks is likely to be well-rewarded in the long run.

There are a number of other skills real estate licensees should have or acquire if they're going to be successful agents:

- **Financial planning.** Most agents work on a commission basis, and in the early months of a real estate career, those commissions can take a long time to make their way into an agent's pocket. It's imperative for agents to use sound financial planning techniques if they want to survive that difficult time period. Real estate agents must be able to budget their income and expenses, and then live within that budget. They should also plan on saving extra money when times are good to help them survive the dry spells.
- **Marketing plans.** Real estate agents must be able to create and execute marketing plans, both for themselves and for the homes they list. They should be adept at using traditional marketing tools (such as yard signs and open houses), as well as newer techniques (such as websites and social media).
- **Accounting.** Those who are paid on a commission basis (rather than a salary) have a lot more work to do with regard to financial recordkeeping and tax planning. If a new agent is unsure about how to go about setting up records and a tax payment system, they should consult an accountant.
- **Technology.** Technology is constantly changing, and real estate agents should keep pace with innovations. While not all high-tech tools are necessary or even effective, many of them will help a licensee be more efficient. Brokerages and multiple listing services are continually refining the software that they provide to agents to help them do their jobs.

Real Estate Firms

Although real estate agents work very independently, an agent's career can be strongly affected by the brokerage they work for. There's a lot of variety among real estate firms, and it's important for an agent to find a good fit.

Types of Firms. Real estate brokerage businesses range from sole proprietorships to very large companies with hundreds of agents and dozens of branch offices. Brokerage firms may be independent or part of a local or national franchise.

Some firms work with all types of property and offer both traditional and nontraditional real estate services, such as sales, property management, escrow, investment counseling, or mortgage brokerage services. Other firms are very specialized, handling only certain types of property or certain types of transactions. For example, a commercial real estate firm might do nothing but tax-deferred exchanges; a residential brokerage might focus strictly on subdivision sales.

The particular type of firm an agent should work for depends entirely on the agent's own preferences and interests. Bigger firms and franchises have some advantages, such as greater name recognition, but there are many small, independent firms with a good clientele and high profits.

Support for Agents. Another way in which real estate firms differ is in the services and support they provide for their agents. When deciding where to work, a new real estate agent should take the following considerations into account.

Training. Real estate is a complicated field, and there's a lot to learn about, from sales techniques to environmental issues. It's also essential to keep up with changes in the laws and regulations that affect real estate. So one of the most important services a firm can offer an agent—particularly a new agent—is ongoing training. Some firms have a formal training program; others simply provide the opportunity to work closely with a more experienced agent. Designated brokers are required by law to review the transactions of brokers with less than two years of experience, but a good brokerage will provide mentoring that goes beyond the minimum requirement. A sink-or-swim approach, where new agents are given little or no guidance, can work out very badly for the agents and for their clients.

Facilities and Expenses. Most firms provide an agent with a telephone, a desk, and access to a computer, fax machine, and copier. It's very useful to have a pleasant office for meeting with clients and customers, where there's a receptionist, secretarial support, and other help. However, an agent will have to pay for those advantages either directly (with a monthly **desk fee**) or indirectly (with a lower commission split). Even if a firm does offer these amenities, individual agents need their own equipment, such as a laptop or tablet and a cell phone.

Almost all real estate firms require agents to pay for the expenses they incur in the course of their business activities, such as the cost of their business cards, car maintenance and gas, and cell phone service. In many cases, agents also bear the cost of advertising their listings and their services, including the cost of "For Sale" signs. An agent should ask about a firm's policy in regard to all of these outlays.

Memberships. In most areas, membership in the local multiple listing service is essential, and some real estate firms provide MLS membership to their agents. Other firms require agents to pay their own membership fees. Some firms offer their agents membership in one or more professional trade associations. These associations typically give their members valuable information and training, and they're a good way to network with others in the real estate business.

Compensation. Some brokerage firms pay their agents with commission splits (for instance, the agent may get 60% of the firm's share of the commission), and other firms charge their agents a substantial monthly desk fee but let them keep 100% of the commissions they earn. Many firms use a combination of these methods. A few firms treat their agents as employees and pay them salaries. Agents should always have a good understanding of the compensation structures offered by the firms they're interested in working for.

Agent's Responsibilities. As we said earlier, real estate agents have a lot of freedom and generally don't have to work on a fixed schedule. However, many firms have some minimal requirements for their agents. For example, an agent might be expected to spend some time on **floor duty** each week. During the hours that an agent is assigned to floor duty, they must be at the office and handle all of the telephone calls and drop-in visits from prospective buyers or sellers. (This isn't just drudgery; if the callers or visitors don't ask to speak with a particular agent, the agent on floor duty can help them and, hopefully, retain them as clients or customers.)

Real estate firms differ in the extent to which they monitor their agents' levels of activity and productivity. Some designated brokers set specific sales goals for their agents to meet, and encourage competition among their agents. An agent who doesn't seem to be working hard enough or getting results may be let go. Other firms allow even new agents to set their own pace, with the understanding that those who aren't getting listings or making sales will eventually drop out on their own. In choosing a firm to work for, agents have to judge whether they will thrive in a high-pressure office or do better in a low-key atmosphere.

Professional Associations and Codes of Ethics

There are numerous professional associations in the real estate industry. They provide their members with information, training, and opportunities for networking. In some cases, they also offer professional designations based on education and experience in particular areas of specialization. The general public often sees membership in a professional association as an indication of competence and trustworthiness.

Some professional associations have adopted codes of ethics for their members. A professional code of ethics sets standards of conduct for the members of a profession to meet in their dealings with the public and with other members of the profession. It provides guidance on how to handle ethical dilemmas with integrity and fairness. Failure to comply with an association's code of ethics can lead to expulsion.

For real estate agents, the code of ethics adopted by the National Association of REALTORS® (NAR) has been especially influential. NAR is the largest and best-known real estate professional association in the United States; there are also affiliated state organizations. (Only licensees who belong to NAR may refer to themselves as "Realtors." That term should not be used interchangeably with "real estate agents.")

Among the many other professional associations in the real estate industry are the National Association of Real Estate Brokers (NAREB), the National Association of Exclusive Buyer Agents (NAEBA), the Real Estate Buyer's Agent Council (REBAC), the Appraisal Institute, the American Society of Appraisers (ASA), the Building Owners and Managers Association (BOMA), the Institute of Real Estate Management (IREM), the Counselors of Real Estate (CRE), and the Real Estate Educators Association (REEA). There's also an organization for real estate regulators, the Association of Real Estate License Law Officials (ARELLO).

Related Careers

If a real estate licensee decides that a career selling real estate is not right for them, there are several related fields that offer opportunities for someone with knowledge about real estate transactions. For instance, property management might be a good choice (and in some cases, also requires a real estate license). Title company employees, escrow officers, and mortgage loan originators all have important roles in real estate transactions, and any of these occupations might be a good fit for a real estate agent looking for another career. (Title insurance companies are regulated by the state insurance commission, and escrow officers and loan originators are regulated by the Department of Financial Institutions.) If a licensee is more interested in the nuts and bolts aspects of real estate, they could become a home inspector. Home inspectors must be licensed by the state and are regulated by the Department of Licensing.

Administration of the License Law

Becoming a successful agent takes more than an outgoing personality and good business skills. Successful real estate agents also take their legal and ethical responsibilities seriously. So let's turn our attention to the real estate license law and the duties and obligations it imposes on real estate agents.

The real estate license law is administered by the Washington State **Department of Licensing**. The Director of the Department of Licensing supervises all divisions within the department, including the Real Estate Division, which is led by the Real Estate Program Manager. The Director and all Real Estate Division staff are employees of the state of Washington.

The Director

The Director of the Department of Licensing is appointed by the Governor. The Director is charged with enforcing all laws, rules, and regulations relating to the licensing of real estate licensees. They have the authority to grant or deny licenses, and to hold disciplinary hearings and impose penalties for violations of the license law. And with the advice and approval of the Real Estate Commission, the Director also issues rules and regulations to govern the activities and practices of real estate licensees.

In fact, the term "real estate license law" is commonly used to refer not only to the statutory provisions adopted by the state legislature, but to the regulations issued by the Director as well. All real estate licensees are required to obtain a copy of the Director's regulations (available from the Department of Licensing), and to keep informed of changes in the regulations.

The Director, while serving in that position, may not have an interest in a real estate business. The same rule also applies to other employees of the Department during their employment. If the Director or a Department employee is a real estate licensee, the license will be placed on inactive status during the period of employment.

The Real Estate Commission

The **Real Estate Commission** is made up of the Director and six commissioners. The commissioners are appointed by the Governor to advise the Director on the real estate industry and profession.

The commissioners are generally required to have at least five years of real estate experience; they are usually real estate managing brokers. Each commissioner serves on a part-time basis for a six-year term. At least two commissioners must be from west of the Cascade mountain range, and two must be from east of the Cascades.

The commissioners are paid a per diem stipend, plus travel expenses, for the days they spend holding public hearings, meeting with the Director, and conducting other Commission business.

The Commission prepares and conducts the real estate license examinations. It's also authorized to hold educational conferences for the benefit of the real estate industry.

The legislature created the **Washington Center for Real Estate Research** to study real estate economics and issues such as affordable housing. The Center advises the Director and the Commission about real estate education and related matters, and it also provides real estate information to the general public, such as a quarterly snapshot of the state's housing market.

The Attorney General

The state Attorney General is the Director's legal advisor on matters relating to the license law. The Attorney General also acts as the attorney for the Director in any legal proceedings involving the Real Estate Division.

Real Estate Licenses

By requiring real estate agents to be licensed, the state tries to ensure that they have at least a minimum level of competence in handling real estate transactions. Licenses also serve as a tool for enforcement of real estate regulations; if an agent fails to comply with the law, their license can be suspended or taken away altogether.

When a License is Required

It's unlawful to perform real estate brokerage services without first obtaining the appropriate license.

The license law defines **real estate brokerage services** as follows:

> "Real estate brokerage services" means any of the following services offered or rendered directly or indirectly to another, or on behalf of another for compensation or the promise or expectation of compensation, or by a licensee on the licensee's own behalf:
>
> a) Listing, selling, purchasing, exchanging, optioning, leasing, or renting of real estate, or any real property interest therein; or any interest in a cooperative; or any interest in a floating home or other floating on-water residence;
>
> b) Negotiating or offering to negotiate, either directly or indirectly, the purchase, sale, exchange, lease, or rental of real estate, or any real property interest therein; or any interest in a cooperative; or any interest in a floating home or other floating on-water residence;
>
> c) Listing, selling, purchasing, exchanging, optioning, leasing, renting, or negotiating the purchase, sale, lease, or exchange of a manufactured or mobile home in conjunction with the purchase, sale, lease, exchange, or rental of the land upon which the manufactured or mobile home is or will be located;
>
> d) Advertising or holding oneself out to the public by any solicitation or representation that one is engaged in real estate brokerage services;
>
> e) Advising, counseling, or consulting buyers, sellers, landlords, or tenants in connection with a real estate transaction;
>
> f) Issuing a broker's price opinion (an oral or written report of property value prepared by a licensee that is not an appraisal);

g) Collecting, holding, or disbursing funds in connection with the negotiating, listing, selling, purchasing, exchanging, optioning, leasing, or renting of real estate or any real property interest;

h) Performing property management services, which includes with no limitation: the marketing, leasing, and renting of real property; the physical, administrative, or financial maintenance of real property; or the supervision of such actions.

Generally, a license is required for the activities listed only if they are performed: 1) on behalf of another person, and 2) for compensation. However, the law states that the definition also applies to "a licensee [acting] on the licensee's own behalf." Thus, real estate agents have to comply with the license law even when they are buying, selling, or leasing property for themselves, not just when they are representing others.

In addition to more traditional real estate transactions, the license law covers business opportunity transactions that include real estate. A **business opportunity** is a business that is for sale or lease (either an existing business, or the equipment, supplies, and services needed to start a new one, as in a franchise arrangement). A person who represents another in the purchase, sale, exchange, or lease of a business opportunity or the goodwill of a business must have a real estate license if the transaction involves real estate.

Also note that the definition of brokerage services may include a person who sells or leases a manufactured home before it has become attached to real property, so long as it is sold or leased at the same time as the land where the home is or will be placed.

Exemptions from Licensing Requirements

There are several exemptions from the real estate licensing requirement. The following people don't need a license, even when their activities fall within the definition of real estate brokerage services.

1. Anyone buying or leasing for themself or selling property they own or co-own; this exemption also covers employees acting on behalf of their employers and others acting on behalf of a group to which they belong.
2. An authorized attorney in fact acting without compensation.
3. An attorney at law, while engaged in the practice of law.

Those are probably the three most important categories. The following people are also exempt from the license law when carrying out duties related to their position:

4. A trustee, a guardian, the personal representative of an estate, or anyone acting under court order.
5. Office personnel performing purely clerical duties.
6. Government employees acquiring property through eminent domain or other means.
7. Owners and managers of self-storage facilities renting storage units.
8. Someone who provides referrals to a real estate licensee but doesn't negotiate or sign documents, and whose compensation isn't contingent on the licensee receiving compensation.
9. Certified public accountants, as long as they don't promote the sale, purchase, or lease of specific properties.
10. Escrow agents who don't promote specific properties.
11. Investment counselors who don't promote specific properties.
12. Community association managers who don't promote specific properties.
13. A property manager who performs only limited tasks, such as providing information about rental units or leases; delivering or accepting lease applications, security deposits, and rent payments; showing units or signing leases under the owner's or real estate firm's direct instructions; or carrying out administrative, clerical, financial, or maintenance tasks.

As we said, the license law definition of real estate brokerage services applies to those who act on behalf of another and for compensation. Thus, someone who acts on their own behalf in a real estate transaction is exempt from the licensing requirement; this is the first exemption on the list above.

Example: Matilda Thorn owns several pieces of property: three single-family homes, a duplex, an apartment building, and two vacant lots. If she decides to sell one of these properties, she can do so without having to obtain a real estate license.

In addition, someone acting on behalf of another but *without compensation* is also exempt; this is the second exemption on the list, the one for an authorized attorney in fact. An **attorney in fact** is not necessarily a lawyer; it is anyone a principal appoints to act as their agent through a power of attorney (see Chapter 3). As long as the attorney in fact is not compensated for services rendered, they are allowed to engage in the activities of a real estate broker without a license.

Example: Suppose Matilda from the previous example is old and unwell. She gives her nephew, Truman, a power of attorney that authorizes Truman to sell Matilda's property for her. As long as Truman is acting without compensation, he doesn't need a real estate license to sell the property.

Unlicensed Assistants. An unlicensed assistant may help a licensee by carrying out various activities, including:

- providing information about a real estate listing or transaction, as written and approved by a real estate licensee;
- writing and placing advertising;
- gathering market analysis information;
- driving people to properties;
- greeting people at an open house and distributing pre-printed material;
- making keys, installing keyboxes, and placing signs on property; and

- telemarketing to seek appointments with prospective clients, as long as the assistant's compensation isn't based on whether the firm is eventually compensated by the client, and the assistant provides no other brokerage services.

Activities that an unlicensed assistant cannot perform include answering questions or interpreting information about a property or its condition (except by providing answers from pre-printed material prepared by a licensee), negotiating prices or other terms of sale, and handling trust funds.

Out-of-State Licensees. A real estate licensee who is licensed in another state may handle transactions concerning commercial real estate in Washington without obtaining a Washington license. (For the purposes of this rule, commercial real estate is any property other than residential property with up to four dwelling units.)

However, the out-of-state licensee must have a written agreement with and work in cooperation with a real estate firm that is licensed in Washington. The Washington firm's name must be included on all advertising, and the Washington firm must have custody of the records for the out-of-state licensee's Washington transactions. The records must be maintained for three years, just like an in-state firm's records.

The out-of-state licensee must provide the Washington firm's designated broker with a copy of their license in good standing and must consent to Washington jurisdiction for any legal disputes that may arise from the transaction.

Types of Licenses

There are three types of real estate licenses in Washington: firm licenses, managing broker licenses, and broker licenses.

Firm. A real estate firm is a business entity (such as a corporation, a partnership, or a sole proprietorship) that conducts real estate brokerage activities in Washington. The firm must name a managing broker as its **designated broker** (see below), who directs the firm. The firm must also provide the Director with the names of the firm's owners and anyone else who has the ability to control the operational and/or financial decisions of the firm.

A firm is authorized to employ managing brokers and brokers. Managing brokers and brokers are sometimes referred to as their firm's **affiliated licensees**. The law defines affiliated licensees as "the natural persons licensed as brokers or managing brokers employed by a real estate firm and who are licensed to represent the firm in the performance of any of the acts" for which a real estate license is required.

A commission or other compensation by clients or by other firms can be paid only to a firm, not directly to affiliated licensees. Managing brokers and brokers may only be paid by or through their own firm, not directly by clients.

Managing Broker. A managing broker's license may be issued only to an individual. The licensee is authorized to work with and represent their firm, to manage other licensees, and to manage a branch office of the brokerage. A managing broker may also be appointed as a firm's designated broker.

A managing broker can be affiliated with only one firm at a time. We will discuss qualifications for a managing broker's license shortly, but to become a managing broker, one usually must have significant experience as a broker first.

Broker. A broker's license can be issued only to an individual. The license authorizes the broker to work with and represent their firm. A broker may be affiliated with only one firm at a time. A broker must be supervised by a designated broker or managing broker, and is not authorized to manage a branch office.

Designated Broker. As mentioned above, a firm license is issued to a business entity, and the firm must have a designated broker. If the firm is a sole proprietorship, the owner is the designated broker. If the firm is some other type of business entity (such as a corporation, a partnership, or a limited liability company), it must name one person to be its designated broker. The designated broker must have a managing broker's license and a controlling interest in the firm (in other words, the authority to control the firm's operational and/or financial decisions). In addition, they must obtain a designated broker's endorsement for their managing broker's license from the Department of Licensing.

Despite the fact that a managing broker can be the affiliated licensee of only one firm at a time, a managing broker may serve as the designated broker for more than one firm at the same time.

Fig. 17.1 Types of Real Estate Licensees

<table>
<tr><th colspan="2">Real Estate Firm</th></tr>
<tr><td colspan="2">• A business entity
• Authorized to provide real estate services and represent clients</td></tr>
<tr><th colspan="2">Affiliated Licensees</th></tr>
<tr><th>Managing Broker</th><th>Broker</th></tr>
<tr><td>• Works for and represents firm
• May be designated broker or manage a branch office</td><td>• Works for and represents firm
• Can't be designated broker or manage a branch office</td></tr>
</table>

A designated broker has the final authority for all activities performed by the real estate firm. This includes ensuring that the firm's records are up-to-date and available to state auditors, that trust accounts are accurate and reconciled, and that procedures are in place to ensure compliance with all laws. A designated broker may delegate these duties to managing brokers and branch managers, but these delegations must be in writing and signed.

When a firm's designated broker changes, the outgoing and incoming designated brokers must submit a statement that lists all outstanding client trust fund liabilities, lists pending transactions, and certifies that sufficient funds are held in trust to cover all client liabilities. If a firm closes down, the designated broker is responsible for submitting a closing firm affidavit to the Director.

Licensing Qualifications and the Application Process

Applicants for real estate licenses must satisfy age and educational requirements and pass an examination. In addition, applicants for a managing broker's license have to meet experience requirements.

All education and experience requirements must be satisfied before applying for the exam.

Managing Broker and Broker Qualifications. The qualifications for the managing broker's license and the broker's license are as follows.

Managing Broker. An applicant for a managing broker's license must:

1. be at least 18 years old;
2. have a high school diploma or the equivalent;
3. have at least three years of experience within the last five years as a full-time real estate broker in this state or another state with similar licensing requirements;
4. have successfully completed 90 clock hours of approved real estate education courses within the previous three years, including one 30-hour course in advanced real estate law, one 30-hour course in brokerage management, and one 30-hour course in business management; and
5. pass the managing broker's examination.

An applicant who lacks three years of experience as a full-time broker may be allowed to take the managing broker's exam if the Director of the Department of Licensing determines that the applicant has other education or experience within the last six years that is a satisfactory substitute. Types of experience that may qualify include:

- post-secondary education with an emphasis on real estate studies, together with one year of experience as a real estate broker;
- at least one year of experience as an attorney specializing in real estate transactions;
- five years of experience as an escrow agent or limited practice officer;
- five years of experience as a mortgage broker or loan originator;
- five years of experience as a real estate appraiser; or
- five years of experience managing, leasing, selling, or buying real estate on behalf of a business entity.

If an applicant who is allowed to take the managing broker's exam based on alternative experience qualifications fails the exam, the applicant cannot re-take the exam without meeting the standard experience requirement (three years of full-time work as a real estate broker within the last five years).

Note that relevant military training or service may also be used to satisfy the experience requirement, upon approval by the Director.

The 90 clock hours of approved courses required for the managing broker's license (number 4 on the list above) are in addition to any courses the Department required the applicant to take for other reasons. For example, if the applicant had to take a 30-hour course to fulfill the continuing education requirement to renew their broker's license, those 30 hours cannot be counted as part of the 90 hours required for the managing broker's license.

If an applicant for a managing broker's license has completed what the Director deems to be equivalent educational coursework at an institution of higher learning or a degree-granting institution, the Director may waive the 90 clock-hour requirement.

Broker. An applicant for a broker's license must:

1. be at least 18 years old;
2. have a high school diploma or the equivalent;
3. have successfully completed a 60 clock-hour course in real estate fundamentals (which must include three hours on fair housing and consumer protection issues) and a 30 clock-hour course in real estate practices; and
4. pass the broker's examination.

After completing the prelicense courses, a student has two years to apply for the broker's license examination before the completion certificates expire.

As with the managing broker's license application, if a broker's license applicant has completed what the Director deems to be the equivalent educational coursework at an institution of higher learning or a degree-granting institution, the Director may waive the 90 clock-hour education requirement.

A managing broker may apply to revert to a broker's license simply by completing the required form and paying any necessary fees. However, a former managing broker who reverted to broker status and now wishes to return to managing broker status must meet all managing broker requirements, including passing the examination again and having three years of experience in the previous five years.

Real Estate Examination. The license law and regulations set forth the requirements for applying for and passing the real estate examination.

Exam Reservations. A person who fulfills the age, education, and (for the managing broker's license) experience requirements may make a reservation to take the exam. All examinations are by reservation only; there are no walk-in exams.

Reservations must be made at least one business day before the desired test date. Applicants must bring a valid piece of government-issued photo identification to the exam with them.

If an applicant fails to show up for the exam without providing adequate notice, they forfeit the exam fee. An applicant who fails either the broker's exam or the managing broker's exam may retake it (more than once, if necessary), but they will have to reapply and pay the fee again.

Prospective licensees who have questions about the examination or the license application process should visit the Department of Licensing website for more information.

Scope of the Examination. The real estate exam tests each applicant for an understanding of:

- real estate conveyances and the legal effect of deeds, finance contracts, and leases;
- real estate investment, property valuation, and appraisals;
- real estate agency relationships;
- real estate practices and business ethics; and
- the real estate license law.

In addition, applicants taking the exam are expected to have basic English language and math skills.

The real estate examination consists of two portions:

1. a national portion consisting of questions that test knowledge of general real estate practices, and
2. a state portion consisting of questions that test knowledge of Washington laws and regulations related to real estate licensing.

Fig. 17.2 Topics on the Real Estate Exam

The Real Estate Exam

- Real estate conveyances:
  - deeds
  - mortgages
  - land contracts
  - exchanges
  - rental and option agreements
  - leases
- Real estate investments and appraisals
- Agency law
- Real estate practices and business ethics
- Real estate license law

Other basic requirements:
English language; arithmetic

To pass, a broker applicant must get a score of at least 70% on each portion of the exam. (Although applicants receive separate scores for the national portion and the state portion, national questions and state questions are intermixed on the exam.) A managing broker applicant must get a score of at least 75% on each portion of the exam. When an applicant passes one portion of the exam but fails the other, the passing score is valid for six months. If the applicant retakes and passes the other portion of the exam within that six-month period, they can then apply for a license.

Licensees from Other Jurisdictions. A license applicant who is actively licensed in the same or greater capacity in another jurisdiction is automatically eligible to take the state portion of the Washington exam. The applicant must submit an application to the Department along with evidence of licensure in the other jurisdiction.

Once this evidence has been verified by the Department, the applicant may take the state portion of the exam. The additional requirements for licensure (education, experience, and passage of the national portion of the exam) are waived.

Obtaining a License. The next step after passing the exam is applying for the real estate license itself. Examination results are only valid for one year. If someone passes the exam, but doesn't become licensed within one year after the exam date, they will be required to pass the exam again before a license can be issued.

Application for License. An application for a managing broker's or broker's license must be approved by the designated broker of the firm the applicant is going to work for. A branch manager may give approval on behalf of the firm's designated broker for licenses issued to that branch office. The application is made online through the Department's website.

Applicants applying for a first broker's license or for a managing broker's license using alternative qualifications must submit fingerprint identification as part of the application. Submission of fingerprints is also required every six years for all licensees, upon license renewal. The fingerprinting process will include a background check through the Washington State Patrol and the Federal Bureau of Investigation. If a fingerprint card is rejected by the Director, the applicant must submit a new fingerprint card within 21 days of receiving written notice of the rejection.

If a firm is applying for a license, certain other information must be submitted, depending on how the firm is organized. For instance, if the firm is a corporation, the applicant must provide a copy of its articles of incorporation and a list of its officers and directors and their addresses. If it is a partnership, the applicant needs to list the partners and their addresses.

Interim License. An applicant for a broker's license who has been notified that they passed the exam may begin working on the date they submit a completed license application form, with the license fee and fingerprint card, to the Department. The completed application serves as an interim license for up to 45 days after submitting the application.

There are no interim licenses for managing broker's license applicants.

License Expiration and Renewal

An individual's initial real estate license expires two years after the issuance of the license. The licensee must apply for renewal and pay a renewal fee. Thereafter, the license must be renewed **every two years** by that same date. If the renewal application is late, the licensee must pay a penalty (in addition to the renewal fee).

If a licensee's name or mailing address changes, the licensee should contact the Department to get the license changed. There is no fee for doing so.

Licenses issued to firms must be renewed every two years. The renewal date for this type of license is the expiration date of the firm's registration or certificate of authority (which is filed with the Secretary of State).

Continuing Education. To renew their licenses, all brokers and managing brokers must submit proof that they have successfully completed a total of **30 clock hours** of approved continuing education courses.

As part of their 30 hours, licensees must complete a three-hour **core curriculum course**. The core curriculum course presents practical information on contemporary real estate issues. The three core curriculum hours may be taken as an independent course or included in a longer course.

Beginning in June 2022, three of the required 30 hours of continuing education must be focused on fair housing and the prevention of unfair practices.

A licensee can use a course to fulfill the continuing education requirement only if they began the course after issuance of their initial license. The licensee must have completed at least 15 of the 30 clock hours (including the three core curriculum hours) within 24 months before the renewal date. The remaining 15 hours can be completed up to 36 months before the renewal date. If the licensee exceeds the 30-hour requirement, up to 15 hours can be carried forward for credit in the next two-year renewal period.

A course the licensee used to fulfill prelicense requirements for either a broker's or a managing broker's license, or to fulfill the requirements for reinstatement (see below), cannot also be used for the continuing education requirement.

Broker's First Renewal. The broker's first renewal has a significant educational requirement. When renewing for the first time, a broker must submit proof of completion of 90 clock hours: a 30 clock-hour course in advanced real estate practices, a 30 clock-hour course in real estate law, and 30 clock hours of other approved continuing education (including the core curriculum).

Cancellation and Reinstatement. If a license isn't renewed within one year after it expires, the license is **canceled**. (In other words, there's a one-year grace period between failure to renew and cancellation.) A license can be **reinstated** within two years after cancellation if the licensee:

- successfully completes 60 clock hours of approved real estate courses (including a 30-hour real estate law course) within one year before applying for reinstatement;
- pays all back renewal fees, plus penalties; and
- pays a reinstatement penalty.

Alternatively, the license will be reinstated if the licensee follows the procedures and satisfies the qualifications for initial licensure. That will mean passing the license exam again. (In some cases, starting over in this way would be less expensive than paying the back fees and penalties.)

If it's been more than two years since the license was canceled, the former licensee can't be reinstated unless they satisfy the qualifications for initial licensure again, including retaking and passing the exam.

Inactive Licenses. An inactive license is a license that has been turned over to the Director temporarily. (The most common reason for this is that the licensee is no longer affiliated with the firm they've been working for.) This process no longer involves surrendering a physical copy of the license; switching to inactive status is done on the Department's website. While someone's license is inactive, they are generally deemed to be unlicensed. In other words, they can't engage in activities requiring a real estate license unless the license is reactivated. They are still subject to disciplinary action for violations of the license law, though.

Although an inactive license must be renewed on its renewal date, the holder is usually not required to comply with the continuing education requirement for renewal. (A licensee is not allowed to use inactive status simply as a means of avoiding the continuing education requirement, however.) Failure to renew an inactive license results in cancellation, just as with an active license.

To reactivate a license that has been inactive for more than three years, the holder must complete a 30 clock-hour real estate course. A single 30 clock-hour course in advanced real estate practices or real estate law may be used both for the reactivation of an inactive license and for the broker's first renewal.

A licensee may not reactivate an inactive license if proceedings to suspend or revoke their license have begun.

License Fees. Fees collected for licensing (application fees, renewal fees, etc.) are placed in the Real Estate Commission Account in the state treasury.

Fig. 17.3 Education Requirements for Renewal

License Renewal (every two years)
First renewal for broker: • 30 clock-hour course in advanced real estate practices, • 30 clock hours in real estate law, and • 30 clock hours of other continuing education, including core curriculum course Subsequent renewals: • 30 clock hours of continuing education, including core curriculum course

Regulation of Business Practices

Many provisions of the license law, as well as other state and federal laws, govern the day-to-day business practices of brokers and managing brokers. There are rules concerning:

- the relationship between licensees and their clients and customers;
  - the relationship between a designated broker and their affiliated licensees;
  - real estate firm offices, trust accounts, and business records; and
  - how real estate transactions are handled.

Agency Relationships

One of a licensee's most important responsibilities is to comply with Washington's real estate agency statute, the Real Estate Brokerage Relationships Act (REBRA). This law determines when and how an agency relationship is formed, the licensee's duties to clients and customers, when an agency relationship terminates, and liability for harm caused while acting as an agent. (For a more detailed discussion of REBRA, see Chapter 7.)

Creating Agency Relationships. Under REBRA, an agency relationship requires a written brokerage services agreement between a firm and a client.. For example, a licensee creates an agency relationship between their firm and a seller when they and the seller sign a listing agreement. A buyer agency relationship is ordinarily created through a written buyer agency agreement, but a licensee creates an agency relationship between their firm and a buyer as soon as they perform any real estate brokerage services for the buyer, unless there is a written agreement to the contrary—that is, unless the licensee is already representing the seller under a listing agreement. If a buyer agency relationship forms through the provision of services, though, the agent and client must still confirm the relationship with a written agreement as soon as reasonably practicable; the buyer's agent cannot continue to provide services without an agreement. (Note that a listing agent who provides substantial services to a buyer could inadvertently create a dual agency; see Chapter 7.)

If the seller's agent and the buyer's agent in a transaction are employed by the same firm, that brokerage firm is acting as a limited dual agent. A limited dual agency arrangement is unlawful without the written consent of both the seller and the buyer, and each of them must have a written agency agreement with the firm.

Agency relationships aren't affected by the payment of compensation. For instance, a buyer's agent may receive compensation from the seller as part of a standard commission split without breaching any duty to the buyer.

Duties Owed by Licensee. REBRA sets forth the duties a licensee owes to any party, and the special duties a licensee owes to a party they represent.

Duties Owed to Any Party. Any licensee owes a number of duties to any party when rendering real estate brokerage services, whether the licensee is acting as a buyer's agent, seller's agent, or limited dual agent. The licensee must:

- exercise reasonable skill and care;
- deal honestly and in good faith;
- present all written communications to and from either party in a timely manner;
- disclose all material facts known to the licensee that wouldn't be readily apparent to a party;
- account in a timely manner for money or property received from or on behalf of either party;
- provide a pamphlet on real estate agency law to all parties for whom the licensee performs real estate brokerage services;
- disclose in writing to anyone they render services to (before that person signs an offer) whether they are representing the buyer, the seller, both parties, or neither one; and
- disclose in writing any compensation that the licensee's firm will receive from another party (such as a buyer's agent being compensated by a seller-paid fee).

The agency disclosure must be made before the party signs an offer in a transaction handled by the licensee. It must be either a separate paragraph entitled "Agency Disclosure" in the purchase and sale agreement, or a separate document entitled "Agency Disclosure."

An agent doesn't owe anyone the duty of independent inspection of the property, independent investigation of either party's financial condition, or independent verification of any statement reasonably believed to be reliable.

Duties Owed to Principal. In addition to the duties owed to any party, a licensee owes certain duties only to their client. The licensee must:

- be loyal to the client, by taking no action that is detrimental to the client's interest;
- disclose any conflicts of interest;
- advise the client to seek expert advice on matters that are outside the agent's knowledge;
- refrain from disclosing confidential information from or about the client; and
- make a good faith and continuous effort to complete the transaction.

It is not a breach of the duty of loyalty for a seller's agent to show or list other properties that are not owned by the seller and that may compete with the seller's property. Similarly, it is not a breach of the duty of loyalty for a buyer's agent to show properties that the buyer may be interested in to other prospective buyers.

Duties Owed by a Limited Dual Agent. A limited dual agent owes the duties just listed to both clients, with one key exception. Since a limited dual agent cannot be completely loyal to both parties, they must instead refrain from taking action that is detrimental to either party's interest in the transaction.

A limited dual agent owes the duty of good faith and continuous effort in both finding a buyer for the seller's property and finding a property for the buyer.

Terminating Agency Relationships. All of the duties owed by the licensee continue until the agency relationship terminates. This occurs upon:

- full performance by the licensee,
- expiration of the agreed-upon term,
- termination by mutual agreement, or
- termination by unilateral action.

The duties of confidentiality and accounting, however, do not expire upon the termination of the agency relationship.

No Vicarious Liability. Under the Real Estate Brokerage Relationships Act, a principal isn't liable for harm caused by any act or omission of an agent or subagent. The two exceptions are: 1) when the principal participated in or authorized the wrongful act, or 2) when the principal benefited from the act and a court determines that the claimant could not enforce a judgment against the agent.

No Imputed Knowledge. Under REBRA, a principal is not held to have notice of any facts known by an agent or subagent that are not actually known by the principal, unless the principal and agent have agreed otherwise in writing. For instance, suppose a property was due to be condemned to build a new freeway on-ramp. The seller did not know about the likely condemnation, but the listing agent did and kept silent about it. If the buyer sued, the seller would not be found liable for the buyer's financial losses caused by the condemnation, although the listing agent could be.

Supervision and Licensee Responsibilities

A designated broker is responsible for the proper supervision of all of their firm's licensees (brokers, managing brokers, and branch managers), whether they are independent contractors or employees. For branch offices, both the branch manager and the designated broker are responsible for all licensees working at the branch.

Any licensee who supervises other licensees must be a managing broker. A broker can't be put in a position of supervising other brokers. For instance, if several licensees form a "team" within a firm, any licensee who supervises other licensees on the team must be a managing broker, not merely a broker. (A team consists of a number of agents within a larger firm who agree to work together with an extra degree of cooperation, in order to increase business; the team may hire shared support staff, such as unlicensed assistants.)

A **fee broker** is a licensed designated broker who does not own or manage a brokerage, but allows another person to operate a brokerage using their name and license, usually for a fee. This arrangement is a violation of the license law, even if the designated broker does not receive any compensation. A designated broker must actively manage and supervise the brokerage, and they can't avoid those responsibilities through any contract, agreement, or understanding with another person.

Liability for Violations by Affiliated Licensees. A designated broker who fails to supervise their affiliated licensees properly may be held responsible for their actions. If an affiliated licensee violates the license law, in addition to other possible consequences for the designated broker, the Director may suspend or revoke the designated broker's license (as well as the licensee's). The same sanctions could also be imposed on a branch manager or any other managing broker who failed to fulfill supervisory responsibilities in the case.

Broker's Responsibilities. Under the license law, a broker's responsibilities include:

- assuring that all brokerage services in which they participate comply with the license law, the Real Estate Brokerage Relationships Act (REBRA), and the Uniform Regulation of Business and Professions Act (URBPA);
- cooperating with the Department of Licensing in an investigation or audit;
- being knowledgeable about the license law, REBRA, and URBPA;
- keeping the Department of Licensing informed of their current mailing address;
- following their firm's written policy regarding referral of home inspectors;
- being appropriately licensed;
- delivering brokerage service contracts and other transaction documents to the designated broker or the appropriate managing broker within two days of mutual acceptance by the parties; and
- following the license law rules regarding trust funds, advertising, and modifying or terminating contracts on behalf of the firm.

A broker who has been licensed for less than two years is subject to one additional responsibility: working under a heightened degree of supervision. This means the broker must participate in all required reviews of contracts by a supervisor (either the designated broker or a managing broker); obtain a supervisor's advice or assistance regarding matters beyond their expertise; submit evidence of completion of required coursework to a supervisor; and submit all contracts, documents, and funds to a supervisor in accordance with the firm's policies. Brokerage service contracts involving a broker licensed for less than two years must be reviewed by a supervising broker within five business days after mutual acceptance by the parties, and documentary proof of review must be kept in the firm's records.

Managing Broker's Responsibilities. A managing broker has all of the same responsibilities as a broker, and may also have additional responsibilities delegated to them by the designated broker. Delegated responsibilities may include ensuring that:

- monthly trust account reconciliations and trial balances are completed, accurate, and show that the trust accounts are in balance;
- policies and procedures are in place for safe handling of client or customer funds and property;
- required records are properly maintained and kept up to date;
- advertising meets legal requirements;

- contracts and other transaction documents are submitted and reviewed in a timely manner;
- the Director's representatives have access to the firm's offices and records; and
- affiliated licensees are following the firm's written policies.

A managing broker serving as a branch manager is responsible for all activity within the branch office, including supervision of all licensees, with heightened supervision for brokers licensed for less than two years. The branch manager is responsible for hiring, releasing, and transferring licensees to and from the branch.

Designated Broker's Responsibilities. A firm's designated broker has additional levels of responsibility beyond those of a managing broker. The designated broker is responsible for ultimate oversight of the entire firm. Among many other responsibilities, this includes maintaining:

- up-to-date written agreements detailing any delegation of supervisory authority to branch managers or other managing brokers; and
- written policies concerning referral of home inspectors, supervision of the firm's brokers, managing brokers, and branch managers, and review of all contracts involving brokers licensed for less than two years.

Affiliations and Termination

A licensed broker or managing broker must be affiliated with a real estate firm in order for their license to be active. A broker or managing broker can't engage in real estate activities except as a representative of a firm and under the supervision of a designated broker. The designated broker has custody of the licenses of their affiliated licensees.

The relationship between a firm and an affiliated licensee may be terminated at any time by either party. Upon termination of the relationship, the broker's or managing broker's license remains inactive until the licensee joins a new firm. (It isn't necessary to notify the Real Estate Commission of the termination.)

Termination of an affiliation is done online. A licensee who is leaving a firm reports the change by updating their license at the DOL website. This immediately places the licensee on inactive status.

When an inactive licensee is going to join a new firm, the new firm must use the DOL website to send an online request to the licensee, who then confirms online that they wish to become affiliated with that firm. The licensee can begin working for the new firm immediately, though a paper copy of the license showing the new affiliation won't arrive for two or three weeks.

When a broker or managing broker has been terminated because of conduct that would be grounds for disciplinary action under the license law, the designated broker must send the Director a written statement of the facts surrounding the termination.

If the firm itself is closing, the designated broker must provide a closing firm affidavit to the Department within five business days.

The designated broker must also give written notice to all parties with pending transactions, and ensure that brokerage service contracts are terminated or transferred to another real estate firm with the parties' written permission. All of the former affiliated licensees will be on inactive status until they join other firms.

Office Requirements

A firm licensed in Washington is required to maintain an office or a records repository in this state. The location must be accessible to the Director's representatives. The office must be identified by a sign displaying the name of the firm or its assumed name.

The firm's license must be prominently displayed at the address appearing on the license, along with the licenses of all of the firm's affiliated licensees. If the firm has more than one office, the firm's license and the designated broker's license are displayed in the main office, and the licenses of affiliated licensees are displayed in the office where they work (which should be the address shown on the license).

If the location of a firm's office changes, within ten days after the move the designated broker must submit a change of address application to the Director, return all licenses (the firm's and those of the affiliated licensees), and pay a fee. The Department will issue licenses for the new address.

Two Businesses in the Same Office. It isn't unusual for a firm to engage in other business activities that are related to—or at least not in conflict with—real estate brokerage activities. For example, a brokerage firm might also act as an escrow agent or as a mortgage broker. A firm can operate two (or more) businesses out of the same office if the brokerage business is carried out separately and apart from other business activities and its records are completely separate.

Branch Offices. There is no limit on the number of branch offices a firm can have, but it must obtain a duplicate license from the Department of Licensing for each branch office. Every branch office is also required to have a branch manager, who must be a managing broker.

A branch office license isn't required for an office located in a subdivision if sales activity there concerns only properties in that subdivision. This exception applies only if the subdivision is within 35 miles of a licensed office or branch office.

Dual-State Firms. A real estate firm that is actively licensed in another state as well as in Washington and has its head office in the other state isn't required to have an office here. However, trust funds for Washington transactions must be kept in a trust account in a Washington depository, and transaction records must be kept at a registered location in this state. Representatives of the Department and also the parties involved in a transaction must be allowed access to the records. The firm's license must be displayed at the same place the records are kept.

If a firm headquartered in another state seeks to operate in Washington, it must obtain a firm license here. As with any other firm, the designated broker must qualify as a managing broker in Washington and have a controlling interest in the firm.

Advertising

Advertising by real estate licensees must be truthful and not misleading. It is a violation of Washington's Consumer Protection Act to place untruthful ads or send misleading email or text messages. Violators can be subject to substantial fines.

A real estate firm may advertise that it pays referral fees to unlicensed persons, so long as the ad complies with all other advertising requirements.

The Department of Licensing has published a booklet (available at its website) with guidelines for advertising by real estate licensees. As the booklet explains, advertising isn't only published ads, but "any activity, public notice, or representation" that promotes a real estate licensee's services or particular properties. For example, business cards, letterhead, yard signs, and open houses are considered forms of advertising.

Firm's Name Required. Advertising placed by a licensee must include the firm's name as licensed (that is, as it appears on the firm's license) in a clear and conspicuous manner. An ad without the firm's name, sometimes called a blind ad, violates the license law. There's one exception to this rule: if a licensee is advertising their own property for sale or lease, the firm's name doesn't have to appear in the ad. The ad must disclose that the seller or landlord holds a real estate license, however.

Before applying for a firm license, the designated broker must obtain approval for the firm's name from the Department of Licensing. A firm may not use a name that is deceptively similar to that of another licensee or firm, nor one that creates the impression that the firm is a nonprofit organization, research organization, or public agency.

A firm may use more than one name in conducting its business, as long as it obtains a separate license for each name. To get a license for an additional name, the designated broker submits an **assumed name** application to the Department. (Assumed name licenses expire at the same time as the firm's main license.) When a firm has more than one licensed name, advertising placed by affiliated licensees will be compliant as long as it includes one of those names.

A broker or managing broker may advertise their own practice using a name or brand without obtaining a license for an assumed name. For instance, as mentioned earlier, some brokers create their own "team" under the broader umbrella of the firm for which they work. The team members can use the team name in their advertising if they also include the firm's licensed name (or assumed name) in the ads. The team name must not suggest that the team is a legal entity separate from the firm; for example, it can't include a designation such as "LLC" or "Inc." or words such as "realty," "real estate," or "firm." The firm's designated broker must give written approval for use of the unlicensed team name or brand.

Advertising and the Internet. The Department of Licensing has adopted guidelines to help licensees use the internet to increase their sales while avoiding violations of advertising rules and regulations.

According to these guidelines, a licensee should be careful to fully disclose their licensed status in all online communications. A full disclosure would include the licensee's own name (as licensed) and the licensed name of the firm with which they are affiliated. If the firm is not licensed in Washington, the disclosure should also include the city and state in which the firm is located.

Note that once a licensee has established an agency relationship with a member of the public, a full disclosure isn't necessary in every online message the licensee sends that person, as long as the licensee fulfilled that disclosure requirement before providing or offering to provide real estate services.

The guidelines include suggestions on how to meet the requirement of full disclosure for each of the following types of online communications:

- **Website:** Whenever a licensee or firm owns a website or controls its contents, every viewable page should include a full disclosure.
- **Email, newsgroups, discussion lists, bulletin boards:** Each should include a full disclosure at the beginning or end of each message, except when the licensee is communicating with a member of the public and the licensee's initial communication contained a full disclosure.
- **Text messages:** A full disclosure is not necessary in this format if the licensee already fulfilled that disclosure requirement in another format before providing or offering to provide real estate services.
- **Chat:** A full disclosure should be made before providing or offering to provide real estate services during the chat session, or it should appear in text visible on the same web page that contains the chat session if the licensee controls the website hosting the chat session.
- **Social media:** A full disclosure should be prominently displayed and be no more than one click away from any viewable page.
- **Multimedia advertising:** This category includes, for example, executable email attachments. A full disclosure should be visible as part of the advertising message.
- **Banner ads:** Each ad should link via a single click to a website that has a full disclosure, unless the banner ad itself has one.

The DOL's guidelines also offer the following advice about prospecting online:

- If listings are maintained on a website, they should be removed in a timely manner after they have expired.
- If a licensee submits listing information to a third-party site, they should provide written communication of any change of listing status to the publisher in a timely manner.
- Licensees should not advertise the listings of other licensees without their written permission. If permission is given, licensees should not alter the online display or any informational part of the listing without the written permission of the listing broker.

- Metatags are descriptive words hidden in a website's code that search engines use to index the website. Sometimes a website owner will insert the name of a competitor into the metatags, so that when a potential customer searches for the competitor's site, the owner's site will also come up as a match. Licensees should avoid this practice, as courts have ruled that it may constitute trademark infringement.
- Licensees should periodically review the advertising and marketing information on their website(s) to make sure that it is current and not misleading.

Trust Accounts

Any funds a licensee temporarily keeps on behalf of clients or customers are **trust funds.** They have been entrusted to the licensee and may not be used for personal benefit. Examples include earnest money deposits, tenant security deposits, and **advance fees,** which are fees a client pays before the licensee provides the services agreed on.

Unless its affiliated licensees never hold trust funds (for example, if earnest money deposits are delivered directly to escrow instead), a real estate firm must maintain one or more **trust accounts** in a recognized financial institution in the state of Washington. Trust funds may never be placed in the firm's general business account or in any licensee's personal bank account; they must not be **commingled** (mixed) with the firm's or a licensee's own money.

A firm's trust account should be opened in the name of the firm as licensed, and specifically designated a trust account.

All funds a licensee is given to hold until a transaction closes (such as earnest money) or until paid to a client (such as rents collected) must be deposited in a trust account no later than the **first banking day after receipt**, unless otherwise specified in the license law. (The license law includes a special rule for earnest money that we'll discuss later in the chapter.) Saturdays, Sundays, and legal holidays are not considered banking days in this context.

Interest-Bearing Accounts. With the exception of property management trust accounts, a real estate firm's trust accounts are required to be interest-bearing accounts that allow withdrawals without delay (other than any minimum notice period required by banking regulations).

A firm is required to put all deposits of **$10,000 or less** into a **pooled account** called the **housing trust fund account**. The interest that accrues on this account, after deducting reasonable bank charges, must be paid to the state treasurer. It will be divided between the Washington **housing trust fund** (75%) and the **real estate education account** (25%).

For deposits **over $10,000**, the client or customer who is turning the funds over to the firm has a choice. With the written consent of the parties, the funds can be deposited in the pooled account, in which case the interest will be paid to the state. Alternatively, the firm can establish a separate trust account for the deposit, with the interest to be paid to the client or customer to whom the funds belong. The designated broker must inform the client or customer of these alternatives in writing.

Fig. 17.4 Rules for Handling Trust Funds

Trust Accounts
• Trust funds must be deposited by the first banking day after receipt • Accounts must be interest-bearing • Deposits of $10,000 or less: – must be placed in pooled account – interest is paid to State • For deposits over $10,000, customer or client chooses to put funds in: – pooled account with interest paid to State, or – separate account with interest paid to customer or client

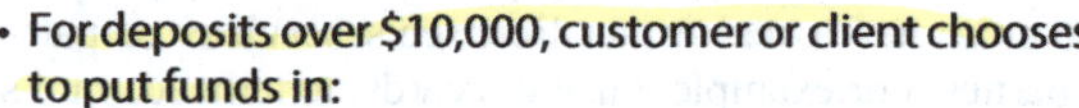

Property Management Trust Accounts. The rules just outlined do not apply to trust funds that a licensee handles in property management transactions (such as rents or tenant security deposits). Property management trust accounts don't have to be interest-bearing accounts, and property management trust funds don't have to be placed in the firm's pooled account. However, a property management account can be interest-bearing, if the firm's written management agreement with the property owner provides for that, and if the firm follows certain special rules in the license law. If any commissions or property management fees are to be paid out of a trust account directly to the firm, they must be removed from the trust account at least once a month.

A firm that manages several rental properties for different owners does not have to open an individual trust account for each one, if all of the owners assign the interest accruing on their funds to the firm.

When the management agreement between the owner and firm terminates, any trust funds associated with that owner that are left in the account will be disbursed according to the agreement's terms; security deposits are disbursed either to the owner or the next property management firm.

Trust Account Procedures. A firm must establish a system of records and procedures that provides an audit trail for all funds received and disbursed, identified to each client. The firm can either follow the procedures that are set forth in the Director's regulations, or submit an alternative system to the Department for approval.

Only trust funds may be maintained in a trust account, with one exception: the firm is allowed to deposit a "minimal amount" of its own funds to open the account, or to maintain a minimum balance to keep the account open. If a client or customer has assigned the interest on a trust account to the firm (in writing), the firm must make arrangements with the financial institution to credit the interest to the firm's general account.

Trust Account Disbursements. As a general rule, a firm may not make any disbursements from a trust account before closing, or before a condition in the purchase and sale agreement has been fulfilled. There are three important exceptions to that rule, however. The designated broker may disburse funds:

1. with the written consent of all parties to the transaction;
2. when the transaction fails to close, if the purchase and sale agreement provides for disbursement in this situation without a written release; or
3. to the closing agent named in the agreement far enough in advance so that the checks will clear by the closing date.

A firm may not pay its own business expenses directly out of a trust account. That includes bank charges for the maintenance of the trust account; these should be paid out of the firm's general business account, not the trust account itself. If a client owes the firm money, the funds must first be transferred from the trust account to the firm's general business account before the firm can use them for business expenses. (See the note on commissions paid from trust accounts below.)

If the parties to a transaction cannot agree on who is entitled to the trust funds, the designated broker must notify all the parties of their intent to disburse the funds. The notice must include the names and addresses of the parties, the amount of money held, to whom it will be disbursed, and the planned date of disbursement.

Commissions Paid from Trust Accounts. Commissions payable to the firm and to other cooperating firms may be paid directly from the trust account. The designated broker must draw a separate check for each commission after the transaction closes.

Commissions the firm owes to its affiliated licensees may not be paid directly out of the trust account. These commissions are handled the same way as the firm's business expenses. Funds must first be transferred to the firm's general business account, and then the firm can pay its affiliated licensees with checks drawn on that account.

Records

The license law requires a real estate firm to keep adequate records of the real estate transactions handled by its affiliated licensees for at least **three years** after closing. (It's wise to keep records for even longer than this minimum requirement, since the statute of limitations for some claims against a firm may not run out for several more years. Also, other state laws and regulations may require firms to keep some records for longer than three years.)

Although a designated broker may delegate recordkeeping duties to someone else, they are still responsible for the custody and accuracy of the required records. They must make the records available to auditors from the Department of Licensing, and provide copies to the Director upon demand.

The firm must maintain an up-to-date log of all agreements and contracts for brokerage services that are submitted by the firm's licensees, and also retain a copy of these documents on file.

For each transaction, a **transaction folder** must be maintained that includes all of the following that apply:

- the listing agreement,
- the purchase and sale agreement,
- the lease or rental agreement,
- any modifications or addenda to those agreements,
- the settlement statement, and
- all other agreements or documents relevant to the transaction.

As we discussed earlier, brokers with less than two years of experience must have their contracts reviewed by the designated broker or a managing broker. Documented proof of the review must be kept on file at the firm's record storage location.

The firm is also required to keep the following **trust account records**:

- a duplicate receipt book or cash receipts journal showing all receipts;
- prenumbered trust account checks with a check register, cash disbursements journal, or check stubs;
- validated duplicate bank deposit slips;
- a client's ledger summarizing all receipts and disbursements for each transaction, property management account, or contract or mortgage collection account;
- separate ledger sheets for each tenant, lessee, vendee, or mortgagor;
- a ledger for interest on the firm's pooled housing trust fund account; and
- reconciled bank statements and canceled checks, including voided checks. (Trust account checks must be prenumbered, so even voided checks must be kept to show that all checks are accounted for.)

All records for recent transactions must be kept at a location where the firm is licensed to have an office. Records for transactions that have been closed for at least one year can be kept at one central facility, as long as the facility is in Washington.

Older transaction records stored in a central location must be retrievable at the request of the Department. A list of all transactions for which records are stored at a remote facility must still be kept at the firm's licensed offices.

Records may be stored electronically, so long as the medium is nonerasable and doesn't allow the documents to be modified. The firm needs to have equipment available at its licensed office to view, retrieve, and print the documents immediately, if Department representatives show up to inspect them. All real estate firms are subject to routine audits even if no wrongdoing is suspected; routine audits occur approximately every three years. Auditors are authorized to arrive unannounced at any time during business hours. The Department does not charge licensees for the costs associated with routine audits.

Commissions

A valid real estate license is a prerequisite to collecting a commission (or any form of compensation) for brokerage services. A firm cannot sue for a commission unless there is proof that the firm and its affiliated licensee were properly licensed before the licensee:

- offered to perform any act or service that requires a license, or
- procured a promise or contract for the payment of compensation for such an act or service.

A Washington firm may share a commission with or pay compensation to any other firm that is licensed in the United States or any foreign jurisdiction with a real estate regulatory program (such as Canada). It may also compensate a licensed manufactured or mobile home dealer, when land is sold or leased in connection with the sale of a mobile home.

A firm may share commissions with, or pay other compensation to, its own affiliated licensees. But it is not allowed to pay any compensation directly to a broker or managing broker licensed with another firm. Payment must be made to the other firm, which then pays its broker or managing broker.

Licensees may receive compensation only from their firm. They cannot collect a commission directly from a client or from another firm. They also are not allowed to share their compensation with other licensees. If two brokers are going to split a commission, for example, the split must be handled by their firm or firms.

Listings, buyer agency agreements, and management agreements are the property of the firm, not the licensee. A broker who changes to a new firm in the middle of a transaction can't bring the transaction to the new firm with them; it belongs to the old firm.

Referral Fees

It's not uncommon for one real estate licensee or firm to pay another licensee or firm a fee for referring a potential customer or client. This type of referral fee between licensees does not violate the license law.

> **Example:** Sheri, a broker with Whitehall Realty, specializes in commercial properties. When a potential client, Jordan, asks her about residential listings, she refers him to Larry, a broker with ABC Homes. In return, Larry agrees to pay Sheri one-third of any commission he receives from working with Jordan. As long as this payment is handled through their firms (and doesn't pass directly from Larry to Sheri), it's legal.

Such a payment also does not violate RESPA, the Real Estate Settlement Procedures Act. Although RESPA generally prohibits referral fees paid by one settlement service provider to another (see Chapter 13), it exempts referral fees paid by one real estate licensee to another real estate licensee.

A real estate licensee or firm may also pay a referral fee to an unlicensed person in exchange for referring a potential customer or client. However, as we mentioned earlier, the real estate license law prohibits such fees if they are contingent on the firm actually receiving compensation.

Handling Transactions

The Director's regulations include several rules governing how licensees serve their clients and customers in a real estate transaction, from preparation of a buyer's offer through closing.

Offers and Document Copies. When involved in negotiations between a buyer and a seller, a licensee must present all written communications, including offers and counteroffers, from one party to the other.

A licensee is also responsible for providing clients and customers with copies of any documents they sign (the listing agreement, purchase and sale agreement, escrow instructions, etc.) within a reasonable time after they sign them.

Earnest Money Deposits. A purchase and sale agreement usually states the amount and form of the buyer's earnest money deposit and who will hold the deposit until closing (see Chapter 9). The license law also affects how a deposit must be handled.

In some cases the agreement provides that the earnest money will take the form of a check to be held by the real estate firm. If so, the buyer's check should be made payable to the firm, and it must be promptly deposited in the firm's trust account.

Alternatively, the agreement may provide that the earnest money check will be held by the closing agent. In that case, the buyer makes out the check to the closing agent, and the check must be promptly delivered to that agent. A dated receipt documenting the delivery must be included in the transaction file.

There's an important exception to these rules, however: the law allows a licensee receiving an earnest money check to hold the check without depositing or delivering it for a certain period or until a particular event occurs (usually until the seller accepts or rejects the buyer's offer), if that's what the agreement directs the licensee to do.

The licensee who receives the earnest money deposit must handle the funds in compliance with these license law rules (although of course the designated broker has ultimate responsibility). This licensee is usually the buyer's agent, who takes the earnest money check from the buyer. In the unlikely case that the purchase and sale agreement doesn't state who the check should be made out to, the law provides that it should be made out to the real estate firm as licensed.

It is a violation of the license law to accept an earnest money deposit in the form of a promissory note (or some other form that is not considered the equivalent of cash) unless the licensee discloses that fact to the seller before the seller accepts the offer. The purchase and sale agreement must also state the form of the earnest money.

Expeditious Performance. When a purchase and sale agreement or other contract obligates a licensee to perform a certain act (for example, ordering an inspection), that act must be performed as expeditiously as possible. Under the license law, a licensee's intentional or negligent delay is considered to be "conduct...that demonstrates bad faith, dishonesty, untrustworthiness or incompetency," and is therefore grounds for disciplinary action.

Closings. The license law makes a licensee who is involved in a sale responsible for ensuring that the parties receive a detailed settlement statement at closing. This requirement has less relevance in residential transactions since, under RESPA, the lender prepares and delivers the closing disclosure (which includes a settlement statement—see Chapter 13). Regardless of who prepares and delivers the settlement statement, however, the licensee must keep a copy in the transaction folder.

Washington's Escrow Agent Registration Act allows a real estate licensee to close a transaction in which they are already representing the buyer or the seller (or both), if the licensee is designated as the closing agent in the purchase and sale agreement. Unless the licensee is a licensed escrow agent, however, they can't charge either party any fee (beyond their brokerage commission) for closing services. Only licensed escrow agents and attorneys can charge a fee for closing real estate transactions. (See Chapter 13 for information about the Washington Escrow Agent Registration Act.)

Property Management Agreements. A firm must have a written property management agreement with the owner or owners of each property it manages. The license law requires the agreement to state all of the following:

- the property manager's compensation;
- the type of property managed (for example, apartment or office building);
- the number of units or square footage;
- whether the firm is authorized to collect and disburse funds, and if so, for what purposes;
- whether the firm is authorized to hold and disburse tenant security deposits, and if so, how; and
- how often the firm is to provide summary statements to the owner.

Note that the property's physical condition does not have to be described in the management agreement.

A **summary statement** is a brief report showing the property's financial status over a certain period of time, such as one month or one quarter. The firm must provide a summary statement to the owner or owners for each property managed as often as the management agreement requires. A summary statement shows:

- the balance carried forward from the last statement;
- the total rent receipts;
- other itemized receipts (for example, from laundry or vending machines);
- contributions from the owner;
- itemized expenditures;
- the ending balance; and
- the number of units or the square footage rented.

The firm must keep a copy of the management agreement and summary statements in its records. The agreement can be modified only in writing, and the modification must be signed by the owner and the firm's designated broker. For all rental properties managed by a firm, the leases or rental agreements must be in writing.

A firm may provide other services to the owner of a property that is being managed, such as janitorial and repair services, with the owner's consent. If the firm uses another company to provide these services, it must make a full written disclosure of its relationship with that company, and disclose the fees that are charged. (Property management is discussed in detail in Chapter 16.)

Disciplinary Action

The Director has the authority to investigate the actions of any real estate licensee and impose penalties, including license suspension or revocation. This is true regardless of whether the licensee was acting on behalf of another or on their own account, and regardless of whether their license is active or inactive.

Grounds for Disciplinary Action

A licensee or a license applicant may be subject to disciplinary action either for engaging in unprofessional conduct in violation of the **Uniform Regulation of Business and Professions Act** (URBPA) or for engaging in one of the activities specifically listed in the license law as grounds for disciplinary action. (The Uniform Regulation of Business and Professions Act applies to all types of professionals regulated by Washington's Department of Licensing, not just to real estate licensees.)

Unprofessional conduct, as defined in the URBPA, includes any of the following conduct, acts, or conditions:

1. the commission of any act involving moral turpitude, dishonesty, or corruption relating to real estate activities, regardless of whether the act constitutes a crime;
2. misrepresentation or concealment of a material fact in obtaining or reinstating a license;
3. false, deceptive, or misleading advertising;
4. incompetence, negligence, or malpractice that harms another or creates an unreasonable risk of harm;
5. having any business or professional license suspended, revoked, or restricted by any government entity;
6. failure to cooperate with the Director of the Department of Licensing in the course of an investigation, audit, or inspection;
7. failure to comply with an order issued by the Director;
8. violating any license law provision or rule made by the Director;
9. aiding or abetting an unlicensed person to perform real estate activities that require a license;
10. practice or operation of a business or profession beyond the scope of practice or operation as defined by law;

11. any type of misrepresentation in the conduct of real estate activities;
12. failure to adequately supervise or oversee staff, whether employees or independent contractors, to the extent that consumers may be harmed or damaged;
13. being convicted of any gross misdemeanor or felony relating to real estate activities;
14. interference with an investigation or disciplinary action by willfully misrepresenting facts, or by threatening, harassing, or bribing customers or witnesses to prevent them from providing evidence; or
15. engaging in unlicensed real estate activities.

Further grounds for disciplinary action are listed in the license law. The first item listed is "Violating any of the provisions of this [statute] or any lawful rules made by the director..." In other words, any violation of the license law is grounds for disciplinary action.

Here is a summary of the items listed in the license law that have not been mentioned elsewhere in this chapter. A licensee is subject to disciplinary action for:

- being convicted of forgery, embezzlement, extortion, fraud, or similar offenses;
- making or authorizing statements that they knew (or could have known by the exercise of reasonable care) were false;
- converting trust funds (misappropriating them for their own use);
- failing to disclose information or to produce records for inspection upon request by the Director;
- selling real estate according to a plan that endangers the public interest, after the Director has objected in writing;
- accepting something other than cash (such as a promissory note) as an earnest money deposit unless that fact is stated in the purchase agreement and the seller has been informed;
- accepting money from more than one party in a transaction without first disclosing this to all interested parties in writing;
- accepting a profit on expenditures made for a principal without disclosing it to the principal;
- accepting compensation for an appraisal contingent on reporting a predetermined value;
- issuing an appraisal for property in which they have an interest without disclosing that interest in the appraisal report;
- falsely claiming to be a member of a state or national real estate association;
- directing a client or customer to a lending institution or escrow company in expectation of a kickback or rebate, without disclosing that expectation to the party they are representing;
- buying, selling, or leasing property (directly or through a third party) without disclosing that they hold a real estate license;
- any conduct in a real estate transaction which demonstrates bad faith, dishonesty, untrustworthiness, or incompetency; and
- discriminating against any person in hiring or in the provision of real estate brokerage services, in violation of antidiscrimination laws.

It is also a prohibited practice, under the license law, for a licensee who has a financial interest in a title insurance company to give a fee or kickback to another real estate licensee for placing business with or referring business to that title insurance company. (Such a kickback would also violate RESPA; see Chapter 13.)

A licensee also may not accept or solicit anything of value from a title insurance company or its representative that it would be illegal for the company to give. In addition, a licensee may not require a client or customer to obtain title insurance from a title insurance company in which the licensee has a financial interest.

The Director is given the power to suspend the license of any real estate licensee who isn't in compliance with a child support or visitation order, as certified by the Department of Social and Health Services. License reinstatement is automatic upon repayment or compliance.

It is also important to note that the state licensing law for attorneys prohibits anyone from practicing law who isn't an active member of the state bar association. Practicing law includes drafting contracts for other people and giving legal advice. Thus, real estate licensees who aren't licensed attorneys should never draw up contracts for their clients and customers, or even draft provisions of any complexity. Agents also should not give opinions about the legal effect of contract provisions or a party's actions. Engaging in the **unauthorized practice of law** is a gross misdemeanor. (However, the parties to a transaction may draft their own contract without violating the rule that prohibits the unauthorized practice of law.)

Disciplinary Procedures

The procedures for disciplinary action are designed to give the licensee notice of the charges and an opportunity to present a defense. The usual procedures include an investigation, a hearing, and, depending on the outcome of the hearing, either no action or some form of sanctions against the licensee. Either party (the licensee or the Department of Licensing) may appeal the result.

Statement of Charges. If, after investigation, it appears that the licensee has violated the license law, the licensee will be served with a statement of charges. The statement of charges includes a notice that the licensee may request a hearing to contest the charges. The licensee must file a request for a hearing within 20 days after receiving the statement of charges. If the licensee fails to request a hearing, the Director may enter a decision on the matter.

Hearing. If the licensee requests a hearing, the Department sets a hearing date. The date must be at least 30 days after the statement of charges was served on the licensee. The only exception to this rule is if the Director issued a summary (immediate) suspension or restriction, in which case the hearing may be held sooner.

The hearing may be conducted by the Director, but in most cases the hearing officer is an administrative law judge. The licensee and the Department of Licensing may each be represented by attorneys in the hearing. The Department and the licensee can present evidence and testimony, cross-examine witnesses for the other side, and present arguments to the hearing officer. A court reporter makes a transcript of the proceedings, just as in a trial.

If the accusation isn't proved by a preponderance of the evidence, no action is taken against the licensee and the case is dismissed. If the accusation is proved, the Director will mail the licensee an order imposing any sanctions. The sanctions take effect as soon as the licensee receives the order.

Appeal. A licensee may appeal the outcome of a disciplinary hearing in superior court. The appeal must be filed within 30 days after the date of the Director's decision and order. The licensee must post a $1,000 appeal bond to cover court costs—in case the judge decides against the licensee—and must also pay for a copy of the transcript of the hearing within 15 days of receiving notice that the transcript has been filed. Filing an appeal does not automatically stay the Director's order. For example, if the Director has suspended the licensee's license, it will remain suspended during the appeal process, unless the Director decides it is appropriate to stay the sanction.

Sanctions for License Law Violations

If a licensee is found to have violated the license law, the Director may impose any or all of the following sanctions:

- revocation of the license for an interval of time;
- suspension of the license for a fixed or indefinite term;
- restriction or limitation of real estate activities;
- satisfactory completion of a specific program of remedial education or treatment;
- monitoring of real estate activities according to the Director's order;
- censure or reprimand;
- compliance with conditions of probation for a designated period of time;
- payment of a fine for each violation found by the Director, of up to $5,000 per violation;
- denial of an initial or renewal license application for an interval of time; or
- other corrective action.

All fines collected are placed in the Real Estate Education Account, to be used for education for the benefit of licensees. If a licensee fails to pay a fine, the Director may enforce the order for payment in superior court.

A **cease and desist order** is issued to stop a licensee (or an unlicensed person) from violating the law. After a disciplinary hearing, the Director might issue a cease and desist order to prevent continuation of an illegal activity. In some circumstances, the Director can issue a temporary cease and desist order even before a hearing is held. The Director may do this only when a delay in issuing the order would result in irreparable harm to the public. The temporary order must advise the licensee that they have a right to a hearing to determine if the order should be canceled, modified, or made permanent. If the licensee requests a hearing, one must be held within 30 days, unless the licensee requests more time.

Alternatively, the Director can ask a court to issue an injunction ordering a licensee or an unlicensed person to stop an ongoing violation. A person who continues to violate an injunction can be fined or found in contempt of court. The Director can also ask the court to appoint a receiver to take over or close a real estate office operating in violation of the law until a hearing can be held.

Criminal Prosecution. Violations of the license law are gross misdemeanors. If the Director decides that criminal charges should be filed against a licensee, the prosecution would ordinarily be handled by the prosecuting attorney in the county where the violation is alleged to have occurred.

Civil Liability. Anyone injured by a licensee's conduct can file a civil lawsuit for damages. (See the discussion of tort suits in Chapter 7.) Note, however, that the Director doesn't have the power to award damages to the victims of real estate fraud or other wrongful actions. Compensation for injured parties is handled through the court system.

Notifying Department of Legal Action. A licensee is required to notify the Department of Licensing's real estate program manager within 20 days after learning of:

- any **criminal complaint**, information, indictment, or conviction in which the licensee is named as a defendant;
- any **civil court order**, **verdict**, or **judgment** entered against the licensee if the case involves any of their real estate or business activities; or
- the suspension or revocation of a professional license or certification held by the licensee (for instance, a real estate license in another state, or a license in another profession such as insurance), or the imposition of a fine connected with a professional license or certification.

Fig. 17.5 Penalties after Disciplinary Action

Sanctions for License Law Violations
• License suspension, revocation, or denial
• Restriction and/or monitoring of real estate activities
• Relevant real estate education
• Censure or reprimand
• Probation
• Fines (up to $5,000 per violation)
• Other corrective action

Chapter Summary

1. Washington's real estate license law is administered by the Director of the Department of Licensing and the Real Estate Commission.
2. It's unlawful to provide real estate brokerage services without a license. There are several important exemptions from the licensing requirement, however, including someone buying or selling on their own behalf, and an uncompensated attorney in fact.
3. There are two types of individual real estate licenses: managing broker licenses and broker licenses. Real estate firms must also be licensed. Managing brokers and brokers may only work when representing a firm. A managing broker is also authorized to manage a branch office, and can be appointed as a firm's designated broker.
4. Any license applicant must be at least 18 years old, have a high school diploma, have completed certain real estate courses, pass an examination, and submit fingerprints. An applicant for a managing broker's license must also have three years of experience as a broker.
5. Licenses must be renewed every two years. For renewal, the licensee must complete 30 clock hours of approved continuing education courses, including the core curriculum. For a first renewal, a broker must have completed 90 clock hours of courses.
6. An agency relationship is formed through a written brokerage services agreement. An agent owes a number of duties to a principal, in addition to the duties any licensee owes to all parties in a transaction. An agency relationship can be terminated through full performance, expiration of the term, mutual agreement, or unilateral action.
7. A designated broker is responsible for the supervision of their affiliated licensees. When an affiliation is terminated, the broker's or managing broker's license is inactive until reissued for affiliation with another firm.
8. A firm is required to maintain an office in Washington that is open to the public, and may have one or more branch offices. Each branch office must be licensed, and each must be managed by a managing broker. An affiliated licensee's license must be displayed in the office where they work.
9. Advertising by real estate licensees must include the firm's name as licensed; blind ads are not allowed. An ad for the licensee's own property does not have to state the firm's name, but it must disclose the licensed status of the seller.
10. Trust funds must be placed in an interest-bearing trust account no later than the first banking day after receipt; deposits of $10,000 or less are placed in a pooled account, with interest paid to the state. (Property management trust accounts do not have to be interest-bearing accounts.) A designated broker may not pay business expenses or an affiliated licensee's share of a commission directly out of a trust account.
11. A firm is required to keep records (including a transaction folder and trust account records) for at least three years after a transaction closes.
12. A valid real estate license is a prerequisite to payment of a commission or other compensation for brokerage services.
13. In handling a real estate transaction, a licensee is required to provide copies to the parties after documents are signed; to perform expeditiously any acts they are obligated to perform by the purchase and sale agreement; and to make sure that the parties receive settlement statements.
14. When a licensee is accused of violating the license law, there is an investigation and usually a disciplinary hearing. The possible sanctions include license suspension, revocation, or denial; fines; relevant coursework; restrictions on or monitoring of real estate activities; censure or reprimand; probation; or other corrective action. Violation of the license law is a gross misdemeanor and may lead to criminal prosecution.

Key Terms

License law—The state statute that governs the licensing and business practices of real estate agents, along with the regulations issued by the Director of the Department of Licensing to implement that statute.

Real Estate Commission—A commission made up of the Director of the Department of Licensing and six commissioners who advise the Director.

Real estate firm—A business entity, such as a corporation or partnership, that is licensed to perform real estate brokerage activities in Washington.

Managing broker—A person who is licensed to represent a firm in real estate transactions and to supervise other licensees or a branch office.

Broker—A person who is licensed to work for and represent a firm in real estate transactions.

Affiliated licensee—A broker or managing broker who is licensed under a particular firm.

Designated broker—The person authorized to have full legal responsibility for a licensed real estate firm and its affiliated licensees.

Business opportunity—A business (including inventory and goodwill) that is for sale, where the transaction includes real property.

Interim license—The completed application form for a broker's license, which serves as a temporary license until the permanent license is issued.

Inactive license—A license in the possession of the Director of the Department of Licensing.

Fee broker—A designated broker who allows another person to use his license to operate a brokerage (which is a violation of the license law).

Blind ad—An advertisement placed by a real estate licensee that does not state the name of the firm as licensed (which is a violation of the license law).

Trust account—A specially designated bank account in a firm's name for funds held by the firm on behalf of clients, to keep those funds segregated from the firm's own money.

Commingling—When someone who is holding trust funds on another person's behalf intentionally or accidentally mixes those funds together with his own money.

Transaction folder—Part of the records a designated broker is required to keep; the contracts and other documents connected with a particular transaction.

Cease and desist order—An order issued by the Director of the Department of Licensing in a disciplinary action, to stop a violation of the license law.

Chapter Quiz

1. **The members of the Washington Real Estate Commission are appointed by the:**
   a) Governor
   b) Real Estate Program Manager
   c) Director of the Department of Licensing
   d) President of the Washington Association of REALTORS®

2. **The Morenos want to sell their house. They gave their friend Jessica Norwood a power of attorney, authorizing her to represent them in the transaction. Norwood doesn't have a real estate license. It's legal for Norwood to represent the Morenos:**
   a) only if she's licensed to practice law
   b) only if she won't be compensated for her services
   c) as long as she obtains a real estate license before the transaction closes
   d) None of the above; it isn't legal for Norwood to represent the Morenos

3. **Mark Cutler doesn't have a real estate license. Which of the following activities can he legally do, for a fee?**
   a) Advise sellers in a real estate transaction
   b) Issue a broker price opinion
   c) Oversee the management of an apartment building for its owner
   d) Lease units in a property he co-owns

4. **Unlike a broker, a managing broker:**
   a) must have at least three years of experience in real estate
   b) can accept compensation directly from a seller
   c) doesn't have to be licensed under a firm
   d) All of the above

5. **Real estate licenses must be renewed:**
   a) annually
   b) every two years
   c) every three years
   d) every five years

6. **Paul Doren's real estate license expired last month, and now he wants to renew it. In order to do so, Doren will be required to:**
   a) complete an additional 60 clock hours of approved real estate courses
   b) pass the license exam again
   c) pay a penalty in addition to the renewal fee
   d) All of the above

7. **To renew a real estate license, a licensee must show that they have taken a certain number of clock hours of approved continuing education courses. The required total is:**
   a) 30 hours commenced within 12 months preceding the licensee's renewal date
   b) 30 hours; at least 15 commenced within 24 months preceding the licensee's renewal date, and the remainder commenced within 36 months preceding the renewal date
   c) 20 hours completed within 24 months preceding the licensee's renewal date
   d) 20 hours completed within 36 months preceding the licensee's renewal date

8. **For their first renewal, real estate brokers must complete:**
   a) 30 clock hours of continuing education
   b) 60 clock hours of continuing education
   c) 90 clock hours of continuing education
   d) 120 clock hours of continuing education

9. **Harrison's license has been canceled. Which of the following does he NOT need to do, in order to get reinstated?**
   a) Complete 60 clock hours of real estate courses, including 30 clock hours of real estate law
   b) Pay all back renewal fees, plus penalties
   c) Pay a reinstatement penalty
   d) Re-take and pass the licensing examination

10. **Jenkins, who lives in Portland, has a valid Oregon real estate license. She decides that she needs a Washington real estate license so she can show some of her Portland customers properties in Vancouver, Washington. Jenkins:**
    a) must fulfill all the normal licensing requirements, just as if she were not already licensed in Oregon
    b) can apply for a Washington real estate license without taking the license exam
    c) only has to take the Washington portion of the real estate exam
    d) can get a special dispensation from the Director and receive a license upon completion of a 30-hour brokerage management course

11. **Peterson hires an assistant to help him with his real estate business. His assistant answers phones, sets up appointments, and files paperwork. Peterson's assistant:**
    a) need not be licensed
    b) must have a real estate license
    c) need not be licensed as long as Peterson has written authorization from his designated broker or branch manager to hire an assistant
    d) must have a real estate assistant license

12. Cortez has one year of experience as a real estate broker. He wants to become a managing broker. He may get the three-year experience requirement waived if he can show:

a) post-secondary education with an emphasis on real estate studies
b) six months of experience as an attorney specializing in real estate transactions
c) three years of experience closing real estate transactions for an escrow company
d) All of the above

13. Although Harper lacked three years of full-time experience as a broker, she was still allowed to take the managing broker's exam because she had other professional experience that was deemed a satisfactory substitute by:

a) Harper
b) her firm's designated broker
c) the Director of the Department of Licensing
d) the Real Estate Commission

14. To pass the managing broker's exam, the applicant must score at least:

a) 70%
b) 75%
c) 80%
d) 85%

15. Which of the following may receive an interim license?

a) A broker applicant who passed the exam
b) A designated broker applicant who passed the exam
c) A managing broker applicant who passed the exam
d) All of the above

16. A limited dual agent may not:

a) disclose a material fact that one party knows and wants to remain confidential
b) disclose one party's intended negotiating position to the other party
c) reveal a latent defect
d) make their agency disclosure before either party has signed an offer in a transaction

17. A seller's broker notices some damage to the foundation of the seller's house, but doesn't tell the buyer about it. The seller won't be liable to the buyer for this failure to disclose if the broker:

a) told the seller, and the seller let the broker decide whether to mention it to the buyer
b) told the seller, and they mutually agreed not to mention it to the buyer
c) didn't tell the seller, but the seller substantially profited from the deal, and the broker is now bankrupt
d) never told the seller about the damage

18. Ellen Kendrick is a licensed broker. She wasn't getting along with her designated broker, so they decided to terminate their affiliation. Which of the following is true?

a) Kendrick's license is inactive
b) Kendrick may continue with real estate transactions that were in progress at the time of her termination
c) Kendrick will be required to take the license exam again in order to reinstate her license
d) All of the above

19. Which of the following statements is true regarding the supervision of brokers? A managing broker must review documents from:

a) all brokers within three days
b) all brokers within five days
c) brokers with less than two years of experience within three days
d) brokers with less than two years of experience within five days

20. The license of a broker who works at a branch office is:

a) kept at their home address
b) displayed at the firm's main office
c) displayed at the branch office where she works
d) kept at the Department of Licensing offices In Olympia

21. Trust funds received by a designated broker in a sales transaction must be placed in an:

a) account that doesn't bear interest, by the third banking day after receipt
b) interest-bearing account, by the second banking day after receipt
c) account that doesn't bear interest, by the first banking day after receipt
d) interest-bearing account, by the first banking day after receipt

22. The license law requires a firm to keep transaction records for:

a) six months
b) one year
c) three years
d) five years

23. A listing was submitted to a multiple listing service. The property was sold by a broker who doesn't work for the listing firm. How will that broker be paid a share of the commission?

a) The listing firm must pay the broker's firm, who will then pay the broker
b) The listing firm must pay the MLS, which will then pay the broker directly
c) The listing firm may either pay the broker's firm or pay the broker directly
d) The listing firm should pay the broker directly

24. Susan Kurosawa, a licensed broker, is advertising her own house for sale. The license law requires the ad to state:

a) that the seller is a licensed real estate agent
b) the name of Kurosawa's firm, as licensed
c) Both of the above
d) None of the above

25. A broker may manage a branch office for their firm:

a) if the broker has at least two years of experience
b) if the broker has taken an approved course in brokerage management
c) if the office is in the broker's residence
d) under no circumstances

26. A broker who is representing a seller is negotiating with a prospective buyer. Before the buyer signs an offer, the broker must:

a) obtain the seller's written consent
b) disclose to the buyer in writing that they are representing the seller
c) explain to the buyer that they are acting as a dual agent
d) have the buyer sign a buyer representation agreement

27. If a licensee accused of violating the license law does not request a hearing within 20 days after receiving the statement of charges:

a) her license is automatically revoked
b) the Director may enter a decision based on the available facts
c) a hearing will automatically be scheduled for the licensee
d) the Director will issue a cease and desist order

28. Howard Gray, a licensed broker, was involved in a traffic accident. The other driver (who was injured) sued Gray for compensation, and a judgment has just been entered against Gray. He is:

a) required to notify the Department of Licensing within five days
b) required to notify the Department of Licensing within 30 days
c) not required to notify the Department of Licensing, because this was not a criminal charge
d) not required to notify the Department of Licensing, because the lawsuit didn't involve Gray's real estate or business activities

29. A firm that is managing property must:

a) have a written property management agreement with the owner
b) keep a copy of all summary statements for the property in its records
c) provide the property owner with a full written disclosure of its relationship with any firm providing services to the property, such as repair services
d) All of the above

30. Barton, a real estate licensee, helps negotiate a sale. The purchase and sale agreement is contingent on a pest inspection, and Barton tells the parties he will arrange for an inspection to be done by August 19. But he forgets to request the inspection before taking his family on a planned vacation. When he gets back into town on August 18, he finally remembers to call the pest inspector. The inspector says she's very busy and won't be able to inspect the home until August 29.

a) Since the pest inspection wasn't an important term in the purchase agreement, Barton hasn't done anything wrong
b) Even though Barton was negligent in failing to perform his duty, he hasn't violated the license law
c) The closing agent will cancel escrow immediately and terminate the sale
d) Barton has failed to perform expeditiously, and may be subject to disciplinary action

Chapter 18:
Real Estate Math

Real estate agents use math from time to time—for example, when calculating their commissions or determining the square footage of homes they are listing or selling. Electronic calculators and real estate software make these calculations much easier than they once were, but it is still helpful to have a grasp of the math used in real estate transactions. (And, of course, the license exam includes some math questions.) This chapter provides step-by-step instructions for solving a wide variety of real estate math problems.

Solving Math Problems

We're going to begin our discussion of real estate math with a simple approach to solving math problems. Master this four-step process, and you'll be able to solve most math problems you are likely to encounter on the state exam.

1. Read the question

The most important step is to thoroughly read and understand the question. You must know what you are looking for before you can successfully solve any math problem. Once you know what you want to find out (for example, the area, the commission amount, or the total profit), you'll be able to decide which formula to use.

2. Write down the formula

Write down the correct formula for the problem you need to solve. For example, the area formula is *Area = Length × Width*, which is abbreviated $A = L \times W$. Formulas for each type of problem are presented throughout this chapter, and there is a complete list at the end of the chapter.

3. Substitute

Substitute the relevant numbers from the problem into the formula. Sometimes there are numbers in the problem that you will not use. It's not unusual for a math problem to contain unnecessary information, which is why it is very important to read the question first and determine what you are looking for. The formula will help you distinguish between the relevant and irrelevant information given in the problem.

In some problems you will be able to substitute numbers into the formula without any additional steps, but in other problems one or more preliminary steps will be necessary. For instance, you may have to convert fractions to decimals.

4. Calculate

Once you've substituted the numbers into the formula, you're ready to perform the calculations to find "the unknown"—the component of the formula that was not given in the problem. Most of the formulas have the same basic form. The problem will give you two of the three numbers (or information to enable you to find two of the numbers) and then you will either have to divide or multiply to find the third number, which is the solution to the problem.

Whether you'll multiply or divide depends on which component in the formula is the unknown. For example, the formula *Area = Length × Width*, or *A = L× W*, may be converted into two other versions of the formula, with the components rearranged. All three versions are equivalent; which arrangement you'll use depends on the component to be discovered.

- If the quantity *A* (the area) is unknown, use *A = L × W*. The number *L* is **multiplied** by *W*. The product of *L* multiplied by *W* is *A*.
- If the quantity *L* (the length) is unknown, use *L = A ÷ W*. The number *A* is **divided** by *W*. The quotient of *A* divided by *W* is *L*.
- If the quantity *W* (the width) is unknown, use *W = A ÷ L*. The number *A* is **divided** by *L*. The quotient of *A* divided by *L* is *W*.

Thus, the formula *A = L × W* may be used three different ways depending on which quantity is unknown. For example, here are the three versions of the formula applied to a rectangle that is 40 feet long, 20 feet wide, and has an area of 800 square feet.

A = L × W	L = A ÷ W	W = A ÷ L
? = 40' × 20'	*? = 800 Sq. ft. ÷ 20'*	*? = 800 Sq. ft. ÷ 40'*
40' × 20'= 800 Sq. ft.	*800 Sq. ft. ÷ 20' = 40'*	*800 Sq. ft. ÷ 40' = 20'*

Once you've performed the calculation, you can check whether you correctly chose to multiply or divide by asking yourself whether you've arrived at a logical number. Does the result make sense? For example, suppose a problem asks you to find the area of a building and gives you the numbers 40 and 20. If you divide 40 by 20 instead of multiplying, the result is 2—in other words, the building's area is only two square feet! You would know right away that you did something wrong. So you should try again, using multiplication this time: 40 × 20 = 800 square feet, a much more likely answer.

Now let's apply the four-step approach to an example. Suppose a room is 10 feet wide and 15 feet long. How many square feet does it contain?

1. **Read the question.** This problem asks you to find the square footage or area of a rectangular room. So you'll need the area formula for a rectangle.
2. **Write down the formula.** *Area = Length × Width*
3. **Substitute.** Substitute the numbers given in the problem into the formula. The length of the rectangle measures 15 feet, and the width measures 10 feet: *A = 15' × 10'.*
4. **Calculate.** Multiply *Length* times *Width* to get the answer: *15' × 10' = 150 Sq. ft.* Thus, *A = 150.* The area of the room is 150 square feet.

Suppose the problem gave you different pieces of information about the same room: the area is 150 square feet and it's 10 feet wide. How long is the room? Again, follow the four-step approach.

1. **Read the question.** You're asked to find the length or width of a rectangle. You'll need the area formula again.
2. **Write down the formula.** *Area = Length × Width*
3. **Substitute.** Substitute the numbers given in the problem into the formula: *150 = L × 10'.*
4. **Calculate.** The length of the rectangle is the unknown. So you'll need to rearrange the basic area formula *(A = L × W)* into a division problem *(A ÷ W = L)* to find the length: *150 Sq. ft. ÷ 10'= 15'.* The quotient of 150 divided by 10 is 15. The length of the rectangle, or of the room, is therefore 15 feet.

Decimal Numbers

To carry out a calculation, it's easier to work with decimal numbers than to work with fractions or percentages. So if a problem presents you with fractions or percentages, you'll usually convert them into decimal numbers.

Converting Fractions. To convert a fraction into decimal form, divide the top number of the fraction (the numerator) by the bottom number of the fraction (the denominator).

> **Example:** To change ¾ into a decimal, divide 3 (the top number) by 4 (the bottom number): *3 ÷ 4 = .75.*

> **Example:** To convert ⅔ into a decimal, divide 2 (the top number) by 3 (the bottom number): *2 ÷ 3 = .66667.*

If you don't already know them, it's useful to memorize the decimal equivalents of the most common fractions:

¼ = .25
½ = .5
¾ = .75

Converting Percentages. To solve a problem involving a percentage, you'll first convert the percentage into a decimal number, then convert the decimal answer back into percentage form.

To convert a percentage to a decimal, remove the percent sign and move the decimal point two places to the left. It may be necessary to add a zero.

> **Example:**
> *98% becomes .98*
> *5% becomes .05*
> *32.5% becomes .325*
> *17.5% becomes .175*

Depending on the type of problem, you may need to convert the decimal answer back into percentage form as a final step. To accomplish that, do just the opposite of what you did in order to convert the percentage into a decimal. Move the decimal point two places to the right, adding a zero if necessary, and add a percent sign.

Example:

.1 becomes 10%
.15 becomes 15%
.08 becomes 08%
.095 becomes 09.5%

The percent key on a calculator performs the conversion of a percentage to a decimal number automatically. On most calculators, you can key in the digits and press the percent key, and the calculator will display the percentage in decimal form.

Decimal Calculations. Calculators handle decimal numbers in exactly the same way as whole numbers. If you enter a decimal number into the calculator with the decimal point in the correct place, the calculator will do the rest. But if you're working without a calculator, you'll need to apply the following rules.

To add or subtract decimals, put the numbers in a column with their decimal points lined up.

Example: To add 3.75, 14.62, 1.245, 679, 1,412.8, and 1.9, put the numbers in a column with the decimal points lined up as shown below, then add them together.

```
     3.75
    14.62
     1.245
   679.0
 1,412.8
+    1.9
 2,113.315
```

To multiply decimal numbers, first do the multiplication without worrying about the decimal points. Then put a decimal point into the answer in the correct place. The answer should have as many decimal places (that is, numbers to the right of its decimal point) as the total number of decimal places in the numbers that were multiplied. So count the decimal places in the numbers you are multiplying and put the decimal point the same number of places to the left in the answer.

Example: Multiply 24.6 times 16.7. The two numbers contain a total of two decimal places.

```
   24.6
 × 16.7
  410.82
```

In some cases, it will be necessary to include one or more zeros in the answer to have the correct number of decimal places.

Example: Multiply .2 times .4. There is a total of two decimal places.

```
   .2
 × .4
  .08
```

A zero has to be included in the answer in order to move the decimal point two places left.

To divide by a decimal number, move the decimal point in the denominator (the number you're dividing the other number by) all the way to the right. Then move the decimal point in the numerator (the number that you're dividing) the same number of places to the right. (In some cases it will be necessary to add one or more zeros to the numerator in order to move the decimal point the correct number of places.)

Example: Divide 26.145 by 1.5. First move the decimal point in 1.5 all the way to the right (in this case, that's only one place). Then move the decimal point in 26.145 the same number of places to the right.

26.145 ÷ 1.5 becomes 261.45 ÷ 15

Now divide. *261.45 ÷ 15 = 17.43*

Remember, this applies only if you are doing calculations by hand; these steps are unnecessary if you're using a calculator. If the numbers are keyed in correctly, the calculator will automatically give you an answer with the decimal point in the correct place.

Area Problems

A real estate agent often needs to calculate the area of a lot, a building, or a room. Area is usually stated in square feet or square yards. The formula to be used for the calculation depends on the shape of the area in question. It may be a square, a rectangle, a triangle, or some combination of those shapes.

Squares and Rectangles

As stated earlier, the formula for finding the area of a square or a rectangle is $A = L \times W$.

Example: A rectangular room measures 15 feet along one wall and 12 feet along the adjoining wall. How many square feet of carpet will be needed to cover the floor?

180
Sq. Feet
15'
12'

1. **Read the question**. You're being asked to find the area (the square footage) of a rectangle.
2. **Write down the formula.** $A = L \times W$
3. **Substitute.** $A = 15' \times 12'$

4. **Calculate.** Since the quantity *A* is unknown, multiply *L* times *W* for the answer: *15′ × 12′ = 180 Sq. ft.* So 180 square feet of carpet will be needed to cover the floor.

Now take the problem one step further. If carpet is on sale for $12 per square yard, how much would it cost to carpet the room?

1. **Read the question.** You're first being asked to determine how many square feet there are in a square yard, and then to determine how many square yards there are in 180 square feet. A square yard is a square that measures one yard on each side. There are three feet in a yard.
2. **Write down the formula.** *A = L × W*
3. **Substitute.** *A = 3′ × 3′*
4. **Calculate.** Since the quantity *A* is the unknown, multiply *L* times *W*: *3′ × 3′ = 9 Sq. ft.*

   So there are 9 square feet in a square yard. Now divide 180 by 9 to see how many square yards there are in 180 square feet: *180 ÷ 9′ = 20 Sq. yd.*

   Now multiply the number of square yards (20) by the cost per square yard ($12): *20 × $12 = $240 Cost to carpet room.*

Triangles

The formula for finding the area of a triangle is:

Height *× ½ Base* *Area*	or	*Area = ½ Base × Height*

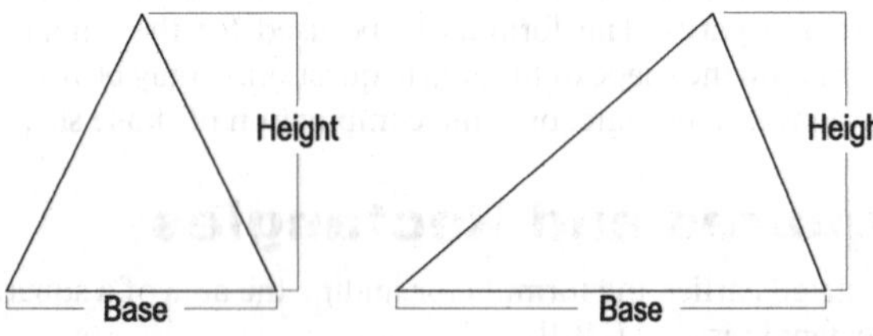

Example: If commercial building lots in a certain neighborhood are selling for approximately $5 per square foot, approximately how much should the lot pictured below sell for?

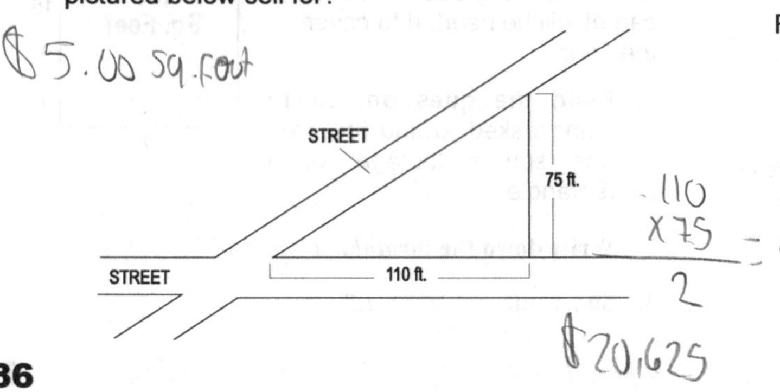

1. **Write down the formula.** *A = ½ B × H*
2. **Substitute.** *Area = 55′ (½ of 110) × 75′*
3. **Calculate.** *75′ × 55′ = 4,125 Sq. ft.*

The order of multiplication doesn't matter. You can multiply 110 times 75 and then divide it in half. Or you can divide 110 by 2 and then multiply the result by 75. Or you can divide 75 by 2 and then multiply the result by 110. Whichever way you do it, the answer will be the same.

	Step 1	Step 2	Answer
a)	110 × 75 = 8,250	8,250 ÷ 2 = 4,125	4,125 Sq. ft.
b)	110 ÷ 2 = 55	55 × 75 = 4,125	4,125 Sq. ft.
c)	75 ÷ 2 = 37.5	37.5 × 110 = 4,125	4,125 Sq. ft.

The lot contains 4,125 square feet. If similar lots are selling for about $5 per square foot, this lot should sell for about $20,625.

4,125	*Square feet*
× $5	*Per square foot*
$20,625	*Selling price*

Odd Shapes

The best approach to finding the area of an odd-shaped figure is to divide it up into squares, rectangles, and triangles. Find the areas of those figures and add them all up to arrive at the area of the odd-shaped lot, room, or building in question.

Example: If the lot pictured below is leased on a 50-year lease for $3 per square foot per year, with rental payments made monthly, how much would the monthly rent be?

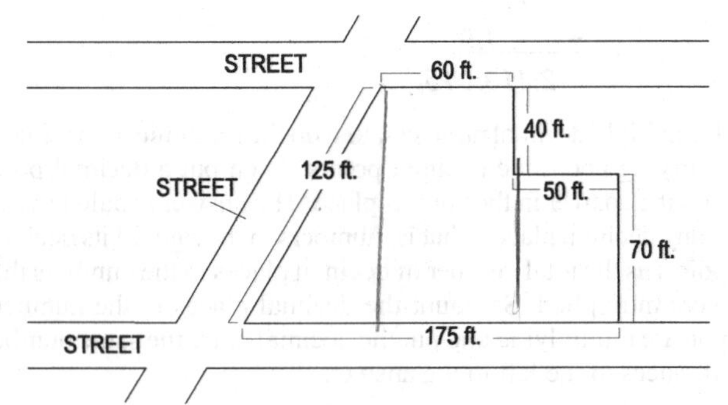

First, divide the lot up into rectangles and triangles.

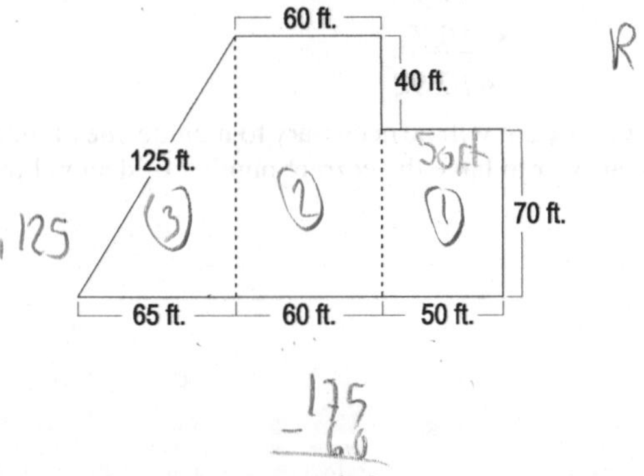

The next step is to find the area of each of the following figures. The height of the triangle is determined by adding together the 70-foot border of the small rectangle and the 40-foot border of the large rectangle, as shown above.

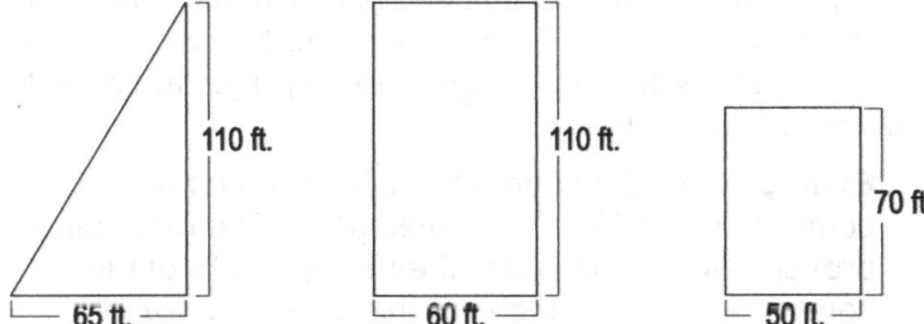

First, find the area of the triangle.

1. **Write down the formula**. A = ½ Base × Height
2. **Substitute**. A = 32.5' (½ of 65') × 110"
3. **Calculate**. 32.5' × 110' = 3,575 Sq. ft.

Then, find the area of the large rectangle.

1. **Write down the formula**. A = Length × Width
2. **Substitute**. A = 110' × 60'
3. **Calculate**. 110' × 60' = 6,600 Sq. ft.

Next, find the area of the small rectangle.

1. **Write down the formula**. A = Length × Width
2. **Substitute**. A = 70' × 50'
3. **Calculate**. 50' × 70' = 3,500 Sq. ft.

Finally, add the three areas together to find the area of the entire lot: *3,575 + 6,600 + 3,500 = 13,675 Total square feet.*

The lot contains 13,675 square feet. At $3 per square foot per year, the annual rent would be $41,025.

13,675	*Square feet*
× $3	*Rent per square foot*
$41,025	*Annual rent*

The monthly rental payment would be one-twelfth of the annual rent: ***$41,025 ÷ 12 = $3,418.75***. Thus, the monthly rental payment for this odd-shaped lot is $3,418.75.

Volume Problems

Occasionally you may need to calculate the volume of a three-dimensional space. Volume is usually stated in cubic feet or cubic yards. A formula for calculating volume can be stated as: *Volume = Length × Width × Height*, or *V = L × W × H*. It's the same as the area formula, except it has one added element: *H*, the height of the space being measured.

Example: The floor of a storage unit measures 13 feet 6 inches by 20 feet, and it has a 12-foot ceiling. What is the volume of the unit in cubic yards?

1. **Write down the formula**. *V = L × W × H*
2. **Substitute**. *V = 20' × 13.5' × 12'*
3. **Calculate**.

Step 1		Step 2	
20'		270	Square feet
× 13.5'		× 12'	
270	Square feet	3,240	Cubic feet

4. **Now convert the cubic feet into cubic yards**. As you saw earlier, a square yard measures 3 feet by 3 feet, or 9 square feet. A cubic yard measures 3 feet by 3 feet by 3 feet, or 27 cubic feet. Divide the volume of the storage area in cubic feet by 27 to find the volume in cubic yards: *3,240 ÷ 27 = 120 Cubic yards*. The volume of the storage space is 120 cubic yards.

Percentage Problems

Many real estate math problems involve percentages. This includes problems about brokerage commissions, interest on mortgage loans, property appreciation or depreciation, and capitalization.

Solving Percentage Problems

To solve percentage problems, you'll usually convert the percentage into a decimal number, calculate, and then, in some cases, convert the answer back into percentage form. As explained earlier, a percentage is converted into a decimal number by removing the percent sign and moving the decimal point two places to the left. If the percentage is a single digit (for example, 7%), it will be necessary to add a zero (.07). To convert a decimal number into a percentage, you reverse those steps: move the decimal point two places to the right and add the percent sign.

In a math problem, whenever something is expressed as a percentage "of" another number, that indicates that you should multiply that other number by the percentage. For instance, what is 75% of $40,000?

Step 1	Step 2
75% becomes .75	$40,000
	× .75
	$30,000

Basically, percentage problems ask you to find a part of a whole. The whole is a larger figure, such as a property's sales price. The part is a smaller figure, such as a broker's commission. The general formula can be stated thus: *A percentage of the whole equals the part.* Written as an equation, this is *Part = Whole × Percentage.*

Example: A house is listed for sale at a price of $172,000, with an agreement to pay a commission of 6% of the sales price. The property sells for $170,000. How much is the commission?

1. **Write down the formula**. *P = W × %*
2. **Substitute**. Change the percentage (6%) into a decimal number (.06) first: *P = $170,000 × .06.*
3. **Calculate**.

$170,000	Sales price
× .06	*Commission rate*
$10,200	*Commission*

The commission is $10,200. (Note that if you divided instead of multiplied, the result would be a $2,833,333 commission. An implausible result like that should prompt you to try the problem the other way, multiplying instead of dividing this time.)

In some percentage problems, the part is given and you're asked to calculate either the whole or the percentage. For those problems, you'll need to rearrange the percentage formula into a division problem. You'll be dividing the value of the part either by the percentage or by the value of the whole. If the whole is the unknown, divide the part by the percentage: *Whole = Part ÷ Percentage.* If the percentage is the unknown, divide the part by the whole: *Percentage = Part ÷ Whole.*

In problems where you're asked to find the percentage, you'll need to decide which of the two numbers given in the problem is the part and which is the whole. This is easy, though: the part will be the smaller number and the whole will be the larger number. Even if you get that wrong, it will be easy to tell: the result will be a percentage that's greater than 100%. Again, that should prompt you to try the problem the other way.

Commission Problems

Like the example above, most commission problems can be solved with the general percentage formula: *Part = Whole × Percentage.*

The percentage is the commission rate, and the whole is the amount that the commission is based on. In most problems, this will be the sales price of a piece of property. The part is the amount of the commission.

Example: A listing agreement provides for a commission of 7% of the sales price. The managing broker has agreed to pay their broker 60% of the commission. How much will the broker receive if the property sells for $580,000?

1. **Write down the formula**. *P = W × %*
2. **Substitute**. Change the percentage (7%) to a decimal number (.07): *P = $580,000 × .07.*
3. **Calculate**. The part is the unknown quantity, so the percentage is multiplied by the whole.

$580,000	*Sales price*
× .07	*Commission rate*
$40,600	*Total commission*

The total commission is $40,600. The broker is entitled to 60% of the total commission. Apply the percentage formula again to determine the amount of the broker's share.

1. **Write down the formula**. *P = W × %*
2. **Substitute**. Convert the percentage (60%) to a decimal number (.60): *P = $40,600 × .60.*
3. **Calculate**.

$40,600	*Total commission*
× .60	*Broker's percentage*
$24,360	*Broker's share*

The following example illustrates another form that commission problems can take.

Example: A listing agreement provided for a two-tiered commission based on the property's sales price. The commission would be 7% of the first $100,000 and 5% of any amount over $100,000. If the commission was $8,250, what was the sales price?

1. **Read the question**. You're given the commission rates and the amount of the commission, and then asked to find the sales price. Your first step in the process is to find out how much of the commission amount is attributable to the first $100,000 of the sales price.
2. **Write down the formula**. *P = W × %*
3. **Substitute**, converting the percentage to a decimal: *P = $100,000 × .07.*
4. **Calculate**. *$100,000 × .07 = $7,000*

So $7,000 of the commission is based on the first $100,000 of the sales price. Next, subtract to find the amount of the rest of the commission.

$8,250	*Total commission*
– 7,000	*Commission from first $100,000*
$1,250	

Now you know that out of the total commission, $1,250 is attributable to the part of the sales price in excess of $100,000. You can use that figure along with the second-tier commission rate (5% of the amount over $100,000) to determine by how much the sales price exceeded $100,000.

1. **Write down the formula**. *P* = *W* × %
2. **Substitute**, converting the percentage to a decimal: *$1,250 = W × .05.*
3. **Calculate**. The quantity *W* (the whole) is the unknown. To isolate the unknown, the basic formula must be turned into a division problem. The part divided by the percentage equals the whole: *$1,250 ÷ .05 = $25,000.*

This shows that the portion of the sales price in excess of $100,000 amounted to $25,000. Thus, the total sales price is $100,000 plus $25,000, or $125,000.

Loan Problems

Loan problems include interest problems and principal balance problems. These can be solved using the general percentage formula: *Part = Whole × Percentage.* Here, the part is the amount of the interest, the whole is the loan amount or principal balance, and the percentage is the interest rate.

Example: Henry borrows $5,000 for one year and agrees to pay 7% interest. How much interest will he be required to pay?

1. **Write down the formula**. *P* = *W* × %
2. **Substitute**. *P = $5,000 × .07*
3. **Calculate**.

$5,000	*Loan amount*
× .07	*Interest rate*
$350	*Interest*

Henry will pay $350 in interest.

Interest Rates. Interest rates are expressed as annual rates. Some problems present you with monthly, quarterly, or semi-annual interest payments instead of the annual amount. In that case, you'll need to multiply the payment amount stated in the problem to determine the annual amount before you substitute the numbers into the formula.

Example: If $450 in interest accrues on a $7,200 interest-only loan in six months, what is the annual interest rate?

1. **Read the question**. You're asked to find the annual interest rate, but the interest amount given in the problem ($450) accrued in only six months. The annual interest amount would be double that, or $900.
2. **Write down the formula**. *P* = *W* × %
3. **Substitute**. For the part (the interest amount), be sure to use the annual figure ($900): *$900 = $7,200 × Percentage.*
4. **Calculate**. Rearrange the formula to isolate the unknown (in this case, the percentage). The part is divided by the whole to determine the percentage: *$900 ÷ $7,200 = .125.*

In this problem, you need to convert the decimal number back into a percentage: .125 becomes 12.5%. Thus, the annual interest rate is 12½%.

Principal Balance. Some loan problems ask you to determine a loan's current principal balance at a certain point in the loan term.

Example: A home loan has monthly payments of $625, which include principal and 9% interest and $47.50 per month for tax and insurance reserves. If $27.75 of the June 1 payment was applied to the principal, what was the outstanding principal balance during the month of May? (Mortgage interest is paid in arrears, so the June payment includes the interest that accrued during May.)

1. **Write down the formula**. *P* = *W* × %. Once again, in this context the part is the amount of interest, the whole is the loan balance, and the percentage is the interest rate.
2. **Substitute**. First, find the interest portion of the payment by subtracting the reserves and the principal portion.

$625.00	*Total June payment*
47.50	*Reserves*
– 27.75	*Principal*
$549.75	*Interest portion of payment*

   Next, multiply the interest portion by 12 to determine the annual interest amount: *$549.75 × 12 = $6,597.*

   Now substitute the annual interest amount and rate into the formula: *$6,597 = W × .09.*

3. **Calculate**. Rearrange the formula to isolate the unknown, *W*. This is a division problem: *$6,597 ÷ .09 = $73,300.*

   The outstanding principal balance for May was $73,300.

Profit or Loss Problems

Profit or loss problems ask you to compare the cost or value of a piece of property at an earlier point in time with its cost or value at a later point. They can be solved using a variation on the percentage formula. Instead of *Part = Whole × Percentage*, the formula is stated like this: *Now = Then × Percentage.*

The *Then* spot in the formula is for the value or cost of the property at an earlier time specified in the problem. The *Now* spot is for the value or cost at a later time. The percentage is 100% plus the percentage of profit or minus the percentage of loss. So, in contrast to other types of percentage problems, in this kind of problem it's common to end up using a percentage greater than 100%.

The idea is to express the value of the property after a profit or loss (*Now*) as a percentage of the property's value before the profit or loss (*Then*). If there is no profit or loss, the *Now* value is exactly 100% of the *Then* value, because the value has not changed. If there is a profit, the *Now* value will be greater than 100% of the *Then* value, since the value has increased. If there is a loss, the *Now* value will be less than 100% of the *Then* value.

Example: Bonnie bought a house five years ago for $450,000 and sold it this year for 30% more than she paid for it. What did she sell it for?

1. **Write down the formula**. *Now = Then × %*
2. **Substitute**. To get the percentage, you must add the percentage of profit to or subtract the percentage of loss from 100%. In this case there is a profit, so you add 30% to 100%, then convert it to a decimal number (130% becomes 1.30): *Now = $450,000 × 1.30.*
3. **Calculate**. *$450,000 × 1.30 = $585,000*

Bonnie sold her house for $585,000.

Example: Paul sold his house this year for $840,000. He paid $1,050,000 for it two years ago. What was the percentage of loss?

1. **Write down the formula**. *Now = Then × %*
2. **Substitute**. *$840,000 = $1,050,000 × %*
3. **Calculate**. The percentage is the unknown quantity; thus, the formula is rearranged to isolate the percentage: *$840,000 ÷ $1,050,000 = .80 or 80%.*

The *Now* value is 80% of the *Then* value. Subtract 80% from 100% to find the percentage of loss: *100% – 80% = 20% Loss.*

Paul took a 20% loss on the sale of his house.

Let's look at another example, except this time there is a profit instead of a loss.

Example: Martha bought her home six years ago for $377,400. She sold it recently for $422,700. What was her percentage of profit?

1. **Write down the formula**. *Now = Then × %*
2. **Substitute**. *$422,700 = $377,400 × %*
3. **Calculate**. Once again, the percentage is the unknown quantity; thus, the formula is rearranged to isolate the percentage: *$422,700 ÷ $377,400 = 1.12 or 112%.*

The *Now* value is approximately 112% of the *Then* value. Subtract 100% from 112%, and you determine Martha received 100% of what she paid for the house, plus a 12% profit. (Note that if you went the other direction and divided $377,400 by $422,700, you would get the answer .89, or 89%. Since any percentage under 100% represents a loss rather than a profit, you would know to discard that answer and try the division step the other way.)

Let's try to solve one last variation on this type of problem.

Example: Ken sold his duplex for $280,000, which represents a 16% profit over what he paid for it five years ago. What did Ken originally pay for the property?

1. **Write down the formula**. *Now = Then × %*
2. **Substitute**. *$280,000 = Then × 116%*
3. **Calculate**. In this instance, the unknown is the price Ken originally paid for the duplex; so you isolate the *Then* part of the equation: *$280,000 ÷ 1.16 = $241,379.31.*

The price paid by Ken was $241,379.31.

Some profit or loss problems involve appreciation or depreciation that has accrued at an annual rate over a specified number of years. You solve this type of problem by applying the *Then* and *Now* formula one year at a time.

Example: A property that is currently worth $174,000 has depreciated 3% per year for the past four years. How much was it worth four years ago?

1. **Write down the formula**. *Now = Then × %*
2. **Substitute**. Because the property is worth 3% less than it was one year ago, the percentage is 97% (100% – 3% = 97%): *$174,000 = Then × .97.*

3. **Calculate**. Rearrange the formula to isolate the unknown, the *Then* value: *$174,000 ÷ .97 = $179,381.44.*

The property was worth $179,381.44 one year ago. Apply the formula to $179,381.44 to determine the property's value two years ago. Repeat the process twice more to find the value four years ago.

$179,381.44 ÷ .97 = $184,929.31

$184,929.31 ÷ .97 = $190,648.77

$190,648.77 ÷ .97 = $196,545.12

The property was worth about $196,545 four years ago.

Capitalization Problems

Capitalization problems involve the income approach to value, a method of real estate appraisal that is discussed in Chapter 12. The capitalization formula is another variation on the percentage formula. Instead of *Part = Whole × Percentage*, the formula is stated like this: *Income = Value × Capitalization Rate.*

The value here is an investment property's value, or the purchase price an investor should be willing to pay for the property in order to obtain a specified rate of return.

The specified rate of return is the capitalization rate. This is the percentage of return the investor desires on the investment. The desired rate of return varies according to many factors. A higher desired rate of return will mean a higher capitalization rate and a lower value for the property.

The income in the capitalization formula is the annual net income produced by the investment property.

Example: A property produces an annual net income of $26,000. If an investor desires an 11% rate of return, what should they pay for the property?

1. **Write down the formula**. *I = V × %*
2. **Substitute**. *$26,000 = V × .11*
3. **Calculate**. Rearrange the formula to isolate *V*, the unknown quantity: *$26,000 ÷ .11 = $236,363.64.*

The investor should be willing to pay approximately $236,364 for the property.

Example: If a property is valued at $1,000,000 using an 8% capitalization rate, what would its value be using a 10% capitalization rate? First, apply the capitalization formula to determine the property's annual net income.

1. **Write down the formula**. *I = V × %*
2. **Substitute**. *I = $1,000,000 × .08*
3. **Calculate**.

$1,000,000	*Value*
× .08	*Capitalization rate*
$80,000	*Annual net income*

The net income is $80,000 annually. Now substitute that figure into the formula to find the value at a 10% capitalization rate.

4. **Substitute**. *$80,000 = V × .10*
5. **Calculate**. Rearrange the formula to isolate *V*, the unknown quantity: *$80,000 ÷ .10 = $800,000.*

So the value of the same property using a 10% capitalization rate is $800,000, compared to $1,000,000 at the 8% rate. As you can see, a higher capitalization rate applied to the same net income results in a lower value for the property.

In some problems, it's necessary to deduct a vacancy factor and operating expenses from gross income to arrive at the net income.

Example: A ten-unit apartment building has six units that rent for $800 per month and four units that rent for $850 per month. Allow 5% for vacancies and uncollected rent. Operating expenses include: annual property taxes of $7,200, monthly utilities of $2,475, and maintenance expenses of approximately $13,600 per year. The owner has an outstanding mortgage balance of $257,000 at 8% interest, with monthly payments of $2,150. If an investor requires a 7.5% rate of return, how much should they offer for the property?

1. **Write down the formula**. *I = V × %*
2. **Substitute**. Remember that the income referred to in the capitalization formula is annual net income. Thus, it's necessary to calculate the annual net income before substituting. The first step in that process is calculating the annual gross income.

$800 × 12 months = $9,600/year × 6 units = $57,600
$850 × 12 months = $10,200/year × 4 units = $40,800
$98,400

The gross income is $98,400 per year.

Next, calculate the vacancy factor and deduct it from the gross income to find the effective gross income. The vacancy factor is 5% of the gross income.

$98,400	*Gross income*
× .05	
$4,920	*Vacancies and uncollected rent*

Thus, the loss to be expected from vacancies and uncollected rent is $4,920 per year.

$98,400	*Gross income*
− 4,920	*Vacancies and uncollected rent*
$93,480	*Effective gross income*

The operating expenses must be deducted from the effective gross income to arrive at the net income. Remember, since you are trying to find annual net income, all the expenses must be annual also.

The operating expenses add up as follows:

$7,200	*Property taxes*
$29,700	*Utilities (at $2,475 per month)*
+ $13,600	*Maintenance*
$50,500	*Annual operating expenses*

The annual operating expenses are $50,500. (The mortgage payments are not treated as operating expenses. See Chapter 12.)

Subtract the operating expenses from the effective gross income to determine the annual net income.

$93,480	*Effective gross income*
– 50,500	*Annual operating expenses*
$42,980	*Annual net income*

Now, substitute the net income and the cap rate into the formula *I= V × %: $42,980 = V × .075.*

3. **Calculate**. Rearrange the formula to isolate *V*, the unknown quantity: *$42,980 ÷ .075 = $573,067.*

The investor should be willing to pay approximately $573,067 for the property.

Example: Continuing with the previous example, if an investor paid $750,000 for the apartment building, what capitalization rate was used? (Assume that the property's income and operating expenses were the same.)

1. **Write down the formula**. *I = V × %*
2. **Substitute**. You already know the net income from the preceding problem: *$42,980 = $750,000 × %.*
3. **Calculate**. Isolate the unknown quantity, the capitalization rate: *$42,980 ÷ $750,000 = .0573 or 5.73%.*

The investor used a capitalization rate of approximately 5.7%.

A capitalization problem may give you the property's **operating expense ratio** (O.E.R.). The O.E.R. is the percentage of the gross income that is used to pay the annual operating expenses. The remainder is the annual net income.

Example: A property's annual gross income is $480,000, and its O.E.R. is 79%. If an investor wants a 10½% return on investment (ROI), how much is the property worth to them?

1. **Write down the formula**. *I = V × %*
2. **Substitute**. Calculate the annual operating expenses using the operating expense ratio. Then subtract the operating expenses from the gross income to arrive at the annual net income.

   $480,000 × .79 = $379,200 Annual operating expenses

   $480,000 – $379,200 = $100,800 Annual net income

   Now substitute the income and the cap rate into the formula: *$100,800 = V × .105.*
3. **Calculate**. Rearrange the formula to isolate *V*, the unknown quantity: *$100,800 ÷ .105 = $960,000 Value.*

The investor should be willing to pay $960,000 for the property.

Tax Assessment Problems

Many tax assessment problems can be solved using this formula: *Tax = Assessed Value × Tax Rate*. You may first have to determine the assessed value before you can carry out the rest of the calculations. Assessed value is a property's value for taxation purposes.

Example: According to the tax assessor, the property's market value is $292,300. The applicable assessment ratio is 85%. If the tax rate is 3%, how much is the annual tax amount?

1. **Multiply** the market value by the assessment ratio to determine the assessed value of the property: *$292,300 × 85% = $248,455 Assessed value.*
2. **Substitute** the assessed value and the tax rate into the formula: *Tax = $248,455 × .03.*
3. **Calculate.**

$248,455	*Assessed value*
× .03	*Tax rate*
$7,453.65	*Annual taxes*

The annual taxes for this property are $7,453.65.

In some problems, the tax rate is not stated as a percentage of the assessed value. Instead, it is expressed as a dollar amount per hundred or per thousand dollars of assessed value.

Example: A property with an assessed value of $173,075 is taxed at a rate of $2.35 per hundred dollars of assessed value. How much is the annual tax amount?

1. **Divide** $173,075 by 100 to determine how many hundred dollar increments there are in the assessed value: *$173,075 ÷ 100 = 1,730.75 or 1,731 $100 increments.* (A partial $100 increment would be taxed as one $100 increment.)
2. **Multiply** the number of hundred dollar increments by the tax rate to calculate the annual tax amount.

1,731	*$100 increments*
× $2.35	*Tax rate*
$4,067.85	*Annual taxes*

The annual tax is $4,067.85.

In other problems, the tax rate is expressed as a specified number of mills per dollar of assessed value. A mill is one-tenth of one cent (.001). Ten mills equals one cent, and 100 mills equals 10 cents.

Example: The property's market value is $310,000 and the assessment ratio is 70%. The tax rate is 21 mills per dollar of assessed value. How much is the annual tax amount?

1. **Multiply** the market value by the assessment ratio to find the assessed value.

$310,000	*Market value*
× .70	*Assessment ratio*
$217,000	*Assessed value*

2. **Multiply** the assessed value by the tax rate to determine the tax. In decimal form, 21 mills is .021.

$217,000	*Assessed value*
× .021	*Tax rate*
$4,557	*Annual tax*

The annual tax is $4,557.

Seller's Net Problems

In a seller's net problem, you're told that a seller wants to take away a specified net amount from closing, after paying the real estate agent's commission and other closing costs. You're then asked to calculate how much the property will have to sell for if the seller is to receive the desired net.

Example: The seller wants to net $50,000 from the sale of their home. They will have to pay off their mortgage balance, which is approximately $126,500, and pay $1,560 for repairs, $2,015 for other closing costs, and a 7% commission. What's the minimum sales price that will net the seller $50,000?

1. **Add** the seller's desired net to the costs of sale, excluding the commission.

$50,000	*Seller's net*
126,500	*Mortgage*
1,560	*Repairs*
+ 2,015	*Closing costs*
$180,075	*Total*

   This figure, $180,075, is the amount that must be left to the seller after the commission has been paid, if they are going to be able to pay all of the listed expenses and still have $50,000 left over.

2. **Subtract** the commission rate from 100%: *100% – 7% = 93%.*

3. **Divide** the total from step one by the percentage from step two. Since the commission rate will be 7% of the sales price, the seller's net plus the other costs will have to equal 93% of the sales price: *$180,075 ÷ .93 = $193,629.*

The property will have to sell for approximately $193,629 for the seller to net $50,000.

This may seem counterintuitive at first. At first glance, it may seem that you're applying the commission rate to the closing costs as well as the selling price. But you aren't. This is best understood by working backwards through the problem. By doing so, you'll see that, as in the real world closing process, the commission is subtracted from the selling price, and then the seller's closing costs are subtracted from those proceeds.

Start by calculating the cost of the 7% commission.

$193,629	*Selling price*
× .07	*Commission*
$13,554	

Now subtract the commission and the other closing costs from the gross proceeds, to find the seller's net proceeds.

$193,629	*Selling Price*
13,554	*Commission*
126,500	*Mortgage*
1,560	*Repairs*
– 2,015	*Closing costs*
$50,000	*Net proceeds*

Proration Problems

Proration is the allocation of an amount of money between two or more parties. As was explained in Chapter 13, prorations are required in real estate closings, where a variety of expenses are prorated based on the closing date.

There are basically three steps in the proration process:

1. Calculate the per diem (daily) rate of the expense.
2. Determine the number of days for which one person is responsible for the expense.
3. Multiply the per diem rate by the number of days to determine the share of the expense that one party is responsible for: *Share = Rate × Days.*

To determine the per diem rate of an annual expense, divide the amount of the expense by 365 days, or 366 in a leap year. Some problems will instruct you to divide by 360 days instead, to simplify the calculation. (A 360-day year is sometimes referred to as a banker's year, as opposed to a calendar year.)

To determine the per diem rate of a monthly expense when you are prorating on the basis of a calendar year, divide the amount of the expense by the number of days in that particular month. Alternatively, to simplify the calculation, you may be instructed to base your prorations on a banker's year, which means that every month is treated as having 30 days, including February.

We'll present examples showing the proration of three types of expenses: property taxes, hazard insurance, and mortgage interest. (See Chapter 13 for more information about these expenses.) In some transactions it's also necessary to prorate property income (rent), so we'll include an example of that type of proration as well.

Property Tax Prorations

Property taxes are an annual expense. At closing, the taxes may or may not have been paid yet. If they've already been paid, the buyer will owe the seller a share of the taxes. If they haven't been paid, the seller will owe the buyer a share. Either way, the proration process is essentially the same.

Example: The closing date is August 3, and the seller has already paid the annual property taxes, which were $2,045. At closing, the seller is entitled to a credit for the tax amount covering the period from August 3 through December 31. The same amount will be a debit for the buyer. How much will the buyer owe the seller for the property taxes? Use a 360-day year with 30-day months for your calculations, and assume the buyer is responsible for the taxes for the day of closing.

1. **Calculate the per diem rate** for the property taxes, using a 360-day year: *$2,045 ÷ 360 = $5.68 per diem.*

2. **Count the number of days** that the buyer is responsible for, using 30-day months.

   28 days August 3 through 30
   30 days September
   30 days October
   30 days November
   + 30 days December
   148 days

3. **Substitute** the rate and number of days into the formula (*S* = *R* × *D*), then calculate.

   148 Days
   × $5.68 Per diem
   $840.64 Credit for seller

   At closing, the buyer will be debited $840.64 and the seller will be credited $840.64 for the property taxes from August 3 through the end of the tax year.

In the following example, the taxes haven't been paid yet. You're given the seller's share of the taxes and asked to calculate the annual tax amount.

Example: The seller hasn't paid any portion of the annual taxes. The closing is scheduled for March 21. At closing, the seller will owe the buyer $663.60 for the taxes. How much was the annual tax bill? This time, use a 365-day year and exact-day months in your calculations. The buyer's responsibility for the taxes begins on the day of closing.

1. **Write down the formula.** *S* = *R* × *D*

2. **Substitute**. First add up the number of days that the seller is responsible for.

   31 days January
   28 days February
   + 20 days March 1 through 20
   79 days

   Substitute the seller's share and the number of days into the formula: *$663.60 = R × 79.*

3. **Calculate**. Rearrange the formula to isolate *R*, the unknown quantity: *$663.60 ÷ 79 = $8.40 Per diem.*

   The per diem rate is $8.40. Multiply that by 365 to arrive at the annual tax amount.

   365 Days
   × $8.40 Per diem
   $3,066 Annual taxes

The annual taxes were $3,066.

Insurance Prorations

A seller is entitled to a refund from the hazard insurance company for any prepaid insurance coverage extending beyond the closing date.

Example: The Morgans are selling their house, and the transaction is closing on May 12. They paid an annual hazard insurance premium of $810 that provides coverage through the end of October. How much of the premium will be refunded to them? Base your calculations on a 360-day year.

1. **Calculate the per diem rate** for the insurance, using a 360-day year: *$810 ÷ 360 = $2.25 Per diem.*

2. **Add up the number of days** for which the sellers are owed a refund, using 30-day months.

   19 days May 12 through 30
   30 days June
   30 days July
   30 days August
   30 days September
   + 30 days October
   169 days

3. **Substitute** the rate and number of days into the formula (*S* = *R* × *D*), then calculate.

   169 Days
   × $2.25 Per diem
   $380.25 Credit for seller

The insurance company will refund $380.25 to the sellers.

Rent Prorations

If the property being sold is rental property, the seller will owe the buyer a prorated share of any rent that has been paid in advance.

Example: A ten-unit apartment building is being sold, with the closing scheduled for April 23. Four of the units rent for $1,500 per month, and the other six rent for $1,200 per month. All of the tenants paid their April rent on time. If the buyer is entitled to the rents for the day of closing, what share of the prepaid rents will the seller owe the buyer at closing?

1. **Determine the total amount** of rent owed for April.

   $1,500 × 4 = $6,000

   $1,200 × 6 = $7,200

   $6,000 + $7,200 = $13,200

2. **Calculate the per diem rate** for the month of April: *$13,200 ÷ 30 = $440 Per diem.*

3. **Determine the number of days** of rent the buyer is entitled to, beginning on the closing date. April 23 through April 30 is eight days. (It doesn't matter whether you use a 360-day or 365-day year here, since either way April has 30 days and we are calculating a prorated share for only part of the month.)

4. **Substitute** and **calculate**.

   $440 Per diem
   × 8 Days
   $3,520 Prorated rent

The seller will owe the buyer $3,520 in prepaid rents at closing.

Mortgage Interest Prorations

Two different types of mortgage interest prorations are necessary in most transactions, one for the seller and one for the buyer. The seller typically owes a final interest payment on the loan they are paying off.

Example: The remaining balance on the seller's mortgage is $317,550, and the interest rate is 8%. The closing date is set for July 6. Because mortgage interest is paid in arrears, the mortgage payment that the seller paid on July 1 covers the interest that accrued during June. At closing, the seller owes the lender interest covering July 1 through the day of closing. How much will that interest payment be? Base your calculations on a calendar year.

1. First calculate the annual interest, using the percentage formula.

   a) **Write down the formula.**
   Payment = Loan balance × Interest

   b) **Substitute**. *P = $317,550 × .08*

   c) **Calculate**.

   $317,550 Loan amount
   × .08 Interest rate
   $25,404 Annual interest

2. Next, find the per diem rate of the expense. Divide the annual rate by 365: *$25,404 ÷ 365 = $69.60 Per diem.*

3. Determine the number of days the seller owes interest for. The lender will charge the seller interest for the day of closing. Thus, the seller owes interest for six days, from July 1 through July 6.

4. Finally, substitute the numbers into the proration formula (*S* = *R* × *D*) and calculate.

   $69.60 Per diem
   × 6 Days
   $417.60 Final interest payment

At closing, the seller will be required to make a final interest payment of $417.60.

The buyer also owes some mortgage interest at closing. This is prepaid interest (interim interest) on the buyer's new loan. Prepaid interest covers the day of closing through the last day of the month in which closing takes place. (See Chapter 13 for more information.)

Example: The principal amount of the buyer's new loan is $230,680. The interest rate is 8%. The transaction closes on June 22. How much prepaid interest will the buyer's lender require the buyer to pay at closing? Base your calculations on a 365-day year.

1. Use the percentage formula to calculate the annual amount of interest.

   a) **Write down the formula.**
   Payment = Loan balance × Interest rate

   b) **Substitute**. *P = $230,680 × 8%*

   c) **Calculate**. *$230,680 × .08 = $18,454.40*

2. Find the per diem rate of the expense. Divide the annual rate by 365: *$18,454.40 ÷ 365 = $50.56.*

3. Determine the number of days the buyer is responsible for. In prepaid interest prorations, the buyer pays for the day of closing. There are nine days: June 22, 23, 24, 25, 26, 27, 28, 29, and 30.

4. Substitute the daily rate and number of days into the proration formula *(S = R × D)* and calculate.

   $50.56 Per diem
   × 9 Days
   $455.04 Prepaid interest

The buyer's interest charge would be $455.04.

Chapter Summary

Converting fractions to decimals:
Divide numerator (top number) by denominator (bottom number).

Converting percentages to decimals:
Move decimal point two places to the left and drop the percent sign.

Converting decimals to percentages:
Move decimal point two places to the right and add a percent sign.

Area formula for squares and rectangles:
Area = Length × Width
$A = L \times W$

Area formula for triangles:
Area = ½ Base × Height
$A = \frac{1}{2} B \times H$

Volume formula:
Volume = Length × Width × Height
$V = L \times W \times H$

Percentage formula:
Part = Whole × Percentage
$P = W \times \%$

Profit or loss formula:
Now = Then × %

Capitalization formula:
Income = Value × Rate
$I = V \times \%$

Proration formula:
Share = Daily Rate × Number of Days
$S = R \times D$

1. *Find annual or monthly amount;*
2. *Find daily rate;*
3. *Determine number of days; and*
4. *Substitute and calculate.*

Chapter Quiz

1. **Christine and Tom bought a condo one year ago for $168,500. If property values in their neighborhood are increasing at an annual rate of 7%, what is the current market value of their condo?**
   a) $180,295
   b) $184,270
   c) $195,980
   d) $198,893

2. **A home just sold for $183,500. The listing firm charged the seller a 6½% commission. The listing firm will pay 50% of that amount to the selling firm, and 25% to the broker who took the listing. How much will the listing broker's share of the commission be?**
   a) $11,927
   b) $5,963
   c) $3,642
   d) $2,982

3. **A rectangular lot that has a 45-foot frontage and contains 1,080 square yards has a depth of:**
   a) 63 feet
   b) 216 feet
   c) 188 feet
   d) 97 feet

4. **An acre contains 43,560 square feet. What is the maximum number of lots measuring 50 feet by 100 feet that can be created from a one-acre parcel?**
   a) Six
   b) Seven
   c) Eight
   d) Nine

5. **Felicia sold a client's building for $480,000 and received a commission of $33,600. What was her commission rate?**
   a) 6.5%
   b) 7%
   c) 7.5%
   d) 8%

6. **Jake bought a lot for $5,000 and later sold it for $8,000. What was his percentage of profit?**
   a) 60%
   b) 75%
   c) 80%
   d) 85%

7. **Diane wants to purchase an income property that has an annual net income of $16,000. If she wants at least an 8% return on her investment, what is the most she should pay for the property?**
   a) $150,000
   b) $175,000
   c) $195,000
   d) $200,000

8. **George purchases a building for $85,000. The building generates a yearly net income of $5,100. What is his rate of return?**
   a) 5.5%
   b) 6%
   c) 6.5%
   d) 7%

9. **How many square yards are there in a rectangle that measures 75 feet × 30 feet?**
   a) 6,750
   b) 2,250
   c) 750
   d) 250

10. **Mike is purchasing an apartment building. The closing date is September 15, and the seller has already collected the monthly rents in the amount of $13,960 for September. They agree that the rents for the day of closing will belong to Mike. At closing, the seller will have to pay Mike a prorated share of the September rents, which will amount to approximately:**
    a) $612
    b) $931
    c) $7,445
    d) $9,035

11. **A triangular lot has a 40-foot base and a 30-foot height. What is the area of the lot?**
    a) 500 square feet
    b) 600 square feet
    c) 750 square feet
    d) 650 square feet

12. **What is the decimal equivalent of five-eighths (5/8)?**
    a) .625
    b) .0825
    c) 1.58
    d) 1.60

13. **Kay has obtained a $112,000 loan at 8.5% interest, as secondary financing to help with the purchase of a home. At closing, the lender will require her to prepay interest for April 26 through April 30. Assuming that the closing agent uses a 365-day year for the proration, how much will that prepaid interest amount to?**

a) $64.35
b) $104.32
c) $130.40
d) $1,403.84

14. **The Binghams are selling their house and paying off the mortgage at closing. The remaining principal balance on the mortgage at closing will be $168,301.50. They will also have to pay interest that accrued over the 7-day period between their last mortgage payment and the closing date. If the annual interest rate on the Binghams' mortgage was 10%, how much will they have to pay in interest at closing? (Use a 365-day year for the proration.)**

a) $85.21
b) $322.77
c) $409.86
d) $694.41

15. **Carol has just paid $460,000 for a building that will bring her a 9.75% return on her investment. What is the building's annual net income?**

a) $34,965
b) $36,750
c) $41,220
d) $44,850

Glossary

The definitions given here explain how the listed terms are used in the real estate field. Some of the terms have additional meanings, which can be found in a standard dictionary.

1031 Exchange—A transaction in which a piece of property held for investment or used in a trade or business is traded for a piece of like-kind property, thus deferring tax on the gain. Sometimes called a Tax-Free Exchange or Tax-Deferred Exchange.

-A-

Abandonment—Failure to occupy and use property, which may result in a loss of rights.

Absolute Fee—The highest and most complete form of ownership, which is of potentially infinite duration. Also called a Fee or a Fee Simple.

Abstract of Judgment—A document summarizing the essential provisions of a court judgment which, when recorded, creates a lien on the judgment debtor's real property.

Abstract of Title— A brief, chronological summary of the recorded documents affecting title to a particular piece of real property.

Abut—To touch, border on, be adjacent to, or share a common boundary with.

Acceleration Clause—A provision in a promissory note or security instrument allowing the lender to declare the entire debt due immediately if the borrower breaches one or more provisions of the loan agreement. Also referred to as a call provision.

Acceptance—1. Agreeing to the terms of an offer to enter into a contract, thereby creating a binding contract. 2. Taking delivery of a deed from the grantor.

Access Easement—An easement that enables the easement holder to reach and/or leave their property (the dominant tenement) by crossing the servient tenement. Also called an easement for ingress and egress.

Accession—The acquisition of title to additional property by its annexation to real estate already owned. This can be the result of human actions (as in the case of fixtures) or natural processes (such as accretion and reliction).

Accord and Satisfaction—An agreement to accept something different than (and usually less than) what the contract originally called for.

Accretion—A gradual addition to dry land by the forces of nature, as when waterborne sediment is deposited on waterfront property.

Accrued Depreciation—Depreciation that has built up or accumulated over a period of time.

Accrued Items of Expense—Expenses that have been incurred but are not yet due or payable; in a settlement statement, the seller's accrued expenses are credited to the buyer.

Acknowledgment—When a person who has signed a document formally declares to an authorized official (usually a notary public) that they signed voluntarily. The official can then attest that the signature is voluntary and genuine.

Acquisition Cost—The amount of money a buyer was required to expend in order to acquire title to a piece of property; in addition to the purchase price, this might include closing costs, legal fees, and other expenses.

Acre—An area of land equal to 43,560 square feet, or 4,840 square yards.

Actual Age—The age of a structure from a chronological standpoint (as opposed to its effective age); how many years it has actually been in existence.

Actual Annexation—When personal property is physically attached to real property, so that it becomes part of the real property.

Actual Authority—Authority actually given to an agent by the principal, either expressly or by implication.

Actual Eviction—Physically forcing someone off of real property (or preventing them from re-entering), or using the legal process to make them leave. *Compare:* Constructive Eviction.

Actual Fraud—Deceit or misrepresentation with the intention of cheating or defrauding another.

Actual Notice—Actual knowledge of a fact, as opposed to knowledge imputed by law (constructive notice).

Ad Valorem—A Latin phrase that means "according to value," used to refer to taxes that are assessed on the value of property.

Ad Valorem Tax—A tax assessed on the value of property.

Addendum—An attachment to a purchase and sale agreement or other contract that contains additional provisions that apply to that transaction.

Adjacent—Nearby, next to, bordering, or neighboring; may or may not be in actual contact.

Adjustable-Rate Mortgage (ARM)—A loan in which the interest rate is periodically increased or decreased to reflect changes in the cost of money. *Compare:* Fixed-Rate Loan.

Adjusted Basis—For income tax purposes, the initial basis plus capital expenditures, less any depreciation deductions.

Adjustment Period—The interval at which an adjustable-rate mortgage borrower's interest rate or monthly payment is changed.

Administrator's Deed—A deed used by the administrator of an estate to convey property owned by the deceased person to the heirs.

Administrator—A person appointed by the probate court to manage and distribute the estate of a deceased person, when no executor is named in the will or there is no will.

Adverse Possession—Acquiring title to real property that belongs to someone else by taking possession of it without permission, in the manner and for the length of time prescribed by statute.

Affidavit—A sworn statement made before a notary public (or other official authorized to administer an oath) that has been written down and acknowledged.

Affiliated Licensee—An individual licensee (either a broker or a managing broker) who is licensed to work for and represent a particular real estate firm.

Affirm—1. To confirm or ratify. 2. To make a solemn declaration that is not under oath.

After-Acquired Title—A rule applicable to warranty deeds; if the title is defective at the time of transfer, but the grantor later acquires more perfect title, the additional interest passes to the grantee automatically.

Age of Majority—The age at which a person becomes legally competent; in Washington, 18 years old. *See:* Minor.

Agency Coupled with an Interest—When an agent has a claim against the property that is the subject of the agency, so that the principal cannot revoke the agent's authority.

Agency—A relationship of trust created when one person (the principal) grants another (the agent) authority to represent the principal in dealings with third parties.

Agent—A person authorized to represent another (the principal) in dealings with third parties.

Agreement—An agreement between two or more persons to do or not do a certain thing, for consideration. Also called Contract.

Air Lot—A parcel of property above the surface of the earth, not containing any land; for example, a condominium unit on the third floor occupies an air lot.

Air Rights—The right to undisturbed use and control of the airspace over a parcel of land; may be transferred separately from the land.

Alienation—The transfer of ownership or an interest in property from one person to another, by any means.

Alienation Clause—A provision in a security instrument that gives the lender the right to declare the entire loan balance due immediately if the borrower sells or otherwise transfers the security property. Also called a due-on-sale clause.

All-Inclusive Trust Deed—A purchase money loan arrangement in which the seller uses part of the buyer's payments to make the payments on an existing loan (called the underlying loan); the buyer takes title subject to the underlying loan, but does not assume it. When the security instrument used for wraparound financing is a deed of trust instead of a mortgage, it may be referred to as a Wrap-around Mortgage.

Amendment—A written modification to a contract that occurs after both parties have signed the document.

Amenities—Features of a property that contribute to the pleasure or convenience of owning it, such as a fireplace, a beautiful view, or its proximity to a good school.

Americans with Disabilities Act (ADA)—A federal law requiring facilities that are open to the public to ensure accessibility to disabled persons, even if that accessibility requires making architectural modifications. The ADA also requires employers to make reasonable accommodations for disabled employees.

Amortize—To gradually pay off a debt with installment payments that include both principal and interest. *See also:* Loan, Amortized.

Amortized Loan—A loan that requires regular installment payments of both principal and interest (as opposed to an interest-only loan). It is fully amortized if the installment payments will pay off the full amount of the principal and all of the interest by the end of the repayment period. It is partially amortized if the installment payments will cover only part of the principal, so that a balloon payment of the remaining principal balance is required at the end of the repayment period.

Annexation—Attaching personal property to real property, so that it becomes part of the real property (a fixture) in the eyes of the law.

Annual Percentage Rate (APR)—All of the charges that the borrower will pay for the loan (including the interest, loan fee, discount points, and mortgage insurance costs), expressed as an annual percentage of the loan amount.

Annuity—A sum of money received in a series of payments at regular intervals (often annually) over a period of time.

Anticipatory Repudiation—When one party to a contract informs the other before the time set for performance that they do not intend to fulfill the contract.

Antitrust Laws—Laws that prohibit agreements that have the effect of restraining trade.

Apparent Agency—When third parties are given the impression that someone who has not been authorized to represent another is that person's agent, or else given the impression that an agent has been authorized to perform acts which are in fact beyond the scope of their authority. Also called ostensible agency.

Apparent Authority—Authority to represent another that someone appears to have and that the principal is estopped from denying, although no actual authority has been granted.

Appeal—When one of the parties to a lawsuit asks a higher court to review the judgment or verdict reached in a lower court.

Appellant—The party who files an appeal because they are dissatisfied with the lower court's decision. Also called the petitioner.

Appellee—In an appeal, the party who did not file the appeal. Also called the respondent.

Apportionment—A division of property (as among tenants in common when the property is sold or partitioned) or liability (as when responsibility for closing costs is allocated between the buyer and seller) into proportionate, but not necessarily equal, parts.

Appraisal—An estimate or opinion of the value of a piece of property as of a particular date. Also called valuation.

Appraiser—One who estimates the value of property, especially an expert qualified to do so by training and experience.

Appreciation—An increase in value; the opposite of depreciation.

Appropriation—Taking property or reducing it to personal possession, to the exclusion of others.

Appropriative Rights—The water rights of a person who holds a prior appropriation permit.

Appurtenances—Rights that go along with ownership of a particular piece of property, such as air rights or mineral rights; they are ordinarily transferred with the property, but may, in some cases, be sold separately.

Appurtenant Easement— An easement that benefits a piece of property, the dominant tenement. *Compare:* Easement in Gross.

Area—1. Locale or region. 2. The size of a surface, usually in square units of measure, such as square feet or square miles.

Arm's Length Transaction—A transaction in which there is no family or business relationship between the parties. *See also:* Normal Market Conditions.

Artificial Person—A legal entity such as a corporation, which the law treats as an individual with legal rights and responsibilities; as distinguished from a natural person, a human being. Sometimes called a legal person.

Assemblage—Combining two or more adjoining properties into one tract. Also called assembly.

Assessed Value—The value placed on property by the taxing authority (the county assessor, for example) for the purposes of taxation.

Assessment—The valuation of property for purposes of taxation.

Assessor—An official who determines the value of property for taxation.

Asset—Anything of value that a person owns.

Assignee—One to whom rights or interests have been assigned.

Assignment of Contract and Deed—The instrument used to substitute a new vendor for the original vendor in a land contract.

Assignment—1. A transfer of contract rights from one person to another. 2. In the case of a lease, when the original tenant transfers their entire leasehold estate to another. *Compare:* Sublease.

Assignor—One who has assigned their rights or interest to another.

Assign—To transfer rights (especially contract rights) or interests to another.

Assumption Fee—A fee paid to the lender, usually by the buyer, when a mortgage or deed of trust is assumed.

Assumption—When a buyer takes on personal liability for paying off the seller's existing mortgage or deed of trust.

Attachment—Court-ordered seizure of property belonging to a defendant in a lawsuit, so that it will be available to satisfy a judgment if the plaintiff wins. In the case of real property, attachment creates a lien.

Attachment Lien—A lien intended to prevent transfer of the property pending the outcome of litigation.

Attorney General—The principal legal advisor for state agencies and employees, including the Department of Licensing.

Attorney in Fact—Any person authorized to represent another by a power of attorney; not necessarily a lawyer (an attorney at law).

Attractive Nuisance—A property feature that is dangerous and inviting to children, and a potential source of liability to the property owner.

Auditing—Verification and examination of records, particularly the financial accounts of a business or other organization.

Automatic Renewal Clause—A lease provision that ensures automatic renewal of the lease unless the tenant or the landlord gives the other party notice of an intent to terminate.

Avulsion—1. When land is suddenly (not gradually) torn away by the action of water. 2. A sudden shift in a watercourse.

-B-

Backup Offer—An offer that's contingent on the failure of an existing sale to close; when a seller accepts a backup offer, the buyer will be able to purchase the property if the first transaction falls through.

Balance Sheet—A brief instrument that is recorded to perfect and give constructive notice of a creditor's security interest in an article of personal property. Also called Financial Statement.

Balloon Mortgage—A partially amortized mortgage loan that requires a large balloon payment at the end of the loan term.

Balloon Payment—A payment on a loan (usually the final payment) that is significantly larger than the regular installment payments.

Bankruptcy—1. When the liabilities of an individual, corporation, or firm exceed the assets. 2. When a court declares an individual, corporation, or firm to be insolvent, so that the assets and debts will be administered under bankruptcy laws.

Base Line—In the government survey system, a main east-west line from which township lines are established. Each principal meridian has one base line associated with it.

Basis—A figure used in calculating a gain on the sale of real estate for federal income tax purposes. Also called cost basis.

Bench Mark—A surveyor's mark on a stationary object at a known point of elevation, used as a reference point in calculating other elevations in a surveyed area; often a metal disk set into cement or rock.

Beneficiary—1. One for whom a trust is created and on whose behalf the trustee administers the trust. 2. The lender in a deed of trust transaction. 3. One entitled to receive real or personal property under a will; a legatee or devisee.

Bequeath—To transfer personal property to another by will.

Bequest—Personal property (including money) that is transferred by will.

Bilateral Contract—A contract in which each party has made a binding promise to perform (as distinguished from a unilateral contract).

Bill of Sale—A document used to transfer title to personal property from one person to another.

Binder—1. An instrument providing immediate insurance coverage until the regular policy is issued. 2. Any payment or preliminary written statement intended to make an agreement legally binding until a formal contract has been drawn up.

Blanket Mortgage—A mortgage that covers more than one parcel of property.

Blind Ad—An advertisement placed by a real estate licensee that does not include the brokerage's name.

Block—In a subdivision, a group of lots surrounded by streets or unimproved land.

Blockbusting—Attempting to induce owners to list or sell their homes by predicting that members of a protected class (another race or ethnic group, or people with some type of disability, for example) will be moving into the neighborhood; this violates antidiscrimination laws. Also called panic selling.

Board of Directors—The body responsible for governing a corporation on behalf of the shareholders, which oversees the corporate management.

Bona Fide—In good faith; genuine; not fraudulent.

Bond—1. A written obligation, usually interest-bearing, to pay a certain sum at a specified time. 2. Money put up as a surety, protecting someone against failure to perform, negligent performance, or fraud.

Boot—In a tax-free exchange, something given or received that is not like-kind property; for example, in an exchange of real property, if one party gives the other cash in addition to real property, the cash is boot.

Boundary—The perimeter or border of a parcel of land; the dividing line between one piece of property and another.

Bounds—Boundaries. *See:* Metes and Bounds.

Branch Manager—A managing broker who is responsible for the operations of a branch office of a real estate firm.

Breach—Violation of an obligation, duty, or law; especially an unexcused failure to perform a contractual obligation.

Broker—An individual licensed to act on behalf of a real estate firm in performing real estate brokerage services.

Broker Price Opinion—Any oral or written report of property value prepared by a real estate licensee. For example, a competitive market analysis is a broker price opinion.

Brokerage— A business entity licensed to offer real estate brokerage services under the supervision and control of its designated broker; also known as a Real Estate Firm.

Brokerage and Affiliated Licensee Contract—An employment contract between a brokerage firm and an affiliated licensee, outlining their mutual obligations.

Brokerage Fee—The commission or other compensation charged for a real estate brokerage's services.

Budget Mortgage—A loan in which the monthly payments include a share of the property taxes and insurance, in addition to principal and interest; the lender places the money for taxes and insurance in a reserve account (impound account).

Buffer—An undeveloped area of land that separates two areas zoned for incompatible uses.

Building Codes—Regulations that set minimum standards for construction methods and materials.

Building Restrictions—Rules concerning building size, placement, or type; they may be public restrictions (in a zoning ordinance, for example) or private restrictions (CC&Rs, for example).

Bump Clause—A provision in a purchase and sale agreement that allows the seller to keep the property on the market while waiting for a contingency clause to be fulfilled; if the seller receives another good offer in the meantime, they can require the buyer to either waive the contingency clause or terminate the contract.

Bundle of Rights—The rights inherent in ownership of property, including the right to use, lease, enjoy, encumber, will, sell, or do nothing with the property.

Business Opportunity—The purchase, sale, exchange, or lease of a business or a business's goodwill, inventory, or other assets. Generally, agents involved in a business opportunity transaction that includes real estate need a real estate license.

Buydown—When discount points are paid to a lender to reduce (buy down) the interest rate charged to the borrower; especially when a seller pays discount points to help the buyer/borrower qualify for financing.

Buyer's Agent—A real estate licensee who is representing a buyer in a transaction, or the firm that licensee works for. Also called the buyer agent or buyer broker.

-C-

Call Provision—A provision in a promissory note or security instrument allowing the lender to declare the entire debt due immediately if the borrower breaches one or more provisions of the loan agreement. Also referred to as an Acceleration Clause.

Called Loan—A loan that has been accelerated by the lender. *See:* Acceleration Clause.

Cancellation—1. Termination of a contract without undoing acts that have been already performed under the contract. *Compare:* Rescission. 2. Termination of a license that has not been renewed in the year following its expiration date.

Capacity—The legal ability or competency to perform some act, such as enter into a contract or execute a deed or will.

Capital—Money (or other forms of wealth) available for use in the production of more money.

Capital Assets—Assets held by a taxpayer other than inventory and depreciable real property used in the taxpayer's trade or business. Thus, real property is a capital asset if it is owned for personal use or for investment.

Capital Expenditures—Money spent on improvements and alterations that add to the value of the property and/or prolong its life.

Capital Gain—Profit realized from the sale of a capital asset.

Capital Improvement—Any improvement that is designed to become a permanent part of the real property or that will have the effect of significantly prolonging the property's life.

Capital Loss—A loss resulting from the sale of a capital asset.

Capitalization Rate—A percentage used in capitalization (Net Income = Capitalization Rate × Value). It is the rate believed to represent the proper relationship between the value of the property and the income it produces; the rate that would be a reasonable return on an investment of the type in question, or the yield necessary to attract investment of capital in property like the subject property.

Capitalization—A method of appraising real property by converting the anticipated net income from the property into the present value. Also called the Income Approach to Value.

Capitalize—1. To provide with cash, or capital. 2. To determine the present value of an asset using capitalization.

Carryback Loan— When a seller extends credit to a buyer to finance the purchase of the property, accepting a deed of trust or mortgage instead of cash. Sometimes called a Purchase Money Mortgage. *Compare:* Purchase Loan.

Carryover Clause—A clause in a listing agreement providing that for a specified period after the listing expires, the brokerage will still be entitled to a commission if the property is sold to someone the brokerage dealt with during the listing term. Also called a safety clause or Extender Clause.

Cash Flow—The residual income after deducting from gross income all operating expenses and debt service. Also called spendable income.

Cash on Cash—The ratio between the cash flow received from an investment in the first year and amount of the cash initially invested.

Caveat Emptor—A Latin phrase meaning "Let the buyer beware"; it expresses the idea that a buyer is expected to examine property carefully before buying, instead of simply relying on the seller to disclose problems.

CC&Rs—A declaration of covenants, conditions, and restrictions; often recorded by a developer to place restrictions on all lots within a new subdivision.

Cease and Desist Order—An order issued by the Director of the Department of Licensing in a disciplinary action, to stop a violation of the license law.

CERCLA—The Comprehensive Environmental Response, Compensation, and Liability Act; a federal law concerning liability for cleanup of contaminated property.

Certificate of Eligibility—A document issued by the Dept. of Veterans Affairs as evidence of a veteran's eligibility for a VA-guaranteed loan.

Certificate of Occupancy—A statement issued by a local government agency (such as the building department) verifying that a newly constructed building is in compliance with all codes and may be occupied.

Certificate of Sale—The document given to the purchaser at a mortgage foreclosure sale, instead of a deed; replaced with a sheriff's deed only after the redemption period expires.

Certified Property Manager (CPM)—A property manager who has satisfied the requirements set by the Institute of Real Estate Management of the National Association of REALTORS®.

Chain of Title—1. The chain of deeds (and other documents) transferring title to a piece of property from one owner to the next, as disclosed in the public record. 2. A listing of all recorded documents affecting title to a particular property; more complete than an abstract.

Civil Law—The body of law concerned with the rights and liabilities of one individual in relation to another; includes contract law, tort law, and property law. *Compare:* Criminal Law.

Civil Rights—Fundamental rights guaranteed to individuals by the law. The term is primarily used in reference to constitutional and statutory protections against discrimination or government interference.

Civil Rights Act of 1866—A federal law guaranteeing all citizens the right to purchase, lease, sell, convey, and inherit property, regardless of race or ancestry.

Civil Rights Act of 1964—A federal law prohibiting discrimination on the basis of race, color, national origin, religion, sex, disability, or familial status in education, employment, access to public accommodations, and in many programs for which the government provides financial assistance.

Civil Rights Act of 1968—The federal Fair Housing Act, which strengthened the protections against discrimination in housing.

Civil Suit—A lawsuit in which one private party sues another private party (as opposed to a criminal suit, in which an individual is sued—prosecuted—by the government).

Civil Wrong—A breach of a duty imposed by law (as opposed to a duty voluntarily taken on in a contract) that causes harm to another person, giving the injured person the right to sue the one who breached the duty. Also called a Tort.

Clear Title—A good title to property, free from encumbrances or defects; marketable title.

Client Ledger—A separate accounting that a real estate firm must keep for each client that the firm is holding trust funds for. The account entries must include the date of deposit, the amount, and a description.

Client—One who employs a real estate agent, lawyer, or appraiser. A real estate agent's client can be a seller, a buyer, a landlord, or a tenant.

Closed End Mortgage—A loan that does not allow the borrower to increase the balance owed; the opposite of an open-end mortgage.

Closed Mortgage—A loan that cannot be paid off early.

Closing—The final stage in a real estate transaction, when the seller receives the purchase money, the buyer receives the deed, and title is transferred. Also called settlement.

Closing Costs—Expenses incurred in the transfer of real estate in addition to the purchase price; for example, the appraisal fee, title insurance premium, brokerage commission, and excise tax.

Closing Date—The date on which all the terms of a purchase and sale agreement must be met, or the contract is terminated.

Closing Disclosure—In a residential transaction subject to RESPA and/or the Truth in Lending Act, a form that the lender must give to the parties before closing, listing the actual closing costs.

Closing Statement—A final, detailed accounting for a real estate transaction, listing each party's debits and credits and the amount each will receive or be required to pay at closing; the closing disclosure includes a settlement statement. Also called a Settlement Statement.

Cloud on Title—A claim, encumbrance, or apparent defect that makes the title to a property unmarketable. *See:* Title, Marketable.

Code of Ethics—A body of rules setting forth accepted standards of conduct, reflecting principles of fairness and morality; especially one that the members of an organization are expected to follow.

Codicil—An addition to or revision of a will.

Collateral—Anything of value used as security for a debt or obligation.

Color of Title— Title that appears to be good title, but which in fact is not; commonly based on a defective instrument, such as an invalid deed.

Commercial Bank—A type of financial institution that has traditionally emphasized commercial lending (loans to businesses), but which also makes many residential mortgage loans.

Commercial Paper—Negotiable instruments, such as promissory notes, sold to meet the short-term capital needs of a business.

Commercial Property—Property zoned and used for business purposes, such as a restaurant or an office building; as distinguished from residential or agricultural property.

Commingled Funds—Funds from different sources that are deposited in the same account and thereby lose their separate character; for example, if a spouse deposits cash that is their separate property in an account with funds that are community property, the entire amount may be treated as community property.

Commingling—Mixing trust funds held on behalf of a client with personal funds; commingling is illegal.

Commission—1. The compensation paid to a brokerage for services in connection with a real estate transaction (usually a percentage of the sales price). 2. A group of people organized for a particular purpose or function; usually a governmental body, such as the Real Estate Commission.

Commission Split—A compensation arrangement in which licensees share a commission paid by the seller.

Commitment—In real estate finance, a lender's promise to make a loan. A loan commitment may be "firm" or "conditional"; a conditional commitment is contingent on something, such as a satisfactory credit report on the borrower.

Common Areas—1. The land and improvements in a condominium, planned unit development, or other housing development that are owned and used collectively by all of the residents, such as parking lots, hallways, and recreational facilities available for common use. Also called common elements. 2. In a building with leased units or spaces, the areas that are available for use by all of the tenants.

Common Law—1. Early English law. 2. Long-established rules of law based on early English law. 3. Rules of law developed through court decisions, as opposed to statutory law.

Common Law Dedication—Involuntary dedication, resulting from a property owner's acquiescence to public use of their property over a long period. Also called implied dedication.

Community Property—Property owned jointly by a married couple in Washington and other community property states, as distinguished from each spouse's separate property; generally, any property acquired through the labor or skill of either spouse during marriage.

Comparable—A recently sold and similarly situated property that is used as a point of comparison by an appraiser using the sales comparison approach.

Compensatory Damages—Damages awarded to a plaintiff as compensation for injuries (personal injuries, property damage, or financial losses) caused by the defendant's act or failure to act.

Competent—1. Of sound mind, for the purposes of entering a contract or executing an instrument. 2. Both of sound mind and having reached the age of majority.

Competitive Market Analysis—A comparison of homes that are similar in location, style, and amenities to the subject property, in order to set a realistic listing price. Similar to the sales comparison approach to value.

Completion Bond— A bond posted by a contractor to guarantee that a project will be completed satisfactorily and free of liens. Also called a performance bond.

Compliance Inspection—A building inspection to determine, for the benefit of a lender, whether building codes, specifications, or conditions established after a prior inspection have been met before a loan is made.

Compound Interest—Interest computed on both the principal and its accrued interest. *Compare:* Interest, Simple.

Comprehensive Environmental Response, Compensation, and Liability Act (CERCLA)— The Comprehensive Environmental Response, Compensation, and Liability Act; a federal law concerning liability for cleanup of contaminated property.

Comprehensive Plan— A long-term plan of development for a community, implemented by zoning and other laws. Also called a general plan or master plan.

Concurrent Ownership— When two or more individuals share ownership of one piece of property, each owning an undivided interest in the property (as in a tenancy in common or joint tenancy, or with community property). Also called co-ownership or co-tenancy.

Condemnation—1. Taking private property for public use through the government's power of eminent domain. 2. A declaration that a structure is unfit for occupancy and must be closed or demolished.

Condition—1. A provision in a contract that makes the parties' rights and obligations depend on the occurrence (or nonoccurrence) of a particular event. Also called a contingency clause. 2. A provision in a deed that makes title depend on compliance with a particular restriction.

Condition Subsequent—An event that will cause a right or interest to be lost if it occurs.

Conditional Commitment— In real estate finance, a lender's promise to make a loan. A loan commitment may be "firm" or "conditional"; a conditional commitment is contingent on something, such as a satisfactory credit report on the borrower. Also known as Commitment.

Conditional Fee—A fee simple estate that carries a qualification, so that ownership may revert to the grantor if a specified event occurs or a condition is not met. Also called a Qualified Fee or Defeasible Fee.

Conditional Sales Contract— A contract for the sale of real property in which the buyer (the vendee) pays in installments; the buyer takes possession of the property immediately, but the seller (the vendor) retains legal title until the full price has been paid. Also called a Conditional Sales Contract, Installment Sales Contract, Land Contract, Real Estate Contract, or Contract for Deed.

Conditional Use Permit—A permit that allows a special use, such as a school or hospital, to operate in a neighborhood where it would otherwise be prohibited by the zoning. Also called a special exception permit.

Condominium—Property developed for concurrent ownership, where each co-owner has a separate interest in an individual unit, combined with an undivided interest in the common areas of the property.

Confidential Information—Information from or concerning a principal that was acquired during the course of an agency relationship, that the principal reasonably expects to be kept confidential, that the principal has not disclosed to third parties, that would operate to the detriment of the principal, and that the principal would not be legally obligated to disclose to the other party.

Conforming Loan—A loan made in accordance with the underwriting criteria of Fannie Mae and Freddie Mac, and which therefore can be sold to those entities.

Consideration—Anything of value given to induce another to enter into a contract, such as money, goods, services, or a promise. Sometimes called valuable consideration.

Conspiracy—An agreement or plan between two or more persons to perform an unlawful act.

Construction Lien—A lien on property in favor of someone who provided labor or materials to improve the property. The term encompasses mechanic's liens (for labor) and materialman's liens (for materials).

Construction Loan—A loan to finance the cost of constructing a building, usually providing that the loan funds will be advanced in installments as the work progresses. Also called an interim loan.

Constructive—Held to be so in the eyes of the law, even if not so in fact. *See:* Constructive Annexation; Constructive Eviction; Constructive Notice; Constructive Severance.

Constructive Annexation—When personal property becomes associated with real property in such a way that the law treats it as a fixture, even though it is not physically attached; for example, a house key is constructively annexed to the house.

Constructive Eviction—When a landlord's act (or failure to act) interferes with the tenant's quiet enjoyment of the property, or makes the property unfit for its intended use, to such an extent that the tenant is forced to move out.

Constructive Fraud—A breach of duty that misleads the person the duty was owed to, without an intention to deceive; for example, if a seller gives a buyer inaccurate information about the property without realizing that it is false, that may be constructive fraud.

Constructive Notice—Knowledge of a fact imputed to a person by law. A person is held to have constructive notice of something when they should have known it (because they could have learned it through reasonable diligence or an inspection of the public record), even if they did not actually know it.

Consumer Financial Protection Bureau—A federal agency that helps enforce a number of consumer financial protection laws, many of which affect the real estate business, such as the Truth in Lending Act.

Consumer Price Index—An index that tracks changes in the cost of goods and services for a typical consumer. Formerly called the cost of living index.

Contiguous—Adjacent, abutting, or in close proximity.

Contingency Clause—1. A provision in a contract that makes the parties' rights and obligations depend on the occurrence (or nonoccurrence) of a particular event. Also called a contingency clause. 2. A provision in a deed that makes title depend on compliance with a particular restriction.

Contour—The shape or configuration of a surface. A contour map depicts the topography of a piece of land by means of lines (contour lines) that connect points of equal elevation.

Contract—An agreement between two or more persons to do or not do a certain thing, for consideration.

Contract for Deed— A contract for the sale of real property in which the buyer (the vendee) pays in installments; the buyer takes possession of the property immediately, but the seller (the vendor) retains legal title until the full price has been paid. Also called a Conditional Sales Contract, Installment Sales Contract, Real Estate Contract, or Land Contract.

Contract of Sale— A contract in which a seller promises to convey title to real property to a buyer in exchange for the purchase price. Also called an Earnest Money Agreement, Deposit Receipt, Sales Contract, or Purchase and Sale Agreement.

Contract Rent—The rent that is actually being paid on property that is currently leased.

Contractor—One who contracts to perform labor or supply materials for a construction project, or to do other work for a specified price.

Conventional Financing— An institutional loan that is not insured or guaranteed by a government agency. Also called Conventional Loan.

Conventional Loan—An institutional loan that is not insured or guaranteed by a government agency.

Conversion—1. Misappropriating property or funds belonging to another; for example, converting trust funds to one's own use. 2. The process of changing an apartment complex into a condominium or cooperative.

Conveyance—The transfer of title to real property from one person to another by means of a written document, especially a deed.

Cooperating Agent—A real estate licensee who shows a buyer a property listed by a different firm that belongs to the same multiple listing service as the firm the licensee works for.

Cooperative—A building owned by a corporation or association, where the residents are shareholders in the corporation; each shareholder receives a proprietary lease on an individual unit and the right to use the common areas.

Cooperative Sale—A sale in which the buyer and the seller are brought together by agents working for different brokerages.

Co-Ownership—When two or more individuals share ownership of one piece of property, each owning an undivided interest in the property (as in a tenancy in common or joint tenancy, or with community property). Also called Concurrent Ownership or Co-Tenancy

Corner Influence—The increase in a property's value that results from its location on or near a corner, with access and exposure on two streets.

Corporation—A business entity owned by shareholders, governed by a board of directors, and managed by corporate officers; the shareholders have limited liability.

Correction Deed—A deed used to correct minor mistakes in an earlier deed, such as misspelled names or typographical errors in the legal description. Also called a deed of confirmation or reformation deed.

Correction Lines—In the government survey system, adjustment lines used to compensate for the curvature of the earth; they occur at 24-mile intervals (every fourth township line), where the distance between range lines is corrected to six miles.

Corrective Maintenance—Ongoing repairs that are made to a building and its equipment in order to restore it to good operating condition.

Cosigner—Someone (usually a family member) who accepts responsibility for the repayment of a mortgage loan along with the primary borrower, to help the borrower qualify for the loan.

Cost—The amount paid for anything in money, goods, or services.

Cost Approach to Value—One of the three main methods of appraisal, in which an estimate of the subject property's value is arrived at by estimating the cost of replacing (or reproducing) the improvements, then deducting the estimated accrued depreciation and adding the estimated market value of the land.

Cost Basis—A figure used in calculating a gain on the sale of real estate for federal income tax purposes. Also called Basis.

Cost of Living Index— An index that tracks changes in the cost of goods and services for a typical consumer. Formerly called the cost of living index. Also called Consumer Price Index.

Co-Tenancy— When two or more individuals share ownership of one piece of property, each owning an undivided interest in the property (as in a tenancy in common or joint tenancy, or with community property). Also called Concurrent Ownership or Co-Ownership.

Counteroffer—A response to a contract offer, changing some of the terms of the original offer; it operates as a rejection of the original offer (not as an acceptance). Also called qualified acceptance.

Course—In a metes and bounds description, a direction, stated in terms of a compass bearing.

Covenant—1. A contract. 2. A promise. 3. A guarantee (express or implied) in a document such as a deed or lease. 4. A restrictive covenant.

Covenant Against Encumbrances—In a warranty deed, a promise that the property is not burdened by any encumbrances other than those that are disclosed in the deed.

Covenant of Quiet Enjoyment—A promise that a buyer or tenant's possession will not be disturbed by the previous owner, the lessor, or anyone else making a lawful claim against the property.

Covenant of Right to Convey—In a warranty deed, a promise that the grantor has the legal ability to make a valid conveyance.

Covenant of Seisin—In a warranty deed, a promise that the grantor actually owns the interest they are conveying to the grantee.

Covenant of Warranty—In a warranty deed, a promise that the grantor will defend the grantee's title against claims superior to the grantor's that exist when the conveyance is made.

Credit—A payment receivable (owed to you), as opposed to a debit, which is a payment due (owed by you).

Credit History—An applicant's record of accruing debts and repaying loans, usually expressed in the form of a personal credit report.

Credit Union—A not-for-profit, cooperative depository institution. Some credit unions serve the members of a particular group or organization.

Creditor—One who is owed a debt.

Criminal Law—The body of law under which the government can prosecute an individual for crimes, wrongs against society. *Compare:* Civil Law.

Curable Depreciation—Deferred maintenance and functional obsolescence that would ordinarily be corrected by a prudent owner, because the correction cost could be recovered in the sales price.

Customer—From the point of view of a seller's agent, a prospective property buyer; from the point of view of a landlord's agent, a prospective tenant.

-D-

Damage Deposit—*See:* Security Deposit.

Damages—In a civil lawsuit, an amount of money the defendant is ordered to pay the plaintiff.

Datum—An artificial horizontal plane of elevation, established in reference to sea level, used by surveyors as a reference point in determining elevation.

Dealer—One who regularly buys and sells real estate in the ordinary course of business.

Dealer Property—Property held for sale to customers rather than long-term investment; a developer's inventory of subdivision lots, for example.

Debit—A charge payable by a party; in a real estate transaction, the purchase price is a debit for the buyer, for example, and the sales commission is a debit for the seller.

Debt Service—The amount of money required to make the periodic payments of principal and interest on an amortized debt, such as a mortgage.

Debtor—One who owes money to another.

Decedent—A person who has died.

Declaration—A written description of a condominium development that addresses various issues, such as designating common areas, how dues are determined, and leasing restrictions.

Declaration of Abandonment—A document recorded by an owner that voluntarily releases a property from homestead protection.

Declaration of Homestead—A recorded document that establishes homestead protection for a property that would not otherwise receive it.

Dedication—A voluntary or involuntary gift of private property for public use; may transfer ownership or simply create an easement.

Deduction—An amount a taxpayer is allowed to subtract from their income before the tax on the income is calculated (as distinguished from a tax credit, which is deducted from the tax owed).

Deed—An instrument which, when properly executed and delivered, conveys title to real property from the grantor to the grantee.

Deed Executed Under Court Order—A deed that is the result of a court action, such as judicial foreclosure or partition.

Deed in Lieu of Foreclosure—A deed given by a borrower to the lender, relinquishing ownership of the security property, to satisfy the debt and avoid foreclosure.

Deed of Reconveyance—The instrument used to release the security property from the lien created by a deed of trust when the debt has been repaid.

Deed of Trust—An instrument that creates a voluntary lien on real property to secure the repayment of a debt, and which includes a power of sale clause permitting nonjudicial foreclosure; the parties are the grantor or trustor (borrower), the beneficiary (the lender), and the trustee (a neutral third party).

Deed Release Provision—1. A clause in a blanket mortgage or deed of trust which allows the borrower to get part of the security property released from the lien when a certain portion of the debt has been paid or other conditions are fulfilled. Often called a partial release clause. 2. A clause in a land contract providing for a deed to a portion of the land to be delivered when a certain portion of the contract price has been paid. Also known as a Release Clause.

Deed Restrictions— A restrictive covenant in a deed. Provisions in a deed that restrict use of the property, and which may be either covenants or conditions.

Default Judgment—A court judgment in favor of the plaintiff due to the defendant's failure to answer the complaint or appear at a hearing.

Default—Failure to fulfill an obligation, duty, or promise, as when a borrower fails to make payments, or a tenant fails to pay rent.

Defeasance Clause—A clause in a mortgage, deed of trust, or lease that cancels or defeats a certain right upon the occurrence of a particular event.

Defeasible Fee—A fee simple estate that carries a qualification, so that ownership may revert to the grantor if a specified event occurs or a condition is not met. Also called a qualified fee.

Defendant—1. The person being sued in a civil lawsuit. 2. The accused person in a criminal lawsuit.

Deferred Maintenance—Physical deterioration of a structure caused by postponed maintenance and/or repairs.

Deficiency Judgment—A personal judgment entered against a borrower in favor of the lender if the proceeds from a foreclosure sale of the security property are not enough to pay off the debt.

Degree—In surveying, a unit of circular measurement equal to $^{1}/_{360}$ of one complete rotation around a point in a plane.

Delegation Agreement—A written agreement in which a designated broker transfers some of their authority and duties to another managing broker, including a branch manager. The agreement doesn't relieve the designated broker of the ultimate responsibility for the delegated function.

Delivery—The legal transfer of a deed from the grantor to the grantee, which results in the transfer of title.

Demand—Desire to own coupled with ability to afford; this is one of the four elements of value, along with scarcity, utility, and transferability.

Demand Note—A promissory note that is due whenever the holder of the note demands payment.

Density—In a land use law, the number of buildings or occupants per unit of land.

Department of Licensing—The state agency in charge of administering the real estate license law in Washington.

Deposit Receipt—A contract in which a seller promises to convey title to real property to a buyer in exchange for the purchase price. Also called an Earnest Money Agreement, Deposit Receipt, Sales Contract, or Purchase and Sale Agreement.

Deposit—Money offered as an indication of commitment or as a protection, and which may be refunded under certain circumstances, such as an earnest money deposit or a tenant's security deposit.

Deposition—The formal, out-of-court testimony of a witness in a lawsuit, taken before trial for possible use later, during the trial; either as part of the discovery process, to determine the facts of the case, or when the witness will not be available during the trial.

Depreciable Property—In the federal income tax code, property that is eligible for depreciation deductions, because it will wear out and have to be replaced.

Depreciation Deductions—Under the federal income tax code, deductions from a taxpayer's income to permit the cost of an asset to be recovered; allowed only for depreciable property that is held for the production of income or used in a trade or business. Also called cost recovery deductions.

Depreciation—1. A loss in the value of improvements to real property due to any cause. 2. For the purposes of income tax deductions, apportioning the cost of an asset over a period of time.

Dereliction— When a body of water gradually recedes, exposing land that was previously under water. Also known as Reliction.

Descent—Acquiring property transferred by intestate succession. A person who receives property by intestate succession is said to receive it by descent.

Designated Broker—A person who is licensed as a managing broker, has a designated broker endorsement added to their license by the DOL, and serves as the designated broker for one or more firms, bearing ultimate responsibility for all firm activities.

Detached Residence—A home physically separated from the neighboring home(s), not connected by a common wall.

Developed Land—Land with man-made improvements, such as buildings or roads.

Developer—One who subdivides or improves land to achieve a profitable use.

Development—1. Any development project, such as a new office park. 2. A housing subdivision. 3. In reference to a property's life cycle, the earliest stage, also called integration.

Devise—1. (noun) A gift of real property through a will. 2. (verb) To transfer real property by will. *Compare:* Bequest; Legacy.

Devisee—Someone who receives title to real property through a will. *Compare:* Legatee Beneficiary.

Devisor—A testator who devises real property in their will.

Disability—According to the Americans with Disabilities Act and Fair Housing Act, a physical or mental impairment that substantially limits a person in one or more major life activities.

Disaffirm—To ask a court to terminate a voidable contract.

Disbursements—Money paid out or expended.

Disclaimer—A denial of legal responsibility.

Discount Points—A percentage of the principal amount of a loan, collected by the lender at the time a loan is originated, to give the lender an additional yield.

Discount—1. (verb) To sell a promissory note at less than its face value. 2. (noun) An amount withheld from the loan amount by the lender when the loan is originated; discount points.

Discount Rate—The interest rate charged when a member bank borrows money from the Federal Reserve Bank.

Discrimination—Treating people unequally because of their race, religion, sex, national origin, age, or some other characteristic.

Disintegration—In a property's life cycle, the period of decline when the property's present economic usefulness is near an end and constant upkeep is necessary.

Disintermediation—When depositors withdraw their savings deposits from financial institutions (such as savings and loan associations and commercial banks) in order to invest the funds directly.

Disposable Income—Income remaining after income taxes have been paid.

Distressed Home—A personal residence that is in danger of foreclosure because the owner is delinquent on mortgage or tax payments.

Distressed Property Law—A state law intended to help protect financially distressed homeowners from foreclosure scams.

Doctrine of Emblements—The legal rule that gives an agricultural tenant the right to enter the land to harvest crops after the lease ends.

Domestic Corporation—A corporation doing business in the state where it was created (incorporated).

Domicile—The state where a person has their permanent home.

Dominant Tenant—A person who has easement rights on another's property; either the owner of a dominant tenement, or someone who has an easement in gross.

Dominant Tenement—Property that receives the benefit of an easement appurtenant.

Double-Entry Bookkeeping—An accounting technique in which an item is entered in the ledger twice, once as a credit and once as a debit; used for settlement statements.

Downpayment—The part of the purchase price of property that the buyer is paying in cash; the difference between the purchase price and the financing.

Downzoning—Rezoning land for a more limited use.

Drainage—A system to draw water off land, either artificially (with pipes) or naturally (such as with a slope).

Due-on-Sale Clause—*See:* Alienation Clause.

Duplex—A structure that contains two separate housing units, with separate entrances, living areas, baths, and kitchens.

Duress—Unlawful force or constraint used to compel someone to do something (such as sign a contract) against their will.

Dwelling—A building or a part of a building used or intended to be used as living quarters.

-E-

Earnest Money—A deposit that a prospective buyer gives the seller as evidence of their good faith intent to complete the transaction.

Earnest Money Agreement— A contract in which a seller promises to convey title to real property to a buyer in exchange for the purchase price. Also called an Deposit Receipt, Sales Contract, Contract of Sale, or Purchase and Sale Agreement.

Easement—An irrevocable right to use some part of another person's real property for a particular purpose.

Easement Appurtenant—An easement that benefits a piece of property, the dominant tenement. *Compare:* Easement in Gross.

Easement by Express Grant—An easement granted to another in a deed or other document.

Easement by Express Reservation—An easement created in a deed when a landowner is dividing the property, transferring the servient tenement but retaining the dominant tenement; an easement that the grantor reserves for their own use.

Easement by Implication—An easement created by law when a parcel of land is divided, if there has been long-standing, apparent prior use, and it is reasonably necessary for the enjoyment of the dominant tenement.

Easement by Necessity—A special type of easement by implication, created by law even when there has been no prior use, if the dominant tenement would be entirely useless without an easement.

Easement in Gross—An easement that benefits a person instead of a piece of land; there is a dominant tenant, but no dominant tenement. *Compare:* Easement Appurtenant.

Economic Life—The period during which improved property will yield a return over and above the rent due to the land itself; also called the useful life.

Economic Obsolescence—Loss in value resulting from factors outside the property itself, such as proximity to an airport. Also called External Inadequacy.

Economic Rent—The rent that a property would be earning if it were available for lease in the current market.

Effective Age—The age of a structure indicated by its condition and remaining usefulness (as opposed to its actual age). Good maintenance may increase a building's effective age, and poor maintenance may decrease it; for example, a 50-year-old home that has been well maintained might have an effective age of 15 years, meaning that its remaining usefulness is equivalent to that of a 15-year-old home.

Effective Gross Income—A measure of a rental property's capacity to generate income; calculated by subtracting a vacancy factor from the economic rent (potential gross income).

Egress—A means of exiting, a way to leave a property; the opposite of ingress. The terms ingress and egress are most commonly used in reference to an access easement.

Ejectment—A legal action to recover possession of real property from someone who is not legally entitled to possession of it; an eviction.

Elements of Comparison—In the sales comparison approach to appraisal, considerations taken into account in selecting comparables and comparing comparables to the subject property; they include date of sale, location, physical characteristics, and terms of sale.

Emblements—Crops that are produced annually through the labor of the cultivator, such as wheat.

Eminent Domain—The government's constitutional power to take (condemn) private property for public use, as long as the owner is paid just compensation.

Employee—Someone who works under the direction and control of another. *Compare:* Independent Contractor.

Encroachment—A physical intrusion onto neighboring property, usually due to a mistake regarding the location of the boundary.

Encumber—To place a lien or other encumbrance against the title to a property.

Encumbrance—A nonpossessory interest in real property; a right or interest held by someone other than the property owner, which may be a lien, an easement, a profit, or a restrictive covenant.

Endorsement—When the payee on a negotiable instrument (such as a check or promissory note) assigns the right to payment to another, by signing the back of the instrument.

Enjoin—To prohibit an act, or command performance of an act, by court order; to issue an injunction.

Environmental Impact Statement (EIS)—A written report analyzing a construction project's impact on the environment; required by Washington's State Environmental Policy Act (SEPA) for projects that are likely to have a significant impact on the environment.

EPA—The federal Environmental Protection Agency.

Equal Credit Opportunity Act—A federal law prohibiting providers of credit from discriminating based on race, color, religion, national origin, sex, marital status, age, or because the applicant receives public assistance.

Equilibrium—In the life cycle of a property, a period of stability, during which the property undergoes little, if any, change.

Equitable Interest or Title— The vendee's interest in property under a land contract. Also may refer to the interest that a purchaser holds before closing. Also called an equitable interest. Also called Equitable Title.

Equitable Lien—A lien arising as a matter of fairness, rather than by agreement or by operation of law.

Equitable Redemption Period—The period between the initial complaint and the sale of a foreclosed property, during which time a borrower may redeem the property by paying the amount of the debt plus costs.

Equitable Remedy—In a civil lawsuit, a judgment granted to the plaintiff that is something other than an award of money (damages); an injunction, rescission, and specific performance are examples.

Equitable Right of Redemption—The right of a mortgagor to redeem property prior to the foreclosure sale.

Equitable Title—The vendee's interest in property under a land contract. Also may refer to the interest that a purchaser holds before closing. Also called an Equitable Interest.

Equity—1. An owner's unencumbered interest in their property; the difference between the value of the property and the liens against it. 2. A judge's power to soften or set aside strict legal rules, to bring about a fair and just result in a particular case.

Erosion—Gradual loss of soil due to the action of water or wind.

Errors and Omissions Insurance—Insurance coverage that will pay for harm caused by an agent's (or firm's) unintentional mistake or negligence.

Escalation Clause—A clause in a contract or mortgage that provides for payment or interest adjustments (usually increases) if specified events occur, such as a change in the property taxes or in the prime interest rate. Also called an escalator clause.

Escheat—The reversion of property to the state after no one with title to the property claims it. (For example, this can happen when a property owner dies without leaving a will and without heirs.)

Escrow—An arrangement in which something of value (such as money or a deed) is held on behalf of the parties to a transaction by a disinterested third party (an escrow agent) until specified conditions have been fulfilled.

Escrow Agent—1. A third party who holds money and documents in trust and carries out the closing process. 2. A company (not a natural person) that is licensed to engage in the escrow business.

Escrow Instructions—A written document that tells the escrow agent how to proceed and states the conditions each party must fulfill before the transaction can close.

Escrow Officer—A person licensed to work for an escrow agent.

Estate—1. An interest in real property that is or may become possessory; either a freehold or a leasehold. 2. The property left by someone who has died.

Estate at Sufferance— When a tenant (who entered into possession of the property lawfully) stays on after the lease ends without the landlord's permission. Also called Tenancy at Sufferance.

Estate at Will— When a tenant is in possession with the owner's permission, but there's no definite lease term; as when a landlord allows a holdover tenant to remain on the premises until another tenant is found. Also called Tenancy at Will.

Estate for Life— A freehold estate that lasts only as long as a specified person lives. That person is referred to as the measuring life. Also called Life Estate.

Estate for Years—A leasehold estate set to last for a definite period (one week, three years, etc.), after which it terminates automatically. Also called a tenancy for years or term tenancy.

Estate of Inheritance—An estate that can pass to the holder's heirs; especially a fee simple.

Estoppel Certificate—A document that prevents a person who signs it from later asserting facts different from those stated in the document. In connection with a mortgage, for example, the term may refer to a document issued by the lender stating the unpaid principal balance of the loan, its interest rate, and so on. Also called an estoppel letter.

Estoppel—A legal doctrine that prevents a person from asserting rights or facts that are inconsistent with their earlier actions or statements.

Et Al.—Abbreviation for the Latin phrase "et alia" or "et alii," meaning "and another" or "and others."

Ethics—A system of accepted principles or standards of moral conduct. *See:* Code of Ethics.

Eviction—Dispossession or expulsion of someone from real property.

Excess Land—That portion of a parcel of land that does not add to its value. For example, where the value of a property lies primarily in its frontage, additional depth beyond the normal lot size would not increase the property's value.

Exchange— A transaction in which a piece of property held for investment or used in a trade or business is traded for a piece of like-kind property, thus deferring tax on the gain. Sometimes called a Tax-Free Exchange, Tax Deferred Exchange, or 1031 Exchange.

Excise Tax—A state tax levied on every sale of real estate, to be paid by the seller.

Exclusive Agency— Either an exclusive agency listing or an exclusive right to sell listing.

Exclusive Agency Listing—A listing agreement that entitles the brokerage to a commission if anyone other than the seller finds a buyer for the property during the listing term.

Exclusive Listing—Either an exclusive agency listing or an exclusive right to sell listing.

Exclusive Right to Sell Listing—A listing agreement that entitles the brokerage to a commission if anyone—including the seller—finds a buyer for the property during the listing term.

Exculpatory Clause—A clause in a contract that relieves one party of liability for certain defaults or problems; such provisions are not always enforceable.

Execute—1. To sign an instrument and take any other steps (such as acknowledgment) that may be necessary to its validity. 2. To perform or complete. *See:* Contract, Executed.

Executed Contract—A contract in which both parties have completely performed their contractual obligations.

Execution—The legal process in which a court orders an official (such as the sheriff) to seize and sell the property of a judgment debtor to satisfy a lien.

Executor—A person named in a will to carry out its provisions.

Executory Contract—A contract in which one or both parties have not yet completed performance of their obligations.

Exemption—A provision holding that a law or rule does not apply to a particular person or group; for example, a person entitled to a tax exemption is not required to pay the tax.

Exit Interview—A final meeting between an agent and a representative of the firm, when the affiliated relationship is terminated; designed to gather feedback for the firm and achieve closure of the relationship.

Express—Stated in words, whether spoken or written. *Compare:* Implied.

Express Contract—A contract that has been put into words, either spoken or written.

Extended Coverage Title Insurance—Title insurance that covers problems that should be discovered in an inspection of the property (such as encroachments and adverse possession), in addition to the problems covered by standard coverage policies. An extended coverage policy is sometimes referred to as an ALTA (American Land Title Association) policy.

Extender Clause—A clause in a listing agreement providing that for a specified period after the listing expires, the brokerage will still be entitled to a commission if the property is sold to someone the brokerage dealt with during the listing term. Also called a safety clause or carryover clause.

External Obsolescence—Loss in value resulting from factors outside the property itself, such as proximity to an airport. Also called economic obsolescence or external inadequacy.

-F-

Face Value—The value of an instrument, such as a promissory note or a security, that is indicated on the face of the instrument itself.

Failure of Purpose—When the intended purpose of an agreement or arrangement can no longer be achieved; in most cases, this releases the parties from their obligations.

Fair Credit Reporting Act—A federal law requiring disclosure if a loan is rejected based on adverse information found in an applicant's credit history; the act also allows consumers to receive periodic free credit reports and to challenge incorrect information in credit reports.

Fair Housing Act—A federal law prohibiting discrimination in the sale or lease of residential property on the basis of race, color, religion, sex, national origin, disability, or familial status.

Fairness in Lending Act—A Washington state law that prohibits redlining.

Fannie Mae—Popular name for the Federal National Mortgage Association (FNMA).

Feasibility Study—A cost-benefit analysis of a proposed project, often required by lenders before they make a loan commitment.

Federal Housing Finance Agency (FHFA)—Regulates Fannie Mae and Freddie Mac.

Federal Reserve System—The government body that regulates commercial banks, and that implements monetary policy in an attempt to control the national economy.

Fed—The Federal Reserve.

Fee Simple Determinable—A defeasible fee that ends automatically, without legal action by the grantor, if the condition is violated or the terminating event occurs.

Fee Simple—The highest and most complete form of ownership, which is of potentially infinite duration. Also called a Fee or a Fee Simple Absolute.

Fee Simple Estate— The highest and most complete form of ownership, which is of potentially infinite duration. Also called a Fee or a Fee Simple Absolute.

Fee Simple Subject to a Condition Subsequent—A defeasible fee that terminates only if the grantor takes legal action to terminate it after the specified condition has come to pass.

FHA—Federal Housing Administration.

FHA Loan—A loan made by an institutional lender and insured by the Federal Housing Administration, so that the FHA will reimburse the lender for losses that result if the borrower defaults.

Fidelity Bond—A bond to cover losses resulting from the dishonesty of an employee.

Fiduciary Relationship—A relationship of trust and confidence, where one party owes the other (or both parties owe each other) loyalty and a higher standard of good faith than is owed to third parties. For example, an agent is a fiduciary in relation to the principal; spouses are fiduciaries in relation to one another.

Finance Charge—Any charge a borrower is assessed, directly or indirectly, in connection with a loan.

Financial Encumbrance—A lien.

Financing Statement—A brief instrument that is recorded to perfect and give constructive notice of a creditor's security interest in an article of personal property.

Finder's Fee—A referral fee paid to someone for directing a buyer or a seller to a real estate agent.

Firm Commitment— In real estate finance, a lender's promise to make a loan. A loan commitment may be "firm" or "conditional"; a conditional commitment is contingent on something, such as a satisfactory credit report on the borrower.

FIRPTA—The Foreign Investment in Real Property Tax Act; this federal law requires withholding funds from a sale of real property when the seller is not a U.S. citizen or a resident alien, in order to prevent tax evasion.

First Lien Position—The position held by a mortgage or deed of trust that has higher lien priority than any other mortgage or deed of trust against the property.

First Mortgage—The mortgage on a property that has first lien position; the one with higher lien priority than any other mortgage against the property.

Fiscal Policy—The federal government's actions in raising revenue (through taxation), spending money, and managing its debt.

Fiscal Year—Any 12-month period used as a business year for accounting, tax, and other financial purposes, as opposed to a calendar year.

Fixed Disbursement Plan—A construction financing arrangement that calls for the loan proceeds to be disbursed in a series of predetermined installments at various stages of the construction.

Fixed Expense— Recurring property expenses, such as general real estate taxes and hazard insurance. In the property management context, the term may refer to a property expense that remains the same regardless of rental income.

Fixed Lease— A lease in which the rent is set at a fixed amount, and the landlord pays all or nearly all of the operating expenses; in some cases the tenant pays for utilities. Also called a Gross Lease, Flat Lease, or Straight Lease.

Fixed Term—A period of time that has a definite beginning and ending.

Fixed-Rate Loan—A loan on which the interest rate will remain the same throughout the entire loan term. *Compare:* Mortgage, Adjustable-rate.

Fixture—An item that used to be personal property but has been attached to or closely associated with real property in such a way that it has legally become part of the real property. *See:* Annexation, Actual; Annexation, Constructive.

For Sale by Owner (FSBO)—A property that is being sold by the owner without the help of a real estate agent.

Foreclosure—When a lienholder causes property to be sold against the owner's wishes, so that the unpaid lien can be satisfied from the sale proceeds.

Foreign Corporation—A corporation doing business in one state, but created (incorporated) in another state, or in another country.

Foreign Investment in Real Property Tax Act (FIRPTA)—Federal law which requires withholding funds from a sale of real property when the seller is not a U.S. citizen or a resident alien, in order to prevent tax evasion.

Forfeiture—Loss of a right or something else of value as a result of failure to perform an obligation or fulfill a condition.

Formal Will—A will that meets the statutory requirements for validity; it must be in writing and signed in the presence of at least two competent witnesses.

Franchise—A right granted by a business to use its trade name and procedures in conducting business.

Fraud—An intentional or negligent misrepresentation or concealment of a material fact, which is relied upon by another, who is induced to enter a transaction and harmed as a result.

Freddie Mac—Popular name for the Federal Home Loan Mortgage Corporation (FHLMC).

Free and Clear—Ownership of real property completely free of any mortgage liens.

Freehold—A possessory interest in real property that has an indeterminable duration; it can be either a fee simple or a life estate. Someone who has a freehold estate has title to the property (as opposed to someone with a leasehold estate, who is only a tenant).

Front Foot—A measurement of property for sale or valuation, with each foot of frontage presumed to extend the entire depth of the lot.

Frontage—The distance a property extends along a street or a body of water; the distance between the two side boundaries at the front of the lot.

Functional Obsolescence—Loss in value due to inadequate or outmoded equipment, or as a result of a poor or outmoded design.

Future Interest—An interest in property that will or may become possessory at some point in the future, such as a remainder or reversion.

-G-

G.I. Loan,— A home loan made by an institutional lender to an eligible veteran, where the Dept. of Veterans Affairs will reimburse the lender for losses if the veteran defaults. Also called VA-Guaranteed Loan.

Gain—Under the federal income tax code, that portion of the proceeds from the sale of a capital asset, such as real estate, that is taxable profit.

Garnishment—A legal process by which a creditor gains access to the personal property or funds of a debtor that are in the hands of a third party. For example, if the debtor's wages are garnished, the employer is required to turn over part of each paycheck to the creditor.

General Agent—An agent authorized to handle all of the principal's affairs in one area or in specified areas.

General Lien—A lien against all the property of a debtor, rather than a particular piece of their property. *Compare:* Specific Lien.

General Partner—A partner who has the authority to manage and contract for a general or limited partnership, and who is personally liable for the partnership's debts.

General Partnership—A partnership in which each member has an equal right to manage the business and share in the profits, as well as equal responsibility for the partnership's debts.

General Plan—A long-term plan of development for a community, implemented by zoning and other laws. Also called a Comprehensive Plan or Master Plan.

General Real Estate Tax—An annual ad valorem tax levied on real property.

General Warranty Deed—A deed in which the grantor warrants the title against defects that might have arisen before or during their period of ownership.

Gift Deed—A deed that is not supported by valuable consideration; often lists "love and affection" as the consideration.

Gift Funds—Money that a relative (or other third party) gives to a buyer who otherwise would not have enough cash to close the transaction.

Ginnie Mae—Popular name for the Government National Mortgage Association (GNMA).

Good Faith Estimate—TILA and RESPA require the lender to make a good faith estimate of loan costs using the loan estimate form.

Goodwill—An intangible asset of a business resulting from a good reputation with the public, serving as an indication of future return business.

Government Lot—In the government survey system, a parcel of land that is not a regular section (one mile square), because of the convergence of range lines, or because of a body of water or some other obstacle; assigned a government lot number.

Government Survey System—A system of grids, made up of range and township lines that divide the land into townships, which are further subdivided into sections; a property is identified by its location within a particular section, township, and range. Also called the rectangular survey system.

Graduated Lease—A lease in which it is agreed that the rental payments will increase at intervals by a specified amount or according to a specified formula.

Graduated Payment Mortgage—A loan in which the payments are increased periodically during the first years of the loan term, usually according to a fixed schedule.

Grant Deed—A deed that uses the word "grant" in its words of conveyance and carries certain implied warranties; rarely used in Washington.

Grantee—One who receives a grant of real property.

Granting Clause—Words in a deed that indicate the grantor's intent to transfer an interest in property.

Grantor—One who grants an interest in real property to another.

Grant—To transfer or convey an interest in real property by means of a written instrument.

Gross Income—A property's total income before making any deductions (for uncollected rent, vacancies, operating expenses, etc.).

Gross Income Multiplier—A figure which is multiplied by a rental property's gross income to arrive at an estimate of the property's value. Also called a Gross Rent Multiplier.

Gross Income Multiplier Method—A method of appraising residential property by reference to its rental value. Also called the gross rent multiplier method.

Gross Lease—A lease in which the rent is set at a fixed amount, and the landlord pays all or nearly all of the operating expenses; in some cases the tenant pays for utilities. Also called a fixed lease, flat lease, or straight lease.

Gross Rent Multiplier—A figure which is multiplied by a rental property's gross income to arrive at an estimate of the property's value. Also called a Gross Income Multiplier.

Ground Lease—A lease of the land only, usually for a long term, to a tenant who intends to construct a building on the property.

Ground Rent—The earnings of improved property attributed to the land itself, after allowance is made for the earnings attributable to the improvement.

Group Boycott—An agreement between two or more business competitors to exclude another competitor from fair participation in business activities.

Growth Management Act—A Washington state law aimed at limiting sprawl and concentrating growth in existing urban areas.

Guaranteed Loan—A loan in which a third party has agreed to reimburse the lender for losses that result if the borrower defaults.

Guardian—A person appointed by a court to administer the affairs of a minor or an incompetent person.

Guide Meridians—In the government survey system, lines running north-south (parallel to the principal meridian) at 24-mile intervals.

-H-

Habendum Clause—A clause included after the granting clause in many deeds; it begins "to have and to hold" and describes the type of estate the grantee will hold.

Hard Money Mortgage—A mortgage given to a lender in exchange for cash, as opposed to one given in exchange for credit.

Hazard Insurance—Insurance against damage to real property caused by fire, flood, theft, or other mishap. Also called casualty insurance.

Heir—Someone entitled to inherit another's property under the laws of intestate succession.

Heirs and Assigns—A phrase used in legal documents to cover all successors to a person's interest in property; assigns are successors who acquire title in some manner other than inheritance, such as by deed.

Highest and Best Use—The use which, at the time of appraisal, is most likely to produce the greatest net return from the property over a given period of time.

Holder in Due Course—A person who obtains a negotiable instrument for value, in good faith, without notice that it is overdue or notice of any defenses against it.

Holdover Tenant—A lessee who remains in possession of the property after the lease term has expired.

Holographic Will—A will written entirely in the testator's handwriting, which may be valid even if it was not witnessed. Not recognized in Washington.

Home Equity Loan—A loan secured by the borrower's equity in the home they already own. *Compare:* Mortgage, Purchase Money.

Home Mortgage Disclosure Act—A federal law requiring institutional lenders to make annual disclosures of all mortgage loans made, as a means of enforcing prohibitions against redlining.

Homeowner's Coverage Title Insurance—Title insurance that covers most of the title problems that an extended coverage policy covers, but protects the buyer instead of the lender.

Homeowner's Insurance—Insurance against damage to the real property and the homeowner's personal property.

Homeowners Association—A nonprofit association made up of homeowners in a subdivision, responsible for enforcing the CC&Rs and managing other community affairs.

Homestead—An owner-occupied dwelling, together with any appurtenant outbuildings and land.

Homestead Law—A state law that provides limited protection against creditors' claims for homestead property.

HUD—The U.S. Department of Housing and Urban Development.

-I-

Implied—Not expressed in words, but understood from actions or circumstances. *Compare:* Express.

Implied Authority—An agent's authority to do everything reasonably necessary to carry out the principal's express orders.

Implied Contract—A contract that has not been put into words, but is implied by the actions of the parties.

Implied Easement— An easement created by law when a parcel of land is divided, if there has been long-standing, apparent prior use, and it is reasonably necessary for the enjoyment of the dominant tenement. Also called Easement by Implication.

Implied Warranty—In a sale or lease of property, a guarantee created by operation of law, whether or not the seller or landlord intended to offer it.

Implied Warranty of Habitability—A warranty, implied by law in every residential lease, that the property is fit for habitation.

Impound Account—A bank account maintained by a lender for payment of property taxes, insurance premiums, and other recurring expenses connected with the security property; the lender requires the borrower to make regular deposits, and pays the expenses out of the account. Also called an Impound Account or Reserve Account.

Improvement Tax—A tax levied only against the properties that have benefited from a public improvement (such as a sewer or a street light), to cover the cost of the improvement; creates a special assessment lien. Also called Special Assessment.

Improvements—Man-made additions to real property.

Imputed Knowledge—A legal doctrine stating that a principal is considered to have notice of information that the agent has, even if the agent never passed that information on to the principal. Washington does not apply this rule in the real estate context.

Inactive License—Any real estate license that has been turned over to the Director temporarily. The holder of an inactive license is not permitted to engage in activities requiring a license.

Inadvertent Dual Agency—Providing agency services to one party without disclosing that you already represent the other party; doing this inadvertently creates an agency with both parties.

Income Approach to Value—One of the three main methods of appraisal, in which an estimate of the subject property's value is based on the net income it produces; also called the capitalization method or investor's method of appraisal.

Income Property—Property that generates rent or other income for the owner, such as an apartment building. In the federal income tax code, it is referred to as property held for the production of income.

Income Ratio—A standard used in qualifying a buyer for a loan, to determine whether they have sufficient income; the buyer's debts and proposed housing expense should not exceed a specified percentage of their income.

Incompetent—Not legally competent; not of sound mind.

Incurable Depreciation—Deferred maintenance, functional obsolescence, or external obsolescence that is either impossible to correct, or not economically feasible to correct, because the cost could not be recovered in the sales price.

Independent Contractor—A person who contracts to do a job for another, but retains control over how they will carry out the task, rather than following detailed instructions. *Compare:* Employee.

Index—A published statistical report that indicates changes in the cost of money; used as the basis for interest rate adjustments in an ARM.

Individual or Sole Proprietorship—A business owned and operated by one person.

Industrial Insurance— State-mandated insurance coverage for injured workers (also known as industrial insurance). Real estate brokerages must pay workers' compensation premiums on all their agents. Also called Workers' Compensation.

Ingress—A means of entering a property; the opposite of egress. The terms ingress and egress are most commonly used in reference to an access easement.

In-House Sale—A sale in which the buyer and the seller are brought together by agents working for the same brokerage.

Initial Basis—The amount of the owner's original investment in the property; what it cost to acquire the property, which may include closing costs and certain other expenses, as well as the purchase price.

Injunction—A court order prohibiting someone from performing an act, or commanding performance of an act.

Installment Note—A promissory note that calls for regular payments of principal and interest until the debt is fully paid.

Installment Sale—Under the federal income tax code, a sale in which less than 100% of the sales price is received in the year the sale takes place.

Installment Sales Contract— A contract for the sale of real property in which the buyer (the vendee) pays in installments; the buyer takes possession of the property immediately, but the seller (the vendor) retains legal title until the full price has been paid. Also called a Conditional Sales Contract, Land Contract, Real Estate Contract, or Contract for Deed.

Institutional Lender—A bank, savings and loan, or similar organization that invests other people's funds in loans; as opposed to an individual or private lender, which invests its own funds.

Instrument—A legal document, usually one that transfers title (such as a deed), creates a lien (such as a mortgage), or establishes a right to payment (such as a promissory note or contract).

Intangible Appurtenances—Rights that go with ownership of a piece of property that do not involve physical objects or substances; for example, an access easement (as opposed to mineral rights).

Integration—In a property's life cycle, the earliest stage, when the property is being developed. Also called development.

Interest—1. A right or share in something (such as a piece of real estate). 2. A charge a borrower pays to a lender for the use of the lender's money.

Interest-Only Loan—Most commonly, a loan that requires the borrower to pay only the interest during the loan term, with the principal due at the end of the term. Also called a term loan.

Interim Interest—Interest on a new loan that must be paid at the time of closing; covers the interest due for the first (partial) month of the loan term. Also called Prepaid Interest.

Interim Loan—A loan to finance the cost of constructing a building, usually providing that the loan funds will be advanced in installments as the work progresses. Also called a Construction Loan.

Interpleader—A court action filed by someone who is holding funds that two or more people are claiming. The holder turns the funds over to the court; the court resolves the dispute and delivers the money to the party who is entitled to it.

Interstate Land Sales Full Disclosure Act—A federal law requiring subdivision developers to make certain disclosures concerning the property to potential buyers.

Intestate Succession—Distribution of the property of a person who died intestate to their heirs.

Intestate—Without a valid will.

Invalid—Not legally binding or legally effective; not valid.

Inventory—The stock-in-trade of a business.

Inverse Condemnation Action—A court action by a private landowner against the government, seeking compensation for damage to property caused by government action.

Inverted Pyramid—A way of visualizing ownership of real property; in theory, a property owner owns all the earth, water, and air enclosed by a pyramid that has its tip at the center of the earth and extends up through the property boundaries out into the sky.

Investment Property—Unimproved property held as an investment in the expectation that it will appreciate in value.

Involuntary Alienation—Transfer of an interest in property against the will of the owner, or without action by the owner, occurring through operation of law, natural processes, or adverse possession.

Involuntary Conversion—For income tax purposes, when an asset is converted into cash without the voluntary action of the owner, such as through a condemnation award or insurance proceeds paid due to destruction of the property.

Involuntary Lien—A lien that arises by operation of law, without the consent of the property owner. Also called a Statutory Lien.

-J-

Joint and Several Liability—A form of liability in which two or more persons are responsible for a debt both individually and as a group.

Joint Note—A promissory note signed by two or more persons with equal liability for payment.

Joint Tenancy—A form of concurrent ownership in which the co-owners have unity of time, title, interest, and possession and the right of survivorship.

Joint Venture—Two or more individuals or companies joining together for one project or a related series of projects, but not as an ongoing business. *Compare:* Partnership.

Judgment—1. A court's binding determination of the rights and duties of the parties in a lawsuit. 2. A court order requiring one party to pay the other damages.

Judgment Creditor—A person who is owed money as a result of a judgment in a lawsuit.

Judgment Debtor—A person who owes money as a result of a judgment in a lawsuit.

Judgment Lien—A general lien against a judgment debtor's property. The lien is created automatically in the county where the judgment was rendered and may be created in other counties by recording an abstract of judgment.

Judicial Foreclosure—1. The sale of property pursuant to court order to satisfy a lien. 2. A lawsuit filed by a mortgagee or deed of trust beneficiary to foreclose on the security property when the borrower has defaulted.

Junior Lienholder—A secured creditor whose lien is lower in priority than another's lien.

Junior Mortgage—A mortgage that has lower lien priority than another mortgage against the same property. Sometimes called a secondary mortgage.

Just Cause—A legitimate reason for terminating a residential tenancy under a just cause eviction law.

Just Compensation—The compensation that the Constitution requires the government to pay a property owner when the property is taken under the power of eminent domain.

-K-

Kickback—A fee paid for a referral (for example, to an appraiser or inspector). The Real Estate Settlement Procedures Act prohibits kickbacks to settlement service providers in most residential mortgage loan transactions.

-L-

Land—In the legal sense, it is the solid part of the surface of the earth, everything affixed to it by nature or by man, or anything on it or in it, such as minerals and water; real property.

Land Contract—A contract for the sale of real property in which the buyer (the vendee) pays in installments; the buyer takes possession of the property immediately, but the seller (the vendor) retains legal title until the full price has been paid. Also called a conditional sales contract, installment sales contract, real estate contract, or contract for deed.

Land Residual Process—A method of appraising vacant land.

Landlocked Property—A parcel of land without access to a road or highway.

Landlord—A landowner who has leased their property to another. Also called a lessor.

Landmark—A monument, natural or artificial, set up on the boundary between two adjacent properties, to show where the boundary is.

Latent Defects—Defects that are not visible or apparent (as opposed to patent defects).

Lateral Support—The support that a piece of land receives from the land adjacent to it.

Lawful Objective—An objective or purpose of a contract that does not violate the law or a judicial determination of public policy.

Lease—A conveyance of a leasehold estate from the fee owner to a tenant; a contract in which one party pays the other rent in exchange for the possession of real estate. Also called a rental agreement.

Leaseback— A form of real estate financing in which the owner of industrial or commercial property sells the property and leases it back from the buyer; in addition to certain tax advantages, the seller/lessee obtains more cash through the sale than would normally be possible by borrowing and mortgaging the property, since lenders will not often lend 100% of the value. Also called Sale-Leaseback.

Leasehold—A possessory interest in real property that has a limited duration, such as an estate for years or a periodic tenancy. Also called a less-than-freehold estate.

Legacy—A gift of personal property by will. Also called a bequest.

Legal Description—A precise description of a parcel of real property; may be a lot and block description, a metes and bounds description, or a government survey description.

Legal Person—A legal entity such as a corporation, which the law treats as an individual with legal rights and responsibilities; as distinguished from a natural person, a human being. Sometimes called an Artificial Person.

Legal Title—The vendor's interest in property under a land contract.

Legatee—Someone who receives personal property (a legacy) under a will.

Lessee—One who leases property from another; a tenant.

Lessor—One who leases property to another; a landlord.

Less-Than-Freehold—A possessory interest in real property that has a limited duration, such as an estate for years or a periodic tenancy. Also called a Leasehold.

Level Payment Mortgage—An amortized loan with payments that are the same amount each month, although the portion of the payment that is applied to principal steadily increases and the portion of the payment applied to interest steadily decreases. *See:* Loan, Amortized.

Leverage—The effective use of borrowed money to finance an investment such as real estate.

Levy—To impose a tax.

Liability—1. A debt or obligation. 2. Legal responsibility.

Liability Insurance—Insurance coverage that will pay for physical harm to a person or property.

Liable—Legally responsible.

License—1. Official permission to do a particular thing that the law does not allow everyone to do. 2. Revocable, non-assignable permission to use another person's land for a particular purpose. *Compare:* Easement.

Lien—A nonpossessory interest in real property, giving the lienholder the right to foreclose if the owner doesn't pay a debt owed to the lienholder; a financial encumbrance on the owner's title.

Lien Priority—The order in which liens are paid off out of the proceeds of a foreclosure sale.

Lien Release—A document removing a lien, given to the borrower by the lender, once a mortgage or deed of trust has been paid off in full.

Lien Theory—The theory holding that a mortgage or deed of trust does not involve a transfer of title to the lender, but merely creates a lien against the property in the lender's favor. *Compare:* Title Theory.

Life Estate—A freehold estate that lasts only as long as a specified person lives. That person is referred to as the measuring life.

Life Tenant—A person who owns a life estate (and who may or may not also be the measuring life).

Life Tenant—Someone who owns a life estate; the person entitled to possession of the property during the measuring life.

Like-Kind Exchange— A transaction in which a piece of property held for investment or used in a trade or business is traded for a piece of like-kind property, thus deferring tax on the gain. Sometimes called a Tax-Free Exchange, Tax-Deferred Exchange, or 1031 exchange.

Limited Common Elements—In a condominium, areas outside of the units (such as balconies or assigned parking spaces) that are designated for the use of particular unit owners, rather than all of the residents.

Limited Dual Agency—When an agent represents both parties to a transaction, as when a brokerage firm represents both the buyer and the seller.

Limited Liability—When a business investor is not personally liable for the debts of the business, as in the case of a limited partner or a corporate shareholder.

Limited Liability Company (LLC)—A form of business entity that offers both limited liability for its owners and certain tax benefits.

Limited Partner—A partner in a limited partnership who is primarily an investor, and who is not personally liable for the partnership's debts.

Limited Partnership—A partnership made up of one or more general partners and one or more limited partners.

Liquid Assets—Cash and other assets that can be readily turned into cash (liquidated), such as stock.

Liquidated Damages—A sum that the parties to a contract agree in advance (at the time the contract is made) will serve as full compensation in the event of a breach.

Liquidity—The ability to convert an asset into cash quickly.

Lis Pendens—A recorded notice stating that there is a lawsuit pending that may affect title to the defendant's real estate.

Listing—A written agency contract between a seller and a real estate brokerage, stipulating that the brokerage will be paid a commission for finding (or attempting to find) a buyer for the seller's property. Also called a listing agreement.

Listing Agent—The real estate licensee who lists a seller's property for sale with the multiple listing service; also called the listing broker. (The firm that this agent works for may also be called the listing agent or listing broker, or the listing brokerage firm.) The listing agent and firm are the seller's agents, but may act as dual agents with the written consent of the seller and a buyer.

Listing Input Sheet—A form used to gather all pertinent information about a listed property, to expedite the process of inputting that data into a multiple listing service database.

Littoral Land—Land that borders on a stationary body of water (such as a lake, as opposed to a river or stream). *Compare:* Riparian Land.

Littoral Rights—The water rights of an owner of littoral land, in regard to use of the water in the lake.

Loan Correspondent—An intermediary who arranges loans of an investor's money to borrowers, and then services the loans.

Loan Estimate—In a residential transaction subject to RESPA and/or the Truth in Lending Act, a form that the lender must give to the buyer (the loan applicant), providing detailed information about the loan and estimates of the closing costs.

Loan Fee—A loan origination fee, an assumption fee, or discount points.

Loan Term—The length of time over which a mortgage will be repaid.

Loan Workout—An alternative to foreclosure in which a lender agrees to a new payment plan for a loan, or to reduction of the loan's interest rate or principal amount.

Loan-to-Value Ratio (LTV)—The relationship between the loan amount and either the sales price or the appraised value of the property (whichever is less), expressed as a percentage.

Lot and Block Description—The type of legal description used for platted property; it states the property's lot number and block number and the name of the subdivision, referring to the plat map recorded in the county where the property is located. Sometimes called a maps and plats description.

Lot—A parcel of land; especially, a parcel in a subdivision.

-M-

Maker—The person who signs a promissory note, promising to repay a debt. *Compare:* Payee.

Managing Broker—An individual with at least three years' experience as a broker who is issued a managing broker's license, which allows their to supervise other licensees, manage a branch office, or be a firm's designated broker.

Man-Made Attachments—An item that used to be personal property but has been attached to or closely associated with real property in such a way that it has legally become part of the real property. *See:* Annexation, Actual; Annexation, Constructive, Fixture.

Maps and Plats—The type of legal description used for platted property; it states the property's lot number and block number and the name of the subdivision, referring to the plat map recorded in the county where the property is located. Sometimes called a Lot and Block Description.

Margin—In an adjustable-rate mortgage, the difference between the index rate and the interest rate charged to the borrower.

Market Data Approach— One of the three main methods of appraisal, in which the sales prices of comparable properties are used to estimate the value of the subject property. Also called the Sales Comparison Approach.

Market Price—1. The current price generally being charged for something in the marketplace. 2. The price actually paid for a property. *Compare:* Value, Market.

Market Value—The most probable price which a property should bring in a competitive and open market under all conditions requisite to a fair sale, the buyer and seller each acting prudently and knowledgeably, and assuming the price is not affected by undue stimulus. (This is the definition used by the federal financial institution regulatory agencies.) Market value is also called Fair Market Value, Value In Exchange, or Objective Value. *Compare:* Market Price.

Marketable Title—Title free and clear of objectionable liens, encumbrances, or defects, so that a reasonably prudent person with full knowledge of the facts would not hesitate to purchase the property.

Master Plan—A long-term plan of development for a community, implemented by zoning and other laws. Also called a General Plan or Comprehensive Plan.

Material Fact—Information that has a substantial negative impact on the value of the property, on a party's ability to perform, or on the purpose of the transaction.

Materialman's Lien—A construction lien in favor of someone who supplied materials for a project (as opposed to labor).

Maturity Date—The date by which a loan is supposed to be paid off in full.

Measuring Life— A freehold estate that lasts only as long as a specified person lives. That person is referred to as the measuring life.

Mechanic's Lien—A construction lien in favor of someone who provided labor for a project (as opposed to materials).

Meeting of Minds—When all parties freely agree to the terms of a contract, without fraud, undue influence, duress, menace, or mistake. Mutual consent is achieved through offer and acceptance; it is sometimes referred to as Mutual Consent.

Merger—1. Uniting two or more separate properties by transferring ownership of all of them to one person. 2. When the owner of one parcel acquires title to one or more adjacent parcels.

Meridian—An imaginary line running north and south, passing through the earth's poles. Also called a longitude line.

Metes—Measurements.

Metes and Bounds Description—A legal description that starts at an identifiable point of beginning, then describes the property's boundaries in terms of courses (compass directions) and distances, ultimately returning to the point of beginning.

Mill—One-tenth of one cent; a measure used to state property tax rates in some cases. For example, a tax rate of one mill on the dollar is the same as a rate of one-tenth of one percent of the assessed value of the property.

Mineral Rights—Rights to the minerals located beneath the surface of a piece of property.

Minor—A person who has not yet reached the age of majority; in Washington, a person under 18.

MIP—Mortgage insurance premium; especially a premium charged in connection with an FHA-insured loan.

Misplaced Improvements—Improvements that do not fit the most profitable use of the site; they can be overimprovements or underimprovements.

Misrepresentation—A false or misleading statement. *See:* Fraud.

Monetary Policy—The Federal Reserve Board's effort to control the supply and cost of money in the United States.

Monopoly—When a single entity or group has exclusive control over the production or sale of a product or service.

Monument—A visible marker (natural or artificial) used in a survey or a metes and bounds description to establish the boundaries of a piece of property.

Mortgage—1. An instrument that creates a voluntary lien on real property to secure repayment of a debt, and which (unlike a deed of trust) does not include a power of sale, so it can only be foreclosed judicially; the parties are the mortgagor (borrower) and mortgagee (lender). 2. The term is often used more generally, to refer to either a mortgage or a deed of trust. Note: If you do not find the specific term you are looking for here under "Mortgage," check the entries under "Loan."

Mortgage Banker—An intermediary who originates and services real estate loans on behalf of investors.

Mortgage Broker—An intermediary who brings real estate lenders and borrowers together and negotiates loan agreements between them.

Mortgage Company—A term that can refer either to a mortgage banker or to a mortgage broker.

Mortgage Insurance—Insurance that protects a lender against losses resulting from the borrower's default.

Mortgage Loan—Any loan secured by real property, whether the actual security instrument used is a mortgage or a deed of trust.

Mortgagee—A lender who accepts a mortgage as security for repayment of the loan.

Mortgaging Clause—A clause in a mortgage that describes the security interest given to the mortgagee.

Mortgagor—A property owner (usually a borrower) who gives a mortgage to another (usually a lender) as security for payment of an obligation.

Multiple Listing—A listing agreement (usually an exclusive right to sell listing) that includes a provision allowing the brokerage to submit the listing to its multiple listing service for dissemination to cooperating agents.

Multiple Listing Service (MLS)—A regional or local cooperative of real estate firms and licensees who exchange listing information and help market the listings of other members. When one firm's listing is shown to buyers by licensees from other firms in the MLS, those licensees are called cooperating agents.

Mutual Consent—When all parties freely agree to the terms of a contract, without fraud, undue influence, duress, menace, or mistake. Mutual consent is achieved through offer and acceptance; it is sometimes referred to as a "meeting of the minds."

Mutual Mortgage Insurance—The mortgage insurance provided by the FHA to lenders who make loans through FHA programs.

-N-

Narrative Report—A thorough appraisal report in which the appraiser summarizes the data and the appraisal methods used, to convince the reader of the soundness of the estimate; a more comprehensive presentation than a form report.

National Association of REALTORS® (NAR)—A trade association of real estate agents. Only members of NAR may call themselves Realtors.

National Environmental Policy Act (NEPA)—A federal law requiring the preparation of an environmental impact statement before any governmental action that would have a significant effect on the environment.

Natural Attachments—Plants growing on a piece of land, such as trees, shrubs, or crops.

Natural Person—A human being, an individual (as opposed to an artificial person, such as a corporation).

Negative Amortization—When unpaid interest on a loan is added to the principal balance, increasing the amount owed.

Negligence—Conduct that falls below the standard of care that a reasonable person would exercise under the circumstances; carelessness or recklessness.

Negotiable Instrument—An instrument containing an unconditional promise to pay a certain sum of money, to order or to bearer, on demand or at a particular time. It can be a check, promissory note, bond, draft, or stock.

Neighborhood Analysis—The gathering of data on home sizes and styles, topography, features, and amenities in a neighborhood, as part of the appraisal or property management process.

Net Lease—A lease requiring the tenant to pay some or all operational expenses (such as taxes, insurance, and repairs), in addition to the rent paid to the landlord.

Net Listing—A listing agreement in which the seller sets a net amount they are willing to accept for the property; if the actual selling price exceeds that amount, the real estate firm is entitled to keep the excess as its commission.

Net Operating Income—The income that is capitalized to estimate the property's value; calculated by subtracting the property's operating expenses (fixed expenses, variable expenses, and reserves for replacement) from the effective gross income. Also called net income.

Net Spendable—The income that remains after deducting operating expenses, debt service, and income taxes from a property's gross income. Also called Spendable Income or Cash Flow.

Net Worth—An individual's financial assets minus their liabilities.

Nominal Interest Rate—The interest rate stated in a promissory note. Also called the note rate or coupon rate. *Compare:* Annual Percentage Rate.

Nonconforming Loan— A loan made in accordance with the underwriting criteria of Fannie Mae and Freddie Mac, and which therefore can be sold to those entities.

Nonconforming Use—A property use that does not conform to current zoning requirements, but is allowed because the property was being used in that way before the present zoning ordinance was enacted.

Nonfinancial Encumbrance—An easement, a profit, or a restrictive covenant.

Nonjudicial Foreclosure—Foreclosure by a trustee under the power of sale clause in a deed of trust.

Nonpossessory Interest—An interest in property that does not include the right to possess and occupy the property; an encumbrance, such as a lien or an easement.

Nonrecognition Transaction—A transaction for which a taxpayer is not required to pay taxes in the year the gain is realized.

Normal Market Conditions—A sale taking place in a competitive and open market, with informed parties acting prudently, at arm's length, and without undue stimulus (such as an urgent need to sell the property immediately).

Notarize—To have the signature(s) on a legal document verified and certified by a notary public.

Notary Public—Someone who is officially authorized to witness and certify the acknowledgment made by someone signing a legal document.

Note—A written promise to repay a debt; it may or may not be a negotiable instrument. Also called Promissory Note.

Notice of Cessation—A notice recorded when work on a construction project has ceased (although the project is unfinished), to limit the time allowed for recording construction liens.

Notice of Completion—A notice recorded when a construction project has been completed, to limit the time allowed for recording construction liens.

Notice of Default—A notice sent by a secured creditor to the debtor, informing the debtor that they have breached the loan agreement.

Notice of Sale—A notice stating that foreclosure proceedings have been commenced against a property.

Notice of Value—A document issued by the Dept. of Veterans Affairs, setting forth the current market value of a property, based on a VA-approved appraisal. Also called a Certificate of Reasonable Value.

Notice to Quit—A notice to a tenant, demanding that they vacate the leased property.

Notice to the World—Constructive notice of the contents of a document provided to the general public by recording the document.

Novation—1. When one party to a contract withdraws and a new party is substituted, relieving the withdrawing party of liability. 2. The substitution of a new obligation for an old one.

Nuisance—A use of property that is offensive or annoying to neighboring landowners or to the community.

Nuncupative Will—An oral will made on the testator's deathbed; valid only as to bequests of personal property worth under $1,000.

-O-

Obligatory Advances—Disbursements of construction loan funds that the lender is obligated to make (by prior agreement with the borrower) when the borrower has completed certain phases of construction.

Obsolescence—Any loss in value (depreciation) due to reduced desirability and usefulness.

Offer—When one person (the offeror) proposes a contract to another (the offeree); if the offeree accepts the offer, a binding contract is formed.

Offeree—One to whom a contract offer is made.

Offeror—One who makes a contract offer.

Officer—In a corporation, an executive authorized by the board of directors to manage the business of the corporation.

Off-Site Improvements—Improvements that add to the usefulness of a site but are not located directly on it, such as curbs, street lights, and sidewalks.

One-Time Agency Agreement—An agreement entered into by a FSBO seller and a buyer's agent: the seller agrees to compensate the agent for bringing them a particular buyer.

Open House—Showing a listed home to the public for a specified period of time.

Open Listing—A nonexclusive listing, given by a seller to as many brokerages as they choose. If the property is sold, a brokerage is only entitled to a commission if it was the procuring cause of the sale.

Open Market Operations—The Federal Reserve's manipulation of the money supply through the purchase and sale of government securities.

Open Mortgage—A mortgage without a prepayment penalty.

Open-End Mortgage—A loan that permits the borrower to reborrow the money they have repaid on the principal, usually up to the original loan amount, without executing a new loan agreement.

Operating Expenses—For income-producing property, the fixed expenses, maintenance expenses, and reserves for replacement; does not include debt service.

Option to Purchase—An option giving the optionee the right to buy property owned by the optionor at an agreed price during a specified period.

Option—A contract giving one party the right to do something, without obligating them to do it.

Optionee—The person to whom an option is given.

Optionor—The person who gives an option.

"Or More"—A provision in a promissory note that allows the borrower to prepay the debt.

Oral Contract—A spoken agreement that has not been written down. Also called a parol contract.

Ordinance—A law passed by a local legislative body, such as a city council. *Compare:* Statute.

Orientation—The placement of a house on its lot, with regard to its exposure to the sun and wind, privacy from the street, and protection from outside noise.

Origination Fee—A fee a lender charges a borrower upon making a new loan, intended to cover the administrative costs of making the loan. Also called a loan fee.

Ostensible Agency—When third parties are given the impression that someone who has not been authorized to represent another is that person's agent, or else given the impression that an agent has been authorized to perform acts which are in fact beyond the scope of their authority. Also called Apparent Agency.

Overimprovement—An improvement that is more expensive than justified by the value of the land.

Overlying Right—A landowner's right to use percolating or diffused groundwater.

Ownership in Severalty—When a piece of property is owned by one individual.

Ownership—Title to property, dominion over property; the rights of possession and control.

-P-

Package Mortgage—A mortgage that is secured by certain items of personal property (such as appliances or carpeting) in addition to the real property.

Panic Selling—Attempting to induce owners to list or sell their homes by predicting that members of a protected class (another race or ethnic group, or people with some type of disability, for example) will be moving into the neighborhood; this violates antidiscrimination laws. Also called Blockbusting.

Par—1. The accepted standard of comparison; the average or typical rate or amount. 2. Face value; for example, a mortgage sold at the secondary market level for 97% of par has been sold for 3% less than its face value.

Parcel—A lot or piece of real estate, especially a specified part of a larger tract.

Partial Reconveyance—The instrument given to the borrower when part of the security property is released from a blanket deed of trust under a partial release clause.

Partial Release Clause—1. A clause in a blanket mortgage or deed of trust which allows the borrower to get part of the security property released from the lien when a certain portion of the debt has been paid or other conditions are fulfilled. Often called a partial release clause. 2. A clause in a land contract providing for a deed to a portion of the land to be delivered when a certain portion of the contract price has been paid. Also known as a Deed Release Provision. or Release Clause.

Partial Satisfaction—The instrument given to the borrower when part of the security property is released from a blanket mortgage under a partial release clause.

Participation Loan—A loan in which the lender receives some yield on the loan in addition to the interest, such as a percentage of the income generated by the property, or a share in the borrower's equity.

Participation Mortgage—A loan made in exchange for a share of the borrower's equity in the property, and/or a share in the earnings of the property.

Partition—The division of a property among its co-owners, so that each owns part of it in severalty; this may occur by agreement of all the co-owners (voluntary partition), or by court order (judicial partition).

Partnership Property—All property that partners bring into their business at the outset or later acquire for their business; property owned as tenants in partnership. *See:* Tenancy in Partnership.

Partnership—An association of two or more persons to carry on a business for profit as co-owners.

Party Wall—A wall located on the boundary line between two adjoining parcels of land that is used by the owners of both properties.

Patent—The instrument used to convey government land to a private individual.

Patent Defect—A problem that is readily observable in an ordinary inspection of the property. *Compare:* Latent Defect.

Payee—In a promissory note, the party who is entitled to be paid; the lender. *Compare:* Maker.

Payment Cap—A limit on the amount an ARM's payments can be increased, either during a given year, or over the entire life of the loan.

Per Diem—Daily.

Percentage Lease—A lease in which the rent is based on a percentage of the tenant's monthly or annual gross sales.

Percolation Test—A test to determine the ability of the ground to absorb or drain water; used to determine whether a site is suitable for construction, particularly for installation of a septic tank system.

Periodic Estate— A leasehold estate that continues for successive periods of equal length (such as from week to week or month to month), until terminated by proper notice from either party. Also called a Month-to-Month (or week-to-week, etc.) Tenancy or Periodic Tenancy. *Compare:* Estate for Years..

Periodic Tenancy—A leasehold estate that continues for successive periods of equal length (such as from week to week or month to month), until terminated by proper notice from either party. Also called a month-to-month (or week-to-week, etc.) tenancy. *Compare:* Estate for Years.

Permanent Loan— Long-term financing used to replace a construction loan (an interim loan) when construction has been completed. Also called a Take-out Loan.

Personal Property—Any property that is not real property; movable property not affixed to land. Also called chattels or personalty.

Personal Use Property—Property that a taxpayer owns for their own use (or family use), as opposed to income property, investment property, dealer property, or property used in a trade or business.

Personalty—Personal property.

Physical Deterioration—Loss in value (depreciation) resulting from wear and tear or deferred maintenance.

Physical Life—An estimate of the time a building will remain structurally sound and capable of being used. *Compare:* Economic Life.

Plaintiff—The party who brings or starts a civil lawsuit; the one who sues.

Planned Unit Development (PUD)—A development (usually residential) with small, clustered lots designed to leave more open space than traditional subdivisions have.

Planning Commission—A local government agency responsible for preparing the community's general plan for development.

Plat—A detailed survey map of a subdivision, recorded in the county where the land is located. Subdivided property is sometimes called platted property.

Plat Book—A large book containing subdivision plats, kept at the county recorder's office.

Pledge—When a debtor transfers possession of property to the creditor as security for repayment of the debt.

Plot Plan—A plan showing lot dimensions and the layout of improvements (such as buildings and landscaping) on a property site.

Plottage—The increment of value that results when two or more lots are combined to produce greater value. Also called the plottage increment.

Point—One percent of the principal amount of a loan.

Point of Beginning (POB)—The starting point in a metes and bounds description; a monument or a point described by reference to a monument.

Points— A percentage of the principal amount of a loan, collected by the lender at the time a loan is originated, to give the lender an additional yield. Also called Discount Points.

Police Power—The power of state and local governments to enact and enforce laws for the protection of the public's health, safety, morals, and general welfare.

Policies and Procedures Manual—Comprehensive handbook that describes a business's goals and objectives, code of conduct in workplace, and the manner in which employees should conduct business with third parties. Also called an employee handbook.

Portfolio—The mix of investments owned by an individual or company.

Possession—1. The holding and enjoyment of property. 2. Actual physical occupation of real property.

Possessory Interest—An interest in property that includes the right to possess and occupy the property. The term includes all estates (leasehold as well as freehold), but does not include encumbrances.

Potential Gross Income—A property's economic rent; the income it could earn if it were available for lease in the current market.

Power of Attorney—An instrument authorizing one person (the attorney in fact) to act as another's agent, to the extent stated in the instrument.

Power of Sale Clause—A clause in a deed of trust giving the trustee the right to foreclose nonjudicially (sell the debtor's property without a court action) if the borrower defaults.

Preapproval—A process that allows a prospective borrower to submit a loan application to a lender and get approved for a loan before beginning the home-buying process.

Prepaid Interest—Interest on a new loan that must be paid at the time of closing; covers the interest due for the first (partial) month of the loan term. Also called interim interest.

Prepayment Penalty—A penalty charged to a borrower who prepays.

Prepayment—Paying off part or all of a loan before payment is due.

Prescription—Acquiring an interest in real property (usually an easement) by using it openly and without the owner's permission for the period prescribed by statute.

Prescriptive Easement—An easement acquired by prescription; that is, by using the property openly and without the owner's permission for the period prescribed by statute.

Preventive Maintenance—A program of regular inspection and care of a property and its fixtures, allowing the prevention of potential problems or their immediate repair.

Price Fixing—The cooperative setting of prices by competing businesses, in violation of antitrust laws.

Primary Mortgage Market—The market in which mortgage loans are originated, where lenders make loans to borrowers. *Compare:* Secondary Mortgage Market.

Prime Rate—The interest rate a bank charges its largest and most desirable customers.

Principal—1. One who grants another person (an agent) authority to represent them in dealings with third parties. 2. One of the parties to a transaction (such as a buyer or seller), as opposed to those who are involved as agents or employees (such as a real estate licensee or escrow agent). 3. In regard to a loan, the amount originally borrowed, as opposed to the interest.

Principal Meridian— In the government survey system, the main north-south line in a particular grid, used as the starting point in numbering the ranges.

Principal Meridian—In the government survey system, the main north-south line in a particular grid, used as the starting point in numbering the ranges.

Principal Residence Property—Real property that is the owner's home, their main dwelling. Under the federal income tax laws, a person can only have one principal residence at a time.

Principle of Anticipation—An appraisal principle which holds that value is created by the expectation of benefits to be received in the future.

Principle of Balance—An appraisal principle which holds that the maximum value of real estate is achieved when the agents of production (labor, coordination, capital, and land) are in proper balance with each other.

Principle of Change—An appraisal principle which holds that property values are in a state of flux, increasing and decreasing in response to social, economic, and governmental forces.

Principle of Competition—An appraisal principle which holds that profits tend to encourage competition, and excess profits tend to result in ruinous competition.

Principle of Conformity—An appraisal principle which holds that the maximum value of property is realized when there is a reasonable degree of social and economic homogeneity in the neighborhood.

Principle of Contribution—An appraisal principle which holds that the value of real property is greatest when the improvements produce the highest return commensurate with their cost (the investment).**Principle of Progression**—An appraisal principle which holds that a property of lesser value tends to be worth more when it is located in an area with properties of greater value than it would be if located elsewhere. The opposite of the principle of regression.

Principle of Regression—An appraisal principle which holds that a valuable property surrounded by properties of lesser value will tend to be worth less than it would be in a different location; the opposite of the principle of progression.

Principle of Substitution—A principle of appraisal holding that the maximum value of a property is set by how much it would cost to obtain another property that is equally desirable, assuming that there would not be a long delay or significant incidental expenses involved in obtaining the substitute.

Principle of Supply and Demand—A principle holding that value varies directly with demand and inversely with supply; that is, the greater the demand the greater the value, and the greater the supply the lower the value.

Prior Appropriation—A system of allocating water rights, under which a person who wants to use water from a certain lake or river is required to apply for a permit; a permit has priority over other permits that are issued later. *Compare:* Riparian Rights.

Private Mortgage Insurance (PMI)—Insurance provided by private companies to conventional lenders for loans with loan-to-value ratios over 80%.

Private Restriction—A restriction imposed on property by a previous owner, a neighbor, or the subdivision developer; a restrictive covenant or a condition in a deed.

Probate—A judicial proceeding in which the validity of a will is established and the executor is authorized to distribute the estate property; or, when there is no valid will, in which an administrator is appointed to distribute the estate to the heirs.

Probate Court—A court that oversees the distribution of property under a will or intestate succession.

Procuring Cause—The real estate agent who is primarily responsible for bringing about a sale; for example, by negotiating the agreement between the buyer and seller.

Profit—A nonpossessory interest; the right to enter another person's land and take something (such as timber or minerals) away from it.

Progressive Tax—A tax, such as the federal income tax, that imposes a higher tax rate on a taxpayer who earns a higher income.

Promisee—Someone who has been promised something; someone who is supposed to receive the benefit of a contractual promise.

Promisor—Someone who has made a contractual promise to another.

Promissory Note—A written promise to repay a debt; it may or may not be a negotiable instrument.

Property—1. The rights of ownership in a thing, such as the right to use, possess, transfer, or encumber it. 2. Something that is owned.

Property Management Agreement—A document that creates an agency relationship between a property owner and property manager and establishes the terms and conditions of the relationship.

Property Management Plan—An outline for a property manager's strategy in meeting the owner's financial goals.

Property Manager—A person hired by a property owner to administer, merchandise, and maintain property, especially rental property.

Property Tax Lien—A specific lien on property to secure payment of property taxes.

Property Tax—1. The general real estate tax. 2. Any ad valorem tax levied on real or personal property.

Property Used in a Trade or Business—Real property and equipment owned by a taxpayer and used to carry out the taxpayer's trade or business.

Proration—The process of dividing or allocating something (especially a sum of money or an expense) proportionately, according to time, interest, or benefit.

Public Offering Statement—A statement required by the Washington Land Development Act, that provides detailed information about the subdivision, such as whether there are any liens, the physical condition of the land, compliance with land use laws, and so on.

Public Record—The official collection of legal documents that individuals have filed with the county recorder in order to make the information contained in them public.

Public Restriction—A law or regulation limiting or regulating the use of real property.

Public Use—A use that benefits the public. For a condemnation action to be constitutional, it must be for a public use.

Puffing—Superlative statements about the quality of a property that should not be considered assertions of fact.

Punitive Damages—In a civil lawsuit, an award added to compensatory damages, to punish the defendant for outrageous or malicious conduct and discourage others from similar conduct.

Purchase and Sale Agreement—A contract in which a seller promises to convey title to real property to a buyer in exchange for the purchase price. Also called an earnest money agreement, deposit receipt, sales contract, or contract of sale.

Purchase Loan—A mortgage loan used to buy the property that is the security for the loan.

Purchase Money Mortgage—When a seller extends credit to a buyer to finance the purchase of the property, accepting a deed of trust or mortgage instead of cash. Sometimes called a carryback loan. *Compare:* Loan, Purchase.

Purchaser's Assignment of Contract and Deed—The instrument used to assign the vendee's equitable interest in a contract to another.

-Q-

Qualified Acceptance— A response to a contract offer, changing some of the terms of the original offer; it operates as a rejection of the original offer (not as an acceptance). Also called Counteroffer.

Qualified Fee— A fee simple estate that carries a qualification, so that ownership may revert to the grantor if a specified event occurs or a condition is not met. Also called a Defeasible Fee.

Qualifying Standards—The standards a lender requires a loan applicant to meet before a loan will be approved. Also called underwriting standards.

Quantity Survey Method—In appraisal, a method of estimating the replacement cost of a structure; it involves a detailed estimate of the quantities and cost of materials and labor, and overhead expenses such as insurance and contractor's profit.

Quiet Enjoyment—Use and possession of real property without interference from the previous owner, the lessor, or anyone else claiming an interest in the property. *See:* Covenant of Quiet Enjoyment.

Quiet Title Action—A lawsuit to determine who has title to a piece of property, or to remove a cloud from the title.

Quitclaim Deed—A deed that conveys any interest in a property that the grantor has at the time the deed is executed, without warranties.

-R-

Range Lines—In the government survey system, the north-south lines (meridians) located six miles apart.

Range—In the government survey system, a strip of land six miles wide, running north and south.

Ratify—To confirm or approve after the fact an act that was not authorized when it was performed.

Ready, Willing, and Able—A buyer is ready, willing, and able if they make an offer that meets the seller's stated terms, and has the contractual capacity and financial resources to complete the transaction.

Real Estate—Land and everything attached to or appurtenant to it. Also called Realty or Real Property. *Compare:* Personal Property.

Real Estate Brokerage Relationships Act—A Washington state law that significantly changed traditional agency law in regard to real estate transactions. It governs when and how real estate agency relationships are created and terminated, the duties owed by real estate licensees to the parties to a real estate transaction, and when and how agency disclosures are to be made.

Real Estate Commission—A commission appointed by the Governor, consisting of the Director of the Department of Licensing and six commissioners; responsible for preparing and conducting the real estate licensing examinations.

Real Estate Contract—1. A purchase and sale agreement. 2. A land contract. 3. Any contract having to do with real property.

Real Estate Firm—A business entity licensed to offer real estate brokerage services under the supervision and control of its designated broker; also known as a brokerage.

Real Estate Investment Trust (REIT)—A real estate investment business with at least 100 investors that qualifies for tax benefits if organized and managed in compliance with IRS rules.

Real Estate Settlement Procedures Act (RESPA)—A federal law that requires disclosure of closing costs to residential mortgage loan applicants and prohibits kickbacks (referral fees) between settlement service providers.

Real Property—Land and everything attached to or appurtenant to it. Also called Realty or Real Estate. *Compare:* Personal Property.

Realization—For income tax purposes, when a gain is separated from an asset, and therefore becomes taxable.

Realtor®—A real estate agent who is an active member of a state and local real estate board that is affiliated with the National Association of REALTORS®.

Realty— Land and everything attached to or appurtenant to it. Also called Real Property or Real Estate. *Compare:* Personal Property.

Recapture—An investor's recovery of money invested in real estate.

Receiver—A person appointed by a court to manage and look after property or funds involved in litigation.

Reconciliation—The final step in an appraisal, when the appraiser assembles and interprets the data in order to arrive at a final value estimate. Also called correlation.

Reconveyance—Releasing the security property from the lien created by a deed of trust, by recording a deed of reconveyance.

Recording—Filing a document at the county recorder's office, so that it will be placed in the public record.

Recording Numbers—The numbers stamped on documents when they're recorded, used to identify and locate the documents in the public record.

Rectangular Survey System—A system of grids, made up of range and township lines that divide the land into townships, which are further subdivided into sections; a property is identified by its location within a particular section, township, and range. Also called the Government Survey System.

Redemption—1. When a defaulting borrower prevents foreclosure by paying the full amount of the debt, plus costs. 2. When a mortgagor regains the property after foreclosure by paying whatever the foreclosure sale purchaser paid for it, plus interest and expenses.

Redlining—When a lender refuses to make loans secured by property in a certain neighborhood because of the racial or ethnic composition of the neighborhood.

Refinancing—When a homeowner takes out a new loan—usually to take advantage of lower interest rates—and uses the loan proceeds to pay off the existing loan.

Reformation—A legal action to correct a mistake, such as a typographical error, in a deed or other document. The court will order the execution of a correction deed.

Reformation Deed— A deed used to correct minor mistakes in an earlier deed, such as misspelled names or typographical errors in the legal description. Also called a Deed of Confirmation or Correction Deed.

Regulation Z—The regulation that implements the Truth in Lending Act.

Reinstate—To prevent foreclosure by curing the default.

Release—1. To give up a legal right. 2. A document in which a legal right is given up.

Release Clause—1. A clause in a blanket mortgage or deed of trust which allows the borrower to get part of the security property released from the lien when a certain portion of the debt has been paid or other conditions are fulfilled. Often called a partial release clause. 2. A clause in a land contract providing for a deed to a portion of the land to be delivered when a certain portion of the contract price has been paid. Also known as a deed release provision.

Reliction—When a body of water gradually recedes, exposing land that was previously under water.

Remainder—A future interest that becomes possessory when a life estate terminates, and that is held by someone other than the grantor of the life estate; as opposed to a reversion, which is a future interest held by the grantor (or the grantor's heirs).

Remainderman—The person who has an estate in remainder.

Remaining Economic Life— The period during which improved property will yield a return over and above the rent due to the land itself; also called the Useful Life or Economic Life.

Remise—To give up; a term used in quitclaim deeds.

Rent—Compensation paid by a tenant to the landlord in exchange for the possession and use of the property.

Rent Roll—A report on rent collections; a list of the total amount of rent earned, both collected and uncollected.

Rental Schedule—A list of rental rates for the units in a given building.

Replacement Cost—In appraisal, the current cost of constructing a building with the same utility as the subject property using modern materials and construction methods.

Reproduction Cost—In appraisal, the cost of constructing a replica (an exact duplicate) of the subject property, using the same materials and construction methods that were originally used, but at current prices.

Rescission—When a contract is terminated and each party gives anything acquired under the contract back to the other party. (The verb form is rescind.) *Compare:* Cancellation.

Reservation—A right retained by a grantor when conveying property; for example, mineral rights, an easement, or a life estate can be reserved in the deed.

Reserve Account—A bank account maintained by a lender for payment of property taxes, insurance premiums, and other recurring expenses connected with the security property; the lender requires the borrower to make regular deposits, and pays the expenses out of the account. Also called an impound account or escrow account.

Reserve Requirements—The percentage of deposits commercial banks must keep on reserve with the Federal Reserve Bank.

Reserves for Replacement—Regular allowances set aside by an investment property owner, a business, or a homeowners association to pay for the replacement of structures and equipment that are expected to wear out.

Residential Landlord-Tenant Act (RLTA)—A Washington state law that regulates landlords and tenants in most residential lease transactions.

Residual Income—The amount of income that an applicant for a VA loan has left over after taxes, recurring obligations, and the proposed housing expense have been deducted from their gross monthly income.

Residual—The property value remaining after the economic life of the improvements has been exhausted.

Residuals—Commissions in the form of delayed payments (when a part of the commission is paid with each installment on an installment sales contract, for example).

Restitution—Restoring something (especially money) that a person was unjustly deprived of.

Restriction—A limitation on the use of real property.

Restrictive Covenant—A promise to do or not do an act relating to real property, especially a promise that runs with the land; usually an owner's promise to not use property in a specified manner.

Retainer—A fee paid up front to a licensee when entering into a real estate agency (usually a buyer agency) relationship.

Return—A profit from an investment. Also referred to as return on investment (ROI). *See also:* Yield.

Reverse Equity Mortgage—An arrangement in which a homeowner mortgages the home to a lender in exchange for a monthly check from the lender.

Reversion—A future interest that becomes possessory when a temporary estate (such as a life estate) terminates, and that is held by the grantor (or their successors in interest). *Compare:* Remainder.

Reversioner—The person who has an estate in reversion.

Rezone—An amendment to a zoning ordinance, usually changing the uses allowed in a particular zone. Also called a zoning amendment.

Right of First Refusal—A right that gives the holder the first opportunity to purchase or lease a particular parcel of real property, should the owner decide to sell or lease it.

Right of Way—An easement that gives the holder the right to cross another person's land.

Right of Survivorship—A characteristic of joint tenancy; surviving joint tenants automatically acquire a deceased joint tenant's interest in the property.

Riparian Land—Land that is adjacent to or crossed by a flowing body of water (a river or stream). *Compare:* Littoral Land.

Riparian Rights—The water rights of a landowner whose property is adjacent to or crossed by a body of water, such as a river or stream. *Compare:* Prior Appropriation.

Risk Analysis—In real estate lending, the process of evaluating a loan application to determine the probability that the applicant would repay the loan, and matching the risk to an appropriate rate of return. Also called Underwriting.

Rule of Capture—A legal rule that gives a landowner the right to all oil and gas produced from wells on their land, even if it migrated from underneath land belonging to someone else.

Running with the Land—Binding or benefiting the successive owners of a piece of property, rather than terminating when a particular owner transfers their interest. Usually said in reference to an easement or a restrictive covenant.

Rural Housing Service Loan—A loan made by the Rural Housing Service, a federal agency, to purchase, build, or rehabilitate homes in rural areas.

-S-

Safety Clause—A clause in a listing agreement providing that for a specified period after the listing expires, the brokerage will still be entitled to a commission if the property is sold to someone the brokerage dealt with during the listing term. Also called a Extender Clause or Carryover Clause.

Sale-Leaseback—A form of real estate financing in which the owner of industrial or commercial property sells the property and leases it back from the buyer; in addition to certain tax advantages, the seller/lessee obtains more cash through the sale than would normally be possible by borrowing and mortgaging the property, since lenders will not often lend 100% of the value.

Sales Comparison Approach—One of the three main methods of appraisal, in which the sales prices of comparable properties are used to estimate the value of the subject property. Also called the market data approach.

Sales Contract—A contract in which a seller promises to convey title to real property to a buyer in exchange for the purchase price. Also called an Earnest Money Agreement, Deposit Receipt, Contract of Sale, or Purchase and Sale Agreement.

Sandwich Lease—When a tenant transfers less than their entire leasehold estate to another person (the subtenant); the subtenant might share possession with the tenant, or have the right to possess only a portion of the leased premises, or have the right to possess the entire premises for only a portion of the remainder of the lease term. Also called a Sublease.

Satisfaction of Mortgage—The document a mortgagee gives the mortgagor when the mortgage debt has been paid in full, acknowledging that the debt has been paid and the mortgage is no longer a lien against the property.

Savings and Loan Association—A type of financial institution that emphasizes home mortgage loans.

Savings Bank—A type of financial institution that emphasizes consumer loans and home mortgages.

Scarcity—A limited or inadequate supply of something; one of the four elements of value (along with utility, demand, and transferability).

Secondary Financing—Money borrowed to pay part of the required downpayment or closing costs for a first loan, when the second loan is secured by the same property that secures the first loan.

Secondary Mortgage— A mortgage that has lower lien priority than another mortgage against the same property. Sometimes called a Junior Mortgage.

Secondary Mortgage Market—The market in which investors (including Fannie Mae and Freddie Mac) purchase real estate loans from lenders.

Secret Profit—A financial benefit that an agent takes from a transaction without informing the principal.

Section—In the government survey system, a section is one mile square and contains 640 acres. There are 36 sections in a township.

Secured Creditor—A creditor with a security interest in or a lien against specific property; if the debt is not repaid, the creditor can repossess the property or (in the case of real estate) foreclose on the property and collect the debt from the sale proceeds.

Securities—Investment instruments, such as stocks and bonds.

Security Agreement—Under the Uniform Commercial Code, a document that creates a lien on personal property being used to secure a loan.

Security Deposit—Money a tenant gives a landlord at the beginning of the tenancy to protect the landlord in case the tenant defaults; the landlord may retain all or part of the deposit to cover unpaid rent or repair costs at the end of the tenancy.

Security Instrument—A document that creates a voluntary lien, to secure repayment of a loan; for debts secured by real property, it is either a mortgage or a deed of trust.

Security Interest—The interest a creditor may acquire in the debtor's property to ensure that the debt will be paid.

Security Property—The property against which a borrower gives a lender a voluntary lien, so that the lender can foreclose if the borrower defaults.

Seisin—Actual possession of a freehold estate; ownership.

Self-Help Eviction—When a landlord uses physical force, a lock-out, or a utility shut-off to evict a tenant, instead of the legal process. This is generally illegal.

Seller Disclosure Statement—A form that state law requires real property sellers to give their buyers, disclosing any problems with the property.

Seller's Agent— A real estate licensee who is representing a seller in a transaction, or the firm that licensee works for.

Senior Mortgage—A mortgage that has higher lien priority than another mortgage against the same property; the opposite of a junior mortgage.

Separate Property—Property owned by a married person that is not community property; includes property acquired before marriage or by gift or inheritance after marriage.

Servient Tenant—The owner of a servient tenement—that is, someone whose property is burdened by an easement.

Servient Tenement—Property burdened by an easement. In other words, the owner of the servient tenement (the servient tenant) must allow someone who has an easement (the dominant tenant) to use the property.

Setback Requirements—Provisions in a zoning ordinance that do not allow structures to be built within a certain distance of the property line.

Settlement—1. An agreement between the parties to a civil lawsuit, in which the plaintiff agrees to drop the suit in exchange for money or the defendant's promise to do or refrain from doing something. 2. Closing.

Settlement Service Provider—Under RESPA, an individual or business that provides services in connection with the closing of a transaction, such as a lender, a mortgage broker, a title company, an escrow agent, or a real estate agent.

Settlement Statement—A final, detailed accounting for a real estate transaction, listing each party's debits and credits and the amount each will receive or be required to pay at closing; the closing disclosure includes a settlement statement. Also called a closing statement.

Severalty—*See:* Ownership in Severalty.

Severance, Constructive—When a landowner enters into a contract to sell an appurtenance or natural attachment, the contract constructively severs the item from the land—making it the personal property of the buyer—even before the buyer has actually taken it off the land.

Severance—1. Termination of a joint tenancy. 2. The permanent removal of a natural attachment, fixture, or appurtenance from real property, which transforms the item into personal property.

Shared Appreciation Mortgage—A mortgage in which a lender is entitled to a share of the increase in the value of the property.

Shareholder—An individual who holds ownership shares (shares of stock) in a corporation, and has limited liability in regard to the corporation's debts. Also called a stockholder.

Sheriff's Deed—A deed delivered, on court order, to the holder of a certificate of sale when the redemption period after a mortgage foreclosure has expired.

Sheriff's Sale—A foreclosure sale held after a judicial foreclosure. Sometimes called an execution sale.

Sherman Act—A federal antitrust law prohibiting any agreement that has the effect of an unreasonable restraint of trade, such as price fixing and tie-in arrangements.

Shoreline Management Act—A Washington state law regulating development within 200 feet of the coast or the shores of larger lakes and streams.

Short Plat—The subdivision of a parcel of land into four or fewer lots.

Short Sale—Selling a home for less than the amount owed, with the lender's consent. The lender receives the sale proceeds and, typically, releases the borrower from the remaining debt.

Simple Interest—Interest that is computed only on the principal amount of the loan, which is the type of interest charged in connection with real estate loans. *Compare:* Compound Interest.

Site Analysis—The gathering of data about the physical characteristics of a property and other factors affecting its use or title, as part of the appraisal process.

Special Agent—An agent with limited authority to do a specific thing or conduct a specific transaction.

Special Assessment—A tax levied only against the properties that have benefited from a public improvement (such as a sewer or a street light), to cover the cost of the improvement; creates a special assessment lien.

Special Warranty Deed—A deed in which the grantor warrants title only against defects that may have arisen during their period of ownership.

Specific Lien—A lien that attaches only to a particular piece of property (as opposed to a general lien, which attaches to all of the debtor's property).

Specific Performance—A legal remedy in which a court orders someone who has breached a contract to actually perform the contract as agreed, rather than simply paying money damages.

Spendable Income—The income that remains after deducting operating expenses, debt service, and income taxes from a property's gross income. Also called net spendable income or cash flow.

Spot Zoning—A proposed rezone that applies only to a small piece of property in an existing zone to benefit a particular landowner; illegal in Washington.

Square Foot Method—In appraisal, a method of estimating replacement cost by calculating the square foot cost of replacing the subject home.

Stable Monthly Income—A loan applicant's gross monthly income that meets the lender's tests of quality and durability.

Standard Coverage Title Insurance—Title insurance that protects against latent title defects (such as forged deeds) and undiscovered recorded encumbrances, but does not protect against problems that could be discovered only through inspection of the property.

State Environmental Policy Act (SEPA)—A Washington state law (analogous to NEPA) that requires an environmental impact statement before property is developed or altered in a way that would have a significant effect on the environment.

Statement of Charges—A document served on a licensee which contains a description of license law violations the Director of the Department of Licensing believes the licensee has committed.

Statement of Disbursements—A list of all of a property's expenses incurred during a specific operating period.

Statement of Operations—A periodic report that shows the total money received and disbursed during a given period, and also describes the overall condition of the property during that period.

Statute—A law enacted by a state legislature or the U.S. Congress. *Compare:* Ordinance.

Statute of Frauds—A law that requires certain types of contracts to be in writing and signed in order to be enforceable.

Statute of Limitations—A law requiring a particular type of lawsuit to be filed within a specified time after the event giving rise to the suit occurred.

Statutory Dedication—A dedication required by law; for example, dedication of property for streets and sidewalks as a prerequisite to subdivision approval.

Statutory Lien— A lien that arises by operation of law, without the consent of the property owner. Also called a Involuntary Lien.

Statutory Redemption Period—The period required by law (one year in Washington) following a sheriff's sale in which a foreclosed borrower may redeem a property.

Statutory Right of Redemption—The right of a mortgagor to get their property back after a foreclosure sale.

Statutory Warranty Deed—A short form of the general warranty deed, in which the covenants are implied (by the use of language specified in the state statute) rather than spelled out.

Steering—Channeling prospective buyers or tenants to or away from particular neighborhoods based on their race, religion, national origin, or ancestry.

Stigmatized Property—A property on which some activity took place (for example, a crime, a death, or drug- or gang-related activity) which might make the property less attractive to certain buyers.

Stockholder—An individual who holds ownership shares (shares of stock) in a corporation, and has limited liability in regard to the corporation's debts. Also called a Shareholder.

Straight Note— A promissory note that calls for regular payments of interest only, so that the entire principal amount is due in one lump sum at the end of the loan term. Also called a Term Note.

Straight Note—A promissory note that calls for regular payments of interest only, so that the entire principal amount is due in one lump sum at the end of the loan term. Also called a term note.

Subagent—A person that an agent has delegated authority to, so that the subagent can assist in carrying out the principal's orders; the agent of an agent.

Subcontractor—A contractor who, at the request of the general contractor, provides a specific service, such as plumbing or drywalling, in connection with the overall construction project.

Subdivision—1. A piece of land divided into two or more parcels. 2. A residential development.

Subdivision Plat—A detailed survey map of a subdivision, recorded in the county where the land is located. Subdivided property is sometimes called Platted Property or Plat.

Subdivision Regulations—State and local laws that must be complied with before land can be subdivided.

Subjacent Support—The support that the surface of a piece of land receives from the land beneath it.

Subject To—When a purchaser takes property subject to a trust deed or mortgage, they are not personally liable for paying off the loan; in case of default, however, the property can still be foreclosed on.

Subjective Value—The value of a property in the eyes of a particular person, as opposed to its market value (objective value).

Sublease—When a tenant transfers less than their entire leasehold estate to another person (the subtenant); the subtenant might share possession with the tenant, or have the right to possess only a portion of the leased premises, or have the right to possess the entire premises for only a portion of the remainder of the lease term. Also called a sandwich lease.

Subordination Clause—A provision in a mortgage or deed of trust that permits a later mortgage or deed of trust to have higher lien priority than the one containing the clause.

Subprime Mortgage—A mortgage loan made to a borrower who doesn't meet the requirements for ordinary mortgage loans, because of problems with credit or financial qualifications, or a lack of documentation. The interest rates and fees for these mortgages are usually higher to offset added risks to the lender.

Subrogation—The substitution of one person in the place of another with reference to a lawful claim or right. For instance, a title company that pays a claim on behalf of its insured, the property owner, is subrogated to any claim the owner successfully undertakes against the former owner.

Substitution of Liability—A buyer wishing to assume an existing loan may apply for the lender's approval; once approved, the buyer assumes liability for repayment of the loan, and the original borrower (the seller) is released from liability.

Succession—Acquiring property by will or inheritance.

Sufferance—Acquiescence, implied permission, or passive consent through a failure to act, as opposed to express permission.

Summary of Operations—The key portion of a property manager's statement of operations, which summarizes income and expenses.

Support Rights—The right to have one's land supported by the land adjacent to it and beneath it.

Surrender—Giving up an estate before it has expired (as occurs, for example, when a landlord and tenant agree to terminate a lease).

Survey—The process of precisely measuring the boundaries and determining the area of a parcel of land.

Syndicate—An association formed to operate an investment business. A syndicate is not a recognized legal entity; it can be organized as a corporation, LLC, partnership, or trust.

-T-

Tacking—When successive periods of use or possession by more than one person are added together to make up the period required for prescription or adverse possession.

Take-Out Loan—Long-term financing used to replace a construction loan (an interim loan) when construction has been completed. Also called a Permanent Loan.

Taking—When the government acquires private property for public use by condemnation, it's called "a taking," and the former owner is entitled to just compensation for the taken property.

Tax Credit—A credit that is subtracted directly from the amount of tax owed. *Compare:* Deduction.

Tax Deed—A deed given to a purchaser of property at a tax foreclosure sale.

Tax Lien—A lien on property to secure the payment of taxes.

Tax Sale—Sale of property after foreclosure of a tax lien.

Tax-Deferred Exchange—A transaction in which a piece of property held for investment or used in a trade or business is traded for a piece of like-kind property, thus deferring tax on the gain. Sometimes called a tax-free exchange or 1031 exchange.

Team—A group of real estate licensees and non-licensees, working in a real estate firm, who collaborate on transactions.

Tenancy—Lawful possession of real property; an estate.

Tenancy at Sufferance—When a tenant (who entered into possession of the property lawfully) stays on after the lease ends without the landlord's permission.

Tenancy at Will—When a tenant is in possession with the owner's permission, but there's no definite lease term; as when a landlord allows a holdover tenant to remain on the premises until another tenant is found.

Tenancy by the Entirety—A form of joint ownership of property by a married couple (in some states that don't use a community property system).

Tenancy for Years— A leasehold estate set to last for a definite period (one week, three years, etc.), after which it terminates automatically. Also called a Term Tenancy or Estate for Years.

Tenancy in Common—A form of concurrent ownership in which two or more persons each have an undivided interest in the entire property, but no right of survivorship. *Compare:* Tenancy, Joint.

Tenant—Someone in lawful possession of real property; especially, someone who has leased property from the owner.

Tender—An unconditional offer by one of the parties to a contract to perform their part of the agreement; made when the offeror believes the other party is breaching, it establishes the offeror's right to sue if the other party doesn't accept it. Also called a tender offer.

Tender Offer— An unconditional offer by one of the parties to a contract to perform their part of the agreement; made when the offeror believes the other party is breaching, it establishes the offeror's right to sue if the other party doesn't accept it. Also called Tender.

Tenure—The period of time during which a person holds certain rights with respect to a piece of real property.

Term—A prescribed period of time; especially, the length of time a borrower has to pay off a loan, or the duration of a lease.

Term Loan— Most commonly, a loan that requires the borrower to pay only the interest during the loan term, with the principal due at the end of the term. Also called an Interest-only Loan.

Term Tenancy—A leasehold estate set to last for a definite period (one week, three years, etc.), after which it terminates automatically. Also called a Tenancy for Years or Estate for Years.

Testament—*See:* Will.

Testate—Refers to someone who has died and left a valid will. *Compare:* Intestate.

Testator—A person who makes a will.

Third Party—1. A person seeking to deal with a principal through an agent. 2. In a transaction, someone who is not one of the principals.

Thrift Institutions—A term used to refer collectively to savings and loan associations and saving banks.

Tie-in Arrangement—An agreement to sell one product only on the condition that the buyer also purchases a different product.

Tight Money Market—When loan funds are scarce, leading lenders to charge high interest rates and discount points.

Time is of the Essence—A clause in a contract that means performance on the exact dates specified is an essential element of the contract; failure to perform on time is a material breach.

Timeshare—An interest in a condominium unit that entitles the holder to occupy the unit during a specified time slot or number of days every year.

Title—Lawful ownership of real property. Also, the deed or other document that is evidence of that ownership.

Title Company—A title insurance company.

Title Insurance— An insurance policy that indemnifies a buyer or a lender against losses resulting from title defects that have not been excepted from coverage. An owner's policy protects the buyer, while a mortgagee's policy protects the buyer's lender.

Title Report—A report issued by a title company, disclosing the condition of the title to a specific piece of property, before the actual title insurance policy is issued.

Title Search—An inspection of the public record to determine all rights and encumbrances affecting title to a piece of property.

Title Theory—The theory holding that a mortgage or deed of trust gives the lender legal title to the security property while the debt is being repaid. *Compare:* Lien Theory.

Topography—The contours of the surface of the land (level, hilly, steep, etc.).

Tort—A breach of a duty imposed by law (as opposed to a duty voluntarily taken on in a contract) that causes harm to another person, giving the injured person the right to sue the one who breached the duty. Also called a civil wrong (in contrast to a criminal wrong, a crime).

Total Interest Percentage—The total amount of interest that the borrower will pay over the loan term, expressed as a percentage of the loan amount.

Township—In the government survey system, a parcel of land 6 miles square, containing 36 sections; the intersection of a range and a township tier.

Township Lines—Lines running east-west, spaced six miles apart, in the government survey system.

Township Tier—In the government survey system, a strip of land running east-west, six miles wide and bounded on the north and south by township lines.

Tract Index—An index of recorded documents in which all documents that carry a particular legal description are grouped together.

Tract—1. A piece of land of undefined size. 2. In the government survey system, an area made up of 16 townships; 24 miles on each side.

Trade Fixtures—Articles of personal property annexed to real property by a tenant for use in their trade or business, which the tenant is allowed to remove at the end of the lease.

Transaction Folder—A record of all documents associated with a particular transaction, such as the listing agreement, the purchase and sale agreement, the settlement statement, and any modifications or addenda.

Transferability—If an object is transferable, then ownership and possession of that object can be conveyed from one person to another. Transferability is one of the four elements of value, along with utility, scarcity, and demand.

Trespass—An unlawful physical invasion of property owned by another.

Triggering Term—Under the Truth in Lending Act, a loan term which, if stated in an advertisement for consumer credit, "triggers" the requirement of full disclosure of repayment terms. Triggering terms include the amount of any finance charge, loan payment, or required downpayment, or the repayment period or number of payments.

Trust—A legal arrangement in which title to property (or funds) is vested in one or more trustees, who manage the property on behalf of the trust's beneficiaries, in accordance with instructions set forth in the document establishing the trust.

Trust Account—A bank account, separate from a real estate licensee's personal and business accounts, used to segregate trust funds from the licensee's own funds.

Trust Deed— An instrument that creates a voluntary lien on real property to secure the repayment of a debt, and which includes a power of sale clause permitting nonjudicial foreclosure; the parties are the grantor or trustor (borrower), the beneficiary (the lender), and the trustee (a neutral third party). Also called Deed of Trust.

Trust Funds—Money or things of value received by an agent, not belonging to the agent but being held for the benefit of others.

Trustee—1. A person appointed to manage a trust on behalf of the beneficiaries. 2. A neutral third party appointed in a deed of trust to handle the nonjudicial foreclosure process in case of default.

Trustee in Bankruptcy—An individual appointed by the court to handle the assets of a person in bankruptcy.

Trustee's Deed—A deed given to a purchaser of property at a trustee's sale.

Trustee's Sale—A nonjudicial foreclosure sale under a deed of trust.

Trustor—The borrower in a deed of trust. Also called the grantor.

Truth in Lending Act (TILA)— A federal law that requires lenders to make disclosures concerning loan costs to consumer loan applicants, and that also requires certain disclosures in advertisements concerning consumer credit.

-U-

Unauthorized Practice of Law—Tasks undertaken by a real estate licensee that can be done legally only by a licensed attorney; for example, drafting special contract language for a client.

Underimprovement—An improvement which, because of deficiency in cost or size, is not the most profitable use of the land; not the highest and best use.

Underwriting—In real estate lending, the process of evaluating a loan application to determine the probability that the applicant would repay the loan, and matching the risk to an appropriate rate of return. Sometimes called risk analysis.

Undivided Interest—A co-owner's interest, giving them the right to shared possession of the whole property, as opposed to separate possession of a particular section of the property.

Undue Influence—Exerting excessive pressure on someone so as to overpower the person's free will and prevent their from making a rational or prudent decision; often involves abusing a relationship of trust.

Unenforceable Contract—An agreement that a court would refuse to enforce; for example, because its contents can't be proven or the statute of limitations has run out.

Uniform Standards of Professional Appraisal Practice—Guidelines for appraisers adopted by the Appraisal Foundation, a nonprofit organization of professional appraiser associations.

Unilateral Contract—A contract that is accepted by performance; the offeror has promised to perform their side of the bargain if the other party performs, but the other party has not promised to do so. *Compare:* Contract, Bilateral.

Unit-in-Place Method—In appraisal, a method of estimating replacement cost by estimating the cost of each component (foundation, roof, etc.), then adding the costs of all components together.

Unity of Interest—In reference to concurrent ownership, when each co-owner has an equal interest (equal share of ownership) in the property. A requirement for joint tenancy.

Unity of Possession—In reference to concurrent ownership, when each co-owner is equally entitled to possession of the entire property, because their interests are undivided. This is a requirement for joint tenancy, but it is also a characteristic of all concurrent ownership.

Unity of Time—In reference to concurrent ownership, when each co-owner acquired title at the same time. A requirement for joint tenancy.

Unity of Title—In reference to concurrent ownership, when each co-owner acquired title through the same instrument (deed, will, or court order). A requirement for joint tenancy.

Universal Agent—An agent authorized to do everything that can be lawfully delegated to a representative.

Unlawful Detainer—A summary legal action to regain possession of real property; especially, a suit filed by a landlord to evict a defaulting tenant.

Upzoning—Rezoning land to allow higher density or more commercial use.

Use Value— The value of a property to its owner or to a user. (A form of subjective value.) Also called Value In Use.

Useful Life—The period during which improved property will yield a return over and above the rent due to the land itself; also called Economic Life.

Usury—Charging an interest rate that exceeds legal limits.

Utility—The ability of an object to satisfy some need and/or arouse a desire for possession; one of the four elements of value, along with scarcity, demand, and transferability.

Utility Value—The value of a property to its owner or to a user. (A form of subjective value.) Also called Value In Use.

-V-

VA—Department of Veterans Affairs.

VA Entitlement—The guaranty amount that a particular veteran is entitled to.

VA-Guaranteed Loan—A home loan made by an institutional lender to an eligible veteran, where the Dept. of Veterans Affairs will reimburse the lender for losses if the veteran defaults.

Vacancy Factor—A percentage deducted from a property's potential gross income to determine the effective gross income; it serves as an estimate of the income that will probably be lost because of vacancies and tenants who don't pay.

Valid—The legal classification of a contract that is binding and enforceable in a court of law.

Valid Contract—A binding, legally enforceable contract.

Valuable Consideration— Anything of value given to induce another to enter into a contract, such as money, goods, services, or a promise. Sometimes called Consideration.

Valuation— An estimate or opinion of the value of a piece of property as of a particular date. Also called Appraisal.

Value—The present worth of future benefits

Value in Exchange— The most probable price which a property should bring in a competitive and open market under all conditions requisite to a fair sale, the buyer and seller each acting prudently and knowledgeably, and assuming the price is not affected by undue stimulus. (This is the definition used by the federal financial institution regulatory agencies.) Also called Fair Market Value, Value in Exchange, Market Value, or Objective Value. *Compare:* Market Price.

Value in Use— The value of a property to its owner or to a user. (A form of subjective value.) Also called Utility Value.

Variable Expenses—Cleaning, supplies, utilities, tenant services, administrative costs, and repairs for income-producing property.

Variable Interest Rate—A loan interest rate that can be adjusted periodically during the loan term, as in the case of an adjustable-rate mortgage.

Variance—Permission (from the local zoning authority) to use property or build a structure in a way that violates the zoning ordinance in a relatively minor way.

Vendee—A buyer or purchaser; particularly, someone buying property under a land contract.

Vendor—A seller; particularly, someone selling property by means of a land contract.

Verify—1. To confirm or substantiate. 2. To confirm under oath.

Vested—A person who has a present, fixed right or interest in property has a vested right or interest, even though they may not have the right to possession until sometime in the future. For example, a remainderman's interest in the property vests when it is granted (not when the life estate ends).

Vicarious Liability—A legal doctrine stating that a principal can be held liable for harm to third parties resulting from an agent's actions.

Void—Having no legal force or effect. *See also:* Void Contract.

Void Contract—An agreement that is not a valid contract, because it lacks a required element (such as consideration) or is defective in some other respect.

Voidable Contract—A contract that one of the parties can disaffirm without liability, because of lack of capacity or a negative factor such as fraud or duress.

Voluntary Alienation—When an owner voluntarily transfers an interest to someone else.

Voluntary Lien—A lien placed against property with the consent of the owner; in the real estate context, either a deed of trust or a mortgage.

-W-

Waiver—The voluntary relinquishment or surrender of a right.

Warranty Deed—1. A general warranty deed. 2. Any type of deed that carries warranties.

Warranty of Habitability— A warranty, implied by law in every residential lease, that the property is fit for habitation.

Washington Human Rights Commission—The state agency that enforces the Law Against Discrimination.

Washington Land Development Act—A Washington state consumer protection law that requires a subdivision developer to provide a public offering statement (which contains information about the development) to prospective purchasers.

Washington Law Against Discrimination—A state law that prohibits discrimination in all real estate transactions (as well as in other contexts) on the basis of race, creed, color, national origin, sex, sexual orientation, gender identity, marital status, familial status, disability, use of a service animal, veteran or military status, and citizenship or immigration status.

Waste—Destruction, damage, or material alteration of property by someone in possession who holds less than a fee estate (such as a life tenant or lessee), or by a co-owner.

Water Rights—The right to use water from a body of water. *See also:* Appropriation, Prior; Littoral Rights; Riparian Rights.

Water Table—The level at which water may be found, either at the surface or underground.

Wild Deed—A deed that won't be discovered in a standard title search, because of a break in the chain of title.

Will—A person's stipulation regarding how their estate should be disposed of after they die. Also called a testament.

Without Recourse—A qualified or conditional endorsement on a negotiable instrument, which relieves the endorser of liability under the instrument.

Workers' Compensation—State-mandated insurance coverage for injured workers (also known as industrial insurance). Real estate brokerages must pay workers' compensation premiums on all their agents.

Wraparound Financing— A purchase money loan arrangement in which the seller uses part of the buyer's payments to make the payments on an existing loan (called the underlying loan); the buyer takes title subject to the underlying loan, but does not assume it. When the security instrument used for wraparound financing is a deed of trust instead of a mortgage, it may be referred to as an all-inclusive trust deed.

Wraparound Mortgage—A purchase money loan arrangement in which the seller uses part of the buyer's payments to make the payments on an existing loan (called the underlying loan); the buyer takes title subject to the underlying loan, but does not assume it. When the security instrument used for wraparound financing is a deed of trust instead of a mortgage, it may be referred to as an all-inclusive trust deed.

Writ of Attachment— Court-ordered seizure of property belonging to a defendant in a lawsuit, so that it will be available to satisfy a judgment if the plaintiff wins. In the case of real property, attachment creates a lien.

Writ of Execution—A court order directing a public officer (usually the sheriff) to seize and sell property to satisfy a debt.

Writ of Restitution—A court order issued after an unlawful detainer action, informing the tenant that they must vacate the landlord's property within a specified period or be forcibly removed by the sheriff. Also called a writ of possession.

-Y-

Yield—The return of profit to an investor on an investment, stated as a percentage of the amount invested.

-Z-

Zone—An area of land set off for a particular use or uses, subject to certain restrictions.

Zoning Amendment—An amendment to a zoning ordinance, usually changing the uses allowed in a particular zone. Also called a Rezone.

Zoning—Government regulation of the uses of property within specified areas.

Appendix

Chapter 1

1. c) Real property is made up of land, everything that is attached to the land (e.g., fixtures), and everything that is appurtenant to the land (e.g., water rights).
2. b) The intention of the party who attached (annexed) the item is the primary consideration in determining whether it is a fixture. The other tests provide evidence of the annexor's intention.
3. b) An article installed by a tenant for use in a business is called a trade fixture, and it remains the tenant's personal property.
4. b) An appurtenance is a right or interest that goes with the property. Riparian rights are an example.
5. a) Riparian rights include the right to reasonable use of the water that flows through a property owner's land.
6. b) When minerals are extracted from the land, they become personal property.
7. a) The rule of capture determines ownership of oil and gas. The rule provides that the landowner owns all the oil and gas removed from a well on his property, even if the oil or gas was originally under someone else's property.
8. d) To obtain a water appropriation permit, it is not necessary to own riparian or littoral land.
9. b) Subjacent support rights involve support from the underlying earth.
10. d) Unlike the other items listed, the kitchen sink is a fixture, and therefore part of the real property.
11. a) The doctrine of emblements allows a tenant farmer to return and harvest crops after the lease expires.
12. c) In the government survey system of land description, one section contains 640 acres.
13. c) A section is one mile on each side, a quarter section is ½ mile on each side, and a quarter of a quarter section is ¼ mile on each side.
14. c) A township measures six miles by six miles.
15. a) Section 36 is always in the southeast corner of a township.

Chapter 2

1. d) A fee simple owner has the full bundle of rights.
2. b) A defeasible fee (or qualified fee) is an estate that will fail if a certain event occurs.
3. b) Although a life estate is a freehold estate, it is not a fee simple estate.
4. d) Baker was entitled to sell his life estate to Clark. Clark can retain possession during Baker's lifetime.
5. d) Smith has possession of the property for the duration of Jones's life, so Smith has a life estate. Cobb has an estate in reversion, because the property will revert to Cobb after Jones's death.
6. b) A life tenant cannot commit waste, which means that the life tenant cannot damage the property or harm the interests of the remainderman. Severely depleting the property's resources—for example, by cutting down all of the timber or extracting all of the minerals—would constitute waste.
7. a) An estate for years has a set termination date.
8. d) A valid joint tenancy requires all four unities: title, time, interest, possession.
9. b) A joint tenant cannot will his interest in the property. The right of survivorship means the surviving joint tenants acquire the deceased tenant's title.

10. c) When C dies, their interest in the property goes to the other joint tenants, A and B. When B sells their interest to D, the joint tenancy is terminated and a tenancy in common is created between A and D.
11. d) Because their interests in the property are unequal, Asher and Blake must be tenants in common.
12. b) A corporation's shareholders have limited liability for the corporation's actions.
13. a) A real estate investment trust must earn most of its income from real estate. The minimum number of investors is 100, not 150.
14. c) In a condominium, residents own their individual units in severalty, but own the common elements as tenants in common.
15. b) A cooperative is owned by a business entity, usually a corporation. Residents purchase shares in the corporation and receive long-term leases, rather than title to their units.

Chapter 3

1. c) The general term for a transfer of ownership of real property from one party to another is alienation.
2. a) The government transfers title to property with a patent.
3. c) The covenant of seisin is a promise that the grantor actually owns the interest that is being conveyed.
4. d) A quitclaim deed is commonly used to clear clouds on title.
5. c) The grantee only has to be identifiable. He does not have to be competent.
6. d) To successfully convey title, the deed must be delivered and accepted.
7. c) A testator is the person who makes a will.
8. b) A holographic will is one that is handwritten by the testator and not witnessed. Generally, holographic wills are not valid in Washington.
9. c) Adverse possession encourages the full use of land by providing a means by which a user may acquire ownership rights.
10. a) A quitclaim deed transfers whatever interest the grantor has. If the grantor has good title, it conveys good title. If the grantor has no interest in the property, it conveys nothing at all.
11. c) A nuncupative will is an oral will; it is valid in Washington under limited circumstances.
12. c) A warranty deed carries no promise that the property is habitable or otherwise suitable for the buyer.
13. a) A quiet title action provides a binding determination of the parties' interests in a piece of real estate.
14. d) All of these are among the requirements for adverse possession, except recording a claim. Although an adverse possessor may perfect title by recording a quitclaim deed after the statutory period ends, that isn't a requirement for adverse possession.
15. c) Standard title insurance coverage insures against title defects related to recorded documents (such as a forged deed), but not against matters that are not part of the public record (such as an adverse possessor or an encroachment), and not against governmental action (such as condemnation).

Chapter 4

1. d) Property tax liens are specific (they attach only to the taxed property) and involuntary.
2. c) In an attachment, a lien is created against the defendant's property, pending the outcome of the lawsuit.
3. a) A lis pendens provides constructive notice of a pending lawsuit that may affect the property described in the document.
4. c) Property tax liens always have priority over other liens.
5. b) The date of recording governs lien priority, rather than the date of execution of the documents.
6. c) The dominant tenement is benefited by the easement; the servient tenement is burdened by the easement. An easement appurtenant is not necessarily an easement for ingress and egress.
7. a) Since you have the right to use another's property to reach your own, you probably own a dominant tenement.
8. d) An easement in gross benefits an individual (the dominant tenant) rather than any parcel of land.
9. c) A commercial easement in gross can be assigned to another party, but a personal easement in gross cannot be.
10. d) Like any other interest in land, an easement must be granted in writing, unless it is created by operation of law.
11. a) An easement by prescription is obtained in much the same way as ownership by adverse possession: the use must be open and notorious, hostile, and continuous for ten years. It does not have to be exclusive, however.
12. b) Merger occurs when one person acquires ownership of both the dominant tenement and the servient tenement. Merger terminates the easement.
13. b) An overhanging porch or balcony is an encroachment.

14. d) A structure built on the property line is an encroachment, not a nuisance. A nuisance is an activity or condition on neighboring property that negatively affects an owner's use and enjoyment of his property.
15. b) CC&Rs are usually imposed by the developer. They run with the land, which means that subsequent owners of the subdivision lots must abide by them.

Chapter 5

1. b) The police power is the government's power to pass laws (such as zoning ordinances) for the protection of the public health, safety, morals, and general welfare.
2. d) Zoning ordinances typically control the height and placement of buildings, as well as type of use.
3. a) Land use controls are not aimed at encouraging the most profitable use of particular properties. In some cases they prohibit more profitable uses that would be detrimental to the public health, safety, or welfare.
4. d) A nonconforming use (a use established before new zoning rules go into effect, which does not comply with those rules) is ordinarily allowed to continue, but the use cannot be expanded, rebuilt after destruction, or resumed after abandonment.
5. c) A rezone is an amendment to the zoning ordinance, giving a particular area a new zoning designation.
6. d) A variance is granted when the property owner shows that strict enforcement of the zoning law would result in undue hardship.
7. b) A variance authorizes the improvement of property in a manner not ordinarily allowed by the zoning ordinance. Most variances permit only minor deviations from the rules.
8. a) Condemnation is an exercise of the power of eminent domain, not the police power.
9. a) When a government body takes property under the power of eminent domain, it is required to pay compensation to the owner. Compensation is not required if a property loses value due to regulation under the police power.
10. a) Radon is an environmental hazard that occurs where uranium deposits are found. As uranium decays, radon gas is released, which can seep into buildings, often through foundation cracks.
11. b) A special assessment is also called an improvement tax; it is levied to pay for a particular public improvement.
12. d) All of these statements concerning general real estate taxes are true.
13. b) CERCLA is the Comprehensive Environmental Response, Compensation, and Liability Act, a federal law enforced by the EPA.
14. a) The real estate excise tax is levied only when title to property is transferred, and it is based on the selling price.
15. c) An EIS is required for all actions by state or local agencies that may have a significant impact on the environment, including state or local approval of private projects.

Chapter 6

1. c) Only certain types of contracts are required to be in writing, but all contracts require consideration, a lawful objective, and offer and acceptance.
2. a) A person has capacity to contract if he has reached the age of majority (in Washington, age 18) and is mentally competent. It isn't necessary to be declared competent by a court, however.
3. b) If the offeree accepts the offer before the offeror revokes it, a binding contract is formed.
4. c) A counteroffer terminates the original offer (operating as a rejection), but if the counteroffer is then accepted, a valid contract is formed.
5. d) All of the answer options are true statements.
6. d) Consideration is almost anything of value: money, goods, services, or a promise to do or not do something.
7. b) An executory contract has not yet been performed; an executed contract is one that has been fully performed.
8. a) A contract that lacks an essential element (such as consideration) is void. It has no legal force or effect, so there is nothing to rescind.
9. b) A voidable contract can be rescinded by the injured party, but unless it is rescinded it will be enforceable.
10. d) The statute of frauds requires certain contracts to be in writing and signed by the party or parties to be bound.
11. d) Performance, cancellation, and novation are all ways of discharging a contract. Breach does not discharge the contract; the breaching party is liable to the other party.
12. a) Novation is the replacement of an existing contract with a new contract, or the replacement of a party to a contract with a new party.
13. c) A contract can be assigned unless otherwise agreed, but the assignor remains secondarily liable to the other party.
14. d) Liquidated damages are an amount the contracting parties agree in advance will be paid as full compensation if one of them breaches the contract.

15. b) If the court granted Jacobsen specific performance, the McClures would be ordered to convey the house as agreed in the contract (as opposed to merely having to pay Jacobsen damages as compensation).

Chapter 7

1. d) An agency relationship may be created by express agreement (written or oral), ratification, estoppel, or implication.
2. b) After an agency relationship terminates, the agent still owes the principal the duty of confidentiality.
3. b) An agency relationship is created by ratification when the principal gives approval to unauthorized actions after the fact.
4. c) The broker was disloyal to their principal and violated their duties by disclosing confidential information to a third party.
5. a) A seller's real estate agent is required to tell the seller if the buyer is related to the agent.
6. a) A principal can't be held liable for harm caused by a licensee unless the act that resulted in harm was authorized by the principal, or unless the principal benefited from the act and there is little chance that the third party will be able to recover damages from the licensee.
7. d) This is an example of puffing, an exaggerated statement that the buyers should realize they can't depend on.
8. b) A listing agent is usually a special agent, with limited authority to represent the principal in a particular transaction. A listing agent is ordinarily not authorized to sign contracts on behalf of the principal.
9. d) Limited dual agency is legal, but only if the seller and the buyer are informed that the agent is representing both of them, and each party has a written agency agreement with the agent.
10. b) A seller's agent can give a buyer information about the seller's property without becoming a limited dual agent.
11. b) This is an in-house transaction, which means that Carter (the designated broker) is a limited dual agent, and so is the brokerage firm itself. Garza (who worked with the buyer) is the buyer's agent. Lee (the listing agent) is the seller's agent.
12. b) If the friend makes an offer on this listing, it will be an in-house transaction. Assuming the listing agreement includes consent to a limited dual agency in this situation, Kelley represents only the buyer and the other Forrest agent (the listing agent) represents only the seller, while Forrest Properties and its designated broker are limited dual agents.
13. c) If the purchased property is listed with the MLS, the buyer brokerage firm receives a share of the commission that the seller owes the listing firm. This compensation arrangement (a commission split) does not create an agency relationship between the seller and the buyer's agent or the buyer brokerage firm.
14. a) A licensee is required to disclose which party they are representing to anyone they render services to in connection with a transaction. The disclosure must be made before that person signs an offer in the transaction.
15. a) A limited dual agent must not disclose confidential information about one party to the other party. This includes information on each party's negotiating position.

Chapter 8

1. c) An exclusive right to sell listing obligates the seller to pay the listing agent a commission if the property sells during the listing period, regardless of who brings about the sale.
2. a) An open listing obligates the seller to pay a commission to the listing agent only if the listing agent was the procuring cause of the sale.
3. d) A net listing is a way of determining the amount of the commission, rather than the circumstances under which a commission is owed.
4. a) Compensation may be (and commonly is) expressed as a percentage of the sales price, rather than a set dollar amount.
5. b) An exclusive agency listing obligates the seller to pay the listing agent a commission if any agent (anyone other than the seller herself) sells the property.
6. c) When the listing agent presents an offer that matches the seller's terms of sale, the listing agent has earned the commission whether or not the seller accepts the offer. The seller is under no obligation to accept the offer.
7. a) In Washington, a listing agreement is not enforceable unless it includes a description of the property that is adequate to identify it.
8. d) An extender clause entitles the listing agent to a commission if the property is sold within a certain time after the listing expires to someone they introduced to the property or negotiated with during the listing period.
9. a) Because the parties voluntarily backed out of the transaction, Ferris Realty is still legally entitled to collect a full commission from Matthews.
10. d) The listing agent under an exclusive right to sell listing has the exclusive right to submit offers to the seller.

11. d) A multiple listing provision typically makes all other MLS members cooperating agents, authorizes the listing agent to submit the listing to the MLS for publication, and states that the MLS is not a party to the contract.
12. a) An open listing is considered to be a unilateral contract, because only the seller promises performance.
13. c) The seller owes the listing agent a commission even when a transaction fails to close, if the failure was the seller's fault. This rule applies in the situation described in the question, where the seller's title turns out to be unmarketable.
14. c) Unlike an open listing, an exclusive listing obligates the listing agent to make a diligent effort to find a buyer for the property.
15. b) The listing agreement is a contract between the seller and the listing agent; it does not create any legal obligations to prospective buyers.

Chapter 9

1. b) The purchase and sale agreement form is used to set forth the buyer's offer. If the seller signs the form, it becomes a binding contract.
2. c) A real estate agent is not allowed to complete a purchase and sale agreement unless she is representing the buyer or the seller (or both parties).
3. c) A purchase and sale agreement is the final contract. It should state all of the terms of sale, including the total purchase price, the method of payment, and the terms on which the buyer will finance the purchase.
4. a) A provision that makes the purchase and sale agreement contingent on the occurrence of a certain event is a contingency clause.
5. b) If the buyer defaults on the purchase and sale agreement, the seller often retains the earnest money deposit as liquidated damages.
6. a) "Time is of the essence" means that the parties must perform by the exact dates specified; failure to meet a deadline in the agreement is a breach of contract.
7. b) The closing date should be far enough off so that all contingencies can be met. If a transaction does not close by the specified date, the contract becomes unenforceable.
8. d) A bump clause allows the seller to keep the property on the market until a contingency is satisfied or waived by the buyer. If a second buyer makes an offer, the seller can ask the first buyer to waive the contingency or terminate their agreement.
9. c) When a contingency in the purchase and sale agreement is not fulfilled, the contract terminates, and the buyer is usually entitled to have the earnest money refunded.
10. c) The parties are required to make a good faith effort to fulfill the conditions in their contract; one party can't deliberately avoid fulfilling a condition and then use that as an excuse for terminating the contract. A contingency clause can usually be waived by the party for whose benefit it was included in the contract.
11. b) It is important to attach to the purchase and sale agreement copies of any financing documents that will be used in a seller-financed transaction.
12. a) When one of the parties to a purchase and sale agreement is married, his or her spouse should always sign the agreement, even if the spouse's signature may not be necessary.
13. c) When a counteroffer is presented, it is much less confusing to use a counteroffer form than to try to change the terms on the original purchase and sale agreement.
14. c) A buyer does not have to pay a penalty for rejecting an inspection report.
15. d) After the purchase and sale agreement has been signed by both parties, the buyer has equitable title to the property (until the seller transfers legal title to the buyer at closing).

Chapter 10

1. d) The Fed lowers interest rates in times of economic downturn in an attempt to stimulate the economy.
2. b) When the Fed buys government securities back from private investors, it puts more money into circulation (increases the money supply).
3. c) Mortgage money comes from the primary market (in the form of savings deposits) and from the secondary market (when investors like Fannie Mae buy mortgages).
4. a) An installment note involves periodic payments that include some of the principal as well as interest.
5. a) An acceleration clause gives the lender the right to declare the entire debt immediately due and payable if the borrower defaults.
6. c) An alienation clause allows the lender to accelerate the loan if the borrower transfers the security property without the lender's approval.
7. c) The statutory redemption period is the period of time after the sheriff's sale in which the borrower has the right to redeem the property by paying off the entire debt, plus costs.
8. d) Any excess proceeds from a foreclosure sale belong to the borrower—that is, to the foreclosed owner.

9. b) When the debt has been fully paid off, a mortgagee gives the mortgagor a satisfaction of mortgage, releasing the property from the lien.
10. d) In the nonjudicial foreclosure of a deed of trust, the trustor is permitted to cure the default and reinstate the loan (as opposed to paying off the loan) before the trustee's sale is held.
11. a) A mortgage given by a buyer to a seller is often called a purchase money mortgage.
12. d) A budget mortgage payment includes a share of the property taxes and hazard insurance as well as principal and interest.
13. d) A blanket mortgage has more than one parcel of property as collateral.
14. b) A subordination clause in the mortgage for the land loan would give it a lower priority than a mortgage executed later on for a construction loan. Lenders generally require first lien position for construction loans, because they are considered especially risky.
15. d) Construction lenders usually delay the final disbursement until no more construction liens can be filed.

Chapter 11

1. d) The mortgage banker is the only primary market lender listed among the options.
2. d) Discount points are a percentage of the loan amount paid at closing to increase the lender's yield on the loan.
3. b) TILA and Regulation Z require lenders to disclose loan costs to loan applicants, but they do not restrict how much a lender can charge in connection with a loan. And while these laws regulate how financing terms are presented in advertising, they do not prohibit advertisement of financing terms.
4. a) The APR is the annual percentage rate, which indicates the relationship between the total cost of the loan and the loan amount.
5. b) Income ratios are used to measure the adequacy or sufficiency of a loan applicant's stable monthly income.
6. a) Fifteen-year mortgages usually have lower interest rates than 30-year mortgages.
7. b) The loan amount is $261,000, because the loan-to-value ratio is based on the appraised value or the sales price, whichever is less. $290,000 × 90% = $261,000.
8. a) Both the interest rate and the payment amount for an ARM are adjusted at specified intervals. The rate and the payment amount may increase or decrease to reflect changes in the index.
9. c) Negative amortization is unpaid interest that is added to the loan balance.
10. d) When the LTV of a conventional loan is more than 80%, PMI is required.
11. b) The FHA only insures loans made by institutional lenders. It does not make loans itself, nor does it buy and sell loans on the secondary market.
12. a) A downpayment is required for an FHA loan.
13. c) A VA loan can be assumed by any buyer, whether or not he's an eligible veteran. The buyer is required to pass a credit check, however.
14. d) An eligible veteran can get a VA loan on a residence with up to four units, as long as the veteran occupies one of the units.
15. c) Predatory lenders are especially likely to target elderly people and other vulnerable groups. Predatory lending is a problem in connection with home purchase loans as well as home equity loans and refinancing. It's especially likely to occur in the subprime market, but it's by no means limited to the subprime market.

Chapter 12

1. c) An appraisal is only an estimate or opinion of value, and it is valid only in regard to a specified date.
2. a) An appraiser is usually asked to determine the subject property's market value (value in exchange).
3. a) The highest and best use is the use that would produce the greatest net return over time, given the current zoning and other restrictions on use.
4. c) Integration is the period during which the property is being developed.
5. d) This is an example of the principle of anticipation, which holds that value is created by the expectation of future benefits to be derived from owning a property.
6. d) The appraiser will be concerned with the principle of contribution. Will the proposed improvement—the swimming pool—contribute enough to the property's value (in the form of higher rents from tenants, and, ultimately, net income to the owner) to justify the expense of installing it?
7. a) The principle of regression holds that association with properties of much lower quality reduces a property's value.
8. c) General data is data concerning factors outside the subject property itself that affect the property's value. A neighborhood analysis involves collection of general data, whereas the site and building analysis involve collection of specific data about the subject property itself.
9. d) In the appraisal of single-family homes, the sales comparison approach is given the most weight.

10. c) A sales comparison appraisal of residential property is usually based on the sales prices of homes that sold within the past six months.
11. b) There is little data available in an inactive market. (However, the appraiser can use older comparable sales if she determines the rate of appreciation or depreciation and adjusts the prices accordingly.)
12. c) Forced sales are never used as comparables for appraisal purposes. Comparable sales must occur under normal market conditions, where neither party was acting under unusual pressure.
13. b) The cost approach involves estimating the current cost of construction, subtracting the amount of accrued depreciation, then adding back in the estimated value of the land. How much the property rents for is irrelevant in the cost approach.
14. b) The cost of producing a replica of an old building at current prices (reproduction cost) is invariably much higher than the cost of constructing a building with the equivalent utility using modern materials (replacement cost). Reproduction cost is not a good indicator of an old building's market value.
15. d) The mortgage payments—referred to as the property's debt service—are not considered operating expenses for the purposes of the income approach.

Chapter 13

1. c) A real estate licensee is exempt from the Escrow Agent Registration Act when handling closing for a transaction in which she is providing brokerage services, as long as the licensee does not charge a separate fee for escrow services.
2. b) A debit on the buyer's side of the statement is a charge that the buyer must pay. In some cases, it is a charge that the buyer must pay to the seller (a refund for taxes paid in advance, for example), but in other cases the buyer owes it to a third party (the loan fee paid to the lender, for example).
3. a) The purchase price is a debit for the buyer and a credit for the seller.
4. d) To help detect money laundering and tax evasion, escrow agents must report large cash payments to the Internal Revenue Service on Form 8300.
5. b) The earnest money deposit is a credit for the buyer, since it has already been paid. It does not appear on the seller's side of the statement, because the full purchase price is listed as a credit for the seller, and the deposit is included in the price.
6. c) A loan the buyer uses to finance the transaction is listed as a credit for the buyer, whatever its source. When the financing comes through the seller (either through an assumption of the seller's loan, or through seller financing) it is a debit for the seller as well as a credit for the buyer.
7. a) The seller almost always pays the real estate commission. The other expenses listed relate to the buyer's loan, and they are ordinarily paid by the buyer.
8. b) The buyer is usually required to pay the premium for the lender's extended coverage title insurance policy.
9. d) Prepaid interest—interest on a new loan to cover the period from the closing date through the last day of the month—is one of the buyer's debits.
10. b) Because mortgage interest is paid in arrears—the month after it accrues—at closing the sellers will be required to pay the interest that has accrued during May. (Their May 1 mortgage payment included the interest that accrued in April.)
11. b) A settlement statement sets forth the charges that must be paid by each party and to each party at closing.
12. b) Prorating an expense is calculating it on the basis of a particular time period, such as number of days.
13. d) All of these are elements of a federally related loan under RESPA.
14. b) When the seller is a foreign investor, FIRPTA generally requires the escrow agent to deduct 15% of the amount realized and send it to the IRS. Different rules apply to less expensive residential properties.
15. b) A real estate agent who isn't also a licensed escrow officer would be violating the Escrow Agent Registration Act if he handled escrow in a transaction he wasn't already involved in as a real estate agent. Also, it would be illegal for the real estate agent to charge a separate fee for escrow services.

Chapter 14

1. d) The cost of installing a deck is a capital expenditure, which would be added to the taxpayer's basis. Remember that principal residences and personal use property do not qualify for depreciation deductions.
2. d) A loss on the sale of a principal residence or personal use property is never deductible.
3. a) If the owner loses money on the sale of the property, she may be able to deduct that loss. Depreciation deductions are not allowed for unimproved investment property, because land is not depreciable. Capital expenditures are not deductible; instead, they increase the taxpayer's basis.

4. c) The like-kind property requirement means that real estate must be exchanged for other real estate.
5. b) Gain is taxed in the year it is realized unless a tax code provision allows deferral of the tax, as with a 1031 exchange.
6. d) To qualify for the exclusion from taxation, the taxpayer must have both owned and used the property as a principal residence for two of the previous five years.
7. c) The initial basis, plus the capital expenditures, less the allowable depreciation deductions, equals an adjusted basis of $480,000.
   $450,000 + $50,000 – $20,000 = $480,000
   (Ignore the increase in market value; it does not affect the taxpayer's basis.)
8. a) A taxpayer can deduct all of the interest paid on a loan of up to $750,000 used to purchase a first or second personal residence. (The limit is $1,000,000 for loans made before 2018.)
9. d) A renovation is a capital improvement, not a repair, so it can't be fully deducted in the year incurred. Instead, the improvement's cost is added to the property's basis and the cost is gradually deducted through annual depreciation deductions.
10. b) Sherrick will realize a $9,180 gain in the transaction. First subtract her selling expenses (the commission and closing costs) from the sales price to determine the amount realized; then subtract her adjusted basis from the amount realized to determine the gain.
   $72,000 × 6% = $4,320 commission
   $4,320 + $2,500 costs = $6,820
   $72,000 – $6,820 = $65,180 (amount realized)
   $65,180 – $56,000 = $9,180 (gain realized)

Chapter 15

1. b) Channeling prospective buyers or tenants away from (or toward) certain neighborhoods based on their race or other protected characteristics is called steering. Steering is a violation of federal and state antidiscrimination laws.
2. c) No residential transaction in which a real estate agent is employed is exempt from the federal Fair Housing Act.
3. a) The Fair Housing Act does not allow an apartment house or a condominium to discriminate on the basis of familial status unless the complex qualifies as "housing for older persons."
4. c) Title VIII of the 1968 Civil Rights Act (better known as the federal Fair Housing Act) prohibits discriminatory practices when selling, renting, advertising, or financing housing.
5. d) The discriminatory practice known as blockbusting is entirely prohibited by the Fair Housing Act.
6. b) The Washington Human Rights Commission is charged with enforcing the Washington Law Against Discrimination.
7. a) The Home Mortgage Disclosure Act helps to enforce the prohibition against redlining by requiring large institutional lenders to file an annual report of all mortgage loans made during that year. Loans are categorized by location, alerting investigators to possible redlining.
8. c) The Fair Housing Act requires a residential landlord to allow a disabled tenant to make reasonable modifications to the property. The landlord must also make reasonable exceptions to the rules to accommodate a disabled tenant.
9. c) A landlord may (and should) base a rental decision on whether the prospective tenant can afford the rent. However, the landlord cannot take into account the prospective tenant's national origin or familial status.
10. a) The Washington Law Against Discrimination protects several more classes of people than the federal Fair Housing Act.
11. b) Discrimination based on sexual orientation in residential sales transactions is generally illegal under both the federal statute and Washington's statute. However, the federal law provides an exemption for the sale of a single-family home, as long as the seller owns no more than three such homes, no real estate agent is involved, and no discriminatory advertising is used. The Washington law, on the other hand, applies to all real estate sales, without any exemptions. So refusal to sell a home (or other real property) based on sexual orientation (or any of the other protected classes) is illegal in this state.
12. a) The Fair Housing Act applies only to residential properties, not to commercial or industrial properties.
13. c) The developer's age limit would violate the Fair Housing Act. Housing for older persons is allowed, but 45 isn't the cutoff age.
14. b) One of the anticompetitive practices prohibited by the Sherman Act is price fixing. An agreement in the brokerage community to charge a standard or fixed commission rate would violate that law.
15. d) Federal antitrust laws were held to apply to the real estate industry in 1950. All real estate agents and all real estate firms are required to comply with them.

Chapter 16

1. b) The lack of liquidity is the main disadvantage of investing in real estate.
2. a) The difference between the value of real estate and the liens against it is the owner's equity.
3. a) Yield is the rate of return on an investment.
4. b) A property manager must try to achieve the property owner's objectives.
5. c) The typical family would be more likely to rent a three-bedroom unit than either a studio or a five-bedroom apartment.
6. a) Because residential lease terms are relatively short, managing residential property tends to involve more marketing than managing other types of property.
7. b) A property management agreement should always include a provision that describes the manager's compensation.
8. c) Rental rates should not be much lower or much higher than the rates for competitive properties.
9. a) The legal process for evicting a tenant is called an unlawful detainer action.
10. c) Fixed expenses remain the same, regardless of rental income. Insurance premiums are fixed expenses.
11. b) A summary of operations is a brief summary of the detailed information in the other sections of the statement of operations.
12. d) A rent roll is a report on the collection of rent.
13. a) Preventive maintenance preserves the physical integrity of the property and reduces the need for corrective maintenance.
14. b) Repairs are classified as corrective maintenance.
15. c) A property manager cannot perform any management functions until she has a written management agreement. The market analysis and the management proposal should also be completed before the manager begins managing the property.

Chapter 17

1. a) The Governor appoints the members of the Real Estate Commission, which includes six commissioners and the Director of the Department of Licensing.
2. b) It is legal for an unlicensed person to represent another in a real estate transaction if authorized to do so by a power of attorney, as long as she is not acting for compensation.
3. d) The co-owner of a rental property can lease property on his own behalf without his actions falling under the definition of brokerage services.
4. a) The required qualifications for a managing broker's license differ from those for a broker's license in that at least three years of real estate experience in the previous five years is required. Just like a broker, a managing broker must be licensed under a firm and cannot accept compensation from anyone other than the firm.
5. b) Real estate licenses must be renewed every two years.
6. c) A real estate license can be renewed within one year after it expires if the licensee pays a penalty in addition to the renewal fee. After one year, the license is canceled, and there are several requirements for reinstatement.
7. b) Renewal requires a total of 30 clock hours of continuing education courses. At least 15 of the 30 hours must have been commenced within 24 months preceding the licensee's renewal date. The remaining hours must have been commenced within 36 months preceding the renewal date.
8. c) Brokers must complete 90 clock hours of continuing education for their first renewal, with courses in advanced real estate practices, real estate law, and elective hours.
9. d) License reinstatement does not require retaking the license exam. A licensee must complete 60 clock hours of coursework, pay the back renewal fees, and pay a reinstatement penalty.
10. c) Those licensed in other jurisdictions must take the Washington portion of the license exam to obtain an equivalent Washington license.
11. a) Assistants need not be licensed, as long as they perform only clerical tasks. If an assistant were to engage in listing or selling activities, the assistant would have to obtain a license.
12. a) One year of experience plus post-secondary education in real estate studies may be sufficient to merit a waiver of the three-year experience requirement.
13. c) An applicant without three years of experience may still sit for the managing broker's exam if the Director of the Department of Licensing determines that her other education or experience is a satisfactory substitute.
14. b) A passing score for the real estate managing broker's exam is 75%. (A passing score for the real estate broker's exam is 70%.)
15. a) Only brokers receive an interim license; managing brokers do not.
16. b) A limited dual agent must not take any action that is detrimental to either party's interest in a transaction, unless it's something the agent is legally required to do (such as disclosing material facts).

17. d) Facts known by a real estate agent that aren't known by the principal are not imputed to the principal.
18. a) When a real estate licensee's affiliation with a firm ends, her license is inactive until she finds another firm to work for and the license is reissued. In the meantime, it's unlawful for the licensee to engage in any activities for which a license is required.
19. d) A managing broker has the responsibility of reviewing documents within five days in transactions that involve a broker with less than two years of experience.
20. c) A real estate license must be prominently displayed in the office where the licensee works.
21. d) Trust funds must be placed in a trust account by the first banking day after receipt, unless the parties have instructed the firm in writing to handle the funds differently. Trust funds received in a sales transaction (or any trust funds other than property management trust funds) must be placed in an interest-bearing account.
22. c) Transaction records and trust account records must be kept for at least three years after a transaction closes (or is otherwise terminated).
23. a) A licensee can only receive compensation through her firm. The listing firm will have to pay the licensee's firm, who will then pay the licensee.
24. a) When advertising their own properties, licensees are required to disclose their licensed status, but the firm's name does not have to be given. (The firm's name as licensed is required in ads for properties a licensee is advertising on behalf of someone else, however.)
25. d) A broker can't manage a branch office; a branch office manager must have a managing broker's license.
26. b) Before the buyer signs an offer, the broker must disclose to the buyer in writing which party he is representing. The agency disclosure may be a separate paragraph in the purchase and sale agreement, or it may be a separate document.
27. b) If the licensee fails to request a hearing within 20 days, she will be considered in default and the Director may enter a decision based on the available facts.
28. d) A licensee has to notify the Department of Licensing of a judgment in a civil lawsuit only if the case involves his real estate activities or other business activities. (With criminal charges, the Department of Licensing must be notified whether or not the charges involve real estate or business activities.)
29. d) A firm that performs property management services must have a written management agreement with the owner, keep summary statements in its records, and fully disclose any interest in businesses that provide ancillary services.
30. d) Real estate licensees must perform their duties as agreed, in a timely manner. Failure to do so may result in disciplinary action.

Chapter 18

1. a) The current market value of Christine and Tom's condo is approximately $180,295. The question asks you to determine the current value of the condo based on its earlier value, so the applicable formula is ***Then* × % = *Now***. Here, the value has increased by 7%, so the appropriate percentage is 107% (100% + 7%), or 1.07 (as a decimal). ***$168,500 × 1.07 = $180,295.***
2. d) The listing broker will get $2,982. This is a percentage question with two parts. First multiply the sales price by the listing firm's commission rate to determine the full commission. ***$183,500 × .065 = $11,927.50.*** Then multiply that number by 25% to determine the listing broker's share: ***$11,927.50 × .25 = $2,981.88.***
3. b) The depth of the lot is 216 feet. The question asks you to determine the length of one of the sides of a rectangle, so the applicable formula is *Area = Length × Width, A = L × W.*

   First convert the area from square yards to square feet, so that it is in the same unit of measurement as the frontage. A square yard is a square that measures 3 feet on each side, or 9 square feet (3 × 3 = 9). Thus, 1,080 square yards is 9,720 square feet (*1,080 × 9 = 9,720*).

   Now substitute the numbers you have into the formula. *9,720 = 45 × L.* Isolate the unknown quantity, *L*, by changing to another version of the same formula: *L = 9,720 ÷ 45.*

   Divide the area, 9,720 square feet, by the width, 45 feet, to determine the length of the rectangle: *9,720 ÷ 45 = 216 feet.*
4. c) There are eight 50′ × 100′ lots in an acre, with one somewhat smaller lot left over. Use the area formula to determine the area of a 50′ × 100′ lot. *A = 50 × 100 = 5,000 square feet.* Thus, each lot will have an area of 5,000 square feet. Now divide the total number of square feet in the acre by the area of each lot: *43,560 ÷ 5,000 = 8.71.*

5. b) Felicia's commission rate was 7%. Use the percentage formula, ***Part = Whole × Percentage,*** ***P = W × %***. You know the part ($33,600) and the total ($480,000), so switch the formula to isolate the percentage, then substitute and calculate.

   P ÷ W = %

   $33,600 ÷ $480,000 = %

   $33,600 ÷ $480,000 = .07

   Thus, the commission rate was 7%.

6. a) Jake's profit on the sale of the lot was 60%. The question asks you to determine what percentage of the original price (the *Then* value) the sales price (the *Now* value) represents. So use the formula *Now = Then × %*, switching it around to isolate the unknown quantity, the percentage:

   Now ÷ Then = %

   $8,000 ÷ $5,000 = 1.60 or 160%

   The *Now* value is 160% of the *Then* value—in other words, 60% more than the *Then* value. Thus, Jake's profit on the sale was 60%.

7. d) Diane could pay $200,000 for the property and get an 8% return on that investment. This is a capitalization problem, so use the capitalization formula, ***Income = Rate × Value, I = R × V.*** You know the net income ($16,000) and the capitalization rate (8%), so switch the formula to isolate the unknown quantity, V:

   I ÷ R = V

   $16,000 ÷ .08 = $200,000

8. b) George has a 6% return on his investment. This problem calls for the capitalization formula again, but this time it's the rate that is unknown. Switch the formula to isolate the rate, R:

   I ÷ V = R

   $5,100 ÷ $85,000 = .06 = 6%

9. d) There are 250 square yards in a 75′ × 30′ rectangle. The area formula, ***A = L × W,*** will give you the area in square feet: ***75 × 30 = 2,250 square feet.*** Then you must convert that figure to square yards. There are 9 square feet in a square yard, so divide 2,250 by 9: ***2,250 ÷ 9 = 250 square yards.***

10. c) Mike, the buyer, is entitled to approximately $7,445 in rent for the period from the closing date through September 30. The proration formula is ***Share = Rate × Days, S = R × D.*** First determine the per diem rate for the rents by dividing the total amount by the number of days in the month: ***$13,960 ÷ 30 = $465.33.*** Next, determine the number of days for which the buyer is entitled to the rent: September 15 through 30 is 16 days. Finally, multiply the rate by the number of days to find the buyer's share: ***$465.33 × 16 = $7,445.***

11. b) The area of the lot is 600 square feet. Since the lot is triangular, the appropriate area formula is ***Area = ½ Base × Height, A = ½ B × H.*** Here, the base is 40 feet, so ½ the base is 20 feet. ***20 feet × 30 feet = 600 square feet.***

12. a) The decimal equivalent of 5/8 is .625. To determine this, divide the numerator of the fraction (the top number, 5) by the denominator (the bottom number, 8). ***5 ÷ 8 = .625.***

13. c) The prepaid interest will be $130.40. First determine the annual interest, using the percentage formula: ***Part = Whole × Percentage, P = W × %.*** The principal (the whole) is $112,000 and the rate (the percentage) is 8.5%. ***$112,000 × .085 = $9,520.*** Next, divide the annual interest by 365 to determine the per diem rate. ***$9,520 ÷ 365 = $26.08.*** Multiply the per diem rate by the number of days for which Kay is responsible for this expense—five days. ***$26.08 × 5 = $130.40.***

14. b) The Binghams will have to pay $322.77 in interest at closing. To find the annual interest amount, use the percentage formula, ***P = W × %. $168,301.50 × .10 = $16,830.15.*** Divide that figure by 365 to determine the per diem rate: ***$16,830.15 ÷ 365 = $46.11.*** Finally, multiply the per diem rate by the number of days: ***$46.11 × 7 days = $322.77.***

15. d) The building's annual net income is $44,850. Use the capitalization formula, ***Income = Rate × Value; .0975 × $460,000 = $44,850.***

Index

Q

R

T

U

V